T0215757

Beginning Java 8
Games Development

Wallace Jackson

Apress®

Beginning Java 8 Games Development

Copyright © 2014 by Wallace Jackson

This work is subject to copyright. All rights are reserved by the Publisher, whether the whole or part of the material is concerned, specifically the rights of translation, reprinting, reuse of illustrations, recitation, broadcasting, reproduction on microfilms or in any other physical way, and transmission or information storage and retrieval, electronic adaptation, computer software, or by similar or dissimilar methodology now known or hereafter developed. Exempted from this legal reservation are brief excerpts in connection with reviews or scholarly analysis or material supplied specifically for the purpose of being entered and executed on a computer system, for exclusive use by the purchaser of the work. Duplication of this publication or parts thereof is permitted only under the provisions of the Copyright Law of the Publisher's location, in its current version, and permission for use must always be obtained from Springer. Permissions for use may be obtained through RightsLink at the Copyright Clearance Center. Violations are liable to prosecution under the respective Copyright Law.

ISBN-13 (pbk): 978-1-4842-0416-0

ISBN-13 (electronic): 978-1-4842-0415-3

Trademarked names, logos, and images may appear in this book. Rather than use a trademark symbol with every occurrence of a trademarked name, logo, or image we use the names, logos, and images only in an editorial fashion and to the benefit of the trademark owner, with no intention of infringement of the trademark.

The use in this publication of trade names, trademarks, service marks, and similar terms, even if they are not identified as such, is not to be taken as an expression of opinion as to whether or not they are subject to proprietary rights.

While the advice and information in this book are believed to be true and accurate at the date of publication, neither the authors nor the editors nor the publisher can accept any legal responsibility for any errors or omissions that may be made. The publisher makes no warranty, express or implied, with respect to the material contained herein.

Managing Director: Welmoed Spahr
Lead Editor: Steve Anglin
Development Editor: Matthew Moodie
Technical Reviewer: Chád Darby
Editorial Board: Steve Anglin, Ewan Buckingham, Gary Cornell, Louise Corrigan, James T. DeWolf,
    Jonathan Gennick, Robert Hutchinson, Michelle Lowman, James Markham, Matthew Moodie,
    Jeff Olson, Jeffrey Pepper, Douglas Pundick, Ben Renow-Clarke, Dominic Shakeshaft,
    Gwenan Spearing, Matt Wade, Steve Weiss
Coordinating Editor: Mark Powers
Copy Editors: Lisa Vecchione, Karen Jameson
Compositor: SPi Global
Indexer: SPi Global
Artist: SPi Global
Cover Designer: Anna Ishchenko

Distributed to the book trade worldwide by Springer Science+Business Media New York, 233 Spring Street, 6th Floor, New York, NY 10013. Phone 1-800-SPRINGER, fax (201) 348-4505, e-mail orders-ny@springer-sbm.com, or visit www.springeronline.com. Apress Media, LLC is a California LLC and the sole member (owner) is Springer Science + Business Media Finance Inc (SSBM Finance Inc). SSBM Finance Inc is a Delaware corporation.

For information on translations, please e-mail rights@apress.com, or visit www.apress.com.

Apress and friends of ED books may be purchased in bulk for academic, corporate, or promotional use. eBook versions and licenses are also available for most titles. For more information, reference our Special Bulk Sales–eBook Licensing web page at www.apress.com/bulk-sales.

Any source code or other supplementary material referenced by the author in this text is available to readers at www.apress.com/9781484204160. For detailed information about how to locate your book's source code, go to www.apress.com/source-code.

This Java 8 Game Development book is dedicated to everyone in the open source community who is working diligently to make professional new media application development software, and content development tools, freely available for all of us rich application developers to utilize to achieve our creative dreams and financial goals. Last, but certainly not least, I dedicate this book to my father Parker, my family, all my life-long friends, and all of my ranching neighbors, for their constant help, assistance, and those smoky late night BBQ parties.

Contents at a Glance

About the Author xix

About the Technical Reviewer xxi

Acknowledgments xxiii

Introduction xxv

■Chapter 1: Setting Up a Java 8 Game Development Environment 1

■Chapter 2: Setting Up Your Java 8 IDE: An Introduction to NetBeans 8.0.......................19

■Chapter 3: A Java 8 Primer: An Introduction to Java 8 Concepts and Principles 43

■Chapter 4: An Introduction to JavaFX 8: Exploring the Capabilities
of the Java 8 Multimedia Engine 75

■Chapter 5: An Introduction to Game Design: Concepts, Multimedia,
and Using Scene Builder...101

■Chapter 6: The Foundation of Game Design: The JavaFX Scene Graph
and the InvinciBagel Game Infrastructure..123

■Chapter 7: The Foundation of Game Play Loop: The JavaFX Pulse System
and the Game Processing Architecture 145

■Chapter 8: Creating Your Actor Engine: Design the Characters for Your Game
and Define Their Capabilities...165

■Chapter 9: Controlling Your Action Figure: Implementing Java Event Handlers
and Using Lambda Expressions..187

■Chapter 10: Directing the Cast of Actors: Creating a Casting Director Engine
and Creating the Bagel Actor Class...207

■Chapter 11: Moving Your Action Figure in 2D: Controlling the X and Y
Display Screen Coordinates..229

■Chapter 12: Setting Boundaries for Your Action Figure in 2D: Using the
Node Class LocalToParent Attribute 251

■Chapter 13: Animating Your Action Figure States: Setting the Image
States Based on KeyEvent Processing 273

■Chapter 14: Setting Up the Game Environment: Creating Fixed Sprite
Classes Using the Actor Superclass 299

■Chapter 15: Implementing Game Audio Assets: Using the JavaFX
AudioClip Class Audio Sequencing Engine 323

■Chapter 16: Collision Detection: Creating SVG Polygons for the Game Actors
and Writing Code to Detect Collision 343

■Chapter 17: Enhancing Game Play: Creating a Scoring Engine,
Adding Treasure and an Enemy Auto-Attack Engine 393

Index 455

Contents

About the Author xix

About the Technical Reviewer xxi

Acknowledgments xxiii

Introduction xxv

■Chapter 1: Setting Up a Java 8 Game Development Environment 1

Prepare a Workstation for Java 8 Game Development 2

Downloading Java JDK 8 and NetBeans 8.0 4

Installing the Java 8 Software Development Environment 6

Installing NetBeans IDE 8.0 8

Installing New Media Content Production Software 11

Downloading and Installing Inkscape 11

Downloading and Installing GIMP 12

Downloading and Installing Audacity 13

Downloading and Installing EditShare Lightworks 14

Downloading and Installing Blender 15

Other Open-Source Software Packages of Interest 16

Organizing Quick Launch Icons in Your Taskbar Area 17

Summary 17

■Chapter 2: Setting Up Your Java 8 IDE: An Introduction to NetBeans 8.0 19

Primary Attributes of NetBeans 8.0: An Intelligent IDE 19

NetBeans 8.0 Is Smart: Put Your Code Editing into Hyperdrive 20

NetBeans 8.0 Is Extensible: Code Editing with Many Languages 20

NetBeans 8.0 Is Efficient: Organized Project Management Tools 21

NetBeans 8.0 Is User Interface Design Friendly: UI Design Tools 22

NetBeans 8.0 Is not Bug Friendly: Squash Bugs with a Debugger 22

NetBeans 8.0 Is a Speed Freak: Optimize the Code with a Profiler 22

Creating Your Java 8 Game Project: The InvinciBagel 23

Compiling Your Java 8 Game Project in NetBeans 8.0 28

Running Your Java 8 Game Project in NetBeans 8.0 29

Profiling Your Java 8 Game Project in NetBeans 8.0 31

Profiling Your Java 8 Game Application CPU Usage 33

Profiling Your Java 8 Game Application Memory Usage 38

Summary 41

■Chapter 3: A Java 8 Primer: An Introduction to Java 8 Concepts and Principles 43

The Syntax of Java: Comments and Code Delimiters 43

Java APIs: Using Packages to Organize by Function 47

Java Classes: Logical Java Constructs to Build On 48

Nested Classes: Java Classes Living Inside Other Classes 49

Inner Classes: Different Types of Nonstatic Nested Classes 50

Java Methods: Core Java Function Code Constructs 51

Creating a Java Object: Invoking a Class's Constructor Method 53

Creating a Constructor Method: Coding an Object's Structure 54

Java Variables and Constants: Values in Data Fields 55

Fixing Data Values in Memory: Defining a Data Constant in Java 56

Java Modifier Keywords: Access Control and More 56

Access Control Modifiers: Public, Protected, Private, Package Private 57

Nonaccess Control Modifiers: final, static, abstract, volatile, synchronized 58

Java Data Types: Defining Data Type in Applications 60

Primitive Data Types: Characters, Numbers, and Boolean (Flags) 60

Reference Data Types: Objects and Arrays 61

Java Operators: Manipulating Data in the Application 61

Java Arithmetic Operators 62

Java Relational Operators 63

Java Logical Operators: 64

Java Assignment Operators 64

Java Conditional Operators 65

Java Conditional Control: Decision Making or Loops 65

Decision-Making Control Structures: Switch-Case and If-Else 66

Looping Control Structures: While, Do-While, and For 68

Java Objects: Virtual Reality, Using Java Constructs 69

Creating an InvinciBagel Object: Attributes, States, and Behavior 69

Creating an InvinciBagel Blueprint: Create the GamePiece Class 72

Creating a GamePiece() Constructor: Overloading a GamePiece 73

Summary 74

■Chapter 4: An Introduction to JavaFX 8: Exploring the Capabilities
of the Java 8 Multimedia Engine 75

Overview of JavaFX: From Scene Graph Down to OS 76

JavaFX Scene Package: 16 Core Java 8 Classes 77

JavaFX Scene Class: Scene Size and Color and Scene Graph Nodes 78

JavaFX Scene Graph: Organizing Scenes, Using Parent Nodes 79

JavaFX Scene Content: Lights, Camera, Cursor, Action! 80

JavaFX Scene Utilities: Scene Snapshots and Antialiasing 81

Scene Subpackages: The 13 Other Scene Packages 82

Other JavaFX Packages: The 15 Top-Level Packages 84

JavaFX Animation for Games: Using javafx.animation Classes 85

JavaFX Screen and Window Control: Using javafx.stage Classes 89

JavaFX Bounds and Dimensions: Using javafx.geometry Classes 95

JavaFX Input Control for Games: Using javafx.event Classes 97

JavaFX Thread Control for Games: javafx.concurrent Package 97

Summary 98

■Chapter 5: An Introduction to Game Design: Concepts, Multimedia, and Using Scene Builder..101

High-Level Concept: Static vs. Dynamic...102

Game Optimization: Balancing Static Elements with Dynamic.........................103

Game Design Concepts: Sprites, Physics, Collision.......................................104

Types of Games: Puzzles, Board Games, Arcade Games, Hybrids...................104

Game Design Assets: New Media Content Concepts.......................................105

Digital Imaging Concepts: Resolution, Color Depth, Alpha, Layers....................106

Digital Video and Animation: Frames, Rate, Looping, Direction.........................113

Digital Audio Concepts: Amplitude, Frequency, Samples................................116

JavaFX Scene Builder: Using FXML for UI Design..120

FXML Definition: Anatomy of an XML UI Definition Construct............................121

Hello World UI FXML Definition: Replicating Your Current UI Design, Using FXML.....121

Summary...122

■Chapter 6: The Foundation of Game Design: The JavaFX Scene Graph and the InvinciBagel Game Infrastructure...123

Game Design Foundation: Primary Function Screens......................................124

Java Class Structure Design: Game Engine Support.......................................125

JavaFX Scene Graph Design: Minimizing UI Nodes..126

Scene Graph Code: Optimizing Your Current InvinciBagel Class.......................127

Scene Graph Design: Streamlining the Existing .start() Method........................128

JavaFX UI Classes: HBox, Pos, Insets, and ImageView..................................129

The JavaFX Pos Class: Generalized Screen Position Constants.........................129

The JavaFX Insets Class: Providing Padding Values for Your UI.........................130

The JavaFX HBox Class: Using a Layout Container in a Design..........................131

The JavaFX Image Class: Referencing Digital Images in a Design......................132

JavaFX ImageView Class: Displaying Digital Images in a Design........................134

The JavaFX TableView Class: Displaying Data Tables in a Design.......................135

Scene Graph Nodes: .createSplashScreenNodes() 136

    Adding Nodes to the Scene Graph: .addStackPaneNodes() 138

Testing the InvinciBagel Application: Pulse the Scene Graph..139

Finishing an InvinciBagel UI Screen Design: Add Images..139

Interactivity: Wiring the InvinciBagel Buttons for Use 140

    Testing the Final InvinciBagel UI Design..142

    Profiling the InvinciBagel Scene Graph for Pulse Efficiency...142

Summary..144

■Chapter 7: The Foundation of Game Play Loop: The JavaFX Pulse System
and the Game Processing Architecture 145

Game Loop Processing: Harnessing a JavaFX Pulse...146

Creating a New Java Class: GamePlayLoop.java..147

Creating the GamePlayLoop Class Structure: Implementing Your .handle() Method................150

Creating a GamePlayLoop Object: Adding Pulse Control 152

Profiling the GamePlayLoop Object: Running NetBeans Profiler 153

Controlling Your GamePlayLoop: .start() and .stop() 154

InvinciBagel Diagram: Package, Classes, and Objects 159

Testing the GamePlayLoop: Animating the UI Container...160

Profiling the GamePlayLoop: Pulse Engine 161

Summary...163

■Chapter 8: Creating Your Actor Engine: Design the Characters for Your Game
and Define Their Capabilities..165

Game Actor Design: Defining the Attributes Up Front..166

The InvinciBagel Sprite Images: Visual Action States..167

Creating an Actor Superclass: Fixed Actor Attributes 168

    Creating an .update() Method: Connect to GamePlayLoop Engine 170

    Adding Sprite Control and Definition Variables to an Actor Class...171

    Accessing Actor Variables: Creating Getter and Setter Methods..174

Creating a Hero Superclass: Motion Actor Attributes 177

    Adding Update and Collision Methods: .update() and .collide() 178

    Adding Sprite Control and Definition Variables to the Hero Class...179

    Accessing Hero Variables: Creating Getter and Setter Methods...182

Updating the Game Design: How Actor or Hero Fit In 185

Summary..186

■Chapter 9: Controlling Your Action Figure: Implementing Java Event Handlers and Using Lambda Expressions...187

Game Surface Design: Adding Resolution Flexibility 188

Finishing the UI Design: Coding a Game Play Button 189

    Testing the Game Play Button: Making Sure Your Code Works...190

    Upgrading the Other UI Button Code: Making ImageView Visible 190

Lambda Expression: A Powerful New Java 8 Feature 191

    Handling NetBeans Unexpected Updates and Incorrect Warnings 194

Event Handling: Adding Interactivity to Your Games..195

    Types of Controllers: What Types of Events Should We Handle?...195

Java 8 and JavaFX Events: javafx.event and java.util 196

    JavaFX Input Event Classes: The javafx.scene.input Package...196

Adding Keyboard Event Handling: Using KeyEvents...199

    Processing Your KeyEvent: Using the Switch-Case Statement...200

    Creating the KeyPressed KeyEvent Handling Structure...202

Adding Alternate KeyEvent Mapping: Using A-S-D-W 204

Updating Our Game Design: Adding Event Handling 205

Summary..206

■Chapter 10: Directing the Cast of Actors: Creating a Casting Director Engine and Creating the Bagel Actor Class 207

Game Design: Adding Our CastingDirector.java class...208

List and ArrayList: Using java.util List Management..208

    The Java Interface: Defining Rules for Implementing Your Class 209

    The List<E> Public Interface: A List Collection of Java Objects 210

Set and HashSet: Using java.util Unordered Sets 212

The java.util HashSet Class: Using Unordered Sets of Objects 212

Creating Your Casting Engine: CastingDirector.java 213

Creating an ArrayList Object: CURRENT_CAST Data Store List 214

Another ArrayList Object: COLLIDE_CHECKLIST Data Store List 218

Creating a HashSet Object: REMOVED_ACTORS Data Store Set<Actor> 219

CastingDirector() Constructor: Having NetBeans Write the Code 221

Creating Our Main Actor: The Bagel Hero Subclass 223

Summary 227

■Chapter 11: Moving Your Action Figure in 2D: Controlling the X and Y Display Screen Coordinates 229

InvinciBagel.java Redesign: Adding Logical Methods 230

The Scene Event Handling Method: .createSceneEventHandling() 231

Adding InvinciBagel: Declare Image, Bagel, and CastingDirector 233

The Actor Image Assets Loading Method: .loadImageAssets() 234

Creating Your InvinciBagel Bagel Object: .createGameActors() 235

Adding Your iBagel to the Scene Graph: .addGameActorNodes() 237

Creating and Managing Your Cast: .createCastingDirection() 238

Create and Start Your GamePlayLoop: .createStartGameLoop 239

Update Splashscreen Scene Graph: .createSplashScreenNodes() 240

Powering the iBagel Actor: Using the GamePlayLoop 242

Moving the iBagel Actor Object: Coding Your .update() Method 243

Testing Our New Game Design: Moving InvinciBagel 246

Summary 249

■Chapter 12: Setting Boundaries for Your Action Figure in 2D: Using the Node Class LocalToParent Attribute 251

InvinciBagel Privatization: Removing Static Modifiers 252

Passing Context from InvinciBagel to Bagel: Using this Keyword 254

Removing a Static iBagel Reference: Revise the Handle() Method 258

Using this in GamePlayLoop() Constructor: GamePlayLoop(this) 260

Removing the Rest of the Static Variables: StackPane and HBox 261

Organizing the .update() Method: .moveInvinciBagel() 265

    Further Modularization of the .update() Method: .setXYLocation() 266

Setting Screen Boundaries: .setBoundaries() Method 267

    Testing the InvinciBagel Sprite Boundaries: Run ➤ Project 270

Summary 270

■Chapter 13: Animating Your Action Figure States: Setting the Image
States Based on KeyEvent Processing 273

InvinciBagel Animation: The .setImageState() Method 274

    The InvinciBagel Wait State: If No Key Pressed Set imageState(0)..274

    The InvinciBagel Run State: If KeyPressed Set imageState(1 & 2) 276

    The InvinciBagel Fly State: If KeyPressed Set imageState(3 & 4)...277

    Mirroring Sprites: Quadrupling Your Image Assets from 9 to 36..278

    Animating Your Run Cycle: Creating a Nested If-Else Structure 279

    Coding Your Run Cycle Throttle: Triple Nested If-Else Structures 283

Adding Event Handling: Giving ASDW Keys Function 289

    Creating ASDW Key Get and Set Methods: NetBeans Insert Code 291

    Adding Jump and Evade Animation: Using the W and S Keys 293

Last Minute Details: Setting the isFlipH Property 294

    Testing the InvinciBagel Sprite Animation States: Run ➤ Project 295

Summary 298

■Chapter 14: Setting Up the Game Environment: Creating Fixed Sprite
Classes Using the Actor Superclass 299

Creating the Prop.java Class: Extending Actor.java 300

    Mirrored Prop Classes: Set the isFlip Property in the Constructor 304

Using the Prop Class: Creating Fixed Scene Objects...310

    Adding Prop and Image Declarations: Prop and Image Objects 310

    Instantiate Image Objects: Using the .loadImageAssets() Method..312

    Adding Fixed Sprites Using Prop Objects: .addGameActors()...312

Using Larger Scene Props: Compositing with JavaFX..317

Summary..320

■**Chapter 15: Implementing Game Audio Assets: Using the JavaFX AudioClip Class Audio Sequencing Engine** **323**

JavaFX AudioClip Class: A Digital Audio Sequencer 324

Creating and Optimizing Digital Audio: Audacity 2.0.6 325

    Optimization Versus Compression: The Audio Memory Footprint 327

Adding Audio to InvinciBagel.java: Using AudioClip 333

    Referencing AudioClip Assets: Using the java.net.URL Class 333

    Adding Your Audio Asset Loading Method: .loadAudioAssets() 335

    Providing Access to Your AudioClip: The .playiSound() Methods 338

Summary 341

■**Chapter 16: Collision Detection: Creating SVG Polygons for the Game Actors and Writing Code to Detect Collision** **343**

The SVG Data Format: Hand Coding Vector Shapes 344

Creating and Optimizing Collision Data: Using GIMP 345

    Creating an Optimized Collision Polygon: Using the Path Tool 352

    Refining SVG Path Collision Shapes in GIMP: Using Import Path 356

Creating and Optimizing Physics Data: Using PhysEd 363

Replacing Dummy Collision Data: InvinciBagel.java 365

Bagel Class Collision Detection: .checkCollision() 370

Locating a Node Object: Using the Bounds Object 372

    Using Node Local Bounds: The .getBoundsInLocal() Method 373

    Using Node Parent Bounds: The .getBoundsInParent() Method 373

    Using Node Intersection: The .intersects(Bounds object) Method 374

Using Shape Class Intersect: The .intersect() Method 374

Overriding the Abstract Hero Class: .collide() Method 375

    If Collision Detected: Manipulating the CastingDirector Object 378

    Removing Actors from the Scene Graph: .getChildren().remove() 380

    Reset the Removed Actor List: .resetRemovedActors() Method 384

    Optimizing Collision Detection Processing: if(collide(object)) 385

Optimizing the Scene Graph: Using the Group Class 386

Creating a Scoring Engine Method: .scoringEngine() 389

Summary 390

■ **Chapter 17: Enhancing Game Play: Creating a Scoring Engine, Adding Treasure and an Enemy Auto-Attack Engine** 393

Creating the Score UI Design: Text and Font Objects 394

Creating a SCORE Label: Adding the Second Text Object 397

Creating the Scoring Engine Logic: .scoringEngine() 399

Optimizing the scoringEngine() Method: Using Logical If Else If 402

Adding Bounty to the Game: The Treasure.java Class..403

Using the Treasure Class: Create Treasure Objects in the Game 404

Adding Treasure Collision Detection: Updating .scoringEngine() 406

Adding Enemies: The Enemy and Projectile Classes 407

Creating Cream Cheese Bullets: Coding a Projectile.java Class 409

Adding an Enemy and Projectiles to the Game: InvinciBagel.java...410

Adding a Background Image: Using .toBack() Method..413

Using Random Number Generators: java.util.Random 416

Mounting the Attack: Coding the Enemy Onslaught 417

The Foundation of an Enemy Class Attack: The .update() Method 418

Attacking on Both Sides of the Screen: .initiateAttack() Method 419

Adding the Element of Surprise: Animating Your Enemy Attack 424

Weaponizing the Enemy: Shooting Projectile Objects 429

Creating a Projectile Infrastructure: Adding Projectile Variables 431

Invoking a .shootProjectile() Method: Setting shootBullet to True..433

Shooting Projectiles: Coding the .shootProjectile() Method 434

Making the Enemy Pause Before Firing: pauseCounter Variable 435

Shoot the Bullet: Pulling the Trigger Using the launchIt Variable..436

Update the .scoringEngine() Method: Using .equals() 437

Adding Bullets to a Clip: Updating .addCurrentCast() 439

Shooting Cream Cheese Balls: Different Bullet Types 443

Tweaking a Game: Fine-Tuning the User Experience 446

    Randomizing an Auto-Attack: Using .nextBoolean with takeSides 447

    Add the Element of Surprise: Randomizing the Attack Frequency 448

    Targeting the InvinciBagel: Adding Enemy Artificial Intelligence 449

Adding Gravity to the Bullets: Intro to Game Physics 451

Summary 453

Index 455

About the Author

Wallace Jackson has been writing for leading multimedia publications about his work in new media content development since the advent of *Multimedia Producer Magazine* nearly two decades ago, when he wrote about advanced computer processor architecture for an issue centerfold (removable "mini-issue" insert) distributed at the SIGGRAPH trade show. Since then, Wallace has written for a number of other popular publications about his work in interactive 3D and new media advertising campaign design, including *3D Artist Magazine, Desktop Publishers Journal, CrossMedia Magazine, AVvideo/Multimedia Producer Magazine, Digital Signage Magazine* and *Kiosk Magazine.*

Wallace Jackson has authored a half-dozen Android book titles for Apress, including four titles in the popular Pro Android series. This particular Java 8 programming title focuses on the Java and JavaFX programming languages **that** are used with Android (and all other popular platforms as well) so that developers can "code once, deliver everywhere."

Wallace Jackson is currently the CEO of Mind Taffy Design, a new media content production and digital campaign design and development agency, located in North Santa Barbara County, halfway between their clientele in Silicon Valley to the North and in Hollywood, "The OC," and San Diego to the South.

Mind Taffy Design has created open source technology-based (HTML5, JavaScript, Java 8, JavaFX 8, and Android 5) digital new media content deliverables for more than two decades (since 1991) for a significant number of leading branded manufacturers worldwide, including Sony, Tyco, Samsung, IBM, Dell, Epson, Nokia, TEAC, Sun, Micron, SGI and Mitsubishi.

Wallace Jackson received his undergraduate degree in **Business Economics** from the University of California at Los Angeles (UCLA). He received his graduate degree in **MIS Design and Implementation** from University of Southern California (USC). Mr. Jackson also received his post-graduate degree in **Marketing Strategy** at USC and completed the **USC Graduate Entrepreneurship Program**. The USC degrees were completed while at USC's night-time Marshall School of Business MBA Program, which allowed Mr. Jackson to work full-time as a programmer, while he completed his graduate and post-graduate business degrees.

About the Technical Reviewer

Chád (shod) Darby is an author, instructor, and speaker in the Java development world. As a recognized authority on Java applications and architectures, he has presented technical sessions at software development conferences worldwide (United Kingdom, United Kingdom, India, Russia, and Australia). In his fifteen years as a professional software architect, he's had the opportunity to work for Blue Cross/Blue Shield, Merck, Boeing, Red Hat, and a handful of startup companies.

Chád is a contributing author to several Java books, including *Professional Java E-Commerce* (Wrox Press), *Beginning Java Networking* (Wrox Press), and *XML and Web Services Unleashed* (Sams Publishing). Chád has Java certifications from Sun Microsystems and IBM. He holds a B.S. in Computer Science from Carnegie Mellon University.

Visit Chád's blog at www.luv2code.com to view his free video tutorials on Java. You can also follow him on Twitter @darbyluvs2code.

Acknowledgments

I would like to acknowledge all my fantastic Editors, and their support staff at Apress, who worked those long hours and toiled so very hard on this book, to make it the ultimate Absolute Beginner Android application production book title.

Steve Anglin, for his work as the **Lead Editor** on the book, and for recruiting me to write programming titles at Apress covering the most popular open source application development platforms (Android and Java).

Matthew Moodie, for his work as the **Development Editor** on the book, and for his experience and guidance during the process of making this book one of the great Java 8 Game Development titles currently on the market.

Mark Powers, for his work as the **Coordinating Editor** on the book, and for his constant diligence in making sure I either hit my chapter delivery deadlines or surpassed them.

Lisa Vecchione and **Karen Jameson**, for their work as the **Copy Editors** for the book, and for their careful attention to excruciatingly minute details, and for conforming the text to the current Apress book writing standards.

Chád Darby, for his work as the **Technical Reviewer** on the book, and for making sure that I did not make any Java programming mistakes, because Java code with mistakes does not run properly, if at all, unless the Java code includes very lucky mistakes, which is quite rare in computer programming these days.

Anna Ishchenko, for her work as the **Book Cover Designer** for the book, and for creating the graphic design for the book cover that brings it into conformance with other popular Apress Java 8 and JavaFX 8 programming titles.

Ira H. Harrison Rubin, a friend and client, and one of the world's finest and most respected comic book and comic strip authors, for allowing us to use some of his BagelToons IP (intellectual property), specifically an InvinciBagel concept, to use as a platform to show our readers how a game can be created around an actual client's intellectual property. Be sure not to create your own InvinciBagel game without checking with Mr. Rubin regarding using his intellectual property!

Patrick Harrington, a friend and client, and one of the world's finest caricature artists, for creating the 2D assets for the InvinciBagel game, and allowing me to use some of them to show how to create a basic Java 8 game engine.

Andreas Loew, a fellow Apress author, for allowing me to use his CodeAndWeb GmbH product PhysicsEditor, or PhysEd, in Chapter 16 of the book to show an alternate professional collision polygon development tool work process.

Finally, I'd like to acknowledge **Oracle** for acquiring Sun Microsystems, and continuing to enhance Java 8, so that it remains the premiere open source programming language, and for acquiring the JavaFX new media engine, and making it a part of Java 8, so that existing Java applications can be "gamified" and made "edutainment" friendly.

Introduction

The Java Programming Language is currently the most popular object-oriented (OOP) programming language in the world today. Java runs on everything from SmartWatches to HD Smartphones to Touchscreen Tablets to eBook Readers to Game Consoles to SmartGlasses to Ultra-High Definition (UHD) 4K Interactive Television Sets, with even more types of consumer electronics devices, such as those found in the automotive, appliances, health care, digital signage, security, and the home automation market, increasingly adopting the open source Java platform for use in their hardware devices as time goes on.

Since there are literally billions of Java compatible consumer electronics devices, owned by billions of users all over the world, it stands to reason that developing popular Java 8 Games for all of these people could be an extremely lucrative undertaking, given that you have the right game concept, artwork, game design, and optimization work process, of course.

Java 8 (and its multimedia engine, JavaFX 8) code can run on just about every operating system out there, including Windows XP; Vista, 7, 8, and 9; all Linux distributions; 32-bit Android 4 and 64-bit Android 5; Open Solaris; Macintosh OS/X, iOS; Symbian, and Raspberry Pi – it's only a matter of time before the other popular OSes add support for this popular open source programming language. Additionally, every popular Internet browser has Java built in! Java provides the ultimate flexibility in installing software, as an application, or in the browser as an applet. You can even drag a Java application right out of the browser, and have it install itself on that user's desktop! Java 8 is a truly remarkable technology.

There are a plethora of embedded and desktop hardware support levels currently for Java 8 (and for JavaFX 8.0) including the full Java SE 8, Java SE 8 Embedded, Java ME (Micro Edition) 8, and Java ME 8 Embedded, as well as Java EE 8 for Enterprise Application Development. Talk about being able to "code once, deliver everywhere!" That is the dream of every programmer, and Oracle is making it a reality with the powerful Java 8 multimedia programming platform.

This book will go a long way toward helping you to learn exactly how to go about developing Java 8 games, using the Java programming language in conjunction with the recently added JavaFX 8.0 multimedia engine. These Java 8 game applications will be able to run across a plethora of Java compatible consumer electronics devices. Developing Java 8 game applications that play smoothly across all of these different types of consumer electronics devices requires a very specific work process, including asset design, game code design, and optimization, all of which I will be covering during this book.

I wrote the Beginning Java 8 Game Development title from scratch, using a real-world client game project that I am actually working on, and will be delivering to the public sometime in 2015. I am targeting those readers who are Beginning Game Developers, and who had not coded in Java 8 and JavaFX 8.0. These readers are technically savvy, but they are not that familiar with object-oriented computer programming concepts and techniques. Since Java is now at Version 8u40, this book will be more advanced than many of the other Java books out there. Java 8 has added some very advanced features, such as the JavaFX 8.0 API, which gives Java 8 its own multimedia engine, supporting SVG, 2D, 3D, audio, and video media.

I designed this book to contain a comprehensive overview of the optimal Java 8 game development work process. Most beginning Java application development books only cover the language, however. If you really want to become that well-known Java game application developer that you seek to become, you will have to understand as well as master all of the areas of game design, including multimedia asset creation, user interface design, Java 8 Programming, JavaFX 8.0 class usage, and data footprint, memory, and CPU usage optimization. Once you've mastered these areas – hopefully, by the end of this book, you will be able to create the memorable user experience that will be required to create popular, best-selling Java 8 games. You can do it; I know you can!

Java 8 games are not only developed using the NetBeans 8.0 Integrated Development Environment (IDE) alone, but also in conjunction with the use of JavaFX 8 and several other different types of new media content development software packages. For this reason, this book covers the installation and use of a wide variety of other popular open source software packages, such as GIMP 2.8 and Audacity 2.0.6, in conjunction with developing Java 8 game applications using the NetBeans 8.0 IDE and the JavaFX new media engine, which brings the "wow factor" to the Java programming language.

I am architecting this book in this fashion so that you can ascertain precisely how your usage of new media content development software will fit into your overall Java 8 game development work process. This comprehensive approach will serve to set this unique book title distinctly apart from all of those other Java 8 game application development titles that are currently out on the market. The book starts out in Chapter 1 with downloading and installing the latest Java 8 JDK as well as the NetBeans 8.0 IDE, along with several popular open source content development applications.

In Chapter 2, you will learn about NetBeans 8.0, and create your first Java 8 game application, and look at useful NetBeans features, such as code completion and code profiling. In Chapter 3, you will learn about the fundamentals of the Java 8 programming language, which you'll be implementing to create a Java 8 game during the remainder of the book.

In Chapter 4, you will learn all about the JavaFX 8.0 new media engine (API) and how its impressive features can take your Java 8 game development and place it into the stratosphere. In Chapter 5, you will learn all about the JavaFX 8 FXML (Java FX Markup Language) and about the underlying concepts of developing new media assets such as digital audio, digital images, digital video, 2D scalable vector graphics (SVG), and 3D geometry, for use with Java 8 games. In Chapter 6, you will learn about game design concepts, and create the foundation for your Java 8 game, its user interface, and a splashscreen. Thus the first third of this book is foundational material, which you'll need to be able to understand how NetBeans 8.0, Java 8, JavaFX 8.0, and various new media asset types supported by the JavaFX engine function together as a platform.

In Chapter 7 we will start to create the various game engines, starting with the game play loop 60 FPS timing engine, and we will learn about the JavaFX 8 Animation, Timeline, KeyFrame, KeyValue, Interpolator, and AnimationTimer classes, which allow the Java 8 game to tap into the JavaFX pulse event timing engine that gives Java 8 its multimedia power.

In Chapter 8, we will create your game Actor and Hero Java abstract classes, the Actor engine, if you will, which will allow us to create the different types of game play components that we will need for the Java 8 game. This will teach you how to create custom foundational classes for a game project, and you will look at the Node, SVGPath, Shape, Image, and ImageView classes as we incorporate these JavaFX class (object) types into our Java 8 Game Actor design.

In Chapter 9, you will learn how to add interactivity to your Java 8 Game projects, using event handling. We will add an event processing engine, which will process all of the different types of action, key, mouse, and drag events that you are likely to utilize in your Java 8 game development work process in the future when you create your own custom games.

In Chapter 10, you will learn about Java List, Set, and Array classes. These are called Java collections, and we will create a custom Actor management engine, which we will call the CastingDirector class, during this chapter. This will allow you to automate the task of keeping track of the cast of your game for each level, and will be used for collision detection.

In Chapter 11 we will start coding our primary Actor class for the InvinciBagel character, and add Java 8 code that controls movement on the screen, so that we can start to work on fusing character animation with game player key use so that we can allow our game players to control the InvinciBagel character completely. This involves "wiring up" the Bagel class to the GamePlayLoop (game play timing class created in Chapter 7) class, so we can start working in the fourth dimension of time.

In Chapter 12 you will use your Actor and Hero abstract classes that you created in Chapter 8 to create the InvinciBagel primary character and his Bagel.java class, as well as learn how to implement code that sets the boundaries for your Java 8 game, so that the Actor does not go off the screen, forcing him stay inside of the field of play for the game.

In Chapter 13 you will add different InvinciBagel sprite image states into your Java 8 game, and when these are combined with the movement you coded in Chapters 11 and 12, allow your InvinciBagel character to run, jump, fly, land, wait impatiently to be moved, and even turn sideways to evade bullets.

In Chapter 14, you will create a series of Prop classes that will allow you to place fixed props and obstacles into your Java 8 game levels. You will learn how to use one digital image asset to create four different scenery props, using the JavaFX ability to flip and mirror your image assets around either (or both of) their X and Y axes.

In Chapter 15, you'll implement your Java 8 game audio engine, using the JavaFX AudioClip class, which allows digital audio sequencing to be integrated into your Java 8 game play, taking it an order of magnitude higher, by stimulating the aural senses of your game player. You'll learn how to optimize digital audio assets so well, that you will not have to use any lossy compression, giving you perfect audio samples, and showing you exactly how much of the system's memory your audio assets will be using.

In Chapter 16, we'll start getting into advanced topics, such as designing collision polygons using SVG data and the GIMP 2.8 and PhysicsEditor software packages. We will also learn about the JavaFX Bounds and Node classes, and how collision detection is accomplished for Java 8 game development, using the .getBoundsInLocal() and .getBoundsInParent() method calls, in conjunction with the Node.intersects() and Shape.intersect() method calls.

In Chapter 17, we will pull everything together, and focus solely on implementing your game play. You will create Actor subclasses for Treasure, Projectile, and Enemy, and create an auto-attack engine that will turn a game player's PC or mobile device into his or her adversary. We look at the most advanced topics, such as physics and AI, during this chapter, after which you will have enough of a foundation to create your own Java 8 games, using your own intellectual property!

This book attempts to be the most comprehensive Java 8 game application development programming title on the market, by covering most, if not all, of the major Java 8 and JavaFX classes that will need to be used to create Java 8 Game Applications. Some of these include the Image, ImageView, Group, Node, StackPane, Scene, Stage, Application, ListArray, HashSet, Arrays, AudioClip, MediaPlayer, URL, Button, Shape, HBox, SVGPath, Insets, AnimationTimer, and more.

If you're looking for the most comprehensive, up-to-date overview of the Java 8 programming language for games, including JavaFX 8.0 and NetBeans 8.0 IDE all seamlessly integrated with new media content development work processes, as well as a "soup to nuts" knowledge about how to optimally use these technologies in conjunction with the leading open source new media game content design and development tools, then this book will really be of significant interest to you.

It is the intention of this book to take you from being a Beginner in Java 8 game application development to a solid intermediate knowledge level regarding Java 8, NetBeans 8, and JavaFX 8.0 game application development. Be advised that this book, even though it's ostensibly a Beginner title, contains a significant amount of technical knowledge. All of the work processes that are described during the book may well take more than one read through to assimilate into an application development knowledge base (your quiver of technical knowledge). It will be well worth your time, however, rest assured.

CHAPTER 1

■ ■ ■

Setting Up a Java 8 Game Development Environment

Welcome to the book *Beginning Java 8 Games Development*! Let's get started by creating a solid development software foundation for use with this book. The core of this foundation will be **Java SDK** (**Software Development Kit**) **8**, also called **JDK** (**Java Development Kit**) **8**. I will also set you up with **NetBeans IDE 8.0** (**Integrated Development Environment**), which will make coding Java 8 games much easier. After that, I will introduce you to the latest open-source new media content creation software packages for digital illustration (Inkscape), digital imaging (GIMP [GNU Image Manipulation Program]), digital video (EditShare Lightworks), digital audio (Audacity), and 3D modeling and animation (Blender). At the end of the chapter, I will also suggest some other professional-level software packages that you should consider adding to the professional game development workstation that you will be creating over the course of this chapter.

To get the best results from all this free, professional-level software, you will want to have a modern, **64-bit** workstation with at least 4GB of system memory (6GB or 8GB would be even better) and a **multicore** processor (central processing unit [CPU]), such as an AMD FX-6300 (hexa-core), AMD FX-8350 (octa-core), or Intel i7 (quad-core). Workstations such as these have become commodity items and can be purchased at Walmart or Pricewatch.com at an affordable price.

The first thing that you will do in this chapter is make sure that you have **removed** any of the **outdated versions** of Java, such as Java 7 or Java 6, or any outdated versions of NetBeans, such as NetBeans 7 or NetBeans 6. This involves **uninstalling** (removing or deleting completely) these older development software versions from your workstation.

You will do this using the Windows program management utility **Programs and Features**, which can be found in the Windows operating system (OS) **Control Panel** suite of **Windows OS Management Utilities**. There are similar utilities on the Linux and Mac platforms, if you happen to be using one of these less commonly used OSs. Because most developers use Windows 7, 8, or 9, you will be using the Windows 64-bit platform for the examples in this book.

Next, I will show you where exactly to go on the Internet to get these software packages, so get ready to fire up your speedy Internet connection so that you can download nearly a gigabyte of all-new game content production software! After you download the latest versions of all this software, you will install the programming and content development packages and configure them for use with this book.

The order in which you perform these software installations is important, because Java JDK 8 and Java 8 Runtime Environment (JRE) form the foundation of NetBeans IDE 8.0. This is because NetBeans IDE 8.0 was originally coded using the Java programming language, so you will see just how incredibly professional a piece of software can be using this language. Thus, the Java 8 software will be the first software you install.

After you install Java 8, you will then install NetBeans 8.0, so that you have a graphical user interface (GUI), on top of the Java programming language, which will make the Java software development work process easier. After you have these two primary software development tools installed, you will get a plethora of new media content creation software packages, which you can use in conjunction with Java 8 and NetBeans 8.0 to create 2D and 3D games.

Prepare a Workstation for Java 8 Game Development

Assuming that you already have a professional-level workstation in place for new media content development and game development, you need to remove all the outdated JDKs and IDEs and make sure that you have the latest V8 (not the drink, silly!) Java and NetBeans software installed on your system and ready to go. If you are new to this and do not have a game-appropriate workstation, go to Walmart or Pricewatch.com, and purchase an affordable multicore (use a 4-, 6- or 8-core) 64-bit computer running Windows 8.1 (or 9.0 if it is available) that has 4GB, 6GB, or 8GB of DDR3 (1333 or 1600 memory access speed) system memory at the very least and a 750GB, or even 1TB, hard disk drive.

The way that you remove old software is through the Windows **Control Panel** and its set of utility icons, one of which is the **Programs and Features** icon (Windows 7 and 8), displayed in Figure 1-1. Note that in earlier versions of Windows, this utility icon may be labeled differently, probably as something like **Add or Remove Programs**.

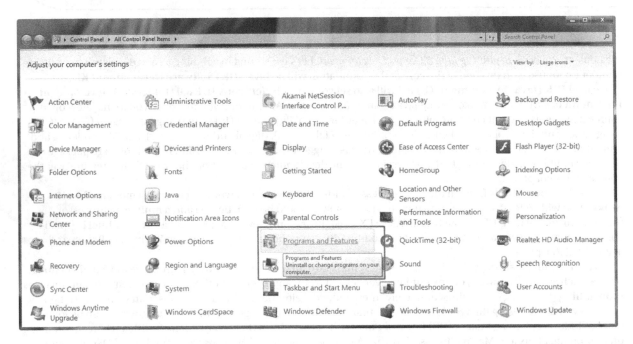

Figure 1-1. *Use the Programs and Features utility icon to uninstall or change programs on your computer workstation*

Click the Programs and Features link, or double-click the icon in previous versions of Windows, to launch the utility. Then, scroll down to see if you have any old versions of the Java development tools (Java 5, Java 6, or Java 7) installed on your workstation. Note that if you have a brand new workstation, you should find no preinstalled versions of Java or NetBeans on your system. If you do find them, return the system, as it may have been used previously!

As you can see in Figure 1-2, on my Windows 7 HTML5 development workstation, I had an older version of Java, Java 7, installed (on November 29, 2013), taking up 344MB of space. To remove a piece of software, **select it** by clicking it (it will turn light blue), and then click the **Uninstall** button, shown at the top of the figure. I left the **tool tip**, which says, "**Uninstall this program**," showing in the screenshot so that you can see that if you **hover** your mouse over anything in the Programs and Features utility, it will tell you what that feature is used for.

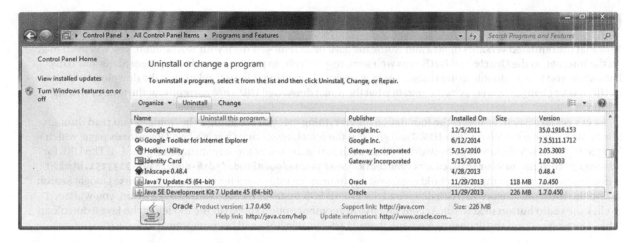

Figure 1-2. *Select any version of Java older than the current version (Java 8), and click the Uninstall button at the top*

Once you click the Uninstall button, the utility will remove the older version of Java. If you want to keep your old Java project files, make sure to back up your Java project files folder (if you have not done so already, that is). Make sure that you back up your workstation's hard disk drive regularly so that you do not lose any of your work.

Also make sure that you uninstall all versions of Java; in my case, there were 64-bit Java 7 update 45 and Java SDK 7u45, used to run or execute IDEs, such as NetBeans (or Eclipse), that were coded using the Java programming language.

Next, you will want to ascertain if there are any older versions of the NetBeans IDE on your workstation. In my case, as you can see in Figure 1-3, there was indeed a NetBeans 7 IDE installation currently on my 64-bit Windows 7 workstation. I selected this for removal and then clicked the **Uninstall/Change** button, shown at left, which brought up a custom **Uninstall Summary** dialog, shown at right.

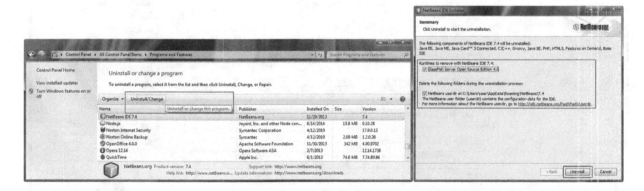

Figure 1-3. *Find and select any version of NetBeans that is older than version 8.0; also, uninstall old GlassFish versions*

Manufacturers (in this case, the NetBeans development team) can create custom Uninstall Summary dialogs for their products to use during the uninstall process, as you can see here. This dialog allows you to select whether you want to uninstall GlassFish Server 4 and the NetBeans **UserDir Configuration** folder. Because you are installing new versions of NetBeans and GlassFish, select both check boxes, and then click the **Uninstall** button.

Downloading Java JDK 8 and NetBeans 8.0

Now that the outdated versions of Java and NetBeans have been removed from your workstation, you will need to go on the Internet, to the **Oracle** and **NetBeans** web sites, respectively, to get the latest development SDKs and IDEs. I will show you how to do this using Google's search engine (I am using this method in case the download links, or URLs, ever change) as well as demonstrate what the direct download URLs are currently, at the time of writing this book.

Let's get Java 8 first, as that is the foundation for everything that you are going to be doing as you read through this book. A Google search for **Java JDK 8** will give you the search result that Oracle's Java **Downloads** page, which is located in the Oracle Technology Network section, as shown at the top of the screenshot in Figure 1-4. The URL for this page is currently **www.oracle.com/technetwork/java/javase/downloads/jdk8-downloads-2133151.html**. It is important to note that this URL could change at any time in the future and that you can always use Google Search to find the latest one. Before you can download the 170MB SDK installer file for Windows 7/8 64-bit, you will need to click the **radio button** next to the **Accept License Agreement** option shown at the top left of the Java 8 download table. Once you accept the license agreement, these 11 OS-specific links will become activated for use.

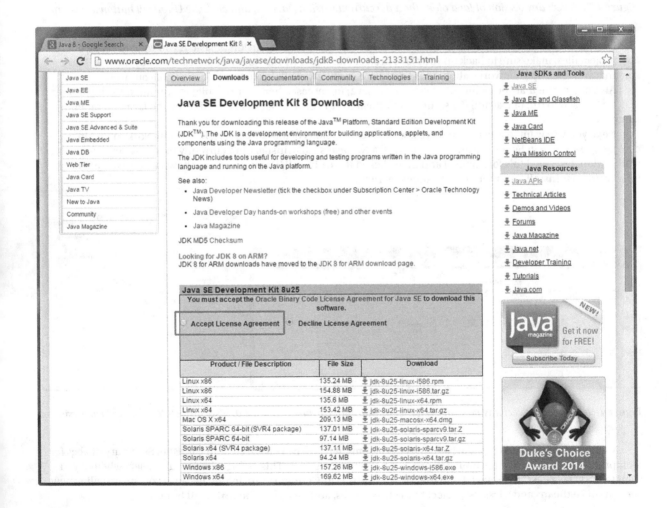

Figure 1-4. *Google the term "Java JDK 8," open the JDK 8 Downloads page, and select Accept License Agreement*

Be sure to match the Java JDK 8 software that you download to your OS and bit level (**x86** signifies a **32-bit**-level OS). Most modern-day workstations use a **64-bit** Linux, Mac, Solaris (Oracle), Windows 7, or Windows 8 OS. This will be specified with the **x64** delineation after the name of the OS.

To find out the bit level of the OS, on **Windows 7**, open the **Start Menu,** right-click the **Computer** entry, and select the **Properties** option, at the bottom of the context-sensitive menu. On Windows 8, you click **Start** (a window pane icon at the bottom left of your desktop if you are in Windows 7 desktop mode) and then the **down-arrow icon** at the bottom left, then click the **PC Settings** purple gear icon and finally the **PC Info** entry at the bottom left of the screen. In both use cases, there should then be a text entry that says **System type** and either **32-bit Operating System** or **64-bit Operating System**.

Now that you have downloaded the Java JDK 8 installer, the next thing that you need to do is download is NetBeans IDE 8.0. Do a Google search for the term **NetBeans 8.0**, as is shown at the top of Figure 1-5, and click the **Download** search result option, which will take you to the NetBeans IDE 8.0.1 Download page (currently `https://netbeans.org/downloads`). If you want to keep both tabs open in the browser, as I did, then right-click the **Download** link, and select the **Open link in new tab** option.

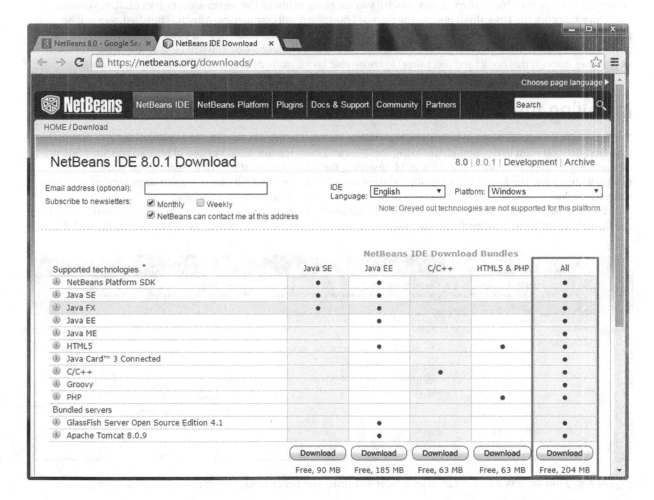

Figure 1-5. *Google the term "NetBeans 8.0," open the NetBeans IDE 8.0.1 Download page, and download all versions*

Once you are on the NetBeans IDE 8.0 Download page, select the **language** and **platform** (OS) that you are using from the drop-down menus at the top right of the page. I chose **English** and **Windows**. Now, you can click one of the three **Download** buttons at the bottom of the page to download a NetBeans IDE 8.0 that supports JavaFX 8 new media (and that will therefore support game development) programming language (application programming interface [API]). You will learn more about what an API is in Chapter 3, when I cover the Java programming language in detail.

If you are only going to develop Java SE (Standard Edition) and JavaFX applications (games) for **individuals**, then click the first button. If you are going to develop Java EE (Enterprise Edition) and JavaFX applications (games) for **enterprise** (business), then click the second button. If you are going to develop both JavaFX and HTML5 applications (games), which is what I do for my business, then you click the fifth **Download** button, and download the "All" version of NetBeans IDE 8.0. This version will allow you to develop in all the programming languages supported by NetBeans!

Because the NetBeans IDE is free, and your workstation hard disk drive can handle huge amounts of data, I recommend that you install this 204MB **All** version of the IDE, in case you ever find that you need any of the other capabilities that NetBeans IDE 8.0 is able to provide for you as a software developer (Java EE, Java ME, PHP, HTML5, Groovy, GlassFish, Tomcat, C++). This is an extra 120MB if you are going to install the client-side, or Java SE IDE, version, but is less than 20MB of extra disk space if you are going to install the server-side, or Java EE IDE, version.

Once you click the **Download** button, the software download will commence. After it is finished, you will be ready to install Java 8 and then NetBeans IDE 8.0. Finally, to complete the setup of your comprehensive Java 8 game development workstation, you will get some ancillary new media content tools. You will be able to use the workstation as you read through this book (and thereafter) to create epic Java 8 game deliverables! This is getting exciting!

Installing the Java 8 Software Development Environment

NetBeans IDE 8.0 requires Java to be installed in order to function (run), so you will need to install the JDK and JRE first. Because you want to develop games using the latest and most feature-filled version of Java, so you are going to be installing Java 8, which was released in 2014. Installing the latest version of software ensures that you have the newest features and the fewest bugs possible. Make sure to check often that you are using the latest version of all your software packages; after all, these are open source and free to download, upgrade, and use!

The first step is to find where you downloaded your installer files to on your system. The default should be set to the **Download** folder in Windows. I downloaded mine to a C:/Clients/Java8 folder, as you can see in Figure 1-6.

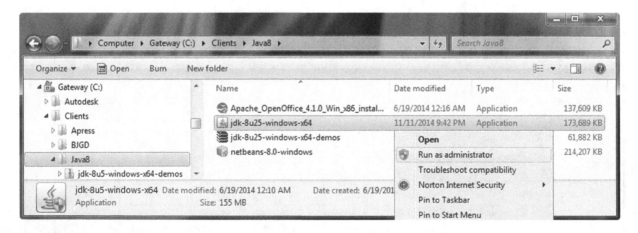

Figure 1-6. _Find the JDK 8 install file on your hard disk drive, right-click it, and select Run as administrator_

The file will be named using the format **jdk-version-platform-bitlevel**, so find the latest version (in this case, it was jdk-8u25-windows-x64). Right-click it, and select the **Run as administrator** option so that the installer has all the OS "permissions" that it needs to create folders, transfer files into them, and the like.

Once you launch the installer, you will see the **Welcome** dialog, shown in Figure 1-7 (left). Click the **Next** button to advance to the **Select Features to Install** dialog, shown in Figure 1-7 (right), and accept the defaults.

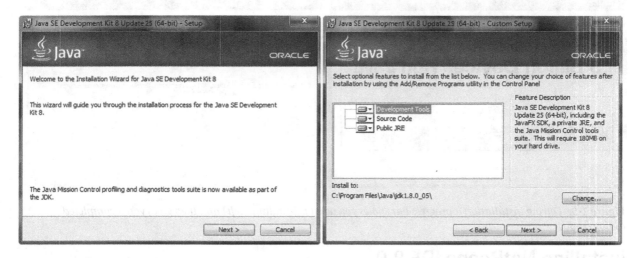

Figure 1-7. *Click Next in the Welcome dialog to advance to the Select Features to Install dialog, and then click the Next button*

As you can see, the installer will install **180MB** of software into the **C:\ProgramFiles\Java\jdk1.8.0_25** folder on your workstation. Click the **Next** button to start the installation process, which will extract the installation files and then copy them onto your system, using an animated progress bar, as displayed in Figure 1-8 (left).

Figure 1-8. *Java 8 installation will extract and copy install files (left) and then suggest the installation directory (right)*

After the Java SDK is installed on your system, you will get the **JRE** installation dialog, which is presented in Figure 1-8 (right). Make sure that you accept the default installation location for this JRE; it should be installed in the **\Java\jre8** folder. It is best to allow Oracle (Java SDK) to put the software in an industry standard folder location, as other software packages that you will be using that use this JRE, such as NetBeans IDE 8.0, will be looking for it there first. Click the **Next** button to install the JRE.

The installation will show a progress bar during the install, as seen in Figure 1-9 (left). When it is finished, it will display the **Successfully Installed** dialog, shown in Figure 1-9 (right). If you want to access tutorials, API documentation, developer guides, version release notes, and so on, you can click the **Next Steps** button.

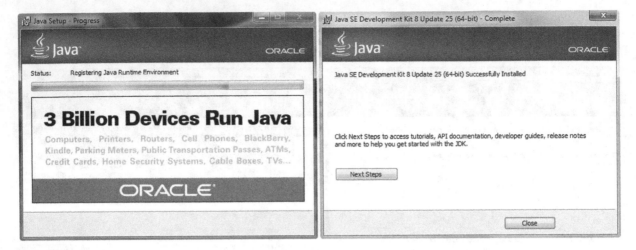

Figure 1-9. *During installation a progress bar shows you what is installing (left) and then gives you a completed dialog (right)*

Installing NetBeans IDE 8.0

Now, you are ready to install NetBeans, so locate your `netbeans-8.0-windows` file (see Figure 1-6. Right-click it, and select the **Run as administrator** option to launch the installer. Once it is launched, you will see the dialog shown in Figure 1-10, which gives you a **Customize** button that you can use to customize the install.

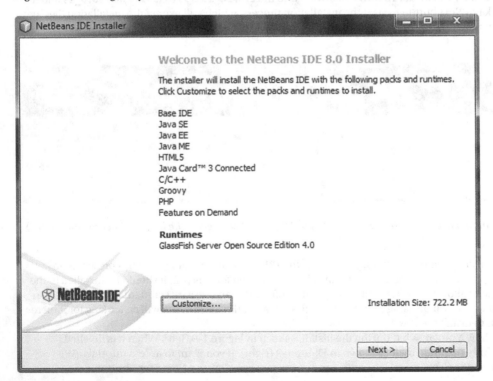

Figure 1-10. *The Welcome to the NetBeans IDE 8.0 Installer dialog*

Click the **Next** button to begin the default (full) installation, and you will get the **NetBeans IDE 8.0 License Agreement** dialog, shown in Figure 1-11 (left). Select the **I accept the terms in the license agreement** check box, and click the **Next** button to advance to the **JUnit License Agreement** dialog, shown in Figure 1-11 (right).

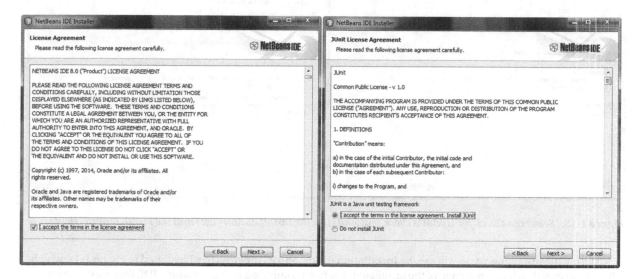

Figure 1-11. *Accept the terms of the license agreement, click the Next button (left), and then do the same for JUnit (right)*

In the JUnit License Agreement dialog, presented in Figure 1-11 (right), click the **radio button** next to the **I accept the terms in the license agreement** statement, and click the **Next** button to proceed with the installation. The next two installer dialogs, illustrated in Figure 1-12, will allow you to specify where NetBeans 8.0 and GlassFish 4.0 will be installed on your system. I suggest accepting the default installation locations in these two dialogs as well. As you will notice, the NetBeans installer has found your Java installation in its default location as well.

Figure 1-12. *Accept the default installation directory suggestions for NetBeans IDE (left) and GlassFish 4.0 (right)*

Once you accept these default installation locations and click the **Next** button to advance through these dialogs, you will get a **Summary** dialog, shown in Figure 1-13 (left). This dialog contains an **Install** button, which will trigger the installation that you have set up over the previous five NetBeans IDE 8.0 installation dialogs.

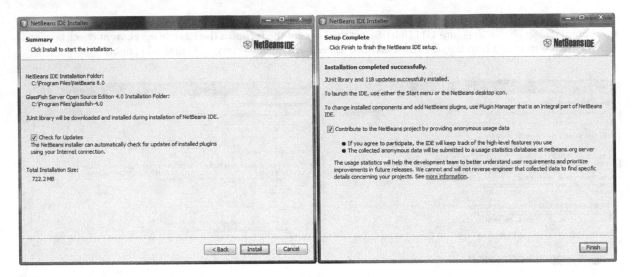

Figure 1-13. *Select the Check for Updates check box, and click the Install button (left) and the Finish button (right)*

During the installation, you will see the **Installation** dialog, and its progress bar, illustrated in Figure 1-14, which will tell you exactly what percentage of the installation has been completed as well as which IDE files are currently being extracted, and installed, on your workstation.

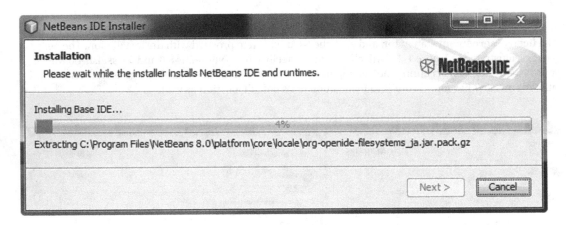

Figure 1-14. *The Installation progress dialog, showing the percentage of install complete*

When the installation process is complete, you will see the **Setup Complete** dialog, which is shown in Figure 1-13 (right). Now, you are ready to develop Java 8 and JavaFX applications (games) on your workstation.

Next, let's download five of the most popular free open-source new media content development software packages so that you have all the tools that you will need for a Java 8 games development business!

After that, you will take a look at some other impressive open-source software that I use on my workstation. That way, if you want to, you can put together the ultimate software development workstation before you have even finished this chapter, creating an incredibly valuable content production workstation for the cost of the hardware (and OS) alone!

Installing New Media Content Production Software

There are a number of "genres" of new media elements, or assets, as I call them, that are supported in JavaFX, which is the new media engine in Java 8 (and Java 7) and thus what you will be using as the foundation for your Java 8 game development. The primary genres of new media, for which you will be installing the leading open-source software in the remainder of this chapter, include digital illustration, digital imaging, digital audio, digital video, and 3D.

Downloading and Installing Inkscape

Because JavaFX supports 2D, or **vector**, technology, commonly used in **digital illustration** software packages, such as Adobe Illustrator and FreeHand, you will download and install the popular open-source digital illustration software package known as **Inkscape**.

Inkscape is available for the Linux, Windows, and Mac OSs, just like all the software packages that you are installing in this chapter, so you can use any platform you like to develop games!

To find the Inkscape software package on the Internet, go to Google Search, and type in **Inkscape**, as shown in Figure 1-15, at the top left. Click the **Download** link (or right-click, and open in a separate tab), and click the icon that represents the OS that you are using. The Penguin signifies Linux (far-left icon), the Window signifies Windows (center icon), and the stylized apple signifies Mac (far-right icon).

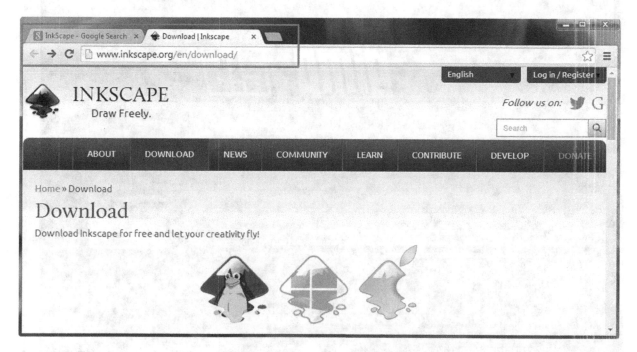

Figure 1-15. *Google the term "InkScape," go to the Inkscape Download page, and click the icon that matches your OS*

If you want to use the 64-bit Windows version of Inkscape, scroll down, and take a look at the text links below these three icons to access that particular OS download. Once you have downloaded the software, right-click it and Run as administrator, and install the software on your workstation. If you have a previous version of Inkscape, the installation will upgrade it to the latest version; you do not need to use the Programs and Features utility that you used earlier in the chapter to uninstall your SDK and IDEs, which do not upgrade previous versions, like new media production software packages tend to do.

After the software is installed, create a Quick Launch icon on your taskbar so that you can launch Inkscape with a single click of the mouse. Next, you will install a popular digital imaging software package, called **GIMP**, which will allow you to create "raster," or pixel-based (bitmap), artwork for your games in JPEG, PNG, or GIF digital image file formats supported by JavaFX. Raster images are different from vector, or shape, illustrations, so you will need GIMP.

Downloading and Installing GIMP

JavaFX also supports 2D images that use **raster** image technology, which represents images as an array of pixels and is commonly used in digital image compositing software packages, such as Adobe Photoshop and Corel Painter. In this section, you will download and install the popular open-source digital image editing and compositing software package called GIMP. This software is available for the Linux, Windows, Solaris, FreeBSD, and Mac OSs.

To find the GIMP software on the Internet, go to Google Search, and type in **GIMP**, as demonstrated in Figure 1-16.

Figure 1-16. *Google the term "GIMP," go to the GIMP Downloads page, and click the Download GIMP link*

Click the **Download** link (or right-click, and open it in a separate tab), and click **Download GIMP 2.8.14** (or the latest version that represents the OS that you are using). The **Downloads** page will automatically detect the OS that you are using and give you the correct OS version; in my case, it is Windows. Download and install the latest version of GIMP, and then create a Quick Launch icon for your workstation taskbar, as you did for Inkscape. Next, you will install a powerful digital audio editing and audio effects software package, called **Audacity**.

Downloading and Installing Audacity

JavaFX supports digital audio sequencing, which uses digital audio technology. Digital audio represents analog audio by taking digital audio **samples**. Digital audio content is commonly created using digital audio composition and sequencer software packages, such as Propellerhead Reason and Cakewalk Sonar. In this section, you will download and install the popular open source digital audio editing and optimization software package known as **Audacity**. Audacity is available for the Linux, Windows, and Mac OSs, so you can use any OS platform that you like to create and optimize digital audio for your Java 8– and JavaFX–based games.

To find the Audacity software package on the Internet, use the Google search engine, and type in **Audacity**, as shown in Figure 1-17, at the top left. Click the **Download** link (or right-click, and open in a separate tab), and click **Audacity for Windows** (or the version that represents the OS that you are using).

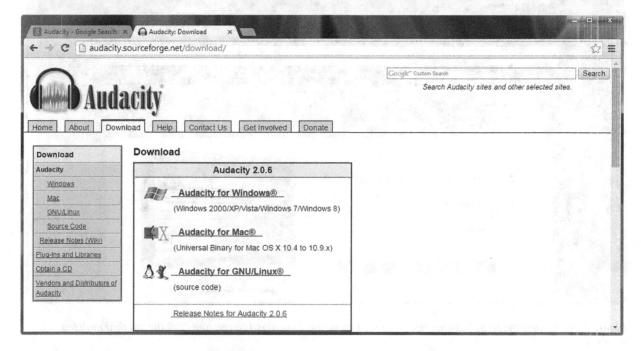

Figure 1-17. *Google the term "Audacity," go to the Audacity Download page, and click a link matching your OS*

Download and install the latest version of Audacity (currently, it is 2.0.6), and then create a Quick Launch Icon for your workstation taskbar, as you did for Inkscape and GIMP. Next, you will install a powerful digital video editing and special effects software package, called **EditShare Lightworks**.

Downloading and Installing EditShare Lightworks

JavaFX also supports digital video, which uses **raster** pixel-based motion video technology. Raster represents video as a sequence of **frames**, each of which contains a digital image based on an array of pixels. Digital video assets are usually created using digital video editing and special effects software packages, such as Adobe After Effects and Sony Vegas. In this section, you will download and install open-source digital video editing software known as **Lightworks**.

EditShare's Lightworks used to be a paid software package until it was made open source. You will have to **register** on the Lightworks web site to download and use the software. This package is available for Linux, Windows, and Mac OSs. To find Lightworks on the Internet, go to Google Search, and type in **Lightworks**, as shown in Figure 1-18, at the top left. Click the **Download** link (or right-click, and open in a separate tab), and click the appropriate **Download** button and the tab that represents the OS that you are using. The **Downloads** page will automatically detect the OS that you are using and select the correct OS tab; in my case, Windows.

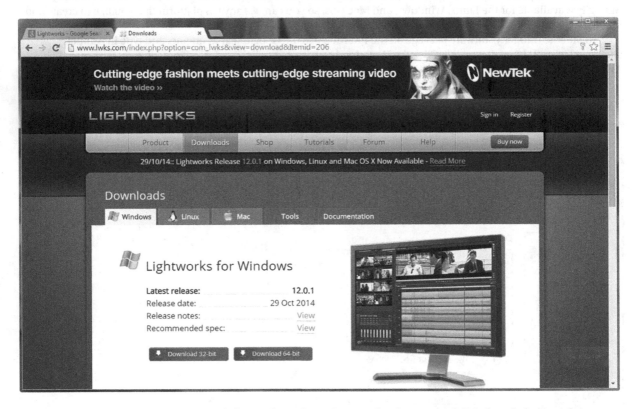

Figure 1-18. *Google the term "Lightworks," go to the Lightworks Downloads page, and click the tab that matches your OS*

Register on the Lightworks web site, if you have not done so already. Once you are approved, you can then download and install the latest version of Lightworks. Install the software, and create a Quick Launch icon for your taskbar, as you did for the other software. Next, you will install a 3D modeling and animation package, called **Blender**.

Downloading and Installing Blender

JavaFX has recently moved to support 3D new media assets that are created outside the JavaFX environment, which means that you will be able to create 3D models, textures, and animation, using third-party software packages, such as Autodesk 3D Studio Max or Maya and NewTek Lightwave 3D. In this section, you will download and install the popular open-source 3D modeling and animation software package known as Blender. Blender is available for the Linux, Windows, and Mac OSs, so you can use any OS platform that you like to create and optimize 3D models, 3D texture mapping, and 3D animation for use in your Java 8 and JavaFX games.

To find the Blender software on the Internet, using the Google search engine, type in **Blender**, as shown in Figure 1-19. Click the correct download link to download and install Blender, and then create the Quick Launch icon.

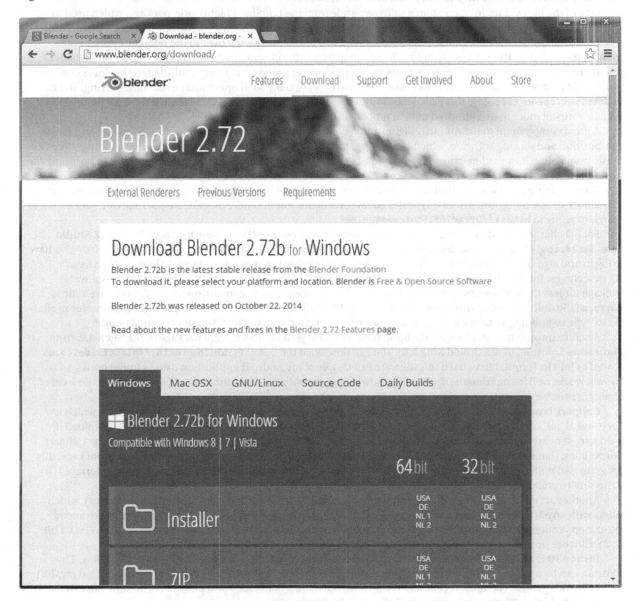

Figure 1-19. *Google the term "Blender," go to the Blender Download page, and click the tab for your OS*

Other Open-Source Software Packages of Interest

There are a number of other professional-level open-source software packages that I use in my new media content production business that I thought I would let you know about, in case you had not heard about them. These will add even more power and versatility to the new media production workstation that you have built up to this point. It is important to note that you have already saved yourself thousands of dollars that would have otherwise been spent on similar paid content production software packages in the process of doing all this extensive downloading and installing. I guess you could say my motto is, "Do it right the first time, and be sure to go all the way," so let me tell you about some of the other free, and even some of the more affordable, new media content production software packages that I have installed on my own content production workstations.

One of the best values in open-source software, aside from the EditShare Lightworks package, which used to cost six figures back in the day, is a **business productivity software suite** that was made open source by **Oracle** after it acquired Sun Microsystems. Oracle transferred its OpenOffice software suite over to the popular Apache open-source project. **OpenOffice 4.1** is an entire office productivity software suite that contains **six** full-fledged business productivity software packages! Because your content production agency is actually a full-fledged business concern, you should probably know about this software, as it is an exceptionally solid open-source software offering. You can find it at **www.openoffice.org**; this popular business software package has been downloaded by savvy professionals such as yourself more than a hundred million times, so it's no joke, as they say!

A great complement to the Audacity digital audio editing software is **Rosegarden** MIDI sequencing and music composition and scoring software, which can be used for music composition and printing out the resulting scores for music publishing. Rosegarden, currently in version 14.02, and being ported from Linux to Windows, can be found via Google Search or at **www.rosegardenmusic.com**.

Another impressive audio, MIDI, and sound design software package is **Qtractor** If you are running the Linux OS, be sure to download and install this professional-level digital audio synthesis software package by doing a Google search or going to **https://Qtractor.SourceForge.net**.

For 3D character modeling and animation, be sure to check out the 3D software packages from **DAZ Studio** (**www.daz3d.com**) when you have the chance. The current version of **DAZ Studio Pro** is 4.6, and yes, it is free! You have to log in and sign up, like you did for EditShare Lightworks, but that is a small price to pay! There is also a free 3D modeling software package on this web site, called **Hexagon 2.5**, and a popular terrain generation software package for less than 20 dollars, called **Bryce 7.1 Pro**. The most expensive software on the DAZ Studio web site is **Carrara** (150 dollars) and **Carrara Pro** (285 dollars). DAZ Studio makes most of its revenue selling **character models** of one type or another, so take a look, as it is a force to be reckoned with in the 3D content (virtual) world!

Another impressive (and free, for the basic version) world generation software package is **Terragen 3.2**, from **Planetside** Software, in the United Kingdom. You can download the basic version from **http://planetside.co.uk** as well as join its forum. I have used this software in a couple of my Android application development books, so I know it works well for multimedia applications and games. It is also used by professional filmmakers, as the level of quality is pristine.

Caligari TrueSpace 7.61 is also excellent, free 3D modeling and animation software. The program, which is "free and alive!" according to the Caligari web site (**https://Caligari.us**), from which you can still download it, used to cost nearly a thousand dollars when it was first developed by Roman Ormandy, the founder of the Caligari Corporation (later purchased by Microsoft). A professional-level 3D modeling and animation software package, this program had millions of users in its heyday. It is a really cool piece of software, with a fun-to-use user interface (UI), so be sure to grab it!

Another 3D rendering software you should take a look at is **POV-Ray** (Persistence of Vision Raytracer), which works with any 3D modeling and animation software package to generate impressive 3D scenes, using advanced ray-traced rendering algorithms. The most recent version on the POV-Ray web site (**www.povray.org**), **3.7**, is **64 bit** and multicore (multithreaded) compatible, and it can be downloaded for free!

Bishop3D is a cool 3D modeling software package that was specifically designed for use with POV-Ray. The software can be used to create custom 3D objects, which can then be imported into POV-Ray (and then into JavaFX) for use in your games. The most recent version, an 8MB download, is **1.0.5.2**, for Windows 7. The software can be found at **www.bishop3d.com** and can currently be downloaded for free!

Yet another free 3D modeling software worth investigating is **Wings 3D**. This software can be used to create custom 3D objects, which can then be imported into JavaFX for use in your games. The most recent version, a **64-bit**, 16MB download, is **1.5.3** and was released in April 2014, for Windows 7, Mac OS X, and Ubuntu Linux. The software can be found at **www.wings3d.com** and can currently be downloaded for free!

For UI design prototyping, the free software package **Pencil 2.0.6**, from **Evolus**, allows you to easily prototype UI designs before you create them in Java, Android, or HTML5. The software is located at **http://pencil.evolus.vn** and is available for Linux, Windows, and Mac OSs.

Next, you will take a look at how I organize some of the basic OS utilities and open-source software on my taskbar.

Organizing Quick Launch Icons in Your Taskbar Area

There are certain OS utilities, such as the calculator, text editor (Notepad), and file manager (Explorer), for which I create Quick Launch icons on my taskbar, as these utilities are used frequently in programming and new media content development work processes. I also keep as Quick Launch icons a wide range of new media development, programming, and office productivity applications. Figure 1-20 displays a dozen of these, including everything that you just installed, in the order in which you installed it, as well as a few others, such as OpenOffice 4.1, DAZ Studio Pro 4.6, and Bryce 7.1 Pro.

Figure 1-20. *Make taskbar Quick Launch icons for key system utilities, NetBeans 8.0, and new media production software*

There are a couple of ways to create these Quick Launch icons: you can drag programs from the start menu and drop them onto the taskbar, or you can right-click icons on the desktop or in the Explorer file manager and select **Pin this program to taskbar** from the context-sensitive menu. Once icons are on the taskbar, you can change their position simply by dragging them to the left or to the right.

Congratulations, you have just set up a new media Java 8 game development workstation that is highly optimized and that will allow you to create any new media Java 8 game that you or your clients can imagine!

Summary

In this first chapter I made sure that you have everything that you need to develop standout Java 8 games, including the latest versions of Java 8, JavaFX, and NetBeans 8.0 as well as all the latest open-source new media software.

You started by downloading and installing the latest Java JDK 8 and NetBeans IDE 8.0 software. Then, you did the same for a plethora of professional open-source new media tools.

In the next chapter, I will show you how to use NetBeans 8.0 to create a Java 8 project.

CHAPTER 2

■ ■ ■

Setting Up Your Java 8 IDE: An Introduction to NetBeans 8.0

Let's get started here in Chapter 2 by considering **NetBeans IDE 8.0**, because that is the primary piece of software that you will be using to create your Java 8 games. Even though Java JDK 8 is the foundation for your Java 8 games, as well as for NetBeans 8.0, you will start your journey by learning about NetBeans, as it is the "front end," the window through which you look at your Java game project.

NetBeans 8.0 is the **official IDE** for Java JDK 8, and, as such, it is what you will be using for this book. That is not to say you cannot use another IDE, such as Eclipse or IntelliJ, which are the official IDEs for Android 4.x (32 bit) and Android 5.x (64 bit) respectively, but I prefer to use NetBeans 8.0 for my new media application and game development for the Java 8, JavaFX 8, HTML5, CSS3 (Cascading Style Sheets 3), and JavaScript software development markup and programming paradigms.

This is not only because NetBeans 8.0 integrates **JavaFX Scene Builder**, which you will be learning about in Chapter 5 of this book, but also because it is an HTML5 IDE, too, and I create everything I design for my clients using Java 8, JavaFX 8, Android 4.x, or Android 5.x as well as HTML5. I do this so that the content works across (on) closed, or proprietary, OSs and platforms. I prefer open-source software and platforms, as you observed in Chapter 1.

First, you will take a look at what is new in NetBeans 8.0. This version of NetBeans was released at the same time as Java 8, and the version number synchronization is no coincidence. You will discover why you will want to use NetBeans 8.0 rather than an older NetBeans version, such as NetBeans 7.4 or earlier.

Next, you will examine the various attributes of NetBeans IDE 8.0 that make it an invaluable tool for Java 8 game development. You will not be able to get hands-on experience with all its features in the chapter, but you will be exploring all the cool things that it can do for you over the course of this book (you will need to put an advanced code base into place to really give some of the features a workout).

Finally, you will learn how to create your Java 8 and JavaFX project, using NetBeans 8.0 so that you progress toward creating the Java 8 game that you will be developing as you read through this book.

Primary Attributes of NetBeans 8.0: An Intelligent IDE

Assuming that you already have a professional-level workstation in place for new media content and game development, you need to remove all the outdated JDKs and IDEs and make sure that you have the latest V8 Java and NetBeans software installed on your system and ready to go. If you are new to this and do not have a game-appropriate workstation, go to Walmart or PriceWatch.com, and purchase an affordable multicore (use a 4-, 6- or 8-core) 64-bit computer running Windows 8.1 (or 9.0 if it is available) that has 4GB, 6GB, or 8GB of DDR3 (1333 or 1600 memory access speed) system memory at the very least and a 750GB, or even 1TB, hard disk drive.

NetBeans 8.0 Is Smart: Put Your Code Editing into Hyperdrive

Although it is true that an IDE is like a word processor, only geared toward writing code text rather than creating business documents, a programming integrated development environment such as NetBeans does a lot more for your programming work process than a word processor does for your document-authoring work process.

For instance, your word processor does not make suggestions in real time regarding the content that you are writing for your business, whereas the NetBeans IDE will actually look at what you are coding while you are writing that code and will help you write your code statements and constructs.

One of the things that NetBeans will do is finish lines of code for you as well as apply color to the code statements to highlight different types of constructs (classes, methods, variables, constants, references, and the like) (for more details, see Chapter 3). NetBeans will also apply the industry standard for **code indenting** to make your code much easier to read (for both yourself and the other members of your game application development team).

In addition, NetBeans will provide **matching** code structure **brackets**, **colons**, and **semicolons** so that you do not get lost when you are creating complex, deeply nested, or exceptionally dense programming constructs. You will be creating constructs such as these as I take you from Java 8 game beginner to Java 8 game developer, and I will point out Java 8 code that is dense, complex, or deeply nested as you encounter it.

NetBeans can also provide bootstrap code, such as the JavaFX game application bootstrap code that you will be creating a bit later in this chapter (see the section "Creating Your Java 8 Project: The InvinciBagel"), as well as code templates (which you can fill out and customize), coding tips and tricks, and code refactoring tools. As your Java code becomes more complex, it also becomes a better candidate for code refactoring, which can make the code easier to understand, easier to upgrade, and more efficient. NetBeans can also refactor your code automatically.

In case you are wondering, **code refactoring** is changing the structure of existing computer code to make it more efficient or scalable without changing its external behavior, that is, what it accomplishes. For instance, you could take Java 6 or Java 7 code and make it more efficient by implementing Lambda Expressions, using Java 8.

Furthermore, NetBeans offers pop-up helper dialogs of various types, containing **methods**, **constants**, asset **references** (see Chapter 3), and even **suggestions** regarding how to construct the code statement, for example, when it might be appropriate to use the powerful new Java 8 **Lambda Expressions** feature to make your code more streamlined and multithread compatible.

NetBeans 8.0 Is Extensible: Code Editing with Many Languages

Another thing that your word processor cannot do is allow you to add features to it, which NetBeans can do using its **plug-in** architecture. The term that describes this type of architecture is **extensible**, which means that if needed, it can be extended to include additional features. So, if you wanted to extend NetBeans 8.0 to allow you to program using Python, for instance, you could. NetBeans 8.0 can also support older languages, such as COBOL and BASIC, in this fashion as well, although with the majority of popular consumer electronics devices using Java, XML, JavaScript, and HTML5 these days, I am not really sure why anyone would want to take the time do this. I did a Google search for this, however, and there are people coding in Python and COBOL in NetBeans 8.0, so there is real-world proof that the IDE is indeed extensible.

Probably because of its extensibility, NetBeans IDE 8.0 supports a number of popular programming languages, including **C**, **C++**, **Java SE**, **JavaScript**, **XML**, **HTML5**, and **CSS** on the **client side** and **PHP**, **Groovy**, **Java EE**, and **JavaServer Pages** (**JSP**) on the **server side**. Client-side software is run on the device that the end user is holding or using (in the case of an iTV); server-side software runs **remotely,** on a server, and talks to the end user over the Internet or a similar network while the software is running on the server. Client-side software is more efficient, as it is **local** to the hardware device that it is running on and thus is more **scalable**: no server is involved to experience overload as more and more people use the software at any given point in time.

NetBeans 8.0 Is Efficient: Organized Project Management Tools

A good programming IDE needs to be able to manage projects that can grow to become quite massive, involving more than a million lines of code contained in hundreds of folders in the project folder hierarchy and thousands of files and new media assets. For this reason, project management features must be extremely robust in any mainstream IDE. NetBeans 8.0 contains a plethora of project management features that allow you to look at your Java 8 game development project, and its corresponding files and their interrelationships, in a number of different ways.

There are four primary project management views, or "panes" that you can use to see the different types of **interrelationships** in your project. (I call them panes, as the entire IDE is in what I call a window). I jumped ahead (to the end of the chapter, once your Java 8 game project has been created) and created the screenshot presented in Figure 2-1. This screenshot displays the four project management panes opened in this new project so that you can see exactly what they will show you.

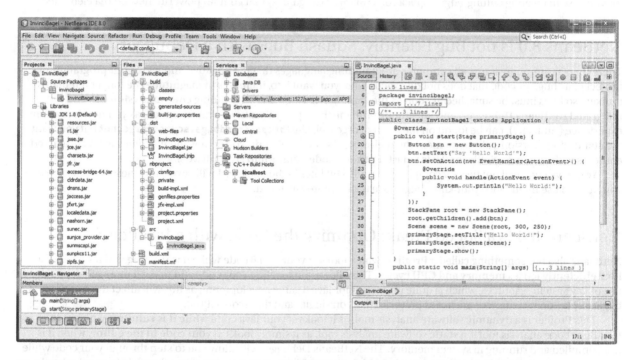

Figure 2-1. *Project management panes, at the left of the IDE, include Projects, Files, Services, and Navigator*

The **Projects** pane, at the left of the screen, shows the Java **Source Packages** and **Libraries** that make up your (game) project. The next pane over is the **Files** pane, which has the **project folder** and **file hierarchy** on your hard disk drive. The **Services** pane contains the databases, servers, repositories, and build hosts, if they are used in the project (these are primarily server-side technologies, and technologies used with a development team, so I am not going to go into these in detail).

The Projects pane should always be left open (as you will see in Figures 2-7 through 2-21). The Projects pane provides you with a primary access point for all the project source code and assets (content) in your Java 8 game project. The Files pane shows not only the project folder and file hierarchy, but also the data and FXML markup (JavaFX) or Java 8 code hierarchy inside each file.

The **Navigator** pane (bottom) shows the **relationships** that exist inside your Java code structures. In this case, these are the InvinciBagel class, the .start() method, and the .main() method (for further information, see Chapter 3).

NetBeans 8.0 Is User Interface Design Friendly: UI Design Tools

NetBeans 8.0 also has **Design a GUI** drag-and-drop design tools for a plethora of platforms, including Java SE, Java EE, Java ME, JavaFX, and Java Swing as well as C, C++, PHP, HTML5, and CSS3. NetBeans provides visual editors that write the application's **UI** code for you, so all you have to do is make the visual on the screen look like what you want it to look like in your game application. Because games use the JavaFX new media (game) engine, you will be learning about the **JavaFX Scene Builder**, an advanced FXML-based visual design editor, in Chapter 5 of this book.

JavaFX has the Prism game engine as well as 3D (using OpenGL ES [**OpenGL for** Embedded Systems]) support, so I will be focusing quite a bit on the JavaFX Scene Graph and JavaFX APIs. The assumption here is that you will want to build the most advanced Java 8 games possible, and leveraging the JavaFX engine, which is now a part of Java 8 (along with Lambda Expressions), is going to be the way to accomplish this. The fastest way to develop a game is to leverage advanced code and programming constructs that the Java 8 and JavaFX environments generously give you for your use in creating cutting-edge applications (in this case, games) that contain powerful new media elements.

NetBeans 8.0 Is not Bug Friendly: Squash Bugs with a Debugger

There is an assumption across all computer programming languages that the negative impact to your programming project of a "bug," or code that does not do exactly what you want it to, increases in magnitude the longer it remains unfixed, so bugs must be squashed as soon as they are "born." NetBeans bug-finding **code analysis** tools, and integrated **NetBeans Debugger**, and integration with the third-party **FindBugs** project, which, as you now know from experience (Audacity), can be found on the SourceForge web site (**http://findbugs.sourceforge.net**) (if you want the stand-alone version), all supplement the real-time, "as you type" code-correcting and efficiency tools I discussed earlier (see the section "NetBeans 8.0 Is Smart: Put Your Code Editing into Hyperdrive").

Your Java code will not be very complicated until a bit later in the book, so I will cover how these tools work when you need to use them, once your knowledge base is a bit more advanced.

NetBeans 8.0 Is a Speed Freak: Optimize the Code with a Profiler

NetBeans also has something called a **Profiler**, which looks at your Java 8 code while it is running and then tells you how **efficiently** it uses **memory** and **CPU** cycles. This allows you to refine your code and make it more efficient in its use of key system resources, which is quite important for Java 8 game development, as this will affect the smoothness of game play on systems that are not as powerful (e.g., on single- and dual-core CPUs).

This Profiler is a **dynamic** software analysis tool, as it looks at your Java code **while it is running**, whereas the FindBugs code analysis tool is a **static** software analysis tool, as it simply looks at your code **in the editor**, when it is not compiled and running in system memory. The NetBeans Debugger will allow you to **step** through your code while it is running, so that tool can be viewed as a **hybrid** that ranges from a static (editing) to a dynamic (executing) code analysis mode.

After you create the foundation for your Java 8 (JavaFX) game engine (in the following sections), you will run the Profiler to see how it works inside NetBeans IDE 8.0. I am going to present as many key features of NetBeans as possible up front so that you get comfortable with this software.

Creating Your Java 8 Game Project: The InvinciBagel

Let's get down to business and create the foundation for your game. I am going to demonstrate how to create an original game so that you can see the process involved in developing a game that does not yet exist, as opposed to most game programming books, which replicate games that are already on the market. I got permission from my client **Ira Harrison-Rubin,** cartoonist/author/humorist for the **BagelToons** franchise, to let readers to see the process of creating his **InvinciBagel** cartoon game during the course of this book.

Click the Quick Launch icon on your taskbar (or double-click the icon on your desktop) to launch NetBeans 8.0, and you will see the NetBeans start-up screen, illustrated in Figure 2-2. This screen contains a progress bar (in red) and will tell you what is being done to configure the NetBeans IDE for use. This involves loading the various components of the IDE into your computer system memory so that they can be used smoothly and in real time during development.

Figure 2-2. *Launch NetBeans 8.0, using the Quick Launch icon*

After NetBeans IDE 8.0 has been loaded into your system memory, the NetBeans 8.0 **start page** will be displayed on your screen, as shown in Figure 2-3. Click the "**x**" at the right of the Start Page tab to close this page.

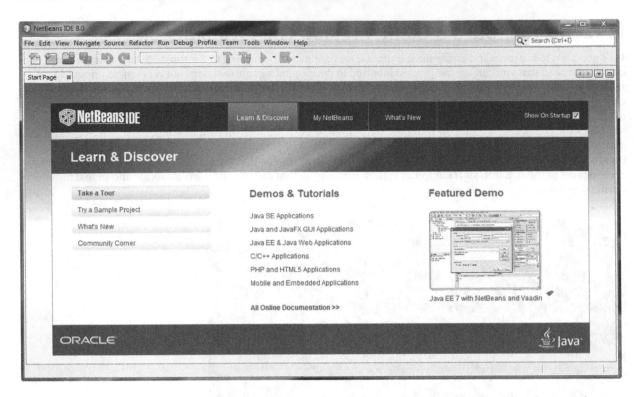

Figure 2-3. *Close the Start Page tab, at the top left of the screen, by clicking the "x" at the right of the tab to reveal NetBeans IDE 8.0*

This will display what I term the virgin IDE, with no projects active. Enjoy this now, as soon you will be filling this IDE with panes for your project components (you can see part of this empty IDE in Figure 2-4, which contains menus and shortcut icons and not much else).

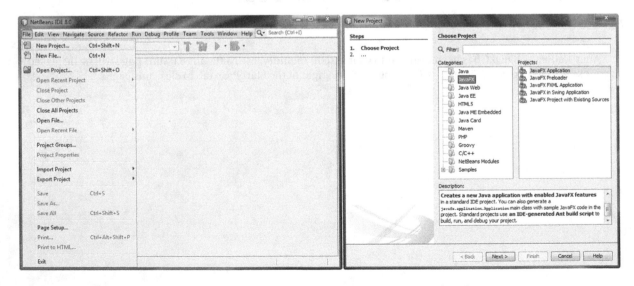

Figure 2-4. *Showing virgin NetBeans 8.0 IDE (left) and a JavaFX New Project dialog (right)*

In case you are wondering, the start page displays every time you start the NetBeans IDE, and if you wanted to open the Start Page tab later on, perhaps to explore the Media Library section (demos) and tutorials, you can! To open the start page at any time, you use the NetBeans IDE 8.0 **Help** menu and the **Start Page** submenu. For future reference, I usually notate a menu sequence like this: **Help ➤ Start Menu**.

The first thing that you will want to do in NetBeans IDE 8.0 is create a new **InvinciBagel game project!** To accomplish this, you will use the NetBeans 8.0 **New Project** series of dialogs. This is one of those helpful Java programming features that I mentioned earlier (see the section "NetBeans IDE 8.0 Is Smart: Put Your Editing into Hyperdrive") that creates a bootstrap project with the correct JavaFX libraries, .main() and .start() methods, and import statements (for more details, see Chapter 3).

Click the **File** menu, at the top-left corner of the DE, as displayed in Figure 2-4 (left), and then select **New Project** (the first menu item). Note that to the right of this selection, there is a keyboard shortcut given (**Ctrl+Shift+N**), in case you want to memorize it.

If you want to use this keyboard short-cut to bring up the New Project series of dialogs, hold down the **CTRL** and **Shift** keys on your keyboard (both at the same time), and while they are depressed (held down), press the **N** key. This will do the same thing as using the **File ➤ New Project** menu sequence.

The first in the series is the **Choose Project** dialog, shown in Figure 2-4 (right). Because you are going to use the powerful JavaFX new media engine in your game, select **JavaFX** from the list of programming language categories in the **Categories** pane, and because a game is a type of application, select **JavaFX Application** from the **Projects** pane.

Remember that Oracle made JavaFX a part of Java 7 and Java 8, so a JavaFX game is also a Java game, whereas before Java 7 (in Java 6), JavaFX was its own separate programming language! The JavaFX engine had to be recoded as a Java (7 and 8) API (set of libraries) for it to become a seamless part of the Java programming language. The JavaFX API replaces AWT (Abstract Windowing Toolkit) and Swing, and although these older UI design libraries can still be used in Java projects, they are normally used only by legacy (older) Java code so that those projects can compile and run in Java 7 and 8. You will be compiling and running the new project you are creating here a bit later in this chapter.

Note that there is a **Description** pane below the other panes that will tell you what your selections will give you. In this case, that would be **a new Java application with enabled JavaFX features**; here, "enabled" indicates that the JavaFX API libraries will be included (and started) in the Java application project's class and methods, as you will soon see in the code (for further information on what the code means, see Chapter 3).

Click the **Next** button to advance to the next dialog in the series, which is the Finding Feature dialog, shown in Figure 2-5. This dialog displays a progress bar while it is "Activating JavaFX 2," which equates to installing the JavaFX API libraries in your project code infrastructure. You will find that sometimes JavaFX 8 is still referred to as JavaFX 2 (2.3 was the latest version of JavaFX before people started using the name JavaFX 8, probably to sync up with Java 8). I have also seen discussion of a JavaFX 3, which is now being called JavaFX 8, and because JavaFX is now a part of Java 8, I am going to refer to it simply as JavaFX for the duration of this book.

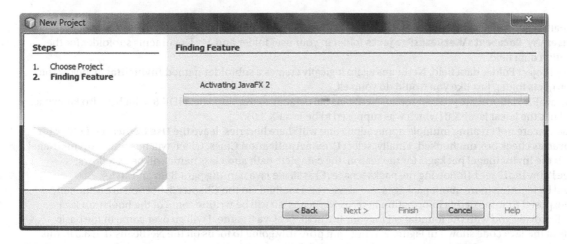

Figure 2-5. *Step 2: Finding Feature dialog, showing the progress bar for the process of activating JavaFX*

Once the Finding Feature dialog has activated JavaFX for your game project, you will get the **Name and Location** dialog, which is presented in Figure 2-6. Name your project **InvinciBagel**, and leave the default **Project Location**, **Project Folder**, **JavaFX Platform**, and **Create Application Class** settings the way that NetBeans 8.0 has configured them.

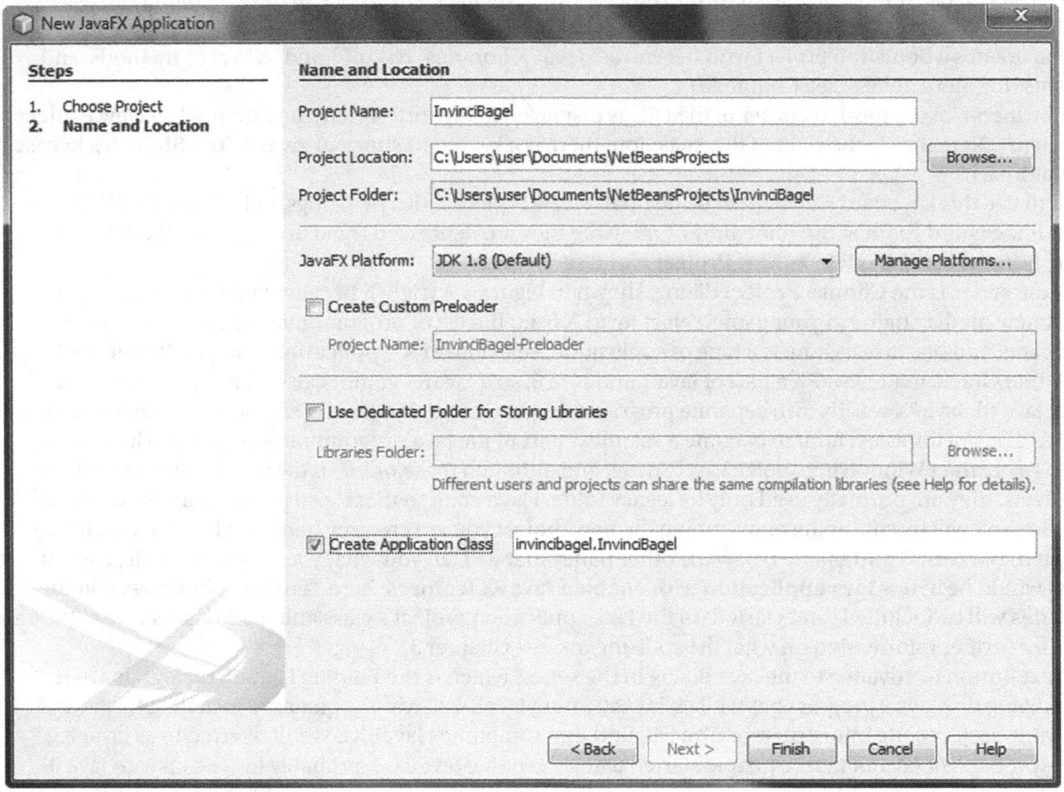

Figure 2-6. Name the project InvinciBagel, and leave the other settings as they are

It is usually a good idea to let NetBeans 8.0 do things for you. As you can see, NetBeans creates the logical **C:\Users\user\My Documents\NetBeansProjects** folder in your user folder and My Documents subfolder for the Project Location data field.

For your Project Folder data field, NetBeans again logically creates a subfolder named **InvinciBagel**, below the **NetBeansProjects** folder, just like you would do yourself.

For the JavaFX Platform drop-down menu, NetBeans 8.0 defaults to the very latest JDK 8, which is also known as JDK 1.8, and has the latest JavaFX 8 (which was supposed to be JavaFX 3.0).

Because you are not creating multiple applications that will share libraries, leave the **Use Dedicated Folder for Storing Libraries** check box **unchecked**. Finally, select **Create Application Class,** which will be named **InvinciBagel** and will be in the **invincibagel** package; for the reason, the complete path and class name will be as follows: invincibagel.InvinciBagel (following the packagename.ClassName Java naming paradigm and style).

(You will be learning more about packages and classes and methods in the Chapter 3, but you are ultimately going to be exposed to some of this information here, as NetBeans 8.0 will be writing some of the bootstrap Java code that will provide you with the foundation for your InvinciBagel Java 8 game. I will go over some of the basic components of the Java code shown in Figure 2-7, but I am primarily going to focus on the NetBeans IDE 8.0 in this chapter and concentrate on the Java 8 programming language in Chapter 3.)

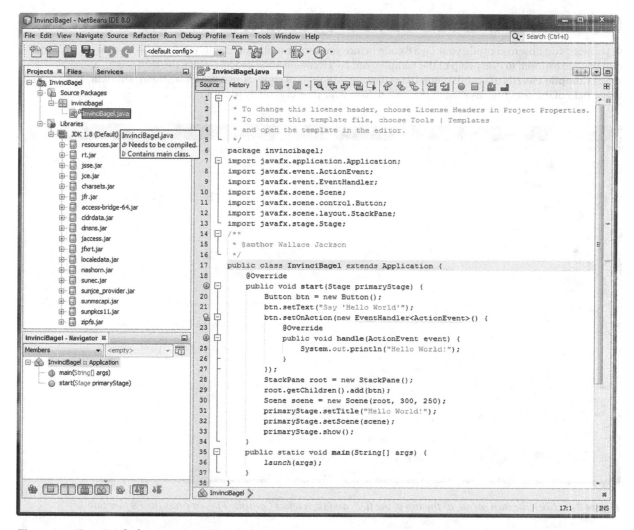

Figure 2-7. *Examine the bootstrap JavaFX code that NetBeans created for you, based on the New JavaFX Application dialog*

As you can see in the figure, NetBeans has written the **package** statement, seven JavaFX **import** statements, the **class** declaration, and the .start() and .main() **methods**. NetBeans 8.0 colors Java key programming **statement words** blue and comments gray. Data values are orange and input/output is green.

Before you can **run** this bootstrap code, to make sure that NetBeans 8.0 wrote code for you that actually works, you will need to **compile** it into an **executable** format, which is run in your system memory.

Compiling Your Java 8 Game Project in NetBeans 8.0

In showing you how to compile your Java 8 code before you run (test) it, I am demonstrating the "long way" here so that you are exposed to every step of the compile/run Java 8 code-testing process. Click the **Run** menu, and then select **Compile File** (the eleventh menu item) to compile your Java code, or use the **F9** keyboard shortcut, as indicated at the right of the selection, as seen in Figure 2-8. Now your project is ready to run!

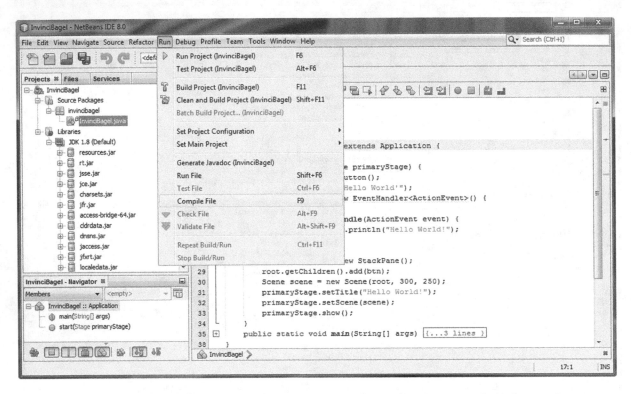

Figure 2-8. *Click the Run menu, at the top of the IDE, and then select Compile File, or press the F9 function key*

Figure 2-9 illustrates the Compile progress bar, which will appear at the bottom of the IDE during compilation.

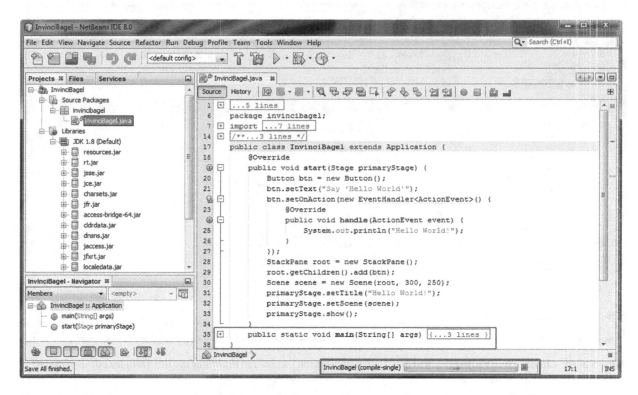

Figure 2-9. *The Compile progress bar is shown at the bottom of the screen, along with expand and collapse icon functionality*

It is also important to note here that NetBeans will compile the project code when you use the **File ➤ Save** menu sequence (or the **CTRL-S** keyboard shortcut), so if you were to use the **Save** feature of the NetBeans IDE right after the bootstrap code is created, you would not have to undertake the compilation process that I just showed you, as this process is done "automagically," (not manually) every time you save a game project.

Also shown in the figure, right above the Compile progress bar, is a highlighted a block of code that was visible in Figure 2-7 but that I have **collapsed**, using the **minus icon** at the left of the code editor pane. You can see three uncollapsed minus icons in the middle of the **code editor** pane (under the InvinciBagel class) as well as three collapsed icons at the top of the **code editor** pane for the two comments and the import statement code block. A minus icon turns into a plus icon so that a collapsed code view can be **expanded**. Now that you have looked at how to compile your project in NetBeans as well as how to collapse and expand the views of logical blocks (components) of your project code, it is time to run the code.

Running Your Java 8 Game Project in NetBeans 8.0

Now that you have created and compiled your bootstrap Java 8/JavaFX game project, it is time to run or execute the bootstrap code and see what it does. You can do this by using the **Run ➤ Run Project** menu sequence (see Figure 2-8), or you can use the shortcut icon at the top of the IDE (resembling a video transport **play** button), displayed in Figure 2-10.

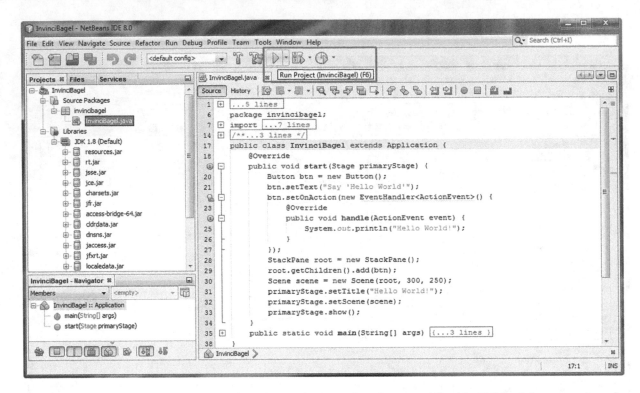

Figure 2-10. *Click the Run Project shortcut icon (green play button), at the top middle of the IDE (tool tip pop-up shown)*

Once you run the compiled Java code, a window will open with your software running in it, at the right of the screen, as seen in Figure 2-11. Currently, the program uses the popular "Hello World!" sample application.

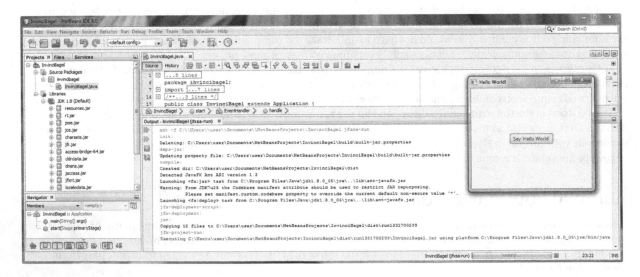

Figure 2-11. *Drag the separator bar upward to reveal the Compile Output area of the IDE (running the application seen at right)*

Click the **divider line** between the **code editor** pane and the **Output tab**, at bottom, and, holding down the mouse button, **drag** this divider line upward, revealing the Output tab contents, as demonstrated in Figure 2-11.

The Output tab will contain different types of output in NetBeans, such as compile operation output from Ant, run operation output (shown in the figure), profiler operation output (which you will be exploring in the next section), and even output from the application itself.

You may have noticed in Figure 2-10 that the code for this bootstrap Java 8/JavaFX application contains a `(System.out.println("Hello World!");` Java statement in line 25, so if you wanted to see the application that you are currently running print to the Output pane (sometimes referred to in programming circles as the Output **Console**), click the **Say "Hello World"** button in the "Hello World!" application (running on top of the IDE).

Once you click this button, **"Hello World!"** will appear in the Output tab, under the red text that says it is executing the **InvinciBagel.jar** file. A `.jar` (Java Archive) file is the **distributable format** for your Java application. Part of the compile process is creating this file, so if your compiled version works, you can have the `.jar` file ready to distribute if your application design and programming are complete!

A `.jar` file does not contain your actual Java 8 code, but rather a compressed, encrypted "Java byte stream" version of the application, which the JRE can **execute and run** (like NetBeans 8.0 is doing now). The path that is attached to the front of the `InvinciBagel.jar` file tells you where the compiled `.jar` file resides and where NetBeans is accessing it from currently to run it. On my system this location was C:\Users\user\Documents\NetBeansProjects\ InvinciBagel\dist\run1331700299\InvinciBagel.jar.

Let's take a look at some of the other Output tab text to see what NetBeans did to get to the point where it could run the `.jar` file for this project. First, the compiler deletes and rebuilds the **build-jar-properties** file, in the **\NetBeansProjects\InvinciBagel\build** folder, based on the unique attributes of your game application.

Next, Ant creates a **\NetBeansProjects\InvinciBagel\dist** distribution folder to hold project `.jar` files and then, detecting JavaFX usage, launches `ant-javafx.jar` to add JavaFX capabilities to the Ant build engine, which will create the `.jar` file. Finally, you will see a warning to change the `manifest.custom.codebase` property from an asterisk value (which means "everything") to a specific value. I may get into the manifest and permissions area of application development later in the book, after you are a bit more advanced. JavaFX is then launched, and the `.jar` file is built.

Ant is the build engine, or **build tool**, that creates your `.jar` file. Other build engines, such as **Maven** and **Gradle**, can also be used in NetBeans, because as you now know, NetBeans is extensible!

Ant is used in the Eclipse IDE as well and is an Apache open-source project that has been around for a very long time. To learn more about the Ant build system and what it does, visit the Ant web site **(http://ant.apache.org)**.

Next, you will explore the profiling capabilities in NetBeans 8.0, which can analyze your code at runtime and let you know how efficiently (or inefficiently) your Java 8 code is running. This is important for a game, especially an arcade game or any game that is moving **sprites** around in real-time on a user's screen. You will be learning game concepts and design in Chapter 6 of this book.

Profiling Your Java 8 Game Project in NetBeans 8.0

To launch the Java 8 code profiling utility, using the Profile menu at the top of the IDE, select Profile Project (InvinciBagel) (the first menu item), as illustrated in Figure 2-12, or use the Profile Project shortcut icon, which is visible in the collapsed screen view given in Figure 2-13 (you can tell that I collapsed the screenshot by the Java code line numbering in the **code editor** pane, which contains only lines 1 and 38, the first and last numbers in the range; I removed lines 2–37, using Photoshop).

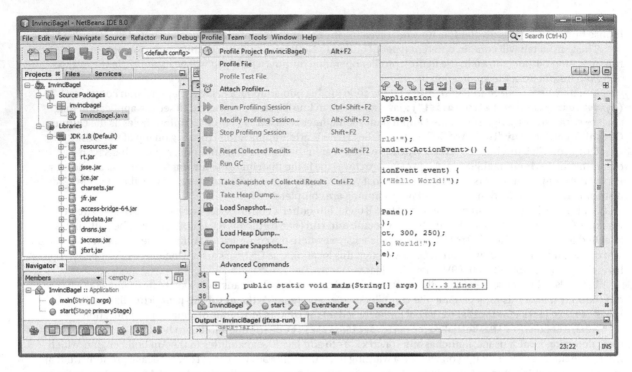

Figure 2-12. *Click the NetBeans IDE 8.0 Profile menu, and select the Profile Project (InvinciBagel) menu option*

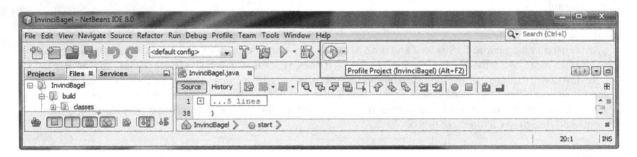

Figure 2-13. *The shortcut icon for the Profile Project utility, with tool tip (screen collapsed)*

As you can see in both the Profile menu and the Profile Project icon tool tip, at the top of the screen, the keyboard shortcut for the Profile Project tool is **ALT+F2** (hold down the **ALT** key on your keyboard, and press the **F2** function key, at the top left of the keyboard, simultaneously).

Profiling Your Java 8 Game Application CPU Usage

Using the Profile Project menu item or shortcut icon will open the **Profile InvinciBagel** (your game project's name) dialog, as shown in Figure 2-14. Let's click the center **CPU** button at the left of the dialog, which will put the dialog in **Analyze Performance** (selection characteristics) mode. You will look at profiling **memory** use a bit later on (see the section "Profiling Your Java 8 Game Application Memory Usage"). The **Monitor** (button) option enables real-time thread monitoring, which can be used while you write your Java code.

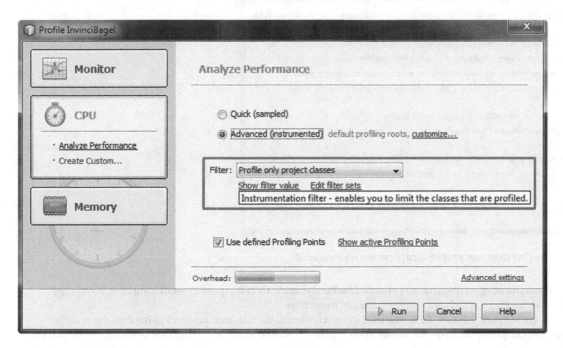

Figure 2-14. *Set the filter, using the drop-down menu in the Profile Project dialog, and select the Advanced (instrumented) output setting*

In this dialog, you can select a **Quick profile** or an **Advanced profile**, which has graphical instruments that show the performance visually. As you can see, this is the option selected as well as the **Profile only project classes** option from the **Instrumentation Filter** drop-down menu. Leave **Use defined Profiling Points** selected to get NetBeans 8.0 to do the maximum amount of profiling work possible. Note as well the **Overhead** gauge (indicator) at the bottom of the dialog, indicating a 50 percent value.

The first time that you run the NetBeans profiling tool, it needs to **calibrate** your workstation, as every workstation will have different characteristics, such as the amount of memory and number of CPU cores, or processors.

Figure 2-15 displays the Calibration Information dialog, which suggests that only NetBeans run on your workstation during the calibration process and tells you how to calibrate again in the future (if you change the system hardware configuration), using the **Profile ➤ Advanced Commands ➤ Manage Calibration Data** menu sequence.

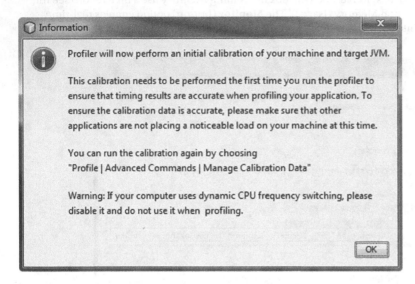

Figure 2-15. *The first time you profile, a calibration is performed*

There is also a warning, saying that you should **disable dynamic CPU frequency switching** (this is typically referred to as overclocking), which is a common feature these days.

Because I want to test for slower CPU speeds, I did not bother to do this, as it involves going into the system BIOS (Basic Input/Output System) on the workstation motherboard and is not something for beginners to be playing around with.

Ultimately, the most thorough way to test a game application is across a wide range of different OSs and hardware configurations, but I wanted to show you this profiling feature, as it is a great way to get a good baseline on your application performance, which you can then improve on as you refine your code (and then run the profiler again and again, comparing the results with the original baseline measurements).

Once you click the OK button, NetBeans IDE 8.0 will calibrate its profiling tool relative to your system hardware characteristics, which should not take long at all on a fast, modern-day, multicore workstation.

If you are running the Windows OS (as seen here, in the 64-bit Windows 7 version), you will probably get a **Windows Firewall has blocked some features of this program** Windows Security Alert dialog. You want to have all the features of NetBeans 8.0 at your disposal, so let's look at how to allow access to the Java SE 8 platform in Windows next.

Unblocking the Java 8 Platform Binary via the Windows Firewall

If you get the dreaded Blocked Features network dialog, presented in Figure 2-16, select the Allow Java Platform SE binary to communicate on Private networks, such as my home or work network check box, and then click the Allow access button, which will allow the Java 8 platform SE binary to communicate through the Windows firewall.

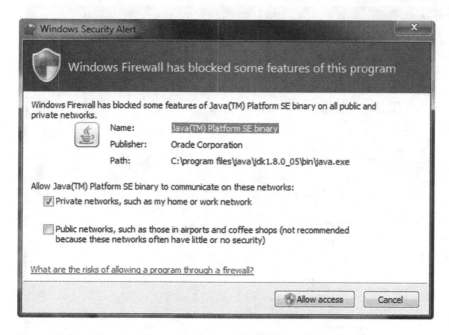

Figure 2-16. *Allow Java features to be used by clicking Allow access*

After you allow access to the **Java 8 platform** SE **binary**, the NetBeans 8.0 profiling tool can (and will) run and will generate **basic profiling telemetry** results. You will take a closer look at these in the following sections, which deal how to analyze profiling results and what they reveal in terms of how your application uses memory and CPU resources.

Analyzing the NetBeans IDE 8.0 Game Project CPU Profiling Tool Results

The NetBeans Profiler essentially looks at **memory usage** and the **CPU time** used to execute your code. The less memory used, and the faster the CPU times (which equates to fewer CPU processing cycles required to execute code), the better optimized your application is. The Profiler also looks at code- (software-) related things, such as method calls and thread states, which you will be learning about over the course of this book.

After you run the NetBeans 8.0 Profiler, you will see that a **Profiler** tab has been added to your Projects, Files, and Services tabs, at the left of the IDE, as illustrated in Figure 2-17. You examined these other three tabs earlier in the chapter (see the section "NetBeans 8.0 Is Efficient: Organized Project Management Tools"), so let's explore the Profiler tab now.

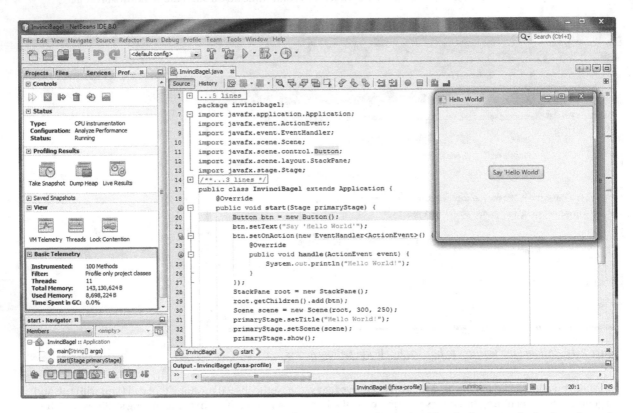

Figure 2-17. *Profile's Basic Telemetry section, at the left of the IDE, under the Profile tab, shows methods, threads, and total and used memory*

At the top of the Profiler tab is the **Controls** section, with **Stop** (Terminate) Profiled Application, **Reset** Collected Profiling Results Buffer, **Garbage Collection**, **Modify** Profiling Session, and **VM Telemetry Overview** icons.

Below these is the **Status** section, showing the **type** of profiling you have selected (in this case, **CPU**), the **configuration** (**Analyze Performance**), and the **Status** (**Running**).

The **Profiling Results** section contains icons that open tabs in the **code editor** section regarding profiling data results (reports), and the **View** section does the same thing for **virtual memory (VM) telemetry**, **threads**, and thread **lock contention**. You will be looking at some of these in the next section, when you profile memory usage (you are currently profiling CPU usage).

You can save **snapshots** of various points in time during your code profiling sessions in the **Saved Snapshots** section. The **Basic Telemetry** section shows **statistics** regarding the profiling session, including number of methods, filter settings, threads running, and memory usage.

Click the **Live Results** icon in the **Profiling Results** section, and open a live profiling result tab, shown in Figure 2-18, at the top, labeled with the CPU time (2:12:09 PM).

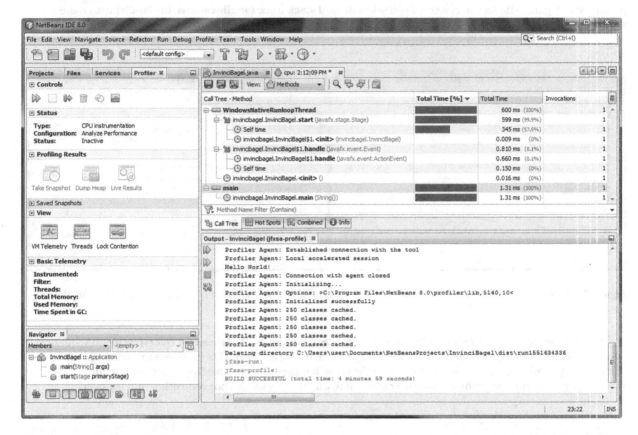

Figure 2-18. *NetBeans Profiler output, shown in the cpu tab, at the top right, and the Output tab, at the bottom right*

As you can see, you are able to open your code hierarchy, including the .main() method, the .start() method, and the .handle() method, and see a visual representation of their percentage of total CPU time used as well as the actual CPU time used, in milliseconds, which is the time value that is employed in Java programming for both Java 8 and JavaFX and even for HTML5, JavaScript, and Android application development.

Finally, as you can see in the **Output** pane at the bottom of the figure, there is also **text output**, just like when this Output pane is used for displaying the compiled, run, and executed code, showing what the Profiler is doing as well. After the "**Hello World!**" that you generated by clicking your application's Say "Hello World" button, you can see the Profiler agent Initializing, caching classes, and so on. There are a ton of tabs and options in this area of NetBeans, and I cannot cover every single one of them in this basic NetBeans overview chapter, so play around with what you see on your screen!

Profiling Your Java 8 Game Application Memory Usage

Let's take a look at **Memory** Profiling next. Click the **Profile Project** icon, and open the **Analyze Memory** dialog, presented in Figure 2-19. As you can see, if you select **Record stack trace for allocations**, the Profiler uses more system **overhead**.

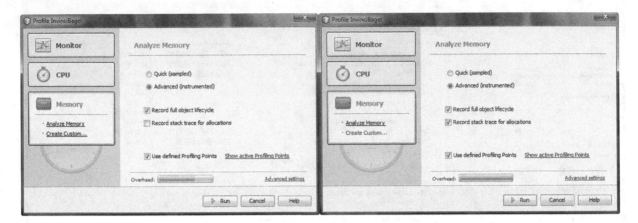

Figure 2-19. *Select the Memory section of the Profile InvinciBagel dialog and select Record stack trace for allocation*

Once the **memory profiler** is running, use a **Window ➤ Profiling ➤ VM Telemetry Overview** menu sequence, shown in Figure 2-20 (top), to open the VM Telemetry Overview tab (bottom). This tab shows **memory allocated** and **memory used**. You can hover the mouse over the visual bar to get an exact reading at any point in time. In programming terms, hovering a mouse over something will be accessed in your code using "mouse-over."

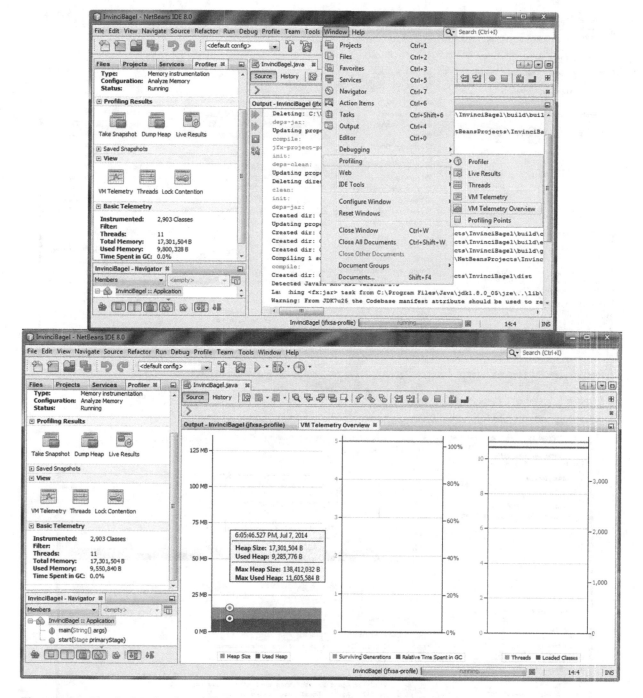

Figure 2-20. *Use the Window ➤ Profiling menu sequence to access the visual profiling tabs*

Check out some of the other visual report tabs in the **Window ➤ Profiling** menu sequence. Presented in Figure 2-21 are the **Threads** tab, showing all **11** threads (see the Basic Telemetry pane, at the left of the screen), including what each thread is doing (what code the thread is running), and the **VM Telemetry** tab, which displays virtual memory usage over time.

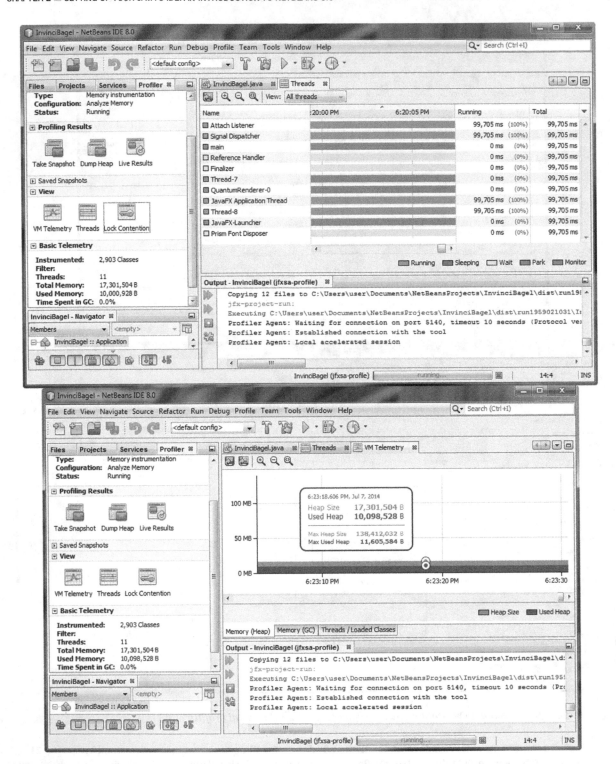

Figure 2-21. *Use the Window ➤ Profiling menu sequence to access the Threads and VM Telemetry tabs*

The NetBeans Profiler is something that you learn how to use over time, first through experimentation and then, as you become familiar with what Profiler can do, by using it with your own projects as they become increasingly complex and observing what your code base does regarding threads, CPU usage, and memory allocation and usage. NetBeans Profiler is a powerful and useful tool of this that is going to serve as the code development foundation for your Java 8 game development. I included it in this chapter to give you a solid overview, as this knowledge base will help you leverage the software, using it to its fullest potential and capabilities.

Clearly, this is an advanced IDE and software development tool that cannot be covered in one short chapter (maybe in a book; however, this is not a NetBeans 8.0 games development title), so you will be learning more about what NetBeans 8.0 can do for you in just about all the chapters in this book, as NetBeans 8.0 and Java 8 (and JavaFX 8) are inexorably intertwined.

Summary

In this second chapter, you learned about NetBeans IDE 8.0, which will serve as the foundation and primary tool for your Java 8 game development work process. This IDE is where your Java 8 (and JavaFX 8) code is written, compiled, run, tested, and debugged as well as where your new media (image, audio, video, 3D, font, shape, and so on) assets are stored and referenced, using your NetBeansProject folder and its subfolders.

You started by taking a look at NetBeans 8.0 and the high-level features that make it the official IDE for Java 8 and that help programmers develop code quickly, efficiently, and effectively (i.e., make code that is bug free) the first time. After this overview, you created your Java 8 game project, using as a model a real-world game project that I am working on for a major client.

You went through the **New Java Application** series of dialogs and created a JavaFX framework for your game, which will allow you to use new media assets, such as images, audio, video, and 3D. Then, you explored how to **compile** and run an application, using NetBeans 8.0. You also studied the Output tab and how that is used for compiler output, runtime output, and profiling output, which you considered next.

You examined both **CPU profiling** and **memory profiling** in NetBeans 8.0; learned how to set up and start up the **Profile Project** tool; and studied some of the output, statistics, and visual reports that the NetBeans Profiler can create for you, based on your Java 8 game project.

In the next chapter, I will present an overview of the Java 8 programming language to make sure that you are up to speed on how Java 8 works; a Java primer chapter, if you will.

CHAPTER 3

■ ■ ■

A Java 8 Primer: An Introduction to Java 8 Concepts and Principles

Let's build on the knowledge you gained about NetBeans IDE 8.0 in the previous chapter by exploring the basic concepts and principles behind the **Java 8** programming language. Java JDK 8 will be the foundation for your Java 8 games, as well as for your NetBeans IDE 8.0, so it is important that you take the time to study this chapter, a Java 8 "primer" that gives you an overview of this internationally popular computer (and device) programming language.

You will of course learn about more advanced concepts, such as **Lambda Expressions**, and about other Java 8 components, such as the recent **JavaFX** multimedia engine, as you progress through the book, so be aware that this chapter will cover the most **foundational** Java programming language concepts, techniques, and principles, spanning the three major versions of Java SE currently in widespread use today, on computers, iTVs, and handheld devices.

These versions of Java, used by billions of users, include **Java 6**, which is used in the 32-bit Android 4.x OS and applications; **Java 7**, which is used in the 64-bit Android 5.x OS and applications; and Java 8, which is used across many popular OSs, such as Microsoft Windows, Apple OS X, Oracle Solaris, and a plethora of popular Linux "distros," or distributions (custom Linux OS versions, such as SUSE, Ubuntu, Mint, Mandrake, Fedora, and Debian).

You will start with the easiest concepts, the highest level of Java, and progress to the more difficult ones, the guts of the Java programming constructs. You will begin, with a study of Java **syntax**, or lingo, including what Java **keywords** are, how Java **delimits** its programming constructs, and how to **comment** your code. Examining this first will give you a head start at being able to read Java code, as it is important to be able to discern the Java code from the commentary regarding that code (which is usually written by the author of the Java code using comments).

Then, you will consider the top-level concept of **APIs**, as well as what a **package** is, and how you can **import** and use the preexisting code that is provided by Java packages. These Java packages are a part of the Java 8 API, and it is important to note that you can create custom Java packages of your own, containing your games or applications.

After that, you will consider the constructs that are held inside of these Java packages, which are called Java **classes**. Java classes are the foundation of Java programming, and can be used to build your applications (in this case, your Java 8 games). You will learn about the **methods**, **variables**, and **constants** that these classes contain, as well as what superclasses and subclasses are, and what nested classes and inner classes are, and how to utilize them.

Finally, you will discover what Java **objects** are, and learn how they form the foundation of **Object Oriented Programming** (**OOP**). You will also come to know what a **constructor** method is, and how it creates the Java object, by using a special kind of method called a **constructor method** that has the same name as the class that it is contained in. Let's get started—we have a lot of ground to cover!

The Syntax of Java: Comments and Code Delimiters

There are a couple of things regarding **syntax**, meaning how Java writes things in its programming language, that you need to consider right off of the bat. These primary syntax **rules** are there to allow the Java **compiler** to understand how you are structuring your Java code. Java **compilation** is the part of the Java programming process, in which the

JDK compiler (program) turns your Java code into **bytecode** that is executed or run by a Java **Runtime** Engine (JRE). This JRE, in this case it is JRE 8, is installed on your end user's computer system. The Java compiler needs to know where your Java code blocks begin and end, where your individual Java programming statements or instructions begin and end within those Java code blocks, and which parts of your code are Java programming logic, and which parts are comments to yourself, or comments (notes) to other members of your game project programming team.

Let's start with comments, as this topic is the easiest to grasp, and you have already seen comments in your InvinciBagel game bootstrap Java code, in Chapter 2. There are two ways to add comments into Java code: single-line, also referred to as **"in-line,"** comments, which are placed after a line of Java code logic, and multiple--line, or **"block,"** comments, which are placed before (or after) a line of Java code or a block of Java code (a Java code structure).

The **single-line comment** is usually utilized to add a comment regarding what that line of Java logic, which I like to call a Java programming **"statement,"** is doing, that is, what that line of Java code is there to accomplish within your overall code structure. Single-line comments in Java start with the **double forward slash** sequence. For instance, if you wanted to comment one of the import statements in the InvinciBagel bootstrap code that you created in Chapter 2, you would add double forward slashes after the line of code. This is what your Java code would look like once it has been commented (see also Figure 3-1, bottom right):

```
import javafx.stage.Stage // This line of code imports the Stage class from JavaFX.stage package
```

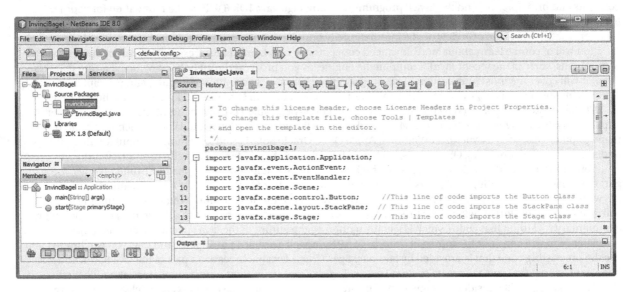

Figure 3-1. *Multiline comments (first five lines of code, at the top) and single-line comments (last three lines of code, at the bottom)*

Next, let's take a look at **multiline comments**, which are shown at the top of Figure 3-1, above the package statement (which you will be learning about in the next section). As you can see, these Java block comments are done differently, using a **single forward slash next to an asterisk** to start the comment and the reverse of that, an **asterisk next to a single forward slash**, to end the multi-line comment.

As you can see in the **InvinciBagel.java** code editing tab in NetBeans 8.0, just as I lined up the single-line comments to look pretty (cool) and organized, so too the Java **convention** in block commenting is to line up the asterisks, with one as the beginning comment delimiter and one as the ending comment delimiter.

■ **Definition**   A "**convention**" in Java programming is the way that most, if not all, Java programmers will implement a Java construct. In this case, this is the way that the Java code block commenting is **styled**.

There is a third type of comment, called a **Javadoc** comment, which you will not be using in your Java 8 game development, as your code is intended to be used to create a game, and not to be distributed to the public. If you were going to write a Java game engine for use by others to create games, that is when you would use Javadoc comments to add documentation to your Java 8 game engine. A Javadoc comment can be used by the **javadoc.exe** tool in the JDK to generate HTML documentation for the Java class containing Javadoc comments, based on the text content that you put inside the Javadoc comment.

A Javadoc comment is similar to a multiline comment, but it uses instead two asterisks to create the opening Javadoc comment delimiter, as shown here:

```
/**  This is an example of a Java Documentation (Javadoc) type of Java code comment.
     This is a type of comment which will automatically generate Java documentation!
*/
```

If you wanted to insert a comment right in the middle of your Java statement or programming structure (which you should never do as a professional Java programmer), use the multiline comment format, like so:

```
import  /* This line of code imports the Stage class */  javafx.stage.Stage;
```

This will not generate any errors, but would confuse the readers of this code, so do not comment your code in this way. The following single line comment way of commenting this code, using the double forward slash, would, however, generate compiler errors in NetBeans 8.0:

```
import  // This line of code imports the Stage class  javafx.stage.Stage
```

Here, the compiler will see only the word **import**, as the single-line comment goes to the end of the line, compared with the multiline comment, which is specifically ended using the block comment delimiter sequence (asterisk and a forward slash). So, the compiler will throw an error for this second improperly commented code, essentially asking, "Import what?"

Just as the Java programming language uses the double forward slash and slash-asterisk pairing to **delimit** the comments in your Java code, so too a couple of other key characters are used to delimit Java programming statements as well as entire blocks of Java programming logic (I often call these Java code structures).

The **semicolon** is used in Java (all versions) to delimit or separate Java programming statements, such as the package and import statements seen in Figure 3-1. The Java compiler looks for a Java keyword, which starts a Java statement, and then takes everything after that keyword, up to the semicolon (which is the way to tell the Java compiler, "I am done coding this Java statement"), as being part of the Java code statement. For instance, to declare the Java package at the top of your Java application, you use the Java **package** keyword, the name of your package, and then a semicolon, as follows (see also Figure 3-1):

```
package invincibagel;
```

Import statements are delimited using the semicolon as well, as can be seen in the figure. The import statement provides the import keyword, the package and class to be imported, and, finally, the semicolon delimiter, as shown in the following Java programming statement:

```
import javafx.application.Application;
```

Next, you should take a look at the **curly { braces ({. . .})** delimiter, which, like the multiline comment delimiter, has an **opening curly brace**, which delimits (that is, which shows a compiler) the start of a collection of Java statements, as well as a **closing curly brace**, which delimits the end of the collection of Java programming statements. The curly braces allow you to use multiple Java programming statements inside a number of Java constructs, including inside of Java classes, methods, loops, conditional statements, lambda expressions, and interfaces, all of which you will be learning about over the course of this book.

As illustrated in Figure 3-2, Java code blocks delimited using curly braces can be nested (contained) inside of each other, allowing far more complex Java code constructs. The first (outermost) code block using curly braces is the InvinciBagel class, with other constructs then nested as follows: the **start()** method, the **.setOnAction()** method, and the **handle()** method. You will be examining what all this code does as this chapter progresses. What I want you to visualize now (with the help of the red squares in Figure 3.2) is how the curly braces are allowing your methods (and class) to define their own code blocks (structures), each of which is a part of a larger Java structure, with the largest Java structure being the **InvinciBagel.java** class itself. Note how each opening curly brace has a matching closing curly brace. Note as well the indenting of the code, such that the innermost Java code structures are indented the farthest to the right. Each block of code is indented by an additional **four characters** or spaces. As you can see, the class is not indented (0), the **start()** method is 4 spaces in, the **.setOnAction()** method is 8 spaces in, and the **handle()** method is 12 spaces in. NetBeans 8.0 will indent each of your Java code structures for you! Also notice that NetBeans 8.0 draws very fine (gray) indentation guide lines in the IDE so that you can line up your code structures visually, if you prefer.

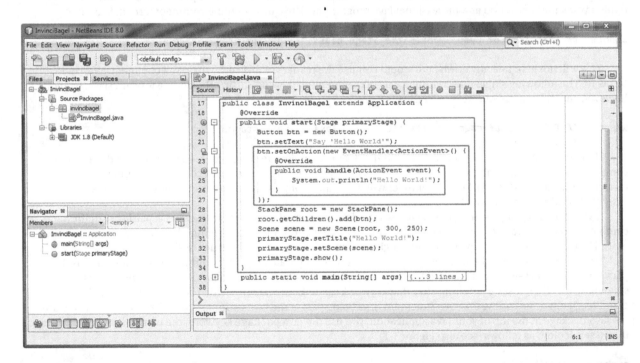

Figure 3-2. *Nested Java code blocks for the InvinciBagel class, start method, setOnAction method, and handle method*

The Java code inside each of the red squares begins with a curly brace and ends with a curly brace. Now that you are familiar with the various Java 8 code commenting approaches, as well as how your Java 8 game programming statements need to be delimited, both individually and as Java code blocks, you will next study the various Java code structures themselves—how they are used, what they can do for your applications and games, and which important Java keywords are employed to implement them.

Java APIs: Using Packages to Organize by Function

At the highest level of a programming platform, such as Google's 32-bit Android 4, which uses Java SE 6; 64-bit Android 5, which uses Java SE 7; and the current Oracle Java SE platform, which was recently released as Java SE 8, there is a collection of packages that contain classes, interfaces, methods, and constants and that together form the **API**. This collection of Java code (in this case, the Java 8 API) can be used by application (in this case, game) developers to create professional-level software across many OSs, platforms, and consumer electronics devices, such as computers, laptops, netbooks, notebooks, tablets, iTV sets, game consoles, smartwatches, and smartphones.

To install a given version of an API level, you install the SDK **(Software Development Kit)**. The Java SDK has a special name, the JDK **(Java Development Kit)**. Those of you who are familiar with Android (Java SE on top of Linux) OS development know that a different API level is released every time a few new features are added. This is because these new **hardware features** need to be supported, not because Google's executives feel like releasing a new SDK every few months. Android has 24 different API levels, whereas Java SE has only eight, and only three of Java's API levels (Java 6, Java 7, Java 8) are in use currently.

Java SE 6 is used with Eclipse ADT (Android Developer Tools) IDE to develop for 32-bit Android (versions 1.5 through 4.5); Java SE 7 is used with IntelliJ IDEA to develop for 64-bit Android (version 5.0 and later); and Java 8 is used with the NetBeans IDE to develop for JavaFX and Java 8 across the Windows, Mac OS X, Linux, and Oracle Solaris OSs. I have three different workstations that are optimized for each of these Java API platforms and IDE software packages so that I can develop applications for Android 4 (Java 6), Android 5 (Java 7), and JavaFX (Java 8) at the same time. Fortunately, you can get a powerful Windows 8.1 hexacore or octacore 64-bit AMD workstation on PriceWatch.com for a few hundred dollars!

Besides API level (the SDK you installed and are using), the highest-level construct in the Java programming language is the **package**. A Java package uses the **package** keyword to declare the application's package at the top of your Java code. This must be the first line of code declared, other than comments (see Figure 3-1; see also Chapter 2). The **New Project** series of dialogs in NetBeans that you used in Chapter 2 will create your package for you and will import other packages that you will need to use, based on what you want to do in your application. In this case, these are JavaFX packages, so you can use the JavaFX new media engine.

As you may have ascertained from the name, a Java package collects all the Java programming constructs. These include classes, interfaces, and methods that relate to your application, so the invinciBagel package will contain all your code, as well as the code that you imported to work with your code, to create, compile, and run the InvinciBagel game.

A Java package is useful for organizing and containing all your own application code, certainly, but it is even more useful for organizing and containing the SDK's (API's) Java code, which you will use, along with your own Java programming logic, to create your Java 8 applications. You can use any of the classes that are part of the API that you are targeting by using the Java **import** keyword, which, in conjunction with the package and class that you want to use, constitutes an **import statement**.

The import statement begins with the **import keyword**, followed by the **fully qualified class name**, which is the **package name,** any **subpackage name,** and the **class name** as a complete **naming reference path** (the full proper name for the class). A **semicolon terminates** an import statement. As you have already seen in Figure 3-1, the import statement used to import the JavaFX **EventHandler** class from the **javafx.event** package should look just like this:

```
import javafx.event.EventHandler;
```

The import statement tells the Java compiler that you will be using methods (or constants) from the class that is referenced, using the import keyword, as well as which package the class is stored in. If you use a class, method, or interface in your own Java class, such as the **InvinciBagel** class (see Figure 3-2), and you have not **declared** the class for use, using the import statement, the Java compiler will **throw** an error until you add the required import statement at the top of the class (after the Java package declaration statement, and before the Java class declaration statement).

■ **Note**   It is possible to use, instead of the Java **import** keyword, the fully qualified class name, that is, to preface the class name with the package name, right inside your Java code. Convention dictates using the import statement; however, line 20 in Figure 3-2 could be written as `javafx.scene.control.Button btn = new javafx.scene.control.Button();` if you wanted to buck standard Java programming convention.

Java Classes: Logical Java Constructs to Build On

The next logical Java programming construct beneath the package level is the Java **class** level, as you saw in the import statement, which references both the package that contains the class and a class itself. Just as a package organizes all the related classes, so too a class organizes all its related methods, variables, and constants and, sometimes, other **nested** classes.

Thus, the Java class is used to organize your Java code at the next logical level of functional organization, and so your class will contain Java code constructs that add functionality to your application. These may include methods, variables, constants, nested classes, or inner classes.

Java classes can also be used to create Java **objects**. Java objects are **constructed**, using your Java class, and have the same name as the Java class and as that class's **constructor method**.

As you saw in Figure 3-2, you **declare** your class, using a Java **class** keyword, along with a name for your class. You can also preface the declaration with Java **modifier** keywords, which you will be studying later in this chapter (see the section "Java Modifier Keywords: Access Control and More"). Java modifier keywords are always placed **before** (or in front of) the Java class keyword, using the following format:

```
<modifier keywords> class <your custom classname goes here>
```

One of the powerful features of Java classes is that they can be used to **modularize** your Java game code so that your core game application features can be a part of a high-level class that can be **subclassed** to create more specialized versions of that class. Once a class has been subclassed, it becomes a **superclass**, in Java class hierarchy terminology. A class will always subclass a superclass using a Java **extends** keyword. If a class does not extend a given superclass in this way, then it automatically extends the Java masterclass: **java.lang.Object**. This is so that every class in Java can create an object by implementing a constructor method.

Using a Java **extends** keyword tells the compiler that you want the superclass's capabilities and functionality added (extended) to your class, which, once it uses this extends keyword, becomes a subclass. A subclass extends the core functionality that is provided by the superclass. To extend your class definition to include a superclass, you add to (or **extend**, no pun intended) your existing class declaration, using the following format:

```
<modifier keywords> class <your custom classname> extends <superclass>
```

When you extend a superclass with your class, which is now a subclass of that superclass, you can use all the superclass's features (nested classes, inner classes, methods, variables, constants) in your subclass, without having them all explicitly written (coded) in the **body** of your class, which would be redundant (and disorganized).

■ **Note** If any of the data fields or methods in the superclass that you are extending (or, if you prefer, subclassing) have been declared using the **private** access control keyword, those variables (or constants) and methods are reserved for use only by (or within) that superclass, and thus will not be accessible to your subclass. The same rules apply to nested and inner classes; these class structures cannot use any code declared as private in the Java constructs that contain them (or that are above them, if you will).

The body of your class is coded inside the curly braces (see Figure 3-2, outermost red box), which follow your class (**and javafx.application.Application superclass**, in this case) declaration. This is why you learned about Java syntax first, and you are building on that with the class declaration and the Java syntax that holds the class definition (variables, constants, methods, constructor, nested classes) constructs.

As you can see in the figure, the **InvinciBagel** class extends an **Application** superclass from the JavaFX package. The inheritance diagram (a tool I will be using throughout the book to show you where things come from in the overall Java and JavaFX API schemas) for your current superclass-to-subclass hierarchy will therefore look like this:

```
> java.lang.Object
  > javafx.application.Application
    > invincibagel.InvinciBagel
```

By extending the javafx.application package and its Application class, you will give the InvinciBagel class everything it needs to host (or run) the JavaFX application. The JavaFX Application class "constructs" an **Application** object so that it can use system memory; call an **.init()** method, to initialize anything that may require initializing; and call a **.start()** method (see Figure 3-2, second-outermost red box), which puts things into place that will ultimately be needed to fire up (start) an InvinciBagel Java 8 game application.

When the end user finishes using the InvinciBagel game **application**, the **Application** object, created by the **Application** class, using the **Application()** constructor method, will call its **.stop()** method and remove your application from system memory, thus freeing up that memory space for other uses by the your end-users. You will be learning about Java 8 methods, constructors, and objects soon, as you are progressing from the high-level package and class constructs, to lower-level method and object constructs, and so you are moving from a high-level overview to lower levels. You may be wondering if Java classes can be **nested** inside each other, that is, if Java classes contain other Java classes. The answer is yes, they certainly can (and do)! Let's take a look at the concept of Java nested classes next.

Nested Classes: Java Classes Living Inside Other Classes

A **nested class** in Java is a class that is defined inside of another Java class. A nested class is part of the class in which it is nested, and this nesting signifies that the two classes are intended to be used together in some fashion. There are two types of nested classes: **static nested classes**, which are commonly referred to simply as nested classes, and **nonstatic nested classes**, which are commonly referred to as **inner classes**.

Static nested classes, which I will refer to as nested classes, are used to create utilities for use with the class that contains them, and are sometimes used only to hold constants for use with that class. Those of you who develop Android applications are very familiar with nested classes, as they are quite commonly employed in the Android API, to hold either utility methods or Android constants, which are used to define things such as screen density settings, animation motion interpolation curve types, alignment constants, and user interface element scaling settings. If you are looking for an understanding regarding the concept of static, it can be thought of as fixed, or not capable of being changed. A photograph is a static image, whereas video is not static. We'll look at this concept often during this book.

A nested class uses what is commonly referred to in Java as **dot notation** to reference the nested class "off of" its master, or parent, containing class. For instance, **MasterClass.NestedClass** would be the referencing format that would be used to reference a nested class via its master class (containing class) name, using generic class type names here. If you created an InvinciBagel SplashScreen nested class to draw the **splash screen** for your Java game, it would be referenced in your Java code as **InvinciBagel.SplashScreen**, using this Java 8 **dot notation** syntax.

Let's take a look at, for example, the JavaFX Application class, which contains a **Parameters** nested class. This nested class **encapsulates**, or contains, the parameters that you can set for your JavaFX application. Thus, this **Application.Parameters** nested class would be a part of the same **javafx.application** package as your **Application** class and would be referenced as **javafx.application.Application.Parameters**, if you were using an import statement.

Similarly, the constructor method would be written as **Application.Parameters()**, because the constructor method must have the exact same naming schema as the class that it is contained in. Unless you are writing code for other developers, which is when nested classes are most often used (such as the JavaFX Application class or the many nested utility or constant provider classes which you will find in the Android OS), you are far more likely to utilize non-static nested classes (commonly referred to as Java **inner classes**).

A nested class can be declared by using the Java **static** keyword. A Java keyword is also sometimes called a Java modifier. Therefore, if you were to do an InvinciBagel.SplashScreen nested class, the InvinciBagel class and its SplashScreen nested class declaration (Java 8 programming structure) would look something like this:

```
public class InvinciBagel extends Application {
    static class SplashScreen {
        // The Java code that creates and displays your splashscreen is in here
    }
}
```

It is important to note if you use, for example, import javafx.application.Application.Parameters to import a nested class, you can reference that nested class within your class, using just the Parameters class name, rather than the full class name path that shows your class's code how to travel through a parent class to its nested class via the Application.Parameter (ClassName.NestedClassName) dot notation syntax reference.

As you will see many times throughout this book, Java methods can also be accessed using the dot notation. So, instead of using **ClassName.NestedClassName.MethodName**, you could, if you had used the import statement to import this nested class, simply use **NestedClassName.MethodName**. This is because the Java import statement has already been used to establish the full reference path to this nested class, through its containing class, and so you do not have to provide this full path reference for the compiler to know what code construct you are referring to!

Next, let's take a look at nonstatic nested classes, which are usually referred to as Java inner classes.

Inner Classes: Different Types of Nonstatic Nested Classes

Java **inner classes** are also nested classes, but they are not declared using the **static** keyword modifier before the class keyword and class name, which is why they are called **nonstatic** nested classes. Thus, any class declaration that is inside another class that does not use the static (keyword) modifier would be termed an inner class in Java. There are three types of inner classes in Java: **member** class, **local** class, and **anonymous** class. In this section, you will discover what the differences are between these inner classes, as well as how they are implemented .

Like nested classes, **member classes** are defined within the body of the containing (parent) class. You can declare a member class anywhere within the body of the containing class. You would declare a member class if you wanted to access data fields (variables or constants) and methods belonging to the containing class without having to provide a path (via dot notation) to the data field or method (**ClassName.DataField or ClassName.Method**). A member class can be thought of as a nested class that does not use the Java static modifier keyword.

Whereas a nested class is referenced through its containing, or top-level, class, using a dot notation path to the static nested class, a member class, because it is not static, is instance specific, meaning that objects (instances) created via that class can be different from each other (an object is a unique instance of a class), whereas a static (fixed) nested class will only have one version, which does not change. For instance, a **private inner class** can only be used by a parent class that contains it. The **SplashScreen** inner class coded as a private class would look something like this:

```java
public class InvinciBagel extends Application {
    private class SplashScreen {
        // The Java code that creates and displays your splashscreen is in here
    }
}
```

Because this class is declared as private, it is for your own application usage (the containing class's usage, specifically). Thus, this would not be a utility or constant class for use by other classes, applications, or developers. You can also declare your inner class without using the **private access modifier keyword**, which would look like the following Java programming construct:

```java
public class InvinciBagel extends Application {
    class SplashScreen {
        // The Java code that creates and displays your splashscreen is in here
    }
}
```

This level of **access control** is called **package** or **package private** and is the default level of access control applied to any class, interface, method, or data field that is declared without using one of the other Java access control modifier **keywords** (public, protected, private). This type of inner class can be accessed not only by the top-level, or containing, class, but also by any other class member of the package that contains that class. This is because the containing class is declared public, and the inner class is declared package private. If you want an inner class to be available outside the package, you declare it to be **public**, using the following Java code structure:

```java
public class InvinciBagel extends Application {
    public class SplashScreen {
        // The Java code that creates and displays your splashscreen is in here
    }
}
```

You can also declare an inner class **protected**, meaning that it can only be accessed by any subclasses of the parent class. If you declare a class inside a lower-level Java programming structure that is not a class, such as a method or an iteration control structure (commonly called a loop), it would technically be referred to as a **local class**. A local class is only visible inside that block of code; thus, it does not allow (or make sense to use) class modifiers, such as static, public, protected, or private. A local class is used like a **local variable**, except that it is a complex Java coding construct rather than a simple a data field value that is used locally.

Finally, there is a type of inner class called an **anonymous class**. An anonymous class is a local class that has not been given a class name. You are likely to encounter anonymous classes far more often than you are local classes. This is because programmers often do not name their local classes (making them anonymous classes); the logic local classes contain is only used **locally**, to their declaration, and so these classes do not really need to have a name—they are only referenced internally to that block of Java code.

Java Methods: Core Java Function Code Constructs

Inside classes, you generally have methods and the data fields (variables or constants) that these methods use. Because we are going from outside to inside, or top-level structures to lower-level structures, I will cover methods next. Methods are sometimes called functions in other programming languages. Figure 3-2 provides an example of the **.start()** method, showing how the method holds the programming logic that creates a basic "Hello World!" application. The programming logic inside the method uses Java programming statements to create a Stage object and a Scene object, place a button on the screen in a **StackPane** object, and define event-handling logic, such that when the button is clicked, the bootstrap Java code writes the "Hello World!" text to your NetBeans IDE output area.

The method declaration starts with an access modifier keyword, either public, protected, private, or package private (which is designated by not using any access control modifier at all). As you can see in the figure, the **.start()** method has been declared, using the public access control modifier.

After this access control modifier, you will need to declare the method's return type. This is the type of data that the method will return after it is called, or invoked. Because the .start() method performs setup operations but does not return a specific type of value, it uses the **void** return type, which signifies that the method performs tasks but does not return any resulting data to the calling entity. In this case, the calling entity is the JavaFX Application class, as the .start() method is one of the key methods (the others being the .stop() and .init() methods) provided by that class to control the life cycle stages of a JavaFX application.

Next, you will supply the method name, which, by convention (programming rules), should start with a lowercase letter (or word, preferably a verb), with any subsequent (internal) words (nouns or adjectives) starting with a capital letter. For instance, a method to display the splash screen would be named **.showSplashScreen()** or **.displaySplashScreen()** and because it does something but does not return a value, would be declared using this code:

```
public void displaySplashScreen() { Java code to display splashscreen goes in here }
```

If you need to pass parameters, which are named data values that have to be operated on within the body of the method (the part inside the curly braces), these go inside the parentheses that are attached to the method name. In Figure 3-2 the **.start()** method for your bootstrap "HelloWorld!" JavaFX application receives a **Stage** object, named **primaryStage**, using the following Java method declaration syntax:

```
public void start(Stage primaryStage) { bootstrap Java code to start Application goes in here }
```

You can provide as many parameters as you like, using the data type and parameter name pairs, with each pair separated by a comma. Methods can also have no parameters, in which case the parameter parentheses are empty, with the opening and closing parentheses right next to each other, for example, .start(), and .stop().

The programming logic that defines your method will be contained in the body of the method, which, as discussed previously, is inside the curly braces that define the beginning and the end of the method. The Java programming logic that is inside methods can include variable declarations, program logic statements, and iterative control structures (loops), all of which you will be leveraging to create your Java game.

Before moving on, let's focus on one other Java concept that applies to methods, namely, **overloading** Java methods. Overloading a Java method means using the same method name, but different parameter list configurations. What this means is that, if you have defined more than one method with the same name, Java can figure out which of your (overloaded) methods to use by looking at the parameters that are being passed into the method being called and then using that parameter list to discern which of the methods (that have the same name) to use by matching the parameter list data types and names and the order in which they appear. Of course, your parameter list configurations must all be unique for this Java method overloading feature to work correctly.

You will be learning how to use and how to code Java methods over the course of this book, beginning in Chapter 4, so I am not going to spend too much time on them here, other than to define what they are and the basic rules for how they are declared, and used, inside Java classes.

One specialized kind of method that I am going to cover in detail, however, is the **constructor method**. This is a type of method that can be used to create objects. Java objects are the foundation of OOP, so you will be taking a look at constructor methods next, as it is important to do so before learning about the Java **object** itself, which you will study later in the chapter (see the section "Java Objects: Virtual Reality, Using Java Constructs").

Creating a Java Object: Invoking a Class's Constructor Method

A Java class can contain a constructor method with the exact same name as the class that can be used to create Java objects using that class. A constructor method uses its Java class like a blueprint to create an **instance** of that class in memory, which creates a Java object. A constructor method will always return a Java object and thus does not use any of the Java return types that other methods will typically use (void, String, and so on). A constructor method is invoked by using the Java **new keyword**, because you are creating a new object.

You can see an example of this in the bootstrap JavaFX code shown in Figure 3-2 (ll. 20, 28, and 30), where **new Button, StackPane, and Scene objects** are created, respectively, by using the following object declaration, naming, and creation Java code structure:

```
<Java class name> <your object instance name> = new <Java constructor method name> <semicolon>
```

The reason that a Java object is declared in this way, using the class name, the name of the object you are constructing, the **Java new keyword**, and the class's constructor method name (and parameters, if any) in a single Java statement terminated with a semicolon, is because a Java object is an **instance** of a Java class.

Let's take a look at, for example, the **Button** object creation from line 20 of your current Java code. Here, via the part of the Java statement on the left-hand side of the equals operator, you are telling the Java language compiler that you want to create a **Button object** named **btn**, using the JavaFX Button class as the object blueprint. This declares the Button class (object type) and gives it a unique name.

The first part of creating the object is thus called the **object declaration**. The second part of creating your Java object is called the **object instantiation**, and this part of the object creation process, seen on the right-hand side of the equals operator, involves a constructor method and the Java new keyword.

To instantiate a Java object, you **invoke** the Java **new** keyword, in conjunction with an object constructor method call. Because this takes place on the right-hand side of the equals operator, the result of the object instantiation is placed in the declared object, which is on the left-hand side of the Java statement. As you will see a bit later in the chapter, when I discuss operators (see the section "Java Operators: Manipulating Data in the Application"), this is what an equals operator does, and a useful operator it is.

This completes the process of **declaring** (class name), **naming** (object name), **creating** (using a **new** keyword), **configuring** (using a constructor method), and **loading** (using the equals operator) your very own custom Java object.

It is important to note that the declaration and instancing parts of this process can be coded using separate lines of Java code as well. For instance, the **Button** object instantiation (see Figure 3-2, l. 20) could be coded as follows:

```
Button btn;
btn = new Button();
```

This is significant, because coding an object creation in this way allows you to declare an object at the top of your class, where each of the methods inside the class that use or access these objects can **see** the object. In Java, unless declared otherwise, using modifiers, an object or data field is only visible inside the Java programming construct (class or method) in which it is declared.

If you declare an object inside your class, and therefore outside all the methods contained in the class, then all the methods in your class can access (use) that object. Similarly, anything declared inside a method is **local to** that method and is only **visible** to other **members** of that method (Java statements inside the method scope delimiters). If you wanted to implement this separate object declaration (in the class, outside the methods) and object instantiation (inside the **.start()** method) in your current InvinciBagel class, the first few lines of Java code for your InvinciBagel class would change to look like the following Java programming logic:

```
public class InvinciBagel extends Application {
    Button btn;
    @Override
    public void start(Stage primaryStage) {
        btn = new Button();
```

```
        btn.setText("Say 'Hello World'");
        // The other programming statements continue underneath here
    }
}
```

When the object declaration and instantiation are split up, they can be placed inside (or outside) methods as needed for visibility. In the preceding code, other methods of your **InvinciBagel** class could call the .setText() method call shown without the Java compiler's throwing an error. The way the **Button** object is declared in Figure 3-2, only the **.start()** method can see the object, and so only the **.start()** method can use this btn.setText() **method call.**

Creating a Constructor Method: Coding an Object's Structure

A constructor method is more a method for creating objects in system memory, whereas other methods (or functions, if using a different programming language) are usually used to perform calculation or processing of one type or another. The constructor method's use in creating Java objects in memory, rather than performing some other programming function, is evidenced by the use of the Java **new** keyword, which creates a new object in memory. For this reason, a constructor method will define the structure of an object as well as allow the calling entity to **populate** the object structure with custom data values, using the constructor method's **parameter list**.

You will create a couple of sample constructor methods in this section to learn the basics of how this is done as well as what a constructor method usually contains. Let's say you are creating an **InvinciBagel** object for your game, so you declare a **public InvinciBagel()** constructor method, using the following Java code structure:

```
public InvinciBagel() {
    int lifeIndex = 1000;  // Defines units of lifespan
    int hitsIndex = 0;    //  Defines units of damage ("hits" on the object)
    String directionFacing = "E";        // Direction that the object is facing
    Boolean currentlyMoving = false;  //  Flag showing if the object is in motion
}
```

This constructor method, when called using an InvinciBagel mortimer = new InvinciBagel(); Java method call, creates an **InvinciBagel** object named **mortimer**, with 1,000 units of life and no hits, that is facing **east** and that is not currently moving.

Next, let's explore the concept of **overloading** the constructor method, which you learned about earlier (see the section "Java Methods: Java Core Function Code Constructs"), and create another constructor method that has parameters that allow you to define the **lifeIndex and directionFacing variables of the InvinciBagel** object while you are creating it. This constructor method looks like this:

```
public InvinciBagel(int lifespan, String direction) {
    int lifeIndex;
    int hitsIndex;
    String directionFacing = null;
    Boolean currentlyMoving = false;
    lifeIndex = lifespan;
    directionFacing = direction;
}
```

In this version the **lifeIndex** and **hitsIndex** variables at the top are initialized to **0,** the default value for an integer, so you do not have to use **lifeIndex = 0 or hitsIndex = 0 in** the code. The Java programming language accommodates method overloading, so if you use an InvinciBagel bert = new InvinciBagel(900, "W"); method call to instantiate **the InvinciBagel object, the correct constructor method will be used to create the object. The InvinciBagel** object named **bert** would have a **lifeIndex** of 900 units of life and no hits on its life, would be facing **West**, and would not be currently moving.

You can have as many (overloaded) constructor methods as you like, so long as they are each 100 percent unique. This means that **overloaded constructors** must have different parameter list configurations, including parameter list length (the number of parameters) and parameter list types (order of data types). As you can see, it is the parameter list (length, data types, order) that allows a Java compiler to differentiate overloaded methods from one another.

Java Variables and Constants: Values in Data Fields

The next level down (progressing from API, to package, to class, to method, to the actual **data values** that are being operated on in Java classes and methods) is the **data field**. Data values are held inside something called a **variable**; if you fix, or make permanent, the data, it is called a **constant**. A constant is a special type of variable (which I will cover in the next section), because declaring a constant correctly is a bit more involved (advanced) than declaring a Java variable.

In the Java lingo, variables declared at the top of a class are called **member variables**, **fields**, or **data fields**, although all variables and constants can be considered data fields, at a fundamental level. A variable declared inside a method or other **lower-level** Java programming structure declared inside a class or method, is called a **local variable**, because it can only be seen locally, inside the programming constructs delimited by curly braces. Finally, variables declared inside a parameter list area of a method declaration or method call are, not surprisingly, called **parameters**.

A variable is a data field that holds an **attribute** of your Java object or software that can (and will) change over the course of time. As you might imagine, this is especially important for game programming. The simplest form of variable declaration can be achieved by using a Java **data type keyword**, along with the name that you want to use for the variable in your Java program logic. In the previous section, using the constructor method, you declared an integer variable named **hitsIndex** to hold the damage, or hits, that your InvinciBagel object will sustain during game play. You defined the variable data type, and named it, using the following Java variable declaration programming statement:

```
int hitsIndex; // This could also be coded as: int hitsIndex = 0; (the default Integer is Zero)
```

As you also saw in that section, you can initialize your variable to a starting value, using an equals operator, along with a data value that **matches up with** the data type declared: for example:

```
String facingDirection = "E";
```

This Java statement declares a **String** data type variable and names it **facingDirection**, on the left side of the equals operator, and then sets the declared variable to a value of "E," which signifies the direction **East**, or right. This is similar to how an object is declared and instantiated, except that the Java new keyword and constructor method are replaced by the data value itself, because now a variable (data field) is being declared instead of an object being created. You will learn about the different data types (I have already covered Integer, String, and Object) later in chapter (see the section "Java Data Types: Defining Data in Applications").

You can also use Java modifier keywords with variable declarations, which I will do in the next section, when I show you how to declare an **immutable** variable, also known as a **constant**, which is fixed, or **locked**, in memory and which cannot be altered.

Now that I am almost finished going from the largest Java constructs to the smallest (data fields), I will start to cover topics that apply to all levels (classes, methods, variables) of Java. These concepts will generally increase in complexity as you progress to the end of this Java 8 primer chapter.

Fixing Data Values in Memory: Defining a Data Constant in Java

If you are already familiar with computer programming, you know that there is often a need to have data fields that will always contain the same data value and that will not change during the duration of your application run cycle. These are called **constants**, and they are defined, or declared, using special Java modifier keywords that are used to fix things in memory so that they cannot be changed. There are also Java modifier keywords that will restrict (or unrestrict) object instances, or access to certain classes inside or outside a Java class or package (which you will be examining in detail in the next section).

To declare Java variables fixed, you must use a Java **final** modifier keyword. "Final" means the same thing as when your parents say that something is final: it is fixed in place, an **FOL (fact of life)**, and not going to change, ever. Thus, the first step in creating a constant is to add this final keyword, placing it in front of the data type keyword in your declaration.

A convention, when declaring a Java constant (and constants in other programming languages), is to use **uppercase characters**, with **underscored characters** between each word, which signifies a constant in your code.

If you want to create **screen width** and **screen height** constants for your game, you do so like this:

```
final int SCREEN_HEIGHT_PIXELS = 480;
final int SCREEN_WIDTH_PIXELS  = 640;
```

If you want all the objects created by your class's constructor method to be able to see and use this constant, you add the Java **static** modifier keyword, placing it in front of the final modifier keyword, like this:

```
static final int SCREEN_HEIGHT_PIXELS = 480;
static final int SCREEN_WIDTH_PIXELS = 640;
```

If you want only your class, and objects created by this class, to be able to see these constants, you declare the constants by placing the Java **private** modifier keyword in front of the static modifier keyword, using this code:

```
private static final int SCREEN_HEIGHT_PIXELS = 480;
private static final int SCREEN_WIDTH_PIXELS = 640;
```

If you want any Java class, even those outside your package (i.e., anyone else's Java classes), to be able to see these constants, you declare the constants by placing the Java **public** modifier keyword in front of the static modifier keyword, using the following Java code:

```
public static final int SCREEN_HEIGHT_PIXELS = 480;
public static final int SCREEN_WIDTH_PIXELS = 640;
```

As you can see, declaring a constant involves a significantly more detailed Java statement than declaring a simple variable for your class! Next, you will take a deeper look at Java modifier keywords, as they allow you to control things such as **access** to your classes, methods, and variables as well as **locking** them from being modified and similar high-level Java code control concepts that are fairly complicated.

Java Modifier Keywords: Access Control and More

Java modifier keywords are reserved Java keywords that modify the access, visibility, or permanence (how long something exists in memory during the execution of an application) for code inside the primary types of Java programming structures. The modifier keywords are the first ones declared outside the Java code structure, because the Java logic for the structure, at least for classes and methods, is contained within the curly braces delimiter, which comes after the class keyword and class name or after the method name and parameter list. Modifier keywords can be used with Java classes, methods, data fields (variables and constants), and interfaces.

As you can see at the bottom of Figure 3-2, for the .main() method, created by NetBeans for your **InvinciBagel** class definition, which uses the public modifier, you can use more than one Java modifier keyword. The **.main()** method first uses a **public** modifier keyword, which is an access control modifier keyword, and then a **static** modifier keyword, which is a nonaccess control modifier keyword.

Access Control Modifiers: Public, Protected, Private, Package Private

Let's cover access control modifiers first, because they are declared first, before nonaccess modifier keywords or return type keywords, and because they are easier to understand conceptually. There are four access control modifier levels that are applied to any Java code structure. If you do not declare an access control modifier keyword, a default access control level of package private will be applied to that code structure, which allows it to be visible, and thus usable, to any Java programming structure inside your Java package (in this case, invincibagel).

The other three access control modifier levels have their own access control modifier keywords, including public, private, and protected. These are somewhat aptly named for what they do, so you probably have a good idea of how to apply them to either share your code publicly or protect it from public usage, but let's cover each one in detail here, just to make sure, as access (security) is an important issue these days, inside your code as well as in the outside world. I will start with the least amount of access control first!

Java's Public Modifier: Allowing Access by the Public to Java Program Constructs

The Java **public** access modifier keyword can be used by classes, methods, constructors, data fields (variables and constants), and interfaces. If you declare something public, it can be accessed by the public! This means that it can be imported and used by any other class, in any other package, in the entire world. Essentially, your code can be used in any software that is created using the Java programming language. As you will see in the classes that you use from the Java or JavaFX programming platforms (APIs), the public keyword is most often used in open-source programming Java platforms or packages that are employed to create custom applications, such as games.

It is important to note that if a public class that you are trying to access and use exists in a package other than your own (in your case, invincibagel), then the Java programming convention is to use the Java import keyword to create an import statement that allows use of that public class. This is why, by the time you reach the end of this book, you will have dozens of import statements at the top of your InvinciBagel.java class, as you will be leveraging preexisting Java and JavaFX classes in code libraries that have already been coded, tested, refined, and made public, using the public access control modifier keyword, so that you can create Java 8 games with them to your heart's content!

Owing to the concept of **class inheritance** in Java, all the public methods and public variables inside a public class will be **inherited** by the subclasses of that class (which, once it is subclassed, becomes a superclass). Figure 3-2 offers an example of a public access control modifier keyword, in front of the InvinciBagel class keyword.

Java's Protected Modifier: Variables and Methods Allow Access by Subclass

The Java **protected** access modifier keyword can be used by data fields (variables and constants) and by methods, including constructor methods, but cannot be used by classes or interfaces. The protected keyword allows variables, methods, and constructors in a superclass to be accessed only by subclasses of that superclass in other packages (such as the invincibagel package) or by any class within the same package as the class containing those protected members (Java constructs).

This access modifier keyword essentially protects methods and variables in a class that is intended to be (hoped to be used as) a superclass by being subclassed (**extended**) by other developers. Unless you own the package that contains these protected Java constructs (which you do not), you must extend the superclass and create your own subclass from that superclass to be able to use the protected methods.

You may be wondering, why would one want to do this, protecting Java code structures in this way? When you are designing a large project, such as the Android OS API, you will often want to have the higher-level methods and variables not be used directly, right out of, or from within, that class, but rather within a more well-defined subclass structure.

You can achieve this direct usage prevention by protecting these methods and variable constructs from being used directly such that they become only a blueprint for more detailed implementations in other classes and are not able to be used directly. Essentially, protecting a method or variable turns it into a blueprint or a definition only.

Java's Private Modifier: Variables, Methods, and Classes Get Local Access Only

The Java **private** access control modifier keyword can be used by data fields (variables or constants) and by methods, including constructor methods, but cannot be used by classes or interfaces. The private modifier can be used by a nested class; however, it cannot be used by an outer or the primary (topmost) class. The private access control keyword allows variables, methods, and constructors in a class to be accessed only inside that class. The private access control keyword allows Java to implement a concept called encapsulation, in which a class (and objects created using that class) can encapsulate itself, hiding its "internals" from outside Java universe, so to speak. The OOP concept of encapsulation can be used in large projects to allow teams to create (and, more importantly, debug) their own classes and objects. In this way, no one else's Java code can break the code that exists inside these classes, because their methods, variables, constants, and constructors are private!

The access modifier keyword essentially privatizes methods or variables in a class so that they can only be used locally within that class or by objects created by that class's constructor method. Unless you own the class that contains these private Java constructs, you cannot access or use these methods or data fields. This is the most restrictive level of access control in Java. A variable declared private can be accessed outside the class if a public method that accesses a private variable from inside the class, called a public .get() method call, is declared public and thus provides a pathway (or doorway) through that public method to the data in the private variable or constant.

Java's Package Private Modifier: Variables, Methods, and Classes in Your Package

If no Java access control modifier keyword is declared, then a **default** access control level, which is also referred to as the **package private** access control level, will be applied to that Java construct (class, method, data field, or interface). This means that these Java constructs are visible, or available, to any other Java class inside the Java package that contains them. This package private level of access control is the easiest to use with your methods, constructors, constants, and variables, as it is applied simply by not explicitly declaring an access control modifier keyword.

You will use this default access control level quite a bit for your own Java applications (game) programming, as usually you are creating your own application in your own package for your users to use in its compiled executable state. If you were developing game engines for other game developers to use, however, you would use more of the access control modifier keywords I have discussed in this section to control how others would use your code.

Nonaccess Control Modifiers: final, static, abstract, volatile, synchronized

The Java modifier keywords that do not specifically provide access control features to your Java constructs are termed **nonaccess control modifier keywords**. These include the often used **final**, **static**, and **abstract** modifier keywords as well as the not so often used **synchronized** and **volatile** modifier keywords, which are employed for more advanced **thread** control and which I will not be covering in this beginner-level programming title, except to describe what they mean and do, in case you encounter them in your Java universe travels.

I will present these concepts in the order of their complexity, that is, from the easiest for beginners to wrap their mind around to the most difficult for beginning OOP developers to wrap their mind around. OOP is like surfing, in that it seems very difficult until you have practiced doing it a number of times, and then suddenly you just get it!

Java's final Modifier: Variables, Methods, and Classes That Cannot Be Modified

You have already explored the **final** modifier keyword as it is used to declare a constant, along with a static keyword. A final data field variable can only be initialized (set) one time. A final **reference variable**, which is a special type of Java variable that contains a reference to an object in memory, cannot be changed (reassigned) to refer to a different object; the data that are held inside the (final) referenced object can be changed, however, as only the reference to the object itself is the final reference variable, which is essentially locked in, using a Java final keyword.

A Java method can also be locked using the final modifier keyword. When a Java method is made final, if the Java class that contains that method is subclassed, that final method cannot be **overridden**, or modified, within the body of the subclass. This basically locks what is inside the method code structure. For example, if you want the .start() method for your **InvinciBagel** class (were it ever to be subclassed) always to do the same things that it does for your InvinciBagel superclass (prepare a JavaFX staging environment), you use the following code:

```
public class InvinciBagel extends Application {
    Button btn;

    @Override
    public final void start(Stage primaryStage) {
        btn = new Button();
        // The other method programming statements continue here
    }
}
```

This prevents any subclasses (public class InvinciBagelReturns extends InvinciBagel) from changing anything regarding how the InvinciBagel game engine (JavaFX) is set up initially, which is what the .start() method does for your game application (see Chapter 4). A class that is declared using a final modifier keyword cannot be extended, or subclassed, locking that class for future use.

Java's Static Modifier: Variables or Methods That Exist in a Class (Not in Objects)

As you have already seen, the static keyword can be used in conjunction with the final keyword to create a constant. The static keyword is used to create Java constructs (methods or variables) that exist independently, or outside, any object instances that are created using the class that static variables or static methods are defined in. A static variable in a class will force all instances of the class to share the data in that variable, almost as if it is a global variable as far as objects created from that class are concerned. Similarly, a static method will also exist outside instanced objects for that class and will be shared by all those objects. A static method will not reference variables outside itself, such as an instanced object's variables.

Generally, a static method will have its own internal (local or static) variables and constants and will also take in variables, using the method parameter list, and then provide processing and computation, based on those parameters and its own internal (static local) constants if needed. Because static is a concept that applies to **instances** of a class, and is thus at a lower level than any class itself, a class would not be declared using a static modifier keyword.

Java's Abstract Modifier: Classes and Methods to Be Extended and Implemented

The Java **abstract** modifier keyword has more to do with protecting your actual code than with code that has been placed in memory (object instances and variables, and so on) at runtime. The abstract keyword allows you to specify how the code will be used as a superclass, that is, how it is implemented in a subclass once it is extended. For this reason, it applies only to classes and methods and not to data fields (variables and constants).

A class that has been declared using the abstract modifier keyword cannot be instanced, and it is intended to be used as a superclass (blueprint) to create (**extend**) other classes. Because a final class cannot be extended, you will not use the final and abstract modifier keywords together at the class level. If a class contains any methods that have been declared using the abstract modifier keyword, the class must itself be declared an abstract class. An abstract class does not have to contain any abstract methods, however.

A method that has been declared using the abstract modifier keyword is a method that has been declared for use in subclasses but that has no current implementation. This means that it will have no Java code inside its method body, which, as you know, is delineated in Java by using curly braces. Any subclass that extends an abstract class must implement all these abstract methods, unless the subclass is also declared abstract, in which case the abstract methods are passed down to the next subclass level.

Java's Volatile Modifier: Advanced Multithreading Control over Data Fields

The Java **volatile** modifier keyword is used when you are developing multithreaded applications, which you are not going to be doing in basic game development, as you want to optimize your game well enough so that it only uses one thread. The volatile modifier tells the Java virtual machine (JVM), which is running your application, to merge the private (that thread's) copy of the data field (variable or constant) that has been declared volatile with the master copy of that variable in system memory.

This is similar to the static modifier keyword, the difference being that a static variable (data field) is shared by more than one object instance, whereas a volatile data field (variable or constant) is shared by more than one thread.

Java's Synchronized Modifier: Advanced Multithreading Control over Methods

The Java **synchronized** modifier keyword is also used when you are developing multithreaded applications, which you are not going to be doing for your basic game development here. The synchronized modifier tells the JVM, which is running your application, that the method that has been declared synchronized can be accessed by only one thread at a time. This concept is similar to that of synchronized database access, which prevents record access **collisions**. A synchronized modifier keyword likewise prevents collisions between threads accessing your method (in system memory) by serializing the access to one at a time so that parallel (simultaneous) access to a method in memory by multiple threads will never occur.

Now that you have studied primary Java constructs (classes, methods, and fields) and basic modifier keywords (public, private, protected, static, final, abstract, and so on), let's journey inside the curly braces now, learning about the tools that are used to create the Java programming logic that will eventually define your game app's game play.

Java Data Types: Defining Data Type in Applications

Because you have already learned about variables and constants encountered in a few of Java's data types, let's explore these next, as it is not too advanced for your current progression from easy to more difficult topics!

There are two primary data type classifications in Java: **primitive data types**, which are the ones that you are the most familiar with if you have used a different programming language, and **reference (object) data types**, which you will know about if you have used another OOP language, such as Lisp, Python, Objective-C, C++, or C# (C Sharp).

Primitive Data Types: Characters, Numbers, and Boolean (Flags)

There are **eight primitive data types** in the Java programming language, as shown in Table 3-1. You will be using these as you work your way through the book to create your InvinciBagel game, so I am not going to go into detail regarding each one of them now, except to say that Java boolean data variables are used for flags or switches (on/off), char is used for Unicode characters or to create String objects (an array of char), and the rest are used to hold numeric values of different sizes and resolutions. Integer values hold whole numbers, whereas a floating point value holds fractional (decimal point value) numbers. It is important to use the right numeric data type for a variable's scope, or range, of use, because, as you can see in Binary Size column in Table 3-1, large numeric data types can use up to eight times more memory than the smaller ones.

Table 3-1. *Java Primitive Data Types, Along with Their Default Values, Size in Memory, Definition, and Numeric Range*

Data Type	Default	Binary Size	Definition	Range
boolean	false	1 bit	True or false value	0 to 1 (false or true)
char	\u0000	16 bit	Unicode character	\u0000 to \uFFFF
byte	0	8 bit	Signed integer value	–128 to 127 (256 total values)
short	0	16 bit	Signed integer value	--32768 to 32767 (65,536 total values)
int	0	32 bit	Signed integer value	–2147483648 to 2147483647
long	0	64 bit	Signed integer value	–9223372036854775808 to 9223372036854775807
float	0.0	32 bit	IEEE 754 floating point value	±1.4E-45 to ±3.4028235E+38
double	0.0	64 bit	IEEE 754 floating point value	±4.9E-324 to ±1.7976931348623157E+308

Reference Data Types: Objects and Arrays

(OOP languages also have **reference data types**, which provide a reference in memory to another structure containing a more complex data structure, such as an **object** or an **array**. These more complex data structures are created using code; in the case of Java, this is a class. There are Java **Array** classes of various types that create arrays of data (such as simple databases) as well as the constructor method in a Java class, which can create the object structure in memory, containing both Java code (methods) and data (fields).

Java Operators: Manipulating Data in the Application

In this section, you will learn about some of the most commonly used **operators** in the Java programming language, especially those that are the most useful for programming games. These include **arithmetic** operators, used for mathematical expressions; **relational** operators, used to ascertain relationships (equal, not equal, greater than, less than, and so on) between data values; **logical** operators, used for boolean logic; **assignment** operators, which do the arithmetic operations and assign the value to another variable in one compact operation (operator); and the **conditional operator**, also called a ternary operator, which assigns a value to a variable, based on the outcome of a true or false (boolean) evaluation.

There are also the conceptually more advanced **bitwise** operators, used to perform operations at the **binary** data (**zeroes and ones**) level, the logic of which is beyond the beginner scope of this book and the use of which is not as common in Java game programming as these other, more mainstream types of operators, each of which you will be using over the course of this book to accomplish various programming objectives in your game play logic.

Java Arithmetic Operators

The Java **arithmetic operators** are the most commonly used in programming, especially in arcade type games, in which things are moving on the screen by a discrete number of pixels. Many more complex equations can be created using these basic arithmetic operators, as you have already learned in math class, from primary school through college.

The only arithmetic operators shown in Table 3-2 that you may not be that familiar with are the **modulus** operator, which will return the remainder (what is left over) after a divide operation is completed, and the **increment** and **decrement** operators, which add or subtract 1, respectively, from a value. These are used to implement your **counter** logic. Counters (using increment and decrement operators) were originally used for loops, (which I will be covering in the next section); however, these increment and decrement operators are also extremely useful for game programming (point scoring, **life span** loss, game piece movement, and similar progressions).

Table 3-2. *Java Arithmetic Operators, Their Operation Type, and a Description of the Arithmetic Operation*

Operator	Operation	Description
Plus +	Addition	Adds the operands on either side of the operator
Minus –	Subtraction	Subtracts the right-hand operand from the left-hand operand
Multiply *	Multiplication	Multiplies the operands on either side of the operator
Divide /	Division	Divides the left-hand operand by the right-hand operand
Modulus %	Remainder	Divides the left-hand operand by the right hand-operand, returning remainder
Increment ++	Add 1	Increases the value of the operand by 1
Decrement --	Subtract 1	Decreases the value of the operand by 1

To implement the arithmetic operators, place the data field (variable) that you want to receive the results of the arithmetic operation on the **left side** of the **equals assignment operator** and the variables that you want to perform arithmetic operations on the right side of the equals sign. Here is an example of **adding** an x and a **y** variable and assigning the result to a z variable:

```
Z = X + Y;   // Using an Addition Operator
```

If you want to **subtract** y from x, you use a **minus** sign rather than a plus sign; if you want to **multiply** the x and y values, you use an **asterisk** rather than a plus sign; and if you want to **divide** x by y, you use a **forward slash** instead of a plus sign. Here is how those operations look:

```
Z = X - Y;   // Subtraction Operator
Z = X * Y;   // Multiplication Operator
Z = X / Y;   //  Division Operator
```

You will be using these arithmetic operators quite a bit, so you will get some great practice with these before you are finished with this book! Let's take a closer look at relational operators next, as sometimes you will want to compare values rather than calculate them.

Java Relational Operators

The Java **relational operators** are used to make **logical comparisons** between two variables or between a variable and a constant, in some circumstances. These should be familiar to you from school and include equals, not equal, greater than, less than, greater than or equal to, **and** less than or equal to. In Java, equal to uses two equals signs side by side between the data fields being compared and an exclamation point before an equals sign to denote "**not equal to**." Table 3-3 shows the relational operators, along with an example and a description of each.

Table 3-3. *Java Relational Operators, an Example in Which A = 25 and B = 50, and a Description of the Relational Operation*

Operator	Example	Description
==	(A == B) **not** true	Comparison of two operands: if they are **equal** then the condition equates to **true**
!=	(A != B) **is** true	Comparison of two operands: if they are **not equal** the condition equates to **true**
>	(A > B) **not** true	Comparison of two operands: if left operand is **greater** than right operand, equates to **true**
<	(A < B) **is** true	Comparison of two operands: if left operand is **less** than right operand, equates to **true**
>=	(A >= B) **not** true	Compare two operands: if left operand is **greater** or equal to right operand equates to **true**
<=	(A <= B) **is** true	Compare two operands: if left operand **less** than or equal to right operand, equates to **true**

The **greater than** symbol is a right-facing arrow-head, and the **less than** symbol is a left-facing arrow-head. These are used before the equals sign to create greater than or equal to and less than or equal to relational operators respectively, as you can see at the bottom of Table 3-3.

These relational operators return a boolean value of true or false, and as such are also used in control (loop) structures in Java quite a bit, and are also used in gameplay programming logic as well to control the path (result) that the gameplay will take. For instance, let's say you want to determine where the left edge of the game screen is so that the InvinciBagel does not travel right off of the screen when he is moving to the left. Using this relational comparison:

```
boolean changeDirection = false; // Create boolean variable changeDirection, initialize to false
changeDirection = (invinciBagelX <= 0); //  boolean changeDirection is TRUE if left side reached
```

Notice that I have used the <= **less than or equal to** (yes, Java supports negative numbers too), so that if the InvinciBagel has gone past **the (x=0) left side of the screen** the **changeDirection** boolean flag will be set to the value of true, and the sprite movement programming logic can deal with the situation, by changing the direction of movement (so InvinciBagel bounces off of the wall) or stopping the movement entirely (so the InvinciBagel sticks to the wall).

You will be getting a lot of exposure to these relational operators during this book as they are quite useful in creating gameplay logic, so we are going to be having a lot of fun with these soon enough. Let's take a look at logical operators next, so we can work with **Boolean Sets** and compare things in groups, which is also important for games.

Java Logical Operators:

The Java **logical operators** are similar to the boolean operations (union, intersection, etc.) that you learned about in school, and allow you to determine if both boolean variables hold the same value (**AND**), or if one of the boolean variables is different (**OR**), from the other. There's also a **NOT** operator that reverses the value of any of the compared boolean operands. Table 3-4 shows Java's three logical operators, and an example of each, along with a description.

Table 3-4. *Java Logical Operators, an Example in Which A = True and B = False, and a Description of Logical Operation*

Operator	Example	Description
&&	(A && B) is false	A logical **AND** operator equates to **true** when **BOTH** operands are the same value.
||	(A || B) is true	A logical **OR** operator equates to **true** when **EITHER** operand is the same value.
!	!(A && B) is true	A logical **NOT** operator **reverses** the **logical state** of the operator (or set) it is applied to.

Let's use logical operators to enhance the game logic example in the previous section by including the **direction** in which the InvinciBagel is moving on the screen. The existing **facingDirection String** variable will control the direction the InvinciBagel is facing (and moving in, if in motion). You can now use the following logical operator to determine if the InvinciBagel is facing left (W, or West); if the **travelingWest** boolean variable is **true**; **AND** if the hit (or passed) boolean variable on the left-hand side of the screen, **hitLeftSideScrn**, is also equal to **true**. The modified code for doing this will include two more boolean variable declarations and initializations and will look like this:

```java
boolean changeDirection = false; // Create boolean variable changeDirection, initialize to false
boolean hitLeftSideScrn = false; // Create boolean variable hitLeftSideScrn, initialize to false
boolean travelingWest = false;   // Create boolean variable travelingWest, initialize to false
hitLeftSideScrn = (invinciBagelX <= 0); //  boolean hitLeftSideScrn is TRUE if left side reached
travelingWest = (facingDirection == "W") // boolean travelingWest is TRUE if facingDirection="W"
changeDirection = (hitLeftSideScrn && travelingWest) // Change Direction, if both equate to TRUE
```

To find out if the InvinciBagel is facing (or traveling, if also moving) **West**, you create another **travelingWest** boolean variable and initialize it (set it equal) to **false** (because your initial facingDirection setting is East). Then, you create a boolean variable called **hitLeftSideScrn**, setting that to the **(invinciBagelX <= 0)** relational operator statement.

Finally, you create a relational operator statement with the `travelingWest = (facingDirection == "W")` logic, and then you are ready to use the **changeDirection** boolean variable with your new logical operator. This logical operator will make sure that **both** the **hitLeftSideScrn** and **travelingWest** boolean variables are set to **true**, using the `changeDirection = (hitLeftSideScrn && travelingWest)` logical operation programming statement.

Now, you have a little practice declaring and initializing variables and using relational and logical operators to determine the direction and location of a primary game piece (called a **sprite** in arcade games; for more on game design lingo, see Chapter 6). Next, let's take a look at assignment operators.

Java Assignment Operators

The Java assignment operators assign a value from a logic construct on the right-hand side of the assignment operator to a variable on the left-hand side of the assignment operator. The most common assignment operator is also the most commonly used operator in the Java programming language, the **equals operator**. The equals operator can be prefaced with any of the arithmetic operators to create an assignment operator that also performs an arithmetic operation, as can be seen in Table 3-5. This allows a more "dense" programming statement to be created when the variable itself is going to be part of the equation. Thus, instead of having to write **C = C + A** , you can simply use **C+=A** and achieve the same end result. You will be using this assignment operator shortcut often in your game logic design.

Table 3-5. *Java Assignment Operators, What Each Assignment Is Equal to in Code, and a Description of the Operator*

Operator	Example	Description
=	C=A+B	Basic assignment operator: Assigns value from right-hand operand to left-hand operand
+=	C+=A equals C=C+A	ADD assignment operator: Adds right-hand operand to left-hand operand; puts result in left-hand operand
-=	C-=A equals C=C-A	SUB assignment operator: Subtracts right-hand operand from left-hand operand; puts result in left-hand operand
*=	C*=A equals C=C*A	MULT assignment operator: Multiplies right-hand operand and left-hand operand; puts result in left-hand operand
/=	C/=A equals C=C/A	DIV assignment operator: Divides left-hand operand by right-hand operand; puts result in left-hand operand
%=	C%=A equals C=C%A	MOD assignment operator: Divides left-hand operand by right-hand operand; puts remainder in left-hand operand

Finally, you are going to take a look at conditional operators, which also allow you to code powerful game logic.

Java Conditional Operators

The Java language also has a **conditional operator** that can **evaluate** a condition and make a variable assignment for you, based on the resolution of that condition, using only one compact programming construct. The generic Java programming statement for a conditional operator always uses the following basic format:

```
Variable = (evaluated expression) ? Set this value if TRUE : Set this value if FALSE ;
```

So, on the left-hand side of the equals sign, you have the variable, which is going to change (be set), based on what is on the right-hand side of the equals sign. This conforms to what you have learned thus far.

On the right-hand side of the equals sign, you have an **evaluated expression**, for instance, "x is equal to 3," followed by a **question mark** and then two numeric values that are separated from each other, using the **colon**, and, finally, a **semicolon to terminate** the conditional operator statement. If you wanted to set a variable **y** to a value of **25** if **x** is equal to **3**, and to **10** if x is not equal to 3, you would write that conditional operator programming statement by using the following Java programming logic:

```
y = (x == 3) ? 25 : 10 ;
```

Next, you are going to look at Java logic control structures that leverage the operators you just learned about.

Java Conditional Control: Decision Making or Loops

As you have just seen, many of the Java operators can have a fairly complex structure and provide a lot of processing power, using very few characters of Java programming logic. Java also has several more complicated **conditional control** structures, which can automatically **make decisions** or **perform repetitive tasks** for you, once you have set up the conditions for those decisions or task repetitions by coding the Java **logic control** structure.

In this section, you will first explore decision-making control structures, such as the Java **switch-case** structure and the **if-else** structure. Then, you will take a look at Java's looping control structures, including **for**, **while**, and **do-while**.

Decision-Making Control Structures: Switch-Case and If-Else

Some of the most powerful Java logic control structures allow you to define **decisions** that you want your program logic to make for you as the application is running. One such structure offers a case-by-case, "flat" decision matrix; the other has a cascading (if this, do this; if not, do this; if not, do this; and so on) type of structure that evaluates things in the order in which you want them examined.

Let's start by looking at the Java **switch** statement, which uses the Java switch keyword and an expression at the top of this decision tree and then uses the Java **case** keyword to provide Java statement blocks for each outcome for this expression's evaluation. If none of the cases inside a switch statement structure (curly braces) are called (used) by the expression evaluation, you can also supply a Java **default** keyword and Java statement code block for what you want done.

The variable used in the case statements can be one of four Java data types: **char** (character), **byte**, **short**, or **int** (integer). You will generally want to add a Java **break** keyword at the end of each of your case statement code blocks, at least in the use case, in which the values being switched between need to be exclusive, and only one is viable (or permissible) for each invocation of the switch statement. The **default** statement, which is the "if any of these do not match" is the last of the statements inside of the switch, and does not need this break keyword.

If you do not furnish a Java **break** keyword in each of your case logic blocks, more than one case statement can be evaluated in the same pass through your switch statement. This would be done as your expression evaluation tree progresses from top (first case code block) to bottom (last case code block or default keyword code block). So if you had a collection of Boolean "flags" such as hasValue, isAlive, isFixed, and so on, these could all be processed on one single "pass" by using a switch-case statement structure that does not use any break statements at all.

The significance of this is that you can create some fairly complex decision trees, based on case statement evaluation order, and whether you put this break keyword at the end of any given case statement's code block.

The **general format** for your switch-case decision tree programming construct would look like this:

```
switch(expression) {
    case value1 :
        programming statement one;
        programming statement two;
        break;
    case value2 :
        programming statement one;
        programming statement two;
        break;
    default :
        programming statement one;
        programming statement two;
}
```

Let's say you want to have a decision in your game as to which InvinciBagel death animation is called when the InvinciBagel is hit (shot, slimed, punched, and so on). The death animation routine (method) would be called, based on the InvinciBagel's state of activity when he or she is hit, such as flying (**F**), jumping (**J**), running (**R**), or idle

(I). Let's say these states are held in a data field called **ibState**, of the type **char**, which holds a single character. The switch-case code construct for using these game-piece state indicators to call the correct method, once a hit has occurred, would be:

```
switch(ibState) {              // Evaluate ibState char and execute case code blocks accordingly
    case 'F' :
        deathLogicFlying();  // Java method controlling death sequence if InvinciBagel flying
        break;
    case 'J' :
        deathLogicJumping(); // Java method controlling death sequence if InvinciBagel jumping
        break;
    case 'R' :
        deathLogicRunning(); // Java method controlling death sequence if InvinciBagel running
        break;
    default :
        deathLogicIdle();      // Java method controlling death sequence if InvinciBagel is idle
```

This switch-case logic construct evaluates the **ibState** char variable inside the evaluation portion of the switch() statement (note that this is a Java method) and then provides a case logic block for each of the game-piece states (flying, jumping, running) and a default logic block for the idle state (which is a logical way to set this up).

Because a game piece cannot be idle, running, flying, and jumping at the same time, you need to use the **break** keyword to make each of the branches of this decision tree unique (exclusive).

The switch-case decision-making construct is generally considered more efficient, and faster, than the if-else decision-making structure, which can use just the **if** keyword for simple evaluations, like this:

```
if(expression = true) {
    programming statement one;
    programming statement two;
}
```

You can also add an **else** keyword to make this decision-making structure evaluate statements that would need to execute if the boolean variable (true or false condition) evaluates to **false** rather than **true**, which makes this structure more powerful (and useful). This general programming construct would then look like this:

```
if(expression = true) {
    programming statement one;
    programming statement two;
} else {                         // Execute this code block if (expression = false)
    programming statement one;
    programming statement two;
}
```

In addition, you can nest **if-else** structures, thereby creating **if{}-{else if}-{else if}-else{}** structures. If these structures get nested too deeply, then you would want to switch (no pun intended) over to the **switch-case** structure, which will become more and more efficient, relative to a nested if-case structure, the deeper the if-else nesting goes. For example, the switch-case statement that you coded earlier for the InvinciBagel game, if translated into a nested if-else decision-making construct, would look like the following Java programming structure:

```
if(ibState = 'F') {
    deathLogicFlying();
} else if(ibState = 'J') {
    deathLogicJumping();
```

```
    } else if(ibState = 'R') {
        deathLogicRunning();
    } else {
        deathLogicIdle();
}
```

As you can see, this if-else decision tree structure is quite similar to the switch-case that you created earlier, except that the decision code structures are **nested** inside each other rather than contained in a flat structure. As a rule of thumb, I would use the if and if-else for one- and two-value evaluations and a switch-case for three-value evaluation scenarios and greater. I use this switch-case structure extensively in my books covering Android.

Next, let's take a look at the other types of conditional control structures that are used extensively in Java, the looping programming structures. These allow you to execute a block of programming statements a predefined number of times (using the **for** loop) or until an objective is achieved (using a **while** or a **do-while** loop).

Looping Control Structures: While, Do-While, and For

Whereas the decision tree type of control structure is traversed a fixed number of times (once all the way through, unless a break [switch-case] or resolved expression [if-else] is encountered), **looping** control structures keep executing over time, which, with respect to the **while** and **do-while** structures, makes them a bit dangerous, as an **infinite loop** can be generated, if you are not careful with your programming logic! The **for** loop structure executes for a **finite number** of loops (the number is specified in the definition of the for loop), as you will soon see in this section.

Let's start with the finite loop, covering the for loop first. A Java for loop uses the following general format:

```
for(initialization; boolean expression; update equation) {
    programming statement one;
    programming statement two;
}
```

As you can see, the three parts of the evaluation area of the for loop are inside the parentheses, separated by semicolons, as each contains a programming statement. The first is a variable declaration and initialization, the second is a boolean expression evaluation, and the third is an update equation showing how to increment the loop during each pass.

To move the InvinciBagel 40 pixels **diagonally** on the screen, along both X and Y, the for loop is as follows:

```
for(int x=0; x < 40; x = x + 1) {    // Note: an x = x + 1 statement could also be coded as x++
    invinciBagelX++;  // Note: invinciBagelX++ could be coded invinciBagelX = invinciBagelX + 1;
    invinciBagelY++;  // Note: invinciBagelY++ could be coded invinciBagelY = invinciBagelY + 1;
}
```

In contrast, the while (or do-while) type of loop does not execute over a finite number of processing cycles, but rather executes the statements inside the loop until a condition is met, using the following structure:

```
while(boolean expression) {
    programming statement one;
    programming statement two;
}
```

To code the for loop to move the InvinciBagel 40 pixels, using a while loop structure, looks like this:

```
int x = 0;
while(x < 40) {
    invinciBagelX++;
    invinciBagelY++;
    x++
}
```

The only difference between a do-while loop and a while loop is that, with the latter, the loop logic programming statements are performed **before**, instead of after, the evaluation. Thus, using a **do-while** loop programming structure, the previous example would be written as follows:

```
int x = 0;
do {
    invinciBagelX++;
    invinciBagelY++;
    x++
} while(x < 40);
```

As you can see, the Java programming logic structure is inside curly braces, following the Java **do** keyword, with the **while** statement **after** the closing brace. Note that the while evaluation statement (and therefore the entire construct) must be terminated with a **semicolon**.

If you want to make sure that the programming logic inside the while loop structure is performed at least one time, use the **do-while**, as the evaluation is performed **after** the loop logic is executed. If you want to make sure that the logic inside the loop is only executed after (whenever) the evaluation is successful, which is the safer way to code things, use the while loop structure.

Java Objects: Virtual Reality, Using Java Constructs

I saved the best, Java objects, for last, because they can be constructed in one fashion or another using all the concepts that I have covered thus far in the chapter and because they are the foundation of OOP language (in this case, Java 8). The fact is, everything in the Java 8 programming language is based on Java's Object superclass (I like to call it the masterclass), which is in the **java.lang** package, so an import statement for it would reference java.lang.Object, the full pathname for the Java Object class.

Java objects are used to "virtualize" reality by allowing the objects you see all around you in everyday life, or, in the case of your game, objects you are creating out from your imagination, to be realistically simulated. This is done by using the data fields (variables and constants) and the methods that you have been learning about in this chapter. These Java programming constructs will make up the object **characteristics**, or **attributes** (constants); **states** (variables); and **behaviors** (methods). The Java class construct organizes each object definition (constants, variables, and methods) and gives birth to an instance of that object, using the constructor method for the class that designs and defines the object via the various Java keywords and constructs.

Creating an InvinciBagel Object: Attributes, States, and Behavior

Let's put together an example of an InvinciBagel object that shows how constants define characteristics, variables define states, and methods define behaviors. We will do this using Java coding constructs that you have learned about thus far in the chapter, including constants, variables, and methods that you have already defined, to some extent.

Let's start with characteristics, which are things about an object that will not change and which are thus represented using constants, variables that will not (cannot) change. An important bagel characteristic is the type (flavor). We all have our favorites; mine are plain, egg, rye, onion, and pumpernickel. Another characteristic is the size of bagel; as we all know, there are minibagels, normal-size bagels, and giant bagels.

```
private static final String FLAVOR_OF_BAGEL = "Pumpernickel";
private static final String SIZE_OF_BAGEL = "Mini Bagel";
```

Thus, constants are used to define the characteristics, or attributes, of an object. If you are defining a car, boat, or plane, the color (paint), engine (type), and transmission (type) are attributes (constants), as they generally do not change, unless you are a mechanic or own a body shop!

Things about an object that will change, such as its location, orientation, how it is traveling (flying, driving, walking, running), and so on are called states and are defined using variables, which can constantly change in real time, based on what is happening in real life. These variables will allow any Java object to mimic, or virtualize, the real-world object that they are creating in your Java universe's virtual reality. This is, of course, especially true in games, which is why the topic of this book, Java and games, is especially relevant and applicable.

There will be more states (variables) than attributes (constants) for the InvinciBagel, as it is the game piece and will be especially active trying to save its hole and score points. Some of the states that you will want to define as variables include screen (x, y) location, orientation, travel direction, travel type, hits taken, and life span used.

```
public int invinciBagelX = 0;              // X screen location of the InvinciBagel
public int invinciBagelY = 0;              // Y screen location of the InvinciBagel
public String bagelOrientation = "side";   //  Defines bagel orientation (front, side, top)
public int lifeIndex = 1000;               //   Defines units of lifespan used
public int hitsIndex = 0;                  //   Defines units of damage (hits taken)
public String directionFacing = "E";       //    Direction that the object is facing
public String movementType = "idle"        //  Type of movement (idle, fly, run, jump)
public boolean currentlyMoving = false;    //   Flag showing if the object is in motion
```

As you progress through this book and create the InvinciBagel game, you will be adding attributes, states, and behaviors that will make the InvinciBagel, as well as its game environment and game play, more realistic, fun, and exciting, just as you would do in real life. In fact, you are using Java objects and Java constructs to model, a realistic virtual world in which InvinciBagel players can triumph over evil and shoot cream cheese balls at delicious targets.

Let's look at a couple of the methods that you might develop to control the InvinciBagel behavior. You will be creating complex methods over the course of this book to accomplish game play objectives, so I am just going to give you an idea here of how methods provide behaviors to objects for the purpose of demonstrating how objects can be created that reflect how real-world objects function.

For your game play of the InvinciBagel, the main behaviors will be 2D movement around the screen, relative to the **x** (width) and y (height) dimension, which will access, use, and update the integer **invinciBagelX**, **invinciBagelY**, and the boolean **currentlyMoving** data fields discussed previously; the InvinciBagel character's orientation (front facing, sideways, facing down, and so on), which will access, use, and update the **bagelOrientation** String field; the life expectancy of the InvinciBagel, which will access, use, and update the **lifeIndex** variable; the health of the InvinciBagel, which will access, use, and update the **hitsIndex** variable; the direction (East or West) in which the InvinciBagel is traveling, which will access, use, and update the **directionFacing** String variable; and the type of movement (flying, jumping, running, idle) that the InvinciBagel is using , which will access, use, and update the **movementType** String variable.

Here is how you declare these methods (behaviors) and pseudocode regarding what they are going to do:

```
public void moveInvinciBagel(int x, int y) {
    currentlyMoving = true;
    invinciBagelX = x;
    invinciBagelY = y;
```

```java
    }

    public String getInvinciBagelOrientation() {
        return bagelOrientation;
    }

    public void setInvinciBagelOrientation(String orientation) {
        bagelOrientation = orientation;
    }

    public int getInvinciBagelLifeIndex() {
        return lifeIndex;
    }

    public void setInvinciBagelLifeIndex(int lifespan) {
        lifeIndex = lifespan;
    }

    public String getInvinciBagelDirection() {
        return directionFacing;
    }

    public void setInvinciBagelDirection(String direction) {
        directionFacing = direction;
    }

    public int getInvinciBagelHitsIndex() {
        return hitsIndex;
    }

    public void setInvinciBagelHitsIndex(int damage) {
        hitsIndex = damage;
    }

    public String getInvinciBagelMovementType() {
        return movementType;
    }

    public void setInvinciBagelMovementType(String movement) {
        movementType = movement;
    }
```

The convention is to create **.get()** and **.set()** methods, as is done here. These allow your Java code to easily access your object states (variables). Now, it is time to install all these attributes (constants), states (variables), and behaviors (methods) into a blueprint for your object. As mentioned earlier, this is done using the Java class programming structure.

Creating an InvinciBagel Blueprint: Create the GamePiece Class

Let's install all this InvinciBagel virtualization code into a **GamePiece** class to create a class and constructor method that is intended for game-piece objects:

```java
public class GamePiece

    private static final String FLAVOR_OF_BAGEL = "Pumpernickel"; // Flavor (or type) of bagel
    private static final String SIZE_OF_BAGEL = "Mini Bagel";     // Size (classification) of bagel

    public int invinciBagelX = 0;                      //  X screen location of the InvinciBagel
    public int invinciBagelY = 0;                      //  Y screen location of the InvinciBagel
    public String bagelOrientation = "side";       //  Define bagel orientation (front, side, top)
    public int lifeIndex = 1000;                    //    Defines units of lifespan used
    public int hitsIndex = 0;                        //    Defines units of damage (hits taken)
    public String directionFacing = "E";         //  Direction that the bagel object is facing
    public String movementType = "idle";         //   Type of movement (idle, fly, run, jump)
    public boolean currentlyMoving = false; //    Flag showing if the object is in motion

    public void moveInvinciBagel(int x, int y) {         // Movement Behavior
        currentlyMoving = true;
        invinciBagelX = x;
        invinciBagelY = y;
    }

    public String getInvinciBagelOrientation() {         // Get Method for Orientation
        return bagelOrientation;
    }

    public void setInvinciBagelOrientation(String orientation) {     // Set Method for Orientation
        bagelOrientation = orientation;
    }

    public int getInvinciBagelLifeIndex() {              // Get Method for Lifespan
        return lifeIndex;
    }

    public void setInvinciBagelLifeIndex(int lifespan) {            // Set Method for Lifespan
        lifeIndex = lifespan;
    }

    public String getInvinciBagelDirection() {           // Get Method for Facing Direction
        return directionFacing;
    }

    public void setInvinciBagelDirection(String direction) {          // Set Method for Direction
        directionFacing = direction;
    }

    public int getInvinciBagelHitsIndex() {              // Get Method for Hits (damage)
        return hitsIndex;
    }
```

```
public void setInvinciBagelHitsIndex(int damage) {          // Set Method for Hits (damage)
    hitsIndex = damage;
}

public String getInvinciBagelMovementType() {           // Get Method for Movement Type
    return movementType;
}

public void setInvinciBagelMovementType(String movement) {   // Set Method for Movement Type
    movementType = movement;
}
}
```

It is important to note that these constants, variables, and methods are for demonstration of how the class, method, and data field keywords let developers create (virtualize) their game components. As you develop the game, these will probably change, as game development is a process of refinement, in which you will be constantly changing and enhancing the Java code base to add features and capabilities.

Now, all you have to do is add your **GamePiece()** constructor method, which will create a new object with the initialized variable settings that you want the default GamePiece to contain. Then, you will create the second **overloaded** constructor method. This second constructor method will allow **parameters** to be passed into a constructor method so that you can provide custom (nondefault) settings to these same variables (states). In this way, if you call GamePiece(), you get a **default object**; if you call GamePiece(parameter list here), you get a **custom object**.

Creating a GamePiece() Constructor: Overloading a GamePiece

Finally, let's create the constructor method (two, actually), which takes the states (variables) from the GamePiece class and creates a default object. You will use this object to create the custom overloaded constructor method. The first constructor method will employ the **package private** access control method, using no access modifier keyword, so that any code in the invincibagel package can call this constructor method. Then, you will set your default variables, using the following Java code:

```
GamePiece() {
    invinciBagelX = 0;
    invinciBagelY = 0;
    bagelOrientation = "side";
    lifeIndex = 1000;
    hitsIndex = 0;
    directionFacing = "E";
    movementType = "idle";
    currentlyMoving = false;
}
```

The overloaded constructor method will have parameters declared in the method parameter list area for those variables that are logical to allow variations for upon object creation. The only two that are not logical to allow variations for are hitsIndex (a new object will not have sustained any damage points and will thus need to be 0) and currentlyMoving (a new object will not be moving when it appears, even if that is only for a fraction of a second) variables, which you will initialize, as you did for the default constructor. The other five variables (states) will be set using parameters passed in via a parameter list, using an equals assignment operator. This is done using the following code:

```
GamePiece(int x, int y, String orientation, int lifespan, String direction, String movement) {
  invinciBagelX = x;
  invinciBagelY = y;
  bagelOrientation = orientation;
  lifeIndex = lifespan;
  hitsIndex = 0;
  directionFacing = direction;
  movementType = movement;
  currentlyMoving = false;
}
```

I bolded the variables in the parameter list, as well as where they are used inside the constructor method, to set the states (variables) for the object. These variables are declared at the top of the GamePiece class, which you have used to design, define, and create the GamePiece object. This second constructor method can be said to **overload** the first constructor method, because it uses the exact same method call (method name), with a different parameter list (full of parameters, versus empty or no parameters). This gives you the default object constructor method as well as a custom object constructor method, so in your game logic, you can create a default GamePiece or a custom GamePiece.

Summary

In this third chapter you took a look at some of the more important concepts and structures found in the Java 8 programming language. Certainly, I cannot cover everything in Java in one chapter, so I stuck with concepts, constructs, and keywords that you will be using to create a game over the course of this book. Most Java books are 800 pages or more, so if you want to get really deep into Java, I suggest *Beginning Java 8 Fundamentals* by Kishori Sharan (Apress, 2014).

You started by taking a high-level view of Java, considering its syntax, including Java **comments** and **delimiters**, APIs, and the Java **packages** that a Java API contains. You also studied Java **classes**, including **nested** classes and **inner** classes, as the Java packages contain Java classes. You then went the next level down in Java, to the **method**, which is like the function in other programming languages, as well as to a special kind of Java method called a **constructor** method.

Next, you explored how Java represents data, using fields, or data fields, examining the different types, such as constants, or fixed data fields, and variables, or data fields that can change their values. After that, you took a closer look at Java **modifier keywords**, including the **public**, **private**, and **protected** access control keywords and the **final**, **static**, **abstract**, **volatile**, and **synchronized** nonaccess control modifier keywords.

After finishing with the basic code structures and how to modify them, you moved on to the primary Java data types, such as **boolean**, **char**, **byte**, **int**, **float**, **short**, **long**, and **double** and then explored the Java operators that are used to process, or bridge, these data types over to your programming logic. You studied **arithmetic** operators, for use with numeric values; **logical** operators, for use with boolean values; **relational** operators, to consider relationships between data values; **conditional** operators, which allow you to establish any conditional variable assignments; and **assignment** operators, which let you assign values to (or between) variables.

Then, you looked at Java **logic control** structures, including decision-making control structures (I like to call them decision trees) and looping, or **iterative**, logic control structures. You learned about the Java **switch-case** structure, the **if-else** structure, the **for** loop structure, and the **do-while** loop structures. Finally, you examined Java objects and discovered how to define object attributes, states, and behaviors, using a Java class, methods, and constructor methods.

In the next chapter, I will give you an overview of the **JavaFX** multimedia engine, and its classes and capabilities, as you will be leveraging JavaFX to add media elements to your games, such as images, video, and audio, and to control your games, using JavaFX object constructs (classes), such as the **Stage**, **Scene**, and **StackPane.**

CHAPTER 4

■ ■ ■

An Introduction to JavaFX 8: Exploring the Capabilities of the Java 8 Multimedia Engine

Let's build on the knowledge of the Java programming language that you gained in the previous chapter here in Chapter 4, by learning about the capabilities, components, and classes that make up the **JavaFX 8** multimedia engine. This amazing JavaFX 8 API was added to Java 8 using the **javafx** package that you saw in Chapters 2 and 3, which was released with Java 8. The JavaFX 8 package is significant to game programming because it contains advanced forms of classes that you will want to harness for game programming, including classes for organizing game components, using a **scene graph**; classes for **user interface** layout and design; classes for 2D **digital illustration** (also called vector graphics); and classes for **digital imaging** (also called raster graphics); 2D **animation**; **digital video**; **digital audio**; **3D**; a **web engine** (WebKit); and much more, all of which I will be covering in this chapter, so that you know exactly what you have available to you, now that these JavaFX 8 libraries have been added into the Java 8 programming language.

The rationale for going into such detail is not only so that you know what JavaFX 8.0 can do for your Java 8 game development, but also so that you have an overview of how the various components of this JavaFX multimedia engine are put together. You will learn about the JavaFX **Quantum** Toolkit, the **Prism** rendering technology, the **WebKit** web engine, the **Glass** Windowing Toolkit, the audio and video **Media** engine, and the Scene Graph API.

The reason you will need this high-level overview of how JavaFX works before you actually start to use it in your games is because it is a fairly complex set of APIs (I like to call it an **engine**). This is due to the power that it brings to implementing user interface (UI) and user experience (UX) "wins" in your Java 8 applications (in this case, games). So, bear with me in these foundational chapters detailing how to master your IDE (NetBeans 8.0), your programming language (Java 8), and this new media engine (JavaFX 8) that is now a part of the Java 8 programming platform that is rapidly growing in power and popularity internationally.

Once you have examined how JavaFX 8.0 comes together at the highest level (just like you did in Chapter 3), you will consider some of those key classes that you might be using to construct Java 8 games, such as the **Node** class as well as the **Stage, Scene, Group, StackPane, Animation, Layout, Shape, Geometry, Control, Media, Image, Camera, Effect, Canvas, and Paint classes**. You have already studied the JavaFX **Application** class (see Chapters 2 and 3), so now you will focus on the classes that can be used to build complex multimedia projects, such as Java 8 games.

Finally, you will take an in-depth look at the bootstrap JavaFX application that you generated in Chapter 2, and at how the Java **.main()** method and the JavaFX **.start()** method create the primaryStage Stage object, using the **Stage()** constructor method, and, inside of that, create your Scene object named **scene**, using the **Scene()** constructor method. You will explore how to use methods from the Stage class to set the **scene** and title and show the **Stage** as well as how to create and use the **StackPane** and **Button** class (objects), and add an **EventHandler** to a **Button**.

Overview of JavaFX: From Scene Graph Down to OS

As in the previous chapter, on Java 8, I am starting this overview of JavaFX at the highest level, with the **Scene Graph API** and with visual editing tools, which are contained in a JavaFX application called **Scene Builder**, which we will not be using (Scene Builder is for application UI design not game design); we will use GIMP instead. As you observed in Chapter 1 (see Figure 1-5), Scene Builder is integrated into NetBeans 8.0 (JavaFX is listed as being supported specifically for use in NetBeans, primarily because Scene Builder has been made an integral part of NetBeans GUI).

As Figure 4-1 demonstrates, these JavaFX application-building tools exist "**on top of**" the **JavaFX 8 API** (a collection of **javafx** packages, such as **javafx.scene** and **javafx.application**), which is what ultimately allows you to build (using Scene Graph) and UI design (using Scene Builder) your JavaFX new media creations (in this case, a Java 8 game). Note that the JavaFX 8.0 API is connected (here, using steel bearings, to denote plugs) not only to Scene Graph and Scene Builder, **above it**, but also to Java JDK 8 and the Quantum Toolkit, **below it**. As you can see, Java JDK 8 (and APIs) then connects the JavaFX new media engine to NetBeans, the JVM, and the various platforms that Java currently supports as well as to future platforms, such as Android 4 (32-bit Android), Android 5 (64-bit Android) and iOS.

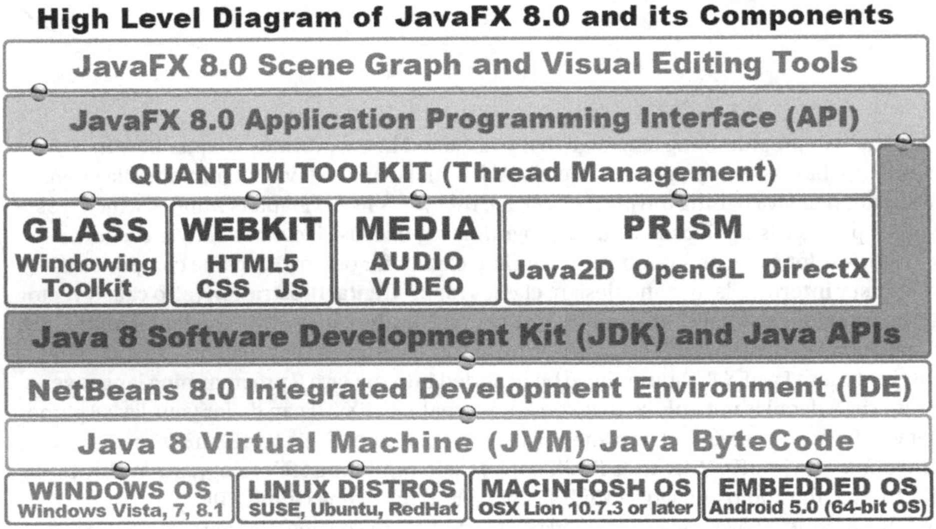

High Level Diagram of JavaFX 8.0 and its Components

Figure 4-1. How JavaFX 8 is stratified, from the Scene Graph at the top down through Java 8, NetBeans 8.0, JVMs, and OSs

The **Quantum Toolkit**, which is connected to the JavaFX 8.0 API, ties together all the powerful new media engines that you are going to be learning about. The Quantum Toolkit also handles the **thread management** for all of these, so your game code, and your game's new media (audio, video, 3D, and so on), can use separate processors on the **dualcore, quadcore, hexacore and octacore** CPUs that are so commonplace in today's computers and consumer electronics devices.

The **Glass Windowing Toolkit** controls **window management** for JavaFX 8.0, and is responsible for all of the discrete areas on the display screen, such as the **stage** and **pop-up** windows, including dialogs. Glass also manages the **event processing queue**, passing events up to JavaFX for processing, and sets up **timers**.

As you can see in the figure, there is also a **WebKit** engine and a **Media** (player) engine, which are managed by the Quantum Toolkit. The WebKit engine renders your HTML5 and CSS3 web content, and the media player media playback engine plays your digital audio and digital video assets, respectively.

The most important new media engine below the Quantum Toolkit is the **Prism** (game) engine, which renders 2D content, using **Java 2D**, and 3D content, using either **OpenGL** (Mac, Linux, Embedded OSs) or **DirectX** if your users are on the Windows Vista, Windows 7, or Windows 8.1 platform. Windows XP support was discontinued in April 2014, as most computers and consumer electronics devices out now are 64-bit capable (XP was 32-bit only).

Prism bridges the powerful 3D game engines (DirectX, OpenGL) that are on the major OS platforms as well as on consumer electronics (embedded) devices so JavaFX 8.0 can **offload** complex rendering task processing to **graphics processing unit (GPU) hardware** from NVIDIA (GeForce), AMD (ATI Radeon), and Intel. This makes JavaFX (and thus Java 8) games faster and allows games to use less CPU processing power for rendering game assets to the screen. This in turn allows more CPU processing power be used for game play logic, such as AI and collision detection. You will be learning about these areas of game design after you master the JavaFX engine in this fourth chapter of the book.

It is important to note that game developers do not need to understand the inner workings of the Quantum (threading), Glass (windowing), or Prism (rendering) engines to be able to take advantage of their amazingly powerful features. Throughout the book, you are going to be focusing on the top level (**Scene Graph** and Scene Builder) as well as the JavaFX and Java 8 **API** levels of the diagram. I will also be covering the NetBeans IDE 8.0 level, which you learned about in Chapter 2 but which you will also be exploring much further during the remainder of this book.

As for the lower levels of the diagram, NetBeans 8.0 will generate a Java **bytecode** file that is read by the custom JVM for each of the OS platforms. The JVM, illustrated at the bottom of the figure, can be installed for any given OS platform by downloading a Java 8 **JRE**, which you already encountered in Chapter 1, when you installed it as part of Java JDK 8.

This JVM layer lets your game be installed as an application across all popular OS platforms as well as on embedded devices, which are also moving to support JavaFX 8. Furthermore, you can generate your Java 8 game as a Java **applet**, which can be embedded in a web site, and there is even a deployment model, in which the application can be dragged out of the web site and onto your desktop, where it is installed as a full-fledged Java 8 application.

In addition, there is already a way to run JavaFX 8 applications on iOS 8, and Android 4.4 and 5.0. If you are interested in the latest information on this, simply google "JavaFX on Android," or "JavaFX on iOS,"; you can bet that by 2015, Android 5.0 and Chrome OS devices will be running JavaFX applications "natively," meaning that you will someday (soon) be able to export Java (and JavaFX engine) applications directly to Android 5.0, using **IntelliJ**, or to Chrome OS, using NetBeans 8.0. You should eventually be able to "code once, run everywhere" with this Java 8 and JavaFX 8.0 dynamic duo! Oracle recently released Java 8 SE Embedded, Java 8 ME and Java 8 ME Embedded versions, all of which support JavaFX.

■ **Note** The **JetBrains IntelliJ IDEA** is now the official IDE used for creating 64-bit Android 5.0 applications. This IDE is examined in my *Android Apps for Absolute Beginners, 3rd Edition* (Apress, 2014), which covers developing 32-bit Android 4.0 applications, using an Eclipse IDE and Java 6, and 64-bit Android 5.0 applications, using an IntelliJ IDEA and Java 7.

Let's start at the top of the diagram, and take a look at the JavaFX Scene Graph and the **javafx.scene** package, which implements Scene Graph in the JavaFX API (you will look at Scene Builder in the next chapter).

JavaFX Scene Package: 16 Core Java 8 Classes

The first thing I want to do after our high-level overview is present one of the most important JavaFX packages, the **javafx.scene** package. In Chapters 2 and 3, you discovered that there is more than one JavaFX package. As you saw in Chapter 3 (see Figure 3-1), the InvinciBagel game application uses four different JavaFX packages. The javafx. scene package contains **16** powerful Java 8 classes (remember, JavaFX was recoded in Java 8), including the **Camera, ParallelCamera** and **PerspectiveCamera, Cursor** and **ImageCursor, LightBase, PointLight,** and **AmbientLight** classes; the *Scene Graph classes* (**Node, Parent, Group,** and **SubScene**); and some utility classes (see Figure 4-2).

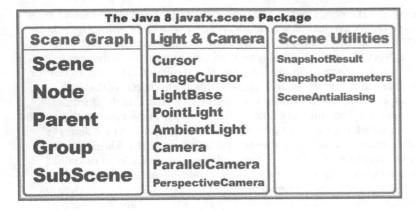

Figure 4-2. The javafx.scene package and its 16-core Scene Graph, Scene utility, Lighting, Camera, and Cursor classes

I have grouped these 16 javafx.scene package classes logically. The Scene class is inside the Scene Graph section of the diagram, because Scene objects, which are created using the Scene class, contain Scene Graph objects, which are created using these four Scene Graph–related classes (Node, Parent, Group, SubScene) and their subclasses. I will be covering the Scene Graph classes in detail later in the chapter (see the section "JavaFX Scene Graph: Organizing Scenes, Using Parent Nodes."

Scene Graph architecting classes in JavaFX start at the highest level, with a **Node** superclass, and its **Parent** class, and include the **Group** and **SubScene** classes, which are subclasses of the Parent class. These core classes are used to create the JavaFX Scene Graph hierarchy and to organize and group objects that have been created using the other JavaFX classes in the JavaFX packages.

There are three Scene utility classes, as I call them, which allow you to take a snapshot (like a screenshot) of your scene or any of its Scene Graph nodes at any time as well as to turn SceneAntialiasing on and off if you are using 3D primitives in a scene. The other half (eight) of the classes in the javafx.scene package are used for scene lighting, scene cameras, and cursor control for your scene. I will be discussing these classes later in the chapter (see the section "JavaFx Scene Content: Lights, Camera, Cursor, Action!"), after you take a look at the Scene Graph classes, which create, group, manage, and manipulate your JavaFX scene content. Thus, I will be covering the javafx.scene package classes shown in the figure, from the left-hand side of the diagram to the right-hand side, in the order in which you are most likely to use them, from least to most.

JavaFX Scene Class: Scene Size and Color and Scene Graph Nodes

The two primary classes in the javafx.scene package are the **Scene** class and the **Node** class. I will be covering the Node class and its **Parent**, **Group**, and **SubScene** subclasses in the next section, as those classes, along with their subclasses (such as the StackPane class used in the InvinciBagel class) are used to implement the Scene Graph architecture in JavaFX. Also, in a sense (and in my diagram) the Node class and its subclasses can be viewed as being below the Scene class, although the Node class is not a subclass of the Scene class. In fact, the Node (Scene Graph) class and subclasses, or rather the objects created using these classes, are contained **inside** the Scene object itself.

For this reason, you will first consider how the Scene class, and its Scene() constructor method, is used to create Scene objects for JavaFX applications. This section will provide reinforcement of what you learned in Chapter 3 regarding overloading constructor methods, as there needs to be several different ways to create a Scene object.

The Scene class is used to create a Scene object, using the **Scene()** constructor class, which takes between one and five parameters, depending on which of the **six** (overloaded) constructor methods you choose to use. These include the following constructor methods, along with their six different (and thus overloaded) parameter list data field configurations:

```
Scene(Parent root)
Scene(Parent root, double width, double height)
Scene(Parent root, double width, double height, boolean depthBuffer)
Scene(Parent root, double width, double height, boolean depthBuffer, SceneAntialiasing aAlias)
Scene(Parent root, double width, double height, Paint fill)
Scene(Parent root, Paint fill)
```

The constructor currently used in your bootstrap Java and JavaFX code is the second one, called as follows:

```
Scene scene = new Scene(root, 300, 250);
```

If you wanted to add a black background to the scene, you would select the **fifth** overloaded constructor method, using a **Color.BLACK** constant from the **Color** class (this is a **Paint** object, because Color is a Paint subclass) as your fill data (in this case, a fill Color). You would do this by using the following Scene() object constructor method call:

```
Scene scene = new Scene(root, 300, 250, Color.BLACK);
```

Note that the **root** object is a **Parent** subclass, called the **StackPane** class, created using the **StackPane()** constructor method (two lines above the Scene() constructor method call) by using the following line of Java code:

```
StackPane root = new StackPane();  // StackPane subclassed from Parent, so Parent root satisfied
```

As you can see, any class can be used in the constructor that is a subclass of the object (class) type that is declared (required) for that constructor parameter position (data). You are able to use Color and StackPane objects in your parameter list because they have superclass origins from the Paint and Parent classes, respectively.

In case you are wondering, the **Boolean depthBuffer** parameter is used for **3D** scene components. Because these scene components are 3D and have depth (a z component, in addition to 2D x **and** y components), you will need to include this parameter, and set it to a value of **true**, if you are creating 3D scenes or combining 2D and 3D scene components. Finally, the **SceneAntialiasing** object (and class) that is passed in the parameter list for the fourth constructor method provides **real-time smoothing** for 3D scene components.

JavaFX Scene Graph: Organizing Scenes, Using Parent Nodes

A scene graph, which is not unique to JavaFX and which can be seen in quite a few new media content creation software packages, is a **data structure** that resembles an upside-down tree, with the **root node** at the top and **branch nodes** and **leaf nodes** coming off the root node. The first time I saw a scene graph approach to design was when I was 3D modeling using a software package on the Amiga called Real 3D from Realsoft Oy. This approach has been copied by many 3D, digital video, and digital imaging software packages since then and now is a part of how JavaFX organizes content and scenes. For this reason, many of you may be familiar (and comfortable) with this design paradigm.

JavaFX Scene Graph data structure allows you not only to architect, organize, and design your JavaFX scene and its content, but also to apply **opacity**, **states**, **event handlers**, **transformations**, and **special effects** to entire logical branches of the Scene Graph hierarchy if you set up the Scene Graph correctly. Figure 4-3 shows the basic Scene Graph tree, with the root node at the top and branch and leaf nodes below it.

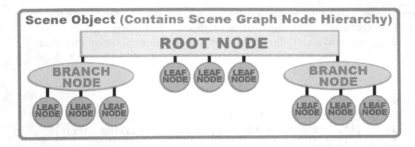

Figure 4-3. *JavaFX Scene Graph hierarchy, starting with the root node and progressing to branch and leaf nodes*

The root node is the topmost node, which is why it is called the root, even though it is at the top, not the bottom, like a root would be in the plant world. A root node has no **parent**, that is, nothing above it in the Scene Graph hierarchy. A root node is itself a parent to the branch nodes and leaf nodes below it.

The next most powerful (and complex) construct in the Scene Graph tree is the branch node, which uses the **javafx.scene.Parent** class as its superclass and which can contain **children** (this is logical, as it extends a class aptly named **Parent**). A branch node can contain other branch nodes, as well as leaf nodes, so it can be used to create some very complicated and powerful Scene Graph hierarchy (or Scene Graph architecture) constructs.

The last level in the hierarchy is the leaf node. A leaf node is the end of the branch and, as such, cannot have children. It is important to note that leaf nodes can come directly off the root node, as you can see in Figure 4-3. Branch nodes can be created by using the **Parent**, **Group**, or **SubScene** classes (see Figure 4-2) or any of their subclasses, such as the **WebView**, **PopupControl**, **Region**, **Pane**, or **StackPane** class.

Examples of leaf nodes include JavaFX classes (as objects), which can be configured using parameters, such as shapes, text, or an ImageView, but which are design or content components, in and of themselves, and have not been designed to have children (child objects).

A leaf node will therefore always contain a JavaFX class that has not been subclassed (extended) from the Parent class, and that has not itself been specifically designed to have child elements (child objects) within it, or below it, in the JavaFX Scene Graph hierarchy.

The four subclasses of the Parent class can all be used as branch nodes and include the **Group** class, for grouping child (leaf node) objects, so that opacity, transforms, and effects can be applied to them; the **Region** class, for grouping child (leaf node) objects to form screen layouts, which can also be styled using CSS; the **Control** class, which can be used to create custom user interface elements (called controls in JavaFX); and the **WebView** class, which is used to contain the JavaFX **WebEngine** class (this class renders HTML5 and CSS3 content into a WebView).

JavaFX Scene Content: Lights, Camera, Cursor, Action!

Next, let's take a look at the eight classes listed in the center column in Figure 4-2. They provide powerful multimedia tools for controlling your application's cursor as well as custom lighting special effects and custom camera capabilities for your 2D and 3D JavaFX applications (in this case, games, but they could also be e-books, or iTV shows, or anything else that requires the powerful new media capabilities that JavaFX offers via the Java language).

The more generalized classes **(Cursor, LightBase, Camera)** in the figure are parent classes, and the more specialized ones **(ImageCursor, PointLight, ParallelCamera**, and so on) listed after each of those are the subclasses of those parent classes. Except the LightBase class, that seems to be stating the obvious!

As you may have guessed (correctly), the JavaFX **Cursor** class can be used to control the application cursor graphic (arrow, hand, closed hand, crosshair, and so on) being used at any given time. The **ImageCursor** subclass can be used to define and supply a custom image-based cursor as well as an x and a y location within the custom cursor image that defines where its point (also called the cursor hot spot) is located.

The **LightBase** class, and its **PointLight** and **AmbientLight** subclasses, can be used to light your scenes. These classes are primarily used for 3D scenes, and they require 3D capabilities on any platform that the game is running on, which is not really a problem these days, as most of the major CPU manufacturers also make (and include) GPUs. Also, it is important to note that the Prism game engine will simulate a 3D environment (GPU), using 3D processing emulation, if one is not available on the platform that is rendering the game. In addition, if you set it up correctly, you can use the lighting classes with your 2D games or use lighting with a hybrid 2D-3D game.

The **Camera** class, and its **ParallelCamera** and **PerspectiveCamera** subclasses, can be used to photograph or video your scene in 3D and 2D (and hybrid) game applications. Two of the camera classes, Camera and ParallelCamera, do not require that 3D (GPU) capabilities be present on the platform that is playing your JavaFX application (in this case, a game).

The subclasses of the Camera class provide two different, specialized types of cameras. The ParallelCamera class can be used for rendering scenes without any depth perspective correction, which in the 3D industry is called an **orthographic projection**. What this means is that this class is perfect for use with 2D scenes (and for 2D games).

The PerspectiveCamera class has a much more complex camera, used for 3D scenes, which will support 3D viewing volumes. Like the LightBase class and its subclasses, the PerspectiveCamera class requires 3D capabilities on the hardware platform that the application (or game) is running on.

The PerspectiveCamera class has a **fieldOfView** attribute (state or variable), which can be used to change its viewing volume, just like a real camera zoom lens, when you zoom it in from wide angle. The default setting for the fieldOfView attribute is an acute angle of 30 degrees. If you remember your geometry from high school, you can visualize this field of view by looking down the **y** (vertical) axis at the camera. As you might expect, there are **.getFieldOfView()** and **.setFieldOfView(double)** method calls to control this camera class attribute.

Next, let's take a closer look at the Scene utility classes. After that, you will examine some of the javafx.scene **subpackages**, such as javafx.scene.text, javafx.scene.image, javafx.scene.shape, and javafx.scene.layout.

JavaFX Scene Utilities: Scene Snapshots and Antialiasing

Finally, you should take a quick look at the three utility classes, shown in the right-hand column in Figure 4-2, as they can be used to improve the quality of scene output on the user's device's screen (using antialiasing) as well as to provide screen capture capabilities to either your user (for social media sharing) or your game play logic itself.

Let's investigate the **SceneAntialiasing** class first. **Antialiasing** is a digital imaging industry term that references an algorithm that smoothes jagged edges where two colors come together, usually on a diagonal line or in the circular area of an image composite. An **image composite** is two separate images placed in **layers** to form one image. Sometimes, the edges between the image components of these two (or more) image layers will need to be **smoothed**. Smoothing (antialiasing) is required so that a final composite looks like it is one seamless image, which is the intention of the artist or game designer. Interestingly, you are already implementing the JavaFX "layer engine" in your InvinciBagel application, using the **StackPane** class (**panes** are **layers**). The "layer stack" image-compositing approach is common in games as well as in software, such as Photoshop and GIMP.

The SceneAntialiasing class offers **antialiasing processing** (algorithm) to 3D scenes so that they can be composited over your 2D scene background, whether that is the default, **Color.WHITE**, or any other color value; a 2D image (creating a hybrid 2D-3D application); or anything else, for that matter. The SceneAntialiasing class allows you to set the **static SceneAntialiasing** data field to a value of **DISABLED** (turn antialiasing off) or **BALANCED** (turn antialiasing on). The balanced option gives a balance of quality and performance, which simply means that the more processing power the device's hardware brings to the table, the more antialiasing quality will be processed.

Next, let's explore the **SnapshotParameters** class (object), which is used to set up (contain) a rendering attribute parameter that will be used by the **SnapshotResult** class (object). The parameters include the type of **Camera** (parallel or perspective) object to be used; whether the **depthBuffer** (used for 3D) is on (true for 3D) or off (false for 2D); a **Paint** object, used to contain the image data; a **Transform** object, used to contain any transform data; and a **Rectangle2D** object, used to define the viewport area to be rendered (i.e., the snapshot dimensions).

You will be looking at all these javafx.scene subpackage classes and concepts in this chapter as well as using many of them over the course of this book. Much of the functionality that you will be tapping into for your Java 8 game development will be found in these JavaFX 8.0 subpackages.

The SnapshotResult class (and, more important, the object created using this class) contains your resulting snapshot image data, the parameters that generated it, and the source node in the scene graph that it was generated from. For this reason, the three methods supported by the class should be obvious: the **.getImage()** method will get a snapshot image, the **.getSource()** method gets the source node information, and the **.getSnapshotParameters()** method will get the SnapshotParameters object contents.

Scene Subpackages: The 13 Other Scene Packages

You may be thinking, "Whew! That was a lot to cover in that javafx.scene package overview!," and indeed the core javafx.scene package has a lot of classes in it, covering scene creation; scene graph organization; and scene utilities, such as lighting, cameras, cursors, and screenshots (or should we call these sceneshots?). There is a lot more in the javafx.scene package, in subpackages, as I call them, or packages that are below the javafx.scene package, referenced using another dot and another package name (description). In fact, there are 13 more javafx.scene packages (see in Table 4-1), covering things such as drawing, painting, charting, UI design, imaging, special effects, media (audio and video) playback, input-output, text, shapes (2D geometry), transforms, and web page (content created with HTML5, JavaScript and CSS3) rendering. You are going to explore these scene package classes in this section.

Table 4-1. *Thirteen Second-Level JavaFX Scene Subpackages, Their Primary Functions, and a Description of Classes*

Package Name	Functions	Description of Contents
javafx.scene.canvas	Drawing	Canvas class (and Canvas object); for a custom drawing surface
javafx.scene.chart	Charting	Chart classes: PieChart, LineChart, XYChart, BarChart, AreaChart, BubbleChart
javafx.scene.control	UI controls	UI control classes: Button, Menu, Slider, Label, ScrollBar, TextField
javafx.scene.effect	Special effects	Special effects classes: Glow, Blend, Bloom, Shadow, Reflection, MotionBlur
javafx.scene.image	imaging	Digital imaging classes: Image, ImageView, WritableImageView, PixelFormat
javafx.scene.input	Input (Events)	Classes related to getting input from the user into the JavaFX application
javafx.scene.layout	UI layouts	UI layout container classes: TilePane, GridPane, FlowPane, Border
javafx.scene.media	Media player	Media playback classes: MediaPlayer, MediaView, Track, AudioTrack, AudioClip
javafx.scene.paint	Painting	Paint classes: Paint, Color, LinearGradient, RadialGradient, Stop, Material, and so on
javafx.scene.shape	Geometry	2D and 3D geometry classes: Mesh, Shape, Shape3D, Arc, Circle, Line, Path, and so on
javafx.scene.text	Text and font	Text rendering and font rendering classes: Font, Text, TextFlow, and so on
javafx.scene.transform	Transforms	Transform classes: Transform, Scale, Rotate, Shear, Translate, Affine
javafx.scene.web	WebKit	Web support classes: WebView, WebEvent, WebEngine, HTMLEditor

Let's start with the packages that have the fewest classes. The table lists subpackages alphabetically, but the first one, javafx.scene.canvas, coincidentally contains only one class, the Canvas class, which, as its name suggests, is employed to create a Canvas object that is used as a canvas for you to create things with! The next subpackage listed is javafx.scene.chart; this has charting classes, such as PieChart, LineChart, XYChart, BarChart, AreaChart, and BubbleChart, for use in business applications, which is a different book entirely, so I will not be covering charting.

The next subpackage, **javafx.scene.control**, offers all the UI **control** ("widget," in Android) classes, such as Button, Menu, CheckBox, RadioButton, DatePicker, ColorPicker, ProgressBar, Slider, Label, Scrollbar, and TextField and about eight dozen others. Because there are approximately a hundred classes in javafx.scene.control, I am not even going to attempt to cover it here; an entire book could probably be written about this subpackage! If you want to review these classes, simply reference "javafx.scene.control" on Google or on the Oracle Java website, and you can peruse what these classes can do for days on end. For this subpackage, "reference" is the key word, as you will want to reference this package and its classes individually at the time you need to implement a given UI element.

The next subpackage, **javafx.scene.effect**, provides all the **special effects** classes, almost two dozen of them. These can be very useful for Java 8 game development, so this is one of the few subpackages that I am going to cover in detail in this section.

The **javafx.scene.image** subpackage is used to implement digital imagery within JavaFX, and it has the **Image**, **ImageView**, **WritableImage**, **PixelFormat**, and **WritablePixelFormat** classes. The ImageView class is what you will normally use to hold your digital image assets, and the more advanced **PixelFormat** classes let you create digital imagery on a **pixel-by-pixel basis** if you want to do more advanced (algorithmic) pixel-based digital image creation.

The **javafx.scene.input** subpackage includes classes that are used to get **input** from the JavaFX application's user. This input is processed using the **event handling** capabilities, which you will be examining in great detail over the course of this book and which you have already experienced in your JavaFX application, in Chapter 3 (see Figure 3-2, ll. 22 to 24).

The **javafx.scene.layout** subpackage contains classes that are used to create UI design **layouts** and that can be used for your screen layout designs as well. These layout classes include classes that control and manage backgrounds; add and style borders; and provide UI pane management, such as **StackPane**, **TilePane**, **GridPane**, **FlowPane**, and **AnchorPane**. These UI classes offer automatic screen layout algorithms for the UI controls in JavaFX. The **Background** class (and subclasses) furnishes **screen background** utilities, and the **Border** class (and its subclasses) supplies **screen border** utilities, which can be used for spicing up the graphics design for your UI screens.

The **javafx.scene.media** subpackage holds classes that are used for the playback of audio or video media, including the **Media**, **MediaPlayer**, and **MediaView** classes. The Media class (or object, actually) references and contains the media (audio or video) asset, MediaPlayer plays that asset, and MediaView (in the case of video) displays the asset. This subpackage also has a **Track** superclass and **AudioTrack**, **VideoTrack**, and **SubtitleTrack** subclasses as well as the AudioClip, AudioEqualizer, and EqualizerBand classes, which provide advanced audio (equalizer) controls and short-form audio clips, or snippets of audio that are perfect for use in games. You will be using the AudioClip class later in the book (see Chapter 15).

The **javafx.scene.paint** subpackage contains a **Stop** class and the **Paint** superclass and its **Color**, **ImagePattern**, **LinearGradient**, and **RadialGradient** subclasses as well as the **Material** superclass and its **PhongMaterial** subclass. Those of you who are familiar with 3D content production will recognize this Phong shader algorithm, which will allow different **surface** looks (plastic, rubber, and so on) to be simulated. The Material and PhongMaterial classes need 3D capabilities to be present on the playback hardware to function successfully, just like the SceneAntialiasing, PerspectiveCamera, and LightBase class (and subclasses). The Paint class creates your Paint object, the Color class colors this object (fills it with a color), the LinearGradient and RadialGradient classes fill the Paint object with color gradients, and the Stop class lets you define where gradient colors start and stop inside the gradients. Finally, there is an ImagePattern class, which can fill a Paint object with a tileable image pattern (this can be quite useful for games).

The **javafx.scene.shape** subpackage provides classes for 2D geometry (commonly referred to as **shapes**) as well as for 3D geometry (commonly referred to as **meshes**). A **Mesh** superclass and its **TriangleMesh** subclass handle 3D geometry, as do the **Shape3D** superclass and its **Box**, **Sphere**, **Cylinder**, and **MeshView** subclasses. The **Shape** superclass has many more subclasses (11); these are 2D geometry elements and include the **Arc**, **Circle**, **CubicCurve**, **Ellipse**, **Line**, **Path**, **Polygon**, **Polyline**, **QuadCurve**, **Rectangle**, and **SVGPath** classes. A path support, a path being defined as an open shape (I like to call it a spline, as I am a 3D modeler), is also supplied by the **PathElement** superclass and its **ArcTo**, **ClosePath**, **CubicCurveTo**, **HLineTo**, LineTo, MoveTo, QuadCurveTo, and VLineTo subclasses, which allows you to draw spline curves to create your own custom shapes!

The **javafx.scene.text** subpackage has classes for rendering text shapes and fonts into your scenes. This includes the **Font** class, for employing any fonts that you may want to use that are not a JavaFX system font, as well as the **Text** class, for creating a text node that will display the text values using this font. There is also a specialized layout container class, called **TextFlow**, which is used to flow text, much like you would see done on a word processor.

The **javafx.scene.transform** subpackage offers classes for rendering 2D and 3D **spatial transformations**, such as the **Scale**, **Rotate**, **Shear**, **Translate**, and **Affine** (3D rotation) subclasses of the **Transform** superclass. These can be applied to any Node object in the Scene Graph. This allows anything in your scene graph (text, UI controls, shapes, meshes, images, media, and so on) to be transformed in any way that you like, which affords JavaFX game developers a ton of creative power. In case you are wondering, translation is linear movement of an entire object; shear is linear movement on a 2D plane in two different directions or movement in one direction when another part of the 2D plane is fixed. Imagine moving the top of a plane, while the bottom remains fixed, such that the square becomes a parallelogram, or moving the top and bottom of the same plane (a square) in different directions.

The **javafx.scene.web** subpackage furnishes classes for rendering web assets into a scene, using a collection of classes, including **WebView**, **WebEvent**, **WebEngine**, **WebHistory**, and **HTMLEditor**. The WebEngine (see, other people call things engines as well) class, as you might imagine, does the processing for showing HTML5 + CSS3 + JS in JavaFX, and the WebView class creates the node for displaying the WebEngine output in the Scene Graph. The WebHistory class (object, ultimately) holds the session history (from WebEngine instantiation to removal from memory) for the web pages visited, and WebEvent bridges the JavaScript web event processing with the JavaFX event processing.

Now that you have looked at a plethora of important and useful classes (objects) in the javafx.scene package and its related subpackages, let's take a look at the 15 top-level JavaFX packages to get a better idea of the key capabilities that JavaFX offers for application development (focusing of course, on those that can be used for game development).

Other JavaFX Packages: The 15 Top-Level Packages

There are 15 top-level packages (javafx.packagename being what I consider a top-level package), some of which have subpackage levels as well, as you have seen with the javafx.scene package and subpackages. Table 4-2 gives an overview of these packages and describes their contents.

Table 4-2. JavaFX Top-Level Packages, Their Primary Functions, and a Description of Their Functional Classes

Package Name	Functions	Description of Contents
javafx.animation	Animation	Timeline, Transition, AnimationTimer, Interpolator, KeyFrame, KeyValue
javafx.application	Application	Application (init, start, stop methods), Preloader, Parameters, Platform
javafx.beans	JavaFX beans	Java interfaces that define the most generic form of observability
javafx.collections	Collections	Java collections that define the most generic form of observability
javafx.concurrent	Threading	Threading classes: Task, Service, ScheduledService, WorkerStateEvent
javafx.css	CSS	Classes related to implementing CSS in JavaFX
javafx.embed	Embeds	Embeds deprecated Java Swing and Java AWT GUI paradigms
javafx.event	Event handler	Event handling classes: Event, ActionEvent, EventType, WeakEventHandler
javafx.fxml	FXML	FXML
javafx.geometry	3D geometry	3D geometry classes

(*continued*)

Table 4-2. (*continued*)

Package Name	Functions	Description of Contents
javafx.print	Printing	Printing classes
javafx.scene	Scene control	Classes related to scene creation, organization, control, and realization
javafx.stage	Stage creation	Stage creation classes
javafx.util	JavaFX utility	JavaFX utility classes
netscape.javascript	JavaScript	Allows Java code to invoke JavaScript methods and examine JavaScript properties

I have discussed some of these already, such as the **javafx.application** package (see Chapters 2 and 3) and the **javafx.scene** package (see the section "JavaFX Scene Package: Sixteen Powerful Java 8 Classes"). There are a few other JavaFX packages that you should take a closer look at here, as they (along with the **javafx.scene** package) contain classes that you will want to use in your Java 8 game development (still others, such as the javafx.print, javafx.fxml, javafx.beans, and javafx.embed packages are not likely to be used in your Java game design and development work process); these are **javafx.animation**, **javafx.stage**, **javafx.geometry**, **javafx.concurrent**, and **javafx.event**. Let's take an in-depth look at what these packages provide for your game development objectives next.

JavaFX Animation for Games: Using javafx.animation Classes

The javafx.animation package contains the **Animation** superclass, which has the **Timeline** and **Transition** subclasses as well as the **AnimationTimer**, **Interpolator**, **KeyFrame**, and **KeyValue** classes. Animation is an important design element in Java 8 games, and these animation classes are already coded for us, thanks to JavaFX, so all you have to do to add animation to your games is use them properly!

The JavaFX Animation Class: The Foundation for Animation Objects

The Animation class (or object, actually) provides the core functionality of animation in JavaFX. The Animation class contains two (overloaded) Animation() constructor methods; these are **Animation()** and **Animation(double targetFramerate)**, and they will create in memory the Animation object, which will control an animation and its playback characteristics and life cycle.

The Animation class contains the **.play()** method, the **.playFrom(cuePoint)** or **.playFrom(Duration time)** method, and a **.playFromStart()** method. These methods are used to start playback for the Animation object. There are also the **.pause()** method, which can pause the animation playback, and a **.stop()** method, to stop animation playback. The **.jumpTo(Duration time)** and **.jumpTo(cuePoint)** methods are used to jump to predefined positions in an animation.

You can set the animation **playback speed** (also called the frame rate or frames per second [FPS]) by using the **rate** property. The **cycleCount** property (variable) allows you to specify how many times an animation will **loop**, and a **delay** property lets you specify a delay time before the animation starts. If your animation is looping, this delay property will specify the delay time between loops, which can help you create some realistic effects.

You can specify a **seamless** animation **loop** by setting the **cycleCount** attribute or property (variable) to **INDEFINITE** and then using the **autoReverse** property (set to **false**), or you can use **pong** (back and forth) animation looping by specifying the **true** value for the autoReverse property. You can also set the cycleCount to a **numeric value** (use 1 if you want the animation to play only one time) if you do not want the animation to loop indefinitely.

The **.setRate()** method sets the animation playback rate property, the **.setDelay()** method sets the delay property, and the **.setCycleCount()** and **.setCycleDuration()** methods control the cycling characteristics. There are also similar **.get()** methods to "get" the currently set values for these Animation object variables (properties, attributes, parameters, or characteristics; however you prefer to look at these data fields is fine).

You can assign an action to be executed when the animation has completed playback, using the **onFinished** property loaded with an ActionEvent object. The action will be executed when the animation reaches the end of each loop, and, as you can imagine, some very powerful things can be triggered in a game with this particular capability.

There are also **read-only** variables (properties), which you can "poll" at any time to find the **status**, **currentTime**, **currentRate**, **cycleDuration**, and **totalDuration** for each Animation object. For example, you can use the **currentTime** property to see the position of the playback head (frame pointer) at any point in time in the animation playback cycle.

The JavaFX TimeLine Class: An Animation Subclass for Property Timeline Management

The JavaFX Timeline class is a subclass of the JavaFX Animation superclass, so its inheritance hierarchy starts with the Java 8 masterclass, java.lang.Object, progressing down to the Timeline class, as follows:

```
> java.lang.Object
  > javafx.animation.Animation
    > javafx.animation.Timeline
```

A Timeline object can be used to define a special kind of Animation object that is composed of JavaFX values (properties) of the object type **WritableValue**. Because all JavaFX properties are of that type, this class can be used to animate anything in JavaFX, which means that its use is limited only by your imagination.

As mentioned earlier, Timeline animations are defined using **KeyFrame** objects, created via the KeyFrame class, which both creates and manages these objects. A KeyFrame object is processed by a Timeline object, according to a **time** variable (accessed via **KeyFrame.time**) and properties to be animated, which are defined using the KeyFrame object's values variable (accessed via **KeyFrame.values**).

It is important to note that you need to set up your KeyFrame objects before you start running the Timeline object, as you cannot change a KeyFrame object within a running Timeline object. This is because it is put into system memory once it has been started. If you want to change a KeyFrame object in a running Timeline object in any way, first, stop the Timeline object; then, make the change to the KeyFrame; and, finally, start the Timeline object again. This will reload the Timeline object and its revised KeyFrame objects into memory with their new values.

The **Interpolator** class interpolates these KeyFrame.values in the Timeline object, based on the timeline **direction**. Interpolation is a process of creating in-between (or tween) frames, based on the beginning and ending values. In case you are wondering how the **direction** is inferred, it is kept in the rate and the read-only currentRate property of the Animation superclass (which is a part of the extended Timeline subclass).

Inverting the value of the rate property (i.e., making it **negative**) will reverse (toggle) the playback direction; the same principle holds when reading the currentRate property (a negative value signifies the reverse, or backward, direction). Finally, the **KeyValue** class (object) is used to hold the values inside the KeyFrame object.

The JavaFX Transition Class: An Animation Subclass for Transition Effects Application

The JavaFX Transition class is a subclass of the JavaFX Animation superclass, so its inheritance hierarchy starts with the Java 8 masterclass, java.lang.Object, progressing down to the Transition class, as follows:

```
> java.lang.Object
  > javafx.animation.Animation
    > javafx.animation.Transition
```

The Transition class is a **public abstract** class, and, as such, it can only be used (subclassed or extended) to create transition subclasses. In fact, ten of these subclasses have already been created for you to use to create your own transition special effects; these are the **SequentialTransition**, **FadeTransition**, **FillTransition**, **PathTransition**, **PauseTransition**, **RotateTransition**, **ScaleTransition**, **TranslateTransition**, **ParallelTransition**, and **StrokeTransition** classes. As a subclass of Animation, the Transition class contains all the functionality of Animation.

Chances are you will end up using the ten custom transition classes directly, as they provide the different types of transitions you are likely to want to use (fades, fills, path based, stroke based, rotate, scale, movement, and so on). I am going to move on to the AnimationTimer class next, as we will be using this class for our game engine during the book.

The JavaFX AnimationTimer Class: Frame Processing, Nanoseconds, and Pulse

The JavaFX AnimationTimer class is **not** a subclass of the JavaFX Animation superclass, so its inheritance hierarchy starts with the Java 8 masterclass, java.lang.Object, and looks like this:

```
> java.lang.Object
  > javafx.animation.AnimationTimer
```

What this means is that the AnimationTimer class is **scratch coded** specifically to offer AnimationTimer functionality to JavaFX and that it is not related to the Animation (or Timeline or Transition) class or subclasses in any way. For this reason, the name of this class may be somewhat misleading if you are mentally grouping the class in with the Animation, Interpolator, KeyFrame, and KeyValue classes that occupy the javafx.animation package with it, as is has no relation to these classes whatsoever!

Like the Transition class, the AnimationTimer class has been declared a **public abstract** class. Because it is an abstract class, it can only be used (subclassed or extended) to create AnimationTimer subclasses. Unlike the Transition class, it has no subclasses that have been created for you; you have to create your own AnimationTimer subclasses from scratch, which we will be doing later on in the book to create our GamePlayLoop.java class.

The AnimationTimer class is deceptively simple, in that it has only one method that you must override or replace, contained in the public abstract class: the .handle() method. This method provides the programming logic that you want to have executed on every frame of the JavaFX engine's stage and scene processing cycle, which is optimized to play at 60FPS (this is perfect for games). JavaFX uses a **pulse** system, which is based on the new Java 8 **nanosecond** unit of time (previous versions of Java used **milliseconds**).

JavaFX Pulse Synchronization: Asynchronous Processing for Scene Graph Elements

A JavaFX pulse is a type of **synchronization** (**timing**) **event**, one that synchronizes the states of the elements that are contained within any given Scene Graph structure that you create for your JavaFX applications (games). The pulse system in JavaFX is administered by the Glass Windowing Toolkit. Pulse uses high-resolution (nanosecond) timers, which are also available to Java programmers using the **System.nanoTime()** method, as of the Java 8 API.

The pulse management system in JavaFX is capped or throttled to **60FPS**. This is so that all the JavaFX threads have the "processing headroom" to do what they need to do. A JavaFX application will automatically **spawn** up to three threads, based on what you are doing in your application logic. A basic business application will probably only use the **primary JavaFX thread**, but a 3D game will also spawn the **Prism rendering thread**, and if that game uses audio or video, or both, which it usually will, it will spawn a **media playback thread** as well.

You will be using audio, 2D, 3D, and possibly video in the course of your game development journey, so your JavaFX game application will certainly be multithreaded! As you will see, JavaFX has been designed to be able to create games that take advantage of multithreading and nanosecond timing capabilities and 3D rendering hardware (Prism) support.

Whenever something is changed in the Scene Graph, such as a UI control positioning, a CSS style definition, or an animation playing, a pulse event is scheduled and is eventually fired to synchronize the states of elements on the Scene Graph. The trick in JavaFX game design is to optimize pulse events so that they are focusing on the game play logic (animation, collision detection, and so on); thus, you will minimize the other changes (UI control location, CSS style changes, and so on) the pulse engine looks at. You will do this by using the Scene Graph as a **fixed** design system, meaning that you will use the Scene Graph to design your game structure but will not manipulate nodes in real time on the Scene Graph, using **dynamic** programming logic, as the pulse system will perform the updates.

A JavaFX pulse system allows developers to handle events **asynchronously**, like a **batch processing** system that schedules tasks on the nanosecond level, instead of once a day, like batch processing schedulers from the old mainframe computer days. Next, let's examine how to schedule code in a pulse, using a **.handle()** method.

Harnessing the JavaFX Pulse Engine: Extending the AnimationTimer Class to Generate Pulse Events

Extending the AnimationTimer class is a great way to get the JavaFX pulse system to process your code for each pulse that it processes. Your real-time game programming logic will be placed inside the **.handle(long now)** method and can be started and stopped at will by using the other two AnimationTimer methods, .start() and .stop().

The **.start()** and **.stop()** methods are called from the AnimationTimer superclass, although the two methods can be overridden as well; just be sure eventually to call **super.start()** and **super.stop()** in your override code methods. If added as an inner class inside your current JavaFX **public void .start()** method structure, the code structure might look as follows (see Chapter 3, Figure 3-2):

```
public void start(Stage primaryStage) {
    Button btn = new Button;
    new AnimationTimer() {
        @Override
        public void handle(long now) {
            // Program logic that gets processed on every pulse that JavaFX processes
        }
    }.start();
}
```

The above programming logic shows how an AnimationTimer inner class would be constructed as well as how Java **dot chaining** works. The .start() method call to the AnimationTimer superclass is appended to the end of the new AnimationTimer(){...} code construct so that the entire AnimationTimer creation (**using new**), declaration (using the curly braces), and execution (using a .start() method call) are chained to the AnimationTimer object construct.

If you want to create a more complex AnimationTimer subclass for something central to your game logic, such as **Collision Detection**, it would be a better idea (Java code design approach) to make this game logic its very own custom AnimationTimer subclass.

This is especially true if you are going to be creating more than one AnimationTimer subclass to do pulse event–controlled high-speed processing. That's right, you can have more than one AnimationTimer subclass running at the same time (just do not get carried away and use too many AnimationTimers). You can accomplish this with the **extends** keyword, creating your own AnimationTimer class, called **GamePlayLoop**, using the following class definition:

```
public class GamePlayLoop extends AnimationTimer {
    @Override
    public void handle(long now) {
        // Program logic that gets processed on every pulse that JavaFX processes
    }
    @Override
    public void start() {
        super.start();
    }
}
```

```
@Override
public void stop() {
    super.stop();
}
}
```

Next, let's investigate the JavaFX Stage class (object),which is passed into your InvinciBagel .start() method!

JavaFX Screen and Window Control: Using javafx.stage Classes

The **javafx.stage** package contains classes that can be considered top level, in terms of the display for your JavaFX application (in this case, a game). This display is at the top of the resulting game play, because it shows your game's scenes to the end user of your application. Inside the Stage object are Scene objects, and inside these are Scene Graph Node objects, which contain the elements that make up an application.

In contrast, the classes that are in this package could be considered fairly **low level**, from an OS perspective; these are the **Stage**, **Screen**, **Window**, **WindowEvent**, **PopupWindow**, **Popup**, **DirectoryChooser**, and **FileChooser** classes as well as the **FileChooser.ExtensionFilter** nested class. These classes can be used to interface with the device's display hardware, and the OS software's windowing management, file management, and directory (folder) management functionality.

To get a description of the display hardware that is being used by the device that a JavaFX application is running on, you will want to use the **Screen** class. This class supports **multiscreen** (commonly referred to as **second screen**) scenarios, using the **.getScreens()** method, which can access an **ObservableList** object that will contain a list (array) with all the currently available screens. A primary screen is accessed using the **.getPrimary()** method call. You can get the **physical resolution** for the primary screen hardware by using a **.getDpi()** method call. There are also **.getBounds()** and **.getVisualBounds()** method calls for usable resolution.

The **Window** superclass, and its **Stage** and **PopupWindow** subclasses, can be used by the JavaFX end user to interact with your application. As you saw in Chapter 3 (see Figure 3-2), this is done using the **Stage** object named primaryStage, which is passed into your .start() method, or using a **PopupWindow** (dialog, tool tip, context menu, notification, and so on) subclass, such as a **Popup** or **PopupControl** object.

You can use the Stage class to create secondary stages within your JavaFX application programming logic. A **primary** Stage object is always constructed by the JavaFX platform, using the **public void start(Stage primaryStage)** method call, as you have already seen in Chapters 2 and 3 in the bootstrap JavaFX application created by NetBeans.

All JavaFX Stage objects must be constructed using, and modified inside the primary JavaFX application thread, which I discussed in the previous section. Because a stage equates to a window on the OS platform it is running on, certain attributes or properties are **read-only**, as they need to be controlled at the OS level; these are **Boolean** properties (variables): **alwaysOnTop**, **fullScreen**, **iconified**, and **maximized**.

All Stage objects have a **StageStyle** attribute and a **Modality** attribute, which can be set using constants. The stageStyle constants are **StageStyle.DECORATED**, **StageStyle.UNDECORATED**, **StageStyle.TRANSPARENT**, and **StageStyle.UTILITY**. The **Modality** constants are **Modality.NONE**, **Modality.APPLICATION_MODAL**, and **Modality. WINDOW_MODAL**. In the next section, I will show you how to do something really impressive using the StageStyle attribute and the TRANSPARENT constant that will make your JavaFX applications stand out from everyone else's in the marketplace.

The Popup class can be used to create custom pop-up notifications, and even custom game components, from scratch. Alternately, you can use the PopupControl class, and its **ContextMenu** and **Tooltip** subclasses, to provide these predefined (coded) JavaFX UI controls.

The **DirectoryChooser** and **FileChooser** classes give support for passing through the standard OS file selection and directory navigation dialogs into your JavaFX applications. The **FileChooser.ExtensionFilter** nested class offers a utility for filtering the files that will come up in the FileChooser dialog, based on file type (file extension).

Next, let's take your current InvinciBagel Stage object to the next level and make it a **windowless** (floating) application. This is one of the impressive features of JavaFX that cannot be matched by Flash or other game engines.

Using a JavaFX Primary Stage Object: Creating a Floating Windowless Application

Let's make the primary **Stage** for your InvinciBagel application transparent so that the **Button** UI control floats right on top of the OS desktop. This is something that JavaFX can do that you do not see very often, and it allows you to create 3D applications that float on top of the OS desktop (for 3D virtual objects, this is called a windowless ActiveX control).

This is accomplished by using the **StageStyle.TRANSPARENT** constant, in conjunction with the **.initStyle()** method, from the **Stage** class. As Figure 4-4 demonstrates, I also used the technique I told you about in Chapter 3 (a technique that does not follow the proper Java coding convention regarding declaring an import statement for classes you are planning to use). In **line 35** of the code, I reference the constant by using the fully qualified class name (package.subpackage.class.constant), **javafx.stage.StageStyle.TRANSPARENT**, inside the **primaryStage. initStyle(StageStyle style)** method call. This is done via the following line of Java code:

```
primaryStage.initStyle(javafx.stage.StageStyle.TRANSPARENT);
```

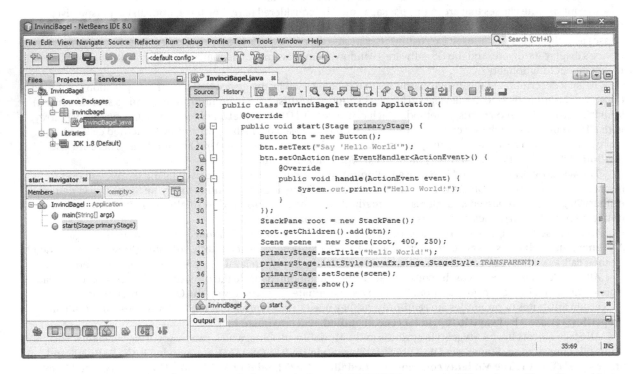

Figure 4-4. *Call an .initStyle() method with the StageStyle.TRANSPARENT constant, off the primaryStage Stage object*

As you can, I clicked the primaryStage Stage object in NetBeans IDE 8.0, in the code editing area, and it shows (tracks) the **usage** of that object in the code. The Stage object is set up (displaying title, style, and scene), using the **.setTitle()**, **.initStyle()**, **.setScene()**, and **.show()** method calls.

I am going to leave the .setTitle() method call in the code, but make a mental note that once you get this windowless application treatment working, the title bar is part of the window's "chrome," or UI elements, and when these are gone (including the title bar), this setting of the title will amount to a moot point.

If you have been worrying about memory optimization, at this point in the application development work process, you would remove the .setTitle() method call, because the title would not be shown using a StageStyle. TRANSPARENT constant for the StageStyle attribute.

90

Next, use the **Run icon** (or **Run menu**), and run the application. As Figure 4-5 illustrates, what you are trying to achieve did not work: the window chrome elements are gone, and the transparency value is not evident.

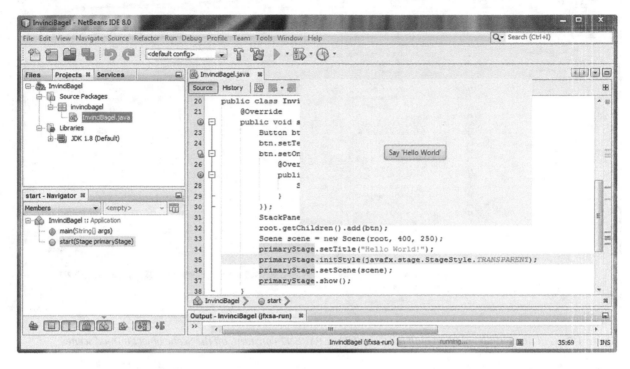

Figure 4-5. *Run the project to see if the Stage object is transparent; clearly, something is set to White*

There must be something else in the processing pipeline that is not yet defining its **background** using the **transparency** value. Transparency is defined using a hexadecimal value of **#00000000**, which signifies that all **AARRGGBB** (alpha channel, red, green, blue) color and opacity values are turned off. You will need to start thinking about the JavaFX components of your application as **layers** (currently, these are **stage-scene-stackPane-button**). You will be learning about digital imaging concepts such as color depth, alpha channels, layers, blending, and all the technical information that relates to processing pixels in a 2D plane as the book progresses.

The next thing you should try to set to this transparent value is the next level down in the JavaFX Scene Graph hierarchy from the stage, which contains the Scene Graph itself. The next most top-level component, as discussed previously, is the **Scene** object, which also has a background color value parameter or attribute.

Like the Stage class (object), the Scene class (object) does not have a style constant of TRANSPARENT, so you will have to approach setting the Scene object's background to a transparency value in a different way, using a different method and constant. One thing you should know is that everything in JavaFX that writes itself to the screen will in some way support transparency to allow multiple-layer **compositing** in JavaFX applications.

If you read the Scene class documentation, you will notice that there is a method, **.setFill(Color value)**, that takes a **Color** (class or object) value, so let's try that next. As Figure 4-6 shows, I called the .setFill() off the Scene object **named scene**, using a `scene.setFill(Color.TRANSPARENT);` statement, which NetBeans helps me construct!

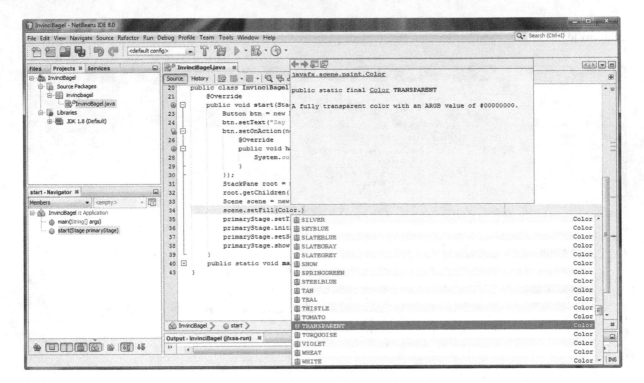

Figure 4-6. *Call the .setFill() method with the Color.TRANSPARENT constant, off the Scene object named scene*

Run the application again, to see if the transparency is showing yet. As you can see in Figure 4-7, it is not!

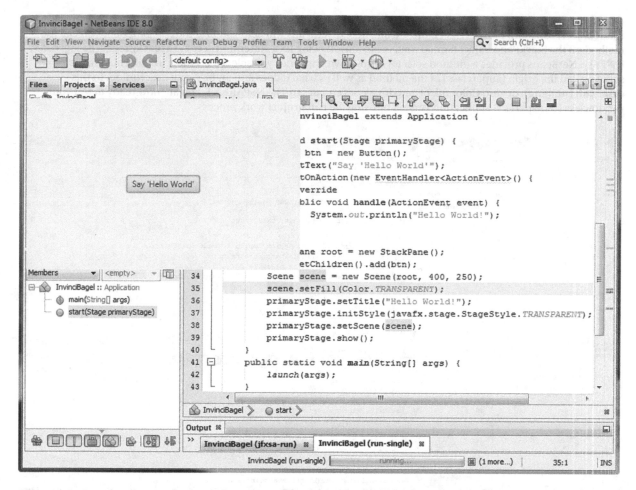

Figure 4-7. *Run the project to look at the transparent Stage object; something is still set to White*

Because you are using a **StackPane** object to implement layers in the InvinciBagel application, this is the next level up that you need to try to set a transparency value for. Evidently, JavaFX uses a Color.WHITE default background color value for all its objects. If I were on the JavaFX design team, I would be arguing for this to be changed to the Color.TRANSPARENT constant, but, of course, this might confuse new users, as alpha channel and compositing layers are advanced concepts.

The **javafx.scene.layout.StackPane** class is subclassed from the **javafx.scene.layout.Region** class, which has a **.setBackground()** method for setting the **Background** (class or object) value. Again, a TRANSPARENT value constant must be available, as you always need to set background values as transparent, especially for Java 8 game design.

Interestingly, things are not always as straightforward and consistent as you would want them to be in Java programming, as, to achieve exactly the same end result (installing a transparent background color/image **plate** for the design element), you have used thus far three different method calls, passing three custom object types: .initStyle(StageStyle object), .setFill(Color object), and .setBackground(Background object).

This time, you are going to call the .setBackground(Background value) method, with yet another Background class (object) constant, **EMPTY**. As Figure 4-8 illustrates, NetBeans will help you find the constant once you call the method off the StackPane object named root, using the following **Java statement: root.setBackground(Background. EMPTY);**. NetBeans provides a method selector drop-down and, once you select a method, an information dialog showing you the origin (superclass) of the method as well as what it does and an in-depth description. In this case, **null** (nothing), or zero Color fill, or zero Image set equates to TRANSPARENT. You are now ready to test your windowless (transparent) application version by using the **run project** work process.

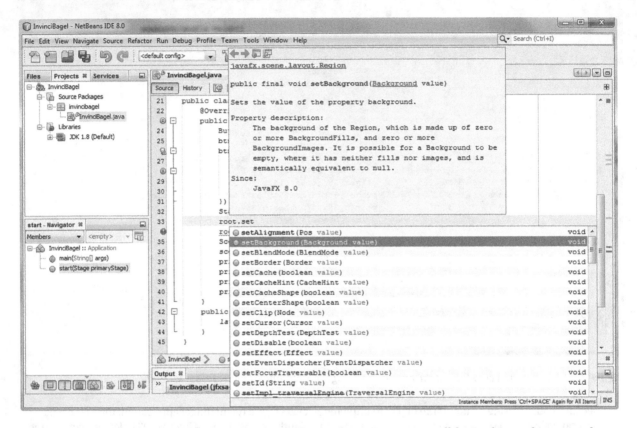

Figure 4-8. *Call a .setBackground() method with a Background.EMPTY constant, off the StackPane object named root*

As you can see in Figure 4-9, you have now achieved your objective, and just the Button object is visible on the desktop. I pulled the top of NetBeans IDE 8.0 down a bit so that you can see how great this works and still see the three lines of Java code that you added to achieve this end result. Using 2D, 3D, and alpha channels, some crazy-cool applications can be created via this **StageStyle.TRANSPARENT** capability, so I thought I would show it to you early on in the book and get some JavaFX application Java coding experience into this JavaFX overview chapter.

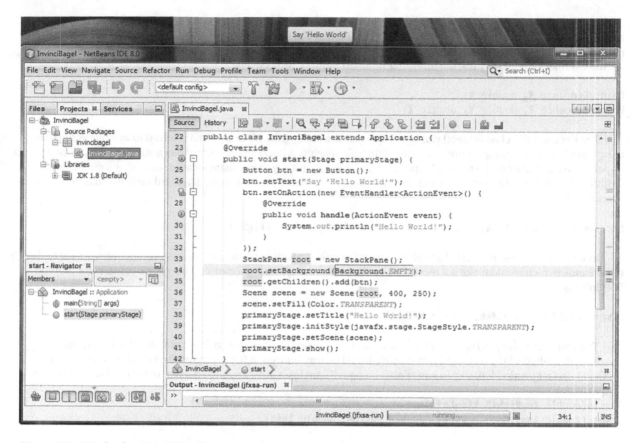

Figure 4-9. *Windowless JavaFX application seen at the top; completed Java and JavaFX code that achieves it seen in the IDE*

Now that you have explored the javafx.stage package, let's examine the javafx.geometry package next!

JavaFX Bounds and Dimensions: Using javafx.geometry Classes

Even though the term "**geometry**" technically applies to 2D and 3D assets, these are contained in a javafx.scene.shape package, which I covered earlier (see the section "**Scene Subpackages: The 13 Other Scene Packages**"). The **javafx. geometry** package could be considered more of a utility package, containing foundational classes for building 2D and 3D constructs from scratch. As such, the package offers classes such as a **Bounds** superclass and its **BoundingBox** subclass as well as **Insets**, **Point2D**, **Point3D**, **Dimension2D**, and **Rectangle2D** geometry content creation utility classes.

All the classes in the javafx.geometry package, except the BoundingBox class, were extended directly from the java.lang.Object master class, meaning that they were each developed (coded) from scratch for providing points (also called vertices), rectangles, dimensions, boundaries, and insets (inside boundaries) for use as geometric utilities for JavaFX application development.

The Point2D and Point3D classes (objects, ultimately) hold **x, y coordinates** for a 2D point on a 2D plane or **x, y, z coordinates** for a 3D point in 3D space. These Point objects will be used to build more complex 2D or 3D structures made up of a collection of points, such as a 2D path or a 3D mesh. The Point2D and Point3D constructor method calls are not overloaded, and they use the following standard formats, respectively:

```
Point2D(double X, double Y)
Point3D(double X, double Y, double Z)
```

The Rectangle2D class (object) can be used to define a rectangular 2D area, often referred to as a plane, and has many uses in graphics programming, as you might well imagine. A Rectangle2D object has a starting point in the upper left-hand corner of the rectangle specified, using an **x** and a **y** coordinate location as well as a dimension (width by height). A constructor method for a Rectangle2D object has the following standard format and is not overloaded:

```
Rectangle2D(double minX, double minY, double width, double height)
```

In addition, a Dimension2D class (object) specifies only the width and height dimensions and does not place the dimensions (which would make it a rectangle) on the screen using an **x, y** location. This class's constructor method is as follows:

```
Dimension2D(double width, double height)
```

The Insets class (object) is like a Dimension2D class, in that it does not provide a location value for the inset but does offer **offsets** for a rectangular inset area, based on **top**, **bottom**, **left**, and **right** offset distances. The Insets method is in fact overloaded, so you can specify an equidistant inset or a customized inset, using the following code:

```
Insets(double topRightBottomLeft)
Insets(double top, double right, double bottom, double left)
```

The Bounds class is a **public abstract** class and will never be an object, but instead is a **blueprint** for creating Node boundary classes, such as its BoundingBox subclass. The Bounds superclass also allows a **negative** value, which is used to indicate that a bounding area is **empty** (think of it as **null**, or **unused**). A BoundingBox class uses the following (overloaded) constructor methods to create a **2D** (first constructor) or **3D** (second constructor) BoundingBox object:

```
BoundingBox(double minX, double minY, double width, double height)
BoundingBox(double minX, double minY, double minZ, double width, double height, double depth)
```

Next, let's take a look at Event and ActionEvent processing in JavaFX, as this will add interactivity to your games.

JavaFX Input Control for Games: Using javafx.event Classes

Because games are interactive by their very nature, let's take a look at the **javafx.event** package next; it provides us with the **Event** superclass and its **ActionEvent** subclass, for handling **ACTION** events, such as UI element use and animation KeyFrame processing. Because you are going to be using ActionEvent in your JavaFX games (applications), I am describing its class inheritance hierarchy here, as this will show you the origins of the Event class as well:

```
Java.lang.Object
  > java.util.EventObject
    > javafx.event.Event
      > javafx.event.ActionEvent
```

Your InvinciBagel game application is already using this **ActionEvent** class (object), with the **EventHandler interface** and its **.handle()** method, which you code yourself to tell your application what to do to "handle" the Event (ActionEvent) once it has occurred (fired). The .handle() method **catches** this **fired** event and then processes it, according to the Java programming logic inside the body of the .handle() method.

A Java **interface** is a class that furnishes **empty** methods, which are declared for use but which do not yet contain any Java programming constructs. The **unimplemented methods** will, at the time of their use, have to be implemented by you, the Java programmer. This Java interface defines only the methods to be implemented (in this case, a method for handling the ActionEvent so that the event gets processed in some fashion). It is important to note that the Java interface defines the method that needs to be coded but does not write the method code for you, so it is a road map of what you must do to complete, or **interface with**, the programming structure that is in place (in this case, the Java programming structure for handling ActionEvent objects, that is, fired action events.

Now, let's take a look at **multithreading** in JavaFX, which is another important concept for advanced games, to conclude this exploration of everything 2D- and 3D- (game) related in the JavaFX API and package hierarchy.

JavaFX Thread Control for Games: javafx.concurrent Package

Games require **background**, or **asynchronous**, processing. This can be done using additional threads besides the JavaFX application thread, Prism rendering thread, and media playback thread, which are all automatically created for you, based on which classes (objects) you are using in your scene graph. Your application programming logic can spawn its own Worker threads for processing so that you do not overload the primary JavaFX application thread. Let's take a look at the **javafx.concurrent** package next, as it provides us with the **Service** superclass and its **ScheduledService** subclass, for creating **Worker** objects, as well as a **Task** class, used for one-off task processing.

Because you are going to be using Service and ScheduledService in your JavaFX games (applications), I am demonstrating the ScheduledService class inheritance hierarchy here, as this will show you the java.lang.Object origins of the Service classes as well:

```
Java.lang.Object
  > javafx.concurrent.Service
    > javafx.concurrent.ScheduledService
```

Whereas Task (class) objects are used only one time, to accomplish a given task, a **service** is ongoing, and a Service object and a ScheduledService (class) object can be reused, that is, they are ready to perform their **service** at any time. This is more appropriate for game play processing, as game play continues for long periods of time, and the assumption here is that the types of game logic processing involved will also need to be calculated as time goes on during game play, and not just one single time, as with the Task class (object).

The **Worker** Java construct is actually an **interface**, and the Task, Service, and ScheduledService classes have been created for you, based on this Worker interface (which is more than can be said for the **EventHandler** interface, which you have to implement yourself!).

A Worker object performs processing, using a background thread, and can be either reusable (such as in the Service class) or not reusable (such as in the Task class). Worker thread states are controlled by the **Worker.State** class (object) and contain the life cycle stages for a Worker thread. These apply across the three primary classes in the javafx.concurrent package, as they implement the Worker interface and its related nested classes. As mentioned in the previous chapter, a nested class is accessed via dot notation, so the State class is thus nested inside the `Worker interface (class)`. Because the states of a Worker thread are very important to understand before you use it, I am going to detail them in the form of a table so that they are crystal clear to you (see Table 4-3).

Table 4-3. *Worker Thread Life Cycle States, as Defined by the Worker.State Nested Class for Use with a Worker Interface*

Worker.State Constant	Significance
READY	Worker object (thread) has been **initialized** (or reinitialized) and is ready to be used.
SCHEDULED	Worker object (thread) has been **scheduled** for execution but is not currently running.
RUNNING	Worker object (thread) is currently **running** and is executing the Java programming logic.
SUCCEEDED	Worker object (thread) has **executed** successfully, and a valid result is in the value property.
FAILED	Worker object (thread) has **failed** to execute successfully because of some unexpected condition.
CANCELLED	Worker object (thread) has been **cancelled** by invoking the **Worker.cancel()** method call.

As with everything else in this JavaFX 8 multimedia engine overview chapter, you will be getting deep into the details of how to use these packages, classes, nested classes, interfaces, methods, constants, and variables over the course of the book, as you apply these JavaFX programming constructs and concepts!

Summary

In this fourth chapter, you took a closer look at some of the more important packages, concepts, components, classes, constructors, constants, and variables (attributes) that can be found in the **JavaFX 8 API**, an impressive collection of **36** javafx.packagename.subpackagename packages, which I outlined in tables and covered, one by one, as needed for multimedia 2D and 3D (and hybrid 2D-3D) game development. When I say, "an overview," I mean an overview!

Certainly, I cannot discuss every functional class in JavaFX in one chapter, so I started with a broad overview of the JavaFX engine and how it integrates with the JavaFX **Scene Builder** tool and the JavaFX **Scene Graph API** above it, and with the **Java 8** API, **NetBeans 8.0**, and target OSs below it, which give JavaFX expansive OS support across so many popular platforms and devices and the leading web browsers.

I presented a high-level technical view of JavaFX, detailing its structures, including **JavaFX Scene Graph**, APIs, **Quantum**, **Prism**, **Glass**, **WebKit**, and **Media** engine. You looked at how these multithreading, rendering, windowing, media, and web engines interface with the **Java 8 API** and **Java JDK 8** as well as with **NetBeans 8.0** and the **JVM** bytecode that it generates, which is read by all the various OS platforms currently running across a dozen different consumer electronics device types.

You also explored JavaFX core concepts, such as the **JavaFX Scene Graph** and the JavaFX **pulse** events system, which you will be leveraging to create a Java 8 game as you work through this book, starting in the next chapter, when I explain how to use the JavaFX Scene Builder visual editing tool in NetBeans.

Then, you dove deep into some of the key JavaFX packages and subpackages for game design, such as **Application, Scene, Shape, Effect, Layout, Control, Media, Image, Stage, Animation, Geometry, Event, and Concurrent**, and their package classes and subclasses and even, in some cases, their interfaces, nested classes, and constants.

You even took a break to add some code to your InvinciBagel application that turned it into a windowless application and learned how to make the **stage, scene, and stackPane** background plates transparent, using alpha channels and hexadecimal #00000000 or Color.TRANSPARENT, Background.EMPTY, and SceneStyle.TRANSPARENT constants. I had to get some work with the NetBeans IDE 8.0, Java 8 programming language, and JavaFX API into this chapter somehow!

In the next chapter, you are going to explore the **JavaFX** Scene Builder, which makes it easy to construct the Scene Graph structures that you learned about in this chapter. You will start to build your game splash screen as well, as I know you are eager to get started on a game infrastructure, even if it is just a splash screen!

■ ■ ■

CHAPTER 5

An Introduction to Game Design: Concepts, Multimedia, and Using Scene Builder

In this chapter, you will build on your knowledge of the JavaFX multimedia engine by learning about the optimal way to use the scene graph paradigm in JavaFX and take a look at JavaFX **Scene Builder** tool and **FXML**, and why (or why not) to use these in certain types of Java game development scenarios. You will also examine basic game design optimization concepts, and the types of games, as well as game engines, that are available for the Java platform, including physics engines, such as JBox2D and Dyn4J, and 3D game engines, such as LWJGL and JMonkey. Finally, you will consider the new media concepts that you will need to understand to integrate digital imaging, digital audio, digital video, and animation into your game production pipeline. We will also look at some of the free open-source multimedia production tools that you installed back in Chapter 1, and can now use to create Java 8 games.

First, you will revisit the underlying concept of **static** (fixed) versus **dynamic** (real time), which was covered in Chapter 3 (constant versus variable) and Chapter 4 (pulse) and which is one of the foundational principles of **game optimization**. This is important, because you will want your game to run smoothly across all the different platforms and devices that are used to play it, even if the device only uses a single processor (which is actually rare these days, with most devices featuring dual core (two processor) or quad core (four processor) CPUs).

Next, you will study the concepts, techniques, and lingo of game design, including sprites, collision detection, physics simulation, background plates, animation, layers, levels, logic, and AI. You will also examine the different types of games that can be designed, and how they differ from each other.

Then, you will explore the role that multimedia assets play in today's visually (and aurally) impressive games. You will learn about the principles of **digital imaging**, **digital video**, and **animation** as well as **digital audio**, as you will be using many of these new media asset types over the course of the book, and will need this foundational knowledge to be able to work with them.

Finally, you will take an in-depth look at the bootstrap JavaFX application code that you generated in Chapter 2 and at how the Java .main() method and the JavaFX .start() method create the primaryStage Stage object, using the **Stage()** constructor method, and, inside that, create a Scene object named scene, using the **Scene()** constructor method. You will look at how to use methods from the Stage class to set the scene, title the stage, and show the stage as well as how to create and use **StackPane** and **Button** class (objects) and how to add an **EventHandler** to a button.

High-Level Concept: Static vs. Dynamic

I want to start out with a high-level concept that touches on everything that I will be talking about in this chapter, from the types of games you can create, to game optimization, to JavaFX Scene Builder and JavaFX Scene Graph. You took a look at this concept back in Chapter 3, whether you realized it or not, while exploring the concept of a Java constant, which is fixed, or **static**, and does not change, versus a Java variable, which is **dynamic** and changes in real time. Similarly, a UI design in JavaFX Scene Graph can be static (fixed and immovable) or dynamic (animated, draggable, or skinnable, meaning that you can change the UI look to suit your personal taste).

The reason these concepts are important in game design and development is that your game's engine, which you design to run or render your game, must constantly check on its dynamic portions to see if they have changed and require a response (update a score, move a sprite position, play an animation frame, change the game piece's state, calculate collision detection, calculate physics, and so on). This checking (and the ensuing processing) on every frame update (called a pulse in JavaFX; see Chapter 4), to make sure that all your variables, positions, states, animations, collisions, physics, and the like are conforming to your Java game engine logic, can really add up, and, at some point, the processor that is doing all this work can get overloaded, which can slow it down!

The result of this overloading of all the real-time, per-frame checking that enhances the dynamics of your game (play) is that the **frame rate** at which your game is running will decrease. That's right, like digital video and animation, Java 8 games have frame rates, too, but Java 8 game frame rates are based upon the efficiency of your programming logic. The lower the frame rate of your game, the less smooth the game play becomes, at least for dynamic, real-time games, such as arcade games; how smoothly a game plays relates to how seamless (enjoyable) the **user experience** is for the customer, the game player.

For this reason, the concept of **static versus dynamic** is very important to every aspect of game play design and makes it easier to achieve a great user experience with certain types of games than with others. I will be discussing different types of games later in the chapter (see the section "Types of Games: Puzzles, Board Games, Arcade Games, Hybrids"), but, as you might imagine, board games are more static in nature, and arcade games are more dynamic. That said, there are optimization approaches that can keep a game dynamic, that is, seem like a lot is going on, when, from a processing point of view, what is really going on is quite manageable. This is one of the many tricks of game design, which, when all is said and done, is about optimization.

One of the most significant static-versus-dynamic design issues in Android (Java) programming is UI design using XML (**static design**) versus UI design using Java (**dynamic design**). The Android platform allows UI design to be done using XML instead of Java so that nonprogrammers (designers) can do the **front-end** design for an application. JavaFX allows exactly the same thing to be done using **FXML**. You have to create an FXML JavaFX application to do this, as you saw in Chapter 2 (see Figure 2-4, right-hand side, third option, "JavaFX FXML Application"). Doing so will add the **javafx.fxml** package and classes to the application, letting you design UIs, using FXML, and later having your Java programming logic "inflate" them so that the design consists of JavaFX UI objects.

It is important to note that using FXML adds another layer, containing the FXML markup and its translation and processing, to the application development and compilation process. I am going to demonstrate later in the chapter how this is done, in case your design team wants to use FXML for the UI design work process, instead of Java (see the section "JavaFX Scene Builder: Using FXML for UI Design"). I am doing this because I want to cover all the design options in JavaFX, including FXML, to make sure that this book is complete in its coverage of what can be done using Java 8 and JavaFX 8.0. At the end of the day, this is a Java 8 programming title, however, so my primary focus during this book will be using Java 8, not FXML.

In any event, the point that I am making regarding using XML (or FXML) to create the UI design is that this approach can be viewed as static, because the design is created beforehand, using XML, and is "inflated" at compile time, using Java. Java inflation methods use the designer-provided FXML structure to create the scene graph, which is filled with JavaFX UI (class) objects, based on the UI design structure (hierarchy) created using FXML. I will give you an overview of how this works later in the chapter so that you have a handle on how this works (see the section "JavaFX Scene Builder: Using FXML for UI Design").

Game Optimization: Balancing Static Elements with Dynamic

Game optimization comes down to **balancing** static elements, which do not require processing in real time, with dynamic elements, which require constant processing. Too much dynamic processing, especially when it is not really needed, can make your game play jerky, or stilted. This is why game programming is an art form: it requires balance as well as great characters, a story line, creativity, illusion, anticipation, accuracy, and, finally, **optimization**.

Some of the different game component considerations for optimization in a dynamic game are listed in Table 5-1. As you can see, there are a lot of areas of game play that can be optimized to make the processor's workload significantly less "busy." If you have even one of these primary dynamic game processing areas "run away" with the processor's precious cycles per frame, this can greatly affect the **user experience** for your game. I will be getting into game terminology (sprites, collision detection, physics simulation, and so on) in the next section of the chapter.

Table 5-1. *Aspects of Game Play That Can Be Optimized to Minimize System Memory and Processor Cycle Usage*

Game Play Aspect	Basic Optimization Principle
Sprite position (Move)	Move sprites by as many pixels as possible to achieve smooth movement on the screen.
Collision detection	Check for collisions between objects on the screen only when necessary (in close proximity).
Physics simulation	Minimize the number of objects in a scene that require physics calculations to be performed.
Sprite animation	Minimize the number of frames that need to be cycled to create an illusion of smooth animation.
Background animation	Minimize background areas that are animated so that the entire background looks animated but is not.
Game play logic	Program game play logic (simulated or AI) to be as efficient as possible.
Scoreboard updates	Update scoreboard only when scoring, and minimize score updates to once per second maximum.
UI design	Use a static UI design so that pulse events are not used for UI element positioning or CSS3.

Considering all these game programming areas makes game programming an extremely tricky endeavor!

It is important to note that some of these aspects work together to create a given illusion for the player. For instance, the sprite animation will create the illusion of a character running, jumping, or flying, but without combining that code with sprite positioning (movement) code, the reality of the illusion will not be achieved. To fine-tune an illusion, the speed of the animation (frame rate) and the distance moved (in pixels per frame) may need to be adjusted (I like to call this tweaked) to get the most realistic result. We will be doing this during Chapter 13.

If you can move game elements (primary player sprite, objectile sprites, enemy sprites, background) a greater number of pixels a fewer number of times, you will save processing cycles. It is the moving part that takes processing time, not the distance (how many pixels are moved). Similarly, with animation, the fewer frames needed to achieve a convincing animation, the less memory will be required to hold those frames. Remember that you are optimizing memory usage as well as processing cycles. Detecting collisions is a major part of game programming logic; it is important not to check for collisions between game elements that are not "in play" (on the screen), or active, and that are not near each other.

Forces of nature (physics simulations) and game play logic if it is not well coded (optimized), are the most processor intensive aspects. These are subjects I will cover later in the book, when you are more advanced (see Chapters 16 and 17).

Game Design Concepts: Sprites, Physics, Collision

Let's take a look at the various game design components that we you will need to understand to be able to build a game, as well as what Java 8 (or JavaFX) packages and classes you can use to implement these aspects of game play, which I like to term components of game play. These can include the game play elements themselves (commonly referred to as **sprites**) as well as processing engines, which you will either code yourself, or import preexisting Java code libraries for, such as **physics simulation** and **collision detection**.

Sprites are the foundation of game play, defining your **main character**, **projectiles** used to damage this main character, and the **enemies** firing these projectiles. Sprites are **2D graphics elements** and can be either static (fixed, a single image) or dynamic (animated, a seamless loop of several images). A sprite will be moved around the screen based on programming logic, which dictates how the game is to function. Sprites need to be composited with background imagery and other game elements as well as other sprites and so the graphics used to create the sprites will need to support **transparent backgrounds**.

In Chapter 4, I introduced you to the concept of alpha channels and transparency. You will need to achieve this same end result with your sprites to create a seamless visual experience with your game. The next most important aspect of game play is **collision detection**, because if your sprites simply flew right past each other on the screen and never did anything cool when they touched, or "intersected" each other, then you really would not have much of a game! Once you add a collision detection engine (composed of **intersection logic** processing routines) your game can ascertain when any two sprites are touching (edges) or overlapping each other. A collision detection will call (trigger) other logic processing routines that will determine what happens when any two given sprites, such as a projectile and the main character, intersect. For example, when a projectile intersects the main character, damage points might accrue, life force index might be decreased, or a death animation may be started. In contrast, if a treasure item intersects with (is picked up by) the main character, power or capability points might accrue, the life force index might be increased, or an "I found it" jubilation animation might be started. As you can see, the collision detection for your game is one of the foundational design elements of your game play, besides the sprites (characters, projectiles, treasures, enemies, obstacles, and so on) themselves, which is why I am covering this concept early on in the book.

The concept next in significance to your game play is **real-world physics simulation**. The addition of things like gravity; friction; bounce; drag; acceleration; motion curves, such as the JavaFX Interpolator class provides; and the like add an additional level of realism on top of the already photo-realistic sprites, synchronized animation sequences, scenic backgrounds, and highly accurate collision detection.

Finally, the most proprietary attribute, or logic construct (Java code), to add to your game play is the **custom game play logic**, which makes your game truly unique in the marketplace. This logic should be kept in its own Java class or methods, separate from physics simulation and collision detection code. After all, Java 8 makes your code modularization well-structured if you learn the OOP concepts and apply them to your programming logic!

When you start to add all these game components together, they begin to make the game more believable as well as more professional. One of the key objectives for a great game is suspension of belief, which means that your player is buying into the premise, characters, objectives, and game play completely. This is the same objective that any content producer, whether he or she be a filmmaker, television producer, author, songwriter, Java 8 game programmer, or application developer, is going for. Games these days have the same revenue-generating capability as any of the other content distribution genres, if not more.

Next, let's take a look at the different types of games that can be created and how these differ in their application of the core game components of sprites, collision detection, physics simulation, and game play logic.

Types of Games: Puzzles, Board Games, Arcade Games, Hybrids

Like everything else I have talked about in this chapter, games themselves can be categorized by using a static-versus-dynamic classification approach. Static games are not processor bound, because they tend to be turn based and not hand-eye coordination based in nature, and so, in a sense, they are easier to get working smoothly; only the programming logic for the rules of game play and the attractive graphics have to be put in place and debugged. A significant opportunity also exists for developing new types of game genres that use a hybrid combination of static and dynamic game play in creative new ways that have never before been seen. I am working on a few of these myself!

Because this is a Java 8 programming title, I am going to approach everything from this standpoint, which happens to be a great way to divide games into discrete categories (static, dynamic, hybrid), so let's cover the static (fixed graphics), turn-based games first. These include **board games**, **puzzle games**, **knowledge games**, **memory games**, and **strategy games**, all of which should not be underestimated in their popularity and marketability.

The thing that is cool about static games is that they can be just as fun to play as dynamic games and have significantly less processing overhead, as they do not have to achieve the 60FPS real-time processing target to achieve smooth, professional game play. This is because the nature of the game is not predicated on motion at all, but rather on making the right **strategic move**, but only when it is your turn to do so.

There can be some forms of collision detection involved in static games regarding which game piece has been moved to a given location on the gameboard or playing surface; however, there is no danger of overloading the processor with collision detection, because the rest of the game board is static, with the exception of the one piece that is being strategically moved during that particular player's turn.

The processing logic for strategy games is more **strategy logic**–based programming, geared toward allowing the players to achieve an end win, given the right sequence of moves, whereas the dynamic game programming logic looks more at what collisions are taking place between game sprites. Dynamic games are focused on point score, dodging projectiles, finding treasures, completing level objectives, and killing enemies.

Complicated strategy games with lots of interrelated rules, such as chess, are likely to have far more programming logic routines than dynamic games. Yet, because the execution of the code is not as time sensitive, the resulting game play will be smooth, no matter how powerful the platform and CPU are. Of course, the game rule set logic must be flawless for this type of game to truly be professional, so, in the end, both static and dynamic games are difficult to code, albeit for different reasons.

Dynamic games could be termed **action games** or **arcade games** and include a lot of movement on the display screen. These highly dynamic games almost always involve shooting things, such as in the first-person shooter (e.g., Doom, Half-Life) as well as in the third-person shooter (Resident Evil, Grand Theft Auto) genres, or stealing things, or evading things. There is also the obstacle course navigation paradigm, commonly seen in platform games, such as Donkey Kong and Super Mario.

It is important to note that any genre of game can be produced using 2D or 3D graphics and assets or even a combination of 2D and 3D assets, which, as I pointed out in Chapter 4, is allowed by JavaFX.

There are so many popular game types that there is always the opportunity to create an entirely new genre of game by using a hybrid approach of a static (strategic) game type and a dynamic (action) game type.

Game Design Assets: New Media Content Concepts

One of the most powerful tools you have to make your game highly professional and desirable to buyers is the **multimedia** production software that you downloaded and installed back in Chapter 1. Before I go any further, I need to spend some time providing you with foundational knowledge regarding four primary types of **new media assets** that are supported in Java 8, using the JavaFX 8 multimedia engine: **digital images**, used for sprites, background imagery, and 2D animation; **vector shapes**, used in 2D illustration, collision detection, 3D objects, paths, and curves; **digital audio**, used for sound effects, narration, and background music; and **digital video**, used in games for animated background loops (birds flying through the sky, drifting clouds, and so on) once highly optimized. As illustrated in Figure 5-1, these four major genres, or areas, are all installed via the JavaFX Scene Graph, using packages that I described in Chapter 4. Some of the primary classes that will be used are **ImageView**, **AudioClip**, **Media**, **MediaView**, **MediaPlayer**, **Line**, **Arc**, **Path**, **Circle**, **Rectangle**, **Box**, **Sphere**, **Cylinder**, **Shape3D**, **Mesh**, and **MeshView**.

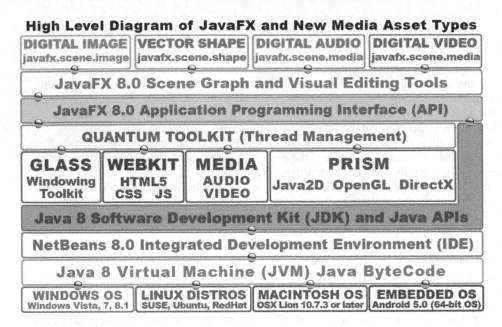

Figure 5-1. *How new media assets are implemented, using Scene Graph through the JavaFX API in Java 8 via NetBeans*

Because you need to have a **technical foundation** before using any of these types of new media elements in a Java 8 game design and programming pipeline, I am going to go over basic concepts for each of these four new media areas, beginning with digital imaging and vector illustration.

Digital Imaging Concepts: Resolution, Color Depth, Alpha, Layers

JavaFX (and therefore Java8) supports a significant number of popular digital imaging file (data) formats, which gives game designers a ton of flexibility. Some of these have been around forever, such as CompuServe's **graphics interchange format** (GIF) and the **Joint Photographic Experts Group** (JPEG) format. Some JavaFX graphics file formats are more modern, such as **portable network graphics** (PNG; pronounced "ping"), which is the file format that you will be using for your games, as it yields the highest quality level and supports image **compositing**. All these mainstream digital image file formats supported in Java are also supported in HTML5 browsers, and because Java applications can be used with HTML applications and web sites, this is a very logical synergy indeed!

The oldest CompuServe GIF format is the **lossless** digital image file format. It is termed lossless because it does not throw away image data to achieve better compression results. The GIF compression algorithm is not as refined (powerful) as that of the PNG format, and GIF only supports **indexed color**, which is how it obtains its **compression** (smaller file size). If your game image assets are already created with the GIF format, you will be able to use them with no problem (other than a less efficient image compression algorithm and no compositing capability) with your Java 8 game applications.

The most popular digital imaging file format that Java 8 (JavaFX) supports is JPEG, which uses a "truecolor" color depth, instead of an indexed color depth, as well as what is termed **lossy** digital image compression, in which the compression algorithm "throws away" image data so that it can achieve a smaller file size (the image data are lost forever, unless you are smart and save your original image!).

If you magnify a JPEG image after compression, you will see a **discolored area** (effect) that clearly was not present in the original imagery. The degraded area or areas in the image are commonly referred to as **compression artifacts**. This will only occur in lossy image compression and is common with JPEG (and Moving Picture Experts Group [MPEG]) compression.

106

■ **Tip** I recommend that you use the **PNG** digital imaging format for your Java 8 games. This is a professional image-**compositing** format, and your games will essentially be a real-time sprite-compositing engine, so you will need to use **PNG32** imagery.

PNG has two truecolor file versions: **PNG24**, which cannot be used in image compositing, and **PNG32**, which carries an alpha channel used to define transparency.

I recommend PNG for your games because it has a decent image compression algorithm and because it is a **lossless** image format. This means that PNG has great image quality as well as reasonable levels of data compression efficiency, which will make your game distribution file smaller. The real power of the PNG32 format lies in its ability to composite with other game imagery, using **transparency** and **antialiasing** (via its alpha channel).

Digital Image Resolution and Aspect Ratio: Defining Image Size and Shape

As you probably know, digital imagery is made up of **2D** (two-dimensional) **arrays** of **pixels** ("pixel" stands for **picture** [pix] **element** [el]). The sharpness of an image is expressed by its **resolution**, which is the number of pixels in the image **width** (or **W**, sometimes referred to as the **x axis**) and **height** (or **H**, sometimes referred to as the **y axis**) dimensions. The more pixels an image has, the higher its resolution. This is similar to how digital cameras work, as the more megapixels in an image capture device (called a camera CCD), the higher the image quality that can be achieved.

To find the total number of image pixels, **multiply** the width pixels by the height pixels. For instance, a wide video graphics array (VGA) 800 × 480 image contains 384,000 pixels, which is exactly three-eighths of a megabyte. This is how you would find the **size** of your image, both in terms of kilobytes (or megabytes) used and height and width on the display screen.

The shape of a digital image asset is specified using the image **aspect ratio**. Aspect ratio is the **width:height** ratio for the digital image and defines the square (**1:1** aspect ratio) or rectangular (also known as **widescreen**) digital image shape. Displays featuring a **2:1** (widescreen) aspect ratio, such as **2,160 × 1,080** resolution, are now available.

A **1:1 aspect ratio** display (or image) is always **perfectly square**, as is a **2:2** or **3:3** aspect ratio image. You might see this aspect ratio on a smart watch, for instance. It is important to note that it is the **ratio** between these two width and height (x and y) variables that defines the shape of an image or screen, not the actual numbers themselves.

An aspect ratio should always be expressed as the **smallest pair of numbers** that can be achieved (reduced) on either side of the **colon**. If you paid attention in high school while you were learning about the lowest common denominator, then an aspect ratio will be very easy for you to calculate. I usually do aspect ratio calculation by continuing to divide each side of the colon by two. For example, if you take the **SXGA 1,280 × 1,024** resolution, half of 1,280 × 1,024 is 640 × 512, and half of 640 × 512 is 320 × 256; half of 320 × 256 is 160 × 128, half of that again is 80 × 64, half of that is 40 × 32, and half of that is 20 × 16; half of 20 × 16 is 10 × 8, and half of that gives you the 5 × 4 aspect ratio for SXGA, which would be signified by using a colon between the two numbers, as in a 5:4 aspect ratio.

Digital Image Color Theory and Color Depth: Defining Precise Image Pixel Colors

The color values for each digital image pixel can be defined by the amount of three different colors, **red**, **green**, and **blue** (**RGB**), which are present in different amounts in every pixel. Consumer electronics display screens leverage additive colors, in which wavelengths of light for each RGB color channel are added together creating **16.8** million different color values. **Additive color** is used in liquid crystal display (LCD), light-emitting diode (LED), and organic light-emitting diode (OLED) displays. It is the opposite of subtractive color, which is used in printing. To show you the different results, under a subtractive color model, mixing red with green (inks) will yield purple colors, whereas in an additive color model, mixing red with green (light) creates a vibrant yellow coloration. Additive color can provide a much broader spectrum of colors than subtractive color.

There are **256 levels** of brightness for each red, green, and blue color value that is held for each pixel. This allows you to set **8 bits** of value-controlling color brightness variation for each of the red, green, and blue values, from a minimum of **0** (#**00**, or off, all dark, or black) to a maximum of **255** (#FF, or fully on, maximum color contributed). The number of bits that are used to represent digital image pixel color is referred to as the **color depth** of the image.

Common color depths used in the digital imaging industry include 8 bit, 16 bit, 24 bit and 32 bit. I will outline these here, along with their formats. The lowest color depth exists in **8-bit indexed color** images. These feature a maximum of 256 color values and use **GIF** and **PNG8** image formats to hold this indexed color type of data.

A medium color depth image will feature a 16-bit color depth and will thus contain 65,536 colors (calculated as 256 × 256). It is supported by the TARGA (TGA) and tagged image file format (TIFF) digital image formats. If you want to use digital image formats other than GIF, JPEG, and PNG in your Java 8 games, import the third-party **ImageJ** library.

Truecolor color depth images will feature **24-bit** color depth and will thus contain more than 16 million colors. This is calculated as **256 × 256 × 256**, which yields **16,777,216** colors. File formats supporting 24-bit color depth include JPEG (or JPG), PNG, BMP, XCF, PSD, TGA, TIFF, and WebP. JavaFX supports three of these: JPG, PNG24 (24 bit), and PNG32 (32 bit). Using 24-bit color depth will give you the highest quality level. This is why I am recommending the use of PNG24 or PNG32 for your Java games. Next, let's take a look at how to represent image pixel transparency values through alpha channels and how these can be used for **compositing** digital imagery in real time in Java 8 games!

Digital Image Compositing: Using Alpha Channels and Transparency in Layers

Compositing is the process of seamlessly **blending** together multiple layers of digital imagery. As you might imagine, this is an extremely important concept for game design and development. Compositing is useful when you want to create an image on the display that appears as though it is one single image (or animation), when it is actually the seamless collection of two or more composited image layers. One of the principle reasons you would want to set up an image or animation composite is to allow programmatic control over various elements in those images, by having them on different layers.

To accomplish this, you need to have an **alpha channel transparency** value, which you can use to control the precision of the blending amount of a given pixel with another pixel (in the same x, y image location) on other layers (above and below it).

Like the other RGB **channels,** an alpha channel has **256 transparency levels**. In Java programming the alpha channel is represented by the **first two slots** in a **hexadecimal representation** of #**AARRGGBB** data values (which I will be covering in detail in the next section). Alpha channel **ARGB** data values use **eight** slots (32 bit) of data rather than the **six data slots** (#**RRGGBB**) used in a 24-bit image, which is really a 32-bit image with zero alpha channel data.

Therefore, a 24-bit (PNG24) image has no alpha channel and will not be used for compositing, unless it is the bottom image plate in a compositing layer stack. In contrast, PNG32 images will be used as compositing layers on top of PNG24 (background plate) or PNG32 (lower, z-order compositing layers), which will need this alpha channel capability to show through (via alpha channel transparency values) in certain pixel locations in the image composite.

How do digital image alpha channels, and the concept of image compositing, factor into Java game design? The primary advantage is an ability to break the game play screen, and the sprites, projectiles, and background graphic elements that it includes, into a number of **component layers.** The reason for doing this is to be able to apply Java 8 programming logic (or JavaFX classes) to individual graphic image elements to control parts of your game play screen that you would not otherwise be able to control individually were it one single image.

Another part of image compositing, called **blending modes**, also factors heavily into professional image-compositing capabilities. JavaFX blending modes are applied by using the **Blend** class with the **BlendMode** constant values found in the **javafx.scene.effect** subpackage (see Chapter 4). This JavaFX blending effect package gives Java game developers many of the same image-compositing modes that Photoshop (and GIMP) afford to a digital imaging artisan. This turns Java 8 (via JavaFX) into a powerful image-compositing engine, just like Photoshop, and the blending algorithms are controllable at a very flexible level, using custom Java 8 code. JavaFX blending mode constants include **ADD**, **SCREEN**, **OVERLAY**, **DARKEN**, **LIGHTEN**, **MULTIPLY**, **DIFFERENCE**, **EXCLUSION**, **SRC_ATOP**, **SRC_OVER**, **SOFT_LIGHT**, **HARD_LIGHT**, **COLOR_BURN**, and **COLOR_DODGE**.

Representing Color and Alpha in Java 8 Game Code: Using Hexadecimal Notation

Now that you know what color depth and alpha channels are, and that color and transparency are represented by using a combination of four different **image channels** (alpha, red, green, and blue [ARGB]) within any given digital image, it is important to understand how, as programmers, you are supposed to represent these four ARGB image color and transparency channel values in Java 8 and JavaFX.

In the Java programming language, color and alpha are used not only in 2D digital imagery (commonly referred to as **bitmap** imagery), but also in 2D illustration (commonly referred to as **vector** imagery). Colors and transparency values are also often used across a number of different color setting options. As you have already seen with the Stage object and the Scene object, you can set a background color (or transparency value) for a stage, scene, layout container (StackPane), or UI control, among other things.

In Java (and thus JavaFX) different levels of ARGB color intensity values are represented using **hexadecimal** notation. Hexadecimal (or hex) is based on the original **Base16** computer notation. This was used long ago to represent **16 bits** of data value. Unlike the more common **Base10**, which counts from 0 to 9, Base16 notation counts from 0 to F, where F represents the Base10 value of 15 (0 to 15 yields 16 data values).

A hexadecimal value in Java always starts with a **0 and an x**, like this: **0xFFFFFF**. This hexadecimal color value represents the Color.WHITE constant and uses no alpha channel. Each of the six slots in this **24-bit hexadecimal representation** stands for a single Base16 value, so to get the 256 values required for each RGB color will take two slots, as 16 × 16 = 256. Therefore, to represent a 24-bit image using hexadecimal notation, you would need to have six slots after the pound sign to hold each of the six hexadecimal data values (data pairs representing 256 levels of value each). If you multiply 16 × 16 × 16 × 16 × 16 × 16 you will get the 16,777,216 colors that are possible using 24-bit, truecolor image data.

The hexadecimal data slots represent RGB values in the following format: **0xRRGGBB**. For the Java constant Color.WHITE, all the red, green, and blue channels in the hexadecimal color data value representation are at the full (maximum color value) luminosity setting. If you add all these colors together, you will get white light.

The color yellow would be represented by the red and green channels' being on, and the blue channel's being off, so a hexadecimal representation for Color.YELLOW would therefore be **0xFFFF00**, where both the red and green channel slots are fully on (FF, or a 255 Base10 data value), and the blue channel slots are fully off (00, or a 0 value).

The eight hexadecimal data slots for an ARGB value will hold data using the following format: **0xAARRGGBB**. Thus, for the Color.WHITE, all alpha, red, green, and blue channels in the hexadecimal color data value representation would be at their maximum luminosity (or opacity), and the alpha channel would be fully opaque, that is, not transparent, as represented by an FF value. Therefore, the hexadecimal value for the Color.WHITE constant would be **0xFFFFFFFF**.

A 100 percent transparent alpha channel can be represented by setting an alpha slot to 0, as you observed when you created a windowless Java 8 application (see Chapter 4). Therefore, you would represent transparent image pixel values using any value between **0x00000000** and **0x00FFFFFF**. It is important to note that if an alpha channel value equates to full transparency, it would follow that the 16,777,216 color values that could be contained in the other six (RGB) hexadecimal data value slots will not matter at all, because that pixel, being transparent, will be evaluated as not being there and thus will not be composited in the final image or animation composite image.

Digital Image Masking: Using Alpha Channels to Create Game Sprites

One of the primary applications for alpha channels in game design is to **mask** out areas of an image or animation (series of images) so that it can be used as a game sprite in a game play image-compositing scenario. **Masking** is the process of cutting subject matter out of a digital image so that the subject matter can be placed on its own virtual layer, using alpha channel transparency values. This is done using a digital imaging software package, such as GIMP.

Digital image–compositing software packages, such as Photoshop and GIMP, feature tools that are included for use in masking and image compositing. You cannot do effective image compositing without doing effective masking, so this is an important area to master for game designers who wish to integrate graphics elements, such as image sprites and sprite animation, into their game designs. The art of digital image masking has been around for a very long time!

Masking can be done for you automatically, using professional blue screen (or green screen) backdrops, along with computer software that can automatically extract those exact color values to create a mask, which is turned into alpha channel (transparency) information (data). Masking can also be done manually, using digital image software, via one of the algorithmic selection tools, in conjunction with various sharpening and blur algorithms.

You will learn a lot about this work process over the course of this book, using common open-source software packages, such as GIMP. Masking can be a complex and involved work process. This chapter is intended to expose you to foundational knowledge that will underlie the processes you undertake while working through the book.

A key consideration in the masking process is getting smooth, sharp edges around a masked object (subject matter). This is so that when you place a masked object (in this case, a game sprite) into (over) new background imagery, it looks as if it were photographed there in the first place. The key to doing this successfully lies in your **selection** work process, which entails using digital image software **selection tools,** such as the **scissors** tool in GIMP, or the **magic wand** tool in Photoshop, in the proper fashion. Choosing the correct work process is critical!

For instance, if there are areas of **uniform color** around the object that you wish to mask (maybe you shot it against a blue screen), you will use a magic wand tool with a proper **threshold** setting to select everything except your object. Then, you **invert** the **selection**, which will give you a **selection set** containing the object. Often, the correct work process requires approaching something in reverse. Other selection tools contain complex algorithms that can look at color changes between pixels. These can be useful for **edge detection**, which you can use for other selection methods.

Smoothing Digital Image Composites: Using Antialiasing to Smooth Image Edges

Antialiasing is a popular digital image–compositing technique, in which two adjacent colors in a digital image are **blended** together along the **edge that** borders the two color areas. This tricks the viewer's eye into seeing a smoother (less jagged) edge when the image is zoomed out, thereby eliminating what has come to be called image jaggies. Antialiasing provides an impressive result by using averaged color values (a color range that is a portion of the way between the two colors coming together), with just a few colored pixels along the edge that needs to be smoothed.

Let's take a look at an example to see what I am talking about. Figure 5-2 shows what appears to be a razor-sharp red circle on one layer, overlaying a yellow fill color on a background layer. I zoomed into the red circle's edge and then made another screenshot, placing it to the right of the zoomed-out circle. This screenshot reveals a range of antialiasing color values (yellow-orange, to orange, to red-orange) right on the edge bordering the red and yellow colors, where the circle meets the background.

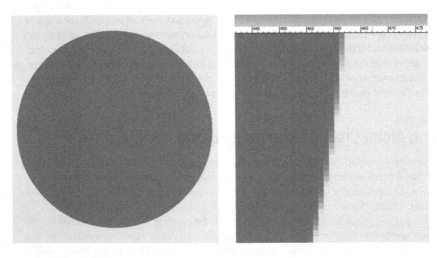

Figure 5-2. *A red circle composited on a yellow background (left) and a zoomed-in view (right) showing antialiasing*

It is important to note that the JavaFX engine will antialias 2D shapes and 3D objects against all background colors and background imagery, using the Java2D software renderer or the hardware rendered with the Prism engine, which can use OpenGL or DirectX. You will still be responsible for correctly compositing, that is, providing antialiasing for your multilayered imagery, using each image's alpha channel.

Digital Image Optimization: Using Compression, Indexed Color, and Dithering

There are a number of factors that affect digital image compression and some basic techniques that you can use to achieve a better-quality result with a smaller data footprint. This is a primary objective in optimized digital imagery; obtaining the smallest possible data footprint for your application (in this case, a game), while achieving the highest quality visual result. Let's start with the aspects that most significantly affect data footprint and examine how each of these contributes to data footprint optimization for any given digital image. Interestingly, their order of significance is similar to the order in which I have presented the digital imaging concepts thus far.

The most critical contributor to a resulting digital image asset file size is what I like to call the **data footprint**, which is the number of pixels, or **resolution** of, a digital image. This is logical, because each of the pixels needs to be stored, along with the color and alpha values that are contained in their three (24 bit) or four (32 bit) channels. The smaller you can get your resolution, while still having the image look sharp, the smaller the resulting file size will be.

Raw (or uncompressed) image size is calculated by **width × height × 3** for 24-bit RBG images, and **width × height × 4** for 32-bit ARGB images. For instance, an uncompressed, truecolor, 24-bit VGA image will have 640 × 480 × 3, equaling **921,600B** of original (raw), uncompressed digital image data. To determine the number of **kilobytes** in this raw VGA image, you would divide as follows: 921,600 ÷ 1,024, the number of bytes that are in a kilobyte, giving you an even **900KB** of data in a truecolor VGA image.

It is important to optimize for raw (uncompressed) image size by optimizing your digital imagery resolution. This is because once an image is decompressed out of a game application file, into system memory, this is the amount of memory that it is going to occupy, as the image will be stored pixel for pixel, using a 24-bit (RGB) or 32-bit (ARGB) representation in memory. This is one of the reasons I use **PNG24** and **PNG32** for my game development, not indexed color (GIF or PNG8); if the OS is going to transmute the color to a 24-bit color space, then you should use that 24-bit color space for quality reasons and deal with (accept) a slightly larger application file size.

Image color depth is the next most critical contributor to the data footprint of a compressed image, because the number of pixels in the image is multiplied by 1 (8 bit), 2 (16 bit), 3 (24 bit), or 4 (32 bit) color data channels. This small file size is the reason 8-bit indexed color images are still widely used, especially with the GIF image format.

Indexed color images can simulate truecolor images if the colors that are used to make up the image do not vary too widely. Indexed color imagery uses only 8 bits of data (256 colors) to define the image pixel color, using a **palette** of up to 256 optimally selected colors, instead of 3 RGB color channels or 4 ARGB color channels, containing 256 levels of color each. Again, it is important to note that once you turn a 24-bit image into an 8-bit image by compressing it using a GIF or PNG8 codec, you only have a potential (maximum) 256 of the original 16,777,216 colors at your disposal. This is why I am advocating using PNG24 or PNG32 imagery rather than GIF or PNG1 (2 color), PNG2 (4 color), PNG4 (16 color), or PNG8 (256 color) images, which JavaFX also supports.

Depending on how many colors are employed in any given 24-bit source image, using 256 colors to represent an image originally containing 16,777,216 colors can cause an effect called **banding**. This is when the transfer between adjoining colors in the resulting (from compression) 256- (or less) color palette is not gradual and thus does not appear to be a smooth color gradient. Indexed color images have an option to correct visually for banding, called **dithering**.

Dithering is an **algorithmic process** of making **dot patterns** along the edges between any adjoining colors within an image to trick the eye into seeing a third color. Dithering will give you a maximum perceptual number of colors (of 65,536; 256 × 256), but this will only occur if each of those 256 colors borders on each of the other 256 colors. Still, you can see the potential for creating additional colors, and you would be amazed at the result that indexed color formats can achieve in some compression scenarios (with certain imagery).

Let's take a truecolor image, such as the one shown in Figure 5-3, and save it as a PNG5 indexed color image format, to show you this dithering effect. It is important to note that PNG5, although supported in Android and HTML5, is not supported in JavaFX, so if you do this exercise yourself, select the 2-, 4-, 16-, or 256-color option! The figure demonstrates the dithering effect on the driver-side rear fender in an Audi 3D image, as it contains a gray gradient.

Figure 5-3. *A truecolor PNG24 image created with Autodesk 3ds Max, which you are going to compress as PNG5*

Interestingly, it is permissible to use **less than the 256**-colormaximum in an 8-bit indexed color image. This is often done to reduce further the imagery's data footprint. For instance, an image that can attain good results using only 32 colors is actually a 5-bit image and would technically be called a PNG5, even though the format itself is generally called PNG8 for the indexed color usage level.

I have set this indexed color PNG image, shown in Figure 5-4, to use 5-bit color (32 color, or PNG5) to illustrate this dithering effect clearly. As you can see in the image preview area, on the left-hand side of the figure, the dithering algorithm makes dot patterns between adjacent colors to create additional colors.

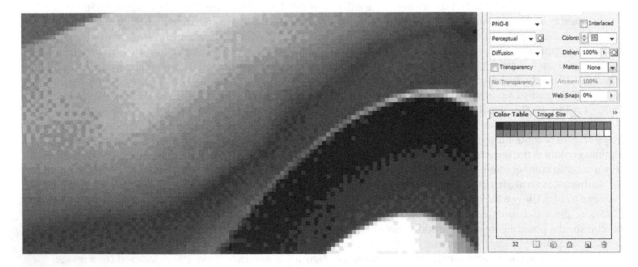

Figure 5-4. *Setting dithering to the diffusion algorithm and 32 colors (5 bit), with 100 percent dithering for PNG5 output*

Also, note that you can set the **percentage of dithering** that is used. I often select either the 0 percent or 100 percent setting; however, you can **fine-tune** the dithering effect anywhere between these two extreme values. You can also choose between **dithering algorithms**, because, as you probably have surmised, the dithering effect is created using dithering algorithms, which are part of the indexed file format (in this case, PNG8) compression routines.

I use **diffusion** dithering, which gives a smooth effect along irregularly shaped gradients, as is seen in the car fender. You can also use a **noise** option, which is more randomized, or a **pattern** option, which is less so. The diffusion option usually gives the best results, which is why I choose it when I am using indexed color (which is not often).

Dithering, as you might imagine, adds data patterns to an image that are more difficult to compress. This is because smooth areas in an image, such as gradients, are easier for the compression algorithm to compress than sharp transitions (edges) or random pixel patterns (e.g., dithering or "noise" from a camera CCD).

Therefore, applying the dithering option will always increase the data footprint by a few percentage points. Be sure to check the resulting file size with and without dithering applied (selected in the Export dialog) to see if it is worth the improved visual result that it affords. Note that there is also a transparency option (check box) for indexed color PNG images but that the alpha channel used in PNG8 images is only 1 bit (on/off), not 8 bit, as with PNG32.

You can also increase the data footprint of your image by adding an alpha channel to define transparency for compositing. This is because by adding an alpha channel you will be adding in another 8-bit color channel (or a transparency channel, actually) to the image being compressed. If you need an alpha channel to define transparency for your image to support future compositing requirements, such as using the image as a game sprite, there is not much choice but to include the alpha channel data.

If your alpha channel contains all zeroes (or uses an all-black fill color), which would define your imagery as being completely transparent, or contains all FF values (or uses an all-white fill color), which would define your image as being completely opaque, you would essentially (in practical terms) be defining an alpha that does not contain any useful alpha data values. The transparent image would therefore need to be removed, and the opaque image would need to be defined as a PNG24 rather than a PNG32.

Finally, most alpha channels that are used to mask objects in the RGB layers of the digital image should compress very well. This is because the alpha channel is primarily areas of white (opaque) and black (transparent), with some medium-gray values along the edge between the two colors to antialias the mask (see Figure 5-2). These gray areas contain the antialiasing values in the alpha channel, and will provide the visually smooth-edge transitions between the object in the RGB layers of the image and any background color or background images that may be used behind it.

The reason for this is that in the alpha channel image mask, an 8-bit **transparency gradient** (from white to black) defines levels of transparency, which could be thought of as per-pixel blending (opacity) strength. Therefore, the medium-gray values on the edges of each object in the mask (which is contained in the alpha channel) will serve essentially to **average** the colors of the object edge, and any target background, no matter what color (or image) value it may contain. This offers real-time antialiasing with any target background that may be used, including animated backgrounds.

Digital Video and Animation: Frames, Rate, Looping, Direction

Interestingly, all the concepts that I have just covered for digital images apply equally well to digital video and animation, as both formats use digital images as the foundation for their content. Digital video and animation extend digital imaging into the fourth dimension (time) by using **frames**. The two formats are composed of an **ordered sequence of frames**, which are displayed rapidly over time.

The term "frame" comes from the film industry, in which, even today, frames of film are run through film projectors at a **rate** of **24 frames per second** (**24FPS**), which creates the illusion of **motion**. Because both digital video and animation are made up of a collection of frames containing digital images, the concept of frame rate, expressed as frames per second, is also very important when it comes to the memory data footprint optimization work process (for animation assets) as well as the digital video file size data footprint optimization work process. As discussed previously, in JavaFX this attribute for animation is stored in the Animation object **rate** variable (see Chapter 4).

The optimization concept regarding frames in an Animation object or digital video asset is very similar to the optimization concept regarding pixels in an image (the resolution of a digital image): the fewer used, the better! This is because the number of frames in an animation or video multiplies both the system memory used and the filesize data footprint with each frame. In digital video, not only does each frame's (image) resolution, but also the frame rate (specified in the **Compression Settings** dialog) impact file size. Earlier in this chapter, you learned that if you multiply the number of pixels in the image by its number of color channels, you will get the raw data footprint for the image. With animation and digital video, you will now multiply that number again by the number of frames that need to be used to create the illusion of motion.

Therefore, if you have an animated VGA (RGB) background plate for your game (remember that each frame is 900KB) that uses five frames to create the illusion of motion, you are using 900KB × 5, or 4,500KB (4.5MB), of system memory to hold that animation. Of course, this is too much memory to use for a background, which is why you will be using static backgrounds with sprite overlays to achieve this exact same end result in less than a megabyte. The calculation for digital video is a bit different, as it has hundreds or thousands of frames. For digital video you would multiply your raw image data size by the number of frames per second (frame rate) at which the digital video is set to play back (this frame rate value is specified during the compression process), and then multiply that result by the total number of seconds of content duration contained in your video file.

To continue with the VGA example, you know that a 24-bit VGA image is 900KB. This makes the calculation to take this to the next level easy. Digital video traditionally runs at 30FPS, so 1 second of **standard definition** raw (uncompressed) digital video would be 30 image frames, each of which is 900KB, yielding a total data footprint of 27,000KB! You can see why having video compression file formats such as MPEG-4 H.264 AVC, which can compress the massive raw data footprint that digital video can create, is extremely important. The JavaFX media package uses one of the most impressive video compression **codecs** ("codec" stands for **code-decode**) which is also supported in HTML5 and Android, the aforementioned MPEG-4 H.264 AVC (advanced video codec). This is quite convenient for developer asset optimization, as one single digital video asset can be used across JavaFX, HTML5, and Android applications. Just in case you want to use digital video in the background of your game (which I do not recommend), I am going to cover the basics of digital video compression and optimization next.

Digital Video Compression Concepts: Bit Rate, Data Streaming, SD, HD, UHD

Let's begin with the primary or standard resolutions that are used in commercial video. These also happen to be common device screen resolutions, probably because if the screen pixel resolution matches the video pixel resolution that is being played full screen on a screen, there will be zero scaling, which can cause **scaling artifacts**. Before high definition came along, video was **standard definition** (**SD**) and used a vertical resolution of **480 pixels**. VGA is an SD resolution, and **720 × 480** could be called **wide SD** resolution. **High definition** (**HD**) video comes in two resolutions, **1,280 × 720**, which I call **pseudo HD**, and **1,920 × 1,080**, which the industry calls **true HD**. Both HD resolutions feature a **16:9** aspect ratio and are used in TVs and iTVs, smartphones, tablets, e-book readers, and game consoles. There is also an **ultra high definition** (**UHD**) resolution out now that features 4,096 × 2,160 pixels.

Video streaming is a more complicated concept than resolution, as it involves playing back video data over a wide expanse, such as the one between your Java 8 game application and the remote video data server that will hold your potentially massive digital video assets. Furthermore, the device that your Java game application is running on will be communicating in real time with remote data servers, receiving **video data packets** as the video plays (it is termed streaming because the video is streaming from the video server, over the Internet, and into the hardware device). Video streaming is supported by the MPEG-4 H.264 AVC format codec (encoder-decoder pair).

The last concept that you need to understand is **bit rate**. Bit rate is the key setting used in the video compression process, as bit rates represent your **target bandwidth**, or the **data pipe size** that is able to accommodate a **certain number of bits streaming through it every second**. The bit-rate setting should also take into consideration the CPU processing power that exists within any given Java-capable device, making your digital video's data optimization even more challenging. Fortunately, most devices these days feature dualcore or quadcore CPUs!

Once the bits travel through a data pipe, they also need to be **processed** and **displayed** on the device screen. Thus, bit rates for digital video assets must be optimized not only for bandwidth, but also in anticipation of variances in CPU processing power. Some single-core CPUs may not be able to decode high-resolution, high–bit rate digital video assets without **dropping** frames, so do make sure to optimize low–bit rate video assets if you are going to target older or less expensive consumer electronics devices.

Digital Video Data Footprint Optimization: Using Codecs and Their Settings

As mentioned earlier, your digital video asset will be compressed, using software utilities called codecs. There are two "sides" to the video codec: one that encodes the video data stream and another that decodes it. The video decoder will be part of the OS, platform (JavaFX), or browser that uses it. The decoder is primarily optimized for speed, as smoothness of playback is a key issue, whereas the encoder is optimized to reduce the data footprint for the digital video asset it is generating. For this reason, the encoding process can take a long time, depending on how many processing cores a workstation contains. Most digital video content production workstations should support eight processor cores, like my 64-bit AMD octacore workstation.

Codecs (the encoder side) are like plug-ins, in that they can be installed into different digital video–editing software packages to enable them to encode different digital video asset file formats. Because Java and JavaFX 8 support the MPEG-4 H.264 AVC format, you need to make sure that you are using one of the digital video software packages that supports encoding digital video data using (or into) this digital video file format. More than one software manufacturer makes MPEG-4 encoding software, so there will be different MPEG-4 AVC codecs that will yield different (better or worse) results, in terms of encoding speed and file size. The professional solution, which I highly recommend that you secure if you want to produce digital video professionally, is called Sorenson Squeeze Pro.

There is also an open-source solution called EditShare LightWorks 12, which is scheduled to support output to the MPEG4 codec natively by 2014. When optimizing (setting compression settings) for digital video data file size, there are many variables that directly affect the digital video data footprint. I will discuss these in their order of importance, in in terms of effect on video file size, from the most important to the least, so that you will know which parameters to tweak to obtain the result you are looking for.

Like with digital image compression, the resolution, or number of pixels, in each frame of video is the optimal place to start the optimization process. If your user is using 800 × 480 or **1,280 × 720** smartphones, e-readers, or tablets, then you do not need to use true HD 1,920 × 1,080 resolution to get good visual results for your digital video assets. With superfine density (small dot pitch) displays out there, you can scale a 1,280 video up 33 percent, and it will look reasonably good. The exception to this may be HD or UHD (popularly termed 4K iTV) games targeted at iTVs; for these huge, 55- to 75-inch (screen) scenarios, you would want to use the industry standard, true HD **1,920 × 1,080** resolution.

The next level of optimization would come in the **number of frames used for each second** of video (or **FPS**), assuming the actual number of seconds in the digital video itself cannot be shortened. As mentioned earlier, this is known as the frame rate, and instead of setting the **video standard 30FPS** frame rate, consider using a **film standard** frame rate of 24FPS or even the **multimedia standard** of **20FPS**. You may even be able to use a **15FPS** frame rate, half the video standard, depending on the amount (and speed) of movement within the content. Note that 15FPS is **half as much data** as 30FPS (a 100 percent reduction in data encoded). For some video content this will play back (look) the same as 30FPS content. The only way to test this is to try frame rate settings during the encoding process.

The next most optimal setting for obtaining a smaller data footprint would be the **bit rate** that you set for a codec to try to achieve. Bit rate equates to the **amount of compression applied** and thus sets a **quality level** for the digital video data. It is important to note that you could simply use 30FPS, 1,920 resolution HD video and specify a low bit-rate ceiling. If you do this, the results will not be as good-looking as if you had experimented with using a lower frame rate and resolution, in conjunction with a higher (quality) bit-rate setting. There is no set rule for this, as every digital video asset contains completely unique data (from the codec's point of view).

The next most effective setting for obtaining a smaller data footprint is the number of **key frames** that the codec uses to **sample** your digital video. Video codecs apply compression by looking at each frame and then encoding only the changes, or **offsets**, over the next several frames so that the codec algorithm does not have to encode every single frame in a video data stream. This is why a talking head video will encode better than a video in which every pixel moves on every frame (such as video that uses fast camera panning, or rapid field of view [FOV] zooming).

A key frame is a setting in a codec that forces that codec to take a **fresh sampling** of your video data assets every so often. There is usually an **auto setting** for key frames, which allows a codec to decide how many key frames to sample, as well as a **manual setting**, which lets you specify a key frame sampling every so often, usually a certain number of times per second or over the duration of the entire video (total frames).

Most codecs usually have either a **quality** or a **sharpness** setting (a slider) that controls the amount of **blur** applied to a video frame before compression. In case you are not familiar with this trick, applying a slight blur to your image or video, which is usually not desirable, can allow for better compression, as sharp transitions (edges) in an image are harder to encode, taking more data to reproduce, than softer transitions. That said, I would keep the quality (or sharpness) slider between 80 percent and 100% percent and try to reduce your data footprint using one of the other variables that I have discussed here, such as decreasing the resolution, frame rate, or bit rate.

Ultimately, there will be a number of different variables that you will need to fine-tune to achieve the best data footprint optimization for any given digital video data asset. It is important to remember that each video asset will look different (mathematically) to a digital video codec. For this reason, there can be no standard settings that can be developed to achieve any given compression result. That said, experience tweaking various settings will eventually allow you to get a feel, over time, for the various settings that you have to change, in terms of the different compressions parameters, to get the desired end result.

Digital Audio Concepts: Amplitude, Frequency, Samples

Those of you who are audiophiles know that sound is created by sending sound waves pulsing through the air. Digital audio is complex; part of that complexity comes from the need to bridge analog audio technology, created with speaker cones, with digital audio codecs. Analog speakers generate sound waves by pulsing them into existence. Our ears receive analog audio in exactly the opposite fashion, catching and receiving those pulses of air, or vibrations with different wavelengths, and then turning them back into data that our brain can process. This is how we "hear" the sound waves; our brain then interprets the different audio sound wave frequencies as different notes, or tones.

Sound waves generate various **tones**, depending on the **frequency** of the sound wave. A wide, or infrequent (long), wave produces a low (bass) tone, whereas a more frequent (short) wavelength produces a higher (treble) tone. Interestingly, different frequencies of light will produce different colors, so there is a close correlation between analog sound (audio) and analog light (color). There are many other similarities between digital images (and video) that will also carry through into your digital new media content production, as you will soon see.

The **volume** of a sound wave will be determined by its **amplitude**, or the **height** (or size) of that wave. Thus, frequency of sound waves equates to how **closely together** the waves are spaced, along the **x axis** if you are looking at it in 2D, and amplitude equates to how tall the waves are, as measured along the **y axis**.

Sound waves can be uniquely shaped, allowing them to "piggyback" various sound effects. A "pure," or baseline, type of sound wave is called a **sine wave** (which you learned about in high school trigonometry, with the sine, cosine, and tangent math functions). Those of you who are familiar with **audio synthesis** are aware that other types of sound waves are also used in sound design, such as the **saw wave**, which looks like the edge of a saw (hence its name), and the **pulse wave**, which is shaped using only right angles, resulting in immediate on and off sounds that translate into pulses (or bursts) of audio.

Even randomized waveforms, such as noise, are used in sound design to obtain edgy sound results. As you may have ascertained by using your recently acquired knowledge of data footprint optimization, the more "chaos," or noise, present in your sound wave (and in new media data in general), the harder it will be to compress for a codec. Therefore, more complex sound waves will result in larger digital audio file sizes, owing to the chaos in the data.

Converting Analog Audio to Digital Audio Data: Sampling, Accuracy, HD Audio

The process of turning analog audio (sound waves) into digital audio data is called **sampling**. If you work in the music industry, you have probably heard about a type of keyboard (or even rack-mounted equipment) called a **sampler**. Sampling is the process of **slicing** an analog audio wave into **segments** so that you can store the **shape** of the wave as digital audio data, using a digital audio format. This turns an infinitely accurate analog sound wave into a discrete amount of digital data, that is, into zeroes and ones. The more zeroes and ones used, the more accurate the reproduction of the infinitely accurate (original) analog sound wave.

Each digital segment of a sampled audio sound wave is called a sample, because it samples that sound wave at an exact point in time. The **sample accuracy** (resolution) you want will determine how many zeroes and ones are used to reproduce analog sound waves, so the **precision** of a sample is determined by the amount of data used to define each wave slice's **height**. As with digital imaging, this precision is termed the **resolution**, or, more accurately (no pun intended), the **sample resolution**. Sample resolution is usually defined using **8-bit**, **12-bit**, **16-bit**, **24-bit**, or **32-bit** resolution. Games mostly leverage 8-bit resolution for effects such as explosions, in which clarity is not as important; 12-bit resolution for crystal-clear spoken dialogue and more important audio elements; and, possibly, 16-bit resolution for background music.

In digital imaging and digital video this resolution is quantified by the number of pixels, and in digital audio, by how many bits of data are used to define each of the analog audio samples taken. Again, as with digital imaging, in which more pixels yields better quality, with digital audio a higher sample resolution yields better sound reproduction. Thus, higher sampling resolutions, using more data to reproduce a given sound wave sample, will produce higher-quality audio playback, at the expense of a larger data footprint. This is the reason that 16-bit audio (commonly referred to as **CD quality audio**) sounds better than 8-bit audio. Depending on the audio involved, 12-bit audio can be a great compromise.

In digital audio there is a new type of audio sample, known as HD audio in the consumer electronics industry. HD digital audio broadcast radio uses a 24-bit sample resolution, so each audio sample, or slice of the sound wave, contains 16,777,216 bits of sample resolution. Some of the newer hardware devices now support HD audio, such as the smartphones you see advertised featuring "HD-quality audio," meaning that they have 24-bit audio hardware. These days, laptops (including PCs), as well as game consoles and iTVs, also come standard with 24-bit audio playback hardware.

It is important to note that HD audio is probably not necessary for Java 8 games, unless your game is music oriented and makes use of high-quality music, in which case you can use HD audio samples via a **WAVE** file format.

Another consideration is digital audio **sampling frequency** (also called the **sampling rate**), This is a measure of how many samples at a particular sample resolution are taken during 1 second of sampling time frame. In terms of digital image editing, sampling frequency is analogous to the number of colors contained in a digital image. You are probably familiar with the term "CD-quality audio," which is defined as using a **16-bit** sample resolution and a **44.1kHz** sampling rate (taking 44,100 samples, each of which has 16 bits of sample resolution, or 65,536 bits of audio data). You can determine the amount of raw data in an audio file by multiplying the sampling bit rate by the sampling frequency by the number of seconds in the audio snippet. Obviously, this can potentially be a huge number! Audio codecs are really great at optimizing data down to an amazingly small data footprint with very little audible loss in quality.

Thus, the exact same trade-off that exists in digital imaging and digital video occurs with digital audio as well: the more data you include, the higher quality the result, but always at the cost of a much larger data footprint. In the visual mediums the size of the data footprint is defined using color depth, pixels, and, in the case of digital video and animation, frames. In the aural medium it is defined via the sample resolution, in combination with the sampling rate. The most common sampling rates in the digital audio industry currently include **8kHz**, **22kHz**, **32kHz**, **44.1kHz**, **48kHz**, **96KHz**, **192kHz**, and even **384kHz**.

Lower sampling rates, such as 8kHz, 11kHz, and 22kHz, are the ones that you are going to use in your games, as, with careful optimization, these can yield high-quality sound effects and arcade music. These rates would be optimal for sampling any voice-based digital audio as well, such as movie dialogue or an e-book narration track. Higher audio sample rates, such as 44.1kHz, would be more appropriate for music, and sound effects that need a high dynamic range (high fidelity), such as rumbling thunder, could use 48kHz. Higher sample rates will allow audio reproduction that exhibits movie theater (THX) sound quality, but this is not required for most games.

Digital Audio Streaming: Captive Audio vs. Streaming Audio

As with digital video data, digital audio data can be either captive within the application distribution file (in the case of Java, a **.JAR** file) or **streamed**, using remote data servers. Similar to digital video, the upside to streaming digital audio data is that it can reduce the data footprint of the application file. The downside is reliability. Many of the same concepts apply equally well to audio and video. Streaming audio will save the data footprint, because you do not have to include all that heavy new media digital audio data in your .JAR files. So, if you are planning on coding a Jukebox application, you may want to consider streaming your digital audio data; otherwise, try to optimize your digital audio data so that you can include them (captive) inside the .JAR file. This way, the data will always be available to the application's users when they need it!

The downside to streaming digital audio is that if a user's connection (or the audio data server) goes down, your digital audio file may not always be present for your end users to play and listen to, using your game application! The reliability and availability of digital audio data are a key factor to be considered on the other side of this streaming-versus-captive trade-off. The same would apply to digital video assets as well.

Again, as with digital video, one of the primary concepts in regard to streaming your digital audio is the bit rate of the digital audio data. As you learned in the previous section, the bit rate is defined during the compression process. Digital audio files that need to support lower bit-rate bandwidth are going to have more compression applied to the audio data, which will result in lower quality. These will stream (play back) more smoothly across a greater number of devices, because fewer bits can be quickly transferred as well as processed more easily.

Digital Audio in JavaFX: Supported Digital Audio Codecs and Data Formats

There are considerably more **digital audio codecs** in JavaFX than digital video codecs, as there is only one video codec, MPEG-4 H.264 AVC. Android audio support includes **.MP3** (**MPEG-3**) files, Windows **WAVE** (**Pulse Code Modulation [PCM]** audio) **.WAV** files, **.MP4** (or .M4A) **MPEG-4 AAC** (**Advanced Audio Coding**) audio, and Apple's **AIFF** (PCM) file format. The most common format supported by JavaFX (and thus Java 8) is the popular .MP3 digital audio file format. Most of you are familiar with MP3 digital audio files, owing to music download web sites, such as Napster or Soundcloud, and most of us collect songs in this format to use on MP3 players and in CD-ROM- or DVD-ROM-based music collections. The MP3 digital audio file format is popular because it has a fairly good compression-to-quality ratio and is widely supported.

MP3 is an acceptable format to use in a Java 8 application, so long as you get the highest quality level possible out of it, using an optimal encoding work process. It is important to note that, like JPEG (used for images), MP3 is a **lossy** audio file format, in which some of the audio data (and thus quality) are **thrown away** during your compression process and cannot be recovered.

JavaFX does have two **lossless** audio compression codecs, AIFF and WAVE. Many of you are familiar with these, as they were the original audio formats used with the Apple Macintosh and Microsoft Windows OSs, respectively. These files use PCM audio, which is lossless (in this case, because there is no compression applied whatsoever!). "PCM," which, as stated, stands for "pulse code modulation," refers to the data format it holds.

PCM audio is commonly used for CD-ROM content as well as telephony applications. This is because PCM WAVE audio is an **uncompressed** digital audio format, with no CPU-intensive compression algorithms applied to the data stream. Thus, decoding (CPU data processing) is not an issue for telephony equipment or for CD players.

For this reason, when you start compressing digital audio assets into the various file formats, you can use PCM as your **baseline** file format. It allows you to look at the difference between PCM (WAVE) and MP3 and MP4 audio compression results to get an idea of how much data footprint optimization you are getting for your JAR file; more important, you can also see how your sample resolution and sample frequency optimization are going to affect the system memory used for your game's audio effects. Even if you used an MP3 or MP4 format, it would still have to be decompressed into memory before the audio asset could be used with the AudioClip class and employed as a sound effect in a Java 8 game.

Because a WAVE or AIFF file will not have any quality loss (as there is also no decompression needed), the PCM data can be placed straight from the JAR file into system memory! This makes PCM audio great for game sound effects that are short in duration (0.1 to 1 second), and it can be highly optimized, using 8-bit and 12-bit sample resolution and 8kHz, 22kHz, or 32kHz sample frequency. Ultimately, the only real way to find out which audio format supported by JavaFX has the best digital audio compression result for any given digital audio data is to encode your digital audio in the primary codecs that you know are supported and efficient. I will be outlining this work process later on, when you add audio to the game, and you will observe the relative data footprint results between the different formats, using the same source audio sample (see Chapter 15). Then, you will listen to the audio playback quality so that you can make your final decision concerning the optimal balance between quality and file size . This is the work process that you will need to go through to develop JavaFX digital audio assets for use in your Java 8 game.

JavaFX also supports the popular MPEG-4 AAC codec. These digital audio data can be contained in MPEG4 containers (.mp4, .m4a, .m4v), or file extensions, and can be played back using any OS. It is important to note that JavaFX does not contain an MPEG-4 decoder, but instead supports what is called a multimedia container, meaning that JavaFX uses the OS's MPEG-4 decoder.

For this reason, and because online listening studies have concluded that the MP3 format has better quality (for music) than the MP4, you will be using the MP3 format for longer-form audio (game background musical loops) via the Media and MediaPlayer classes. You will use the PCM WAVE audio format for short-form (1 second or less) audio (game sound effects, such as shots, bells, yelps, grunts, laughter, cheering, and other such digital audio assets), which you will use via the AudioClip digital audio sequencing engine (class) that JavaFX so generously provides.

Digital Audio Optimization: Start with CD-Quality Audio, and Work Backward

Optimizing your digital audio assets for playback across the widest range of hardware devices on the market is going to be easier than optimizing your digital video or digital imagery (and thus animation) across these devices. This is because there is a much wider disparity between target screen resolutions and display aspect ratios than there is between types of digital audio playback hardware support across hardware devices (with the possible exception of new hardware featuring 24-bit HD audio playback hardware compatibility). All hardware plays digital audio assets well, so audio optimization is a "one audio asset hits all devices" scenario, whereas with the visual (video, image, animation) part of the equation, you have display screens as large as 4,096 × 2,160 pixels (4K iTV Sets) and as small as 320 × 320 pixels (flip phones and smart watches).

It is important to remember that the user's ears cannot perceive the same quality difference with digital audio that the user's eyes can with digital imagery, 2D animation, and digital video. Generally, there are three primary "sweet spots" of digital audio support across all hardware devices that you should target for support for Java game audio.

Lower-quality audio, such as short narration tracks, character exclamations, and short-duration sound effects, can achieve remarkably high quality by using a sampling rate of **8kHZ** or **22kHz**, along with **8-bit** or **12-bit** sampling resolution. Medium-quality audio, such as long narration tracks, longer-duration sound effects, and looped background (ambient) audio, can achieve a very high quality level by using a **22kHz** or **32kHz** sampling rate, along with a **12-bit** or **16-bit** sampling resolution.

The high-quality audio assets, such as music, should be optimized approaching **CD-quality audio** and will use a **32kHz** or **44.1kHz** sampling rate, along with the **16-bit** data sampling resolution. For **HD**-quality audio, being at the ultra-high end of this audio spectrum, you would use the **48kHz** sampling rate, along with the **24-bit** digital audio data sampling resolution. There is also an unnamed, "somewhere in the middle" high-end audio specification, using a **48kHz** sampling rate, along with a **16-bit** data sampling resolution, which just happens to be what Dolby THX used to use for its high-end audio experience technology in movie theaters (back in the day).

Ultimately, it comes down to the quality–file size balance results that emerge from the digital audio data footprint optimization work process, which can be amazing. Therefore, your initial work process for optimizing your digital audio assets across all these hardware devices is going to be to create baseline 16-bit assets, at either 44.1kHz or 48kHz, and then optimize (compress) them, using the different formats supported in JavaFX. Once that work process is completed, you can see which resulting digital audio assets provide the smallest data footprint, along with the highest quality digital audio playback. After that, you can reduce your 44.1KHz or 48kHz data to 32kHz and save that out ,using first 16-bit and then 12-bit resolution. Next, reopen the original 48kHz data, downsample to 22kHz sample frequency, and export that, using 16-bit and 12-bit resolution, and so on. You will be performing this work process later on, when you add digital audio assets to the Java 8 game, so you will see the entire process (see Chapter 15).

Next, let's take a look at JavaFX Scene Builder and how it uses FXML to allow designers to design Java FX applications visually. I am not going to be using Scene Builder or FXML (just Java 8 code and JavaFX classes) over the course of this book, so pay attention!

JavaFX Scene Builder: Using FXML for UI Design

JavaFX **Scene Builder** is a visual design tool that generates an **FXML** (JavaFX markup language) UI Scene Graph construct to define your JavaFX application's front-end design. This FXML **UI definition** can then be "inflated" in Java 8 to create your application's JavaFX Scene Graph, nodes, groups, and SubScene objects filled with javafx. scene.control package classes (objects) defining your UI design. Oracle's intention in offering both a Scene Builder visual development tool and FXML is to allow nonprogrammers, ostensibly UI designers, to design the front-end UIs for their Java 8 applications so that the Java programmers can then focus on back-end functional application task processing logic.

Because FXML and Scene Builder are optimized for UI design (arranging controls, such as buttons, text entry fields, radio buttons, check boxes, and so on), I am not going to use Scene Builder and FXML over the course of this book. I am, however, going to cover it in this chapter so that you know how to use it if you want to for your other JavaFX applications. My reasoning is that, other than the initial game splash screen, which contains a few UI Button objects, which show game instructions, list the contributors, track the high scores, save a current game state, and start game play, UI design will not be a major focus of this book.

To use FXML, and soon after use of the Scene Builder visual UI design tool, you must create a special kind of FXML application, as you learned in Chapter 2 (see Figure 2-4), when you created the JavaFX game. Creating an FXML application imports the **javafx.fxml** package and classes. This allows the Java 8 code to **inflate** FXML constructs created by the UI designers so that they can be used by the programmers to attach Java logic to the various UI controls. The Android OS does this as well, using basic XML, but in Android this approach is not optional; it is part of the way things are done. In JavaFX 8 (as you saw in Figure 2-4), it is simply one option. If you want to research XML-based UI design further for Android, check out my book *Pro Android UI* (Apress, 2014).

The Scene Builder visual layout tool that writes **FXML** UI design constructs for you is a **WYSIWYG drag and drop** interface design tool. All a designer has to do is drag and drop any of the JavaFX UI controls onto the editing screen from a UI Control **panel** that contains every Control class (object) in the **javafx.scene.control** package (see Chapter 4). This Scene Builder is integrated into NetBeans 8.0 for easy access and integration with JavaFX, in case programmers also need to use it to quickly prototype UI designs for their clients. There is also a stand-alone version of the Scene Builder tool, at version 2.0, for designers who do not want to work inside the NetBeans IDE.

You can switch back and forth from FXML editing and previewing in real time and see UI design and layout changes without having to compile the Java application. You can also apply all **CSS styles** to the Scene Builder tool and FXML structure in real time and see the results of those coding changes as well, again, without any Java compilation! In addition, you can add custom UI controls to the UI Control panel library, using third-party JAR files or FXML definitions.

The **Scene Builder Kit API** is open source. This lets you customize your own integrations of Scene Builder's UI panels and controls, allowing you to integrate Scene Builder into other IDEs, such as Eclipse or IntelliJ IDEA. A rich text TextFlow container has recently been added into the GUI component (Control) library, affording **rich text– editing** capabilities. With these new capabilities, you can build multiple-node, rich text constructs that can integrate other UI elements, or new media element types, with the TextFlow elements.

For you 3D "aficionados," 3D is also fully supported in the Scene Builder visual design editor and in FXML. A 3D object can be loaded and even saved out using the Scene Builder tool, and all of the object's properties can be edited (and viewed) in real time, using the **Inspector panel**. It is not yet possible to create from scratch 3D objects using Scene Builder, and you cannot yet assign or edit complex Mesh or Materials properties at this time, but I am sure that these features will come, along with the advanced 3D OpenGL ES power that is scheduled to be added into JavaFX 8.

Next, let's take a look at FXML markup language specifically, at an in-depth level. After that, you will examine an actual FXML UI definition structure, and you will see exactly how the current JavaFX application's UI design would be structured using an FXML UI definition construct. As you will see, FXML makes UI design a lot easier!

FXML Definition: Anatomy of an XML UI Definition Construct

The FXML structure is based on the JavaFX classes (objects), and their attributes, that the FXML **tags,** and **parameters** structures, which you can easily create, allow you to "mock up" a front-end UI more easily, using a mark-up language. The FXML structure lets you more easily construct your Scene Graph hierarchy, and the FXML tags and their parameters, which you will be looking at in the next section, match up 1:1 with the JavaFX API classes.

Once you create your UI design, the Java programmers can use **javafx.fxml** classes and methods to inflate your UI layout container and UI control arrangement into a JavaFX scene and Scene Graph structure, based on Java objects. Then, the UI design can be used in the application Java code. As mentioned earlier, FXML is most useful for designing complex, static (fixed) UI design layouts containing lots of buttons, forms, check boxes and the like.

Hello World UI FXML Definition: Replicating Your Current UI Design, Using FXML

The first thing that you define in the FXML structure is the FXML **processing instructions**. Each processing instruction starts with a less-than sign, question mark sequence (**<?**) and ends with the reversal of that sequence (question mark, greater-than sign [**?>**]). The first processing instruction is a declaration of the XML language use, its **version** (1.0), and the **text character set** language-encoding format that you want to use (in this case, **UTF-8** [**universal** character set **transformation format, 8 bit**]). Because it is 8 bit, there are 256 characters in this international character set, which was designed to span the many languages based on Germanic characters, that is, languages that use an A to Z alphabet (including accented characters).

Following the declaration of an XML language and a character set are processing instructions. These **import** the Java language, utilities, and **javafx.scene package** as well as the **javafx.scene.layout** and **javafx.scene.control** packages, which are used to design the UI layout and the UI controls that the layout contains.

For example, the StackPane UI layout container that you are using in the current application is in the javafx. scene.layout package, and the button UI control element is in the javafx.scene.control package. Because the <StackPane> FXML UI layout container is the **parent** element in this structure, it goes first, or **outside** the **nested** FXML UI definition structure that you are about to create.

Inside the <StackPane>, you will nest **children** of the StackPane class (object), using the **<children>** tags (XML tags are coded using **<arrowHeadBrackets>**). Nested inside these <children> tags are the UI control elements (in this case, a button control, so you would use the <Button> tag). Note that the class (object) proper name is used inside the arrowhead brackets to create the FXML tag, so this is very logical and should be quite easy to learn and assimilate into your UI design work process:

```
<? xml version="1.0" encoding="UTF-8" ?>
<? import java.lang.* ?>
<? import java.util.* ?>
<? import javafx.scene.* ?>
<? import javafx.scene.layout.* ?>
<? import javafx.scene.control.* ?>

<StackPane id="root" prefHeight="250" prefWidth="300" >
    <children>
        <Button id="btn" text="Say 'Hello World'" layoutX="125" layoutY="116" />
    </children>
</StackPane>
```

Next, let's take a look at the tag and parameter syntax so that you always know how to construct FXML UI layout and control definition files. A UI element that has no children, such as the prior <Button> UI control, will use a shorthand tag open-and-close syntax, using the **<ClassName** opening tag and forward slash, greater-than sign closing tag (**/>**), like this:

```
<Button  id="btn"  text="Say 'Hello World'"  layoutX="125"  layoutY="116"  />
```

Note that the **parameters** that configure the tag, which would equate to the attributes of the object (or the variables in the class that creates the object) are (yet again) **nested** inside the tag itself and use the **variable name** and **equals** operator, along with the **data value** specified in quotation marks, as shown in the previous code.

A FXML tag that has <children> objects nested inside it will use this different **<ClassName>** opening tag. Following the nested tags listed inside (after) this tag is a **</ClassName>** closing tag. This allows the tag syntax to specify (become) the **container** for the <children> tags inside it, as you can see in the example here, in which the opening and closing FXML tags are ordered according to their nesting (inside) hierarchy:

```
<StackPane id="root" prefHeight="250" prefWidth="300" >
    <children>
        <Button id="btn" text="Say 'Hello World'" layoutX="125" layoutY="116" />
    </children>
</StackPane>
```

As you can see, the parameters can be put inside the opening tag for a parent tag by placing them **between** the <ClassName part of the opening tag and the greater-than sign. This is how you would configure the parent tag for any parameters if you needed to do so, as when you specified the StackPane size and name (called an **id** in FXML).

Summary

In this fifth chapter, you took a closer look at some of the more important game design and new media concepts that you will be using in your Java 8 game development work process so that you have the foundational knowledge necessary to create your game. You also studied JavaFX Scene Builder and FXML, just to get those concepts under your belt and out of the way, as I am going to do everything in this book using Java 8 code and JavaFX classes to comply with the requests I get from readers of my Android books ("How do we do this using only Java code? We don't want to use XML to create our applications!" is the mantra that I am constantly hearing these days).

First, you examined the key concept of static versus dynamic and how this is important for both game design and game optimization, as too much dynamics can overload older single-core and even dualcore CPUs if game optimization is not an ongoing consideration throughout the game design, development, and optimization process.

Next, you explored some of the key components of **game design** (and development), such as **sprites**, **collision detection**, **physics simulation**, **background animation**, **UI design**, **scoring engines**, and **game play logic**. You took a look at how these applied to static games, or games without continuous movement, such as strategy games, board games, puzzles, knowledge games, memory games, and dynamic games, and games using continuous movement, such as platformers, arcade games, first-person shooters, third-person shooters, driving games, and the like.

You took a high-level technical overview of new media asset types and the concepts and terminology across digital imaging, animation, digital video, and digital audio. You learned about pixels; resolutions; and how aspect ratios define the shape of an image, animation, or video and about color depth and alpha channel transparency and how to define these, using hexadecimal notation. Then, you investigated the fourth dimension of time and learned about frames, frame rates, and bit rates, and you looked at digital audio, sample frequency, and sample resolution. Finally, you studied JavaFX Scene Graph and FXML how these work and how they can be used in your current game.

In the next chapter, you are going to examine **JavaFX** Scene Graph and create the **infrastructure** for your Java 8 game application, including the splash screen (your game's home screen and primary UI).

■ ■ ■

The Foundation of Game Design: The JavaFX Scene Graph and the InvinciBagel Game Infrastructure

In this chapter, you will start to design the infrastructure of your InvinciBagel game, both from the **user interface** (UI) and **user experience** standpoint as well as from the "under the hood" **game engine**, **sprite engine**, **collision engine**, and **physics engine** standpoint. You will keep optimization in mind, as you must do as you work through the rest of the book, so that you do not get a **scene graph** that is so extensive or complicated that the **pulse** system cannot update everything efficiently. This means keeping primary game UI screens (**Scene** or **SubScene nodes**) to a minimum (three or four); making sure that the 3D and Media engine (digital audio and digital video) use their own threads; and checking that the functional "engines" that drive the game are all coded logically, using their own classes and proper Java 8 programming conventions, structures, variables, constants, and modifiers (see Chapter 3).

First, you will learn about the **top-level**, **front-facing** UI screen design that your game will offer the user, including the InvinciBagel "branding" splash screen he or she sees when launching the application. This screen will have Button controls on it, accessing other information screens, which you will want to minimize in number, as they will be either Scene nodes (primary game play screen) or ImageView nodes (the other information screens). These game support screens will contain things that the user needs to know to play the game effectively, such as game instructions and a high scores screen. You will also include a legal disclaimers screen (to keep your legal department happy), which will also have credits for the various programmers and new media artisans who worked on the creation of the game engine and game assets.

The next level down of the InvinciBagel game design foundation that you will develop is the **under the hood**, or **back-facing** (unseen by the game user), game engine component Java class design aspects for the InvinciBagel game. These include a **game play engine**, which will use a **javafx.animation.AnimationTimer** class to control the game play updates to the game play interface screen; a **sprites engine**, which will use Java **list** arrays and **sets** to manage game sprites; a **collision engine**, which will detect and respond when a collision has occurred between two sprites; a **physics engine**, which will apply force and similar physics simulations to the game play so that sprites **accelerate** and **react to gravity** realistically; and an **actor engine**, which will manage each of the characteristics of individual actors in the InvinciBagel game.

Finally, you will modify your existing InvinciBagel.java Application subclass to implement a new splash screen and buttons for the game play screen and for the other three functional information screens needed to provide these top-level UI features and the foundational UI screen infrastructure for this InvinciBagel game application. This will ultimately get you into some Java and JavaFX programming, as you create the foundation for the game.

Game Design Foundation: Primary Function Screens

One of the first things you want to design is the top-level, or **highest-level**, UIs that your game's users will interface with. These will all be accessed using the InvinciBagel splash (branding) screen, contained in the primary **InvinciBagel.java** class code. As discussed previously, this Java code will extend the **javafx.application.Application** class and will launch the application, displaying its splash screen, along with options to review instructions, play the game, see the high scores, or review the game's legal disclaimers and game creator credits (programmer, artist, writer, composer, sound designer, and so on). A high-level diagram showing the game, starting with functional UI screens at the top and progressing down to the OS level, can be seen in Figure 6-1.

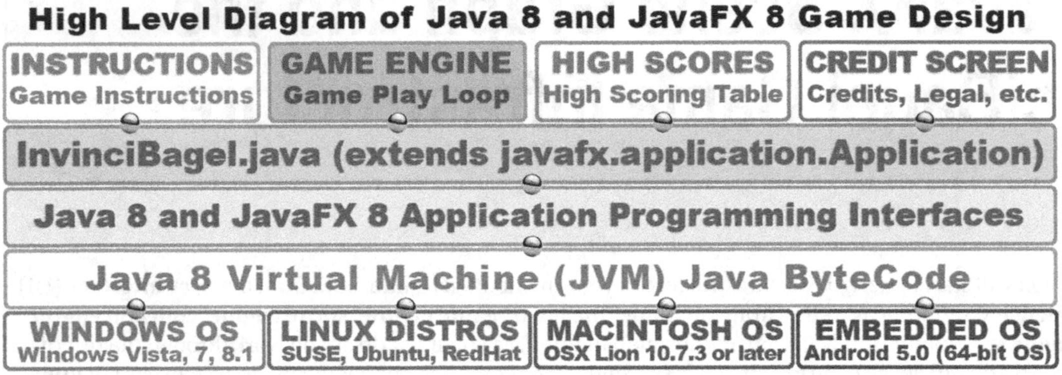

High Level Diagram of Java 8 and JavaFX 8 Game Design

INSTRUCTIONS	GAME ENGINE	HIGH SCORES	CREDIT SCREEN
Game Instructions	Game Play Loop	High Scoring Table	Credits, Legal, etc.

InvinciBagel.java (extends javafx.application.Application)

Java 8 and JavaFX 8 Application Programming Interfaces

Java 8 Virtual Machine (JVM) Java ByteCode

WINDOWS OS	LINUX DISTROS	MACINTOSH OS	EMBEDDED OS
Windows Vista, 7, 8.1	SUSE, Ubuntu, RedHat	OSX Lion 10.7.3 or later	Android 5.0 (64-bit OS)

Figure 6-1. *Primary game functional screens and how they are implemented through Java and JavaFX API, using a JVM*

This will require adding three more **Button** nodes to your **StackPane** layout container **Parent** node as well as an **ImageView** node for the splash screen background image container. The ImageView node will have to be added to the StackPane first to be the **first child node** in the StackPane (**z-order = 0**), as this ImageView holds what I call the **background plate** for the splash screen UI design. Because it is in the background, the image would need to be behind the Button UI control elements, which will have z-order values of 1 through 4.

This means that you will be using six Node objects (one parent node and five child nodes) in your application's scene graph just to create your InvinciBagel splash screen! The instructions and credit screens will use another ImageView node, so you are up to six nodes already, and the high scores screen will likely use another two (ImageView and TableView) nodes, so you likely have more than eight nodes in the Scene Graph for creating the game support infrastructure before you have even considered adding the nodes for the game play screen, which is, of course, where you want to get the best performance possible for your game.

This really is not so bad if you think about it, as these screens are all **static** and do not need to be updated, that is, the (UI) elements they contain are fixed and do not require updates using the pulse system, and so you should essentially still have **99 percent** of the power of the JavaFX **pulse** engine left over to process an InvinciBagel game **GamePlayLoop** engine. In fact, as Java 8 and JavaFX 8 continue to improve the efficiency of their platform APIs and classes, you may actually have even more processing power left over for game play (sprite movements, collisions, physics, animation, and so on) and thus will be in good shape.

The GamePlayLoop will process the game code for you, using the **javafx.animation** package and its **AnimationTimer** class. You will always need to be cognizant of how many **Scene Graph Node** objects you are asking the pulse engine to process, because, if this number gets to be too large, it will start to affect the game's performance.

Java Class Structure Design: Game Engine Support

Next, let's take a look at how the functional structure of the InvinciBagel game will need to be put together under the hood, so to speak, within your Java 8 game programming code, which is what this book is all about! There is really no correlation between what the front-facing UI screens look like and what the underlying programming logic looks like, as the majority of the programming code will go toward creating the game play experience on the game play screen. The game instructions and legal and credits screens will just be images (ImageView) and will either have the text embedded in the image (resulting in fewer Scene Graph nodes used) or composite a transparent TextView on top of the ImageView. The high scores screen will take a little bit of programming logic, which you will do toward the end of the game development, as the game logic has to be created and played for high scores to even be generated in the first place (see Chapter 17)!

Figure 6-2 displays the primary functional area components required for the InvinciBagel game to be complete. The diagram shows an InvinciBagel Application subclass at the top of the hierarchy, creating the top level and the scene, and the Scene Graph contained below (or inside) it.

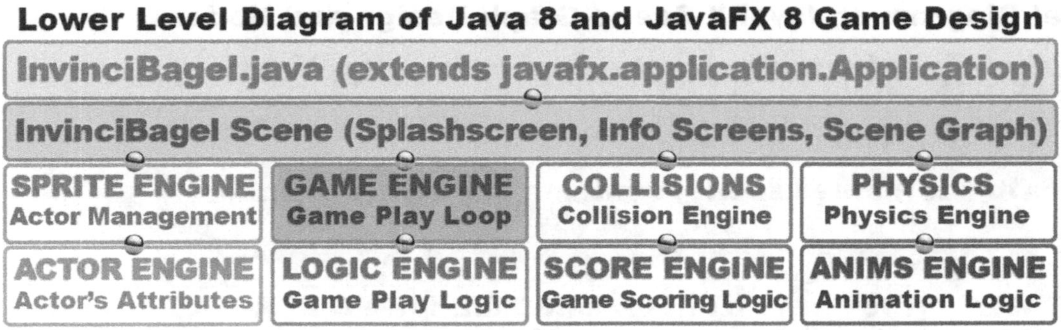

Lower Level Diagram of Java 8 and JavaFX 8 Game Design

InvinciBagel.java (extends javafx.application.Application)			
InvinciBagel Scene (Splashscreen, Info Screens, Scene Graph)			
SPRITE ENGINE Actor Management	**GAME ENGINE** Game Play Loop	**COLLISIONS** Collision Engine	**PHYSICS** Physics Engine
ACTOR ENGINE Actor's Attributes	**LOGIC ENGINE** Game Play Logic	**SCORE ENGINE** Game Scoring Logic	**ANIMS ENGINE** Animation Logic

Figure 6-2. *Primary game functional classes and how they are implemented under the Scene and Scene Graph levels*

Below the InvinciBagel Scene object, which is actually created inside this InvinciBagel Application subclass, is the broader structural design for functional classes that you will need to code over the course of the remainder of the book. The engines (classes) shown in the figure will create your game functions, such as **game engine** (gameplay loop), **logic engine** (game play logic), **sprite engine** (actor management), **actor engine** (actor attributes), **score engine** (game-scoring logic), **animation engine** (animation logic), **collision detection**, and **physics simulation**. You will have to create all these Java class functions to fully implement a comprehensive, 2D game engine for the InvinciBagel game.

The game engine, which I call the GamePlayLoop class, is the primary class that creates the AnimationTimer object that invoke the pulse events that continually process the gameplay loop. This loop, as you know, will call the **.handle()** method, which will in turn contain method calls, which will ultimately access the other classes that you will be creating to manage actors (sprite engine); move them around the screen (actor engine); detect any collisions (collision engine); apply the game logic after collisions have been detected (logic engine); and apply the forces of physics to provide realistic effects, such as gravity and acceleration, to the game play (physics engine).

From Chapter 7 on, you will be building up these various engines, which will be used to create the game play experience. I will stratify chapter topics, based on each of these engines and what they need to do, so that everything is structured logically from a learning as well as coding perspective.

JavaFX Scene Graph Design: Minimizing UI Nodes

The trick to **minimizing** the Scene Graph is to use as few nodes as possible to implement a complete design, and, as you can see in Figure 6-3, this can be accomplished with one StackPane **root** node, one VBox **branch** (parent) node, and seven **leaf** (children) nodes (one **TableView**, two **ImageView**, and four **Button** UI controls). When you get into coding the Scene Graph next (finally!), you will use only 14 objects, and import only 12 classes, to make the entire top level for your InvinciBagel game, which you designed in the previous section, a reality. The TableView will overlay the ImageView composite, which contains the information screen layers of the design. This TableView object will be added in later stages of your game design. An ImageView **backplate** will contain the InvinciBagel artwork; an ImageView **compositing** layer will contain three different transparent images, which will seamlessly overlay the backplate image, based on the ActionEvents (clicks of the Button controls); and a **VBox** Parent UI layout container will contain the four Button controls. You will also create an **Insets** object to hold the **padding** values to fine-tune the button bank alignment.

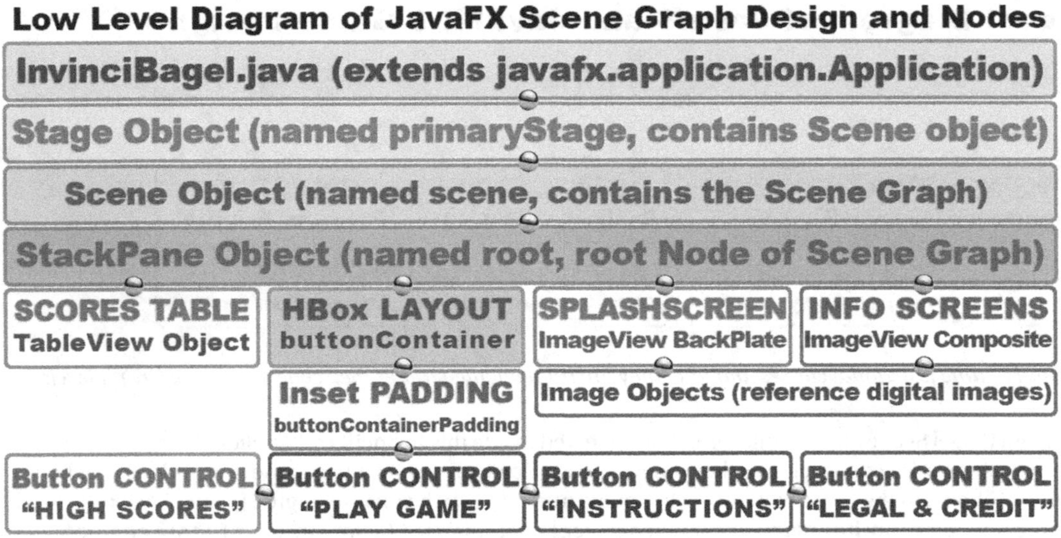

Low Level Diagram of JavaFX Scene Graph Design and Nodes

InvinciBagel.java (extends javafx.application.Application)

Stage Object (named primaryStage, contains Scene object)

Scene Object (named scene, contains the Scene Graph)

StackPane Object (named root, root Node of Scene Graph)

SCORES TABLE TableView Object	**HBox LAYOUT** buttonContainer	**SPLASHSCREEN** ImageView BackPlate	**INFO SCREENS** ImageView Composite

Inset PADDING
buttonContainerPadding   Image Objects (reference digital images)

Button CONTROL "HIGH SCORES"	**Button CONTROL** "PLAY GAME"	**Button CONTROL** "INSTRUCTIONS"	**Button CONTROL** "LEGAL & CREDIT"

Figure 6-3. *Primary splash screen Scene Graph node hierarchy, the objects it contains, and the assets it references*

Because a Button object cannot be positioned individually, I had to use the **HBox** class, along with an **Insets** class and a **Pos** class, to contain and position the Button controls. I will be going over the classes you will be using for this high-level design in this chapter so that you have an overview of every class that you are going to be adding to your InvinciBagel class to create this top-level UI design.

The way I optimized the Scene Graph use for the four different screens needed to match the four different buttons was to use one ImageView as a **backplate** to contain the InvinciBagel splash screen artwork and then one more ImageView to contain different **composite images** (overlays) that use transparency (alpha channel). In this way, you can simulate four different screens, using only two ImageView Scene Graph Node objects.

Finally, a TableView Scene Graph node will contain the table structure for the high scores table. This will be created via the score engine, which you will be creating last, after you finish your entire game design and programming. For now, you will leave the High Scores and Play Game button code unimplemented.

Scene Graph Code: Optimizing Your Current InvinciBagel Class

I know you are eager to work on the InvinciBagel class code, so let's clean up, organize, and optimize the existing Java code to implement this top-level UI screen design. First, put the object declaration and naming Java code at the top of the InvinciBagel class. This is more organized, and all the methods that are inside your class will be able to see and reference these objects without using Java modifier keywords. As you can see in Figure 6-4, these include your existing scene Scene object, root StackPane object, and btn Button object (which I am renaming gameButton). I added three other Button objects, named **helpButton**, **scoreButton**, and **legalButton**, all declared and named using a single line of Java code, as well as two ImageView objects, named **splashScreenbackplate** and **splashScreenTextArea**. You also need to create four Image objects to hold digital image assets, which will be displayed in the ImageView nodes; I have named these **splashScreen**, **instructionLayer**, **legalLayer**, and **scoresLayer** and declared them, using one **compound** Java statement. Finally, you declare and name the **buttonContainer** VBox object and the **buttonContainerPadding** Insets object. NetBeans will write import statements for you, so long as you use the Alt+Enter keyboard shortcut, selecting the correct javafx package and class path. The imports are shown at the top of the figure.

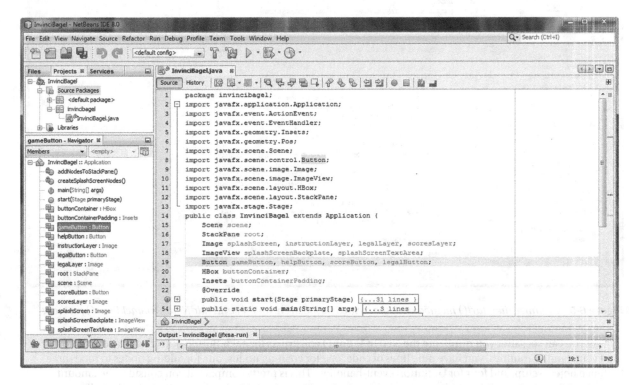

Figure 6-4. *Declaring and naming the 14 objects that will make up your Scene Graph hierarchy at the top of the class*

You will be taking a look at all these JavaFX classes in detail in this chapter so that you learn what they are used for and what they can do for your Java applications.

Scene Graph Design: Streamlining the Existing .start() Method

Now, you can optimize the .start() method so that it only has one or two dozen lines of code. First, modularize the Scene Graph node creation Java routines into their own **createSplashScreenNodes()** method, which will be called at the top of the .start() method, as can be seen in Figure 6-5. After all the nodes are created in this method, create an **addNodesToStackPane()** method to add the nodes to the StackPane root node, and then have the three primaryStage lines of code configuring and managing the Stage object and, finally, the ActionEvent handling code routines that "wire" the Button UI controls to the Java code to be executed when they are clicked.

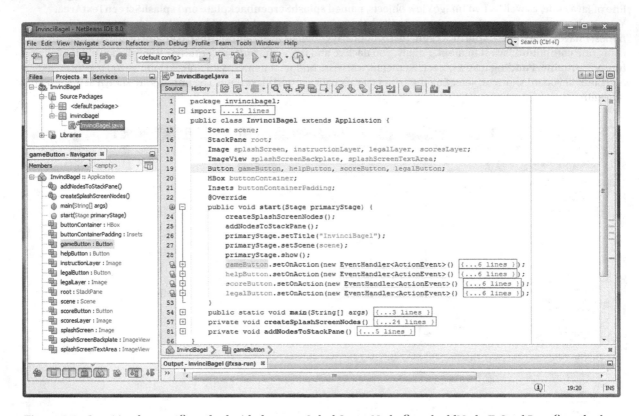

Figure 6-5. *Organize the .start() method with the createSplashScreenNodes() and addNodesToStackPane() methods*

As you can see, after you **duplicate** the **.setOnAction()** constructs for each Button object, when you collapse the EventHandler routines, you have nine lines of code: one for creating nodes, one for adding nodes to root, three for Stage object setup, and four for UI Button event-handling. This is pretty compact, if you consider the amount of functionality you are adding to the top level of your game structure (game play, instructions, legal, credits, scoreboard).

It is important that you do things in the correct order, as some Java code is predicated on other Java code. For this reason, the object declarations come first; then, inside the .start() method, you create (instantiate) the nodes. Once these are declared, named, and instantiated (created), you add them to the StackPane root node and then configure (using the .setTitle() method) and add the scene Scene object to the primaryStage Stage object, using the .setScene() method. After your objects are in system memory, only then will you be able to process ActionEvent handling routines, which are attached to your four Button UI controls. Next, let's make sure that your digital image assets, which will be referenced in the **createSplashScreenNodes()** method, are in the proper NetBeans folder.

Scene Graph Assets: Installing the ImageView's Image Assets in Your Project

To reference the digital image assets inside the JAR file in your Java code, you have to insert a forward slash before the file name. Before you can reference the files, however, you must copy these image files from the book repository into the **Computer/ComputerName/Users/user/MyDocuments/NetBeansProjects/InvinciBagel/src** folder, as shown on the left-hand side (and the top) of Figure 6-6. You can also see how these digital image assets will composite, as the background plate invincibagelsplash PNG24 has a spot for the other three PNG32 images to overlay (cover). The white areas seen in the composite ImageView assets are actually transparent! Now, you are ready!

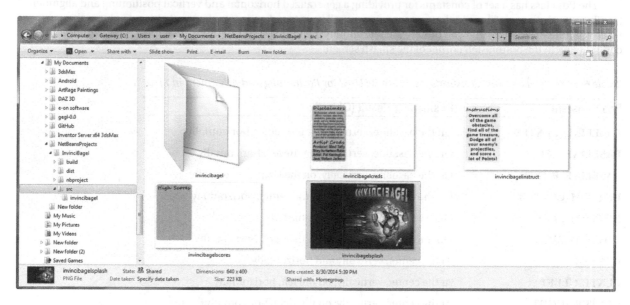

Figure 6-6. *Windows 7 Explorer file management utility, showing a PNG24 splash screen and three PNG32 overlays*

JavaFX UI Classes: HBox, Pos, Insets, and ImageView

Let's take a break from coding for an in-depth look at some of the new classes you are going to use to complete your top-level game application UI design. These include the Pos class (positioning); the Insets class (padding); the HBox class (UI layout container); the Image class (digital image container); the ImageView class (digital image display); and the TableView class (table data display), which you will study here but implement in code later in your game development once the game is completely finished. You will examine these in order, from simplest (Pos) to most complex (TableView), and then code the **.createSplashScreenNodes()** and **.addNodesToStackPane()** methods, which use these new classes (objects).

The JavaFX Pos Class: Generalized Screen Position Constants

The **Pos** class is an **Enum<Pos>** class, which stands for "enumeration." This class contains a list of **constants** that are translated into integer values for use in the code. The constant values (in this case, positioning constants, such as TOP, CENTER, and BASELINE) make it easier for programmers to use these values in their code.

The Java class extension hierarchy for the Pos class starts at the java.lang.Object masterclass and progresses to the java.lang.Enum<Pos> class, finally ending with the **javafx.geometry.Pos** class. As Figure 6-4 demonstrates (l. 6), Pos is in the JavaFX geometry package and uses the following subclass hierarchy structure:

```
java.lang.Object
  > java.lang.Enum<Pos>
  > javafx.geometry.Pos
```

The Pos class has a set of constants for providing a generalized horizontal and vertical positioning and alignment (see Table 6-1). As you will see in the next section, you will have to use an Insets class and object to obtain the pixel-accurate positioning that you desire. You will employ the BOTTOM_LEFT constant to position the Button control bank in the bottom-left corner of the splash screen.

Table 6-1. *Pos Class Enum Constants That Can Be Used for Positioning and Alignment in JavaFX*

Pos Constant	Positioning Result (Object)
BASELINE_CENTER	On the baseline, vertically; at the center, horizontally
BASELINE_LEFT	On the baseline, vertically; on the left, horizontally
BASELINE_RIGHT	On the baseline, vertically; on the right, horizontally
BOTTOM_CENTER	On the bottom, vertically; at the center, horizontally
BOTTOM_LEFT	On the bottom, vertically; on the left, horizontally
BOTTOM_RIGHT	On the bottom, vertically; on the right, horizontally
CENTER	At the center, vertically and horizontally
CENTER_LEFT	At the center, vertically; on the left, horizontally
CENTER_RIGHT	At the center, vertically; on the right, horizontally
TOP_CENTER	At the top, vertically; at the center, horizontally
TOP_LEFT	At the top, vertically; on the left, horizontally
TOP_RIGHT	At the top, vertically; on the right, horizontally

Because the Pos class offers generalized positioning, it should be used in conjunction with the **Insets** class to effect pixel-precise positioning. Let's take a look at the Insets class next, as it is also in the **javafx.geometry** package.

The JavaFX Insets Class: Providing Padding Values for Your UI

The **Insets** class is a **public** class that directly extends the java.lang.Object masterclass, meaning that the Insets class was coded from scratch to provide insets, or **offsets** inside a rectangular area. Imagine a picture frame in which you place a mat, or an attractive border between the frame on the outside and the picture on the inside. This is what the Insets class does with two constructor methods: one provides **equal**, or even, insets, and the other, **unequal**, or uneven, insets.

You will be using the constructor that offers **unequal** insets values, which would look very unprofessional if you were framing a picture! The Java class hierarchy for the Insets class starts with the **java.lang.Object** master class and uses this class to create the **javafx.geometry.Insets** class. As Figure 6-4 illustrates (l. 5), Insets is contained in the JavaFX geometry package, just like the Pos class, and uses the following class hierarchy structure:

```
java.lang.Object
  > javafx.geometry.Insets
```

The Insets class furnishes a set of four double offset values specifying the four sides (**top**, **right**, **bottom**, **left**) of a rectangle, which should be specified in that order within the constructor method. You will be using the Insets class (object) to fine-tune the position of the Button control bank, which you will be creating using the HBox layout container. Think of these Insets objects as a way to draw a box inside another box, which shows the spacing that you want the objects inside the rectangle to "respect" around its edges. The simple constructor for an Insets object would use the following format:

```
Insets(double topRightBottomLeft)
```

This constructor uses a single value for all the spacing sides (topRightBottomLeft), and an overloaded constructor allows you to specify each of these values separately, like this:

```
Insets(double top, double right, double bottom, double left)
```

These values need to be specified in this order. An easy way to remember this is by using an analog clock. A clock has "12" at the top, "3" at the right, "6" at the bottom, and "9" at the left. So, starting at high noon (for you western genre lovers out there), always work clockwise, the way the hands move around a clockface, and you will have a great way to remember how to specify the Insets values in the "uneven values" constructor method. You will soon be using the Insets class to position the Button control bank, which are initially "stuck" in the bottom-left corner of the splash screen design, away from the left-hand side and bottom of the screen, using two of these four insets positioning parameters.

The JavaFX HBox Class: Using a Layout Container in a Design

Because Button objects cannot be positioned easily, I will be placing the four Button objects in a **layout container** from the **javafx.scene.layout** package called **HBox**, which stands for **Horizontal Box**. This **public** class arranges things in a row, and because you want the buttons to be aligned at the bottom of the splash screen, you use the Parent node for four Button control nodes, which will become children (**leaf** nodes) of this HBox **branch** node. This will create a bank of UI buttons that can be positioned (moved around) together as a single unit of the splash screen design.

An **HBox** class is a **public** class that directly extends the javafx.layout.Pane superclass, which in turn extends a javafx.layout.Region superclass. The javafx.layout.Region superclass extends a javafx.scene.parent superclass, which in turn extends a javafx.scene.Node superclass, which extends the java.lang.Object masterclass. As Figure 6-4 shows (l. 11), HBox is contained in the javafx.scene.layout package, just like the StackPane class, and it uses the following class hierarchy structure:

```
java.lang.Object
  > javafx.scene.Node
    > javafx.scene.Parent
      > javafx.scene.layout.Region
        > javafx.scene.layout.Pane
          > javafx.scene.layout.HBox
```

If an HBox has a **border** or a **padding** value specified, the contents of your HBox layout container will respect that border or padding specification. A padding value is specified using the Insets class, which you will be using for exactly this fine-tuned UI control bank application.

You will use the HBox class (object), along with the Pos class constant and the Insets class (object), to group the UI Button objects together and, later, to fine-tune their position as a Button control bank. This HBox layout container will thus become the Parent node (or a branch node) for the Button UI controls (or leaf nodes).

Think of an HBox object as a way to **array** children objects **horizontally**, in a row. These could be your image assets, which would use the basic HBox constructor (with zero spacing), or UI controls, such as buttons, arranged next to each other but spaced apart, using one of the overloaded constructors. The simplest constructor for an HBox object creation would use the following **empty** constructor method call format:

```
HBox()
```

The overloaded constructor that you will be employing for your HBox object creation will use a spacing value to put some space between the child Button objects inside the HBox, with the following constructor method call format:

```
HBox(double spacing)
```

There are also two other overloaded constructor method call formats. These will allow you to specify the children Node objects (in this case, Button objects) inside the constructor method call itself, as follows:

```
HBox(double spacing, Nodes... children)  - or, with zero spacing value in between Node objects:
```

```
HBox(Nodes... children)
```

You are going to be using the "long form," and **.getChildren().addAll()** method chain, in your code, but you could also declare the HBox, and its Button Node objects, by using the following constructor:

```
HBox buttonContainer = new HBox(12, gameButton, helpButton, scoreButton, legalButton);
```

The HBox layout container will control resizing of child elements, based on different screen sizes, aspect ratios, and physical resolutions if the child objects are set to be resizable. If the HBox area will accommodate the child objects' preferred widths, they will be set to that value. In addition, a **fillHeight** attribute (boolean variable) is set to **true**, as the default value, specifying whether a child object should fill (scale up to) the HBox height value.

Alignment of an HBox is controlled by the **alignment** attribute (property or variable), which defaults to the **TOP_LEFT** constant from the Pos class (**Pos.TOP_LEFT**). If an HBox is sized above its specified width, the child objects use their preferred width values, and the extra space goes unused. It is important to note that the HBox layout engine will lay out the managed child elements, regardless of their **visibility** attribute (property or variable) setting.

Now that I have discussed the JavaFX geometry and layout classes, which you will be using to create the UI (a bank of Button objects) design, let's take a look at the digital image–related classes, from the javafx.scene.image package, which will allow you to implement the digital image–compositing pipeline that you will put in place behind these four JavaFX Button UI control element objects held inside an HBox UI layout container object.

The JavaFX Image Class: Referencing Digital Images in a Design

The **Image** class is a **public** class that directly extends the java.lang.Object masterclass, meaning that the Image class was also coded from scratch to provide image loading (referencing) and scaling (resizing). You can lock the aspect ratio for scaling and specify the scaling algorithm (quality) as well. All URLs that are supported by the java.net.URL class are supported. This means that you can load images from the Internet (`www.servername.com/image.png`); from the OS (file:image.png); or from the JAR file, using a forward slash (/image.png).

The Java class hierarchy for the Image class starts with the **java.lang.Object** master class and uses this class to create the **javafx.scene.image.Image** class. As Figure 6-4 shows (l. 9), Image is contained in the JavaFX image package, just like the ImageView class, and uses the following class hierarchy structure:

```
java.lang.Object
  > javafx.scene.image.Image
```

The Image class supplies six different (overloaded) **Image()** constructor methods. These take anything from a simple URL to a set of parameter values specifying the **URL**, **width**, **height**, **aspectRatioLock**, **smoothing**, and **preload** options. These should be specified in that order within the constructor method, as you will soon see, when you write an Image() constructor using the most complicated of all the constructor methods, which has the following format:

```
Image(String url, double requestedWidth, double requestedHeight, boolean preserveRatio, boolean smooth, boolean backgroundLoading)
```

The simple constructor for an Image object specifies only the URL and uses the following format:

```
Image(String url)
```

If you want to load an image and also have the constructor method scale the image to a different width and height (usually, this is smaller, to save memory), while locking (preserving) the aspect ratio, using the highest-quality resampling (smooth-pixel scaling), that Image object constructor uses the following format:

```
Image(String url, double scaleWidth, double scaleHeight, boolean preserveAspect, boolean smooth)
```

If you want to load an image in the background (**asynchronously**), using its "native," or physical, resolution and native aspect ratio, the Image() constructor uses the following format:

```
Image(String url, boolean backgroundLoading)
```

Two Image() constructor methods also use the java.io.InputStream class, which furnishes a real-time stream (like streaming video or audio, only customized for a Java application) of input data to the Image() constructor method. These two Image object constructor formats take the following formats (simple and complex):

```
Image(InputStream is) // This is the simple format. The complex format would thus be as follows:
```

```
Image(InputStream is, double newWidth, double newHeight, boolean preserveAspect, boolean smooth)
```

Therefore, the Image class (object) is used to prepare a digital image asset for use, that is, to read its data from a URL; resize them, if necessary (using whatever smoothing and aspect ratio lock you like); and load them asynchronously, while other things are going on in your application. It is important to note that the Image class (or object) does not display an image asset: the Image class just loads it; scales it, if needed; and places it in system memory to be used in your application.

To display an Image object, you will need to use a second class (object), called an ImageView class. The ImageView object can be used as a node on your Scene Graph and references and then "paints" the Image object data onto the layout container, which holds the ImageView node (in this case, a StackPane Scene Graph root and Parent node to the leaf ImageView node). I will be covering the ImageView class in the next section.

From a digital image–compositing perspective, the StackPane class (object) is the image-compositing engine, or layer manager, if you will, and each ImageView object represents an individual layer in the layer stack. An Image object contains the digital image data in the ImageView layer or in more than one ImageView, if needed, as the Image objects and the ImageView objects are decoupled and exist independently of each other.

133

JavaFX ImageView Class: Displaying Digital Images in a Design

The **ImageView** class is a **public** class that directly extends the javafx.scene.Node superclass, which is an extension of the java.lang.Object (see Chapter 4). The ImageView object is therefore a type of **Node** object in the JavaFX Scene Graph that is used for painting a view, using the data contained in an Image object. The class has methods that allow image resampling (resizing), and, as with the Image class, you can lock the aspect ratio for scaling as well as specify the resampling algorithm (smoothing quality).

The Java class hierarchy for the ImageView class starts with the **java.lang.Object** master class and uses this class to create the **javafx.scene.Node** class, which is then employed to create an ImageView Node subclass. As Figure 6-4 illustrates (l. 10), like the Image class, ImageView is contained in the JavaFX image package. The ImageView class uses the following Java class inheritance hierarchy structure:

```
java.lang.Object
  > javafx.scene.Node
  > javafx.scene.image.ImageView
```

The ImageView class provides three different (overloaded) **ImageView()** constructor methods. These range from an empty constructor (which is the one you are going to use later on, in your code); to one that takes an Image object as its parameter; to one that takes a URL String object as the parameter and creates the Image object automatically. To create an ImageView object, the simple (empty) ImageView() constructor method uses the following format:

```
ImageView()
```

You will be employing this constructor method so that I can show you how to use the **.setImage()** method call to load an Image object into an ImageView object. If you want to avoid using the .setImage() method call, you can use the overloaded constructor method, which has the following format:

```
ImageView(Image image)
```

So, to set up an ImageView "explicitly" and wire it to the Image object looks like this:

```
splashScreenBackplate = new ImageView();       // This uses the empty constructor method approach
splashScreenBackplate.setImage(splashScreen);
```

You can condense this into one line of code, using an overloaded constructor method, structured as follows:

```
splashScreenBackplate = new ImageView(splashScreen);  // using the overloaded constructor method
```

If you want to bypass the process of creating and loading an Image object, there is a constructor method for that as well, which uses the following format:

```
ImageView(String url)
```

To load an image in the background (**asynchronously**), using its native (default) resolution and native aspect ratio, the Image() constructor uses the following format:

```
splashScreen = new Image("/invincibagelsplash.png", 640, 400, true, false, true);
splashScreenBackplate = new ImageView();
splashScreenBackplate.setImage(splashScreen);    // uses the empty constructor method approach
```

If you did not want to specify the image dimensions, background image loading, and smooth scaling, or lock the aspect ratio for any scaling, you could condense the previous three lines of Java code into the following constructor:

```
splashScreenBackplate = new ImageView("/invincibagel.png");    // uses third constructor method
```

At least initially (for learning purposes), I am going to do this the long way, and I will always explicitly load Image objects, using the Image() constructor method, so that you can specify all the different attributes and see all the different image assets that you are using in this Java programming logic. I want to show you the shortcut code here, because you will be using this approach later in the book, once you start using ImageViews as sprites (see Chapter 8). You can use this shortcut approach with your sprites because you will not be scaling them and because they are so highly optimized that background loading will not be necessary.

Next, let's take a quick look at the TableView class, which will hold the high scores table. Although you will not be implementing this here, I will cover the class, as it is part of the top-level UI design that you are creating and implementing in this chapter.

The JavaFX TableView Class: Displaying Data Tables in a Design

The **TableView** class is a **public** class that directly extends the **javafx.scene.control.Control** superclass, which is an extension of javafx.scene.layout.Region. javafx.scene.layout.Region is an extension of the javafx.scene.Parent, which is an extension of the javafx.scene.Node Scene Graph superclass (see Chapter 4). A TableView<S> object is therefore a type of UI control (a table) and a Node object in the JavaFX Scene Graph that is used for constructing a table, using S objects, each of which contains data to be displayed in a table. You will be writing data into a TableView<S> object later in the book, using these S objects, after scores have been achieved that eclipse those currently listed in the table.

The Java class hierarchy for the TableView class starts with the **java.lang.Object** master class and uses this class to create the **javafx.scene.Node** class, which is then used to create a Parent class. This is used to create a Region class, which in turn creates a Control class, which is used to create the TableView class. The TableView class has the following Java class inheritance hierarchy structure:

```
java.lang.Object
  > javafx.scene.Node
    > javafx.scene.Parent
      > javafx.scene.layout.Region
        > javafx.scene.control.Control
          > javafx.scene.control.TableView<S>
```

The TableView class provides two different (overloaded) **TableView()** constructor methods, an empty constructor and a constructor that takes an **ObservableList<S>** object, filled with Table data items as a parameter. A simple (empty) TableView() constructor method to create an empty TableView object will use the following format:

```
TableView()
```

The second constructor type uses an **ObservableList<E>** class (object) from the **javafx.collections** package, which is a type of list that allows a data change event listener to track any changes in the list as they occur. This TableView object constructor method call uses the following format:

```
TableView(ObservableList<S> items)
```

I think that is enough class background information for now, so let's get into writing the code for your first **.createSplashScreenNodes()** method, which will instantiate and set up all the Node objects for your Scene Graph!

Scene Graph Nodes: .createSplashScreenNodes()

The first thing you will want to do with your createSplashScreenNodes() method is code the empty method structure and add the Node object creation code that already exists in the bootstrap code that was generated for you by NetBeans in Chapter 2. This includes the Node objects for the Button node, the StackPane root node, and the Scene object named scene. You will keep the primaryStage code in the .start() method because that object is created using the .start(Stage primaryStage) constructor method call. The Button object has already been renamed gameButton (it was btn), so you have three lines of object instantiation code and a line of configuration code, as follows:

```
root = new StackPane();
scene = new Scene(root, 640, 400);
gameButton = new Button();
gameButton.setText("PLAY GAME");
```

It is important to note that because the root StackPane object is used in the constructor method call for the scene Scene object, this line of code needs to come first (your root object has to be created before it is used!). The next thing you need to create is the HBox layout container object that will hold your four Button UI controls. You will also set the alignment attribute for the HBox; add an Insets object to contain the padding values; and then add this padding to the4 HBox object, using these four lines of Java code:

```
buttonContainer = new HBox(12);
buttonContainer.setAlignment(Pos.BOTTOM_LEFT);
buttonContainerPadding = new Insets(0, 0, 10, 16);
buttonContainer.setpadding(buttonContainerPadding);
```

Next, let's take a handy programmers' shortcut and copy and paste the two gameButton (instantiation and configuration) lines of code below the HBox code (because the buttons are inside the HBox, this is just for visual organization, not to make the code work) and then copy and paste them three more times, on separate lines. This will allow you to change the game to help, score, and legal, respectively, by creating the following four button Java codes:

```
gameButton = new Button();
gameButton.setText("PLAY GAME");
helpButton = new Button();
helpButton.setText("INSTRUCTIONS");
scoreButton = new Button();
scoreButton.setText("HIGH SCORES");
legalButton = new Button();
legalButton.setText("LEGAL & CREDITS");
```

Now that you have created the HBox Button UI control layout container and buttons, you still need to write one more line of code to fill the HBox with Button objects, using the .getChildren().addAll() method chain, like this:

```
buttonContainer.getChildren().addAll(gameButton, helpButton, scoreButton, legalButton);
```

Next, let's add your image-compositing Node objects (Image and ImageView) so that you can add the artwork for your InvinciBagel splash screen as well as the panel overlays that will decorate your instructions, legal disclaimers and production credits and a background and screen title for your (eventual) game high scores table. I use two ImageView objects to contain these two layers; let's set up the bottommost backplate image layer first by using the following Java code to instantiate the Image object and then the ImageView object and wire them together:

```
splashScreen = new Image("/invincibagelsplash.png", 640, 400, true, false, true);
splashScreenBackplate = new ImageView();
splashScreenBackplate.setImage(splashScreen);    // this Java statement connects the two objects
```

Finally, let's do the same thing for the image-compositing plate, that is, the ImageView that will hold the different Image objects containing the alpha channel (transparency) values that will create an overlay of panel images for the InvinciBagel splash screen artwork (which was created by the talented 2D artist Patrick Harrington):

```
instructionLayer = new Image("/invincibagelinstruct.png", 640, 400, true, false, true);
splashScreenTextArea = new ImageView();
splashScreenTextArea.setImage(instructionLayer); // this Java statement connects the two objects
```

As Figure 6-7 demonstrates, your Scene Graph node creation (seen at the top of the InvinciBagel class) and the Node object instantiation and configuration (seen in the createSplashScreenNodes() method) are in place and error free. You still need to add in the Image objects for the other two screens, but there is enough code here to be able to add these Node objects to the Scene Graph, using the **addNodesToStackPane()** method, and then test the code to make sure that it is working. According to the NetBeans IDE, this code is error free!

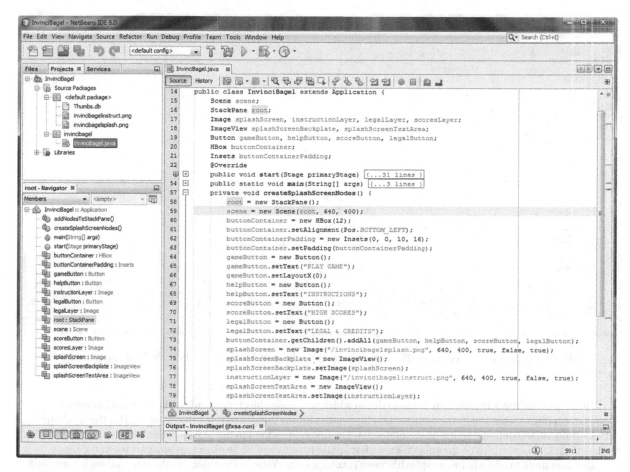

Figure 6-7. *Coding the createSplashScreenNodes() method; instantiating and configuring the nodes in the Scene Graph*

Next, let's add the Node objects to the StackPane Scene Graph root object in an addNodesToStackPane() method.

Adding Nodes to the Scene Graph: .addStackPaneNodes()

Finally, you have to create a method that will add the Node objects that you have created to the Scene Graph root, which, in this case, is a StackPane object. You will use the .getChildren().add() method chain to add the children Node objects to the parent StackPane root Scene Graph node. This is done via three simple lines of Java code, like this:

```
root.getChildren().add(splashScreenBackplate);
root.getChildren().add(splashScreenTextArea);
root.getChildren().add(buttonContainer);
```

As you can see in Figure 6-8, the Java code is error free, and the root object sees its declaration at the top of the class. Clicking the root object in the code creates this highlighting, which traces the use of the object through the code. This is a pretty cool NetBeans 8.0 trick that you should use whenever you want to track an object in code.

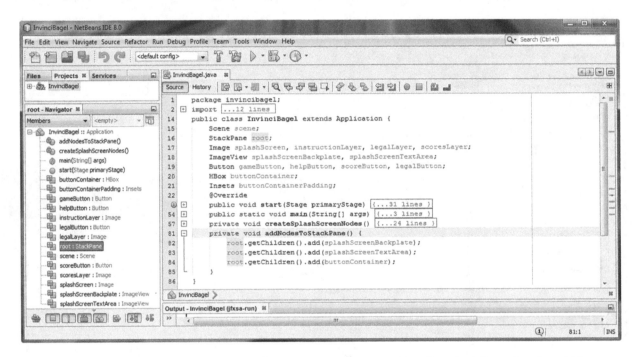

Figure 6-8. *Coding the addNodesToStackPane() method, using the .getChildren() method chained to the .add() method*

The important thing to note here is the **order** in which the Node objects were added to the StackPane root Scene Graph object. This affects the compositing layer order for the image compositing, as well as for the UI element compositing, on top of these digital image elements. The first node added to the StackPane will be on the **bottom** of the layer stack; this needs to be the **splashScreenBackplate** ImageView Node object, as you can see in the figure.

The next node to add will be the **splashScreenTextArea** ImageView Node object, as the transparent images with the panel overlays need to go right on top of Pat Harrington's InvinciBagel splash screen 2D artwork. After this, you can place the UI design, which, in this case can be done in one fell swoop, using the **buttonContainer** HBox Node object, which contains all the Button objects. Note that you do not have to add buttons to this StackPane root Scene Graph object, because you have already used the **.getChildren().addAll()** method chain to add your Button UI controls to the Scene Graph hierarchy below an HBox (Parent object) Node branch object. Now, you are ready to test!

Testing the InvinciBagel Application: Pulse the Scene Graph

Click the green **Play** arrow at the top of the NetBeans IDE, and **run** the **project**. This will bring up the window illustrated in Figure 6-9 (I have removed the Java code added in Chapter 4, demonstrating how to create a windowless application). So, you have window "chrome" back, at least for now. As you can see, you are getting a very good result, using only a dozen import statements (external classes), a few dozen lines of Java code, and a half a dozen child nodes below the Scene Graph root (StackPane) object. As you can see, JavaFX does a great job of compositing the backplate, composite image overlays, and button bank overlay into one seamless, professional result!

Figure 6-9. *Run the InvinciBagel application, and make sure that the StackPane compositing class is working correctly*

Because you only copied and pasted the EventHandler routines for each button, and changed your Button objects' names but not the code inside these routines, the Button objects will still work properly (writing text to the console) and not cause compiler errors. However, they will not do what you want them to do, which is to change an image overlay so that the panel on the left-hand side of the design holds a title and text that you want it to show a user.

This will be done using a call to the .setImage() method, which will set the splashScreenTextArea ImageView object to the instructionLayer, scoresLayer, or legalLayer Image object, based on which Button UI control is clicked by the user. You cannot implement this event-handling code until you add the last two Image object instantiations!

Finishing an InvinciBagel UI Screen Design: Add Images

Let's finish with the createSplashScreenNodes() method by adding two more lines at the end of the method that add two more Image objects, referencing the **invincibagelcreds.png** and **invincibagelscores.png** 32-bit PNG32 digital image assets. This is done by employing the following two lines of Java object instantiation code using the new keyword:

```
legalLayer = new Image( "/invincibagelcreds.png", 640, 400, true, false, true );
scoresLayer = new Image( "/invincibagelscores.png", 640, 400, true, false, true );
```

As Figure 6-10 shows, the code is error free, because you have copied the four PNG files into your project's /src folder. You do not need the other lines of code (ImageView object instantiation, .setImage()), because you will be using the splashScreenTextArea ImageView object to hold these last two Image objects. Thus, you are saving on Scene Graph Node objects used, as you are using a single ImageView Scene Graph Node object to display three different Image objects (overlays), based on button events.

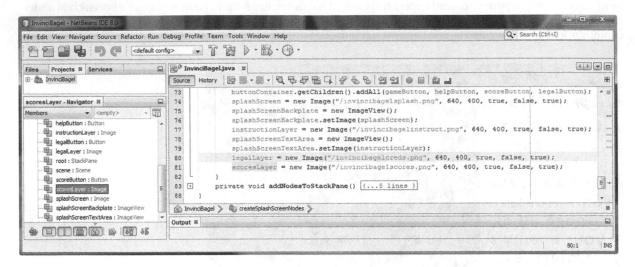

Figure 6-10. *Adding legalLayer and scoresLayer Image object instantiations to add the other image composite plates*

This means that the **splashScreenTextArea.setImage()** method calls you will make off the **splashScreenTextArea** ImageView object will be placed inside the ActionEvent EventHandler programming constructs for the three Button objects that trigger image composite overlays when they are clicked. The fourth Button object will start up game play, so, for now, you will just have a Java comment in that button event-handling structure, making it an "empty" logic structure. Now, let's take a look at how to finish coding these EventHandler constructs so that you can finish this UI design and get on with creating the game play engines mentioned earlier.

Interactivity: Wiring the InvinciBagel Buttons for Use

You need to replace the system writing to the console code in all these duplicated button event-handling structures with calls to the .setImage() method so that you can set the image-compositing plate ImageView to the Image object that holds the digital image asset you want to overlay the InvinciBagel backplate artwork created by Pat Harrington. You have already written this code construct twice in the createSplashScreenNodes() method, so you can copy the line of code directly above the two Image object instantiations you just wrote, if you want a shortcut.

The **.setOnAction()** event-handling Java code structures would therefore look like this:

```
helpButton.setOnAction(new EventHandler<ActionEvent>() {
    @Override
    public void handle(ActionEvent event) {
        splashScreenTextArea.setImage(instructionLayer);
    }
});
```

```
scoreButton.setOnAction(new EventHandler<ActionEvent>() {
    @Override
    public void handle(ActionEvent event) {
        splashScreenTextArea.setImage(scoresLayer);
    }
});
legalButton.setOnAction(new EventHandler<ActionEvent>() {
    @Override
    public void handle(ActionEvent event) {
        splashScreenTextArea.setImage(legalLayer);
    }
});
```

As Figure 6-11 demonstrates, your event-handling code is error free, and you are ready to run and test again!

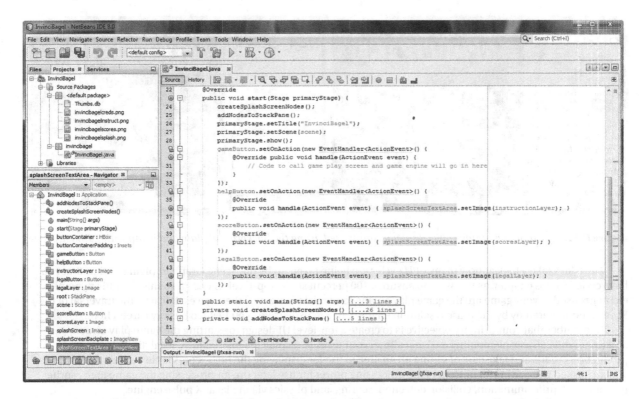

Figure 6-11. *Modify the body of the .handle() method for each of four Button controls to complete the infrastructure*

As you can see, you are leaving the gameButton.setOnAction() event-handling structure empty for now; in the next chapter, you will create the primary game play surface and a pulse event-processing engine (structure) that will run this game by calling the various functional engines that you will be writing over the course of the book.

You are leaving the bottom part of the high scores screen blank for now as well so that you can overlay the two ImageView layers with a TableView Node object in your Scene Graph root StackPane. You will complete this composite for the High Scores button UI element later on after you finish developing your Java 8 game.

Now, it is time for the final testing of the top-level UI part of your game application to make sure that all the UI button elements (objects) function properly and do what you have designed (coded) them to do. After that, you will be running the NetBeans 8.0 Profiler again to ensure that the Scene Graph hierarchy that you have just created is indeed leaving 99 percent of the available CPU processing power for the game engines that you will be creating from here on.

Testing the Final InvinciBagel UI Design

Again, click the green **Play** arrow at the top of NetBeans IDE 8.0, and **run** your **project**. This will bring up the windows demonstrated in Figure 6-12. As you can see, when you click the **Legal and Credits** button UI element, the overlay makes a seamless composite with the InvinciBagel artwork backplate, as shown on the left-hand side of the figure, and when the **High Scores** button UI element (control) is clicked, the high scores table background is put in place, as displayed on the right-hand side of the figure. As you can see, the classes from the **javafx.image** package provide a pristine result with regard to compositing

Figure 6-12. *The other two Image objects shown composited, using the background plate and compositing ImageViews*

Next, let's take a look at how many CPU cycles are being taken up by the Scene Graph implementation that you have coded in this chapter, as you want to ensure a 100 percent static, top-level UI design so that the only dynamic elements used in your game are the game play engine (and related engines) themselves. Because the traversal of the Scene Graph hierarchy by the pulse resolution engine can get "expensive," you need to be very careful here!

Remember that your primary objective is to create a top-level UI design for starting the game play screen and loop, while also implementing a UI that allows your users to display the instructions, legal disclaimers, and production credits and take care of setting up an area to use for displaying the high scores table. At the same time, you are tasked with saving 99 percent of the processing power for use later on, for processing the game logic, sprite movements, sprite animation, collision detection, scoring, and physics via the JavaFX pulse engine.

Profiling the InvinciBagel Scene Graph for Pulse Efficiency

It is important that the game UI design not take any processing power away from the CPU, as the game engine is going to need all of it. As Figure 6-13 reveals, you can use the **Profile > Profile Project (InvinciBagel)** menu sequence to run the Profiler and take a screenshot of the CPU statistics for the current (top-level UI) application.

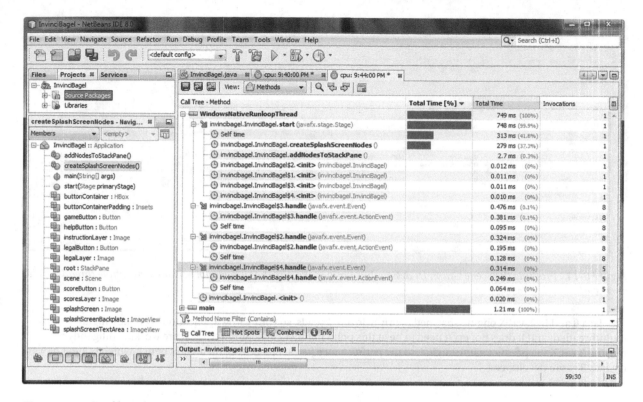

Figure 6-13. *Profiling the Scene Graph UI design thus far to make sure that it does not use any perceptible CPU cycles*

As you can see in the **Total Time** column, on the right-hand side of the figure, the createSplashScreenNodes() method takes 279 milliseconds, or approximately three-tenths of a second, to execute, and your Scene Graph is created. The addNodesToStackPane() method takes approximately 3 milliseconds, or three one-thousandths of a second, to execute.

If you look at the threads profiling output and click the UI button elements, you will see a blip of color appear on the thread, showing the processing overhead of a button click, which, as you can see, is less than one-tenth of a second per click (look at the **Invocations** column, on the far right, to see how many times I tested the button click functions). I highlighted the threads view, where I clicked High Scores, and then the Legal and Credits button UI elements (see Figure 6-14). As you can see in this view as well, the current design is using minimal resources.

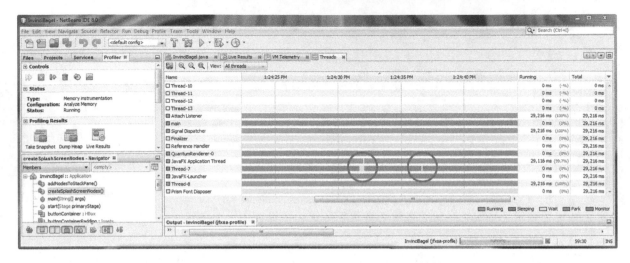

Figure 6-14. *Profiling the Scene Graph UI design thus far to make sure that it does not use any perceptible thread overhead*

Java 8 and its JavaFX engine spawned nearly a dozen threads, so your game application is already highly multithreaded, and it does not even need to be at this point in time! The teams at Oracle are working diligently at making JavaFX the premier game engine, so the performance just keeps getting better and better, which is great news for Java 8 game developers!

Summary

In this sixth chapter, you got your hands dirty doing the actual **top-level UI design** for your game as well as outlining the underlying **game engine component design** and figuring out the most efficient **Scene Graph node design**. Then, you got back into Java 8 game programming and redesigned your existing bootstrap Java 8 code, originally created by NetBeans 8.0.

Because this NetBeans-generated Java code design was not optimal for your purposes, you rewrote it completely to make it more organized. You did this by creating two custom Java methods, **.createSplashScreenNodes()** and **.addNodesToStackPane()**, to **modularize** the Scene Graph node creation process as well as the adding of the three Parent (and leaf) Node objects to the Scene Graph **root** (in this case, the **StackPane** object, which you are using for its multilayer UI object-compositing capability).

Next, you learned about some of the JavaFX classes for implementing these new methods, including the **Pos** class and the **Insets** class, from the **javafx.geometry** package; the **Image** and the **ImageView** class, from the **javafx.scene. image** package; the **HBox** class, from the **javafx.scene.layout** package; and the **TableView** class, from the **javafx. scene.control** package. You coded the new .createSplashScreenNodes() method, which instantiated and configured the HBox object, using the Insets object, and then the Image and ImageView objects and the four Button objects. Once all these Scene Graph nodes were instantiated and configured, you wrote an .addNodesToStackPane() method to add Node objects to the StackPane root object so that they would be displayed by the Stage object, which references the Scene Graph's root object. Next, you tested your top-level game application UI design. Then, you added in the last couple of Image objects and added ActionEvent EventHandler program logic. Finally, you profiled the application to make sure it was efficient.

In the next chapter, I will present the **JavaFX** pulse engine and the AnimationTimer class so that you can create the **infrastructure** for your Java 8 game engine, which will process your game events in real time.

■ ■ ■

The Foundation of Game Play Loop: The JavaFX Pulse System and the Game Processing Architecture

Now that you have created the top-level UI screens needed for your user to learn how to play the game, start the game, view high scores, and review the legal disclaimers and Ira H. Harrison Rubin's InvinciBagel intellectual property game production credits, let's get down to business and create the game play timing loop for your InvinciBagel game. This is of the greatest importance from a **user experience** standpoint, and is also critical to the proper functioning of the different **game engines** that you will be creating over the course of the remainder of this book, including the **sprite engine**, **collision detection engine**, **animation engine**, **scoring engine**, and **physics engine**. You will always keep **smoothness** of game play in mind; the efficient, optimal implementation of the JavaFX **pulse** system is of paramount importance at this stage of the game (no pun intended). For this reason, I will be going into great detail in this chapter regarding the **javafx.animation** package, and how all of its functional classes differ from each other.

First, you will explore the two **Animation superclasses** in the javafx.animation package: **Animation** and **AnimationTimer**. After that, you will take a look at Animation, **Timeline**, and **Transition** and how these classes, and any of their subclasses, such as **PathAnimation** and **TranslateAnimation**, will allow you to access the JavaFX **pulse event timing system**. Now, you need to use pulse, if you want to create an action-oriented arcade type Java 8 game!

You will also be taking a closer look at the overall structure of the entire javafx.animation package, because you'll need to use one of these classes for your Java 8 game play loop. You will do this by using a diagram of the entire package, so that you can get an overview of how all its classes interrelate. You will then examine the class hierarchies among all of the JavaFX Animation classes, in detail. With the exception of **AnimationTimer**, **Interpolator**, **KeyFrame**, and **KeyValue**, all of these javafx.animation package classes are subclassed (using the Java extends keyword) using the JavaFX Animation superclass.

Finally, you will be adding the new **GamePlayLoop.java** class into your invincibagel package, which will be created as a GamePlayLoop object in the InvinciBagel.java Application subclass, implementing the **timing loop**. This GamePlayLoop class will contain a **.handle()** method, as well as a **.start()** method and a **.stop()** method, which will allow you to control your GamePlayLoop **timing events** when the GamePlayLoop is operational, and to determine when it is latent (stopped or paused).

I will create a diagram that will show the class and object hierarchy for this InvinciBagel game, so that you can start to visualize how these classes that you are coding, and objects that you are creating, will all fit together. It is almost as if the coding of a game using Java 8 and JavaFX is in itself a (puzzle) game! Pretty cool stuff.

Game Loop Processing: Harnessing a JavaFX Pulse

One of the primary questions, even among Oracle employees on the development teams, is which **design approach** to implementing a **game timing loop** engine should be used with classes that are contained in the JavaFX animation package (suite of classes). Indeed, this is precisely what this chapter is all about: using the **javafx.animation** package and its classes, which tap into the **JavaFX pulse event timing engine**. At the top level of the class hierarchy for the package, shown in Figure 7-1, the **AnimationTimer** and **Animation** classes provide the primary way to grab hold of these pulse events so that they do your real-time processing for you. In this section, you will see how they differ and what they have been designed for, including the kinds of games they should be used for. With the exception of **Interpolator** (motion curve application), **KeyFrame** (keyframe definition), and **KeyValue** (keyframe customization), all the classes in the javafx.animation package can be used to harness pulse events.

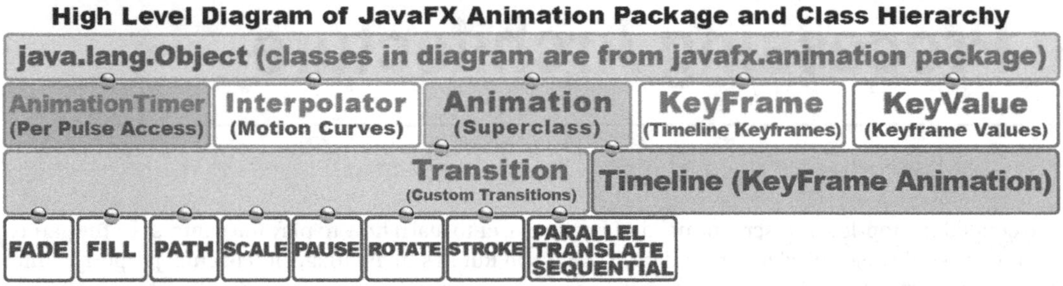

High Level Diagram of JavaFX Animation Package and Class Hierarchy

java.lang.Object (classes in diagram are from javafx.animation package)				
AnimationTimer (Per Pulse Access)	**Interpolator** (Motion Curves)	**Animation** (Superclass)	**KeyFrame** (Timeline Keyframes)	**KeyValue** (Keyframe Values)
		Transition (Custom Transitions)	**Timeline (KeyFrame Animation)**	
FADE FILL PATH SCALE PAUSE ROTATE STROKE		PARALLEL TRANSLATE SEQUENTIAL		

***Figure 7-1.** Javafx.animation package subclass hierarchy; top level classes all coded from scratch with java.lang.Object*

There are four basic approaches to implementing (accessing) the JavaFX pulse event timing system to create a game timing loop. These different approaches apply to the different types of game play, which I discussed previously (see Chapter 5). These game play types range from static games (board games, puzzle games) that need to use the pulse event engine to implement special effects (**Transition** subclasses) or custom animations (**Timeline** class, in conjunction with the **KeyFrame** class and possibly the **KeyValue** class) to highly dynamic games that need no-frills core access to the pulse event system at the full 60 times per second game play refresh rate (**AnimationTimer** class).

The highest level (visually, the lowest level, shown at the bottom left of the figure) is the use of **prebuilt Transition subclasses** in the javafx.animation package, such as the **PathTransition** class (or object), for the path of the game sprites or projectiles, or TranslateTransition, which translates (moves) things on the screen. All these Transition subclasses are coded for you; all you have to do is use them, which is why I am labeling this the highest functional level, in this particular discussion. With this high level of prebuilt functionality comes a memory and processing price; this is because, as you know from what you learned about Java inheritance (see Chapter 3), the PathTransition class contains all its methods, variables, and constants as well as those from all the classes above it in the class hierarchy.

This means that the entire PathTransition class, the Transition superclass, the Animation superclass, and the java.lang.Object masterclass are all contained within the memory footprint for this class and potentially the processing overhead, too, depending on how the object is implemented using the class. This is something to consider, as the lower down you go in the JavaFX animation package, the more expensive it is and the more control you give the code that has been written for you rather than custom code you are writing yourself.

The next-highest-level approach to coding custom game loops is to subclass the **javafx.animation.Transition** class to create your own customized Transition subclass. Both this and the previous level are what would be considered the top-level approaches and would be best applied to games that are static yet animated, or that have a less dynamic game play.

The middle-level solution is to use the **Timeline** class and its related **KeyFrame** and **KeyValue** classes, which are great for implementing the type of timeline-based animation that you see in drag-and-drop tools, such as Flash. As you will find, if you look online at JavaFX game engine discussions, this is a popular approach, as many animations are implemented by creating a single KeyFrame object and then using a TimeLine object to process the pulse events.

Using the Timeline object approach allows you to specify a frame **rate** for processing your game loop, such as 30FPS. This would be appropriate for less dynamic games that can use a lower frame rate, because they do not involve a lot of interframe game processing, such as sprite movement, sprite animation, collision detection, or physics calculation. It is important to note that if you use a **Timeline** object (class), you will be defining variables in system memory for **frame rate** and at least one **KeyFrame** object reference (these are part of the Timeline class definition) as well as properties (variables) inherited from the Animation superclass, such as **status**, **duration**, **delay**, **cycleCount**, **cycleDuration**, **autoReverse**, **currentRate**, **currentTime**, and an **onFinished** (ActionEvent) ObjectProperty.

If you are familiar with creating animations, you will see that Timeline, along with at least one KeyFrame object and potentially a large number of KeyValue objects stored inside each KeyFrame object, is clearly designed for (optimized toward) creating timeline-based animation. Although this is a very powerful feature, it also means that using a Timeline and KeyFrame object for game loop processing will create close to a dozen areas of memory allocation that you may not even use in your game or that may not be designed (coded) optimally for your game design implementation.

Fortunately, there is another javafx.animation package timing-related class that carries none of this prebuilt class overhead, and so I term this the lowest-level approach, in which you have to build all your game processing logic yourself, inside one simple **.handle()** function, which accesses the JavaFX pulse engine on every pass it makes.

The low-level solution involves using the **AnimationTimer** class, so named because Java (Swing) already has a **Timer** class (javax.swing.Timer), as does Java's utility class (java.util.Timer), which you could also use if you were an advanced enough programmer to deal with all the thread synchronization issues (and coding).

Because this is a beginner-level book, you will stick with looping your game using the Java 8 game engine (JavaFX 8). JavaFX has its own Timer class, in the javafx.animation package, called AnimationTimer so as not to cause confusion with Swing GUI Toolkit's Timer class (which is still supported, for legacy code reasons). Many new developers are confused by the "Animation" part of this class name; do not assume that this Timer class is for Animation; it is, at its core, for timing purposes. This class is the lowest-level class in the javafx.animation package, in terms of accessing a JavaFX pulse timing system, and essentially serves just to access the pulse timing system. Absolutely everything else is stripped away.

The AnimationTimer class is therefore the class that will provide you with the least system overhead (memory used) to implement. At the full 60FPS speed, it will have the highest performance, assuming that all the code inside the .handle() method is well optimized. This is the class to use for a fast, high-dynamics game, such as an arcade game or a shooter game. For this reason, this is the class that you are going to use for your game, as you can continue to build a game engine framework and add features without running out of power.

You will use the lowest-level approach throughout this book just in case you are pushing your Java 8 game development to the very limit and are creating a highly dynamic, action-filled game. The JavaFX AnimationTimer superclass is perfect for this type of game application, as it processes its .handle() method on every single JavaFX pulse event. A pulse event is currently throttled at 60FPS, the standard frame rate (also called a refresh rate) for professional action games. You will subclass your GamePlayLoop.java class from the AnimationTimer superclass.

Interestingly, most modern iTV LCD, OLED, and LED display screen products also update at this exact **refresh rate** (60Hz), although newer displays will update at twice this rate (120Hz). Displays with a 240Hz refresh rate are also coming out, but because these 120Hz and 240Hz refresh rate displays use an even multiple (2× or 4×) of 60Hz, 60FPS is a logical frame rate for developing games for today's consumer electronics devices. Next, let's implement the **GamePlayLoop.java** class in your game, which will subclass AnimationTimer to access pulses.

Creating a New Java Class: GamePlayLoop.java

Let's use the AnimationTimer superclass from the javafx.animation package to create a custom **GamePlayLoop** class (and, eventually, object) and the required .handle() method to process your game play calculations. As Figure 7-2 demonstrates, this is done in NetBeans 8.0 by right-clicking the **invincibagel** package folder in your **Projects** hierarchy pane. This will show NetBeans where you want the new Java class to be placed after it is created.

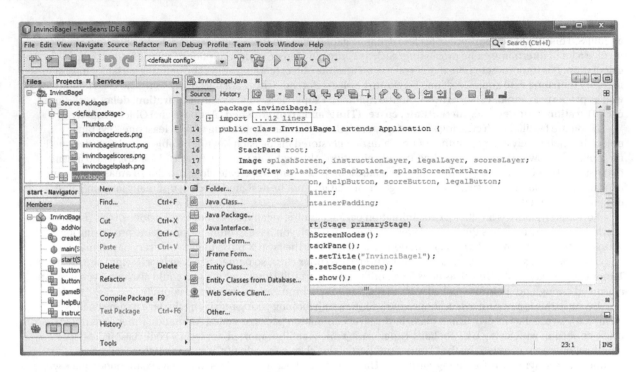

Figure 7-2. *Right-click the invincibagel package folder, and use the New ➤ Java Class menu sequence*

Click **New ➤ Java Class**, which will open the **New Java Class** dialog, seen in Figure 7-3. Name the class **GamePlayLoop**, and leave the other defaults, which NetBeans set, based on your right-clicking the invincibagel package folder, and click **Finish**.

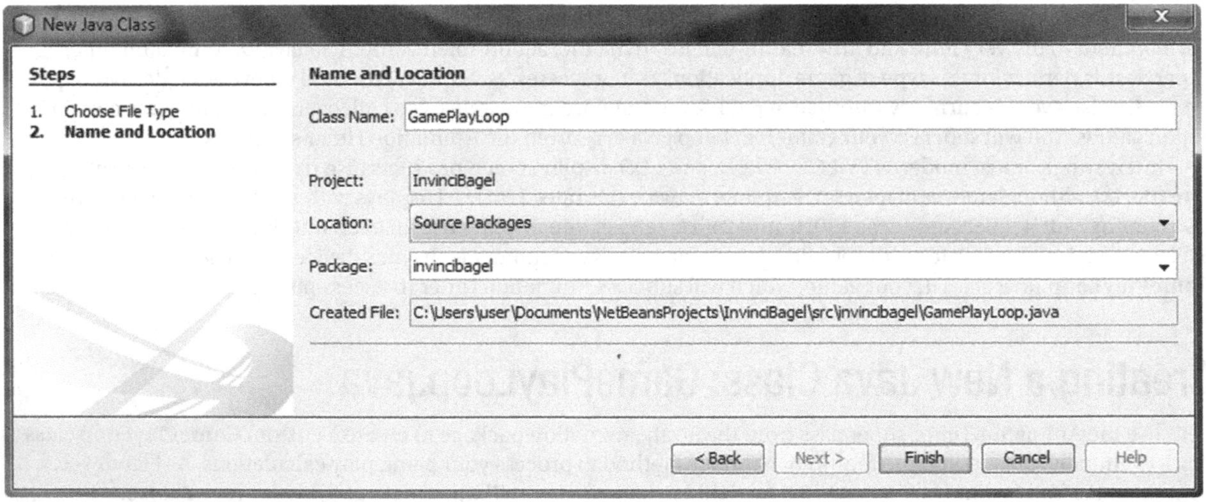

Figure 7-3. *Name the new Java class GamePlayLoop, and let NetBeans set up the other fields*

NetBeans will create a bootstrap infrastructure for the GamePlayLoop.java class, with a package and a class declaration, as illustrated in Figure 7-4. Now, you add an **extends** keyword and AnimationTimer.

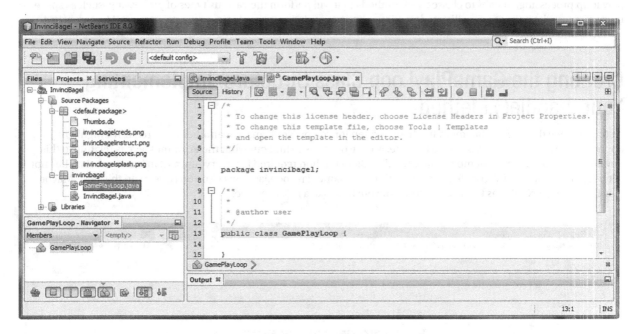

Figure 7-4. *NetBeans creates a GamePlayLoop.java class and opens it in an editing tab in the IDE, for you to edit*

Mouse over the error, press **Alt+Enter**, and select **Add import**, as displayed in Figure 7-5.

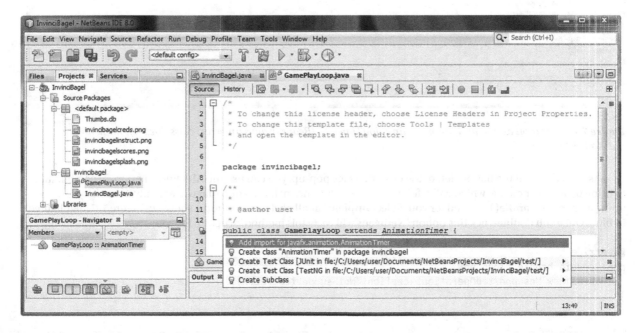

Figure 7-5. *Subclass an AnimationTimer superclass with an extends keyword: press Alt+Enter, and select Add import*

Once NetBeans adds the import javafx.animation.AnimationTimer; programming statement, you will be ready to start creating this class, which will harness the JavaFX pulse engine for you and contain all your core game play loop processing, or calls to classes and methods that will perform the various types of processing, such as sprite movement, sprite animation, collision detection, physics simulation, game logic, audio processing, AI, scoreboard updates, and the like.

Creating the GamePlayLoop Class Structure: Implementing Your .handle() Method

Note that once the import statement has been written for you by NetBeans, yet another wavy red error highlight appears below the GamePlayLoop class name. Mouse over this to find out what the error message is relating to this newest error. As Figure 7-6 demonstrates, the **.handle()** method required for every AnimationTimer subclass has not yet been implemented (also called overridden) in this GamePlayLoop.java class, so you have to do this next. Maybe you can even get NetBeans to write the code for you; let's take a look, and see!

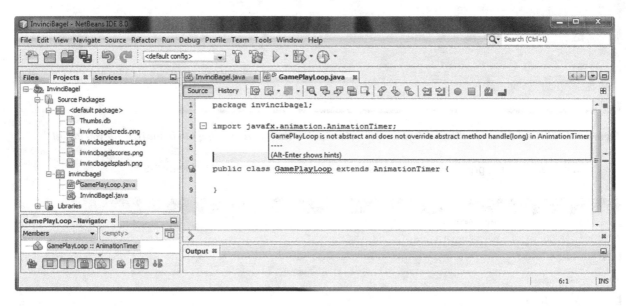

Figure 7-6. *Once you extend and import AnimationTimer, NetBeans throws an error: class does not implement the .handle()*

As you can see at the bottom left of the error message pop-up, you can use the **Alt+Enter** keystroke combination to bring up a helper dialog, which will offer you several solutions, including one that will actually write the unimplemented **.handle()** method for you. Select **Implement all abstract methods**, shown in Figure 7-7, highlighted in blue. Once you double-click this option, NetBeans will write this method structure for you:

```
@Override
public void handle (long now) {
    throw new UnsupportedOperationException("Not supported yet.");
}
```

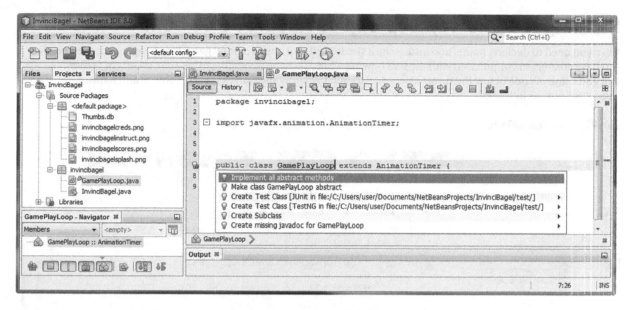

Figure 7-7. *Take a coding shortcut: press Alt+Enter to bring up a helper dialog, and select Implement all abstract methods*

Note that the an **@Override** keyword precedes the **public void handle** method access keyword, return type keyword, and method name. This tells the Java compiler that your .handle() method is going to replace (override) AnimationTimer's .handle() method, which is why the error indicates that you have to **override abstract method .handle(long)**.

You certainly do not want your .handle() method to throw 60 UnsupportedOperationException() errors every single second of your game loop; however, you are going to leave this in there for now so that you can see what it does and also learn a bit more about the NetBeans error console.

As Figure 7-8 demonstrates, once you select the Implement all abstract methods option, the Java code is error free, and the basic package-import-class-method structure for the class is in place. Now, you should be able to create a GamePlayLoop object using this class, so let's switch gears and do some programming in the InvinciBagel Java class, in which you create a GamePlayLoop object, and then profile the application to see what it does.

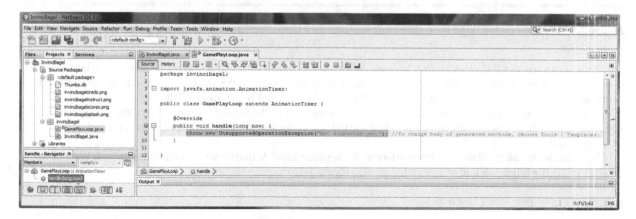

Figure 7-8. *NetBeans creates a public void handle(long now) bootstrap method with UnsupportedOperationException*

Creating a GamePlayLoop Object: Adding Pulse Control

Next, you need to declare, name, and instantiate a GamePlayLoop object named **gamePlayLoop**, using the new class you have created, in conjunction with the Java **new** keyword. Click the InvinciBagel.java tab, shown in Figure 7-9, and add a line of code below the Insets object declaration declaring the GamePlayLoop object, and name it gamePlayLoop, as follows:

```
GamePlayLoop gamePlayLoop;
```

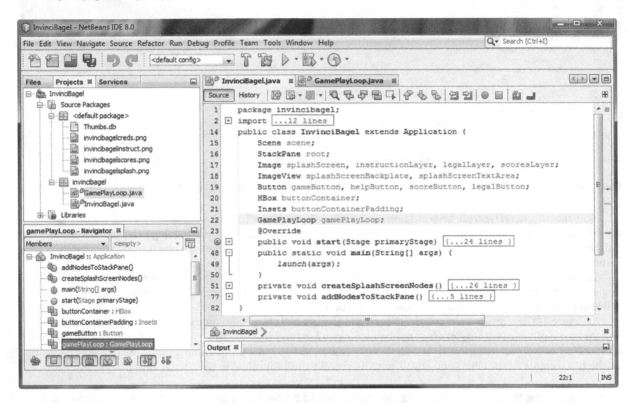

Figure 7-9. *Click the InvinciBagel.java editing tab, and declare a GamePlayLoop object named gamePlayLoop at the top*

As you can see, the code is error free, because NetBeans has found your GamePlayLoop class, which contains the overridden .handle() method and whose parent AnimationTimer class has a constructor method that can create an AnimationTimer (type of) object, using the GamePlayLoop class, extending AnimationTimer.

Now, you have to instantiate, or create, an instance in memory of the GamePlayLoop object, using the Java new keyword. This is done once, when the game is first started, which means that the instance needs to go in the .start() method.

You can do this **after** all the other Scene Graph Node objects and ActionEvent EventHandler objects have been created, using the following line of Java code (see also Figure 7-10):

```
gamePlayLoop = new GamePlayLoop();
```

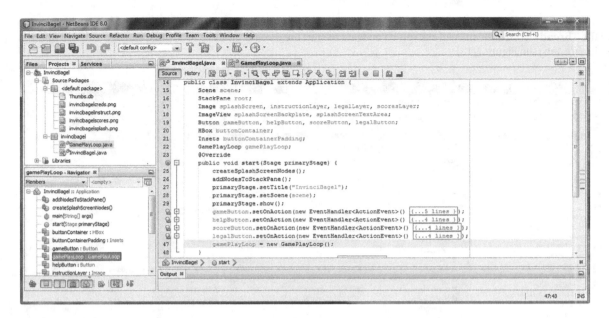

Figure 7-10. *At the end of the .start() method, instantiate the gamePlayLoop object by using the Java new keyword*

The logic of this code placement (at the end), is to set up all your static objects, in terms of creation and configuration, and then create the dynamic object at the end that will be processing the pulse-related logic.

Profiling the GamePlayLoop Object: Running NetBeans Profiler

Let's run NetBeans Profiler, using a **Profile ➤ Project Profile** menu sequence, to determine if you can see the GamePlayLoop object that you have created in any of the profiling views. As Figure 7-11 demonstrates, the GamePlayLoop **<init>** call takes less than 2 milliseconds to set up the GamePlayLoop object in memory for your use, using very little overhead.

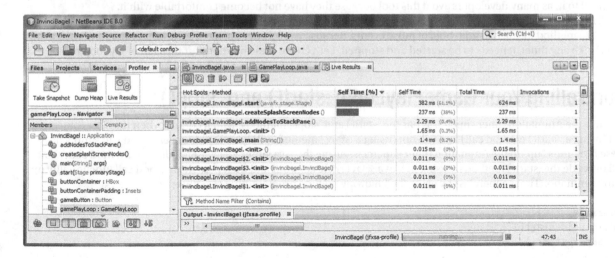

Figure 7-11. *Use a Profile ➤ Profile Project menu sequence to start the Profiler and look at GamePlayLoop memory use*

Next, let's study the threads analysis pane by scrolling down in the Profiler tab, shown at the top left of Figure 7-11. Find the **Threads** iconNetBeans will ask you if you want to start the threads analysis tool; once you agree, it will open the Threads tab (see Figure 7-12).

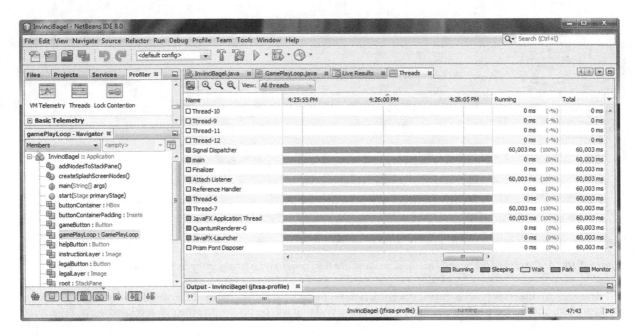

Figure 7-12. *Click the Threads icon, seen at the left of the screen, and open the Threads tab; the same eleven threads are running*

In case you are wondering why you are not seeing any "blips" in the Thread objects shown in Figure 7-12, like you did when you clicked the Button objects in the previous chapter, you are correct in your assumption that you should see the JavaFX pulse engine timing events somewhere in this diagram Yet, all the thread bars are solid colored, so no action or pulse events are firing. I am going to have you use the NetBeans profiling utility as often as necessary to get you used to it, as many developers avoid this tool because they have not become comfortable with it.

This reason you do not see any events is that simply creating the GamePlayLoop object is not enough for the .handle() method inside it to grab hold of pulse events. Because it is a Timer object of sorts (an AnimationTimer, to be exact), like any timer, it needs to be **started** and **stopped**. Let's create these methods for the GamePlayLoop next.

Controlling Your GamePlayLoop: .start() and .stop()

Because the AnimationTimer superclass has the .start() and .stop() methods, which control when the class (object) will (using a .start() method call) and will not (using a .stop() method call) handle pulse events, you will simply pass these functions "up" to the AnimationTimer superclass, using the Java **super** keyword inside your method code. You will override the .start() method by using the Java **@Override** keyword and then pass the method call functionality up to the AnimationTimer superclass by using the following method programming structure:

```
@Override
public void start() {
    super.start();
}
```

The .stop() method structure will be overridden, and the method functionality, passed up to the superclass, in exactly the same fashion, using the following Java method programming structure:

```java
@Override
public void stop() {
    super.stop();
}
```

As Figure 7-13 reveals, the GamePlayLoop class code is error free, and you can now write the code in the InvinciBagel class that starts the GamePlayLoop AnimationTimer object so that you can see pulse objects when you profile the application.

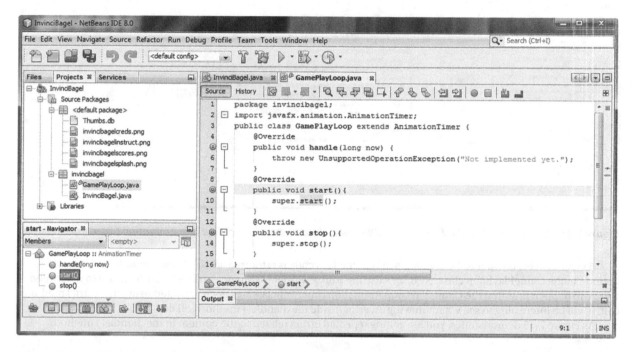

Figure 7-13. *Adding .start() and .stop() methods to the GamePlayLoop class and using the Java super keyword properly*

You will need to call this .start() method off the GamePlayLoop object named **gamePlayLoop**, using the new .start() method that you just created. Click the InvinciBagel.java tab, shown in Figure 7-14, and add a line of code below the GamePlayLoop object instantiation, calling the .start() method off the GamePlayLoop object named gamePlayLoop, as follows:

```java
gamePlayLoop.start();
```

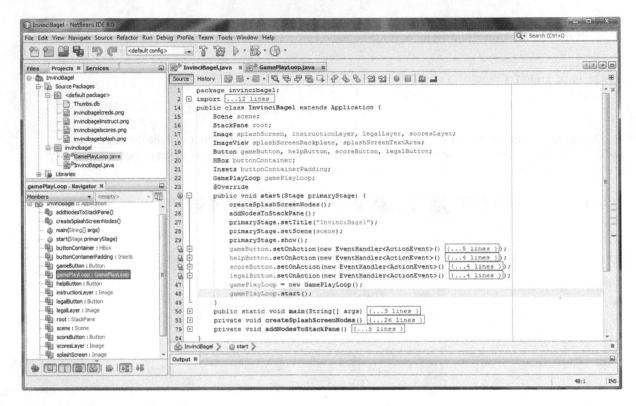

Figure 7-14. *Call a .start() method off the gamePlayLoop object to start GamePlayLoop AnimationTimer*

As you can see, the method call is in place, and the Java code is error free, as NetBeans can now find the .start() method in the GamePlayLoop class. Next, let's use the **Run ➤ Project** sequence and test a pulse or two to determine what will happen now that the GamePlayLoop AnimationTimer subclass has been activated using the .start() method call. It will be interesting to see what throwing an error inside the .handle() method will do!

As Figure 7-15 demonstrates, you are getting repeated errors related to the content in the .handle() method.

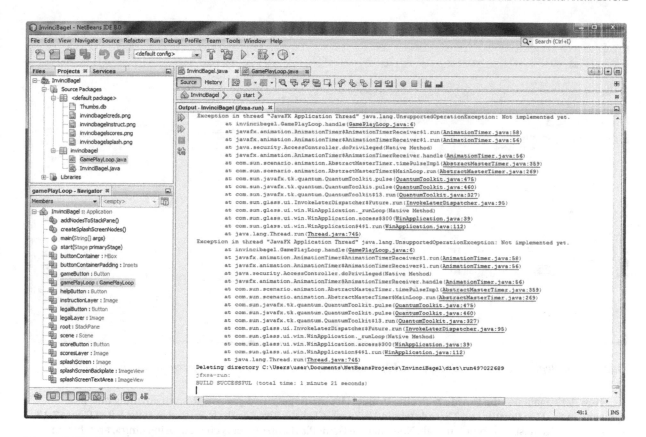

Figure 7-15. *Click Run ➤ Project, and open the Output pane to see errors being generated in .handle()*

Clearly, NetBeans 8.0 does not always write optimal code for the bootstrap methods that it codes for us, so let's remove the `throw new UnsupportedOperationException("Not implemented yet.");` line of code (see Figure 7-13). In its place, you will insert a Java comment, which creates for now what is termed an **empty method**, shown in Figure 7-16. This should allow your game application to run. Although the game application window did launch with the thrown errors, the components of the Scene Graph were not written to the scene, and only a default white background color could be seen. You will observe this if you are following along in NetBeans.

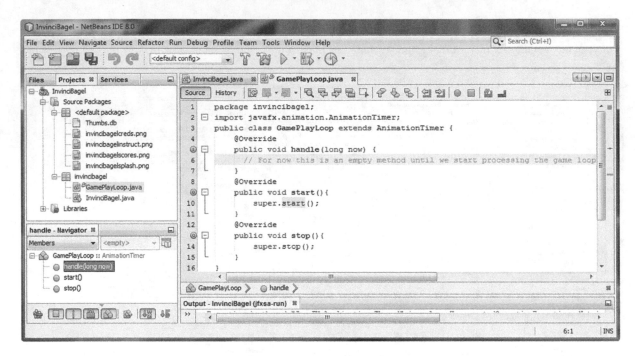

Figure 7-16. *Replace throw new UnsupportedOperationException(); with a comment, creating an empty method*

Now, let's again use the **Profile ➤ Profile Project (InvinciBagel)** work process to see if anything new has appeared in the **Live Results** and **Threads** tabs in NetBeans. Click the Live Results icon, shown at the left of Figure 7-17, and start the Live Results Profiler in a tab. Note that the GamePlayLoop object is created, using <init>, and that an AnimationTimer is started, using the **invincibagel.GamePlayLoop.start()** entry in the Profiler output.

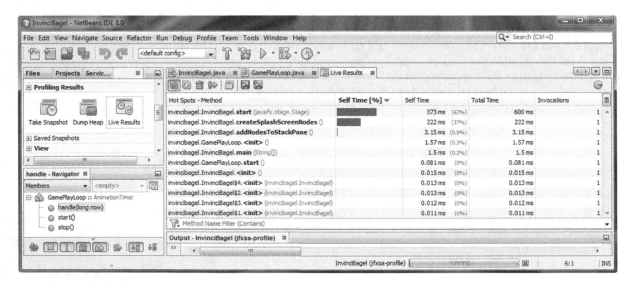

Figure 7-17. *Use a Profile ➤ Profile Project menu sequence to start the Profiler, and look at GamePlayLoop memory use*

As you can see, it only takes a fraction of a millisecond to initialize each of the event queues, including the pulse event, and all four ActionEvent EventHandler event processing queues. This is in keeping with our maximum game optimization approach, using static Scene Graph nodes and not doing anything inside the GamePlayLoop that will use up any more system resources (memory and processing cycles) than are absolutely necessary to accomplish the various tasks that you will be building up as you create your action-filled arcade game.

Now that you have created and started your GamePlayLoop object, let's take a look at the Threads Profiler!

Again, scroll down in the Profiler tab, shown at the top left of Figure 7-17, and find the **Threads** icon, which is displayed at the top- left of Figure 7-18. NetBeans will ask you if you want to start the threads analysis tool; once you agree, it will open the Threads tab. As Figure 7-18 illlustrates, the pulse engine is running, and several pulse events are shown for Thread-6. Interestingly, once JavaFX ascertains that the .handle() method is empty, the pulse event system does not continue to process this empty .handle() method and use unnecessary pulse events, indicating that the JavaFX pulse event system has some modicum of intelligence.

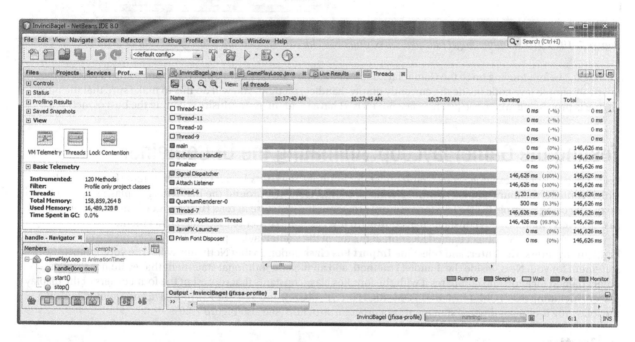

Figure 7-18. *Click the Threads icon, seen at the left side of the screen, and open a Threads tab; AnimationTimer pulses can be observed on Thread-6*

InvinciBagel Diagram: Package, Classes, and Objects

Next, let's take a look at your current package, class, and object hierarchy, in the form of a diagram (see Figure 7-19), to see where you are in terms of creating your game engine. At the right of the diagram is the InvinciBagel class, which holds the Scene Graph, and Stage, Scene, and StackPane objects, which hold and display your splash screen UI design. At the left of the diagram is the GamePlayLoop class, which will contain the game processing logic calls and which gets declared and instantiated as a gamePlayLoop object in the InvinciBagel class but is not part of the Scene Graph hierarchy. Soon, you will start building the other functional areas displayed in the diagram so that you can control your sprites, detect collisions between the sprites, and simulate real-world forces of physics to make the game more realistic. You will see additions to this diagram as you progress through the book and create your Java 8 game.

Diagram of invincibagel package and InvinciBagel Class (and Object) Hierarchy

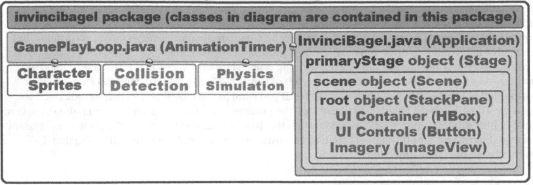

Figure 7-19. Current invincibagel package, class, and object hierarchy, after addition of the GamePlayLoop

Next, , before moving on to the GamePlayLoop AnimationTimer class and object, you are going to place some relatively simple Java code inside the currently empty .handle() method. You will do this to make sure that the pulse engine is processing and to see just how fast 60FPS is! (I have to admit, my curiosity is getting the best of me!).

Testing the GamePlayLoop: Animating the UI Container

Let's move one of the existing Scene Graph nodes, for example, the **HBox** layout container parent (branch) node, which contains the four UI Button control elements, counterclockwise around the InvinciBagel splash screen. You will do this by using a simple **if-else** Java loop control programming structure to read (using a **.get()** method) and control (using a **.set()** method) Pos constants that control (in this case) the corner of the screen placement.

First, declare a Pos object named location at the top of the GamePlayLoop class. Then, click on the error message highlighting, press **Alt+Enter**, and select the **Import Pos class** option so that NetBeans will write your import statement for you. Next, inside the .handle() method, add an if-else conditional statement that evaluates this Pos object named location and compares it with the four Pos class constants that represent the four corners of the display screen, including BOTTOM_LEFT, BOTTOM_RIGHT, TOP_RIGHT, and TOP_LEFT. Your Java code should look like the following if-else conditional statement Java program structure (see also Figure 7-20):

```
Pos location;
@Override
public void handle(long now) {
  location = InvinciBagel.buttonContainer.getAlignment();
    if (location == Pos.BOTTOM_LEFT) {
        InvinciBagel.buttonContainer.setAlignment(Pos.BOTTOM_RIGHT);
    } else if (location == Pos.BOTTOM_RIGHT) {
        InvinciBagel.buttonContainer.setAlignment(Pos.TOP_RIGHT);
    } else if (location == Pos.TOP_RIGHT) {
        InvinciBagel.buttonContainer.setAlignment(Pos.TOP_LEFT);
    } else if (location == Pos.TOP_LEFT) {
        InvinciBagel.buttonContainer.setAlignment(Pos.BOTTOM_LEFT);
    }
}
```

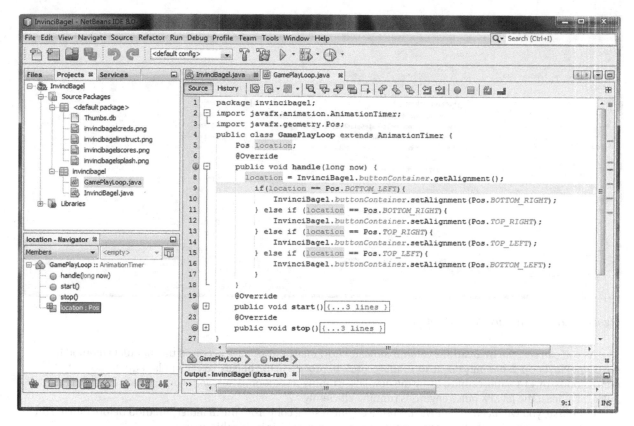

Figure 7-20. *Create an if-else loop that moves the HBox UI counterclockwise around the four corners of a splash screen*

As the figure illustrates, your code is error free, and you are ready to use the **Run ➤ Project** work process and watch the 60FPS fireworks! Get ready for some blinding speed!

Next, let's run the **Live Results** Profiler and **Threads Profiler** one last time to see if your pulse engine is cranking! Once you do this, you will know that you have successfully implemented your GamePlayLoop timing engine for your game, and you can then shift your focus to developing your game sprites, collision detection, physics, and logic!

Profiling the GamePlayLoop: Pulse Engine

Now, let's use the **Profile ➤ Profile Project (InvinciBagel)** work process one final time to see if anything new has appeared in the **Live Results** and **Threads** tabs in NetBeans. Click the Live Results icon, shown at the left of Figure 7-21, and start the Live Results Profiler in a tab. Note that the GamePlayLoop object is created, using <init>; that an AnimationTimer is started, using the **invincibagel.GamePlayLoop.start()** entry in the Profiler output; and that there is an **invincibagel.GamePlayLoop.handle(long)** entry as well, which means that your game timing loop is being processed.

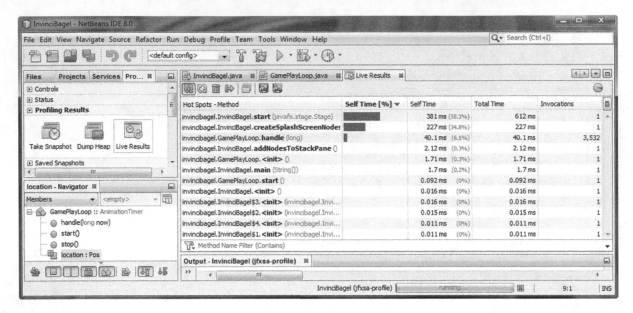

Figure 7-21. *Run the Live Results Profiler*

As you can see, the **Invocations** column indicates how many pulses have accessed the .handle() method in the GamePlayLoop. It has only taken **40.1** milliseconds to process **3,532** pulses, so each pulse equates to **0.0114** milliseconds, or **114** nanoseconds, using the new Java 8 timing resolution. Thus, your current code for testing the pulse, or at least the JavaFX pulse engine, is running efficiently.

Of course, you will need to remove this pulse engine testing code from the .handle() method before moving on to the next chapter, when you will start processing game assets and logic inside this method.

Next, let's scroll down one last time in the Profiler tab, displayed at the top left of Figure 7-21, and click the **Threads** icon, which is shown at the top left of Figure 7-22, to open the Threads tab. As you can see, the pulse engine is running, and pulse events can be seen processing in Thread-6 as well as the JavaFX Application Thread.

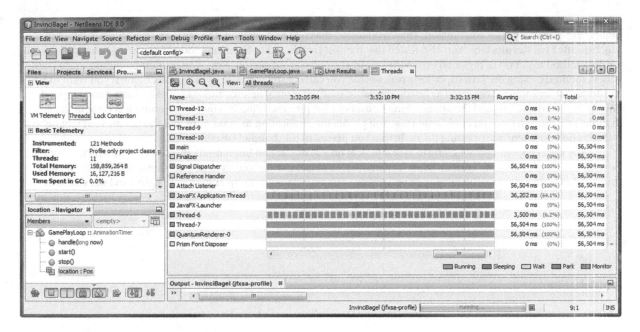

Figure 7-22. *Run the Threads Profiler*

Given the empty .handle() method processing from the GamePlayLoop object in Thread-6 (see Figure 7-18), you can assume that the pulse events in Thread-6 are from the GamePlayLoop AnimationTimer subclass. This means that the pulse events showing in the JavaFX Application Thread are showing where the .handle() method is accessing a buttonContainer HBox object contained in a stackPane Scene Graph root in the InvinciBagel class.

Now, you have a low-overhead, extremely fast game processing loop in place, and you can start to create your other (sprite, collision, physics, scoring, logic, and so on) game engines! One down, and a whole bunch to go!

Summary

In this seventh chapter, you wrote the first of the many game engines that you will be designing and coding over the course of this book, the GamePlayLoop game play timing class and object, which allow you to tap into the powerful JavaFX pulse event processing system.

First, you examined the different classes in the javafx.animation package and the different ways to use the **Animation**, **Transition**, **Timeline**, and **AnimationTimer** classes to harness the JavaFX pulse event processing system.

After that, you learned how to create a **new Java class** in NetBeans and then **extended** the AnimationTimer superclass to create the **GamePlayLoop** subclass, which will process your game play logic at 60FPS. You saw how to use NetBeans to help you write the majority of the code for this new subclass, including the package and class statement, the import statement, and the bootstrap .handle() method.

Next, you went into the InvinciBagel.java class and declared and named a new gamePlayLoop GamePlayLoop object, using the new class you created. Then, you tested the code and profiled it to see if any new entries appeared in the **Threads Live Results** tabs. You also tested the .handle() method that NetBeans coded for you and changed it to an empty method to get rid of repeated errors thrown by the pulse event engine. Next, you implemented the .start() and .stop() methods, using the Java super keyword, so that you can control your use of the pulse engine if you want to add in additional Java statements, such as saving the game state, later on, when the pulse engine is started and stopped. You again tested and profiled the application to observe your progress. Finally, you placed some test code in the .handle() method so that you could again test and profile the application to make sure that the pulse event engine was quickly and consistently processing the code that you placed in the .handle() method.

In the next chapter, you are going to take a look at how to create and implement abstract classes which will later be used to create your game **sprites**. Once we have that in place, it will allow us to display them, animate them, and process their movement on the display screen inside your new gamePlayLoop engine in real time in later chapters.

■ ■ ■

Creating Your Actor Engine: Design the Characters for Your Game and Define Their Capabilities

Now that we have created the game play timing loop in Chapter 7, let's get into some scratch coding here in Chapter 8, and create the **public abstract class** framework that we can use to create the different types of **sprites** that we will be using in our InvinciBagel game. This essentially equates to your "**Actor Engine**" for your game, as you'll define and design the various types of game components that your game will include as actors, and these two classes will be used to create all of the other classes that will be used to create the objects (components) that are in your game. These would include things such as the InvinciBagel himself (the Bagel class), his adversaries (the Enemy class), all the treasure he looks for during the game (the Treasure class), things that are shot at him (the Projectile class), things that he navigates over and around (the Prop classes), all providing game objectives that InvinciBagel must try and achieve.

During this chapter, we will create **two** public abstract class constructs. The first, the **Actor** class, will be the superclass of the other, the **Hero** subclass. These two abstract classes can be used during the book to create both our **fixed sprites**, which are sprites that do not move (obstacles and treasure), using the Actor superclass, and sprites that move around the screen, using a **Hero** subclass of the Actor class. The Hero class will provide additional methods and variables for motion sprites (the superhero, and his arch enemies in the multi-player version of the game). These will track things like collision and physics characteristics, as well as Actor animation (motion states). Having lots of motion on the screen will make game play more interesting, and allow us to make the game more challenging for the player.

Creating the Actor Engine up front will give you experience in creating public abstract classes. As you recall from Chapter 3, public abstract classes are used to create other class (and object) structures in Java, but are not used directly in the actual game programming logic. This is the reason I am terming creating these two "blueprint" classes creating the Actor Engine, as we are essentially defining the lowest level of the game, the "actors" during this chapter.

As we progress in the design of the game during the book, we'll create the **Treasure** subclass using the **Actor** (fixed sprite) class, for "fixed" treasures that will get picked up by InvinciBagel during the game play. We'll also create the **Prop** class using this Actor superclass, for the obstacles in the game that InvinciBagel has to navigate up, over, under, around, or through, successfully. We'll also create sprites that move around on the screen using the Hero subclass of the Actor superclass, such as the **Bagel** class. We'll eventually create an **Enemy** class and **Projectile** class.

Besides designing the two key public abstract Actor classes during this chapter, we will also define our main InvinciBagel character's **digital image states** using less than ten **PNG32** digital image assets. We will do this during this chapter so that this is in place before we'll want to use these classes and sprite image states in the next chapter of the book, when we'll look at event handling, so that the player can control where the InvinciBagel goes around the screen and what states (stand, run, jump, leap, fly, land, miss, crouch, etc.) he is using to navigate the obstacles in his world.

Game Actor Design: Defining the Attributes Up Front

The foundation of any popular game is the characters – the Hero and his Arch Enemies – as well as the game's obstacles, armory (projectiles), and treasures. Each of these "actors" need to have attributes, defined using variables in Java, that keep track of what is going on with each of these actors during game play in real time, using areas of system memory. I am going to try to do this right the first time, in the same sense that you want to define a database record structure to hold the data you will need out into the future correctly the first time that you define your database. This can be a challenging stage of your game development, as you need to look out into the future and ascertain what features you want your game and its actors to have, and then put those into your actor's capabilities (variables and methods) up front. Figure 8-1 gives you an idea of some of the two dozen attributes that we will be installing for the game actors over the course of the chapter as we create over a hundred lines of code to implement our actor engine for the game.

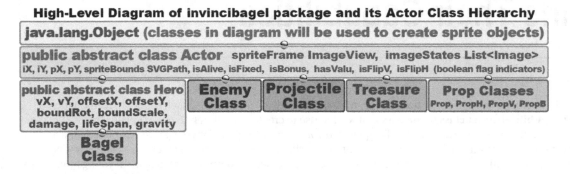

Figure 8-1. *Design a public abstract Actor superclass and a public abstract Hero subclass to use to create sprite classes*

As you can see, I'm trying to get a balanced number of variables; in this case it's about a dozen each, between the fixed sprite Actor class and the motion sprite Hero class. As you know from Chapter 3, because the Hero subclass we'll be creating **extends** the Actor superclass, it actually has two dozen attributes or characteristics, as it assumes all of the superclass variables, in addition to having its own. A design challenge will be to put as many of these attributes in the Actor superclass as possible, so that fixed sprites have as much flexibility as possible. A good example of this is that in the first rounds of design I had the **pivot point** (**pX** and **pY** variables) in the Hero class, but then I thought about it and thought "what if I want to rotate fixed sprites (obstacles and treasure) later on for more level design efficiency" so I placed these variables in the Actor superclass, giving this pivot (rotate) capability to **both** fixed and motion sprites.

Another variable that I had in the Hero class that I moved "up" into the Actor superclass is the List<Image> property. I thought to myself during this design process, "What if for some reason I want my fixed sprites to have more than one image state?" I also upgraded the Actor class from using a simple Rectangle Shape object to using a **SVGPath** Shape subclass, so that I can define **collision geometry** (which is what a spriteBounds variable is) using more complex shapes than a **Rectangle** to support advanced obstacle constructs in later levels of the game that are more complex.

Also note that I have the **spriteFrame ImageView**, which holds the sprite image assets, in the Actor class, as both fixed and motion sprites use images, so I can put the ImageView into the Actor superclass. I use the **imageStates List<Image>** in the Actor superclass, so that fixed sprites have access to different "visual states" just like the motion sprites do. As you may have guessed, List<Image> is a Java List object filled with JavaFX Image objects. The iX and iY variables in the Actor class are image (or initial) placement X and Y locations, which place a fixed sprite on your game level layout, but will also hold current sprite position for motion sprites, when assumed by the Hero subclass. Other variables hold Boolean states (alive/dead, etc.) and lifespan, damage, offset, collision, or physics data we'll need later.

The InvinciBagel Sprite Images: Visual Action States

Besides designing the optimal Actor Engine classes to use to implement characters, treasure, and obstacles in a game, the other important thing to optimize is the main character for the game, and the different **states** of animation that a character will move between, based on the movement of the character by the player. From a memory optimization standpoint, the fewer image frames that we can accomplish all of this in, the better. As you can see in Figure 8-2, I will provide all of the InvinciBagel character motion states using only nine different sprite image assets; some of these can be used in more than one way: for instance, by using the **pX** and **pY** variables, which will allow us to rotate these sprite frames around any pivot point that we choose. An example of this is **center pivot point placement** for the **FLY** state, seen in the middle of Figure 8-2, which gives us a take-off (fly up), flying, and landing (fly down) simply by rotating this image **50** degrees clockwise (to a horizontal orientation) to **100** degrees clockwise (tilting to fly down, instead of up).

Figure 8-2. *The nine primary character motion sprites for the InvinciBagel character that will be used during the game*

Even though we are providing **offset** and **pivot point** capabilities in our sprite Actor Engine abstract classes, that doesn't mean that we should not make sure that our motion sprite image states are well **synchronized** with each other. This is so that we do not routinely have to use these pivot or offset capabilities to get good visual results. This is what I term **sprite registration**, and involves **positioning** the different sprite states optimally relative to each other.

Some examples of sprite registration between sprite frames that will be used with each other can be seen in Figure 8-3. For instance, the starting to run imageStates[1] sprite should start its run cycle with the same foot position as a standing (or waiting) imageStates[0] sprite, as seen on the left side of Figure 8-3. Also, the running imageStates[2] sprite should keep its body portion as still as possible, relative to the imageStates[1] starting to run sprite. A preparing to land imageStates[6] sprite should change foot positioning realistically relative to the landed imageStates[7] sprite.

Figure 8-3. *Sprite registration (alignment) to make sure the transition motion is smooth*

What you want to do to optimize sprite registration, relative to all of the other sprites, is to put all of your digital image sprites into the same square 1:1 aspect ratio resolution image format, and place them all in **layers** in a digital image compositing software package, such as GIMP or Photoshop. Then use the **move tool** and **nudge** (single pixel movements using arrow keys on keyboard) each sprite into position, relative to whichever two layers you have visibility (toggled on/off using the eye icon on the left of each layer) turned on for. The result is shown in Figure 8-3.

Creating an Actor Superclass: Fixed Actor Attributes

Let's get down to scratch coding our public abstract Actor class that will be the foundation for all sprites we will be creating for the game during this book. I won't revisit how to create a new class in NetBeans (see Figure 7-2) as you've already learned that in Chapter 7, so create an **Actor.java** class, and declare it using **public abstract class Actor** and place the first five lines of code at the top of the class, declaring a List<Image> named **imageStates**, and creating a **new ArrayList<>** object, as well as an ImageView named **spriteFrame**, an SVGPath named **spriteBound**, and double variables **iX** and **iY**. Make all of these **protected**, so that any subclasses can access them, as is shown in Figure 8-4. You'll need to use the **Alt-Enter** work process for the red error underlining relating to the **import** statements you will need for the List class (object), ArrayList class (object), Image class (object), ImageView class (object), and SVGPath class (object). Once NetBeans writes these for you, the dozen or so lines of code declaring the List<Image> ArrayList, spriteFrame ImageView, SVGPath collision Shape object and double variables containing the sprite's X and Y location should look like the following Java class structure:

```java
package invincibagel;
import java.util.ArrayList;
import java.util.List;
import javafx.scene.image.Image;
import javafx.scene.image.ImageView;
import javafx.scene.shape.SVGPath;
public abstract class Actor {
    protected List<Image> imageStates = new ArrayList<>();
    protected ImageView spriteFrame;
    protected SVGPath spriteBound;
    protected double iX;
    protected double iY;
}
```

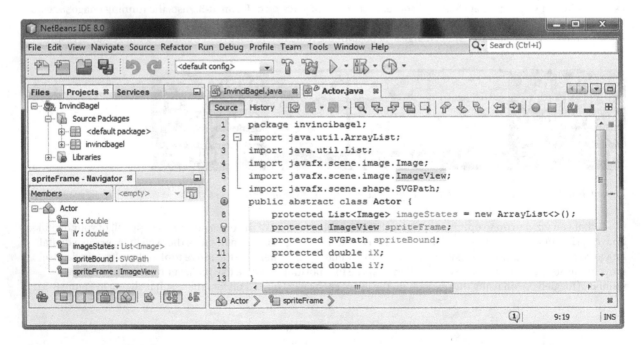

Figure 8-4. *Create a New Class in NetBeans, name it public abstract class Actor, and add in the primary Actor variables*

These five variables or attributes hold the "core" properties for any sprite; the spriteFrame ImageView and the List<Image> ArrayList of Image assets (one to many visible states) that it holds (this defines what the sprite looks like), the spriteBound collision Shape area (defines what is deemed to have intersected with the sprite), and the X, Y location of the sprite on the display screen.

These are also the five variables that will be configured using your Actor() constructor method, as well as your Hero() constructor method later on. First we will create the Actor() constructor; after that, we will add in all the other variables that we will need every Actor subclass to include.

After we create all of the other variables for the Actor class, which are not set using the Actor() constructor method, we will initialize these to hold their default values inside of the constructor method, and finally we will have NetBeans create **.get()** and **.set()** methods for our variables using an automatic coding function which you'll really like.

The parameters that we will code to pass into this Actor() constructor will include the **String** object named **SVGdata,** which will contain a string of text defining the SVGPath collision shape, as well as the sprite X, Y location, and a comma delimited List of Image objects. The SVGPath class has a .setContent() method that can read or "parse" raw SVG data strings, and so we will use this to turn the String SVGdata variable into our SVGPath collision Shape object.

We will not be implementing the collision code, or SVGPath Shape object during this chapter, or the next for that matter, but we need to put them in place, so we can use them later during Chapter 16 on collision detection processing and how to create collision polygon data using the GIMP and PhysEd (PhysicsEditor) software packages.

The Actor constructor method that we will be creating will follow the following constructor method format:

```
public Actor(String SVGdata, double xLocation, double yLocation, Image... spriteCels)
```

Later on if we need to create more complex Actor() constructor methods, we can "overload" this method by adding other more advanced parameters, such as pivot point pX and pY, for instance, or the isFlipH or isFlipV boolean values, to allow us to mirror fixed sprite imagery horizontally or vertically. Your Java code will look like the following:

```
public Actor(String SVGdata, double xLocation, double yLocation, Image... spriteCels) {
    spriteBound = new SVGPath();
    spriteBound.setContent(SVGdata);
    spriteFrame = new ImageView(spriteCels[0]);
    imageStates.addAll(Arrays.asList(spriteCels));
    iX = xLocation;
    iY = yLocation;
}
```

Notice that the ImageView constructor, invoked using the Java **new** keyword, passes the **first frame** (Image) of the List<Image> ArrayList data you are passing in using a comma delimited list by using a **spriteCels[0]** annotation. If you were to create an **overloaded method** that allowed you to set up the pivot point data, it might look like this:

```
public Actor(String SVG, double xLoc, double yLoc, double xPivot, double yPivot, Image... Cels){
    spriteBound = new SVGPath();
    spriteBound.setContent(SVG);
    spriteFrame = new ImageView(Cels[0]);
    imageStates.addAll(Arrays.asList(Cels));
    iX = xLoc;
    iY = yLoc;
    pX = xPivot;
    pY = yPivot;
}
```

As you can see in Figure 8-5, you will need to use the **Alt-Enter** work process, and have NetBeans code your import statements for the **Arrays** class for you. Once you do this, your code will be error free.

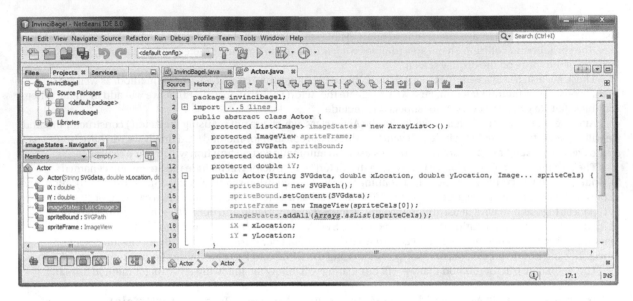

Figure 8-5. *Create a constructor method to set up fixed Actor sprite subclasses with collision shape, Image list, location*

Next, let's code the other crucial method for this class, the abstract **.update()** method, and then we can add the rest of the Actor class fixed sprite attributes that we will need. After that, we can initialize the additional variables inside of the Actor() constructor method. Finally we will learn how to create "getter and setter" methods for the Actor class, before we move on to use this new custom Actor superclass to create our other Hero motion sprites subclass.

Creating an .update() Method: Connect to GamePlayLoop Engine

The most important method for any sprite class, other than the constructor method that births it into existence, is the **.update()** method. The .update() method will contain the Java 8 code that tells the sprite what to do on every pulse of the GamePlayLoop. For this reason, this .update() method will serve to "wire" the Actor sprite subclasses created using our Actor superclass and Hero subclass into the GamePlayLoop timing engine that we created in Chapter 7.

Because we need to have an .update() method as part of every Actor object (actor sprite) in our game, we'll need to include an "empty" (for now) abstract .update() method in the Actor superclass we are coding currently.

As you learned in Chapter 3, this public abstract method is left empty, or more accurately, **unimplemented**, in the Actor superclass, but will need to be (that is, will be required to be) implemented (or alternatively, to again be declared as an abstract method) in any Actor subclass, including the Hero subclass we are going to be coding later on.

The method is declared **public abstract void**, as it does not return any values (it is simply executed on each JavaFX pulse event) and does not include the {...} curly braces, as it does not (yet) have any body of code inside of it! The single line of code that declares the public abstract (empty or unimplemented) method should look like this:

```
public abstract void update();
```

As you can see in Figure 8-6, the method is very simple to implement, and once you add this new method under your Actor() constructor method, your Java 8 code is again error free, and you will be ready to add more code.

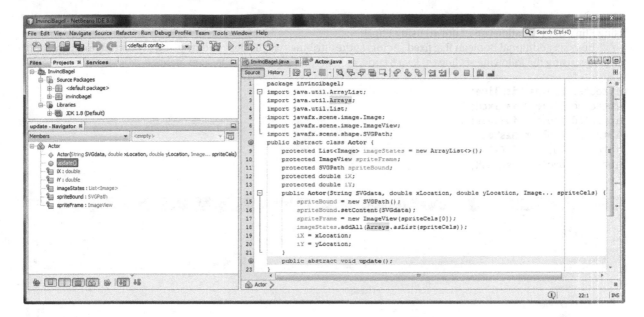

Figure 8-6. *Add an Arrays import statement to support constructor method; add a public abstract .update() method*

Next, we will add the rest of the attributes (or variables) for our fixed sprite Actor superclass, which requires us to think ahead, regarding what we want to be able to accomplish with our sprites during the creation of this game.

Adding Sprite Control and Definition Variables to an Actor Class

The next part of the process is easy, from a coding standpoint, as we will be declaring some more variables at the top of the Actor class. From a design standpoint, this is more difficult, however, as it requires that we think ahead as far as possible, and speculate about what variable data we will need for our sprite actors, both fixed and motion sprites, to be able to do everything that we want to during the construction of this game, as well as during its game play.

The first additional variables I am going to declare after the iX and iY variables are the **pX** and **pY** pivot point variables. I had originally placed these in the Hero subclass, which we're going to create next, once we are done with the creation of this Actor superclass. The reason I moved these "up" to the Actor superclass level is because I wanted to have the flexibility of rotating fixed sprites (treasure and obstacles) as well as motion sprites. This gives me more power and flexibility where level and scene design purposes are concerned. These pivot point X and Y variables would be declared as **protected double** data variables, and would be done using the following two lines of Java code:

```
protected double pX;
protected double pY;
```

Next, we need to add some boolean "**flags**" to our Actor class (object) definition. These will indicate certain things about the sprite object in question, such as if it is **Alive** (for fixed sprites this will always be false) or **Dead**, or if it is **Fixed** (for fixed sprites this will always be true, and true for motion sprites that are not in motion) or **Moving**, or **Bonus** objects, indicating additional points (or lifespan) for their capture (collision), or **Valuable**, indicating additional powers (or lifespan) for their acquisition (collision). Finally, I'm defining a **Flip Horizontal** and **Flip Vertical** flag, to give me four times the flexibility with (fixed or motion) sprite image assets than I would have without these flags in place.

Since JavaFX can flip or mirror images on the X or Y axis, this means I can reverse a sprite direction (left or right) using FlipV or orientation (up or down) using FlipH.

These six additional Boolean flag fixed (Actor) sprite attributes will be declared by using **protected boolean** data variables, using the following six lines of Java 8 code, as is shown (error free, no less) in Figure 8-7:

```java
protected boolean isAlive;
protected boolean isFixed;
protected boolean isBonus;
protected boolean hasValu;
protected boolean isFlipV;
protected boolean isFlipH;
```

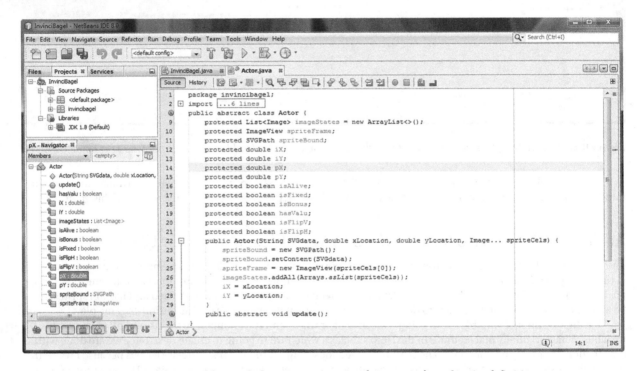

Figure 8-7. *Add the rest of the variables needed to support rotation (pivot point), and sprite definition states*

Next, we'll initialize these variables, inside the Actor() constructor method. If you wanted to pass settings to any of these Boolean flags into the Actor() constructor method using the parameter list, remember that you're able to create as many **overloaded** constructor method formats as you like, as long as the parameter list for each one is 100% unique. We may well do this later on during the book, if, for instance, we need a constructor method that pivots our fixed sprites for layout design purposes, for instance, or one that flips it around a given axis, for instance, for the same exact purpose, or one that does both of these, which would give us a nine parameter Actor() constructor method call.

Initializing Sprite Control and Definition Variables in an Actor Constructor Method

For now we are going to initialize our pivot point **pX** and **pY** to **0** (the upper left corner origin) and all of our Boolean flags to a value of **false** except for the **isFixed** variable, which for a fixed sprite will always be set to a value of **true**. We will do this using the following eight lines of Java code inside of the current Actor() constructor method and underneath the initial four lines of code in the method that deal with configuring the Actor object using the method parameters:

```
pX = 0;
pY = 0;
isAlive = false;
isFixed = true;
isBonus = false;
hasValu = false;
isFlipV = false;
isFlipH = false;
```

We could also do this using **compound initialization statements**. This would reduce the code to three lines:

```
px = pY = 0;
isFixed = true;
isAlive = isBonus = hasValu = isFlipV = isFlipH = false;
```

As you can see in Figure 8-8 we have now coded nearly three dozen lines of error-free Java 8 code, and we are ready to create the rest of the .get() and .set() methods that will make up the public abstract Actor superclass.

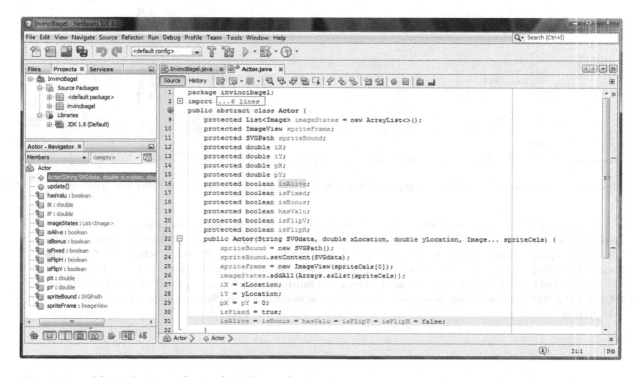

Figure 8-8. *Add initialization values to the eight new fixed sprite pivot and state definition variables you just declared*

The remaining methods in the Actor class will be what are commonly termed "getter" and "setter" methods because these methods provide access to the data variables inside of the class. Using **getter** and **setter** methods is the correct way to do things, because doing this implements the Java concept (and advantage) of **encapsulation**, which allows Java objects to be self-contained vessels of object attributes (variable data values) and behaviors (methods).

Accessing Actor Variables: Creating Getter and Setter Methods

One of the really powerful (and time saving, as you are about to see) features of NetBeans is that it will write all of your .get() and .set() methods for each of your object and data variables for you automatically. We will be using this handy feature during this book whenever possible, so you can get used to using this time saving feature to write lots of Java 8 code for you, accelerating your Java 8 game code production output! You access this auto-coding feature by using the **Source** menu, and its **Insert Code** submenu, as can be seen in Figure 8-9. As you can see, there is also a keyboard short-cut (**Alt-Insert**); using either of these will bring up a floating **Generate** menu, which is shown highlighted in red in the bottom center of Figure 8-9.

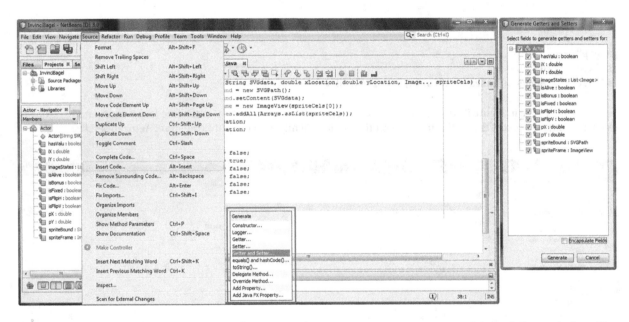

Figure 8-9. *Use Source ➤ Insert Code menu (or Alt+Insert) to bring up a Generate Getter and Setter dialog and select all*

Click on the **Getter and Setter** option, shown highlighted in the middle of the Generate floating menu, and a **Generate Getters and Setters** dialog will appear, which is shown on the right side of Figure 8-9. Make sure that the hierarchy is open, and that the check box next to Actor is selected, which will automatically select all of the variables inside of the class, in this case, a dozen variables also shown selected on the right hand side of Figure 8-9.

Once all of these are selected, click on the **Generate** button at the bottom of the dialog and generate the 24 .get() and .set() methods that you would have to type in manually if NetBeans 8.0 did not offer this handy IDE feature.

These **.get()** and **.set()** methods, which are generated by the NetBeans 8.0 **Source ➤ Insert Code ➤ Generate ➤ Getters and Setters** menu sequence, will give you the following **twenty-four** Java method code constructs, which equates to two methods for each of the twelve variables that we defined within the public abstract Actor class:

```java
public List<Image> getImageStates() {
    return imageStates;
}

public void setImageStates(List<Image> imageStates) {
    this.imageStates = imageStates;
}

public ImageView getSpriteFrame() {
    return spriteFrame;
}

public void setSpriteFrame(ImageView spriteFrame) {
    this.spriteFrame = spriteFrame;
}

public SVGPath getSpriteBound() {
    return spriteBound;
}

public void setSpriteBound(SVGPath spriteBound) {
    this.spriteBound = spriteBound;
}

public double getiX() {
    return iX;
}

public void setiX(double iX) {
    this.iX = iX;
}

public double getiY() {
    return iY;
}

public void setiY(double iY) {
    this.iY = iY;
}

public double getpX() {
    return pX;
}

public void setpX(double pX) {
    this.pX = pX;
}

public double getpY() {
    return pY;
}
```

```java
public void setpY(double pY) {
    this.pY = pY;
}

public boolean isAlive() {
    return isAlive;
}

public void setIsAlive(boolean isAlive) {
    this.isAlive = isAlive;
}

public boolean isFixed() {
    return isFixed;
}

public void setIsFixed(boolean isFixed) {
    this.isFixed = isFixed;
}

public boolean isBonus() {
    return isBonus;
}

public void setIsBonus(boolean isBonus) {
    this.isBonus = isBonus;
}

public boolean hasValu() {
    return hasValu;
}

public void setHasValu(boolean hasValu) {
    this.hasValu = hasValu;
}

public boolean isFlipV() {
    return isFlipV;
}

public void setIsFlipV(boolean isFlipV) {
    this.isFlipV = isFlipV;
}

public boolean isFlipH() {
    return isFlipH;
}

public void setIsFlipH(boo lean isFlipH) {
    this.isFlipH = isFlipH;
}
```

Notice that in addition to the .get() and .set() methods generated, for the boolean variables there is also an additional .is() method that is generated instead of the .get() method. Since I already named the boolean flags using the "is" preface, I am going to remove the second "Is" so that these "double is" methods are more readable. I am also going to do this to the hasValu method, so that inquiring as to the boolean setting in the method call is more natural, for instance, .hasValu(), isFlipV(), isBonus(), isFixed() or .isFlipH() for instance. I suggest that you perform the same edits with your code, for readability purposes.

Now we are ready to create our **Hero subclass**, which will add another eleven attributes to the thirteen we have created in the Actor class, bringing the total to an even two dozen. These additional eleven attributes held in the Hero class will be used with movable sprites that can move around the screen (I like to call these motion sprites). Our InvinciBagel character will be the primary Hero Actor object in the single-player version of our game, and for a future multi-player version, this would include the InvinciBagel Hero Actor object and the Enemy Hero Actor object as well.

Creating a Hero Superclass: Motion Actor Attributes

Let's create our **public abstract Hero** class next! This class will be the foundation for **motion sprites** that we will be creating for the game during this book. Create your **Hero.java** class in NetBeans, and declare it as **public abstract class Hero extends Actor**. Since we have done a lot of the "heavy lifting" in the Actor class, you will not have to create an ImageView to hold the sprite Image assets, or the List<Image> ArrayList object loaded with a List object filled with Image objects, or an SVGPath Shape object to hold the collision shape SVG polyline (or polygon) path data.

Since we don't have to declare any primary attributes, as those are inherited from the Actor superclass, the first thing we are going to do is to create a **Hero()** constructor method. This will contain your collision Shape data in a **String** object, the sprite **X, Y** location, and the **Image** objects that will be loaded into the List<Image> ArrayList object. After we create a basic Hero() constructor method, we will finish figuring out the other attributes (or variables) that your motion sprites will need to contain, just like we did when we designed the Actor superclass.

Remember that you already have the spriteBound SVGPath Shape object, imageStates List<Image> ArrayList object, SpriteFrames Image object and iX and iY variables constructed in the Actor class using Actor() method. We will also need these to be in place in order to be able to code our Hero() constructor method. Since these are all already in place, due to the java **extends** keyword in the Hero class declaration, all we have to do is use the **super()** constructor method call and pass these variables from the Hero() constructor up to the Actor() constructor. This will automatically pass these variables up into the Hero class for our use, using the Java **super** keyword.

Therefore, we have everything we need to be able to code our core Hero() constructor method, so let's get into that now. The Hero() constructor will take in the same number of complex parameters as the Actor() constructor. These include your collision shape data, contained in the String object named **SVGdata**, an "initial placement" X and Y location for the sprite, and a comma separated list of the Image objects (cels or frames) for the sprite, which I named Image... spriteCels. This **Image...** designation, which needs to be at the end of your parameter list, because it is "open ended," means that the parameter list will pass in one or more Image objects. Your code will look like the following:

```
public void Hero(String SVGdata, double xLocation, double yLocation, Image... spriteCels) {
    super(SVGdata, xLocation, yLocation, spriteCels);
}
```

By using super() to pass your core constructor work up to the Actor superclass Actor() constructor method, your code that you wrote earlier, inside of the Actor() constructor, will create the **spriteBound** SVGPath Shape object using the Java **new** keyword and the **SVGPath** Shape subclass, and will uses a SVGPath class **.setContent()** method in order to load the SVGPath Shape object with your collision shape to be used with the sprite image states. The **iX** and **iY** initial locations are set, and the **imageStates** List<Image> array is loaded with sprite **Image** objects, passed in from the end of the parameter list.

It's important to note that since we're setting this up in this way that the Hero class has access to everything that the Actor class has (thirteen powerful attributes). Actually, it may be more "salient" to look at this the other way around, that the Actor (fixed sprites) class has every capability that the Hero (motion sprites) class. This power should be leveraged for level design wow factor, including multi-image states (List<Image> Array), custom SVGPath collision shape capability, custom pivot point placements, and the ability to flip (mirror) sprite imagery around either the X axis (FlipV = true) or the Y axis (FlipH = true) or both axes (FlipH = FlipV = true). Putting these capabilities into place in your Actor Engine (Actor and Hero abstract superclasses) is only the first step; using them brilliantly for your game's design and programming, as time goes on and you continue to build and refine the game, is the ultimate goal for putting this foundation into place during this chapter. As you can see in Figure 8-10 our basic (core) constructor code is error free.

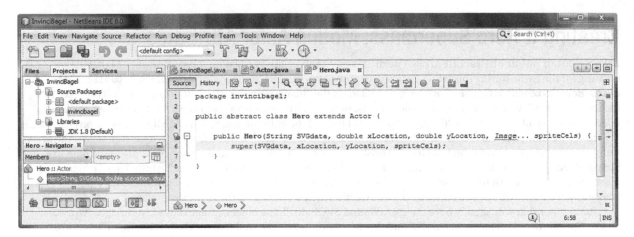

Figure 8-10. *Create a public abstract class Hero extends Actor and add a constructor method and a super() constructor*

Adding Update and Collision Methods: .update() and .collide()

Now that we have a basic constructor method, which we'll be adding to a bit later, let's add the required abstract **.update()** method, as well as a **.collide()** method, as motion sprites are moving, and therefore can collide with things! First let's add in the **public abstract void .update();** method, as it is required by our Actor superclass. Doing this essentially passes down (or up, if you prefer) the implementation requirement for this .update() method, from Actor superclass to Hero subclass, and on to any future subclasses of Hero (which will make Hero into a superclass, and more reflective of its name). Future non-abstract (functioning) classes will implement this .update() method, which will be utilized to do all the heavy lifting for the game programming logic. As you can see in Figure 8-11, motion sprites (Hero subclasses) will also need to have a collision detection method, which I will call **.collide()**, as that is a shorter name, and that, at least for now, will remain **unimplemented** except for returning a boolean **false** (no collision here, Boss!) boolean data value. Your Java code for the .collide() method structure will take an **Actor object** as its parameter, since that is what your Hero object will be colliding with, and should look like the following:

```
public boolean collide(Actor object) {
    return false;
}
```

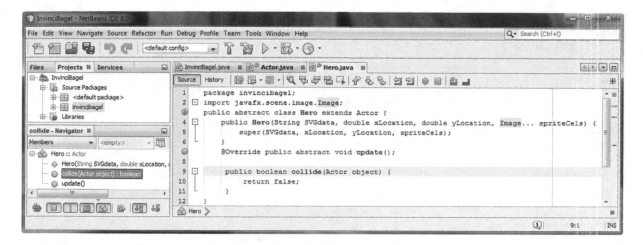

Figure 8-11. *Add the @Override public abstract void .update() and public boolean .collide(Actor object) methods*

Next, let's add another eleven variables into this Hero class. These will hold data values that apply to motion sprites, which have to deal with colliding with things, and obey the laws of physics. We will also need things such as a **lifespan** variable, and one that holds the accumulation of **damage** (points), which may be incurred if enemies shoot at each other. We'll add protected variables such as X and Y **velocity**, X and Y **offset** (for fine-tuning positioning of things relative to a sprite), **and** collision shape **rotation** and **scaling** factors, and finally, **friction**, **gravity,** and **bounce** factors.

Adding Sprite Control and Definition Variables to the Hero Class

The next thing that we need to do is to make sure that all of the variables that we will need to hold data for motion sprites are defined at the top of the Hero class, as seen in Figure 8-12. This information will be used by NetBeans to create getter and setter methods for the Hero class. The Java code should look like this:

```
protected double vX;
protected double vY;
protected double lifeSpan;
protected double damage;
protected double offsetX;
protected double offsetY;
protected double boundScale;
protected double boundRot;
protected double friction;
protected double gravity;
protected double bounce;
```

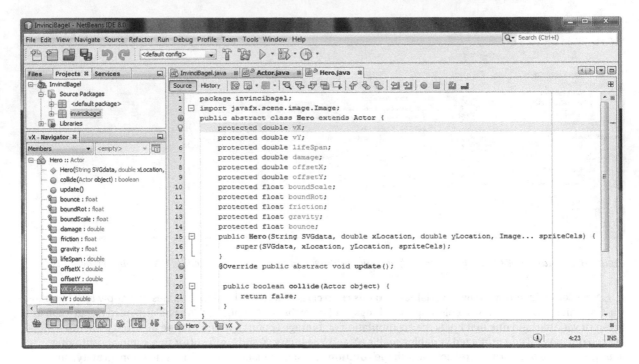

Figure 8-12. *Add eleven variables at the top of Hero class defining velocity, lifespan, damage, physics, collision*

Before we add all **22** of your getter and setter methods, which would be 11 .get() and 11 .set() methods, to match our new Hero class variables, let's go back and finish our **Hero()** constructor method, and initialize these eleven variables that we just added at the top of the Hero class.

Initializing the Sprite Control and Definition Variables in the Hero Constructor

Let's give our Hero Actor objects (motion sprites) a lifespan of 1000 units, and set the other variables to zero, which you can see that I have done using compound initialization statements to save eight lines of code. As you can see in Figure 8-13, the code is error free, and the Java programming statements should take the following format:

```
lifespan = 1000;
vX = vY = damage = offsetX = offsetY = 0;
boundScale = boundRot = friction = gravity = bounce = 0;
```

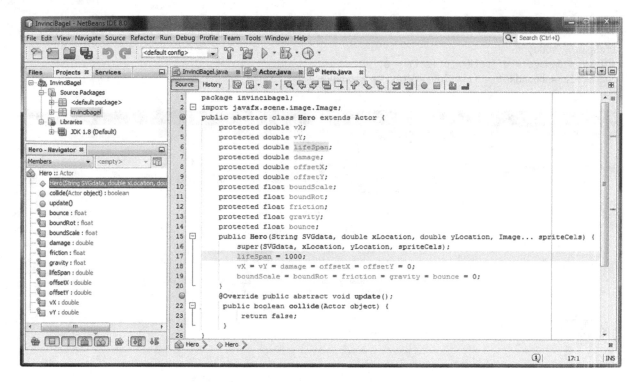

Figure 8-13. Add initialization for your eleven variables inside of your constructor method using compound statements

Before we generate our getter and setter methods, let's take a look at how we can use a combination of compound variable declaration statements and the knowledge of what default variable type values Java will set for our variables if we do not explicitly specify them to reduce the amount of code that it takes to write the entire Hero class from its 25 lines of code (or 33 if we didn't use compound variable initialization statements) to 14 lines of code.

If you don't count lines of code with one curly brace on them (three) we are talking less than a dozen lines of Java statements, including package, class and import declarations, to code this entire public abstract class. This is pretty impressive, given how much motion sprite power and capabilities the core class gives us. Of course, after we add the 22 getter and setter methods, which are 3 lines of code each, we will have about 80 lines of total code, sans spacing. It is important to note that NetBeans will be writing more than 75% of this class's code for us! Pretty cool.

Optimizing the Hero Class Via Compound Statements and Default Variable Values

I am going to do two major things to reduce the amount of code in this primary portion of the Hero class, before we have NetBeans write our getter and setter methods for us. The first is to use compound declaration for all of our similar data types, declaring the protected double and protected float modifiers and keywords first, and then listing all of the variables after those, separated by commas, which is called "comma delimited" in programming terms. The Java code for the eleven Hero class variable declarations will now look like the following:

```
protected double vX, vY, lifeSpan, damage, offsetX, offsetY;
protected float boundScale, boundRot, friction, gravity, bounce;
```

As you can see in Figures 8-13 and 8-14, we did the same type of compound statement for the initializations:

```
lifeSpan = 1000;
vX = vY = damage = offsetX = offsetY = 0;
boundScale = boundRot = friction = gravity = bounce = 0;
```

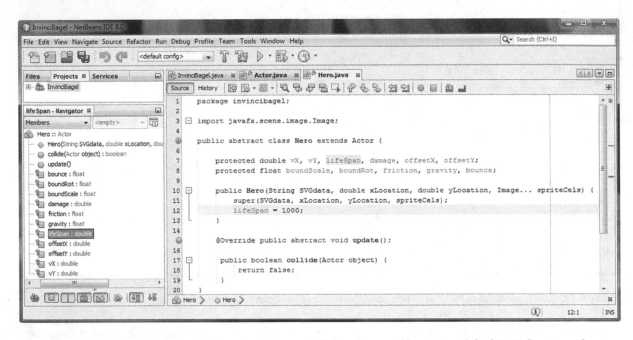

Figure 8-14. *Optimize your Java code by using compound declarations, and leveraging default initialization values*

This could also be done using only two lines of code, if you happen to be editing on an HDTV display screen:

```
lifeSpan = 1000;
vX = vY = damage = offsetX = offsetY = boundScale = boundRot = friction = gravity = bounce = 0;
```

Next, if we depend on the Java compiler to initialize our variables to zero, as double and float variables will be initialized to if no initialization value has been specified, we can reduce these two lines of code to one line of code:

```
lifeSpan = 1000;
```

Now that we've finished the "core" of our Hero() constructor method, let's have NetBeans write some code!

Accessing Hero Variables: Creating Getter and Setter Methods

Create a line of space after your .collide() method, and place your cursor there, which will show NetBeans where you want it to place the code that it is about to generate. This is shown in Figure 8-15 by a light-blue shaded line seen behind the Source menu. Use a **Source > Insert Code** menu sequence or the **Alt-Insert** keystroke combination, and when the **Generate** floating pop-up menu appears under this blue line (this shows the selected line of code), select the **Getter and Setter** option, shown highlighted in Figure 8-15, and select all of the Hero classes. Make sure that all of the Hero class variables are selected, either by using the Hero class master selection check box, or by using the check box UI elements for each variable, as is shown on the right hand side of Figure 8-15.

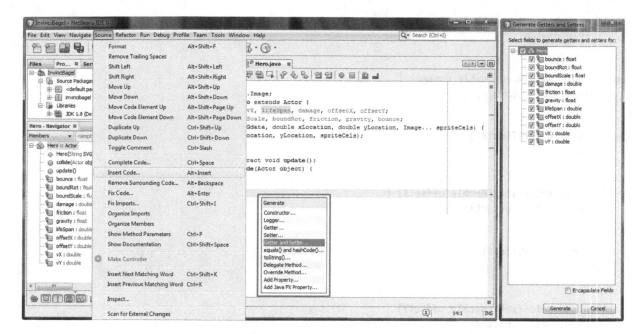

Figure 8-15. *Use the Source ➤ Insert Code ➤ Generate ➤ Getter and Setter menu sequence and select all class variables*

After you click on the **Generate** button at the bottom of the Generate Getters and Setters dialog, you will see the 22 new methods, all shiny and new and coded for you by NetBeans. The methods will look like the following:

```java
public double getvX() {
    return vX;
}

public void setvX(double vX) {
    this.vX = vX;
}

public double getvY() {
    return vY;
}

public void setvY(double vY) {
    this.vY = vY;
}

public double getLifeSpan() {
    return lifeSpan;
}

public void setLifeSpan(double lifeSpan) {
    this.lifeSpan = lifeSpan;
}
```

```java
public double getDamage() {
    return damage;
}

public void setDamage(double damage) {
    this.damage = damage;
}

public double getOffsetX() {
    return offsetX;
}

public void setOffsetX(double offsetX) {
    this.offsetX = offsetX;
}

public double getOffsetY() {
    return offsetY;
}

public void setOffsetY(double offsetY) {
    this.offsetY = offsetY;
}

public float getBoundScale() {
    return boundScale;
}

public void setBoundScale(float boundScale) {
    this.boundScale = boundScale;
}

public float getBoundRot() {
    return boundRot;
}

public void setBoundRot(float boundRot) {
    this.boundRot = boundRot;
}

public float getFriction() {
    return friction;
}

public void setFriction(float friction) {
    this.friction = friction;
}

public float getGravity() {
    return gravity;
}
```

```
public void setGravity(float gravity) {
    this.gravity = gravity;
}

public float getBounce() {
    return bounce;
}

public void setBounce(float bounce) {
    this.bounce = bounce;
}
```

It is important to note that objects created using the Hero class also have access to the getter and setter methods that we generated earlier for the Actor class. In case you are wondering what the Java keyword **this** means in all of these .set() methods, it is referring to the current object that has been created using the Actor or Hero class constructor method. Thus if you call the .setBounce() method off of the iBagel Bagel object (which we will soon be creating in Chapter 10), this keyword is referring to this (iBagel) Bagel object instance. So if we wanted to set a 50% bounce factor, we would make the following method call using our new .setBounce() setter method:

```
iBagel.setBounce(0.50);
```

Next let's take a look at how these sprite Actor classes fit in with the other classes we have coded during the book so far. After that, we will summarize what we have learned so far during this chapter, and we can move on into the future chapters in this book, and use these classes to create sprites for our game, as we learn how to use sprites for game play.

Updating the Game Design: How Actor or Hero Fit In

Let's update the diagram that I introduced in Chapter 7 (Figure 7-19) to include the Actor.java and Hero.java classes. As you can see in Figure 8-16, I had to switch the .update() physics and .collide() collision parts of the diagram, as the Actor class only includes the .update() method, and the Hero class includes both of these methods. Since the .collide() method will be called in the .update() method, I connected these two parts of the diagram with a chrome sphere as well.

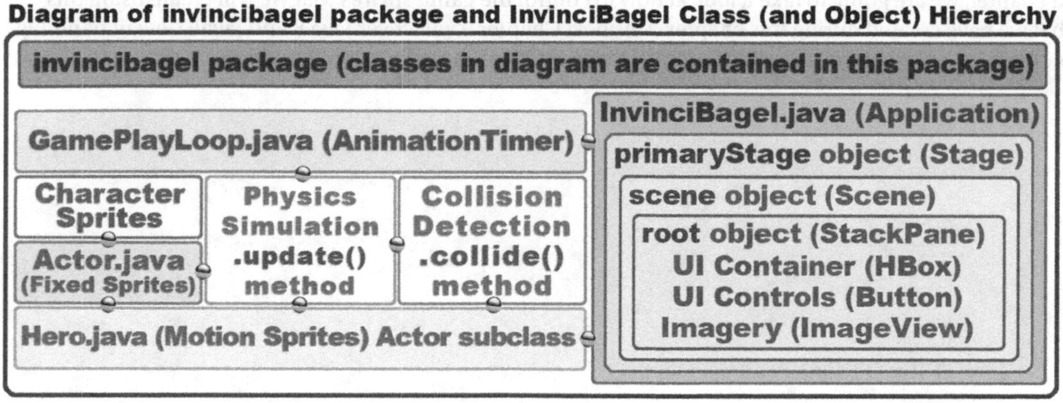

Diagram of invincibagel package and InvinciBagel Class (and Object) Hierarchy

invincibagel package (classes in diagram are contained in this package)

GamePlayLoop.java (AnimationTimer)

Character Sprites

Actor.java (Fixed Sprites)

Physics Simulation .update() method

Collision Detection .collide() method

Hero.java (Motion Sprites) Actor subclass

InvinciBagel.java (Application)

primaryStage object (Stage)

scene object (Scene)

root object (StackPane)

UI Container (HBox)

UI Controls (Button)

Imagery (ImageView)

Figure 8-16. *The current invincibagel package class (object) hierarchy, now that we have added Actor and Hero classes*

The **.handle()** method in a GamePlayLoop object will call these **.update()** methods, so there is a connection there as well. There are connections between the Actor and Hero classes with the InvinciBagel class, as all your game sprite objects created using these abstract classes will be declared and instantiated from within a method in this class.

We are making great progress on developing our game engine framework, while at the same time, seeing how some of the core features of the Java 8 programming language can be implemented to our advantage. We will be looking at the powerful new Java 8 **lambda expressions** feature in the next chapter on event handling as well, so more knowledge regarding leading-edge Java 8 features is right around the (game) bend. I hope you are as excited as I am!

Summary

In this eighth chapter, we wrote the second round of the several game engines that we will be designing and coding during this book, the **Actor** (fixed sprites) superclass, and its **Hero** (motion sprites) subclass. Once we start creating our game sprites in Chapter 10 and subsequent chapters, the Hero class will also become a superclass. Essentially, during this chapter you learned how to create **public abstract classes**, which will be used to define our sprite objects from here on out during the book. What this amounts to is doing all the heavy lifting (sprite design and coding work) up front for all of the actors (sprites) in our game, making the creation of powerful fixed and motion sprites for our game much easier for us to do from here on out. We are building both our knowledge base and our game engine framework first!

We first took a look at how these Actor and Hero classes would be designed, as well as what types of actual sprite classes we would be creating with them. We looked at nine sprite Image assets, and how these covered a wide range of motions by using only nine assets, and looked at how to "register" the sprite "states" relative to each other.

Next, we designed and created our Actor superclass, to handle fixed sprites such as props and treasure, creating the basic List<Image>, ImageView, SVGPath, iX and iY variables and a constructor method that used these to define the fixed sprite appearance, position, and collision boundaries. Then we added some additional variables that we will be needing for future game design aspects, and learned how to have NetBeans write .get() and .set() methods.

Next, we designed and created our Hero subclass, which extends Actor to handle motion sprites such as the InvinciBagel himself and his enemies, as well as projectiles and moving challenges. We created the basic constructor method that sets the variables from the Actor superclass, this time to define a motion sprites imagery, initial position, and collision boundaries. Then we added some additional variables, which we will be needing for future game design aspects, and again saw how NetBeans will write our .get() and .set() methods for us, which is always fun to watch!

Finally, we took a look at an updated invincibagel package, class and object structure diagram, to see just how much progress we have made so far during the first eight chapters of this book. This is getting pretty exciting!

In the next chapter, we are going to take a look at how to control the game **sprites** that we will create using this Actor engine that we have created during this chapter. This next Chapter 9 will cover Java 8 and JavaFX event handling, which will allow our game player to manipulate (control) these actor sprites using event handling.

CHAPTER 9

■ ■ ■

Controlling Your Action Figure: Implementing Java Event Handlers and Using Lambda Expressions

Now that we have created the public abstract Actor and Hero classes, which I call the "actor engine," in Chapter 8, let's get back into our **InvinciBagel.java** primary application class coding here in Chapter 9, and create the **event handling** framework that we can use to control the primary hero for our game, the InvinciBagel himself. The event handling that implements the interface between the player and your game programming logic could be looked at as the **"interactivity engine"** for your game, if we follow the engine paradigm we have been using thus far. There are many ways to interface with a game, including **arrow keys** (also known as a **DPAD** for consumer electronics devices), the **keyboard**, a **mouse** or trackball, a **game controller**, **touchscreen**, or even advanced hardware, such as **gyroscopes** and **accelerometers**. One of the choices you will make for your game development will be how a player will **interface** with the game, using the hardware device they are playing the game on, and the **input capabilities** it supports.

During this chapter, we will be doing a number of **upgrades** to your InvinciBagel.java class. The first is to add support for the game **WIDTH** and **HEIGHT** variables in the form of Java **constants**. These will allow us to change the width and height of the game play surface, which is the area inside of the game window that pops up, or the entire screen, if your game player is using a consumer electronics device.

The second upgrade we will do is to add the Java code that will create a **blank white screen** for us to design the game over (on top of) during the next several chapters. We'll do this by installing a **Color.WHITE** background color in the Scene() constructor method call (along with our new width and height variables), and then installing Java code into our Button control event handler structure that are already in place, to **hide** the two ImageView "plates" we are using for image compositing of our splash screen UI design. We can also use these two ImageView Node objects later on to hold background imagery for our game play, once we get into that level of design. Remember it is important to keep the number of Nodes in the Scene Graph to a minimum, so we will **reuse** Node objects, instead of adding more.

The third upgrade we'll add is to add **keyboard event handling** routines to our Scene object that will handle the arrow key support that we will use for the game, to span any hardware device that has an arrow key pad or DPAD. This will handle any events at the top-level of the Scene down to the StackPane (Scene Graph) hierarchy. This will pass the arrow key values pressed by the user to our Node objects. This will eventually allow **motion control code** to move the actors around the game, which is something we will be getting involved with in greater detail in the next chapter.

Besides upgrading our InvinciBagel.java code, and adding keyboard event handling, we will also be learning about **lambda expressions** during this chapter, just to make sure I get everything that is new in Java 8 covered during this book. These lambda expressions are somewhat advanced to be covered in this beginner level book, but since they are a major new feature of Java 8, and provide multi-threading support as well as more compact code structures, I am going to cover them here in this chapter, partly because NetBeans 8 (no surprise here) is willing to code them for you!

Game Surface Design: Adding Resolution Flexibility

The first thing that I want to do to the InvinciBagel.java code, which should already be open in a tab in NetBeans (if it is not, use the right-click and **Open** work process), is to add **WIDTH** and **HEIGHT** constants for the game application. The reason for doing this is that you may want to provide custom versions for netbooks or tablets (1024 by 600), or iTV set or eReaders (1280 by 720) or HDTV usage (1920 by 1080) or even for new 4K iTV sets (4096 by 2160). Having a height and width variable allows you to not have to change your **Scene()** constructor method call later, and to do certain screen boundary calculations using these variables rather than "hard coded" numeric values throughout your code. As you can see at the top of Figure 9-1, I have created a **constant** declaration for these two variables using a single line of Java code, which is known as a **compound statement**, as you learned in the previous chapter. The Java code for this declaration can be seen at the top of the class in Figure 9-1, and should look like the following:

```
static final double WIDTH = 640, HEIGHT = 400;
```

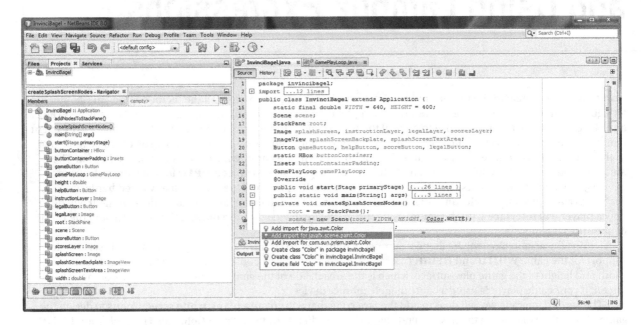

Figure 9-1. *Add private static final double WIDTH and HEIGHT constants; install these, and Color.WHITE, in Scene()*

The next thing that we will want to do is the upgrade our Stage() constructor method call, to use one of the other overloaded constructor methods that allows us to also specify the **background color** value. Let's use the **Color** class constant of **WHITE**, and our new width and height display screen size constants, and create this new constructor method call, using the following line of Java code, which is also shown (laden with errors) at the bottom of Figure 9-1:

```
scene = new Scene(root, WIDTH, HEIGHT, Color.WHITE);
```

As you can see in Figure 9-1, you will have a wavy red error underline under your **Color** class reference, until you use the **Alt-Enter** work process to bring up the helper dialog (as shown), and select the option that specifies "Add import for javafx.scene.paint.Color" in order to have NetBeans write the Java import statement for you. Once you do this, your code will be error free, and we will be ready to write some code that will put this background color in place.

To do this, we'll need to hide the ImageView Node objects that hold our full screen (splashScreenbackplate) and overlay (splashScreenTextArea) image assets. We will do this by setting the **visible** attribute (or characteristic, or parameter, if you prefer) to a value of **false**, which will allow the white background color that we set to show through.

Finishing the UI Design: Coding a Game Play Button

The next thing that we will need to do is to finish the Button control event handling code so that when we click on the **GAME PLAY** Button object, the white background is revealed for us to develop our game over. Later on we can use the ImageView plates that we use for our splash screen support to provide background image compositing for the game to make it more interesting visually. The way that we are going to hide the two ImageView Node objects in the Scene Graph is by calling the **.setVisible()** method off of each of these objects inside of the .handle() method that is attached to the PLAY GAME UI Button object. This can be seen in the bottom portion of Figure 9-2, and would be implemented using the following two lines of Java code, inside of the **.handle()** EventHandler<ActionEvent> method structure:

```
splashScreenBackplate.setVisible(false);
splashScreenTextArea.setVisible(false);
```

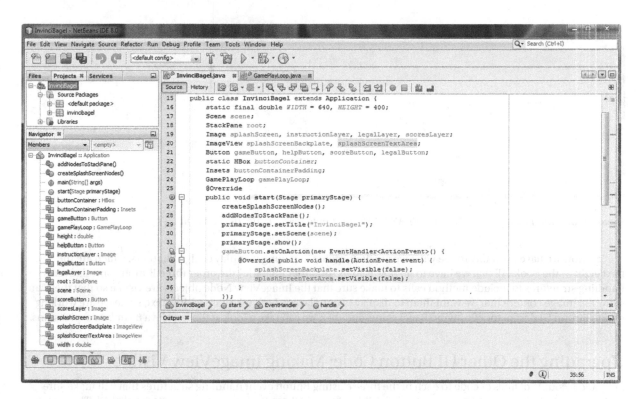

Figure 9-2. *Use a .setVisible() method for the ImageView class to hide background image plates and reveal White color*

As you can see, there is also a wavy yellow warning highlight under the EventHandler<ActionEvent> part of this event handling structure which relates to Java lambda expressions. After we finish implementing all of the final UI design code for the Buttons that controls what is visible to the player, and which imagery it is showing them, I will get into lambda expressions, and we will get rid of these warning messages in your code as well. After that, we'll move on to implement arrow key event handling structures, so that the user can navigate the InvinciBagel around the screen.

First, let's test the code that we put into the previously empty PLAY GAME Button event handling structure.

Testing the Game Play Button: Making Sure Your Code Works

Use the **Run ➤ Project** (or the Run icon at the top of the IDE that looks like a video play transport button) to launch your InvinciBagel game and click on the **PLAY GAME** Button on the bottom left of the window. As you can see in Figure 9-3, the screen turns white because the two ImageView image plates are not visible anymore and your white background color is shining through! You will notice if you click on the other three Button controls that they do not work anymore. Actually they are working, but they are not visible anymore, so the UI design now seems to be broken!

Figure 9-3. *Run the Project, and test the PLAY GAME Button to reveal white background*

So now we have an ability to see what we are doing going into our game play design chapters, which are the next eight in the book. All that we have to do now is to fix (or rather upgrade) the other three Button controls event handling structures to include method calls to make sure that the ImageView Node objects are visible so that they can show the image content that we want them to display to our players. Let's take care of this next, since we are working on the Button UI design for our InvinciBagel game, and then we can take a look at the new Java 8 lambda expressions.

Upgrading the Other UI Button Code: Making ImageView Visible

Let's add a couple of lines of code to each of the three existing Button event handling structures that will make sure that both ImageView image plates are set to be visible whenever these Button control objects are clicked. The reason that we need to put this code into each of the three other UI Button event handling structures is because we do not know what order the user will click on the Buttons, so we need to put these statements into each Button event handler. If the ImageView Node objects are already set as visible when these statements are triggered, then they will simply remain visible, because they were already previously visible! The Java method calls will look like the following:

```
splashScreenBackplate.setVisible(false);
splashScreenTextArea.setVisible(false);
```

As you can see highlighted in Figure 9-4, I've installed these (identical, except for the Image object that they reference) two statements inside of the other three Button event handling structures. These statements can go either before or after the existing method calls inside each of these .handle() methods.

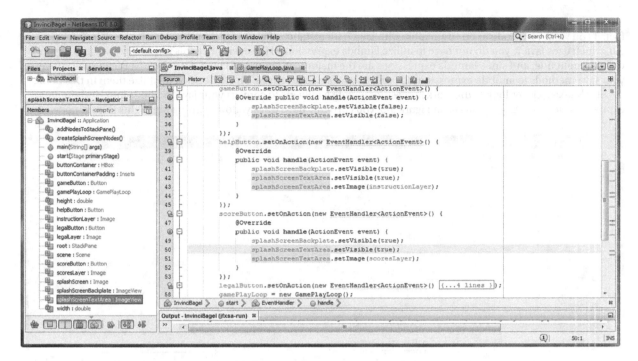

Figure 9-4. *Add in the .setVisible(true) method calls for the splashScreenBackplate and splashScreenTextArea objects*

Now you will see that when you use your **Run ➤ Project** work process, that all of your Button UI controls will do what they are supposed to do, and will display either a white background for the game or information screens that have the InvinciBagel splash screen artwork behind them. Now we are ready to learn about Java lambda expressions.

Lambda Expression: A Powerful New Java 8 Feature

One of the major new features that was recently released in Java 8 during 2014 is the **lambda expression**. Using the lambda expression can make your code more compact, and allows you to turn a method into a simple Java statement using Java 8's new lambda -> "arrow" operator. The lambda expression provides a Java code shortcut to structure one single method interface by instead using a lambda expression.

The Java 8 lambda expression has the same features as a Java method structure, as it requires a list of parameters to be passed in, as well as the code "body" to be specified. The code that the lambda expression calls can be a single java statement, or a block of code, containing multiple Java programming statements. This statement (or statements) will be expressed utilizing the parameters passed into the lambda expression. The basic Java 8 syntax for the **simple lambda expression** should be written as follows:

```
(the parameter list) -> (a Java expression)
```

You can also create a **complex lambda expression** by using the **curly braces** that are used in Java to define an entire block of Java code statements in conjunction with the lambda expression. This would be done by using the following format:

```
(the parameter list) -> { statement one; statement two; statement three; statement n; }
```

191

It is important to note that you do not have to use lambda expressions to replace traditional Java methods! In fact, if you want your code to be compatible with Java 7, for instance, if you want your code to also work in Android 5.0, which uses Java 7, you do not have to utilize lambda expressions. However, since this is specifically a Java 8 game development title, and since lambda expressions are the major new feature of Java 8, and since NetBeans will convert your Java methods to lambda expressions for you, as you are about to see, I have decided to utilize them in this book.

Let's take a closer look at the work process for getting NetBeans to convert your Java methods into lambda expressions for you. As you can see in Figure 9-5, you currently have wavy yellow warning highlights in your code.

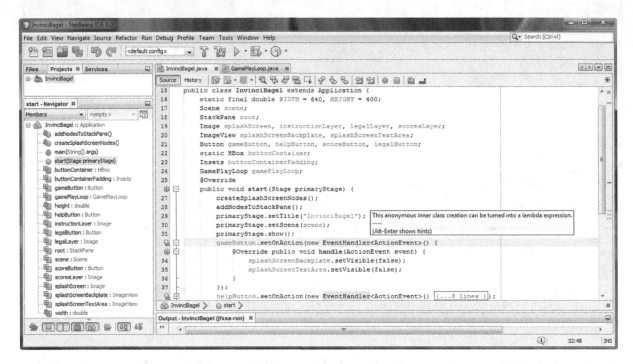

Figure 9-5. *Mouse-over wavy yellow warning highlight, and reveal a "inner class can be turned into a lambda" pop-up*

When you mouse-over these, they will give you a "This anonymous inner class creation can be turned into a lambda expression," message. This lets you know that NetBeans 8.0 may be willing to write some lambda expression code for you, which is really nifty.

To find out, you'll need to leverage your trusty **Alt-Enter** work process, and as you can see there is a lambda expression option that will have NetBeans rewrite the code as a lambda expression. The original code looked like this:

```
gameButton.setOnAction(new EventHandler<ActionEvent>() {
    @Override public void handle(ActionEvent event) {
        splashScreenBackplate.setVisible(false);
        splashScreenTextArea.setVisible(false);
    }
});
```

The lambda expression that NetBeans codes is much more compact and looks like the following Java 8 code:

```
gameButton.setOnAction((ActionEvent event) -> {
    splashScreenBackplate.setVisible(false);
    splashScreenTextArea.setVisible(false);
});
```

As you can see in Figure 9-6, this lambda expression that NetBeans wrote for you is not without warnings itself, as there is a "Parameter event is not used" warning, so we will be removing the **event** next, to make the lambda expression even more compact! At some point in time, Oracle will update this code that writes lambda expressions so that it looks inside of your method code block, sees that there is no event object referenced, and will remove this as well, and the warning will no longer be generated. Until that time comes, we'll need to edit NetBeans' code ourselves.

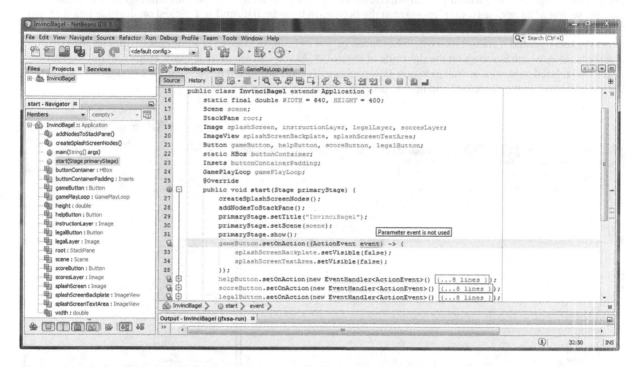

Figure 9-6. *The lambda expression that NetBeans writes for you has a warning message "Parameter event is not used"*

Since we are not using the event variable inside of the code body of this lambda expression, we can remove it, giving us this following final Java 8 lambda expression code, which is quite a bit more simple than the original code:

```
gameButton.setOnAction((ActionEvent) -> {
    splashScreenBackplate.setVisible(false);
    splashScreenTextArea.setVisible(false);
});
```

As you can see the lambda expression requires that the Java compiler create the ActionEvent object for you, replacing a **new EventHandler<ActionEvent>()** constructor method call with the **ActionEvent** object it creates. If you are wondering why lambda expressions were added to Java 8, and how they make it better, they allow a Java function (method), especially a "one shot" or inner method, to be written like a statement. They also facilitate multi-threading.

Before we get into event handling classes in Java 8 and JavaFX, let's take a look at an update I encountered as I was writing this chapter, as well as a couple of warning highlights that are appearing, which are not accurate.

Handling NetBeans Unexpected Updates and Incorrect Warnings

As I was "upgrading" my UI Button event handling code structures to use lambda expressions, as shown in Figure 9-7, I noticed a couple of things I wanted to take a couple of pages to address before I proceed to get into event handling. First of all, there is an incorrect warning "Parameter ActionEvent is not used," which is incorrect, as an event handling construct inherently uses an ActionEvent object, and besides that, why don't the other identical constructs above and below this exhibit the same warning? I ran the code and it all works great, so I am ignoring this highlight in NetBeans. I also am seeing a "39 updates found" message at the bottom-right of the IDE, and so I clicked on the blue link that said "click here to make your IDE up to date," and I took a couple of screen shots showing the work process I went through to get my IDE updated. I am not sure where NetBeans got the 39 from, as there were hundreds of updates listed in an installer dialog, which is shown on the right side of Figure 9-7. As you can see there are numerous updates to JavaFX, Java 8 and related packages, as well as to non-Java packages that are supported by NetBeans 8. I clicked on the **Next** button and invoked the download and update process, which took several minutes.

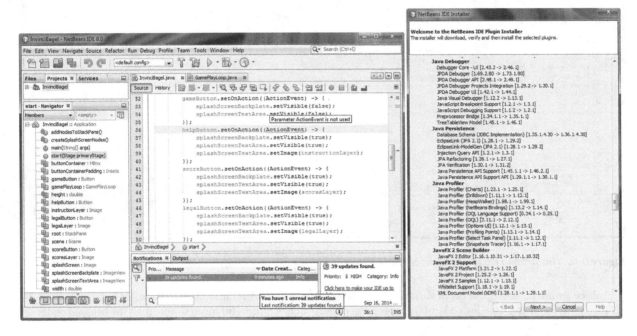

Figure 9-7. *Showing the incorrect lambda expression warning message and the 39 updates found notification message*

As you can see on the left-hand side of Figure 9-8, you will have to read and then accept all of those relevant licensing agreements that are required for you to download and install all of the software package upgrades which you will be upgrading to since you initially installed Java 8 and NetBeans (or since you last updated your IDE).

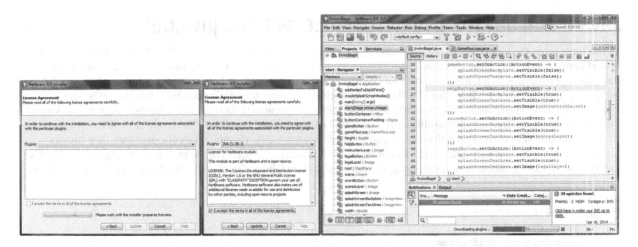

Figure 9-8. *Showing the License Agreement dialog (left) and the download and update progress bar (right) in NetBeans*

Select the "I accept the terms in all of the license agreements" checkbox, and click on the **Update** button, to start the downloading and installation process. As you can see on the bottom-right of Figure 9-8, a progress bar will tell you exactly how much has been downloaded, as well as what is being downloaded and installed onto the system.

Let's spend the remainder of this chapter taking a look at event handling, and the event-related classes in Java and JavaFX that we can use to provide different types of event handling to our Java 8 game development efforts.

Event Handling: Adding Interactivity to Your Games

One could argue that event handing is at the very foundation and core of game development, as without a way to interface with the game play logic and actors, you really don't have much of a game at all. I am going to cover the Java and JavaFX event handling related classes during this section of the chapter, and then we'll implement keypad event handing, so that we can support using the **arrow keys** to navigate our InvinciBagel character around the screen. After that, we'll turn that Java 7 compatible code into Java 8 compatible lambda expressions, and then we will be ready to cover sprite movement around the screen during the next chapter of the book. The first thing I want to talk about before we start dissecting Java and JavaFX classes is the different types of events that are handled for games, from the arrow keys (DPAD on Smartphones) to keyboard (or remotes for iTV) to mouse (or trackball on Smartphones) to touchscreen (Smartphones and Tablets) to game controllers (Game Consoles and iTV Sets) to gyroscopes and accelerometers (Smartphones and Tablets) to motion controllers such as the Leap Motion and Razer Hydra Portal.

Types of Controllers: What Types of Events Should We Handle?

One of the key things to look at is what is the most logical approach to supporting game play related events, such as arrow keys; mouse clicks; touchscreen events; game controller buttons (A, B, C and D); and more advanced controllers, such as gyroscopes and accelerometers that are available on Android, Kindle, Tizen, and iOS consumer electronics devices. This decision will be driven by the hardware devices that a game is targeted to run on; if a game needs to run everywhere, then code for handling different event types, and even different programming approaches to event handling, will ultimately be required. We'll take a look at what input events are currently supported in Java 8.

It is also interesting to note that Java 8 and JavaFX apps are already working on these embedded platforms, and I'd put money on **native support** on **open platforms** (Android, Tizen, Chrome, Ubuntu), and proprietary platforms that currently support Java technology (Windows, Blackberry, Samsung Bada, LGE WebOS, Firefox OS, Opera, etc.), at some point in time in the near future. The future of Java 8 is bright, thanks to JavaFX and hardware platform support!

Java 8 and JavaFX Events: javafx.event and java.util

As you have seen, the **javafx.event** package's **EventHandler** public interface, which extends the **java.util** package's **EventListener** interface, is the way that **Event** objects are created and handled, either using an anonymous inner class (Java 7) structure, or a lambda expression (Java 8). You have become familiar now with how to code both of these types of event handling structures, and I will continue during this book to initially code methods using the Java 7 (anonymous inner class) approach, and I will then use NetBeans to convert them to Java 8 lambda expressions so that you can create games that are compatible with both Java 7 (Android) and Java 8 (PC OS) game code delivery pipelines.

The **ActionEvent** class (and objects) that you've used thus far during the book for your user interface Button control event handling is a subclass of the **Event** superclass, which is a subclass of the **java.util** package's **EventObject** superclass, which is a subclass of the java.lang.Object master class. The entire class hierarchy is structured as follows:

```
java.lang.Object
  > java.util.EventObject
    > javafx.event.Event
      > javafx.event.ActionEvent
```

The ActionEvent class is also in the javafx.event package, along with the EventHandler public interface. All of the other event-related classes that we will be using from here on out are contained in a **javafx.scene.input** package. I am going to focus on the javafx.scene.input package for the rest of this chapter, as you have already learned how to use the EventHandler<ActionEvent> {...} structure for Java 7 and the (ActionEvent) -> {...} structure for Java 8, so it is time to learn how to use other types of events, called **input events**, in our Java 8 game development work process.

Let's take a look next at this important JavaFX Scene input event package, and the twenty-five input event classes that it provides us to use for our Java 8 game development.

JavaFX Input Event Classes: The javafx.scene.input Package

Even though it is the java.util and javafx.event packages that contain the core **EventObject**, **Event** and **EventHandler** classes that "handle" the events, at the foundational level of making sure that the events get processed (handled), there is another JavaFX package called **javafx.scene.input** which contains the classes that we will be interested in using to process (handle) our player's input for the different types of games that you might be creating. I will call these "input events," because they are different events than the action events and pulse (timing) events that we have encountered thus far in the book. Once we've covered input events in this chapter, you will be familiar with many of the different types of events that you will want to use in your own Java 8 games development. Later on in the chapter we will also implement a KeyEvent object to handle arrow keypad (or DPAD and game controller) usage in our game.

It's interesting to note that a number of the input event types that are supported in the javafx.scene.input package are more suited to consumer electronics (the industry term is "embedded") devices, such as smartphones or tablets, which tells me that JavaFX is being positioned (designed) for use on open source platforms such as Android or Chrome. JavaFX has specialized events such as **GestureEvent**, **SwipeEvent**, **TouchEvent**, and **ZoomEvent**, that support specific features in the new embedded devices marketplace. These input event classes support advanced touchscreen device features, such as gestures, page swiping, touchscreen input handling, and multi-touch display that are required features for these devices, which support advanced input paradigms such as two-finger (pinching in or spreading out) touch input, for instance, to zoom in and out of the content on the screen.

We will be covering the more "universal" input types in this book, which are supported across both personal computers (desktops, laptops, notebooks, netbooks, and the newer "pro" tablets, such as the Surface Pro 3) as well as embedded devices, including smartphones, tablets, e-Readers, iTV sets, game consoles, home media centers, Set-Top Boxes (STBs), and so forth. These devices will also process these more widespread (in their implementation) **KeyEvent** and **MouseEvent** types of input events, as mouse and key events are always supported for legacy software packages.

It is interesting to note that a touchscreen display will "handle" mouse events as well as touch events, which is very convenient as far as making sure that your game works across as many different platforms as possible. I often use this approach of using mouse event handling in my Android book titles, so that both the touchscreen and a DPAD center (click) button can be used by the user to generate a mouse click event without having to specifically use touch events. Another advantage of using mouse (click) events where possible for touchscreen users is that if you use touch events, you cannot go in the other direction, that is, your game application will only work on touchscreen devices and not on devices (such as iTV sets, laptops, desktops, netbooks, and the like) that feature mouse hardware of some type.

This same principle applies to key events, especially the arrow keys we will be using for this game, as these keys can be found on the arrow keypad on keyboards and remote controls, on game controllers, and on the DPAD on most smartphones. I will also show you how to include alternate key mapping so that your players can decide which input method they prefer to use to play your Java 8 game. Let's take a look at the KeyCode and KeyEvent classes next.

The KeyCode Class: Using Enum Constants to Define Keys Players Use for Game

Since we are going to use the **arrow keypad** for our game, and possibly the **A-S-D-W** keys, and in the future, the game controller's **GAME_A, GAME_B, GAME_C** and **GAME_D** buttons, let's take a closer look at the **KeyCode** class first. This class is a public **Enum** class that holds **enumerated constant** values. This class is where the KeyEvent class goes to get the KeyCode constant values that it uses (processes) to determine which key was used by the player for any particular key event invocation. The Java 8 and JavaFX class hierarchy for the KeyCode class looks like the following:

```
java.lang.Object
  > java.lang.Enum<KeyCode>
  > javafx.scene.input.KeyCode
```

The constant values contained in the KeyCode class use **capital letters**, and are named after the key that the keycode supports. For instance, the a, s, w, and d keycodes are **A, S, W,** and **D**. The arrow keypad keycodes are **UP, DOWN, LEFT,** and **RIGHT**, and the game controller button keycodes are **GAME_A, GAME_B, GAME_C,** and **GAME_D**.

We will be implementing KeyCode constants along with the KeyEvent object in the EventHandler object in a bit, after we cover these foundational packages and classes for input event handling. As you will soon see, this is done in much the same way that an ActionEvent is set up to be handled, and KeyEvents can be coded using the Java 7 inner class approach, or by using a Java 8 lambda expression.

We will set up our KeyEvent object handling in a very **modular** fashion, so that an event KeyCode evaluation structure sets Boolean flag variables for each KeyCode mapping. The nature of event processing is that it is a real-time engine, like the pulse engine, so these Boolean **flags** will provide an accurate "view" of what keys are being pressed or released by the player during any given nanosecond. These Boolean values can then be read and acted upon, by using Java game programming logic in our other game engine classes, which will then process these key events in real time.

The KeyEvent Class: Using KeyEvent Objects to Hold KeyCode Players Are Using

Next, let's take a closer look at the **KeyEvent** class. This class is designated **public final KeyEvent,** and it extends the **InputEvent** superclass, which is used to create all of the input event subclasses that are in the javafx.scene. input package. The KeyEvent class is set into motion using the EventHandler class, and handles **KeyCode** class constant values. This class's hierarchy starts with the java.lang.Object master class and goes through the java. util.EventObject event superclass to the javafx.event.Event class, which is used to create the javafx.scene.input. InputEvent class that the KeyEvent class extends (subclasses). It is interesting to note that we are spanning four different packages here!

The Java 8 and JavaFX class hierarchy for the KeyEvent class jumps from the java.lang package to the java.util package to the javafx.event package to the javafx.scene.input package. The KeyEvent class hierarchy looks like the following:

```
java.lang.Object
  > java.util.EventObject
    > javafx.event.Event
      > javafx.scene.input.InputEvent
        > javafx.scene.input.KeyEvent
```

The generation of a KeyEvent object by the EventHandler object indicates that a keystroke has occurred. A KeyEvent is often generated in a Scene Graph Node, such as an editable text UI control, but in our case we are going to attach our event handling above the Scene Graph Node hierarchy directly to the Scene object named **scene**, hoping to avoid any Scene Graph processing overhead that would be incurred by attaching event handling to any of the Node objects in the Scene Graph (in our case, this is currently the StackPane object named **root**).

A KeyEvent object is generated whenever a key is **pressed** and held down, **released**, or **typed** (pressed and immediately released). Depending on the nature of this key pressing action itself, your KeyEvent object is passed into either an **.onKeyPressed()**, an **.onKeyTyped()** or an **.onKeyReleased()** method for further processing inside the nested .handle() method, which is what will hold your game-specific programming logic.

Games typically use key-pressed and key-released events, as users typically press and hold keys to move the actors in the game. Key-typed events on the other hand tend to be "higher-level" events and generally do not depend upon the OS platform or the keyboard layout. Typed key events (.onKeyTyped() method calls) will be generated when a Unicode character is entered, and are used to obtain **character input** for UI controls such as text fields, and are used for business applications, such as calendars and word processors, for instance.

In a simple case, the key-typed event will be produced by using a single key press and its immediate release. Additionally, alternate characters can be produced using combinations of key press events, for instance, the capital A can be produced using a SHIFT key press and an 'a' key-type (press and immediate release).

A key-release is not usually necessary to generate a key-typed KeyEvent object. It is important to notice that there are some fringe cases where a key-typed event is not generated until the key is released; a great example of this is the process of entering **ASCII character code sequences**, using that old-school **Alt-Key-with-Numeric-keypad** entry method, which was used "back in the day," with DOS and held over into Windows OSes.

It is important to note that no key-typed KeyEvent objects will be generated for keys that do not generate any Unicode characters. This would include action keys or modifier keys, although these do generate key-pressed and key-released KeyEvent objects, and could thus be used for game play! This would not represent a good user interface design (or user experience design) approach, generally speaking, as these keys are used to modify other key behavior.

The KeyEvent class has a **character** variable (I am tempted to call this a character characteristic, but I won't) which will always contains a valid **Unicode character** for a key-typed event or **CHAR_UNDEFINED** for a key-pressed or key-released event. Character input is only reported for key-typed events, since key-pressed and key-released events are not necessarily associated with character input. Therefore, the character variable is guaranteed to be meaningful only for key-typed events. In a sense, by not using key-typed events, we are saving both memory and CPU processing, by not having to process this Unicode character variable.

For key-pressed and key-released KeyEvent objects, the **code** variable in the KeyEvent class will contain your KeyEvent object's keycode, defined using the KeyCode class you learned about earlier. For key-typed events, this code variable always contains the constant **KeyCode.UNDEFINED**. So as you can see, key-pressed and key-released are thus designed to be used differently than key-typed, and that's the reason we are using these for our game event handling.

Key-pressed and key-released events are low-level, and depend upon platform or keyboard layout. They are generated whenever a given key is pressed or released, and are the only way to "poll" the keys that do not generate character input. The key being pressed or released is indicated by the **code** variable, which contains a virtual KeyCode.

Adding Keyboard Event Handling: Using KeyEvents

I think that is enough background information for us to move on to implementing KeyEvent processing for the game, so add a line of code after your screen WIDTH and HEIGHT constant declarations, and declare four Boolean variables named **up**, **down**, **left**, and **right**, using a single compound declaration statement, shown in Figure 9-9. Since the default value for any Boolean value is **false** (which will signify a key which is not being pressed, that is, a key which is currently released), we do not have to **explicitly initialize** these variables. This is done by using the following line of Java code, which is also shown error-free at the top of Figure 9-9:

```java
boolean up, down, left, right;
```

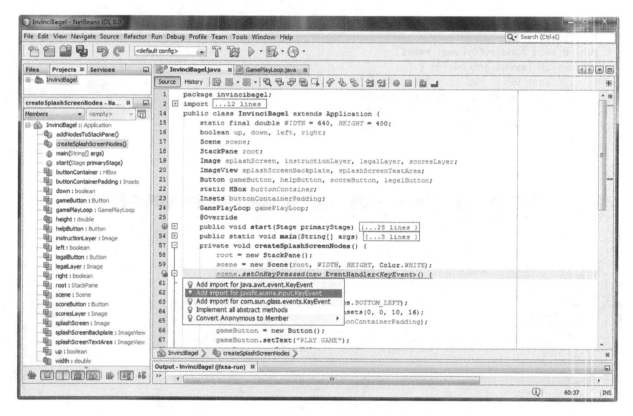

Figure 9-9. *Add a .setOnKeyPressed() function call off a scene object and create a new EventHandler<KeyEvent> object*

As you can see at the bottom of Figure 9-9, I put the foundation for my KeyEvent (pressed) handling using the .setOnKeyPressed() method call off of the Scene object named scene, which I have instantiated in the previous line of code. Inside of this method call I create a new EventHandler<KeyEvent> just like we did for our action events. The code, which as you can see has an error message attached to it until you import a **KeyEvent** class, looks like this:

```java
scene.setOnKeyPressed(new EventHandler<KeyEvent>() { your .handle() method will go in here });
```

Use an **Alt-Enter** work process to select an **import javafx.scene.input.KeyEvent** option seen in Figure 9-9, to remove this error message. Next, let's take a look at the .handle() method we need to write to process the KeyEvent.

Processing Your KeyEvent: Using the Switch-Case Statement

KeyEvent object processing is a perfect application for implementing Java's highly efficient **switch-case** statement. We can add a **case** statement for each type of KeyCode constant that is contained inside of any KeyEvent (named **event**) that is passed into the .handle() method. A KeyCode can be extracted from a KeyEvent object using a **.getCode()** method. This method is called on the KeyEvent object named event, inside of the switch() evaluation area. Inside of the switch{} body, the case statements compare themselves against this extracted KeyCode constant, and if there is a match, the statements after the colon are processed. The break; statement allows processing to exit the switch-case evaluation, as an optimization.

This event handling switch-case structure should be implemented by using the following Java programming structure, which is also shown highlighted in Figure 9-10:

```java
scene.setOnKeyPressed(new EventHandler<KeyEvent>() {
    @Override
    public void handle(KeyEvent event) {
        switch (event.getCode()) {
            case UP:    up    = true; break;
            case DOWN:  down  = true; break;
            case LEFT:  left  = true; break;
            case RIGHT: right = true; break;
        }
    }
});
```

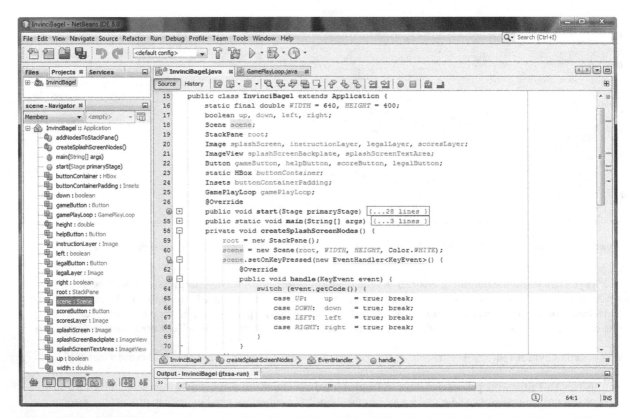

Figure 9-10. *Add a switch-case statement inside of the public void handle() method setting Boolean direction variables*

Now we have the basic **key-pressed** event handling structure, which we'll be adding to a bit later, let's have NetBeans turn this Java 7 code into a Java 8 lambda expression for us! After that, we can create a **key-released** event handling structure by using a block copy and paste operation, turning the .setOnKeyPressed() to .setOnKeyReleased(), and the true values to false values. Programming shortcuts are almost as cool as having NetBeans write code for us!

Converting the KeyEvent Handling Structure: Using a Java 8 Lambda Expression

Next let's have NetBeans recode our EventHandler<KeyEvent> code structure as a lambda expression, which will simplify it significantly, reducing it from a three-deep nested code block to one that is nested only two deep, and from eleven lines of code to only eight. These lambda expressions are really elegant for writing tight code, and they are designed for multi-threaded environments, so whenever possible their usage could result in more optimal Thread usage! The resulting Java 8 lambda expression code structure should look like the following, as shown in Figure 9-11:

```java
scene.setOnKeyPressed(KeyEvent event) -> {
    switch (event.getCode()) {
        case UP:    up    = true; break; // UP, DOWN, LEFT, RIGHT constants from KeyCode class
        case DOWN:  down  = true; break;
        case LEFT:  left  = true; break;
        case RIGHT: right = true; break;
    }
});
```

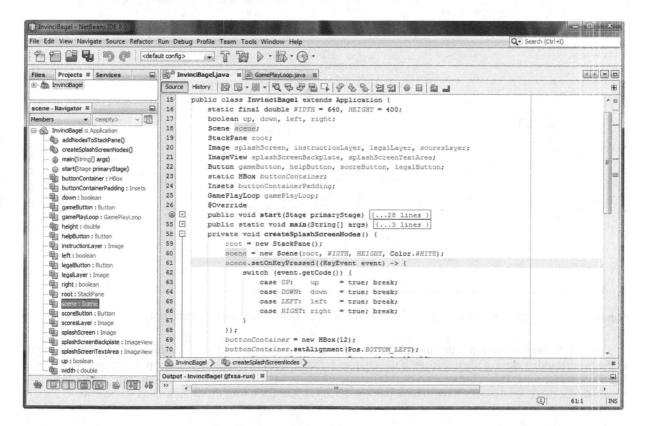

Figure 9-11. *Convert the KeyEvent method to a lambda expression; notice that the event variable is used in the switch*

Next, let's use a block copy and paste operation, and copy the .OnKeyPressed() KeyEvent handing structure underneath itself, changing it to be an .OnKeyReleased KeyEvent handling structure, with false values instead of true.

Creating the KeyPressed KeyEvent Handling Structure

The next thing that we will need to do is to create the polar opposite of the OnKeyPressed structure, and create the OnKeyReleased structure. This will use the same code structure, except that the true values will become false values, and the .setOnKeyPressed() method call will instead be a .setOnKeyReleased() method call. The easiest way to do this is to select the .setOnKeyPressed() structure, and copy and paste it underneath itself. The Java code, which is shown in Figure 9-12, should look like this Java structure:

```java
scene.setOnKeyReleased(KeyEvent event) -> {
    switch (event.getCode()) {
        case UP:    up    = false; break;
        case DOWN:  down  = false; break;
        case LEFT:  left  = false; break;
        case RIGHT: right = false; break;
    }
});
```

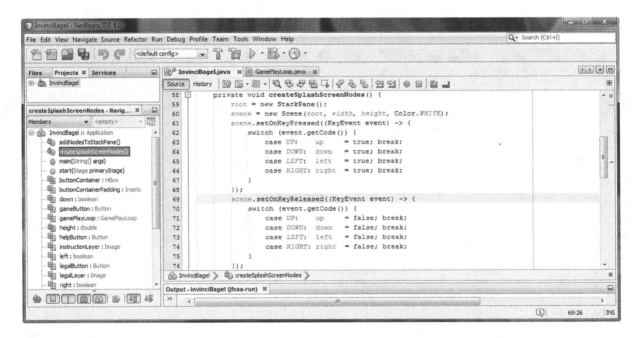

Figure 9-12. *Use a block copy and paste operation to create .setOnKeyReleased() code block, using .setOnKeyPressed()*

One of the interesting things that using lambda expressions does by "implicitly" declaring and using classes, such as the EventHandler class in the instances in this chapter, is that it **reduces the number of import statements** in the top of your class code. This is because if a class is not specifically used (its name written) in your code, the import statement for that class does not have to be in place at the top of your code with the other import statements.

Also, notice that the code-collapsing plus and minus icons in the left margin of NetBeans are also gone! This is because a lambda expression is a basic Java code statement, and not a construct, such as a method or inner class as it was before you converted it to a lambda expression. If you look at Figure 9-12, your event handling code is looking very clean and well-structured, and yet, in just over a dozen lines of code, it is actually doing quite a lot for your game.

Next, let's take a look at your import statements code block (especially if you have your import code block collapsed), since you had NetBeans 8 create lambda expressions for you. Let's see if you have any unneeded imports!

Optimizing Import Statements: Remove the EventHandler Class Import Statement

Click the + plus icon at the top-left of NetBeans and expand your import statement section and see if you now have an unused import javafx.event.EventHandler statement with wavy yellow underline warning highlighting underneath it. I have this, as you can see in Figure 9-13, and when I mouse-over it I get the "Unused Import" warning message. I used the **Alt-Enter** work process to bring up the solutions options helper dialog, and sure enough, there was a "Remove Import Statement" option. So NetBeans will unwrite code for you as well as writing it for you! Pretty amazing feature!

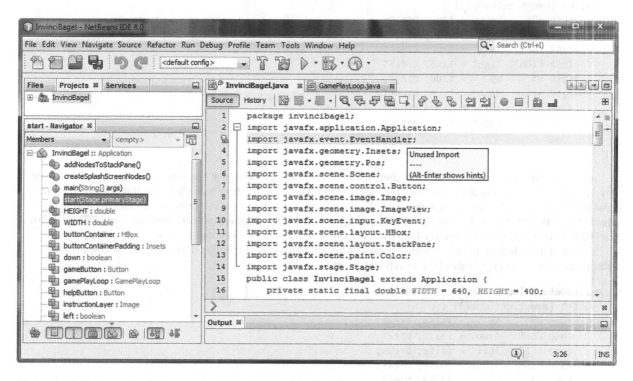

Figure 9-13. Mouse-over the import EventHandler warning highlight, and display the pop-up "Unused Import" warning

Next, let's add the traditional ASDW game play key event handling, to give our users an option to use those keys or to use two hands for their game play! This will show you how to add alternate key mapping support to your existing event handling code, using only a few more lines of code in the highly efficient switch-case statement.

Adding Alternate KeyEvent Mapping: Using A-S-D-W

Now that we have these KeyEvent handling structures in place, let's take a look at how easy it is to add an alternate key mapping to the ASDW keys often used for game play. This is done by adding in a few more case statements for the A, S, D, and W characters on the keyboard, and setting them to the UP, DOWN, LEFT, and RIGHT Boolean equivalents that we have set up already. This will allow users to use the A and D characters with their left hand and the UP and DOWN arrows with their right hand for easier game play, for instance.

Later on, if you wanted to add more features to your game play, using your game controller, and its support for the KeyCode class's **GAME_A (Jump)**, **GAME_B (Fly)**, **GAME_C (climb)**, and **GAME_D (crawl)** constants, all that you would have to do is to add these new features into your game would be to add another four Boolean variables (jump, fly, climb, and crawl) to the up, down, left, and right at the top of the screen, and add in another four case statements.

These four W (UP), S (DOWN), A (LEFT), and D (RIGHT) case statements, once added to the switch statement, would bring your KeyEvent object and its event handling Java code structure to only a dozen lines of Java code. Your new .setOnKeyPressed() event handling structure would look like this block of code after you make this modification:

```
scene.setOnKeyPressed(KeyEvent event) -> {
    switch (event.getCode()) {
        case UP:    up    = true; break;
        case DOWN:  down  = true; break;
        case LEFT:  left  = true; break;
        case RIGHT: right = true; break;
        case W:     up    = true; break;
        case S:     down  = true; break;
        case A:     left  = true; break;
        case D:     right = true; break;
    }
});
```

As you can see, now the user can use either set of keys, or both sets of keys at the same time, to control the game play. Now that you have made the .setOnKeyPressed() event handling structure more flexible (and powerful) for the game player, let's do the same thing to the .setOnKeyReleased() event handling structure, which will instead set a **false** value to the up, down, left and right Boolean flag variables when the user has **released** the A or LEFT, W or UP, S or DOWN, or D or RIGHT keys on the keyboard, remote control, or device keyboard and keypad.

Your .setOnKeyReleased() event handling Java code should look like the following once you add these case statements at the end of the body of the switch statement:

```
scene.setOnKeyReleased(KeyEvent event) -> {
    switch (event.getCode()) {
        case UP:    up    = false; break;
        case DOWN:  down  = false; break;
        case LEFT:  left  = false; break;
        case RIGHT: right = false; break;
        case W:     up    = false; break;
        case S:     down  = false; break;
        case A:     left  = false; break;
        case D:     right = false; break;
    }
});
```

Now that you have added another set of player movement control keys for your player to use to control the game play, your code is error free, and has a simple, effective structure, as is shown in Figure 9-14. We are handling the events one time at the very top of the Scene object named scene, not involving any Scene Graph Node objects in this event handling "calculation," and are using only a few bytes of memory to hold eight Boolean (on/off) values.

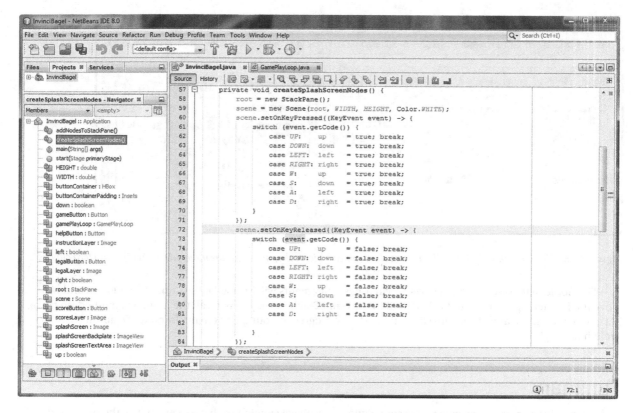

Figure 9-14. *Add the case statements for ASDW keys to give users two key options, or to allow two-handed game play*

This is in keeping with our objective of optimizing both memory and CPU cycles, so that these are available for the more advanced parts of our game play, such as the game play logic, collision detection, or physics calculation.

We also added constants that will allow us to later scale this 640 by 400 game prototype to fit display screens of different resolutions such as Pseudo HD (1280 by 720), True HD (1920 by 1080), and UHD (4096 by 2160). These can also be used in the game logic, to calculate the size of the screen area to determine movement boundaries.

So far, we have added our actor and supporting cast engine, as well as our basic event handling processing, so that we can start to determine how this InvinciBagel game hero is going to move around on the screen in the next chapter. We have .handle() as well as .update() and .collide() methods in place to hold the code, which will animate a character, and eventually enemies, in both the single-player as well as a future multi-player version of this game.

Next, let's revisit our overview diagram of this game design, and take a look at the InvinciBagel package, the InvinciBagel.java class, and the GamePlayLoop and Actor and Hero classes, which provide the foundation for our game play processing and actor (and projectiles, treasure, enemy and obstacles or "props") creation.

Updating Our Game Design: Adding Event Handling

Let's update the diagram that I introduced in Chapter 7 (Figure 7-19) and updated in Chapter 8 (Figure 8-17) to include the ActionEvent and KeyEvent handling by the EventHandler class. As you can see in Figure 9-15, I added the EventHandler event handling class to the diagram as well as the ActionEvent objects that handle our UI design control and the KeyEvent that we are going to use to move the InvinciBagel actor around the screen. Since the .setOnKeyPressed() and .setOnKeyReleased() methods are called off of the scene Scene object named scene, and the ActionEvent is also contained under the Scene object, I placed these inside of the Scene object in the diagram.

Diagram of invincibagel package and InvinciBagel Class (and Object) Hierarchy

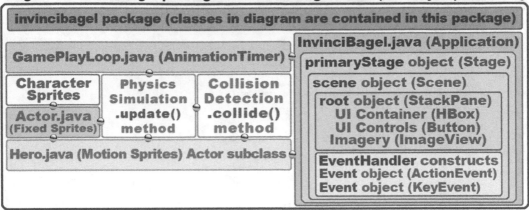

Figure 9-15. *The current InvinciBagel package class (object) hierarchy, now that we have added Actor and Hero classes*

The Boolean flags set by the KeyEvent switch-case statements will be used in the .update() method and will move the InvinciBagel. The .handle() method in the GamePlayLoop object will call the .update() method, so there is a connection there as well. We are still making steady progress on our game engine framework, adding event handling!

Summary

In this ninth chapter, we added constants to our game Scene object creation so that we can change the supported display resolution at any time in the future, as well as adding a Color.WHITE background color using one of the other overloaded Scene() constructor methods. We did this so that we could finish our UI design and implement the PLAY GAME UI Button control so that it would hide the two ImageView image compositing plates that currently hold splash screen assets, and which can later hold game background digital image assets.

We learned about the ImageView class (and object) **visible** characteristic (or attribute, or variable), and how to use the **.setVisible()** method call to toggle the visibility of a given ImageView image plate using true or false values. Since we turned the ImageView image compositing plate's visibility off in the ActionEvent handling structure for the PLAY GAME Button, we then of course had to make sure that the visible attribute was set back to **true** (on or visible) for the other three Button UI controls in case your game player wanted to review any of these screens at a later time.

Next we covered how to turn Java 7 compatible anonymous inner class event handling structures into a Java 8 lambda expression using NetBeans. I wanted to cover Java 8 **lambda expressions** in this book, even though they are an advanced feature, because they are one of the major new features in Java 8, and this is a Java 8 programming title.

Finally we got into adding new features to our Java 8 game programming infrastructure, and learned about **input event** (InputEvent) classes and subclasses and about how the event handler (EventHandler) class structures are set up, and how they span across the java.lang, java.util, javafx.event and javafx.scene.input packages. We took a look at **KeyCode** constants and at the **KeyEvent** class, and then implemented this KeyEvent handing in our Java game code, using **.setOnKeyPressed()** and **.setOnKeyReleased()** event handler structures for both Java 7 and Java 8 compatibility.

In the next chapter, we are going to take a look at how to move a game sprite around your screen using this KeyEvent event handling structure that we have created during this chapter, as well as how to ascertain the boundary (edges) of the screen, character direction, movement velocity, and related animation and movement considerations.

Directing the Cast of Actors: Creating a Casting Director Engine and Creating the Bagel Actor Class

Now that we have created the public abstract Actor and Hero classes (the Actor Engine) in Chapter 8, and some basic KeyEvent handling in Chapter 9, it is time to put more of our game infrastructure in place here in Chapter 10. We are going to create yet another Java class to manage our cast of actors, called **CastingDirector.java** (the Casting Engine). We will do this so that we can keep track of the Actor objects on the game play screen that have been created using our Actor and Hero abstract classes. It is important to know what game components (actors) are currently on the screen (or stage, or set, if you like the film production lingo that we are using) at any given time (or level) in the game.

In this chapter, we'll also need to learn more about, and use, the **List** and **ArrayList** classes as well as the **Set** and **HashSet** classes. These Java "collection" classes will manage the List objects and Set object that we'll use to **track** the current Actor objects that are involved in the game play on the screen. We'll cover these **java.util** package classes in detail early on during this chapter, so get ready to learn about Java Array objects, and some other fairly advanced Java programming concepts that may be a challenge for the beginner. However, they will be very useful for you to use in your Java 8 game title development work process, so I have decided to include them in this book.

We will also want to create our first actor for the game, the InvinciBagel character actor, since I don't want to get too far removed from the code that we wrote in Chapter 8 without implementing it (using it to create an actor). We will accomplish this by creating a **Bagel.java** class that will use the Java **extends** keyword to subclass a Hero.java abstract class. This makes Bagel.java into a subclass, and makes Hero.java a superclass.

Once we have a Bagel.java class in place, we will then use the Java **new** keyword and the Bagel() constructor method for the Bagel class to create a Bagel object named **iBagel**. We will load the iBagel object with some temporary SVG data, at least until we get into how to create complex SVG collision shape data in Chapter 16 covering collision detection. We will also pass an X and Y coordinate, to put the iBagel actor in the middle of the screen, and finally the 9-character movement sprite "cels," which we first looked at during Chapter 8.

We will do this so you can start to utilize the primary data fields (variables, properties, or attributes) that we installed in a public abstract Actor and Hero class infrastructure, which we so painstakingly (or, should I say, lovingly) designed back in Chapter 8.

We will also be working in our **InvinciBagel.java** primary application class again here in Chapter 10, and will create our **iBagel** Bagel (Hero) object in a new **.createGameActor()** method we will be coding, so that we can wire our main character up to the GamePlayLoop class's .handle() method. This will then access (call) the Bagel class .update() method, so that we can start to control the movements for the primary hero for our game, the InvinciBagel himself.

Game Design: Adding Our CastingDirector.java class

The first thing that I want to do to is to update our invincibagel package and class structure diagram to show you the new actor (sprite) management class that we are going to develop during this chapter using Java **ArrayList** and **HashSet** classes (objects). As you can see in Figure 10-1, I am going to name this class **CastingDirector.java** because it will act just like a Casting Director would for any entertainment project, adding Actors to the project, and removing them when the scene is finished. This class will also contain a Java **collection** (a Java ListArray is an ordered collection and a Java HashSet is an unordered collection) that will be used when we start to implement collision detection later on during the book. As your game levels and scenes get more complicated, you will be glad to have a CastingDirector class that keeps your game actors organized and adds and removes actors from the game as needed by your game's programming logic. It is important to keep track of exactly how many Actor (fixed sprites) and Hero (motion sprites) objects are in the scene, so that you only involve the fewest possible number of actors in your collision detection code (algorithms). This is a function of optimizing your game programming logic so the game plays well across all platforms.

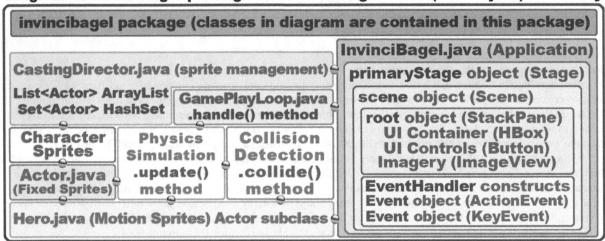

Diagram of invincibagel package and InvinciBagel Class (and Object) Hierarchy

Figure 10-1. *Create a CastingDirector.java actor casting and tracking engine to keep track of Actor and Hero objects*

Before we code our CastingDirector.java class, let's take some time to learn about Java collections, generics, and the List, ListArray, Set and HashSet classes that we are going to use to create these actor management tools.

List and ArrayList: Using java.util List Management

First, let's cover the **public** class **ArrayList<E>** because it is a class, and then we will look at List as that is an Interface, and not a Java class. In case you are wondering what the **<E>** stands for, it stands for **Element**, if you see a **<K>** that stands for **Key**, if you see a **<T>** that stands for **Type**, and if you see a **<V>** that stands for **Value**. The <E> gets replaced by an element (object) that you're using in an ArrayList. In our case that is ArrayList<Actor> as CastingDirector.java class ArrayList (and Set) will reference Actor objects (subclasses of Actor superclass). The class hierarchy is as follows:

```
java.lang.Object
  > java.util.AbstractCollection<E>
    > java.util.AbstractList<E>
      > java.util.ArrayList<E>
```

This class is a member of the **Java Collections Framework**, as you might have surmised, as a List, as well as an Array, both contain collections of data, much like a data structure (or a data store) does, only in a simpler format. An ArrayList<E> class can **"implement"** or support the following Java Interfaces: Serializable, Cloneable, Iterable<E>, Collection<E>, List<E>, and RandomAccess. We will be using the List<E> or, in our case, List<Actor> Java interface, which we will be looking at in the next section on List<E> when we will learn about **Java Interfaces**.

Essentially the ArrayList class (and object) creates a **resizable Array** implementation of the List<E> interface. An ArrayList object thus implements all optional List operations, and permits all types of List elements, including **null**. In addition to implementing the List<E> Java interface, this class also provides method calls, including a **.removeAll()**, **.addAll()**, and **.clear()**, which we will be using in our class, to manipulate both the List content as well as the size of the ArrayList object that is used internally to store the List of Actors (for List<Actor>) or Images (for List<Image>) used.

Each ArrayList object instance has a capacity. The capacity is the size of the Array used to store the elements (objects) in the List<E> implementation: in our case, a List<Actor>. The capacity will always be at least as large as the List size. As elements (Actor objects) are added to an ArrayList, its capacity will grow automatically, which makes it perfect for our CastingDirector class, as we can make levels of the game more and more complex that is, it can utilize more Actor objects in the ArrayList<Actor> of List<Actor>.

It is important to note that the List<E> implementation is not **synchronized** (capable of running on multiple threads simultaneously). If you need to have multiple threads access an ArrayList instance concurrently (at the same exact time), and at least one of these multiple threads modifies your List<Actor> structure, it must be synchronized externally (manually, using your code). We are going to call the CastingDirector class specifically when an enemy is killed, or a projectile is shot, or a treasure is found (collected) and will not have it being continually called on a pulse.

A structural modification of an ArrayList object is an operation that adds or removes one or more elements; merely setting the value of an element (Actor) in the ArrayList would not be considered to be structural modification.

The Java Interface: Defining Rules for Implementing Your Class

Before we look at the List<E> Java interface, let's take a look at what Java interfaces do in general, as we did not have enough pages to cover all of the Java programming language back in Chapter 3. So I am going to cover some of the more advanced Java topics as we need to learn them during the book. A good example of this is lambda expressions in Chapter 9 and Java interfaces here in Chapter 10. The reason for using a Java interface is to make sure that other programmers who are going to use your code implement it correctly; that is, include everything necessary for the code to work properly.

Essentially, all an interface specifies is the group of related methods that is needed for another developer to implement your class. These are specified with "empty method" code bodies. If you wanted to have other developers use the Hero class, for instance, you would specify a Hero interface. This would be done using the following Java code:

```
public interface Hero {
    public void update();
    public boolean collide(Actor actor);
}
```

As you can see, this is similar to what we did with the .update() method in the Actor superclass, as there is no {code body} specified as there usually is in a method. Thus, in a sense, a Java interface is also used in an abstract fashion to define what needs to be included in a class that "implements" the Java interface. As you probably have guessed, you would thus use the Java **implements** keyword in your class declaration to implement a Java interface.

So, if you had defined a Hero interface, and wanted to implement it in one of your classes, in which case the Java compiler would watch over the code and make sure that you are implementing the necessary method structures, the class definition line of code and the methods inside the body of the class would look something like the following:

```
public class SuperHero implements Hero {
    protected boolean flagVariable1, flagVariable2;
    public void update() {
        // Java statements to process on each update
    }
    public boolean collide(Actor actor) {
        // Java statements to process for collision detection
    }
}
```

So with the java.util ArrayList class that we looked at earlier, the technical class definition is as follows:

```
public class ArrayList<E> extends AbstractList<E> implements List<E>
```

The ArrayList<E> class also implements RandomAccess, Cloneable, and Serializable, but we will not be using those at this time so I am just showing you the parts of the ArrayList<E> class definition that pertain to what we will be learning during this chapter, not the full **public class ArrayList<E> extends AbstractList<E> implements List<E>, RandomAccess, Cloneable, Serializable** class definition, as you would see if you look at the Java class documentation for the ArrayList<E> class online.

It is important to notice that the **.addAll()**, **.removeAll()** and **.clear()** method calls that we will use with the ArrayList<E> class are implemented because the List<E> Java interface demands that they be implemented, so that is the connection between the classes and why we will specify the declaration of the ArrayList<> object using this code:

```
private List<Actor> CURRENT_CAST = new ArrayList<>();
```

You may be wondering why we will not need to explicitly specify the Actor object type on both sides of this declaration and instantiation statement. Prior to Java 7, you would have needed to specify your Actor object type on both sides of this statement, inside of the ArrayList<>() constructor method call. So, if you are writing game code that needs to be compatible with Java 5 and Java 6, you would code this statement using the following line of Java code:

```
private List<Actor> CURRENT_CAST = new ArrayList<Actor>();
```

Now that we have learned what a Java interface is, let's take a look at the List<E> public interface in detail.

The List<E> Public Interface: A List Collection of Java Objects

The **List<E> public interface** is also a member of the Java Collections Framework. The Java public interface List<E> extends the Collections<E> public interface, which extends the Iterable<T> public interface. Thus, the super interface to sub interface hierarchy would look something like this following List<E> Java interface hierarchy:

```
Interface Iterable<T>
  > Interface Collection<E>
    > Interface List<E>
```

A List<E> is an **ordered** Collection<E> and could also be thought of as a **sequence** of objects. In our case, the List<Actor> will be an ordered sequence of Actor objects. A user of the List interface has precise control over where in the List each element (in our case, Actor object) is inserted. The user can access elements using an **integer index**, that is, the position in the List, using a **parenthesis** after the name of the List. You can also search for elements in a List.

For instance, in the Actor.java class, we have the following line of code we declared at the top of the class:

```
protected List<Image> imageStates = new ArrayList<>();
```

To access the first Actor class imageState Image object List sprite, we will use the following Java statement:

```
imageStates.get(0);
```

Unlike Set objects, which we will be learning about in the next section of the chapter, your List<E> interface conformant ArrayList objects will typically allow duplicate elements. An example of this for a game application might include projectiles (say, bullets) if you have coded the game to allow the Enemy object to shoot at the Bagel object. We will, of course, try to keep duplicate elements in our game to a minimum for optimization purposes, but it is nice to have this capability in the List<Actor> implementation if we need to have duplicate elements in a game scene.

The List<E> interface provides four methods for positional (indexed) access to List elements (objects) using the integer index in the method call. These include the **.get(int index)** method, to get an object from the List; the **.remove(int index)** method, to remove an object from the List; the **.set(int index, E element)** method, which will replace an object within the List; and a **.listIterator()** method, which returns a **ListIterator** object from the List. A ListIterator object allows you to perform an operation (add, remove, set/replace) on more than one List element at a time, in case you might be wondering what a ListIterator is utilized for.

The List interface provides this special Iterator<E> implementation, called a **ListIterator<E>**, which is a sub interface of the Iterator<E> super interface, to allow multiple element insertion and replacement. A ListIterator<E> also provides bidirectional List access, in addition to the normal operations that the Iterator<E> interface provides.

The .listIterator() method that we discussed earlier was provided to obtain a ListIterator object that starts at a specified position in the list. So using an imageStates List<Image> ArrayList object, a imageStates.listIterator() method call would produce a ListIteration object containing an iteration over an entire imageStates ArrayList<Image> object. This would give us imageStates(0), the starting List element, as well as the remainder of this List<Image> in an ArrayList<Image> construct, which would be referenced as imageStates(1), imageStates(2), and the last one would be referenced as imageStates(8). Java List class use **() parens** to reference List objects, whereas Java Array classes use the **[] square brackets**. A Java List is "dynamic" (luckily, we have discussed static versus dynamic); that is, it's open-ended, whereas a Java Array is "static," or fixed, which means that its length needs to be defined when it is created.

Objects that implement List<E> start their numbering schema using a zero, just like all Java Array objects. This is not out of the ordinary, as most Java programming constructs will also start counting at zero instead of using one. It is important to note from an optimization standpoint that **iterating** over the elements in List<E> is typically preferable (more optimal) to indexing through it by number, for instance using a for loop, which is probably why support for this ListIterator interface is a part of the List<E> interface specification, and therefore is a part of the ArrayList class, which has no choice but to implement the List<E> interface specification because it uses the Java implements keyword.

The List<E> interface also provides three methods allowing access to the List using a specified object. These include **.indexOf(Object object)**, **.contains(Object object)**, and **.remove(Object object)**. Again, looking at it strictly from a performance standpoint, these methods should be used with caution, because having to compare an "input" object to every object inside of the List is going to take way more memory and CPU cycles than simply using the index for the object in the List. After all, that is what an index is for! In many implementations this will perform a costly "linear" object search, starting at ListElement[0] and going through the entire list comparing objects. If your object is at the "head" of this List, this would not be costly at all. One the other hand, if your object is at the end of a List containing a great many object elements, you may well observe a performance hit using these "object oriented" methods. Well, all methods are object oriented, so, let's cleverly call these methods "object parameterized" instead!

The List<E> interface also provides two methods to efficiently read or remove multiple List elements at an arbitrary point within the List. The **.removeRange(int fromIndex, int toIndex)** removes a range of List elements, and the **.subList(int fromIndex, int toIndex)** returns a view of the portion of the List between the specified fromIndex and the toIndex. The fromIndex is included in the returned sub-list, however, the toIndex is not included.

Finally, the List<E> interface provides three methods that manipulate the entire List using a single method. Since we are using the List to manage all of the Actor objects currently in the scene, we will primarily be using these methods, which were mentioned earlier in the ArrayList section of the chapter and include .addAll(), .removeAll(), and .clear(). We will also be using the **.add(E element)** method to add a single Actor object to our CURRENT_CAST List.

Finally, while it is technically permissible for a List<E> to contain itself as an element, this is not viewed as being a "good" programming practice, so I do not recommend doing this. You should use extreme caution if you are going to try doing this, because the **equals** and **hashCode** methods will no longer be "well defined" in such a List.

Set and HashSet: Using java.util Unordered Sets

The **Set<E> public interface** is also a member of the Java Collections Framework. The Java public interface Set<E> extends the Collections<E> public interface, which extends the Iterable<T> public interface. Thus, the super interface to sub interface hierarchy for Set<E> is the same as it is for List<E> and looks like the following interface hierarchy:

```
Interface Iterable<T>
  > Interface Collection<E>
    > Interface Set<E>
```

A Set<E> is an **unordered** Collection<E> and could also be thought of as a random collection of objects in no particular order. A Set<E> collection may contains **no duplicate elements**, and will throw an error, called an "exception," if a duplicate element is added to the Set<E> or if any "mutable" (elements than can change into something else) element is changed into an element that duplicates another element already in the Set<E>. This no duplicates rule also means that at the most, a Set<E> can contain only **one single null** element. As all of you who are well versed in mathematics may have surmised already, this Set<E> interface is modeled after the **mathematical set** you learned about in school.

The Set<E> interface places additional stipulations beyond those that are "inherited" from the Collection<E> super interface, on the "contracts" (requirements for all of you non-legal types) for all constructor methods, as well as on the contracts (requirements) of the **.add()**, **.equals()**, and **.hashCode()** related methods.

The additional stipulations on these constructor methods is, according to rule, that all constructors must create a Set<E> containing zero duplicate elements.

As mentioned earlier, you must be careful regarding what you are doing if mutable (changeable) objects are used as elements in a Set<E> collection. The behavior of the Set<E> is not specified if the value of an object is changed in a manner that affects the .equals() method comparisons while the mutable object is an element in that Set<E>. The special case of this prohibition is that it is not permissible for a Set<E> to contain itself as an element, as a List<E> can.

The java.util HashSet Class: Using Unordered Sets of Objects

Next, let's cover the **public** class **HashSet<E>** that is a member of the Java Collections Framework as well. This class that provides a HashSet object container for the Set<E> interface specification is similar to the way that the ArrayList<E> class creates an ArrayList object container for the List<E> interface. The HashSet class can "**implement**" or support the following Java Interfaces: Serializable, Cloneable, Iterable<E>, Collection<E>, and Set<E>. We will be using the Set<E>, or in our case, Set<Actor> interface, in our CastingDirector.java class. The Set<E> class hierarchy is as follows:

```
java.lang.Object
  > java.util.AbstractCollection<E>
    > java.util.AbstractSet<E>
      > java.util.HashSet<E>
```

The HashSet class implements the Set<E> interface in the form of a **hash table**, which is actually an instance of a **HashMap**. The HashSet makes no guarantees as to the iteration order of the Set<E> of objects; in particular, it does not guarantee that the order will remain constant over time. This class permits the use of one null element.

It is important to note that the Set<E> implementation is **not synchronized**. If multiple threads access your HashSet object concurrently, and at least one of these threads modifies your Set<E>, then it should be synchronized externally. This is typically accomplished by synchronizing on some object that naturally encapsulates the Set<E> such as the HashSet. We are using the HashSet in a very basic fashion: to hold objects that are removed from the game play for one reason or another, such as treasure being found; enemies being eliminated; or similar game design scenarios.

One of the advantages of the HashSet class (and object) offers is a constant time performance for your basic dataset operations such as the .add(), .remove(), .contains(), and .size() methods. Iteration over a HashSet object will require a time period proportional to the sum of the Set<E> object instance size, which is determined by the number of elements currently in the Set<E> combined with the "capacity" of the backing HashMap object instance.

Creating Your Casting Engine: CastingDirector.java

Now that you have some background on Java interfaces, the Java Collection Framework, and its List<E> and Set<E> interfaces implemented by the ArrayList<E> and HashSet<E> classes, we can move on to create our basic CastingDirector class. The class will keep a List object of what Actor objects are currently "in play" in the current scene and another List object of what Actor objects should be checked for collisions. There will also be a Set object to hold Actor objects that need to be removed. Right-click on the **invincibagel** package folder in the NetBeans Projects pane, and select the **New ➤ Java Class** menu sequence to bring up the **New Java Class** dialog, which is shown in Figure 10-2. Name the new class **CastingDirector** and leave the other fields in the dialog, which are automatically set by NetBeans.

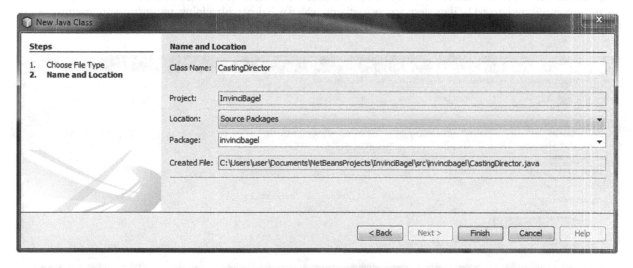

Figure 10-2. *Create a New Java Class in the invincibagel package; name it CastingDirector for the InvinciBagel Project*

We will start by creating the **List<Actor> ArrayList<Actor>** objects first, one to hold the current cast for your scene and then a second List<Actor> to hold objects to be checked for collision detection. After that we will create the **Set<Actor> HashSet<Actor>** object, which will provide an unordered Set object, which will collect those Actor objects that need to be removed from the scene. Let's get started creating the body of our public CastingDirector class.

Creating an ArrayList Object: CURRENT_CAST Data Store List

The first thing that we need to add to the CastingDirector class is a private List<Actor> ArrayList<Actor> object that I am going to name CURRENT_CAST as it contains the Actor objects that are currently on the Stage, which is the current cast. Although it is not technically a constant as far as using static and final keywords in its declaration, it is acting (no pun intended) as a database of sorts, and so I am using ALL_CAPS so that it stands out in the code as being a data structure. I'm also going to add a basic .get() method to access the ArrayList<Actor> structure using a Java **return** keyword to return an object to the calling entity. The code for the declaration and instantiation of the CURRENT_CAST ArrayList object and the body of the .getCurrentCast() method structure should look like the following Java code:

```
package invincibagel;
public class CastingDirector {

    private List<Actor> CURRENT_CAST = new ArrayList<>();

    public List<Actor> getCurrentCast() {
        return CURRENT_CAST;
    }
}
```

As you can see in Figure 10-3, there is wavy red error highlighting under your List interface reference as well as your ArrayList reference in the line of code that declares and instantiates the CURRENT_CAST object, so you'll need to use the **Alt-Enter** work process, and have NetBeans 8 write the **import java.util.List;** statement at the top of your class. The **.getCurrentCast()** will be the easiest method to code, as it simply **returns** your entire **CURRENT_CAST** ArrayList<Actor> object to whatever Java entity may be calling the method. Next, we'll take a look at how to code the more complicated ArrayList data store access methods, which will deal with adding, removing, and resetting (clearing) the Actor objects from this CURRENT_CAST ArrayList<Actor> object.

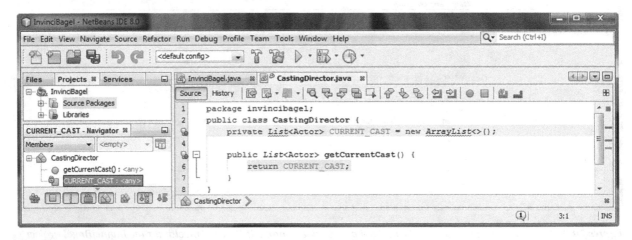

Figure 10-3. *Inside the CastingDirector class, add a CURRENT_CAST List<Actor> object, and a .getCurrentCast() method*

The first method that we will code is the **.addCurrentCast()** method, which will pass in a comma delimited List of Actor objects to the List (and the ArrayList class that implements List) interfaces **.addAll()** method call. As you have learned already, a comma delimited List is passed at the end of the method parameter list, unless, as it is in this case, it is the only parameter.

To show the .addCurrentCast() method that we are going to pass more than one Actor object into the body of the method, we used the **Actor...** annotation, and I am going to name the (more than one) Actor objects variable **actors**. Inside of the body of the .addCurrentCast() method we will call an **.addAll()** method off of the CURRENT_CAST object using dot notation.

Inside of the .addAll() method we will nest another Java statement that will create an **Arrays** object from the comma delimited List using the **.asList()** method called off the **Arrays** class reference and pass the actors Actor... comma delimited list into that method. This is all done using the following Java method construct:

```java
public void addCurrentCast(Actor... actors) {
    CURRENT_CAST.addAll( Arrays.asList(actors) );
}
```

As you can see in Figure 10-4, you will get a wavy red error highlighting under the Arrays class, so use the **Alt-Enter** work process and have NetBeans write your **import java.util.Arrays;** statement for you. Now we are ready to write the other two methods relating to the CURRENT_CAST data store that will remove Actor objects from the List<Actor> ArrayList<Actor> data store object, and one that will clear it out entirely (reset it to being unused).

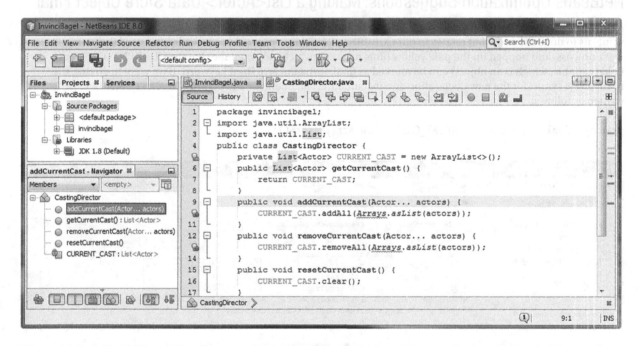

Figure 10-4. *Add .addCurrentCast(), removeCurrentCast(), and resetCurrentCast methods to the CastingDirector class*

The second method that we will code is the **.removeCurrentCast()** method, which will also pass in a comma delimited List of Actor objects to the List (and ArrayList class implementing List) interfaces **.removeAll()** method call.

To show this .removeCurrentCast() method that we are going to pass more than one Actor object into the body of the method, we again use the **Actor...** annotation, and I am going to again name this variable **actors**. Inside of the body of the .removeCurrentCast() method we will again call the .removeAll() method off of the CURRENT_CAST object, and inside of the .removeAll() method we'll nest another Java statement that will create an Arrays object from the comma delimited List using the .asList() method called off the Arrays class reference, again passing the Actor... comma delimited list named actors into the method. This is done using the following Java method seen in Figure 10-4:

```java
public void removeCurrentCast(Actor... actors) {
    CURRENT_CAST.removeAll( Arrays.asList(actors) );
}
```

Now all you have left to code is a simple .resetCurrentCast() method, which invokes the .clear() method call:

```java
public void resetCurrentCast() {
    CURRENT_CAST.clear();
}
```

Next let's take a look at one more issue in our CastingDirector.java code thus far, and then we can move on.

NetBeans Optimization Suggestions: Making a List<Actor> Data Store Object Final

As you can see in Figure 10-5, your code is error-free, but is not warning free, so let's take a look at what NetBeans wants us to do to the code that relates to our CURRENT_CAST List<Array> data store object. I used the mouse-over work process, and popped up the pale yellow hints message, which informed me that the CURRENT_CAST data field (variable, which is an object) can be marked as final, using the Java **final** keyword. If we were to do this, the basic Java 8 syntax for the new declaration and instantiation statement for the CURRENT_CAST object will be written as follows:

```java
private final List<Actor> CURRENT_CAST = new ArrayList<>();
```

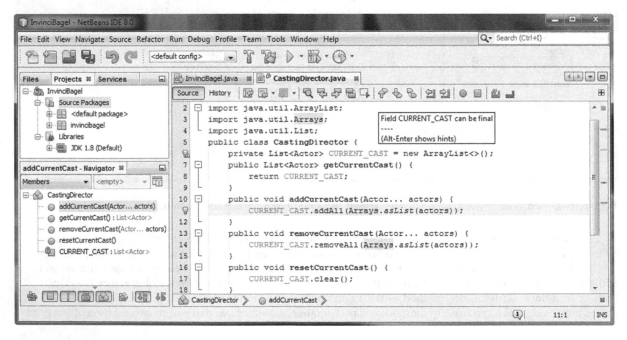

Figure 10-5. Mouse-over yellow warning highlight under CURRENT_CAST, and use the Alt-Enter dialog to fix problem

Often there is a misunderstanding as to the use of this Java modifier keyword **final** with regard to **objects**. It is true that with most Java variables (numeric, Boolean, and String) when made final, the variable value itself can't be changed. Many assume that a final modifier when used with a Java object (variable declaration) also makes the object itself "final," and therefore "immutable," or not changeable in memory.

Generally in Java the final keyword when used with an object variable refers to **memory references**, and the **immutable** keyword applies to those objects themselves, and means that they can't be changed. Therefore, an object (reference) that is declared as final can still contain an object that is **mutable** (can be changed, as we wish to do here).

In fact, what the final modifier keyword does regarding Java objects in memory, such as our CURRENT_CAST ArrayList<Actor> object, is to make the **reference** to where it's being kept in memory locked, that is, finalized. So what NetBeans is suggesting here is an **optimization** that will allow your CURRENT_CAST data store object to remain where it is in memory all of the time (after it is created).

This does not mean that your List<Actor> ArrayList<Actor> object itself can't change. Your game's Java code can expand, contract, and clear (reset) a List<Actor> ArrayList<Actor> object that has been declared final at any time, based upon your game's invocation of the .addCurrentCast(), .removeCurrentCast(), and .resetCurrentCast() methods.

The optimization theory here would be the more a JVM can "lock down" memory locations "up front" (upon program launch, when loading into memory), the better it can optimize memory, as well as the CPU cycles that are needed to access this memory. If you think about it, if the CPU does not have to "look" for an object in memory, then it will be able to access it faster. A final object can also be used more optimally in a **multi-threaded** environment.

If, however, you do not want to make your object references final, you can optionally turn this feature off in NetBeans. This can be done using the **Tools ➤ Options** menu sequence, seen on the left side of Figure 10-6, in order to access the **Options** dialog, which is shown in the right side of Figure 10-6. As you can see along the top of this Options dialog, NetBeans has organized it's hundreds of preferences (also known as options) into ten specific areas, and even has a Search Filter, seen at the top right of the dialog as well, in case you don't know exactly where to look for a given option. If any of these sections have too many options to display on the dialog screen, there will be tabs (the **hints** tab is shown selected in Figure 10-6), which you can use to navigate to an area you want to visit. We're going to the **Hints** section, and selecting the **Java** Language from the drop-down, and then finally opening up the **Threading** section.

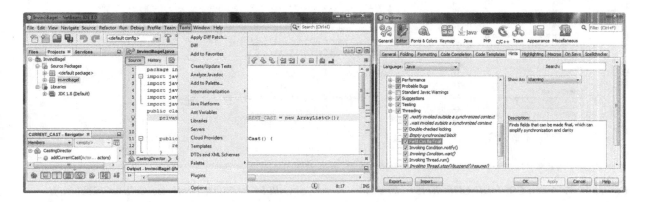

Figure 10-6. *Setting Editor Hints Preferences using the Tools ➤ Options menu and the Editor ➤ Hints ➤ Java ➤ Threading*

Now that we have covered the final object variable issue, and shown you both ways of dealing with it, let's continue on, and create a second ArrayList<Actor> object named COLLIDE_CHECKLIST to store complex collision data.

Another ArrayList Object: COLLIDE_CHECKLIST Data Store List

Now let's create our second List<Actor> ArrayList data store object and call it COLLIDE_CHECKLIST since it will eventually be accessed in the .collide() method; this will happen if you implement complex multiple object collision lists in later advanced stages of game development. We will not get to the advanced level that will require implementation of this during this book, but I wanted to show you how to put a complete CastingDirector class together, so that you will have it in place when you need it for your game development, as you add more advanced features into your game. This object will hold the most current copy of the CURRENT_CAST ArrayList<Actor> and will have two methods. The .getCollideCheckList() method will return the COLLIDE_CHECKLIST object, and the .resetCollideCheckList() will reset the COLLIDE_CHECKLIST, by using the .clear() method call, and for now, we will use the .addAll() method to load COLLIDE_CHECKLIST ArrayList<Actor> object with the current version of the CURRENT_CAST ArrayList<Actor> object. Later we can use this List to hold a custom collision checklist, that groups together only objects that can collide with each other into one List. The Java code, which can be seen in Figure 10-7, needed to declare and instantiate the object, should look like the following:

```java
private final List<Actor> COLLIDE_CHECKLIST = new ArrayList<>();
```

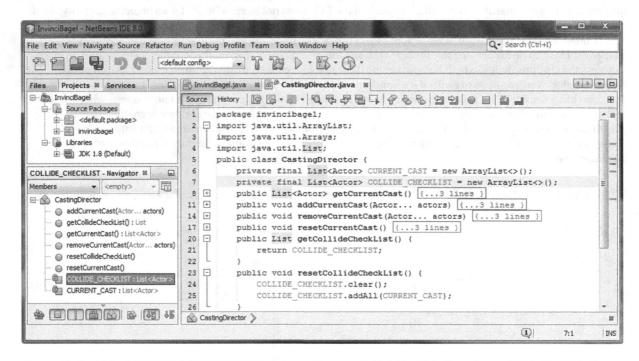

Figure 10-7. *Add a COLLIDE_CHECKLIST List<Actor> object, .getCollideCheckList(), and resetCollideCheckList() methods*

A .getCollideCheckList() method uses a **return** keyword, to give access to the COLLIDE_CHECKLIST, like this:

```java
public List getCollideCheckList() {
    return COLLIDE_CHECKLIST;
}
```

A .resetCollideCheckList() method uses a **.clear()** method to clear out the COLLIDE_CHECKLIST and then uses an **.addAll()** method to add (insert) the contents of the CURRENT_CAST object into the COLLIDE_CHECKLIST object.

```java
public void resetCollideCheckList() {
    COLLIDE_CHECKLIST.clear();
    COLLIDE_CHECKLIST.addAll(CURRENT_CAST);
}
```

Now that we have our ArrayList<Actor> objects set up to hold cast members and advanced collision list data sets, let's create a HashSet<Actor> object. This Set object will be used to collect Actors that for one reason or another need to be removed from the game play (the Scene and the Stage).

Creating a HashSet Object: REMOVED_ACTORS Data Store Set<Actor>

Now let's create our third Set<Actor> HashSet data store object, and let's call it **REMOVED_ACTORS**, since it will be used to hold a collection of Actor objects that have been removed from the current Stage. This Set<Actor> object will hold all of the Actor objects that for whatever reason need to be removed from the CURRENT_CAST List. The REMOVED_ACTORS data store (data set) will have three associated methods.

The .getRemovedActors() method will return the REMOVED_ACTORS object, the .addToRemovedActors() will be the "core" method that will add Actor objects to the REMOVED_ACTORS Set<Actor> object as things happen during game play (finding treasure, killing enemies, etc.) that eliminate an Actor object from the Stage and Scene, and the .resetRemovedActors() that will use the .removeAll() method to remove Actors from the CURRENT_CAST ArrayList<Actor> object, and then reset the REMOVED_ACTORS data set, by using the .clear() method call on the REMOVED_ACTORS HashSet object. The code, seen in Figure 10-8, needed to declare and instantiate the HashSet object using the Java new keyword, looks like this:

```java
private final Set<Actor> REMOVED_ACTORS = new HashSet<>();
```

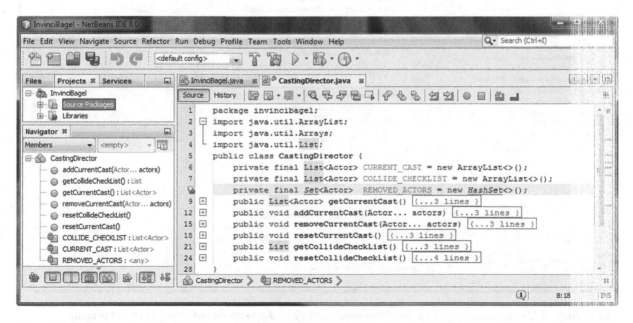

Figure 10-8. *Add a private final Set named REMOVED_ACTORS and use the Java new keyword to create a HashSet<>*

The easiest of these three methods to write is the .getRemovedActors() method, which simply uses a **return** keyword to pass the entire HashSet<Actor> Set object to a calling entity. This provides access to **REMOVED_ACTORS** to other methods, such as the ones we will be writing later on in this section. The Java code should look just like this:

```java
public Set getRemovedActors() {
    return REMOVED_ACTORS;
}
```

The next method we'll need to code is the most complicated as well as the most often used, as it will be the one you use when something in your cast has changed: for instance, a killed enemy, such as an InvinciBagel, a spent projectile, such as a bullet, consumed food, such as a ball of cream cheese, or found treasure, such as a gift box.

The **.addToRemovedActors()** method uses the **if-else** statement, to ascertain if multiple Actor objects have been passed in the parameter list (the first or if part of the construct) or if just one Actor object needs to be removed (the second or else part of the construct). The first part of the if-else statement uses the **.length()** method to ascertain if more than one Actor objects has been passed into the method call parameter list using **if(actors.length > 1)** since an **Actor...** parameter allows more than one Actor object to be submitted to the method, as seen in Figure 10-9.

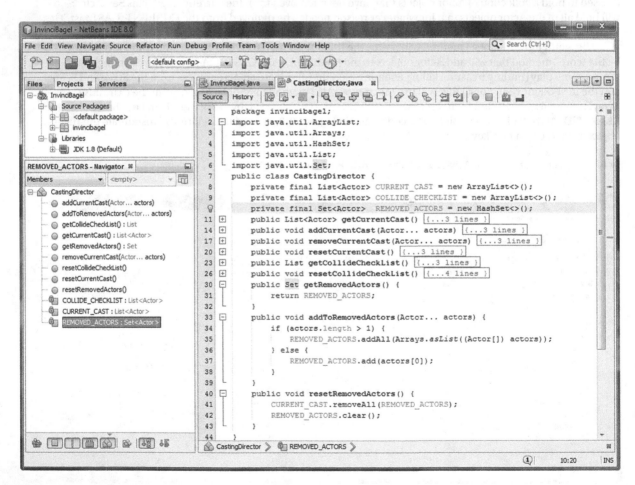

Figure 10-9. *Add .getRemovedActors(), .addToRemovedActors(), and .resetRemovedActors() method structures*

If there are multiple Actor objects to be processed the inside of an **if{...}** construct, use the **.addAll()** method to add the contents of the parameter list to your **REMOVED_ACTORS** Set<Actor> object. This is accomplished by using the **Arrays.asList((Actor[]) actors))** construct inside of the .addAll() method call, which constructs the Actor[] Array named **actors** that is compatible with (necessary for) using an .addAll() method call with a Set<E> object type. The second **else{...}** portion of this method body adds one single Actor object, since the actors.length was not greater than one, by using an **actors[0]** annotation (first Actor parameter) and an .add() method call using the following code:

```
public void addToRemovedActors(Actor... actors) {
    if (actors.length > 1) { REMOVED_ACTORS.addAll(Arrays.asList((Actor[]) actors)); }
    else {                    REMOVED_ACTORS.add(actors[0]);                           }
```

Notice that since we have converted the Actor... parameters (which are destined for a List, but are not one yet) into an Array (because the compiler can count the fixed number of items), so we can use the **actors[0]** notation.

Now that we have a way to add one or more Actor objects to the REMOVED_ACTORS Set<Actor> HashSet, let's create a .resetRemovedActors() to clear out the REMOVED_ACTORS data set. Before we clear the Set<Actor> object we need to make sure all of the Actor objects contained within it are removed from the CURRENT_CAST Actor List object, since that is what it is there for, so the first part of this method will call the .removeAll() method off of the CURRENT_CAST ArrayList<Actor> object and inside of this method pass over the REMOVED_ACTORS Set<Actors> object. After that we can use the .clear() method call off of the REMOVED_ACTORS object to reset it back to being empty, so that it can be used all over again to collect Actor objects that need to be disposed of. The Java code, which is shown in Figure 10-9, should look like the following:

```
public void resetRemovedActors() {
    CURRENT_CAST.removeAll(REMOVED_ACTORS);
    REMOVED_ACTORS.clear();
}
```

Next, we are going to look at how we can get NetBeans to code our **CastingDirector()** constructor method!

CastingDirector() Constructor: Having NetBeans Write the Code

There is a way that you can get NetBeans to write a **constructor method** for you, and since it is a little bit "hidden," I'll show you how to find it! I left the **insertion-bar cursor** in Figure 10-10, to show you that I clicked on the **final** keyword and the yellow light bulb **"tip"** icon that appears, and the pale yellow pop-up tooltip message that I get when I mouse-over the tip light bulb. The message that I get is the "Move initializer to constructor(s)," and so I hit the **Alt-Enter** key combo that is suggested. Sure enough, there is an option for NetBeans to write this constructor method code for me.

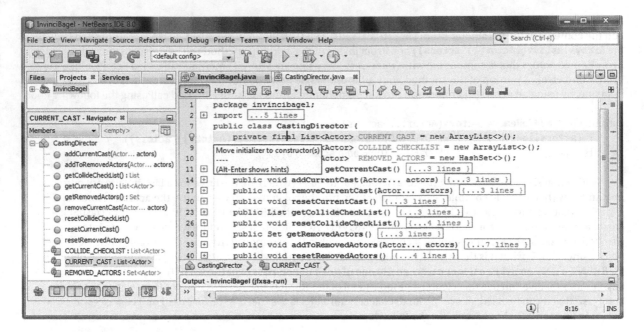

Figure 10-10. *Mouse-over the yellow light bulb icon in the line number area of the pane and reveal the constructor tip*

For the first final keyword that you click on, and Alt-Enter, and have NetBeans write your CastingDirector() constructor method for, it will code the **public CastingDirector(){...}** structure for you, and add the first instantiation statement. As you can see in Figure 10-11, once you click on each of the three final keywords at the top of your class and use the same work process, you can have NetBeans write the entire constructor method for you. The Java code that NetBeans generates uses the Java **this** keyword (so that the CastingDirector object can refer to itself) to preface each of the three data store objects, as well as using the Java **new** keyword to create new instances of ArrayList<E> and HashSet<E> should look like the following:

```java
public CastingDirector() {
    this.CURRENT_CAST = new ArrayList<>();
    this.COLLIDE_CHECKLIST = new ArrayList<>();
    this.REMOVED_ACTORS = new HashSet<>();
}
```

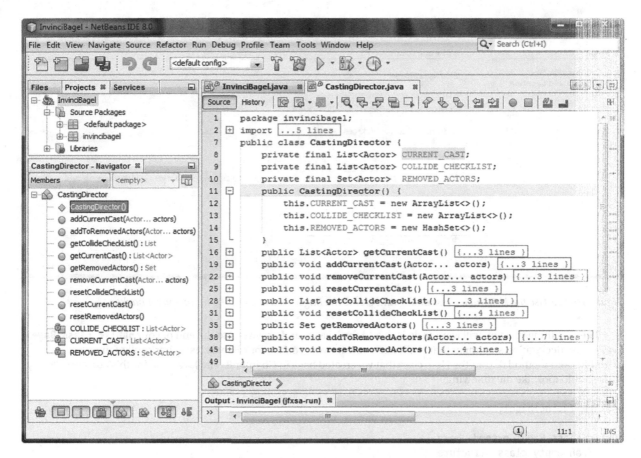

Figure 10-11. *Use Alt-Enter, and have NetBeans write your CastingDirector() constructor method Java code for you*

We should probably create at least one Actor class (object) for our game's star character, the InvinciBagel himself, before we close out this chapter. Let's use our Hero abstract class to create a Bagel class so that later we can create an iBagel object. We will use this code in the next chapter, where we will learn how to move this InvinciBagel character around the Stage, as well as optimizing the structure of our InvinciBagel.java class a bit more as well.

Creating Our Main Actor: The Bagel Hero Subclass

Let's create a **Bagel.java** class by right-clicking on the **invincibagel** package folder in the NetBeans Projects pane on the left side of the IDE, and select the **New ➤ Java Class** menu sequence to bring up the **New Java Class** dialog, shown in Figure 10-12. Name the class **Bagel** and accept the other default Project, Location, Package and Created File option fields, by clicking on the **Finish** button, which will create the new Bagel.java class, and open it up in a tab in NetBeans.

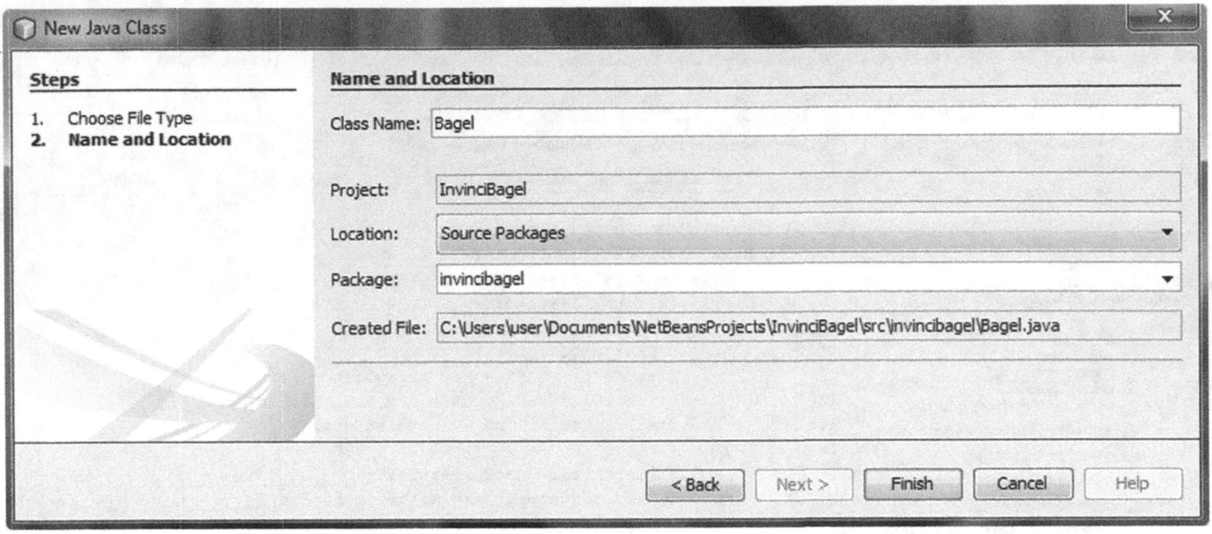

Figure 10-12. *Use the New Java Class dialog and create the Bagel.java class in the invincibagel package*

The first thing that you will want to do is to add the Java **extends** keyword to the end of your **public class Bagel {...}** class declaration statement that NetBeans wrote for you, so that your Bagel class inherits all of the power (variables and methods) from the Hero class that we created back in Chapter 8. The Java code for this currently empty class should look like the following:

```
package invincibagel;

public class Bagel extends Hero {
    // an empty class structure
}
```

The first thing that we will want to write is the Bagel() constructor method, since we want to create a Bagel character to place onto the screen so that we can start to work on movement code, and later collision code. This code will take in the same exact parameters that the Hero class Hero() constructor method needs to receive, and will pass them "up" to the Hero class Hero() constructor using the Java **super** keyword (I like to call this a **super constructor**) in the form of a **super()** constructor method call. Your Java code for this **Bagel()** constructor method should look just like the following Java class and constructor method structure:

```
public class Bagel extends Hero {
    public Bagel(String SVGdata, double xLocation, double yLocation, Image... spriteCels) {
        super(SVGdata, xLocation, yLocation, spriteCels);
    }
}
```

As you can see in Figure 10-13, there is a wavy red error underline highlight, under the Bagel class name. If you mouse-over this you will see the "Bagel is not abstract and does not override abstract method .update() in Hero," which tells you that you either need to make Bagel a public abstract class, which we are not going to do because we wish to actually use this class to hold a character (object) and its attributes (variables) and capabilities (methods), so the other option to eliminate this error is to add in your **@Override public void update() {...}** method structure, even if it is an empty method for now.

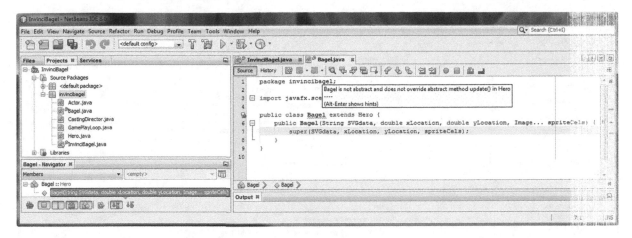

Figure 10-13. *Code a public Bagel() constructor method that calls a super() constructor method (from Hero superclass)*

The code to implement the (currently) empty .update() method uses a Java **@Override** keyword, and once it is in place the error will disappear, and the code will be error-free, as seen in Figure 10-14. The code looks like this:

```
@Override
public void update() { // empty method structure }
```

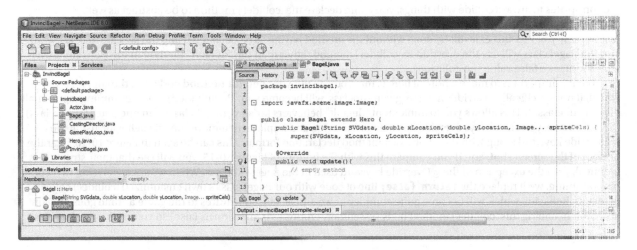

Figure 10-14. *Add a public void .update() method to override the public abstract void update method in the Hero class*

Notice at the top of Figure 10-14 that you will have to add the **import javafx.scene.image.Image;** code statement in order to be able to use the **Image...** annotation in your **public Bagel()** constructor method parameter list.

Just to be thorough, let's **override** a public Boolean **.collide()** method as well, so that we have it in the Bagel class. You may be wondering why NetBeans did not give us an error in Figure 10-14 when we did not add the .collide() method to the Bagel class. As you can see in Figure 10-15, which shows the public abstract Hero class, we didn't make the .collide() method a public abstract method, like we did with the .update() method. This is why NetBeans 8 did not generate any error highlighting, because we're not required to implement the .collide() method in all Hero subclasses.

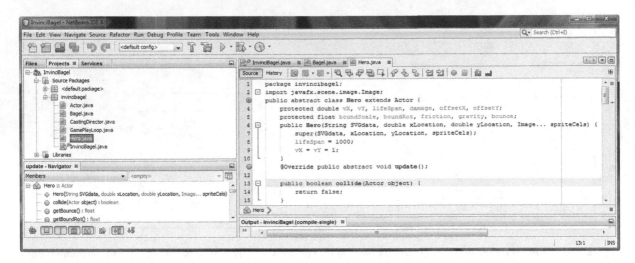

Figure 10-15. *The Hero abstract class has a public boolean collide() method but since it is not abstract it is not required*

You might be wondering why we didn't make .collide() into an abstract method, which it's important to note that we could do, at any point in time in the future. The reason is that we might want to have (add in) motion sprites that do not collide with anything in the scene (game play) at some point in your future game development, perhaps to add in visual detail elements, such as a bird flying across the top of the screen. The choice is yours to make, so if you want motion sprites to always collide with things, you could declare the .collide() method to be abstract as well.

The important thing to note is that **we can still override the .collide() method**, which I am going to do next, just to show you that this can still be done without the method having to be declared using the Java abstract keyword and the Bagel class will use the overridden .collide() method rather than the "default" method in the Hero superclass, which returns a false value (no collision).

What is important to make a note of here is that you can put your **default method code** into the superclass, which, if not specifically overridden in any given subclass, will become your default method programming logic for all of your subclasses. This allows you to implement "default" behaviors for all your subclasses, in one place (superclass).

Of course, you can always override this default behavior, and implement a more specific behavior, using the @Override keyword along with the same exact method declaration format. This can be seen in Figure 10-16, near the bottom of the screen shot, and if you compare this with the bottom of Figure 10-15, you will see that their structure is identical, with the exception of the @Override keyword used in the Bagel subclass. When we cover collision detection programming, we'll replace the **return false;** line of code with our Bagel class's own customized .collide() collision detection behavior, which will become quite complex as we add advanced features to the game as time goes on. For now I am installing this .collide() method body (essentially empty, as it just returns false) so you see a complete class.

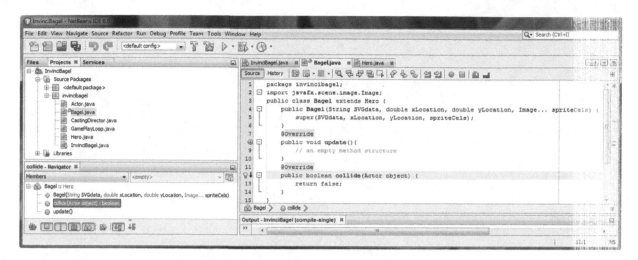

Figure 10-16. *Override public boolean .collide() method body, for our use later on during a collision detection chapter*

We have made a lot of good progress in this chapter, creating a Casting Director and the Star for your game!

Summary

In this tenth chapter, we added two key classes to the game: the CastingDirector.java class and the Bagel.java class. The first performs a cast management and collision management functionality, and the second adds the primary actor for the game, so that we can start to work on how the InvinciBagel moves around the screen. We looked at a diagram of our current package and class structure and how the new classes are going to fit into an overall game engine design strategy that we are implementing during this book.

We learned what a Java **interface** is, and how Java interfaces will allow us to control what's implemented by other developers regarding our classes. We also learned about the **Java Collection Framework**, which provides things such as Arrays, Lists and Sets to use to provide data store functionality for our Java 8 and JavaFX applications (games).

We learned about the java.util package and its **List<E>** interface, as well as the **ArrayList<E>** class, and how the ArrayList<E> class implements this List<E> interface. We learned about **<E> Elements**, **<K> Keys**, **<V> Values**, and **<T> Types**. We learned that the List and ArrayList objects have a structure and an order, whereas the Set and HashSet objects do not have a specific order, and cannot have duplicate elements.

Next we created your **CastingDirector.java** class, to manage the Actor objects that will need to be added to the game and removed from the game. This class will also maintain the List<Actor> structure that will be used for the collision detection logic that we will be adding later on during the book in Chapter 16.

Finally, we created our first Actor related class, the Bagel class, which extends the Hero superclass and will allow us to put the primary InvinciBagel Actor object character into our game Scene and onto the Stage. We created the Bagel() constructor method and used the **@Override** keyword to override the **.update()** and **.collide()** methods, so that we have someplace to construct our programming logic relating to this character during the rest of the book.

In the next chapter, we're going to take a look at how to move the game **sprite** around the screen using this KeyEvent event handling structure that we have created during this chapter, as well as how to ascertain the **boundary** (edges) of the screen, character direction, movement velocity, and related animation and movement considerations.

CHAPTER 11

■ ■ ■

Moving Your Action Figure in 2D: Controlling the X and Y Display Screen Coordinates

Now that we have created the public CastingDirector class, which I call the "casting engine," in Chapter 10, we need to get back into our **InvinciBagel.java** primary application class coding here in Chapter 11, and create our **iBagel** primary game play Actor (character) in the **.createGameActors()** method. We will also create the **castDirector** object using the CastingDirector.java class and its CastingDirector() constructor method, which we created in Chapter 10, as well as creating the **.createCastingDirection()** method, which will manage our casting direction class-related features.

After we finish adding the code into our InvinciBagel.java class that will create the iBagel Bagel object, and create a **castDirector** CastingDirector object, we will reorganize our code into **logical method structures** for the major task areas that need to be addressed in the InvinciBagel class. After we do this, we'll have eight logical method areas. These methods will then serve as "guides" to the functional areas that we will need to keep updated (add statements to) as we develop our game over the rest of the book. For instance, if we add an Actor to the game, we will do this by adding (instantiating) an Actor object inside of a .createGameActors() method, and then add the Actor object to a cast object created using our new CastingDirector() constructor method inside of a new .createCastingDirection() method.

In addition to the .createGameActors() and .createCastingDirector() methods, our new methods will include the **.loadImageAssets()** method, the **.createSceneEventHandling()** method, the **.createStartGameLoop()** method, and the **.addGameActorNodes()** method. So, we will be creating half a dozen new methods for your InvinciBagel. java class during this chapter, to significantly "beef up" the top-level organizational structure for our game's core class as well as its "top-level" .start() method. There's only one method that will survive this process without any modifications; that will be the .addNodesToStackPane() method, that you created in Chapter 6 (see Figure 6-8 to refresh your memory).

After we have reorganized our InvinciBagel.java code infrastructure, we can move on and start to create the program logic that will be used to create, and later control, the primary hero for our game, the InvinciBagel himself. This will involve using the Bagel() and CastingDirector() constructor methods, and then adding the **iBagel** Bagel object to the Scene Graph (StackPane **root** object) and CastingDirector **castDirector** object, using the **.add()** method call and the **.addCurrentCast()** method call respectively.

After we have the iBagel Actor created, we will wire up its .update() method to the GamePlayLoop .handle() method, at which point we can start to build the programming logic that will move this InvinciBagel around on your Stage. At this point, things get more interesting, as we can start to define the movement boundaries for the Stage, the sprite image states (the nine different character positions), and how these relate to X (left-right) and Y (up-down) key usage. For instance, no movement will be standing, left and right will use running, up will use jump, down will land, or later on in the game design, certain key combinations can cause an InvinciBagel to fly and so on as we refine the code.

InvinciBagel.java Redesign: Adding Logical Methods

The first thing that I want to do regarding the InvinciBagel.java code, which should already be open in a tab in NetBeans (if it is not, use the right-click and **Open** work process), is to reorganize the current code using a half-dozen new methods that logically contain, as well as show, the different areas that we will need to address in order to add new Actors to our game. These include things such as managing event handling, adding new Image asset references, creating the new game Actor objects, adding the new actors to the Scene Graph, adding the new Actor objects to the CURRENT_CAST List we created in Chapter 10, and starting the GamePlayLoop AnimationTimer pulse engine. The first thing that we should do is to put those Java statements that need to be done first and that need to be in the .start() method itself at the top of the code. These create the Scene Graph root, a Scene object, and set up the Stage object:

```
primaryStage.setTitle(InvinciBagel);
root = new StackPane();
scene = new Scene(root, WIDTH, HEIGHT, Color.WHITE);
primaryStage.setScene(scene);
primaryStage.show();
```

As you can see in Figure 11-1, we are taking the root and scene object instantiations out of the method that is called .createSplashScreenNodes(), and putting these at the top of the .start() method. I am doing this because they are foundational to our InvinciBagel game (class). Next, we are also going to add six all-new method structures to our existing code. The only method that will remain untouched during this process is your **.addNodesToStackPane()**. You can see I'm calling the methods in a logical order: add events, add images, add actors, add Scene Graph, and add cast.

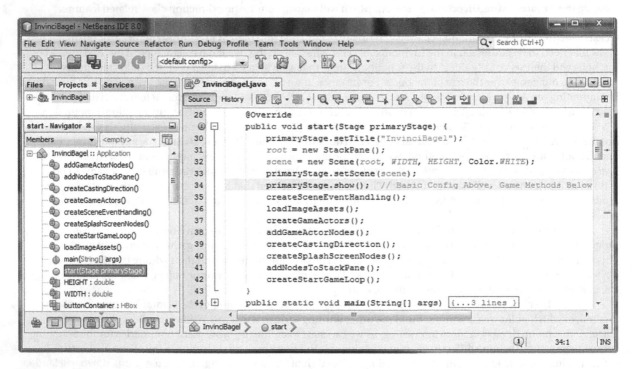

Figure 11-1. *Place basic configuration statements at top of the .start() method, and then the eight game method calls*

The method calls that we are going to put into place during the first part of this chapter involve creating the event handlers for the Scene object, which we will do right after we have set-up that Scene object named scene. The next thing that we will need to do in the process of adding to the game is to load the Image object assets (digital image references), which is what your .loadImageAssets() method will do. Once your Image objects are declared and instantiated, we can then create the game actors using the .createGameActors() method and the constructor method calls that we created in our custom Actor and Hero subclasses, such as the Bagel.java class we created in Chapter 10. Once we have the actors created, we can add them to the Scene Graph using .addGameActorNodes() as well as adding them to the game cast using the .createCastingDirection() method. At the end, we create and start the GamePlayLoop object by calling the .createStartGameLoop() method. The .createSplashScreenNodes() and .addNodesToStackPane() are at the end, as they won't be added to now that the splashscreen content production work has been completed. The method call code that we'll add during this chapter looks like the following:

```
createSceneEventHandling();
loadImageAssets();
createGameActors();
addGameActorNodes();
createCastingDirection();
createSplashScreenNodes();
addNodesToStackPane();
createStartGameLoop();
```

Let's get down to business and start implementing this code redesign process for the InvinciBagel.java class.

The Scene Event Handling Method: .createSceneEventHandling()

The first thing that we will want to do is to move the event handling for our game play into its own method, which we will call **.createSceneEventHandling()**. The reason that I am creating a method for the creation of Scene object event handling is because if later on you wanted to add other types of input events into your game, such as mouse events or drag events, you will have a logical method already in place which can hold this event-related Java code.

This new Java code, which can be seen in Figure 11-2, will involve taking your **scene.setOnKeyPressed()** and **scene.setOnKeyReleased()** method handling structures, created in Chapter 9, out of your .createSplashScreenNodes() method, and placing them into their own method structure. Later we'll relocate all ActionEvent handlers, which are in the .start() method, and actually belong inside the .createSplashScreenNodes() method where they would be grouped with the other splashscreen objects. This new event handling code structure should look like the following Java code:

```
private void createSceneEventHandling() {
    scene.setOnKeyPressed((KeyEvent event) -> {
        switch (event.getCode()) {
            case UP:    up    = true; break;
            case DOWN:  down  = true; break;
            case LEFT:  left  = true; break;
            case RIGHT: right = true; break;
            case W:     up    = true; break;
            case S:     down  = true; break;
            case A:     left  = true; break;
            case D:     right = true; break;
        }
    });
```

```java
        scene.setOnKeyReleased((KeyEvent event) -> {
            switch (event.getCode()) {
                case UP:    up    = false; break;
                case DOWN:  down  = false; break;
                case LEFT:  left  = false; break;
                case RIGHT: right = false; break;
                case W:     up    = false; break;
                case S:     down  = false; break;
                case A:     left  = false; break;
                case D:     right = false; break;
            }
        });
    }
```

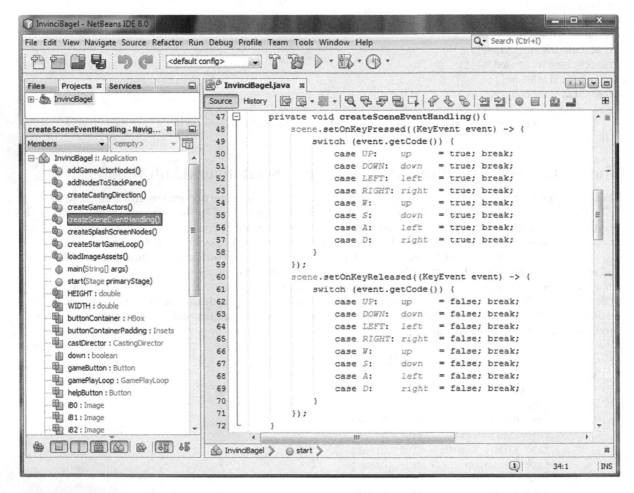

Figure 11-2. *Create private void createSceneEventHandling() method for OnKeyReleased and OnKeyPressed event handling structures*

Now that the event handling for the game play is where it needs to be, before we can write the rest of the method structures for adding Image, Actor, and CastingDirector objects, we'll need to declare these objects for use at the top of our InvinciBagel.java class. Let's do this work that sets up the rest of the methods we'll need to code next.

Adding InvinciBagel: Declare Image, Bagel, and CastingDirector

Since we are going to start to get our InvinciBagel character on the game play screen during this chapter, and bring together all of the code we wrote during previous chapters creating our GamePlayLoop class (Chapter 7), Actor and Hero classes (Chapter 8), event handling (Chapter 9), and CastingDirector class (Chapter 10), we need to declare some object variables at the top of the InvinciBagel.java class, before we can instantiate and use these objects during the chapter. We will declare the Bagel object named **iBagel** using the **static** keyword, as we will be calling the iBagel object's .update() method from the GamePlayLoop object's .handle() method, and this will make the iBagel "visible" across (or between) these two classes. We will also declare the nine Image (sprite state) objects, iB0 through iB8, by using a compound declaration. Finally, we will declare a CastingDirector object, which we will name **castDirector**. The declaration statements, which we need to add at the top of our InvinciBagel.java class, can be seen in Figure 11-3. They include the following Java variable declaration statements, located at the top of your InvinciBagel.java class:

```
static Bagel iBagel;
Image iB0, iB1, iB2, iB3, iB4, iB5, iB6, iB7, iB8;
CastingDirector castDirector;
```

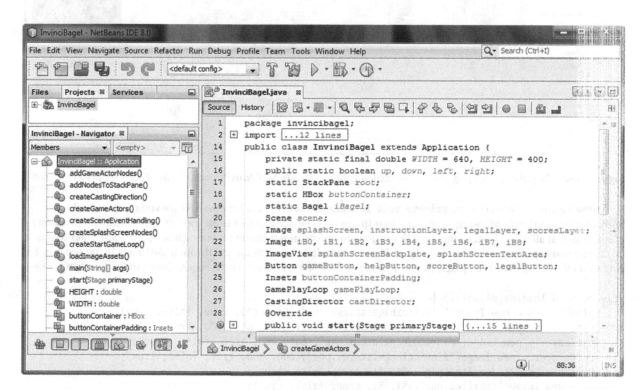

Figure 11-3. *Add static Bagel iBagel, CastingDirector castDirector and Image object declaration named iB0 through iB8*

Now that we've declared the object variables that we will need to implement the InvinciBagel Actor object instantiation in the .createGameActors() method and CastingDirection engine in the createCastingDirection() method, let's move on to creating the first of our new methods, the **.loadImageAssets()** method, which will contain all of your Image object instantiation calls to the Image() constructor. We will put all Image object instantiations in this method.

The Actor Image Assets Loading Method: .loadImageAssets()

Now that we have declared the nine Image objects for use at the top of our InvinciBagel.java class, the next thing that we will need to do is to copy the nine PNG32 sprite images, which are named sprite0.png through sprite8.png, into the /src folder for our InvinciBagel NetBeans project. This is done using the file management utility for your operating system; in the case of my 64-bit Windows 7 OS it is the Windows Explorer utility, shown in Figure 11-4, with the Image assets copied into the **C:/Users/user/MyDocuments/NetBeansProjects/InvinciBagel/src** folder. All of the PNG image assets are **PNG32** (24-bit RGB true color data with a 8-bit 256 gray level alpha channel) except for the back plate for the splashscreen, which is a PNG24, as it does not need an alpha channel because it is a background image plate.

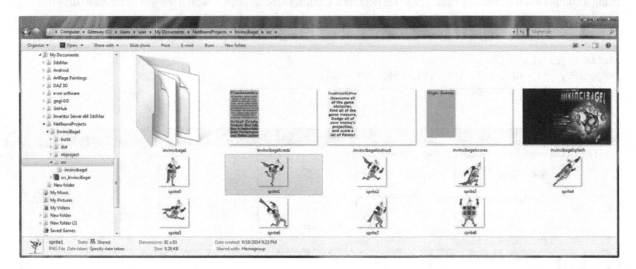

Figure 11-4. *Copy the sprite0.png through sprite8.png files into your NetBeansProjects/InvinciBagel/src project folder*

Now we are ready to code the **private void loadImageAssets(){...}** method. Once you create a method body (declaration), you will want to copy the four Image object instantiations from your .createSplashScreenNodes() method so that all of the Image object loading is done in one central location for your game application. After that is done, you can copy and paste the scoresLayer Image instantiation and create iB0 through iB8 Image instantiations. Be sure to set the image size to **81** pixels (X and Y) and use the correct file name references, shown in the following code:

```
private void loadImageAssets() {
    splashScreen = new Image("/invincibagelsplash.png", 640, 400, true, false, true);
    instructionLayer = new Image("/invincibagelinstruct.png", 640, 400, true, false, true);
    legalLayer = new Image("/invincibagelcreds.png", 640, 400, true, false, true);
    scoresLayer = new Image("/invincibagelscores.png", 640, 400, true, false, true);
    iB0 = new Image("/sprite0.png", 81, 81, true, false, true);
    iB1 = new Image("/sprite1.png", 81, 81, true, false, true);
    iB2 = new Image("/sprite2.png", 81, 81, true, false, true);
    iB3 = new Image("/sprite3.png", 81, 81, true, false, true);
    iB4 = new Image("/sprite4.png", 81, 81, true, false, true);
    iB5 = new Image("/sprite5.png", 81, 81, true, false, true);
    iB6 = new Image("/sprite6.png", 81, 81, true, false, true);
    iB7 = new Image("/sprite7.png", 81, 81, true, false, true);
    iB8 = new Image("/sprite8.png", 81, 81, true, false, true);
}
```

As you can see in Figure 11-5, your code is error-free, which means that you have copied your sprite assets into the proper /src folder, and you now have more than a dozen digital image assets installed for use in your game.

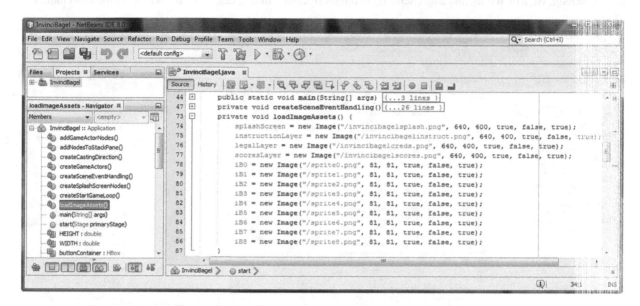

Figure 11-5. *Create a private void loadImageAssets() method, add the iB0 through iB8 and splashScreen Image objects*

Now that the assets you need to call your Bagel() constructor method that you created in Chapter 10 are in place, we can move on to creating a method that holds our game asset creation Java code. This amounts to calling the constructor methods for each of the Actor subclasses we eventually create, the first of which was the Bagel class, which we created first so that we can start to work on getting our primary character moving around the screen.

Creating Your InvinciBagel Bagel Object: .createGameActors()

The next step in the game actor creation process after loading your image assets is to call the constructor method for the game actor. To be able to do this, you must first subclass either the Actor superclass (for fixed game actors, which could be called "props") or the Hero superclass (for motion game actors, such as the Hero, his enemies, and the like). I am going to create a .createGameActors() method to hold these instantiations, because even though initially there is only going to be one line of code inside of the body of this method, eventually, as the game becomes more and more complex, this method will serve as a "roadmap" regarding what game actor assets we have installed. This method will be declared as a **private** method, since the InvinciBagel class will be controlling the creation of these game actors, and will feature a **void** return type, because the method doesn't return any values to the calling entity (the .start() method in this case). Inside of the method we'll call the Bagel() constructor method, using some "placeholder" SVG path data, as well as a 0,0 initial X,Y screen location, and finally, the nine sprite cels using a comma-delimited list at the end of the constructor method call. The method body and object instantiation will use the following three lines of Java code:

```
private void createGameActors() {
    iBagel = new Bagel("M150 0 L75 500 L225 200 Z", 0, 0, iB0,iB1,iB2,iB3,iB4,iB5,iB6,iB7,iB8);
}
```

As you can see in Figure 11-6, the code is error-free, and you now have an iBagel Bagel object that you can now use to start to develop the InvinciBagel sprite movement around the game play stage, which is usually the entire display screen. We'll be wiring this Bagel Actor up to the JavaFX pulse timing engine a bit later on during this chapter.

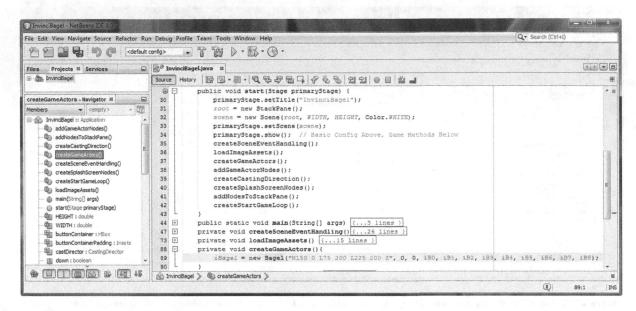

Figure 11-6. *Add a private void createGameActors() method; add an iBagel object instantiation via Bagel() constructor*

In case you're wondering what the SVGdata String object "M150 0 L75 200 L225 200 Z" does, it is shorthand for the following line drawing instructions (commands). The M is a "Move Absolute" command and tells the line draw (or in this case a path draw) operation to start at location 150,0. The L is a "Line Draw To" command and tells the SVG data to draw a line from 150,0 to 75,200. The second L draws a line from 75,200 to 225,200, giving us two sides of the triangle shape. The Z is a "Close Shape" command, which, if the shape is open, as ours is currently, will draw a line to close the shape. In this case, that would equate to drawing a line from 225,200 to 150,0, giving us three sides to our triangle shape, closing the open path, and giving us a valid collision detection boundary.

We will be replacing this with a more complex collision shape later on, during Chapter 16 covering collision detection polygon creation, SVG data, and collision detection logic. Our actual collision polygon will contain many more numbers, making our Bagel() constructor method call unwieldy. As you might imagine, at that point in the game (no pun intended), I will probably create a work process that will be used specifically for constructing collision shapes. This work process will show you how to generate SVG polygon data using GIMP so that you can place SVG data into its own String object, and reference that in your Actor object constructor. If you wanted to turn collision data creation into its own method as well, this is how that would look, using a (theoretical) .createActorCollisionData() method:

```
String cBagel; // Create String variable named cBagel (collision data Bagel) at top of class

private void createActorCollisionData() {
    cBagel = "M150 0 L75 500 L225 200 Z";
}
private void createGameActors() {
    iBagel = new Bagel(cBagel, 0, 0, iB0,iB1,iB2,iB3,iB4,iB5,iB6,iB7,iB8);
}
```

You could also, later on, create a method for Image sprite List<Actor> object loading. This would pass the ArrayList as a parameter, instead of a comma-delimited List. Note that if you did this, you would also need to change your Actor abstract class constructor to take in an ArrayList<Actor> object, instead of an Image... List of Image objects.

Next, let's take a look at how we add our newly created iBagel object into our game's Scene Graph object, which is currently a Stackpane object named root.

Adding Your iBagel to the Scene Graph: .addGameActorNodes()

One of the steps that JavaFX application developers often forget is to add their objects that will need to be displayed in the Scene (and on the Stage that the Scene object is attached to) to the root object of the Scene Graph. In our case, this is a **StackPane** object named **root**. We will need to use the same **root.getChildren().add()** method call chain that we did in Chapter 6, when we started developing our Splashscreen, to add our iBagel object ImageView, which is referenced using **iBagel.spriteFrame**, to the Scene Graph root object. I am going to add a method at this stage that will ensure that we never forget this important **add to Scene Graph** step in our work process. I am going to specifically address this stage in the Actor creation work process by making it into its own method, which I am going to call **.addGameActorNodes()**. The creation of this method body, and our first add Actor to Scene Graph programming statement, would be accomplished using the following Java code, which is also shown (highlighted) in Figure 11-7:

```
private void addGameActorNodes() {
    root.getChildren().add(iBagel.spriteFrame);
}
```

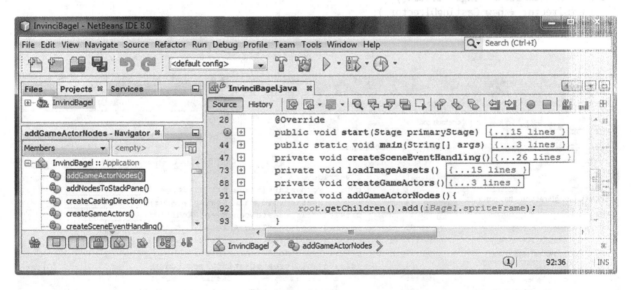

Figure 11-7. *Create a private void addGameActorNodes() method; .add() iBagel.spriteFrame ImageView to root object*

It is important to note that I am calling this .addGameActorNodes() method, at the top of the InvinciBagel class, inside of the .start() method, before I call the .addNodesToStackPane() method. There is a very good reason for doing this, and it goes back to what you learned about JavaFX in Chapter 4. Remember the objects that you add to the StackPane layer management object are displayed using a **Z-index** (or **Z-order**), which means that they are "stacked" on top of each other. If any of these layers do not have an **alpha channel**, which we learned about in Chapter 5, then nothing behind them will be able to show through! For this reason, the easiest way to get our Splashscreen to overlay our game at any point in time that a player clicks the INSTRUCTIONS Button control object is to add these assets last.

By having your .addNodesToStackPane() method called **after** your .addGameActorNodes() method, you will guarantee that your game assets will always be at a **lower Z-index** than your Splashscreen assets. This means that the **SplashScreenBackplate** and the **SplashScreenTextArea** ImageView "plates" will always be at the **top Z-index layers** in the StackPane, and thus, when these are displayed (made visible), they will completely cover your game play. This is because the SplashScreenBackplate ImageView contains an opaque PNG24 image asset that is the same size as your Scene (and Stage) object.

We will be seeing the result of this method order reorganization later on when we test the new InvinciBagel game application, and you will see that we have resolved this problem of the game actor(s) displaying on top of the Splashscreen. We accomplished this simply by changing the order that your programming code is executed in. This should also point out to you that the order that the Java programming code is executed in is almost as important as the Java programming logic itself!

Creating and Managing Your Cast: .createCastingDirection()

Now the time has come to implement the other class that we created in Chapter 10, the CastingDirector.java class, and its CastingDirector() constructor method. We will do this inside of another new custom method we will create called **.createCastingDirection()**. This method will contain the initial instantiation of a CastingDirector object named castDirector, which we will create by using the Java **new** keyword and the CastingDirector() constructor method, as well as adding the iBagel Actor object to the castDirector object, using the **.addCurrentCast()** method that we created in Chapter 10. The Java method structure, which is shown error-free in Figure 11-8, should look like the following:

```java
private void createCastingDirection() {
    castDirector = new CastingDirector();
    castDirector.addCurrentCast(iBagel);
}
```

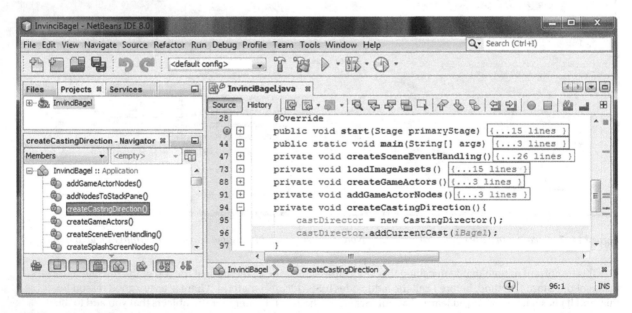

Figure 11-8. *Create private void createCastingDirection() method with castDirector and .addCurrentCast() statements*

Now that we have put our Image assets into place, created our Actor object, added him to the Scene Graph, created a CastingDirector engine, and added our iBagel to the cast, we're ready to deal with the Game Timing Engine.

Create and Start Your GamePlayLoop: .createStartGameLoop

I am going to jump ahead of the .createSceneGraphNodes() method, which is still our most complex method body and which I am saving for last, and create a new method called .createStartGameLoop(). Inside of this method we're going to create, and then start, our GamePlayLoop object, which we created back in Chapter 7 using the GamePlayLoop.java class. This class extends the JavaFX AnimationTimer superclass to provide access to the JavaFX pulse timing engine for our game. Inside of the .createStartGameLoop() method we are going to use the Java new keyword to create a pulse engine for our game named gamePlayLoop using the GamePlayLoop() constructor method. After that, we are going to call the .start() method off of this gamePlayLoop object to start the pulse event timing engine. This call is done by using the following four lines of Java programming logic, which are also shown error-free in Figure 11-9:

```java
private void createStartGameLoop() {
    gamePlayLoop = new GamePlayLoop();
    gamePlayLoop.start();
}
```

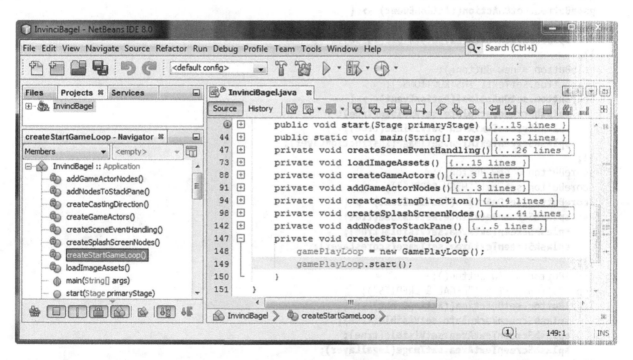

Figure 11-9. *Create a private void createStartGameLoop() method, and create and .start() the gamePlayLoop object*

As you can see at the bottom of Figure 11-9, I have collapsed the other method structures, and I have them in the same order in the code that they are called within the .start() method, for organization purposes. I start a game play loop last because I want to make sure I have done absolutely everything else that I need to do to set up the game environment first, before I start the JavaFX pulse engine firing and launch the game. As you can see, I'm using the Java method names, and my game code design, to keep me reminded about what I need to do every time that I add some new game actor, which now that our hero is in place, could be game props, projectiles, enemies, treasure, and so on.

Update Splashscreen Scene Graph: .createSplashScreenNodes()

Now the time has come to reorganize our .createSplashScreenNodes() method body, and then we will be ready to get into "wiring up" the JavaFX pulse engine that we created in our GamePlayLoop.java class to the Actor object that we created using our Actor.java, Hero.java and Bagel.java classes. We have already removed four lines of code from the end of the .createSplashScreenNodes() method, and placed them into the .loadImageAssets() method, where they more logically belong. The other thing that we need to do to try and streamline our .start() method is to group the ActionEvent handling structures with each of their respective object instantiations and configuration Java statements. Thus, your **gameButton** object instantiation, configuration, and event handling will all be kept together in one place, for instance. We will do the same thing for the **helpButton**, **scoreButton**, and **legalButton** objects. The event handling structures that I copied from the .start() method into the .createSplashScreenNodes() method are shown here in bold. The new .createSplashScreenNodes() method body will contain the following three dozen lines of Java code:

```
private void createSplashScreenNodes() {
    buttonContainer = new HBox(12);
    buttonContainer.setAlignment(Pos.BOTTOM_LEFT);
    buttonContainerPadding = new Insets(0, 0, 10, 16);
    buttonContainer.setPadding(buttonContainerPadding);
    gameButton = new Button();
    gameButton.setText("PLAY GAME");
    gameButton.setOnAction((ActionEvent) -> {
        splashScreenBackplate.setVisible(false);
        splashScreenTextArea.setVisible(false);
    });
    helpButton = new Button();
    helpButton.setText("INSTRUCTIONS");
    helpButton.setOnAction((ActionEvent) -> {
        splashScreenBackplate.setVisible(true);
        splashScreenTextArea.setVisible(true);
        splashScreenTextArea.setImage(instructionLayer);
    });
    scoreButton = new Button();
    scoreButton.setText("HIGH SCORES");
    scoreButton.setOnAction((ActionEvent) -> {
        splashScreenBackplate.setVisible(true);
        splashScreenTextArea.setVisible(true);
        splashScreenTextArea.setImage(scoresLayer);
    });
    legalButton = new Button();
    legalButton.setText("LEGAL & CREDITS");
    legalButton.setOnAction((ActionEvent) -> {
        splashScreenBackplate.setVisible(true);
        splashScreenTextArea.setVisible(true);
        splashScreenTextArea.setImage(legalLayer);
    });
        buttonContainer.getChildren().addAll(gameButton, helpButton, scoreButton, legalButton);
        splashScreenBackplate = new ImageView();
        splashScreenBackplate.setImage(splashScreen);
        splashScreenTextArea = new ImageView();
        splashScreenTextArea.setImage(instructionLayer);
    }
```

Notice that since the .loadImageAssets() method is called **before** the .createSplashScreenNodes() method, that we can still keep the last four lines of code in the method body that reference the loaded Image assets in place. This is because the splashScreen and instructionLayer Image objects have been created, and loaded with their digital image assets, in the top part of the .loadImageAssets() method. Since this method is called inside the .start() method before the .createSplashScreenNodes() method is called, these objects can be safely used inside of this method body.

As you can see in Figure 11-10, the new method is error-free and all of the objects, including the HBox named buttonContainer, Button(s) named gameButton, helpButton, scoreButton and legalButton, and ImageView(s) named splashScreenBackplate and splashScreenTextArea, are all logically grouped together, and are now well organized.

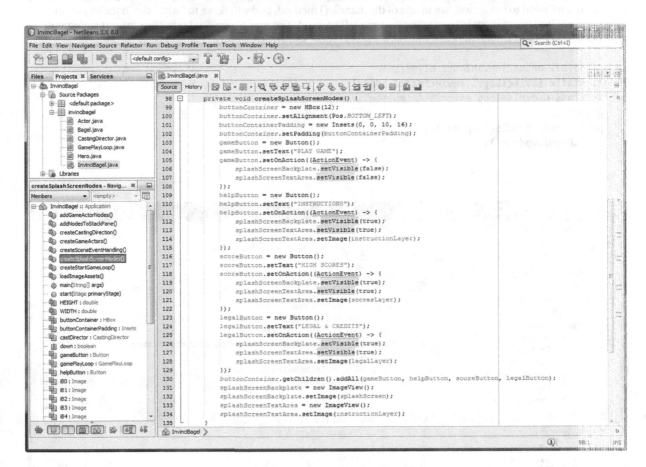

Figure 11-10. *Copy .setOnAction() event handlers from the .start() method into the .createSplashScreenNodes() method*

Since we don't have to do anything to your **.addNodesToStackPane()** method, we are finished with the code reorganization that we needed to do here, before we take this game to the next level of complexity! Every now and then, you need to go back and make sure that your programming logic is optimally structured, so that when you build more complex structures, you have a solid foundation to build upon, just like you're building a real building structure.

Powering the iBagel Actor: Using the GamePlayLoop

Next let's "wire up" or make the connection between these game engines that we have been putting into place in our game code infrastructure during the first half of the book. The first thing that we will need to do is to tell our GamePlay Engine in the GamePlayLoop AnimationTimer subclass that we want to have it look at (update) the iBagel Bagel object on every pulse. There are two major lines of code that we will need to install in the GamePlayLoop.java class for this to happen. The first is a reference to the **static** Bagel object named iBagel that we declared in the code that is shown in Figure 11-3 using the **import static invincibagel.InvinciBagel.iBagel** Java statement. The second line of code that we need to install will live inside of the .handle() method, and will serve to "wire" the .handle() method (the pulse engine) to the iBagel object using its .update() method. The new GamePlayLoop class import statements and .handle() method should look like the following Java code, shown error-free in Figure 11-11:

```java
import javafx.animation.AnimationTimer;
import static invincibagel.InvinciBagel.iBagel;
public class GamePlayLoop extends AnimationTimer {
    @Override
    public void handle(long now) {
        iBagel.update();
    }
}
```

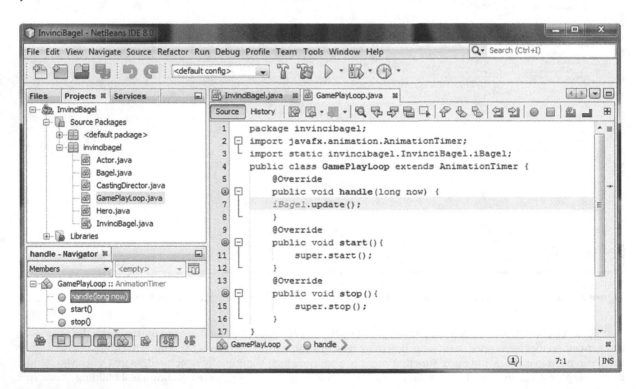

Figure 11-11. *Add a Java statement inside of the GamePlayLoop .handle() method invoking an iBagel.update() method*

What the **iBagel.update()** Java statement does is to call the .update() method for the Bagel object named iBagel on every pulse event. Anything that you put into this .update() method will be executed 60 times every second. Any other Actor object that you want processed at 60 FPS, simply add a similar .update() call to this .handle() method.

Moving the iBagel Actor Object: Coding Your .update() Method

Now we are ready to start developing the code that will move our InvinciBagel Actor object around the screen. We will be refining this Java code during the remainder of the book, as everything revolves around this primary Actor object, and his movement. This includes where he moves (boundaries and collisions), how fast he moves (speed and physics), and what he looks like when he moves (animating between sprite image cels or "states"). All of this code will originate inside of the iBagel object's **.update()** method, and so we are going to start this lengthy journey by adding some basic code that looks at the Boolean variables that are in our InvinciBagel.java class, and which hold the arrow (or ASDW keys) key pressed and released states, and then process these states using **conditional If statements**. The results of this conditional statement processing will then move the InvinciBagel character on the screen (initially, later we will add more advanced programming logic). We will eventually make this movement and interaction more and more "intelligent." The first thing that we will want to do is to make the Boolean variables for up, down, left, and right visible to the Bagel class using import static statements, as we did earlier in the chapter, to make the iBagel object visible to the GamePlayLoop class .handle() method. The four added import static statements will look like this:

```
package invincibagel;
import static invincibagel.InvinciBagel.down;
import static invincibagel.InvinciBagel.left;
import static invincibagel.InvinciBagel.right;
import static invincibagel.InvinciBagel.up;
import javafx.scene.image.Image;
public class Bagel extends Hero {...}
```

As you can see in Figure 11-12, there are no error or warning highlights regarding this code, and we're ready to move on and add the conditional programming logic that will look at which of these four variables are set to true, or KeyPressed, and which are set to false, or KeyReleased. Inside of these conditional statements we'll place the code that will move the **iX** and **iY** (Actor location) variables, based on the **vX** and **vY** (Actor velocity of movement) variables.

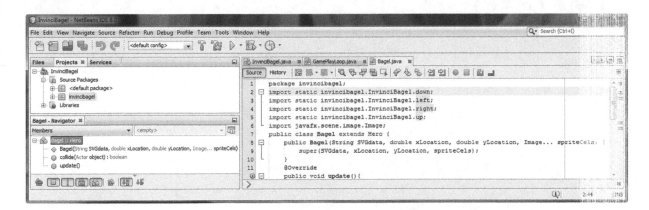

Figure 11-12. *Add import static invincibagel.InvinciBagel references to static boolean down, left, right, and up variables*

Since we are writing this code inside of the Bagel object (in our case, we instantiated and named it iBagel), we will have a chance to utilize and understand the iX and iY variables, which we will be doing in the next section of this chapter, when we develop the code statements that access and change the iBagel Bagel object's iX and iY location attributes, as well as adding code that accesses and utilizes the iBagel Bagel object's vX and vY velocity attributes.

Building the .update() Method: Using If Statements to Determine X or Y Movement

Now it is time to add some basic Java programming logic inside of the Bagel class .update() method that will move the iBagel object along the X or Y axis (or both, if multiple keys are being pressed). Since our iX and iY variables hold the Actor location on the screen, we will use these inside of each if statement, and add (or subtract) the velocity variable amount for each axis (vX if we are dealing with iX, vY if we are dealing with iY) respectively. We have initially set the vX and vY values at one, which would equate to a relatively slow movement. If the vX and vY were set to 2, the iBagel would move twice as fast (it would move by two pixels on each pulse event, instead of by one pixel).

If the **right** Boolean variable is true, we want your iBagel object to move in the positive direction along the X axis, so we would use an **if(right){iX+=vX}** programming statement to add the vX velocity value to the iX location value using the += operator we learned about in Chapter 3. Similarly, if the **left** Boolean variable is true, we would use an **if(left){iX-=vX}** programming statement, which will subtract the vX velocity value from the iX location value, using the -= Java operator.

We will do essentially the same thing along the Y axis when the up and down (or W and S) keys are pressed. If the **down** Boolean variable is true, we want the iBagel object to move in the positive direction along the Y axis. Thus we would use an **if(down){iY+=vY}** programming statement, which will add the vY velocity value to the iY location value, using the += operator. In JavaFX, a positive X value goes from the 0,0 origin to the right, while positive Y values go from 0,0 down. Finally, to move the iBagel up, we will use an **if(up){iY-=vY}** programming statement, which will subtract the vY velocity value from the iY location value, using the -= operator. The basic Java code to perform these four conditional if statement evaluations, and their respective X or Y sprite movement calculations inside of the Bagel class .update() method, is shown in Figure 11-13, and should look like the following method body structure thus far:

```
@Override
public void update() {
    if(right) { iX += vX }
    if(left)  { iX -= vX }
    if(down)  { iY += vY }
    if(up)    { iY -= vY }
}
```

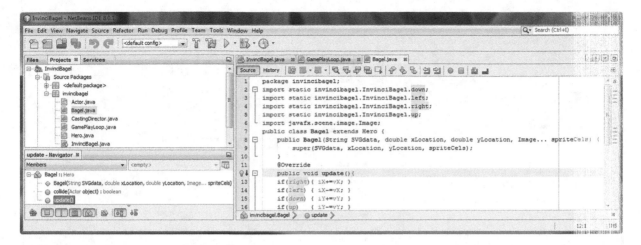

Figure 11-13. *Add four if statements to the .update() method, one for each right, left, down, and up boolean variable*

Next, let's move an iBagel on the screen using the ImageView .setTranslateX() and .setTranslateY() methods.

Moving a Scene Graph ImageView Node: .setTranslateX() and .setTranslateY()

Now that we have the conditional statements in place that will process where our InvinciBagel is supposed to be on the screen based on what arrow keys (or ASDW keys) are being held down (or not held down) by the player, let's add the Java programming statements that will take this data from our InvinciBagel iX and iY variables, and pass this sprite location information to the **spriteFrame** ImageView Node object, to actually have it reposition the Node on the display screen. The **.setTranslateX()** and **.setTranslateY()** methods are part of the **Node** superclass's **transformation** methods. These methods also include method calls that will **rotate** and **scale** a Node object; in this case, it is the Actor spriteFrame ImageView Node that contains one of the Image assets held in your List<Image> ArrayList object.

When we call these .setTranslate() methods, off of our iBagel object's spriteFrame ImageView Node object, we are referring to the spriteFrame ImageView object that we installed inside of the abstract Actor superclass. Since an Actor superclass was used to create the Hero superclass, which was used to create the Bagel class, the spriteFrame ImageView object can be referenced inside of the Bagel class by using a **spriteFrame.setTranslateX(iX)** statement, as is shown in the following Java code for the completed .update() method, which is also shown in Figure 11-14:

```java
public void update() {
    if(right) { iX += vX }
    if(left)  { iX -= vX }
    if(down)  { iY += vY }
    if(up)    { iY -= vY }
    spriteFrame.setTranslateX(iX);
    spriteFrame.setTranslateY(iY);
}
```

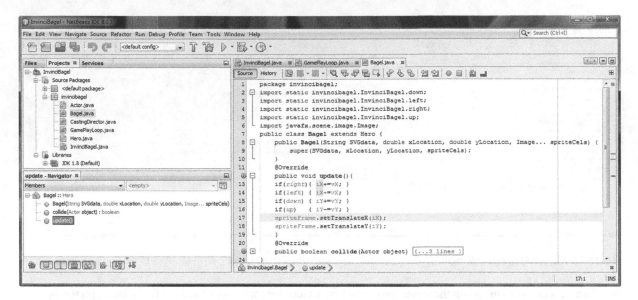

Figure 11-14. *After the four if statements, add statements calling the .setTranslate() methods off of the spriteFrame*

As you can see in Figure 11-14, the code is error- and warning-free, and we're ready to test the code that we have written during the chapter, including a reorganized InvinciBagel.java class and its six new methods, the updated Bagel.java class and its .update() method, and the updated GamePlayLoop.java class, and its .handle() method.

Testing Our New Game Design: Moving InvinciBagel

We have made significant changes to our game application during this chapter, especially to the structure of the InvinciBagel.java class, adding six all-new methods, and moving our event handling code around completely. We created an iBagel Bagel object, and a castDirector CastingDirector object, using classes that we created in Chapter 10. We wired up our GamePlayLoop object and one of our Actor objects (an iBagel Bagel object) by using the JavaFX pulse engine .handle() method in the GamePlayLoop.java class and the .update() method in the Bagel.java class. Now the time has come to use our **Run ➤ Project** work process and make sure that all of the Java code that we have put into place during this chapter does what it is supposed to do: that is, what we think that it should do. After all, that is what the programming practice is all about: writing code that we think will do something, running it to see if it does, and then debugging it to find out why it is not working, if in fact it is not. Once you click on the Play button at the top of the NetBeans IDE and invoke the **Run ➤ Project** process, the code will compile and the InvinciBagel game window seen in Figure 11-15 will open up on your desktop. The first thing that you should notice is that the InvinciBagel sprite is nowhere to be seen, since we added it to the root StackPane object first instead of last, and so the splashscreen and game user interface design is still working as intended.

Figure 11-15. *Use Run ➤ Project to start the game and click the PLAY GAME Button*

Next, let's test your ActionEvent handling, and later, the KeyEvent handling, by clicking on the **PLAY GAME** Button control object. This should hide the splashScreenBackplate and splashScreenTextArea ImageView objects, and reveal the white background color which is set for the Scene object named scene using the Color.WHITE constant.

As you can see, on the left half of Figure 11-16, this is indeed the case, and our InvinciBagel character is on the screen, and we are ready to test the KeyEvent handling that we put into place in Chapter 9, and see if we can get the InvinciBagel (iBagel Bagel object) character to move around on the screen. This is starting to get more and more exciting with each successive chapter that we finish!

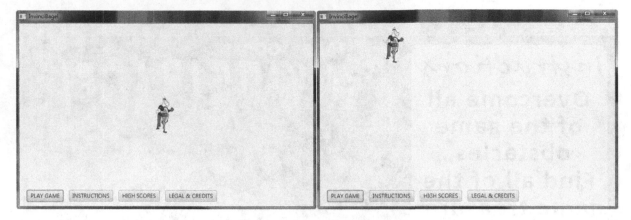

Figure 11-16. *Hold a left arrow (or A) and up arrow (or W) key down at the same time, and move the Actor diagonally*

Let's test the worst case scenario first, and see how powerful the JavaFX pulse event and key event handling infrastructure really is. Press the up key and the left arrow key, or the A key and the W key, **at the same time**. As you can see, the InvinciBagel character moves smoothly and steadily on a diagonal vector, up and to the left. The result of this can be seen on the right half of Figure 11-16. Try using the individual keys as well, to make sure they are working.

As you play around with your now motion-enabled InvinciBagel sprite, notice that you are able to move him behind the UI buttons at the bottom of the screen, as seen on the left half of Figure 11-17. This happens because you have your .addGameActorNodes() method called before your .addNodesToStackPane() method is called, which gives everything in your game a lower Z-index than everything in your user interface design. Also notice that you can move the InvinciBagel off of the screen (out of view of the player), which we are going to address in Chapter 12, when you will add to the existing code to establish boundaries and implement other advanced movement features. Finally, note that if you use the left and right arrow keys (not the ASDW keys), the Button control focus (the blue outline) moves as well, which means that we will also have to fix this in a future chapter, by having our KeyEvents "consumed." As you can see, there is lots of really cool code to write and things about Java 8 and JavaFX 8.0 to learn before we're finished!

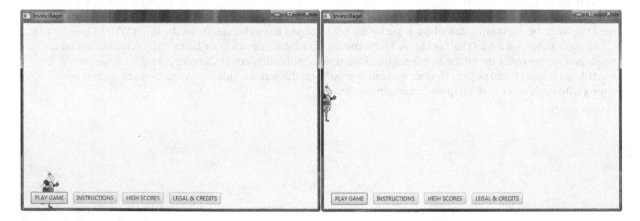

Figure 11-17. *Notice the InvinciBagel character is using a lower Z-index than the UI elements, and can move off-screen*

Yet again you have made a ton of progress during this chapter in getting your primary InvinciBagel.java class optimized, implementing all of the classes that you have coded thus far in this book, wired the game play loop engine into your primary game character, tested all of your ActionEvent and KeyEvent handling, and had an all-around good time doing it! I would call that a pretty successful chapter, and we will continue to have a good time in every chapter!

Summary

In this eleventh chapter, we reorganized our primary InvinciBagel.java class to extract the five key game creation Java statements, and then organized the rest of the Java code into eight logical methods (routines), six of them which we created from scratch during this chapter. The six new methods serve to parcelize things such as adding Image assets, creating new Actor objects, adding Actors to the Scene Graph, adding Actors to the Cast, creating and starting the Game Engine, and implementing the game key event handling routines. We added object declarations so that we could create a new iBagel Bagel object for our game's primary character, and also created a castDirector CastingDirection engine so that we could manage our cast members as we add them to the game in later chapters.

We learned about import static statements, and we saw how to use them to wire our iBagel Bagel object to the GamePlayLoop.java engine .handle() method. We also used these import static statements to allow our Bagel.java class to process the Boolean up, down, left, and right variables in the .update() method.

Next, we covered how to use conditional if statements to determine which key events (held in four Boolean variables) were being used by the game player. We placed this logic inside of the Bagel class .update() method, which as we know is being rapidly executed 60 times per second by the GamePlayLoop .handle() JavaFX pulse engine.

Finally we tested all of the new methods and Java statements that we added during the chapter to see if the basic game sprite movement works. We observed some of the things that we will need to address in future chapters, and thoroughly tested the existing KeyEvent handling methods and iX, iY, vX, and vY attributes of the abstract Actor class that we created as the foundation for all of our game actor assets.

In the next chapter, we are going to take a closer look at the JavaFX Node class and also take a look at advanced concepts regarding moving the game **sprite** around your screen, as well as how to ascertain the boundary (edges) of the screen, character direction, movement velocity, and related animation and movement considerations.

■ ■ ■

Setting Boundaries for Your Action Figure in 2D: Using the Node Class LocalToParent Attribute

Now that we have organized your Java code into logical methods in the InvinciBagel.java class, and wired up the GamePlayLoop .handle() method to the Bagel .update() method in Chapter 10, to make sure that our KeyEvent handlers will move our InvinciBagel character around the screen, it is time to establish some **boundaries** for our game hero, so that he does not leave the field of play, so to speak. To do this, we will need to dive into the JavaFX Node superclass at a much deeper level of detail then we did in Chapter 4. We will look at how **transforms** are performed, and more important, how they function **relative** to the Parent Node, which is located above them in the Scene Graph. For our Actor ImageView Node(s), that Parent Node would be the Scene Graph **root** StackPane Node.

Before we start getting into code complexities such as absolute or relative transformation, which we will be looking at during this chapter, and things such as collision detection and physics simulation, which we will cover later in Chapters 16 and 17, we will need to get back into our **InvinciBagel.java** primary application class Java code here in Chapter 12, so that we can do a few more things that will optimize the Java 8 foundation for our game. We have been putting our game engines into place during the first part of this book, and I want to make sure that everything is "up to snuff" before I start to build complex code structures on top of what we have put into place so far. We're going to make sure everything is "locked down tightly!"

For this reason, I am going to spend the first few pages of this chapter getting rid of those **import static** Java statements, which although they work just fine, as you have seen, they are not what is termed **"best practice"** in Java programming. There is a more complex and involved way to talk between classes, involving a Java "this" keyword, so I am going to show you how to implement far more **private** variables (and far less static variables), and then I will teach you how to use reference objects, represented by the Java **this** keyword, to send object data variables between classes.

This is a somewhat advanced topic for a beginner level book, but it will allow you to write more professional and "industry standard" Java 8 code, so it will be worth the extra effort. Sometimes, the right way to do things is more involved and detailed than the basic (simple) way to get things coded. The assumption here is that you are going to be producing a commercially viable game, so you will need a rock solid foundation to build increasingly complex code on.

After we finish adding additional code refinements in our InvinciBagel.java class, which will implement Java "encapsulation" using **private** variables wherever possible, and the **this** keyword where needed to provide access to the InvinciBagel object to other related classes—in this case, the GamePlayLoop and Bagel classes for now—we will begin to add complexity to the sprite movement code that is in our Bagel class .update() method.

We will add code that will tell your InvinciBagel character where the ceiling and floor of his Scene and Stage are located, and where the left and right sides of the screen are, so that he does not fall off of his flat 2D world. We will also organize the methods in the Bagel.java class, so that the .update() method only calls higher-level methods that contain all of the Java programming logic in an exceptionally well organized fashion.

InvinciBagel Privatization: Removing Static Modifiers

The first thing that I want to do regarding the InvinciBagel.java class Java code, as well as the GamePlayLoop.java class code and the Bagel.java class code that both reference the InvinciBagel up, down, left, and right Boolean variables by using import static statements, is to **remove** these import static statements from the top of both of these "worker" classes, and instead pass an InvinciBagel class (**context**) object, using the Java **this** keyword, in the Bagel() constructor method as well as in the GamePlayLoop() constructor method. The first step in this process, which will span the next several pages of the chapter, is to change the **public static boolean** variable declaration compound statement to not use a static modifier, and instead of the public access control modifier, to use the **private** keyword, as is shown here:

```
private boolean up, down, left, right;
```

As you can see in Figure 12-1, this doesn't generate any red errors or yellow warning highlights in the code; however, it does generate wavy grey underlining. This signifies that the code that is highlighted is not currently being used. Since the "convention" or general rule in Java regarding static modifier keywords is to use them with constants, such as we are in the first line of code, and thus, I am going to try and "encapsulate" the code in this InvinciBagel.java class as much as possible, by removing the static modifiers (first), and making many of the other declarations **private**.

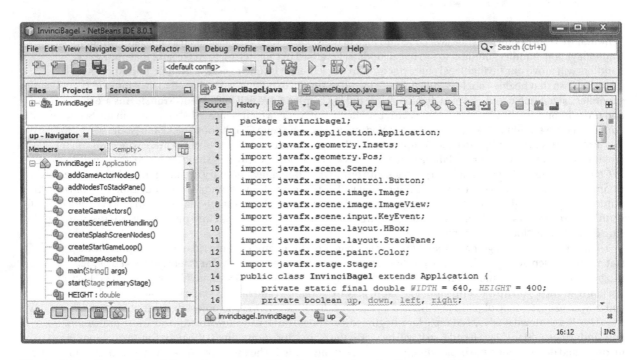

Figure 12-1. *Change the public static access modifiers for the boolean KeyEvent variables to be private access control*

The code that we are going to put into place next will eliminate this wavy grey highlighting, and in fact, we are going to have NetBeans write that code for us using the **Source ➤ Insert Code ➤ Getters and Setters** work process, which we learned about in Chapter 8, when we created our Actor and Hero superclasses. The **.is()** and **.set()** methods, which we are about to generate next, are the solution that allows us to eliminate the public static variable declaration that was allowing your classes external to InvinciBagel.java to "reach inside" (think of this as a security breach) to grab these four Boolean variables. Making these variables **private** prevents this. So, we need to put .is() and .set() methods into place which force external classes and methods to "request" this information, using a more "formal" method call.

This time, we are going to use the NetBeans **Generate Getters and Setters** dialog, which is shown in Figure 12-2, to selectively write the getters (the .is() methods) and the setters (the .set() methods), which will access the four Boolean variables. Technically, right now we only need to use the getter .is() methods, so you could use the **Generate ➤ Getter** menu option, shown in the middle (pop-up or floating) Generate menu, above the selected Getter and Setter option, in the middle (encased with a red line) of Figure 12-2. I prefer to generate both of these method "directions," just in case, later on in the software development process, I need to set these variables (externally, in another class) for some programming reason relating to the game play logic development.

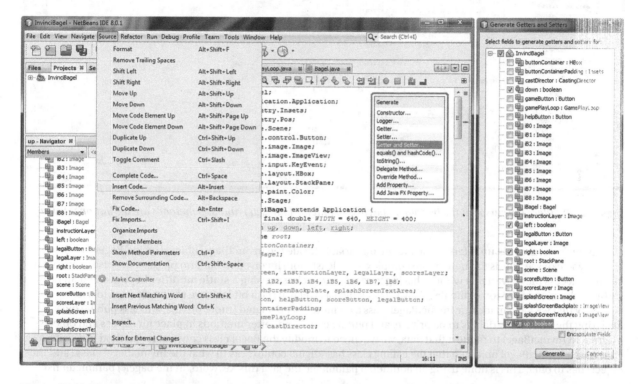

Figure 12-2. *Use the Source ➤ Insert Code ➤ Getter and Setter dialog to create methods for the four boolean variables*

Select the four Boolean **down**, **left**, **right**, and **up** variables in the Generate Getters and Setters dialog, shown on the far right side of Figure 12-2, click your cursor so that it is in front of the final } curly brace in your class (this will tell NetBeans that you want it to write, or place, this code at the end of the current class structure), and then click the **Generate** button at the bottom of this dialog, to generate the eight new Boolean variable access method structures.

As you can see in Figure 12-3, there are eight new methods at the bottom of your InvinciBagel.java class. It is important to note that the .set() methods all use the Java **this** keyword to set the Boolean variable that you pass in to the method to the up, down, left, or right (private) variables. The .setUp() method, for instance, would look like this:

```java
public void setUp(boolean up) {
    this.up = up;
}
```

Figure 12-3. *Place the cursor at the bottom of the class so that the four .set() and .is() methods are the last ones listed*

In this case, the **this.up** refers to the private up variable inside the InvinciBagel object (InvinciBagel class).

As you can see, this is the new (more complex, or at least more involved to put into place, code-wise) way that we can now access the up variable without having to reach across classes using a **static modifier keyword** and an **import static** declaration at the top of the Bagel.java class, which as you will see a bit later, we no longer need to use.

Now that we have made our InvinciBagel class a bit more encapsulated (more private, and less public) by declaring the Boolean variables to be private, and putting getter and setter methods in place for classes and objects external to InvinciBagel to request that data, we will need to modify the Bagel class constructor method to receive a copy of the InvinciBagel object so that the calling class has "digital context" as to what the InvinciBagel class (and thus object) has to offer. This is done using an additional parameter, the Java **this** keyword, in the Bagel() parameter list.

Passing Context from InvinciBagel to Bagel: Using this Keyword

The final piece in the puzzle regarding how to eliminate static import statements, and reach between classes (objects) in a legitimate fashion, is to pass the InvinciBagel class's current configuration, held in a contextual object reference, which the **this** keyword actually represents, over to the Bagel class (object) using the Bagel() constructor method. Once the Bagel class has received this **contextual information** regarding how the InvinciBagel class (object) is set up, what it includes, and what it does (hey, I have not called this object reference a "contextual" object reference for no reason), it will be able to use the .isUp() method to "see" the value of a Boolean up variable, without having any static declaration in place anywhere other than for constants, which is what an import static reference should be used for.

The first thing that we need to do to upgrade your Bagel class is to set up a variable to hold this InvinciBagel contextual object reference information, and modify our current Bagel() constructor method so that it can receive an InvinciBagel object reference. We'll need to add a **protected InvinciBagel invinciBagel;** statement, at the top of the class, to create an invinciBagel reference object (the variable will hold a reference to this object in memory) to hold this information. The reason I am making this **protected access** is so that if we make any subclass using Bagel, it will have access to this contextual object reference information. This object declaration would use the following Java statement, located at the very top of the Bagel.java class, as shown in Figure 12-4:

```
protected InvinciBagel invinciBagel;
```

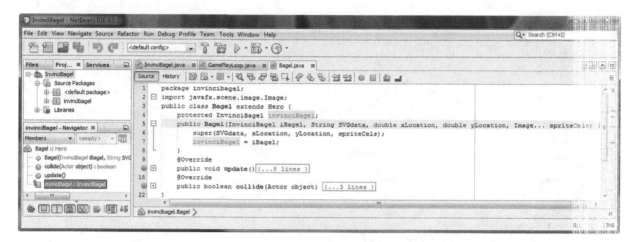

Figure 12-4. *Add an InvinciBagel object variable named invinciBagel, and add the object into the constructor method*

Next, let's add the InvinciBagel context object into the front of the Bagel() constructor's parameter list, since we can't put it at the end of the parameter list, because we're using the end of the parameter list to hold our Image... List (or Array, at some point in the code it is both of these) specification. Inside of the constructor method itself, you'll set the InvinciBagel reference object, which is passed into the constructor method using the name **iBagel**, to equal an **invinciBagel** variable, which you have already declared at the top of the Bagel.java class. This would all be done using the following modified Bagel() constructor method structure, which can be seen highlighted at the top of Figure 12-4:

```
public Bagel(InvinviBagel iBagel, String SVGdata, double xLocation, double yLocation,
             Image... spriteCels) {
    super(SVGdata, xLocation, yLocation, spriteCels);
    invinciBagel = iBagel;
}
```

As you can see in Figure 12-4, our code is error-free, and we are ready to go back into our InvinciBagel.java class and add the Java **this** keyword into the Bagel() constructor method call. Doing this will pass an InvinciBagel class (object) reference object over to the Bagel.java class (object) so that we will be able to use the .is() and .set() methods from the InvinciBagel class without having to specify any import statements whatsoever. You can also delete the four import static statements at the top of your Bagel.java class. As you can see in Figure 12-4, I have deleted these static import statements already.

Now let's go back into the InvinciBagel.java NetBeans editing tab, and finish wiring the two classes together.

Modifying the iBagel Instantiation: Adding a Java this Keyword to the Method Call

Open up your .createGameActors() method structure using the + expand icon on the left side of NetBeans. Add a **this** keyword at the "head" or front of the list of parameters that you are passing into the Bagel() constructor method call. Your newly revised Java statement should look like the following code, which is also shown highlighted in Figure 12-5:

```java
iBagel = new Bagel(this, "M150 0 L75 200 L225 200 Z", 0,0, iB0,iB1,iB2,iB3,iB4,iB5,iB6,iB7,iB8);
```

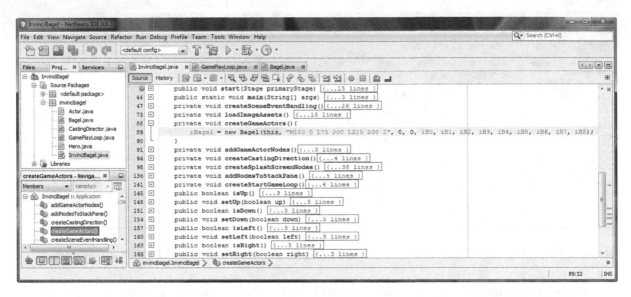

Figure 12-5. *Modify the iBagel instantiation to add a Java this keyword to the Bagel() constructor method parameters*

As you can see in Figure 12-5, your Java code is error-free, which means that you have now passed a copy of your InvinciBagel.java class's (or the object created by it, however you prefer to look at it) context into the Bagel class (or more precisely, into the object which is created by your use of the Bagel() constructor method). What is contained in the digital context structure of the **this** object is beyond the scope of a beginner book, but suffice it to say that the **this** keyword will pass over a complete structural reference to an object. This reference contains all of the contextual information which would be needed to give the object that it is being passed to enough information to be able to put everything into "digital perspective" (context) regarding the class that is passing the this reference object over, in our case, this will be the InvinciBagel class (object) passing contextual information about itself to the Bagel class (object). This will include your object structure (variables, constants, methods, etc.) for the object as well as state information relating to more complex things that relate to use of system memory and thread usage. Think of passing one object's context information to another object using the Java **this** keyword as wiring them together, so to speak, so that your receiving object can peer into the sending object by using the **this** object reference.

Now that the **this** reference (contextual object) for the InvinciBagel class (object) has been passed to the Bagel class (object) by using the Java **this** keyword inside of the Bagel() constructor method, we have now create a far more industry standard link between these two classes. We can now proceed to change our Bagel .update() method so that it uses the new **.is()** method calls to get the four different Boolean variable values (states) from the InvinciBagel object reference that it now has. We will need this data to be able to move our InvinciBagel character around on the screen.

Using Your New InvinciBagel .is() Methods: Updating Your Bagel .update() Method

The next step in our elimination of using import static references and static variables will be to rewrite the conditional if statements using the .isUp(), isDown(), isLeft() and isRight() method calls. Since we're not using static variables to reach across classes (objects) anymore, we'll need to replace these actual **up**, **down**, **left**, and **right** static variables that are currently used inside the if() statements in the Bagel class .update() method. These will no longer work, because they are now encapsulated in the InvinciBagel class, and are private variables, so we will have to use .isUp(), isDown(), isLeft(), and isRight() "getter" methods instead, to politely knock on the InvinciBagel's door, and ask for these values!

We will call our four .is() methods "off of" the InvinciBagel reference object (using dot notation), which we have declared and named **invinciBagel** at the top of the Bagel.java class. This variable (object reference) contains the InvinciBagel class context, which we sent from the InvinciBagel class into the Bagel class using the Java **this** keyword. What this means is that if we say **invinciBagel.isRight()** in our code, our Bagel class (object) now knows that to mean: go into the invinciBagel InvinciBagel object using "this" reference object (just trying to be cute here), which will now show the Bagel class (object) how, and where, to get to, and to execute, the **public void .isRight() {...}** method structure, which will pass over the **private boolean right** variable encapsulated in an InvinciBagel object. This is included here as a demonstration of the Java OOP concept of "encapsulation."

Your new .update() method body will use the same six lines of Java code, modified to call the **.is()** methods on the inside of the **if(condition=true)** evaluation portion of your existing conditional if structure. The new Java code, which is also shown in Figure 12-6, should look like the following:

```java
public void update() {
    if(invinciBagel.isRight()) { iX += vX; }
    if(invinciBagel.isLeft())  { iX -= vX; }
    if(invinciBagel.isDown())  { iY += vY; }
    if(invinciBagel.isUp())    { iY -= vY; }
    spriteFrame.setTranslateX(iX);
    spriteFrame.setTranslateY(iY);
}
```

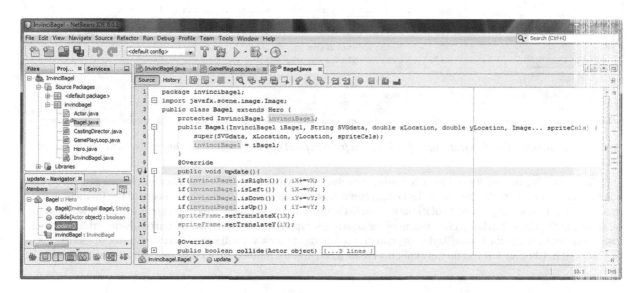

Figure 12-6. *Insert the invinciBagel.is() method calls inside of the if statements, where the boolean variables used to be*

As you can see in Figure 12-6, the code is error-free, and you now have an .update() method that accesses the Boolean variables from your InvinciBagel.java class without having to use any import static statements to do so.

You might be thinking, well, since this is a great way to get rid of import static statements in my Bagel.java class, why don't I use this same approach to also get rid of the **static Bagel iBagel** declaration in my InvinciBagel.java class, as well as the **import static** statement that is used in the GamePlayLoop.java class to access the static iBagel Bagel object? Wow, that is a fantastic idea, folks, I just wish that I had thought of it! In fact, let's do that right now!

Removing a Static iBagel Reference: Revise the Handle( ) Method

As you can see in Figure 12-7, we still have quite a few InvinciBagel variables declared using the static keywords that are not, in fact, constants. Before this chapter is over we will have eliminated these, so that only our WIDTH and HEIGHT constants use the static modifier keyword. Since we are going to pass the InvinciBagel object reference to the GamePlayLoop class using the Java this keyword inside of the GamePlayLoop() constructor method, which means that we can remove the static keyword from the Bagel iBagel object declaration statement at the top of the InvinciBagel class. This can be accomplished using the following variable declaration, which is shown (highlighted) in Figure 12-7:

Bagel iBagel;

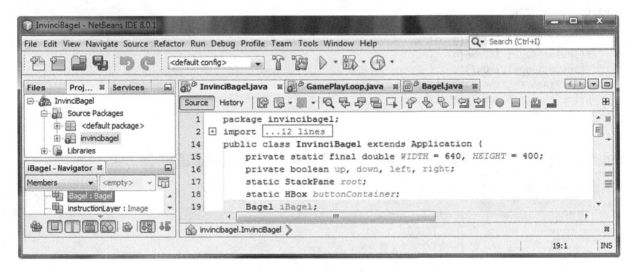

Figure 12-7. *Remove the Java static modifier keyword from in front of your Bagel iBagel object declaration statement*

The next thing that we'll need to do to makes sure that our InvinciBagel and GamePlayLoop classes (objects) can talk to each other is to make the GamePlayLoop() constructor method compatible with (accept in the InvinciBagel **this** context reference object inside of its parameter list) the InvinciBagel class's **this** object reference that we need to send over to the GamePlayLoop class inside of the constructor method call. Since we are currently depending on the Java compiler to create the GamePlayLoop() constructor method for us, we will need to create one for ourselves! As you learned in Chapter 3, if you do not explicitly create a constructor method for a class, one will be created for you.

Enhancing GamePlayLoop.java: Creating a GamePlayLoop() Constructor Method

Let's perform a similar work process in the GamePlayLoop.java class to what we did in the Bagel.java class. Add a **protected InvinciBagel invinciBagel;** statement at the top of the class. Next, create a **public GamePlayLoop()** constructor method, with an **InvinciBagel** object named **iBagel** inside the parameter list. Inside the GamePlayLoop() constructor method, set the **iBagel** InvinciBagel object reference equal to the protected InvinciBagel **invinciBagel** (reference) variable so that we can use the new invinciBagel InvinciBagel object reference inside of the GamePlayLoop .handle() method. This will allow us to call the .update() method off of the iBagel Bagel object using the invinciBagel InvinciBagel reference object. The GamePlayLoop class and constructor method structure, along with a new .handle() method body, which includes a revised **invinciBagel.iBagel.update()** method call path (object referencing structure), are shown error-free in Figure 12-8, and should look like the following Java code:

```java
public class GamePlayLoop extends AnimationTimer {
    protected InvinciBagel invinciBagel;
    public GamePlayLoop(InvinciBagel iBagel) {
        invinciBagel = iBagel;
    }
    @Override
    public void handle(long now) {
        invinciBagel.iBagel.update();.
    }
}
```

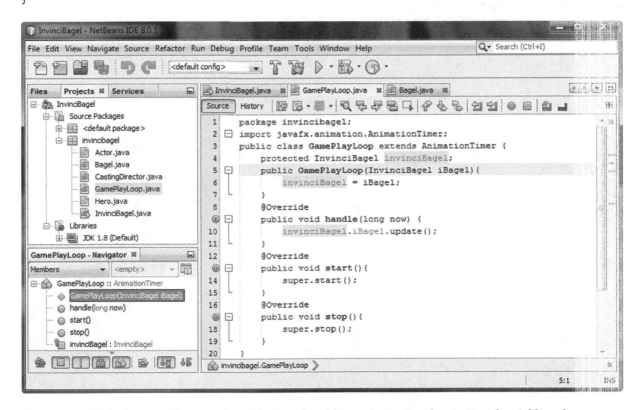

Figure 12-8. *Make the same change to GamePlayLoop by adding an invinciBagel InvinciBagel variable and constructor*

As you can see in Figure 12-8, I have clicked on the invinciBagel variable (InvinciBagel object reference) so it is highlighted, and you can see its usage across the two methods. The declaration is used in the GamePlayLoop class, the instance inside of the GamePlayLoop() constructor method is set using the InvinciBagel class this keyword (using the iBagel parameter), and the variable reference inside of the .handle() method accessed the Bagel class .update() method using the iBagel Bagel object and the invinciBagel InvinciBagel reference object. Java is advanced, but cool.

Now that we have created our custom GamePlayLoop() constructor method that accommodates the receipt of the InvinciBagel object reference named iBagel, and then assigns it to the invinciBagel variable, it is time to return to the InvinciBagel.java code (editing tab in NetBeans).

The final piece of this (second) puzzle of removing the **static Bagel iBagel;** declaration is to add the Java **this** keyword in the GamePlayLoop() constructor method call. After we do this, our InvinciBagel, Bagel and GamePlayLoop will all be wired up to each other, without using any static variables (other than the WIDTH and HEIGHT constants).

Using this in GamePlayLoop() Constructor: GamePlayLoop(this)

Open up your **.createStartGameLoop()** method structure, using the + expand icon on the left side of NetBeans, as shown in Figure 12-9. Add the Java **this** keyword in the parameter area, so that you are again passing the InvinciBagel object reference, this time into the GamePlayLoop() constructor method call. This will give that class a reference to your InvinciBagel class and its context and structure, just like you did with the Bagel class. Your newly revised Java method body and constructor method call will look like the following code, which is shown highlighted in Figure 12-9:

```
private void createStartGameLoop() {
    gamePlayLoop = new GamePlayLoop(this);
    gamePlayLoop.start();
}
```

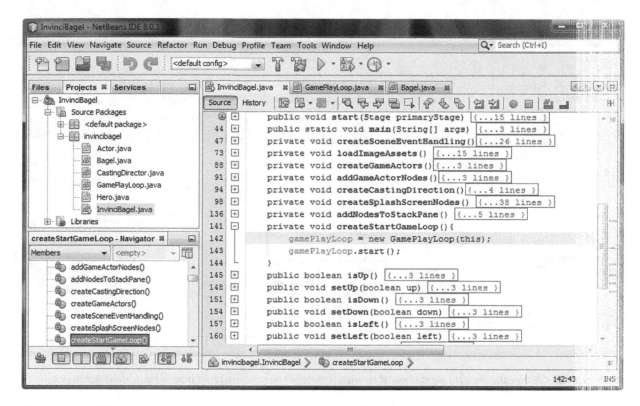

Figure 12-9. *Add a Java this keyword inside of the GamePlayLoop() constructor method call to provide a context object*

As long as we are making our InvinciBagel.java class completely encapsulated, let's make the StackPane root variable private as well, and get rid of the static modifier. Since I have moved the StackPane object named root back up into the .start() menu from the **.createSplashScreenNodes()** method, there is no good reason for a static modifier keyword. I am trying to remove all static modifiers (that are not constants) and "privatize" this class as much as I can.

Removing the Rest of the Static Variables: StackPane and HBox

Now I am going to start going right down the variable declaration lines of code at the top of the InvinciBagel.java class starting with the Boolean variables that we made private (which were public static), and see which of these variables I can make private instead of **package protected static** (which StackPane and HBox are currently), or which are package protected, and can be made **private**. A private variable "encapsulates" that variable's data inside of the class (object) itself; in this case, this would be the **InvinciBagel.java** code that we're currently refining. A package protected variable encapsulates the data inside of the package; in this case that would be the **invincibagel** package. The new Java statement for declaring the StackPane object named root, which is a root element of the Scene Graph, to be a private member of the InvinciBagel.java class (only), would be accomplished using the following code, shown in Figure 12-10.

private StackPane root;

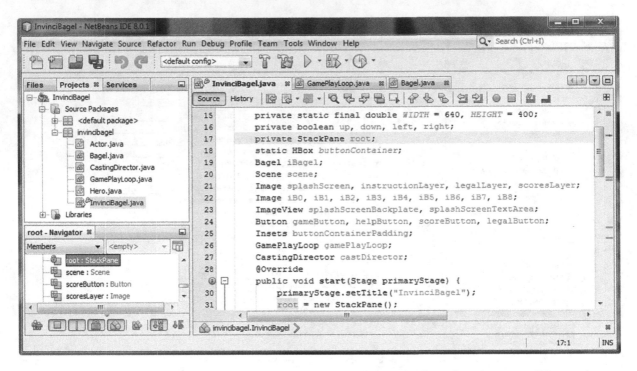

Figure 12-10. *Change the declaration statement for the StackPane object named root from a static modifier to private*

The next static variable down in the declarations at the top of the class is static HBox buttonContainer; and I am also going to change this variable declaration to be a private variable, using the following Java statement:

private HBox buttonContainer;

Let's make sure that the Java statements inside of the .createSplashScreenNodes() method can still "see" or reference this buttonContainer HBox object, which as you can see in Figure 12-11, they can. I also clicked on the HBox object in NetBeans so that it showed me the object references throughout my code (this is a really useful feature that you should use to visualize how objects relate between different Java 8 programming statements inside of your code). This selected object highlighting is shown in your code inside of NetBeans 8 by using a yellow field highlighting color.

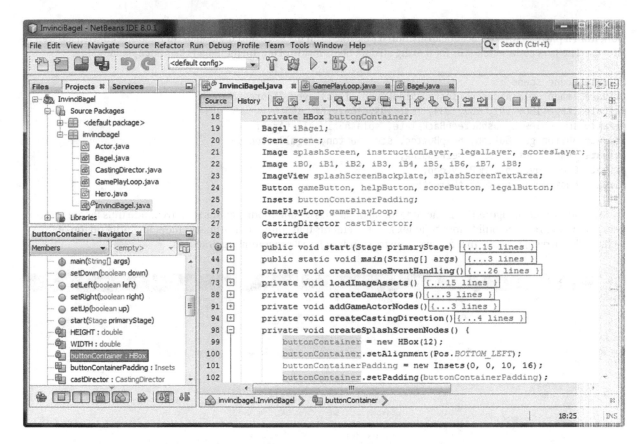

Figure 12-11. *Change declaration statement for HBox object named buttonContainer from a static modifier to private*

I had originally declared these fields static because I had read on the Internet, on several of the Java coding sites, that this is an "optimization trick," which allows the JVM to set aside fixed areas of memory, and make the code run more optimally. I have decided to make the objects for my game as encapsulated as possible first, here during the development process, and then look at optimization later on, if and when it becomes necessary.

As long as we are making our InvinciBagel.java class completely encapsulated, let's make the other variables private as well. I tested this game after making each of the variables (after the Bagel iBagel declaration) private, and it ran just fine. When I make the Bagel iBagel private, the game hangs on a white (background color) screen, so I left the Bagel iBagel declaration **package protected** (no access control modifier keyword signifies package protected access).

Making the Remaining Variables Private: Finish Encapsulating InvinciBagel Class

My work process for making the other eight lines of variable declarations private rather than package protected was to place the private Java access control keyword in front of the (simple or compound) variable declaration, and then use the **Run ➤ Project** work process (or click the green play icon at the top of NetBeans, which is faster) to test the code and see if all of the features, including the Button UI, splashscreens and character movement, work as they have been, using package protected access control. If for some reason at a later point in the software development we need to remove the private modifier or replace it with a different modifier keyword for any reason, we can, but it is best to work from a place of total object encapsulation if possible from the start, and then open up the object if we need to later on. The Java code statements for making all data fields inside of our InvinciBagel class encapsulated are:

```java
private Scene scene;
private Image splashScreen, instructionLayer, legalLayer, scoresLayer;
private Image iB0, iB1, iB2, iB3, iB4, iB5, iB6, iB7, iB8;
private ImageView splashScreenBackplate, splashScreenTextArea;
private Button gameButton, helpButton, scoreButton, legalButton,;
private Insets buttonContainerPadding;
private GamePlayLoop gamePlayLoop;
private CastingDirector castDirector;
```

As you can see in Figure 12-12, the code for all of the classes and modifications we have made thus far are error-free, and we are ready to build more complex Java statements that control our primary character sprite on top of technically correct Java code that follows industry standard Java 8 programming practices.

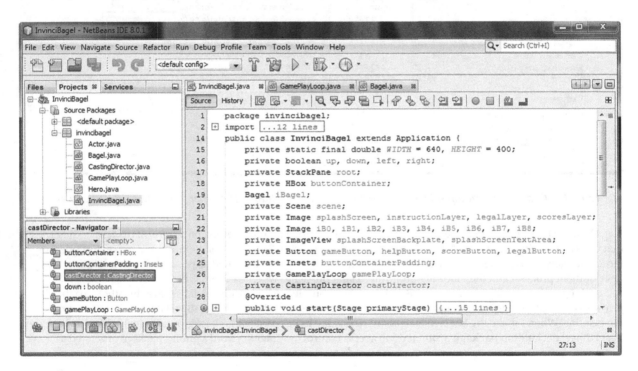

Figure 12-12. *Make all of the variable declarations after the iBagel Bagel object declaration use private access control*

Next, we will get back into our Bagel.java class, and the .update() method, and start to refine (and organize) that code into more logical methods, so that our .update() method becomes more of a "top-level" method, that calls lower-level method "Java code blocks" that implement things such as key event processing, character movement, screen boundaries, sprite Image state, and so on.

This will allow us to put a more complex "workload" on the Bagel character's .update() method by calling logical methods such as **.setXYLocation()**, **.moveInvinciBagel()**, and **.setBoundaries()**, and later on during this book, **.setImageState()**, **.checkForCollision()** and **.playAudioClip()** for example. In this way, your .update() method calls other methods containing logical code blocks. This keeps your Java code well organized and makes programming logic easier to visualize.

Organizing the .update() Method: .moveInvinciBagel()

Since we are going to be adding more and more Java programming logic into the .update() method of the Bagel class during the remainder of the book, I want to put into place some "method modularization" that will be quite similar to what we did for the InvinciBagel class in Chapter 11 when we added the six new logical method structures. Since we will be performing a number of complex operations inside of the .update() method as the game becomes more and more complex, it is logical that the .update() method should contain calls to other methods that logically organize the tasks that we will need to do on each frame, such as determining keys pressed (or not pressed), moving the InvinciBagel character, looking to see if he has gone off the screen (setting boundaries), and eventually controlling his visual states, detecting collision, and applying physics effects. The first thing that I want to do is to "extract" the movement of the sprite into a .moveInvinciBagel() method that will perform any translation transforms that need to be implemented using a **moveInvinciBagel(iX, iY);** method call. This means that we will have to create the **private void moveInvinciBagel(double x, double y){...}** method structure and place the .setTranslate() method calls inside of it, replacing them in the .update() method with the .moveInvinciBagel() method call. The basic Java code to perform these changes to the Bagel.java class are shown in Figure 12-13, and will look like this Java code:

```java
@Override
public void update() {
    if(invinciBagel.isRight()) { iX += vX }
    if(invinciBagel.isLeft())  { iX -= vX }
    if(invinciBagel.isDown())  { iY += vY }
    if(invinciBagel.isUp())    { iY -= vY }
    moveInvinciBagel(iX, iY);
}
private void moveInvinciBagel(double x, double y) {
    spriteFrame.setTranslateX(x);
    spriteFrame.setTranslateY(y);
}
```

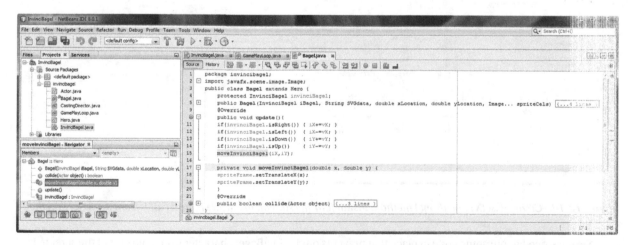

Figure 12-13. *Create a .moveInvinciBagel() method for .setTranslate() method calls, and call if from .update() method*

Next, let's move an iBagel on the screen using the ImageView .setTranslateX() and .setTranslateY() methods.

265

Further Modularization of the .update() Method: .setXYLocation()

You might think that the KeyEvent handling Boolean variables need to be processed inside of the .update() method, but since they are simply evaluated and then increment the Bagel object's iX and iY properties, this can be placed into its own .setXYLocation() method as well, leaving us with only top-level method calls inside of our .update() method. This will make further sprite manipulation and game play development much more organized, and will also help us to see what code is being performed at what stages in the .update() cycle. What we are going to do, which is also shown in Figure 12-14, is to create a .setXYLocation() method, which we will call first in our .update() method, and then place the four conditional if() statements inside of this new **private void setXYLocation(){...}** method structure. The new three method structure for our Bagel.java class .update() "chain of command" will utilize the following Java code:

```
public void update() {
    setXYLocation();
    moveInvinciBagel(iX, iY);
}
private void setXYLocation() {
    if(invinciBagel.isRight()) { iX += vX }
    if(invinciBagel.isLeft())  { iX -= vX }
    if(invinciBagel.isDown())  { iY += vY }
    if(invinciBagel.isUp())    { iY -= vY }
}
private void moveInvinciBagel(double x, double y) {
    spriteFrame.setTranslateX(x);
    spriteFrame.setTranslateY(y);
}
```

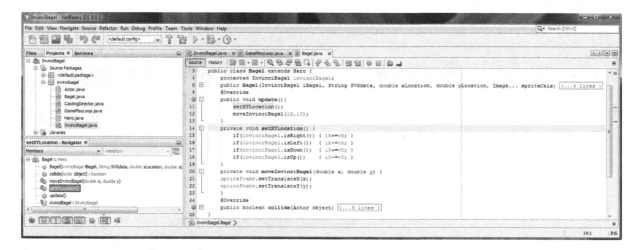

Figure 12-14. *Create a .setXYLocation() method, install four if() statements inside it, and call it from .update() method*

Next, we need to put some code in place that prevents our InvinciBagel character from going off of the screen, in case our game player does not reverse his direction in time. Later when we implement scoring, we could add in code that subtracts points for going "out of bounds," but for now we are simply going to stop the movement, as if there was an invisible barrier in place at the edges of the game play area (the Stage and Scene size boundaries).

Setting Screen Boundaries: .setBoundaries() Method

The next most important thing to do for our InvinciBagel game is to make sure that the character does not disappear off the edge of the screen by placing a **.setBoundaries()** method call between the .setXYLocation() method, which evaluates arrow (or ASDW) keypress combinations, and increments the iX and iY Bagel object properties accordingly, and the .moveInvinciBagel() method, which actually executes the movement. By placing the .setBoundaries() method before the sprite movement is invoked, we can make sure that the sprite is not off the screen (and if he is, move him back onto the screen) before we actually call the move function (method). The first step in writing this code is to define the sprite size in pixels so that we can calculate this along with our WIDTH and HEIGHT Stage size constants to determine the boundary variable values that we will need to check our iX and iY sprite location against inside of the .setBoundaries() method and its conditional if() statement structures. As you can see in Figure 12-15, I define these sprite pixel size constant declarations at the top of the Bagel.java class, by using the following two lines of Java code:

```
protected static final double SPRITE_PIXELS_X = 81;
protected static final double SPRITE_PIXELS_Y = 81;
```

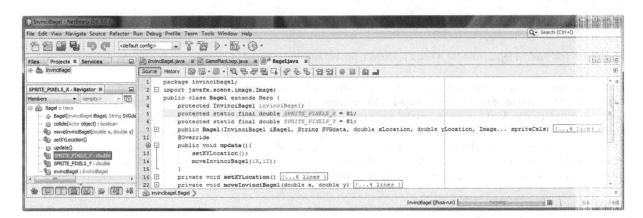

Figure 12-15. *Declare protected static final double SPRITE_PIXELS_X and SPRITE_PIXELS_Y constants at the top of class*

Next, we need to calculate the four screen boundary values using the WIDTH and HEIGHT constants in the InvinciBagel class and the SPRITE_PIXELS_X and SPRITE_PIXELS_Y constants we just defined at the top of this class. As you may have noticed from our 0,0 initial X,Y Bagel object location coordinates putting our sprite in the center of the screen, JavaFX is using a centered X axis and Y axis screen addressing paradigm. This means there are four quadrants, and that negative values (which mirror positive values) move left and up, and positive values move right and down. We can actually use this paradigm later on to quickly ascertain which quadrant of the screen the character is in. The way we would thus calculate the boundaries is to take half of the screen width and subtract half of the sprite width to find the right (positive) boundary value and simply take the negative of this for the value for the left boundary limit. A similar calculation applies to the top and bottom boundary value limit, for which we will take half of the screen height and subtract half of the sprite height to find the bottom (positive) boundary value and simply take the negative of this for the value for the top boundary limit value. The Java code for these calculations should look like the following:

```
protected static final double rightBoundary  =  WIDTH/2  - SPRITE_PIXELS_X/2;
protected static final double leftBoundary    = -(WIDTH/2  - SPRITE_PIXELS_X/2);
protected static final double bottomBoundary =  HEIGHT/2 - SPRITE_PIXELS_Y/2;
protected static final double topBoundary     = -(HEIGHT/2 - SPRITE_PIXELS_Y/2);
```

As you can see in Figure 12-16, NetBeans is having trouble seeing the constants inside the InvinciBagel class.

Figure 12-16. *Hold a left arrow (or A) and up arrow (or W) key down at the same time, and move the Actor diagonally*

Mouse-over the wavy red error highlighting in NetBeans that is underneath the WIDTH constant, and select the **import static invincibagel.InvinciBagel.WIDTH;** option so that NetBeans will write this import statement for you. The industry standard way to "correctly" utilize import static (or static imports, if you wish) are for the import and use of constants, so we are in top conformance with Java programming standard procedures here. Perform that same work process again for the red error highlighting underneath the HEIGHT constant reference, and then add the .setBoundaries() method call in between the .setXYLocation() and .moveInvinciBagel() method calls in your .update() method. This would be done using the following Java method call in the .update() method, shown in Figure 12-17:

```
setBoundaries();
```

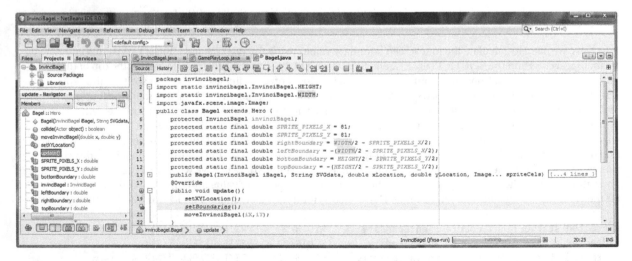

Figure 12-17. *Create rightBoundary, leftBoundary, bottomBoundary and topBoundary constants at the top of the class*

As you can see in Figure 12-17, this will generate an error under the method call, until we code the method.

Create a **private void setBoundaries(){...}** empty method structure underneath the .setXYLocation() method structure, so that your methods are in the same order that we will call them from inside of your .update() method. Next you will place your four conditional if() structures, one for each screen boundary, starting with the X axis related right and left screen boundaries, and then for the Y axis related bottom and top screen boundaries. The first if statement needs to look at the rightBoundary value and compare the current iX location to that value. If the iX value **is greater than or equal to** the rightBoundary value limit, then you want to set the iX value to the rightBoundary value. This will keep the InvinciBagel locked into position right at the boundary. The reverse of this logic will also work for the left side of the screen; if the iX value **is less than or equal to** the rightBoundary value limit, then you will want to set the iX value equal to the leftBoundary value.

The third if statement needs to look at the bottomBoundary value and compare the current iY location to that value. If the iY value **is greater than or equal to** the bottomBoundary value limit, then you will want to set the iY value to the bottomBoundary value. This will keep your InvinciBagel locked into position at the bottom of the screen boundary. The reverse of this logic will also work for the top of the screen; if the iY value **is less than or equal to** the topBoundary value limit, then you will want to set the iY value equal to the topBoundary value. The Java code for the .setBoundaries() method including the four if() statements is shown in Figure 12-18, and should look like the following:

```
private void setBoundaries() {
    if (iX >= rightBoundary)  { iX=rightBoundary;  }
    if (iX <= leftBoundary)   { iX=leftBoundary;   }
    if (iY >= bottomBoundary) { iY=bottomBoundary; }
    if (iY <= topBoundary)    { iY=topBoundary;    }
}
```

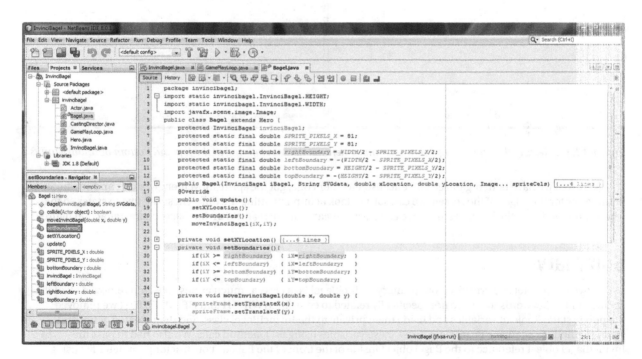

Figure 12-18. *Create a private void .setBoundaries() method and four if() statements to ascertain and set boundaries*

Next, let's test all of this code to see if it does what we think that it logically should do! The code is quite well organized and very logical, so I don't see any problems with it, but testing it in NetBeans is the only real way to find out for sure! Let's do that next. This is getting kind of exciting!

Testing the InvinciBagel Sprite Boundaries: Run ➤ Project

Now it is time to use the NetBeans **Run ➤ Project** work process and test the .setBoundaries() method, which now gets called after the .setXYLocation() method but before the .moveInvinciBagel() method. So the logical progression as it sits now is check keypressed and set X and Y location based on that, then check to make sure you have not gone past any boundaries, then position the sprite.

As you can see in Figure 12-19, the InvinciBagel character now stops at all four edges of the screen. On the left and right sides he stops a short distance away from the side of the screen because the sprite is centered in the ImageView area, but once we get him running, which we will be doing in the next chapter covering how to animate the character's movements, this will look at lot closer to the edge of the screen. We always have the option to adjust our leftBoundary and rightBoundary variable algorithms at the top of the Bagel.java class, which allows us to "tweak" the boundary limits value later on, as we continue to refine our code.

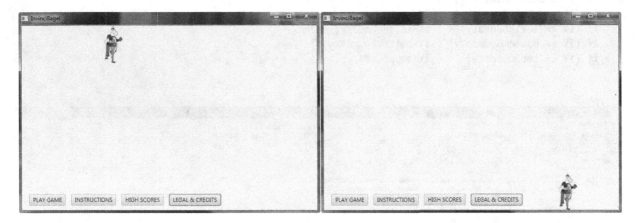

Figure 12-19. *Testing the InvinciBagel character movement; shown as stopping at the top and bottom boundary limits*

Now that we have both organized and encapsulated our code, got the sprite movement working and set the boundaries for the edges of the screen, we can start to look at implementing the different sprite image states so that when combined with the key movement, we can start to create a more realistic InvinciBagel character action figure!

Summary

In this twelfth chapter, we privatized our primary InvinciBagel.java class as much as possible, and removed all of the static modifier keywords that were not specifically related to constants (WIDTH and HEIGHT). First we removed the public static Boolean variables and made them private to the InvinciBagel class, and then created getter and setter methods to allow the Bagel class to use these variables using .is() method calls. We also had to pass the InvinciBagel object reference to the Bagel object inside of the front of the Bagel() constructor parameter list using the Java **this** keyword. We made these same changes to the static Bagel iBagel object declaration, removing the static modifier keyword and passing the InvinciBagel object context using the Java **this** keyword, this time inside of the GamePlayLoop() constructor method call. To do this we had to create our own custom GamePlayLoop() constructor method rather than using the one that is created by the compiler (JVM) if we do not specifically provide one.

After that we removed the other two static modifier keywords on the StackPane and HBox objects, and made all of the rest of the variables private, at least for now, to provide the greatest level of encapsulation for the InvinciBagel (primary) game class.

Next, we reorganized the code in the Bagel.java class relating to the .update() method. We created specific methods for polling the keypressed values and setting the iX and iY properties for the object, which we called the .setXYLocation() method, as well as creating the .moveInvinciBagel() method for calling the .setTranslate() methods.

Finally, we created a new .setBoundaries() method in the Bagel.java class, which is called after the .setXYLocation() method but before the .moveInvinciBagel() method that makes sure that our main character stays on the screen at all times.

In the next chapter, we are going take a look at advanced concepts regarding animating the game sprite as it **is moved** around your screen using the List<Image> ArrayList<Image> object, so that we get more realistic sprite animation before we get into advanced topics such as digital audio, collision detection, and physics simulation.

CHAPTER 13

■ ■ ■

Animating Your Action Figure States: Setting the Image States Based on KeyEvent Processing

Now that we have also organized your Java code into logical methods in the Bagel.java class, as well as making sure that all of our Java code is standards compliant in Chapters 11 and 12, it is time to get into some more complicated code structures that will animate our InvinciBagel character on the screen as the user moves the character. For instance, if the character is traveling due East or due West (using only left or right keypresses, to travel in a straight line), he should be running (alternating between the imageStates(1) and imageStates(2) List<Image> elements). If the up key is also pressed, he should be leaping up in the direction of the left or right keypress, and if the down key is pressed, he should be preparing to land in the direction of the left or right keypress.

We will also need to implement the Actor class's **isFlipH** property or attribute, so that the character is facing the right way based upon the direction he is traveling. Instead of using another image for that, we will use the JavaFX capability to "flip" or "mirror" any image around its central Y axis (isFlipH) or around its central X axis (isFlipV). Once a sprite animation state is combined with the movement code that you put into place in the previous chapter, you'll be amazed at how realistic this character will become, and we are still using only nine sprite state images (under 84KB of total data footprint used for our new media assets so far).

We will do all of this character animation during this chapter using only Java code, and using only the JavaFX **AnimationTimer** (GamePlayLoop) superclass. This way, we are optimizing the use of the JavaFX pulse engine for our game by accessing the pulse event timing engine using only the **javafx.animation** package's class that uses the least amount of memory overhead. The AnimationTimer class is the most simple class, with no class variables, and only a **.handle()** method to implement, and yet it is also the most powerful, because it lets you write all of your own code.

This approach allows us to write custom code to animate a character based on keys pressed and movement, rather than triggering predefined Timeline objects based on KeyFrames (and their KeyValues) along that Timeline. I am keeping it simple on the game engine side, and putting all of the complexity into our custom game play code. This will save us a lot of headaches later on, trying to "synchronize" keyframe-based and timeline-based linear animations, which puts us into a linear timeline-based paradigm, such as Flash uses. This 100% Java 8 coding approach is certainly more difficult, from a Java coding perspective, but gives us an order of magnitude more power, to achieve a seamless integration of event processing, screen movement, character animation, physics, and collision detection. Setting up a multitude of prebuilt JavaFX Animation subclasses would presumably allow the same results in the end, but the code would be less elegant, and probably much more difficult to build future versions of the game play on top of.

All of our character state animation will be created using a **.setImageState()** method that will be called from inside of the .update() method, so, we will continue to be organized in the movement and animation of our character.

InvinciBagel Animation: The .setImageState() Method

In this chapter, we are going to create one (fairly complex) method called **.setImageState()**, which will set our InvinciBagel character's animation or motion state based upon which keys are being pressed at any given moment. Calling a .setImageState() method right before the .moveInvinciBagel() method in the .update() method will serve to combine one of the character's nine image cels (frames) with the motion of the character. This will create the illusion of animation, and will achieve this without using any animation timelines whatsoever. From a game optimization standpoint, this means that the JavaFX engine that is running our GamePlayLoop can focus its resources on just that single animation (pulse) engine. As you can see in Figure 13-1, we need to add a **.setImageState();** method call, inside of the .update() method before the .moveInvinciBagel() method call and after the .setBoundaries() method call. After you do this, you'll have to create an empty method to get rid of the error highlight. The Java code looks like this:

```
private void setImageState() { The Method Body we'll develop in this chapter goes in here }
```

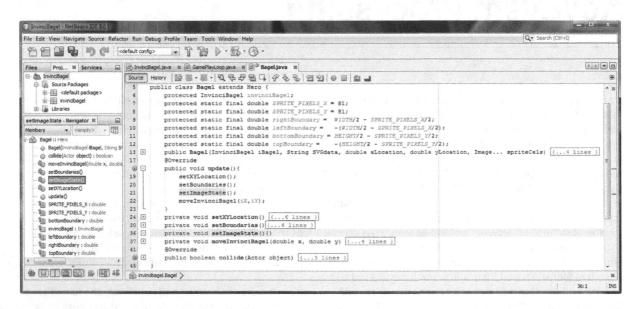

Figure 13-1. *Create the private void setImageState( ) method; place a setImageState( ) method call in .update( ) method*

As you can see in Figure 13-1, this empty code framework doesn't generate any red error or yellow warning highlights in the code. We are currently very organized, accomplishing all our KeyEvent handling, boundary detection, sprite animation, and sprite movement, by using only four method calls inside of this Bagel class .update() method.

The first thing that we want to check for is no movement: that is, no keys pressed, so that we can correctly implement the "waiting" InvinciBagel state we used in the previous chapter to develop a sprite movement algorithm.

The InvinciBagel Wait State: If No Key Pressed Set imageState(0)

The first conditional if( ) statement that we put into place will be the default or "no keys pressed" state, which is sprite zero that shows the InvinciBagel waiting impatiently to be moved and animated. What we want to look for inside of the if evaluation area inside of the parenthesis is a false value for each of the up, down, left, and right variables, all at the same moment of time. Up until now, we have been looking for a **true** value, using the .isUp(), .isDown(), .isLeft(), and .isRight() method calls off of the invinciBagel object reference. In this situation we want to look for a **false** value.

To accomplish this, we need to use the Java **Unary Exclamation Point !** operator. This reverses the Boolean value, so in our case, a false value from one of these method calls would be represented by a **!invinciBagel.isUp()** construct, for instance. To find out if more than one value is false at the same time, we'll need to implement the Java **Conditional AND** operator, which uses **two consecutive ampersand** characters, like this && so; in this case, we will be using three of these && Conditional AND operators, to tell the Java compiler that we want **Right AND Left AND Down AND Up** to all be **false**. All of this logic will go inside of the if() evaluation area (inside of the parenthesis). Inside of the curly braces, where the statements go if the if() evaluation area is met (if up, down, left and right are all false), we will set the **spriteFrame** ImageView object equal to the **first** Image object in the **imageStates** List<Image> object using the **.setImage()** method call. Inside of that method call, we will use the **.get()** method call on the imageStates List<Image> object, to get the first Image reference imageStates(0) from the List<Image> object. This is the "waiting" sprite cel for the InvinciBagel, which shows him waiting impatiently to be moved (animated). The Java code for the construct would look like the following Java programming structure (I have indented this for easier readability and learning purposes):

```java
if( !invinciBagel.isRight() &&
    !invinciBagel.isLeft()  &&
    !invinciBagel.isDown()  &&
    !invinciBagel.isUp()       ) {
    spriteFrame.setImage(imageStates.get(0)); }
```

As is seen in Figure 13-2, this first if() statement, representing "if none of the arrow keys are being pressed," is error-free. If you use the **Run ➤ Project** work process, and test this code, you'll get the same result as you did in the previous chapter! To see if this code works we must first make the InvinciBagel run, so that when we stop moving him using the arrow keys, we get this impatient "waiting" state, which actually makes it a lot more effective (funny), when this wait is in the context of all this animated movement we're about to implement during the course of the chapter!

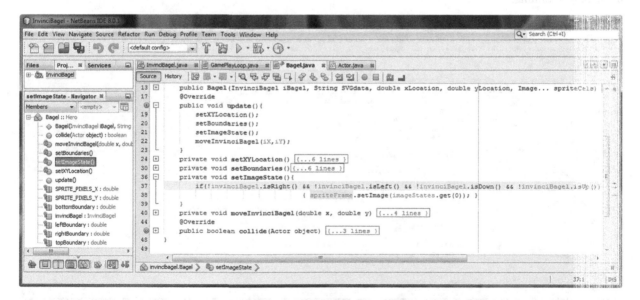

Figure 13-2. *Add a conditional if() statement that checks for no movement, and sets the wait sprite image state (zero)*

Next let's start to implement some of the other character image cels to try and get our character animating!

The InvinciBagel Run State: If KeyPressed Set imageState(1 & 2)

As you have seen in Chapter 8, I am going to try and achieve an animated run state for the character using only two sprite cels, imageState(1) and imageState(2). This is about as optimized as you can get, both from an Image assets standpoint, as well as from a coding standpoint, as you are about to see. This is especially true given that you can't animate anything such as a run cycle using a single image state. That said, we are going to create a lot of very realistic animation during this chapter by using single cel, well-designed, sprite states, in combination with the sprite motion code that we put into place in Chapter 12. The **if(invinciBagel.isRight())** and **if(invinciBagel.isLeft())** statement constructs will initially be quite easy and straightforward, but these will grow far more complex as we add refining features during the course of this chapter. We will put the foundation into place for these first, then add the up and down conditional if() statements, and then later, we will refine the right and left KeyEvent handling. Inside of the if() constructs for the left and right arrow key (and A and D key movement), we will use the same **chained method** call that we used in the first (impatiently waiting state) if() construct, only here we will call the imageStates(1) or imageStates(2) sprite cels, from the List<Image> object, instead of using the imageStates(0) sprite cel. The Java code to change the sprite Image states to state 1 or 2, if the right or left key is pressed (true), should look like the following:

```java
if(invinciBagel.isRight()) {
    spriteFrame.setImage(imageStates.get(1));
}
if(invinciBagel.isLeft()) {
    spriteFrame.setImage(imageStates.get(2));
}
```

As you can see in Figure 13-3, the Java code is error-free, and we are ready to use the **Run > Project** work process test this preliminary run mode. If you quickly press the left and right arrow keys in succession, you'll see the InvinciBagel running!

Figure 13-3. *Add conditional if() statements that check for left/right movement, and sets the run sprite image states*

Since this is not how we want to make our game player make the InvinciBagel run (because the very nature of it stops his movement around the screen, and because it's just plain lame), let's quickly put into place your up and down key support, so that we can come back and work on the left and right keys so we can make the run cycle work!

The InvinciBagel Fly State: If KeyPressed Set imageState(3 & 4)

The **if(invinciBagel.isDown())** and the **if(invinciBagel.isUp())** conditional if() structures are identical to the left and right key structures, except that they call **imageStates(3)** and **imageStates(4)** List elements, to allow the InvinciBagel character to "come in for landing" (cel 3), and "take off flying" (cel 4). As we add more of the imageStates during this chapter, and combine this cel animation code with our motion and boundary code, you are going to have more and more fun testing this chapter's coding results! If you want to take a programmer's shortcut, copy and paste the .isRight() and .isLeft() constructs underneath themselves, and simply change the .get(1) and .get(2) to .get(3) and .get(4). As you can see in Figure 13-4, the code is currently very compact and well organized; structured; and logical; and in only half a dozen lines of Java code, we have now implemented more than half of our nine image states already! Of course, we still have to add refinement code, to implement sprite mirroring for direction changes and run-cycle timing refinement. The Java code for the .isUp() and .isDown() method structures should look like the following:

```java
if(invinciBagel.isDown()) {
    spriteFrame.setImage(imageStates.get(3));
}
if(invinciBagel.isUp()) {
    spriteFrame.setImage(imageStates.get(4));
}
```

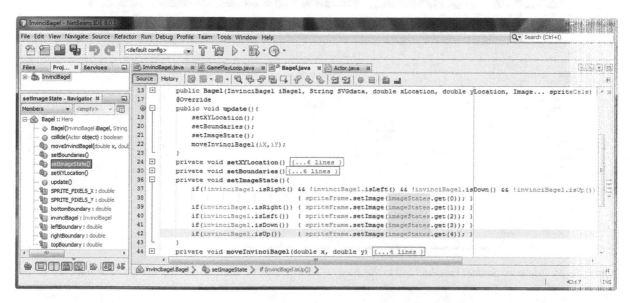

Figure 13-4. *Add conditional if() statements that check for up/down movement and sets jump/land sprite image state*

As you can see in Figure 13-4, our code is error-free, and we are ready to add several layers of complexity to the left and right arrow key event processing code, since these two keys are defining the direction (East and West) the InvinciBagel is traveling. For this reason, these two conditional if() statement structures, in particular, need to become more complex, because traveling East (to the right) will use original (isFlipH = false) sprites, and traveling West (to the left) will utilize a mirrored version (isFlipH = true) of each sprite, "flipping" the Image assets around the central Y axis.

Mirroring Sprites: Quadrupling Your Image Assets from 9 to 36

Now let's go back into the existing .isLeft() and .isRight() conditional evaluation statements, which are going to become quite "robust" (complicated) over the course of this chapter, and let's add our spite mirroring capability. The JavaFX API has its mirroring capability "hidden" in the ImageView class's .setScaleX() method call. Although we are not going to scale our Image assets, as doing so causes artifacts in our pristine PNG32 image assets, there is a little known trick that you can pass a **-1** (negative 100% scaling factor) value into a .setScaleX() method, to flip or mirror the Image asset around the Y axis (or into the .setScaleY() method, to flip or mirror around the X axis). Clearly we will need to also "undo" this in the other conditional if() structure by passing a 1 (positive 100% scaling factor) into the same method call, which does not make a whole lot of sense (normally) as our Image scale is already 100% (not scaled) but in light that the -1 scale-flip factor might have been set previously, this is how we make sure that mirroring is disabled and we are again using our original sprite Image assets for that particular state. Your newly upgraded Java statements implementing sprite mirroring should now look like the following code, which is also shown highlighted in Figure 13-5:

```java
if(invinciBagel.isRight()) {
    spriteFrame.setImage(imageStates.get(1));
    spriteFrame.setScaleX(1);
}
if(invinciBagel.isLeft()) {
    spriteFrame.setImage(imageStates.get(1));
    spriteFrame.setScaleX(-1);
}
```

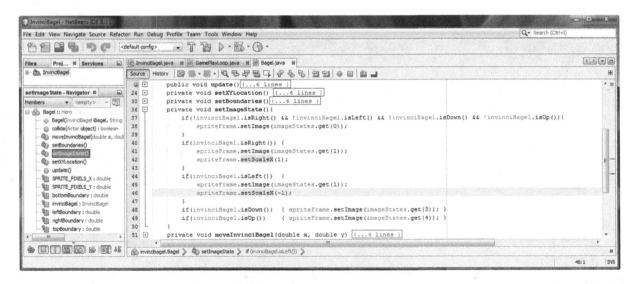

Figure 13-5. *Add a .setScaleX() method call to the .isRight() and .isLeft() evaluations to flip the sprite around the Y axis*

As you can see in Figure 13-5, your Java code is still error-free. It is interesting to note that we are calling the sprite mirroring method on the **spriteFrame ImageView** object, and not on the Image assets inside of this ImageView. This is of tantamount importance, because it means that we can use this one single line of code inside of .isRight() and .isLeft() to flip whatever sprite state (image) is showing inside of an ImageView! That's highly optimized programming!

Now that our sprite mirroring code is in place, we need to take care of the issue of having the run cycle that is implemented by alternating imageStates(1) and imageStates(2) accomplished using our conditional if() processing.

Animating Your Run Cycle: Creating a Nested If-Else Structure

The next step in our sprite animation for this chapter is to actually animate a run cycle for our character, which we would normally do with JavaFX KeyFrame and Timeline classes, but which we will do here in little more than a dozen lines of code. Since we are already using the AnimationTimer class, this is the optimal approach, and can be done using only a single Boolean variable. Since we have two cels for our run cycle, we can use this Boolean variable and alternate its value between true and false. If this Boolean value, which we will call **animator**, is false, we will show the cel in imageStates(1), which is our starting to run position (foot touching the ground). If animator is true, we will show the cel in imageStates(2), which is our full-out run position (both feet in full motion). Create the Boolean animator variable at the top of the Bagel.java class. NetBeans was giving me a "variable not initialized" warning, so I explicitly set it equal to the default Boolean value of **false**, as I want the run cycle to always start with a foot pushing off of the ground. The variable declaration statement should look like the following, and is shown at the very top of Figure 13-6:

```
boolean animator = false;
```

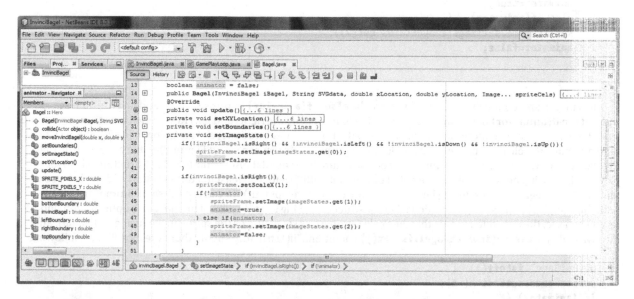

Figure 13-6. *Nest an if-else logic structure alternating between sprite cels 1 and 2 using the boolean animator variable*

Since we want the run cycle to always start with the imageStates(1) foot pushing off the ground cel, we will add an **animator=false;** line of code inside of our "no arrow keys pressed" code statement. This statement will now do two different things: setting the imageStates(0) waiting sprite Image reference; and making sure that the animator variable is initialized to a false value, which ensures the run cycle starts with a foot on the ground, just like it would in real life. The new Java code for the "no arrow keys pressed" conditional if() structure should look like the following:

```
if( !invinciBagel.isRight()   &&
    !invinciBagel.isLeft()   &&
    !invinciBagel.isDown()   &&
    !invinciBagel.isUp()         ) {
    spriteFrame.setImage(imageStates.get(0));
    animator=false;                  }
```

The Java code for the **.isRight()** and **.isLeft()** conditional if() structures is going to become significantly more robust now, as we will have to **nest** another if-else conditional statement inside of the one that determines if the right arrow key is pressed. If right is true, it will set the ScaleX property to 1 (not mirrored), and then adds a conditional if() statement that looks to see if the value of the **animator** Boolean variable is **false**. If animator is false we use the handy method chain to get imageStates(1), and set this Image asset as the cel that the spriteFrame ImageView will use. After that, we need to set the animator variable to a **true** value, so that later on the imageStates(2) full run sprite image can be set. If animator is true, the else-if portion of the structure then looks to confirm animator is true, and if it is, again uses the **spriteFrame.setImage(imageStates.get(2));** method chain to get imageStates(2) and sets animator to false. The new code for the statement, which is also shown in Figure 13-6, should look like the following:

```
if(invinciBagel.isRight())  {
    spriteFrame.setScaleX(1);
    if(!animator) {
        spriteFrame.setImage(imageStates.get(1));
        animator=true;
    }   else if(animator)   {
        spriteFrame.setImage(imageStates.get(2));
        animator=false;
    }
}
```

It is important to note that you could remove the **else if(animator)** in this situation, and just use an **else** without the **if(animator)** part. However, we're going to be making the right (and left) KeyPressed construct even more complex, by nesting even more code even deeper in the if-else-if-else structure, so I am going to leave it this way both for readability as well as for future code development purposes. As you can see in Figure 13-6, the code is error-free.

You can now implement the same exact code structure into your **.isLeft()** conditional if() structure. Since the player will be using either the left or the right key (but not both together, at least not until we start adding those cool hidden "Easter egg" features during later stages of the game development) we can use the same **animator** variable in both the .isRight() and .isLeft() conditional if() constructs, allowing us to do a bit of memory-use optimization here. As you can see, the only difference is that the ScaleX property is set to mirror the sprite image (using a -1 value), and the Java code for **the if(invinciBagel.isLeft())** conditional if() structure should therefore look like the following:

```
if(invinciBagel.isLeft())  {
    spriteFrame.setScaleX(-1);
    if(!animator) {
        spriteFrame.setImage(imageStates.get(1));
        animator=true;
    }   else if(animator)   {
        spriteFrame.setImage(imageStates.get(2));
        animator=false;
    }
}
```

As you can see in Figure 13-7, this Java code is error-free, and you are ready to use your **Run > Project** work process, and test the InvinciBagel run cycle so you can see just how fast your superhero can run (or how fast the pulse engine in JavaFX can be, using the AnimationTimer superclass for your GamePlayLoop class). When you test your Java code, you will see that your superhero character is running much faster than humanly possible (and much faster than a bagel can run); in fact, the sprite animation cels are alternating so fast, that it looks like one blurred run animation!

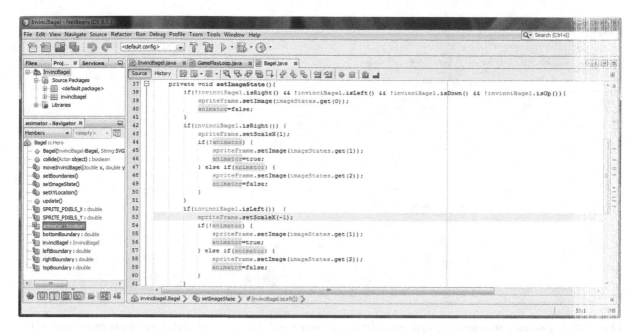

Figure 13-7. *Duplicate the nested if-else statement in .isLeft() structure, so InvinciBagel character runs both directions*

The next thing that we'll need to is to add some Java code to control the running speed of your InvinciBagel sprite. We will do this using two Integer variables: one to serve as a framecounter and the other to hold the running speed value, which we can change later on based on our vX (velocity along the X axis) variable to get a realistic match between the speed the run cycle is animating at and the speed the sprite is being moved across the screen.

Controlling Run Cycle Speed: Setting Up Your Animation Throttle Program Logic

In order to be able to "throttle" our run cycle sprite animation to achieve different speeds, we need to introduce a "counter" variable called **framecounter**, which will count up to a certain number of frames before we change a false (sprite cel 1) animator value to true (sprite cel 2). We will also use a **runningspeed** variable, so that our animation speed is not hard-coded, and exists in a variable that we can change later on. This allows us to have fine-tuned control over the speed (realism) of this run-cycle animation. Declare these two Integer (int) variables at the top of the Bagel. java class and initialize the framecounter variable to zero and set the runningspeed variable to a value of 6. Since both the false (!animator) and true (animator) second-level if() structures will use this "count up to 6" variable, the math for what we are doing would equate to 6+6=12, divided into the 60FPS pulse timing loop, means that we are slowing down the unthrottled animation by 500% (five times, because 60/12=5). The variable declaration statements at the top of the Bagel class should look like the following Java code, and are also shown in the middle of Figure 13-8:

```
int framecounter = 0;
int runningspeed = 6;
```

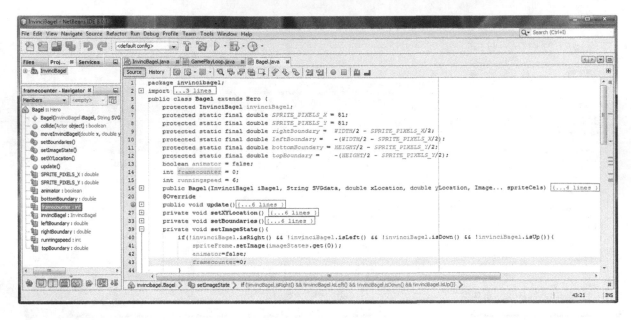

Figure 13-8. *Add int variables at top of the class for framecounter and runningspeed and set to zero in no movement if*

As you can see in Figure 13-8, I've clicked on the framecounter variable, so it is highlighted, and you can see its use in an initialization statement that we'll need to put into the "no arrow keys pressed" conditional if() structure, just as we did with the animator variable. The code for this if() structure is shown in Figure 13-8, and looks like this:

```
if( !invinciBagel.isRight() &&
    !invinciBagel.isLeft()  &&
    !invinciBagel.isDown()  &&
    !invinciBagel.isUp()        ) {
    spriteFrame.setImage(imageStates.get(0));
    animator=false;
    framecounter=0;
}
```

Just like we want the **animator** Boolean variable to be reset to the **false** value any time that all of the arrow keys are not in use, so to do we want the **framecounter** integer variable to be reset to a **zero** value, any time that the arrow keys are not in use (that is, are in a released state all at the same time). As you can see, we not only are setting our sprite's waiting image state in this conditional statement, we are also using it to reset our other variables as well.

Now we are ready to make our .isRight() and .isLeft() conditional if structures even more complicated, as we will be nesting our Java logic three-nested conditional if structures deep, to allow us to incorporate the framecounter and runningspeed integer variables into our conditional if() structure. This will make our animation code "wait" for six pulse event cycles before it changes the animator false value to true, and then wait for another six pulse event cycles before changing it back to false.

This is fairly complicated Java code, at least for a beginner Java 8 title, but game programming is inherently a complex undertaking, so let's go ahead and learn how to code this throttle mechanism for our run-cycle animation.

I want to teach you about advanced topics during this book, and this one (implementing a speed throttle) is one that we simply can't avoid, as this run speed using a simple Boolean alternating image state logic structure is not feasible to use in our game, given the incredible speed of the JavaFX pulse event timing engine and its "console game" 60FPS frame rate, which is making our InvinciBagel sprite run cycle look not only unrealistic, but painful to look at!

That said, this is about as complex as our Java 8 coding is going to get during this chapter, at least, so hang on tight, and enjoy the ride (or rather, the run) as we create a 16 lines of Java code, nested conditional if() structure, in the next section. It will be a lot of work, but the resulting run-cycle throttle control will be well worth the effort!

Coding Your Run Cycle Throttle: Triple Nested If-Else Structures

The modification we are going to make to our Boolean animator if() structure is to place an **if(framecounter >= runningspeed){...}** structure "around" the **animator=true;** statement, so that the animator does not become true until six pulse event loops have transpired. If the framecounter is equal to (or for some reason, greater than) six, animator becomes true, and the framecounter gets reset to zero and imageStates(2) is used. If framecounter is less than six, the **else** part of the statement increments the framecounter by one with a **framecounter+=1;** statement. We wrap framecounter code around both the **if(animator)** code in both parts of this structure, as shown in Figure 13-9:

```
if(invinciBagel.isRight())  {
    spriteFrame.setScaleX(1);
    if(!animator) {
        spriteFrame.setImage(imageStates.get(1));
        if(framecounter >= runningspeed) {
            animator=true;
            framecounter=0;
        } else { framecounter+=1; }
    }   else if(animator) {
        spriteFrame.setImage(imageStates.get(2));
        if(framecounter >= runningspeed) {
            animator=false;
            framecounter=0;
        } else { framecounter+=1; }
    }
}
```

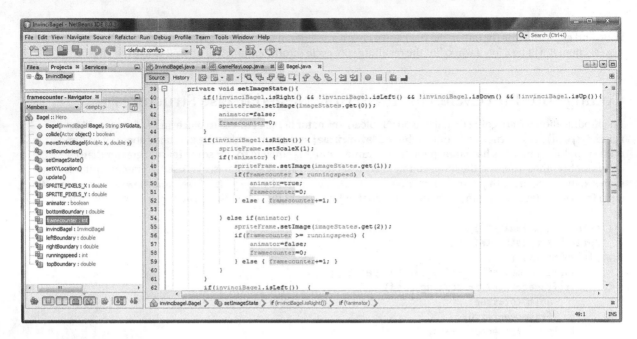

Figure 13-9. *Add a third level of if-else nesting that prevents cels from alternating too quickly by using a framecounter*

Now make the same modifications to the **if(invinciBagel.isLeft())** conditional if() structure. The only difference will be the **ScaleX** property being **-1** (mirrored sprite image) as shown in the following code in Figure 13-10:

```
if(invinciBagel.isLeft()) {
    spriteFrame.setScaleX(-1);
    if(!animator) {
        spriteFrame.setImage(imageStates.get(1));
        if(framecounter >= runningspeed) {
            animator=true;
            framecounter=0;
        } else { framecounter+=1; }
    } else if(animator) {
        spriteFrame.setImage(imageStates.get(2));
        if(framecounter >= runningspeed) {
            animator=false;
            framecounter=0;
        } else { framecounter+=1; }
    }
}
```

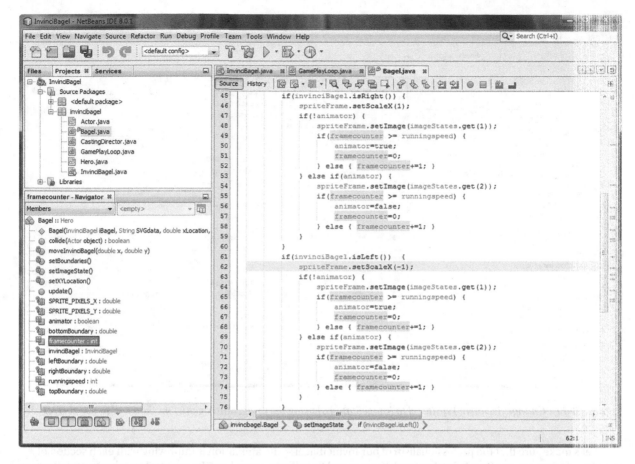

Figure 13-10. *Duplicate the if-else structure from the isRight() structure into the isLeft() structure using framecounter*

Now the time has come again to use the **Run ➤ Project** work process and test the run-cycle code, which now exhibits a smooth, even, realistic run cycle. You can fine tune the running speed to slightly slower with a 7 or 8 value or slightly faster with a 4 or 5 value. As we add faster vX values for running (say vX = 2) we can set the runningspeed to 3 or 4 to match this and make the game far more realistic.

One additional thing that I noticed as I was testing the code during this chapter that I want to correct here is the sprite cel image for landing. I have been using imageStates(3), which is the "landed" image, which should actually be better utilized with a collision situation. Let's save this sprite cel image state for use later, in the collision detection code development phase, to signify a collision with a surface (just landed or on impact image). The image I want to use while the down arrow key is pressed is actually **imageStates(6)**, which is the "preparing to land" image. The revised Java code will look like the following, and is shown highlighted in Figure 13-11:

```
if(invinciBagel.isDown()) {
    spriteFrame.setImage(imageStates.get(6));
}
```

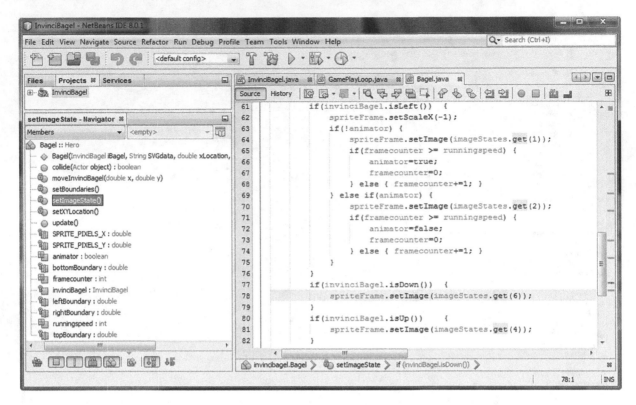

Figure 13-11. *Change .isDown() sprite cel to imageStates(6) using the imageStates.get(6) method call to use correct cel*

Let's make sure that the professionalism of our InvinciBagel sprite animation is improving with each section of this chapter, and use the **Run ➤ Project** work process and test all four arrow keys. Be sure and test the up and down keypresses with the left and right keypresses (left-up, left-down, right-up, and right-down) to really see what the Java code that you have put into place so far is capable of. We have a long way to go, but very impressive results already!

Optimizing Run-Cycle Processing: Turning Off Processing for Fly and Land States

The next thing that I want to do is also advanced conceptually, but uses far less code. As an optimization nut, what is concerning me is that the animator, framecounter, and runningspeed variables and the programming logic that uses them might be taking up memory when the player is using the up and down arrow keys, so I want to put a statement in the top of the conditional if() structure that leaves the .setScaleX() sprite mirroring code intact but turns off the rest of the processing logic if the up and down keys are being used. The Java code for excluding the run-cycle logic should be based on the up and down arrow key variables both showing as false, indicating the player is using the left or right keys **only**. This exclusion logic is seen in Figure 13-12, and looks like the following Java code (shown in bold) addition:

```
if(invinciBagel.isRight())  {
    spriteFrame.setScaleX(1);
    if( !animator && ( !invinciBagel.isDown() && !invinciBagel.isUp() ) ) {
        spriteFrame.setImage(imageStates.get(1));
        if(framecounter >= runningspeed) {
            animator=true;
```

```
        framecounter=0;
    } else { framecounter+=1; }
}   else if(animator) {
    spriteFrame.setImage(imageStates.get(2));
    if(framecounter >= runningspeed) {
        animator=false;
        framecounter=0;
    } else { framecounter+=1; }
  }
}
```

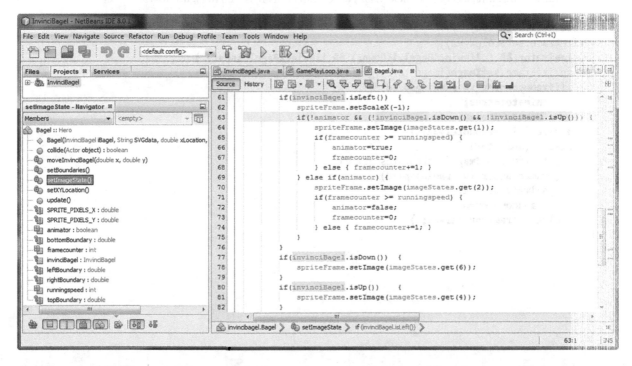

Figure 13-12. *Add if() statement logic to exclude processing of nested if-else hierarchy if down or up keys being pressed*

The reason that I'm doing this is because when either the up or down key is being pressed, the jump (or fly) or preparing to land sprite cel image is showing. For this reason, optimization dictates that I need to turn off all of the "alternating between sprite cel 1 and sprite cel 2" processing code. I want to do this so that this constant processing is not going on in memory and in the thread (CPU) when the imageStates(1) and imageStates(2) are not even being used (displayed) inside of the spriteFrame ImageView "container."

To achieve this optimization objective, I added a new level of evaluation to the outside of the second nested if() loop. This is the level that contains all of the sprite cel changes (1 to 2 and back) using the animator, framecounter, and runningspeed variables and related processing. This new more complex evaluation statement guarantees that all of this run-cycle processing logic will not be executed if this the new condition is being met.

What this new condition says specifically, is that if the animator variable is false **AND** the up **AND** down keys are both not being used (are false) then to process the rest of the logic, which switches between the two sprite image states (as well as waiting a certain number of pulse events before each switch). What this means is that if either of the up or down keys are being pressed (thus showing the fly or land sprite cel image state), none of the programming logic past that point will be processed at all, saving CPU processing cycles for the many other things that we are going to be adding into the game play that will need to use this "saved" processing overhead for other game play-related logic.

You may be wondering why I have not added this same extended condition to the **else if(animator)** portion of this programming structure. The reason is that this portion of the loop will never be executed unless the first part, which we are excluding with this new statement, is processed. This is because inside of the first part of this loop, we set **animator=true;** and this will never happen (now that we have added the extended condition) if the up or down key is being pressed.

What is really cool about this is that the **if(invinciBagel.isRight())** and **if(invinciBagel.isLeft())** conditional if() structures can now be used to mirror all sprite cel state Image assets, when your player uses the left or right key to set the direction that the character is traveling in, and only when the left and right keys (only) are used to make the character run will the run-cycle part of this Java code processing take place.

Make sure that you implement this same exact extended condition in your **if(invinciBagel.isLeft())** part of the conditional if() structure, as is shown below, and which can be seen as well in Figure 13-13.

```
if(invinciBagel.isLeft()) {
    spriteFrame.setScaleX(-1);
    if( !animator && ( !invinciBagel.isDown() && !invinciBagel.isUp() ) ) {
        spriteFrame.setImage(imageStates.get(1));
        if(framecounter >= runningspeed) {
            animator=true;
            framecounter=0;
        } else { framecounter+=1; }
    }   else if(animator) {
        spriteFrame.setImage(imageStates.get(2));
        if(framecounter >= runningspeed) {
            animator=false;
            framecounter=0;
        } else { framecounter+=1; }
    }
}
```

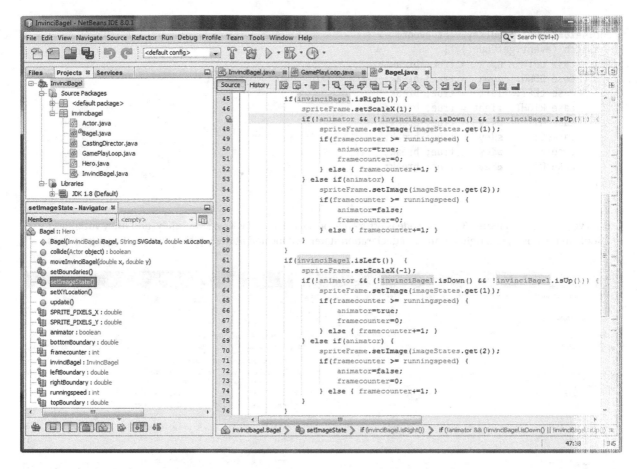

Figure 13-13. *Add if() statement logic to exclude processing of nested if() hierarchy if down/up keys pressed to isRight()*

Next, let's make the ASDW keys their own sprite control keys, instead of having them mimic the arrow keys.

Adding Event Handling: Giving ASDW Keys Function

Since I have a few more sprite states that I want to implement, I'm going to upgrade the event handler to use a two-handed play scenario, using arrow keys with ASDW, or ABCD (color) game controller buttons, using this code upgrade:

```
scene.setOnKeyPressed(KeyEvent event) -> {
    switch (event.getCode()) {
        case UP:    up    = true; break;
        case DOWN:  down  = true; break;
        case LEFT:  left  = true; break;
        case RIGHT: right = true; break;
        case W:     wKey  = true; break;
        case S:     sKey  = true; break;
        case A:     aKey  = true; break;
        case D:     dKey  = true; break;
    }
```

```
});
scene.setOnKeyReleased(KeyEvent event) -> {
    switch (event.getCode()) {
        case UP:    up    = true; break;
        case DOWN:  down  = true; break;
        case LEFT:  left  = true; break;
        case RIGHT: right = true; break;
        case W:     wKey  = true; break;
        case S:     sKey  = true; break;
        case A:     aKey  = true; break;
        case D:     dKey  = true; break;
    }
});
```

As you can see in Figure 13-14, the code is error-free, because I added wKey, sKey, aKey, and dKey variables to the Boolean up, down, left, right compound declaration statement located at the top of the InvinciBagel.java class.

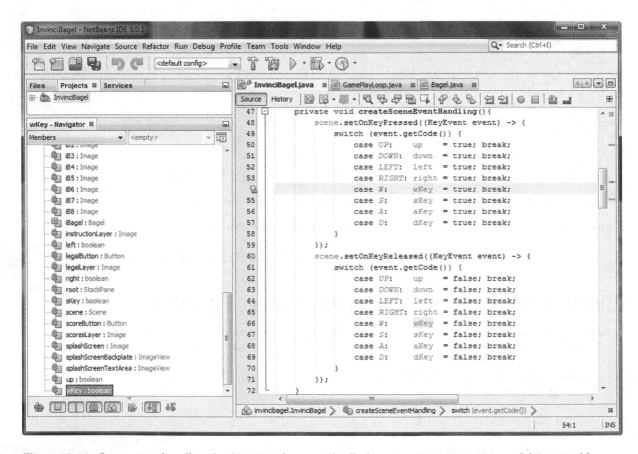

Figure 13-14. *Create event handling for the WSAD keys specifically, by using wKey, sKey, aKey, and dKey variables*

Next, we need to use the **Source ➤ Insert Code ➤ Generate ➤ Getters and Setters** work process, to have NetBeans write the eight .is() and .set() methods for us, so that we can access the variables in our Bagel.java class.

Creating ASDW Key Get and Set Methods: NetBeans Insert Code

Place your cursor in front of the closing } curly brace for the InvinciBagel.java class, as shown by the light blue area in Figure 13-15, and use the **Source** menu to select the **Insert Code** option. In the **Generate** floating menu select the **Getter and Setter** option and aKey, dKey, sKey and wKey options, shown in Figure 13-15, so NetBeans will generate eight .is() and .set() methods, based on this new Boolean declaration statement, also shown at the top of this Figure:

```java
private boolean up, down, left, right, wKey, aKey, sKey, dKey;
```

The eight method structures NetBeans generates at the end of your class look like the following Java code:

```java
public boolean iswKey() {
    return wKey;
}
public void setwKey(boolean wKey) {
    this.wKey = wKey;
}
public boolean isaKey() {
    return aKey;
}
public void setaKey(boolean aKey) {
    this.aKey = aKey;
}
public boolean issKey() {
    return sKey;
}
public void setsKey(boolean sKey) {
    this.sKey = sKey;
}
public boolean isdKey() {
    return dKey;
}
public void setdKey(boolean dKey) {
    this.dKey = dKey;
}
```

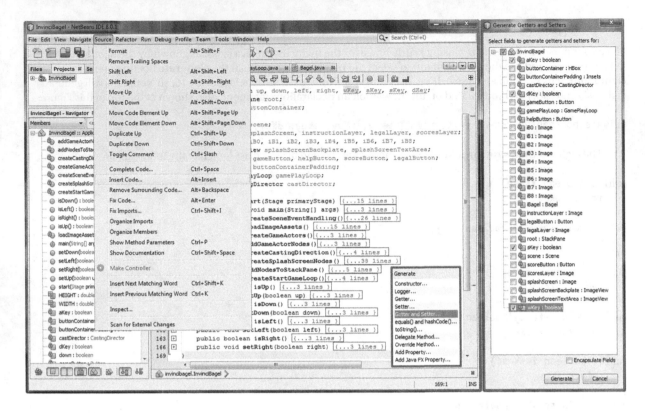

Figure 13-15. *Use the Source ➤ Insert Code ➤ Generate ➤ Getter and Setter sequence and select aKey, dKey, sKey, wKey*

As you can see in Figure 13-16, NetBeans has created all eight of our getter and setter methods for the new KeyEvent processing variables that we have added to the InvinciBagel.java class. The code is error-free, and we are ready to go back into the Bagel.java class, and utilize some of these new method calls to implement **jump** and **evade**.

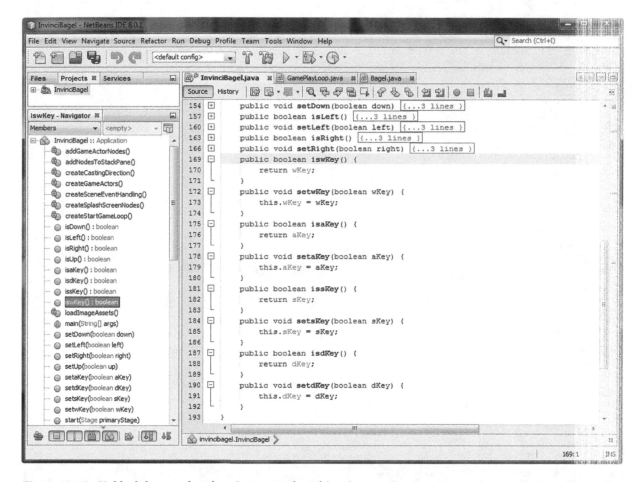

Figure 13-16. *Hold a left arrow (or A) and up arrow (or W) key down at the same time, and move the Actor diagonally*

Adding Jump and Evade Animation: Using the W and S Keys

Let's start to put into place the infrastructure for using another set of four keys to give our players more flexibility in implementing sprite (character) actions (animation). Using the keyboard, these would use the ASDW keys, and using a game controller, these would use the JavaFX KeyCode class constants GAME_A, GAME_B, GAME_C, and GAME_D. I'll be adding game controller event handling a bit later on during my game development after I add in more game play logic. The implementation of the basic jump and evade (projectiles) sprite cel Image assets would be accomplished by using the following two basic Java conditional if() structures for using the W key via **if(invinciBagel.iswKey())** and the S key via **if(invinciBagel.issKey())** processing structures, which are shown below, as well as in Figure 13-17:

```
if(invinciBagel.iswKey()) {
    spriteFrame.setImage(imageStates.get(5));
}
if(invinciBagel.issKey()) {
    spriteFrame.setImage(imageStates.get(8));
}
```

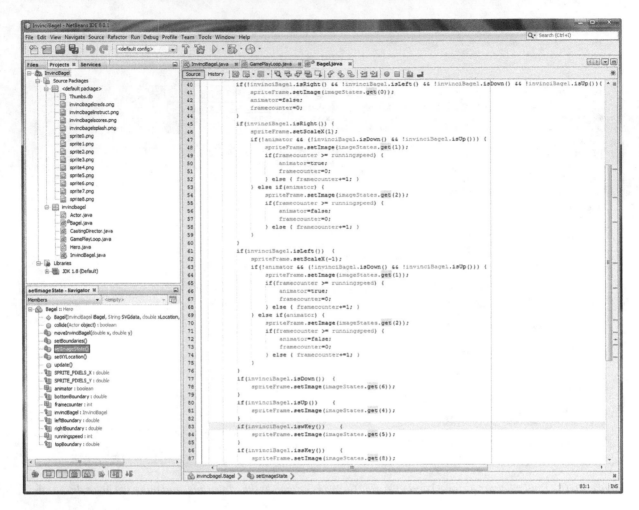

Figure 13-17. *Add if() statements at the bottom of the method for .iswKey() and issKey for Jump and Evade animation*

Now we have implemented imageStates(0), imageStates(1), imageStates(2), imageStates(4), imageStates(5), imageStates(6), and imageStates(8) in our game event handling and character animation processing. The other sprites are better suited for use with collision detection, so let's save those for later chapters in the book.

Last Minute Details: Setting the isFlipH Property

Next, I want to add in two more lines of code for what I call "bookkeeping," because we have installed isFlipH and isFlipV properties in our Actor superclass, so if we mirror sprites around the X or Y axis, we need to be sure to set these variables correctly, to reflect that (no pun intended) change to the Actor object, so that we can use this information in other areas of our game application programming logic. We will do this using the Java **this** keyword, to refer to the iBagel object that we are coding for in the Bagel.java class, and call the **.setIsFlipH()** method, using a false value if ScaleX property has been set to 1, or a true value if the ScaleX property has been set to a value of -1. It is important to note that we don't absolutely have to use the Java this keyword; I am using it for clarity of meaning, and so you could also simply utilize the method call without using dot notation, like this: **setIsFlipH(false);** if you like. The Java code for doing this simple bookkeeping addition can be seen highlighted in Figure 13-18, and looks like this:

```
if(invinciBagel.isRight())  {
    spriteFrame.setScaleX(1);
    this.setIsFlipH(false);         // nested conditional if() processing ommitted for brevity
} if(invinciBagel.isLeft())  {
    spriteFrame.setScaleX(-1);
    this.setIsFlipH(true);          // nested conditional if() processing ommitted for brevity
}
```

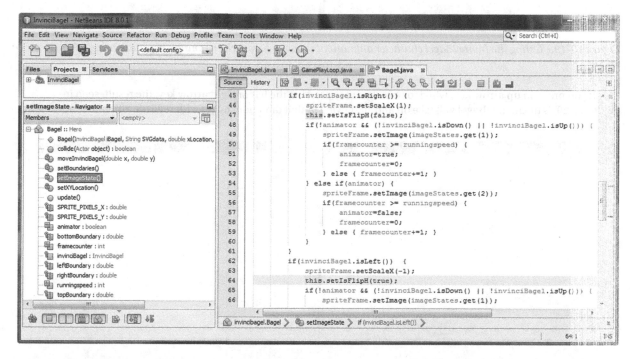

Figure 13-18. *Be sure to set the isFlipH property for the Bagel object using .setIsFlipH() called off of the this (object)*

Next, let's test all of the new sprite animation code to see if it does what we think that it logically should do! The code is complex, at least for the primary left and right arrow key character movement, but is quite well organized, and very logical, and I don't see any problems with it from a logic standpoint, but testing it thoroughly using NetBeans is the only way to find out! Let's do that next. To review the sprite image states, refer back to Chapter 8 (Figure 8-2).

Testing the InvinciBagel Sprite Animation States: Run ➤ Project

Now it is time to use the NetBeans **Run ➤ Project** work process and test the **.setImageState()** method, which now gets called after the .setXYLocation() and .setBoundaries() methods, but before the **.moveInvinciBagel()** method. So the logical progression as it sits now is check keypressed, set X and Y location based on that, check to make sure you have not gone past any boundaries, set the sprite animation (Image) state, and then position the sprite. As you can see in Figure 13-19, the InvinciBagel character now runs realistically across the screen when you use **left** or **right** arrow keys.

Figure 13-19. *Testing the InvinciBagel character animation; showing here is the running animation using isFlipH mirror*

If you press an **up** arrow key, while (or after) you are pressing the left or right arrow key, the result, seen in Figure 13-20, is the InvinciBagel will take off and start flying in that direction, again with realistic animated movement.

Figure 13-20. *Testing the InvinciBagel character animation; showing here is the leap up animation, using isFlipH mirror*

If you press the **down** arrow key, while (or even after) you're pressing the left or right arrow key, the result, seen in Figure 13-21, is the InvinciBagel will descend while preparing to land, again with realistic animated movement.

Figure 13-21. *Testing the InvinciBagel character animation; showing here is the landing animation, using isFlipH mirror*

Now that our arrow keys are invoking the primary run-leap-fly-land game play states, let's test this new **S** and **W** key logic that we put into place at the end of this chapter, so that we can invoke some of the less-often used (evade bullet and jump over) sprite cel states, which will add even more diversity to this character animation which we have put into place during this chapter using only around five dozen lines of code (two dozen in InvinciBagel.java and three dozen in Bagel.java). As you can see in Figure 13-22 on the left side, when we use the S key the InvinciBagel character turns sideways so that the bullets fly past (in front of) him, and on the right side of the screen shot, you can see that when we press the W key, the InvinciBagel character will hurdle over objects!

Figure 13-22. *Testing InvinciBagel character animation; shown here is the evade (left) animation, and jumping (right)*

You have added quite a significant amount of "wow factor" into this game's primary InvinciBagel character, during this chapter covering animation. This will go a long way toward making this a popular game across age groups.

Summary

In this thirteenth chapter, we implemented sprite animation across the InvinciBagel application using highly optimized code. We combined seven basic sprite shapes with the key movement that we developed in Chapter 11 and the boundary detection that we developed in Chapter 12 to create a fully animated InvinciBagel character that really comes alive, and does so based on the use of six basic game play control keys (up, down, left, right, W, and S).

We learned how to use the JavaFX ImageView class ScaleX property with its special **-1** use case setting to flip or **mirror** the Image asset that is inside of the ImageView "Image container" around the Y axis. This allows us to create 36 sprite image states using only 9 basic sprite states, which we have imported as Image assets, into a List<Image> ArrayList object. This is a form of optimization, as it allows us to use less than 84KB of image assets instead of 336KB of Image assets for our primary game superhero, the InvinciBagel character.

Next, we learned how to implement a Boolean **animator** variable, which we used to animate between two different sprite cel run states, imageStates(1) and imageStates(2) in our List. The resulting run cycle was too rapid for professional use, so next, we then added a **framecounter** variable, to slow the movement down, and a **runningspeed** variable, allowing us to implement a fine-tuned control over the sprite's running speed, which we will be able to take advantage of in later on in our game play logic.

Next we optimized our code so that the variables and processing code used for the run cycle were not used if the run cycle was not showing, that is, if the InvinciBagel is flying or landing. We also made sure to set the isFlipH property in our Actor superclass (and therefore in our Bagel object) using the **this.setIsFlipH()** method call.

Next we added four new game play control keys in our event handling code in the InvinciBagel.java class, and added four new private Boolean variables aKey, sKey, dKey, and wKey, and had NetBeans create Getter and Setter methods for them automatically. After we made that enhancement, we added the sprite evade action image to the S key and the sprite jump over action image to the W key to make our game a two-hand game and to get ready to make the game prepared to use professional game controller hardware.

Finally, we tested this new sprite animation code with the rest of the event handling, Actor and Hero class, CastingDirector class, GamePlayLoop class, and Bagel class sprite movement and boundary code that we have written over the previous six chapters (Chapters 7 through 12). Our sprite movement and animation work together seamlessly to provide a professional result when navigating our InvinciBagel character around the game play Stage.

In the next chapter, we are going take a look at how to add fixed game sprite (Prop Actor) objects into the game, so that we have something to work with when we get into collision detection, and so we can start to really use our recent **CastingDirector** class.

■ ■ ■

Setting Up the Game Environment: Creating Fixed Sprite Classes Using the Actor Superclass

Now that we made a significant amount of progress creating your primary InvinciBagel character, using a number of key methods in the Bagel.java class, as well as the Actor and Hero superclasses, all of which we put into place along with the GamePlayLoop class and CastingDirector class in Chapters 7 through 13, it is time to add fixed sprite objects, which I will call "Props," into the Scene and on the Stage (on the screen). These fixed objects are almost as important to the game as the main character himself, as they can be used to provide obstacles, barriers, protection from the enemy, and various challenges for the primary game hero character to overcome. We will also need these fixed objects in the Scene to use in our collision detection program logic, and to test our CastingDirector class (object).

If you remember, back in Chapter 8, we created the **Actor** superclass with fixed sprites in mind and the **Hero** superclass with motion sprites in mind. I started out with the motion sprites, because the primary game character is a motion sprite, and even though motion sprites are more complex, by their very nature, they are also a lot more fun to play around with! Now I need to take a chapter and put the Actor superclass into action and create some **Prop**-related subclasses. We will use these Actor subclasses to populate our Scene (Stage) with things such as platforms, obstacles, barriers, bridges, treasure, and similar game play fixed location objects that you will want to add into the Scene (on the Stage) to create a game world and enhance the game play experience (also known as user experience).

We'll create four fixed **Prop** subclasses, using the Actor superclass, which will make it easy to construct fixed scenes (also called levels, when you have created more than one). The **Prop.java** class will use your fixed sprite Image assets "as-is," while the **PropH.java** class will set the **isFlipH** property to **true** and mirror the image asset around the Y axis, using a JavaFX **spriteFrame.setScaleX(-1);** Java statement. The **PropV.java** class will set the **isFlipV** property to **true** and mirror the image asset around the X axis, using a JavaFX **spriteFrame.setScaleY(-1);** Java statement. The **PropB.java** class (B stands for "both") will set both the **isFlipV** property and **isFlipH** property to **true**, which would mirror an image asset around both the X and Y axis, using two JavaFX **spriteFrame.setScale(-1);** Java statements.

Once we have created these four Prop-related Actor subclasses, we will use them to place fixed objects into the Scene to create the first level of this game. That way, when we get into the collision detection chapter, everything that would be in a real game will be in place, and we will be able to start coding the collision detection logic; and then, eventually, an auto-attack engine; and then game play logic, which dictates how the scoring engine is implemented.

This chapter will be valuable in creating a more feature-filled game. A major part of any game design, in this case, it is Ira H. Harrison Rubin's InvinciBagel character and game, is building the environment that the characters (the hero and his or her enemies, whether in a single-player or a multi-player game) engage in is critical to the success and popularity of the game, since these fixed elements are a major part of creating the game play challenge for the player.

Creating the Prop.java Class: Extending Actor.java

Open up the InvinciBagel project in NetBeans 8, and **right-click** on the **invincibagel** (package) folder that contains your .java files and select the **New ➤ Java Class** menu sequence. In the **New Java Class** dialog, shown in Figure 14-1, name the class **Prop**, and accept the other default settings, suggested by NetBeans, and then click on the **Finish** button.

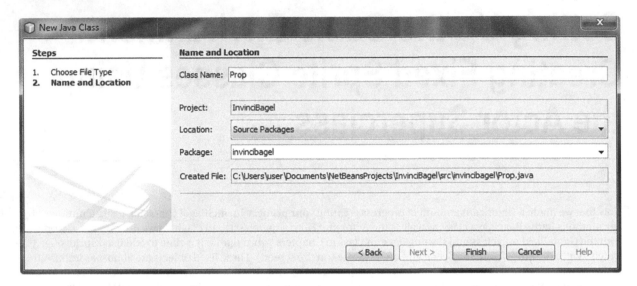

Figure 14-1. Right-click on the project folder and select New ➤ Java Class; using a New Java Class dialog, name it Prop

Once NetBeans creates a bootstrap class, add the Java **extends** keyword and **Actor**, as shown in Figure 14-2.

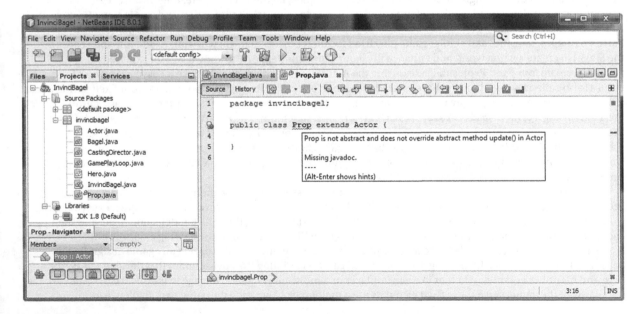

Figure 14-2. Add a Java extends keyword and the Actor superclass. Mouse-over the error highlighting underneath Prop

Use a suggested **Alt-Enter** work process, shown in Figure 14-3, and select "Implement all abstract methods."

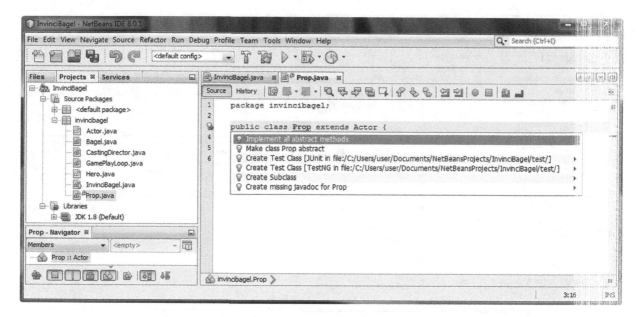

Figure 14-3. *Use the Alt-Enter work process to pop up a helper dialog filled with suggestions regarding fixing the error*

Remove the **throw new UnsupportedOperationException()** and create an empty .update() method for now.

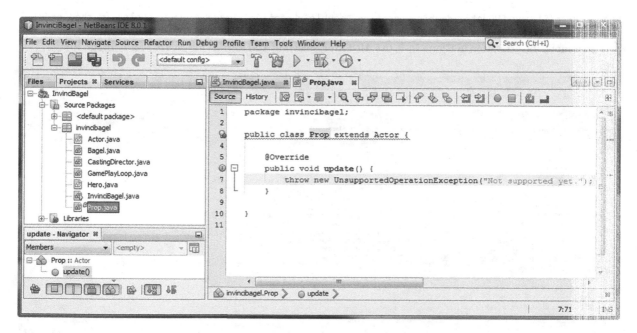

Figure 14-4. *NetBeans generates abstract method for you; remove the throw new statement; create an empty method*

The Java code still has a wavy red error highlight under the class declaration statement, seen in Figure 14-5.

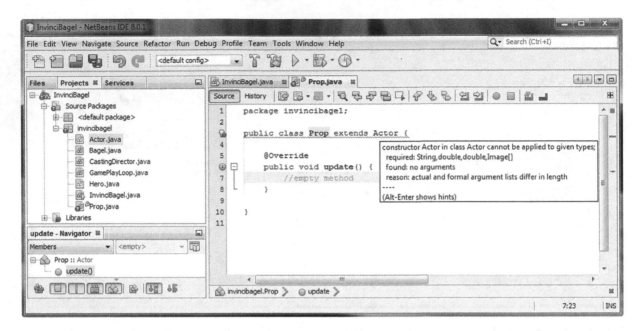

Figure 14-5. *Overriding .update() method doesn't remove the error, so mouse-over again, to reveal needed constructor*

Mouse-over this and you'll see you need to code a **Prop()** constructor method using the following Java code:

```
public Prop(String SVGdata, double xLocation, double yLocation, Image... spriteCels) {method code}
```

To remove the error seen in Figure 14-6, use **Alt-Enter**, selecting **Add import for javafx.scene.image.Image**.

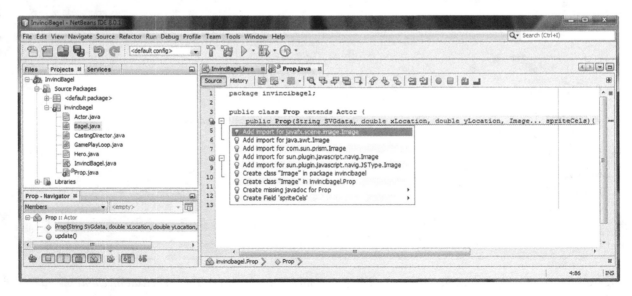

Figure 14-6. *Add a public Prop() constructor, and mouse-over the error highlight, and select Add import for Image class*

If you still see that wavy red error highlight, once you have imported the Image class reference, it is because you need to pass the parameter list in your Prop() constructor method definition "up to" the Actor class. This is done using the Java **super** keyword, sometimes called a **super()** constructor (method), using the following Java statement:

```
super(SVGdata, xLocation, yLocation, spriteCels);
```

Since this Prop class uses a default, or unflipped (unmirrored) imageStates(0) image for the class, this is the first thing that we need to do to make a usable Prop class that is in conformance with the abstract Actor class. Also, remember that the Actor class initializes all of the flag properties for us, thanks to a detailed design process. The Java code for the class, which now includes the basic super constructor, and is now error-free, can be seen in Figure 14-7:

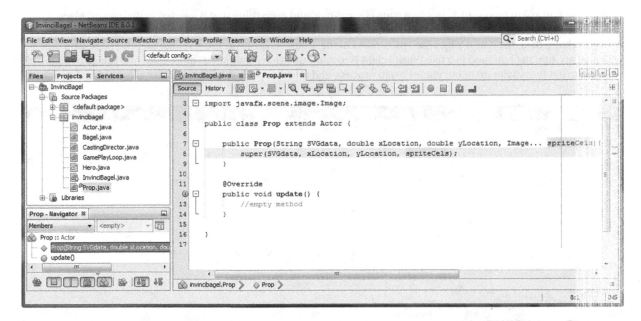

Figure 14-7. *Add the super() constructor method call inside of the Prop() constructor, to get rid of the error highlight*

The next thing that we will need to do, to position the fixed sprite, using the xLocation and yLocation values that are passed into the constructor method, is to use the .setTranslateX() and .setTranslateY() methods. Remember that you utilized these methods in Chapter 12 in the .moveInvinciBagel() method. We'll use these again, in this Prop() constructor method, to position these fixed sprites on the Stage where your constructor method parameters instruct the object constructor to locate them on the screen.

It is important to remember that because of the work we did in Chapter 8 that the Actor superclass's Actor() constructor method already performs the **iX=xLocation;** and **iY=yLocation;** sprite iX and iY property setting for us. Thus, all that we have to do in the Prop() constructor method is to call **spriteFrame.setTranslateX(xLocation);** and **spriteFrame.setTranslateY(yLocation);** inside of the constructor method, and after our **super()** constructor method call. Notice in the code that the xLocation and yLocation variables are utilized in both the super() constructor method call to set the iX and iY properties for the Prop Actor as well as inside the .setTranslateX() and .setTranslateY() method calls, to position the fixed sprites on the Stage during the Prop object instantiation, so that we do not have to do this somewhere else in our code. The Java code for the class, and constructor method, will look like the following:

```
package invincibagel;
import javafxscene.image.Image;
public class Prop extends Actor {
```

```java
public Prop(String SVGdata, double xLocation, double yLocation, Image... spriteCels) {
    super(SVGdata, xLocation, yLocation, spriteCels);
    spriteFrame.setTranslateX(xLocation);
    spriteFrame.setTranslateY(yLocation);
}
@Override
public void update() {
    // empty method
}
}
```

As you can see in Figure 14-8, this Java code is error-free, and everything that is needed to define and place a prop in the Scene (on the Stage) is in place, thanks to good design of the Actor (fixed) sprite class. This includes SVG collision shape data, the X and Y location (placement in the scene), and one or more Image assets. The reason that we included an .update() method in a fixed sprite class is to allow us to have animated (more than one Image cel) props if we want to get fancy later on in our game design process, and ratchet up the wow factor of the game's visual design.

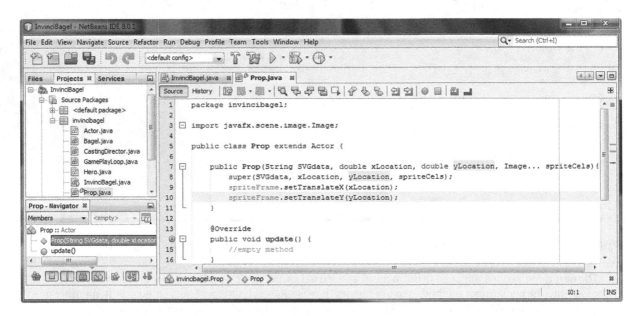

Figure 14-8. *Position a fixed sprite on the Stage in the constructor method using a .setTranslateX() and .setTranslateY()*

Next let's create **PropH**, **PropV**, and **PropB** (which stands for "both") classes. These will automatically mirror props for us around the X, Y or X and Y axes using the constructor method, so the object will inherently mirror images.

Mirrored Prop Classes: Set the isFlip Property in the Constructor

To make our process of building scenes easier, since everything (collision, location, animation) is part of a constructor method call, the difference between props is how they are mirrored (X or Y axis, or both axes). In this section, we are going to create variants of the Prop class that flip sprites for us, inside of a constructor method, so that all we have to do to get the effect we want is create that PropX object type. Create the first **PropH** class, as is shown in Figure 14-9.

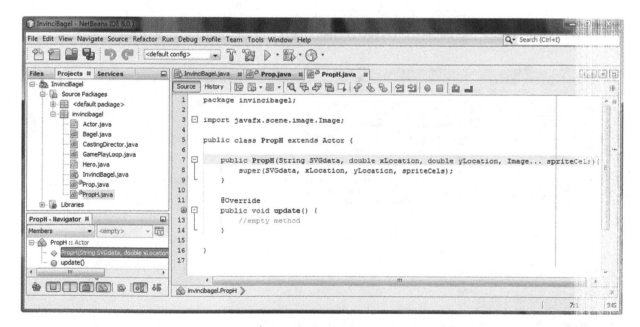

Figure 14-9. *Right-click on the project folder and select New ➤ Java Class; using a New Java Class dialog, name it* PropH

Copy the contents of the basic Prop class that you created in the previous section, including the package, import and super() constructor, into the PropH class, and then change **Prop** to **PropH**, as is shown in Figure 14-10.

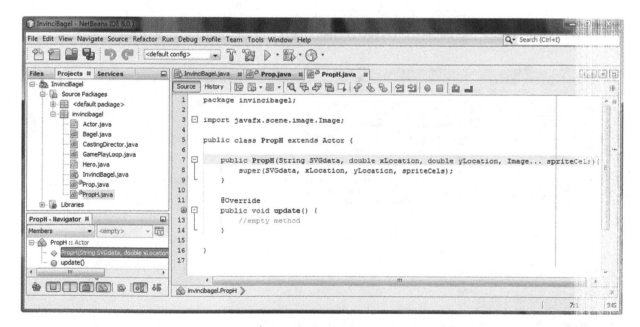

Figure 14-10. *Create a PropH class structure identical to the Prop class structure, except using PropH, instead of Prop*

Add the Java **this** keyword to your PropH() constructor method on a new line under the super() constructor, and then use (type) the **period** key to open up the handy NetBeans method selector pop-up, as seen in Figure 14-11.

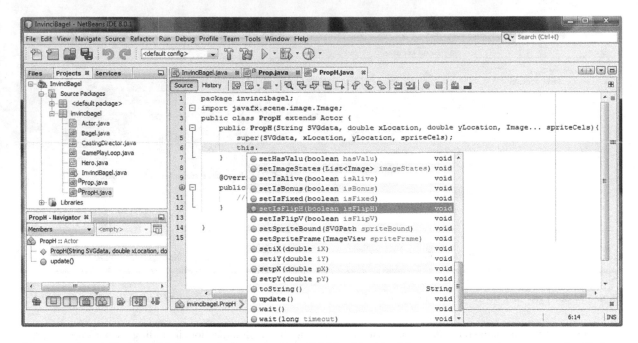

Figure 14-11. *Add a Java this keyword reference to PropH (object) inside of the constructor and open up method helper*

Double-click on the **.setIsFlipH** method, shown highlighted in Figure 14-11, and insert a **true** value inside the method call parameter area. The finished **this.setIsFlipH(true);** Java statement can be seen in Figure 14-12.

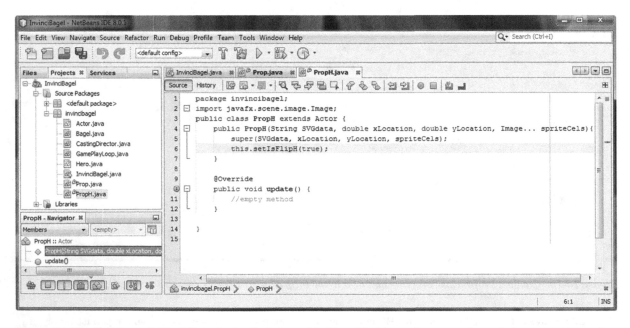

Figure 14-12. *Call the .setIsFlipH() method, off of a Java this (PropH) object reference, and pass it the true setting value*

It is important to note that if we only use the **this.setFlipH(true);** method invocation in the constructor method, we would still need to observe that **isFlipH** is set this way, and invoke your **.spriteFrame.setScaleX(-1);** method call, somewhere else in the code. Let's go ahead and put this method call in your constructor method as well, so that all our PropH objects automatically will have their Image assets flipped around the Y axis. In case you might be wondering why the .setScaleX(-1) method mirrors the Image asset around the Y axis, that is something that I was also wondering about, but what I did was match the isFlipH with the .setScaleX(-1) (since X is an H or horizontal axis). That said, I would have made .setScaleY(-1) mirror around the vertical Y axis, which makes more sense to me. Add another line of code and type **spriteFrame** and hit the **period** key, and select **.setScaleX** in the pop-up, as seen in Figure 14-13.

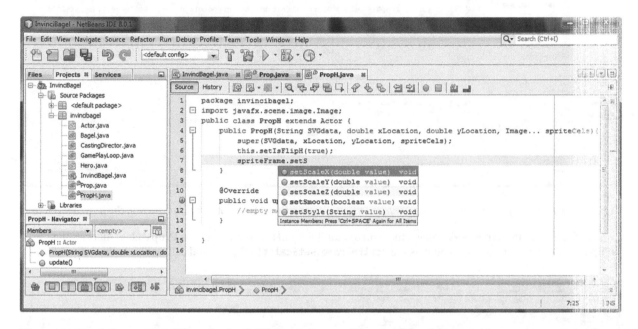

Figure 14-13. *Call a .setScaleX() method, off of the spriteFrame object variable reference, and pass it a -1 setting value*

Double-click on the **setScaleX(double value) void** option in the pop-up method selector and then add the -1 value, completing the method call. Now all PropH objects will automatically have the Image asset Y axis mirrored! The final code for the PropH constructor, once you add in the .setTranslateX() and .setTranslateY() method calls that will actually position the fixed sprite location on the Stage, is seen in Figure 14-14, and looks like the following Java code:

```java
import javafxscene.image.Image;
public class PropH extends Actor {
    public PropH(String SVGdata, double xLocation, double yLocation, Image... spriteCels) {
        super(SVGdata, xLocation, yLocation, spriteCels);
        this.setIsFlipH(true);
        spriteFrame.setScaleX(-1);
        spriteFrame.setTranslateX(xLocation);
        spriteFrame.setTranslateY(yLocation);
    }
}
```

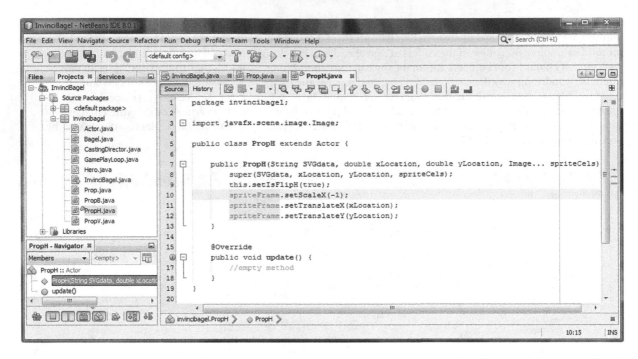

Figure 14-14. *A completed PropH() constructor method creates a fixed PropH object flipped along the horizontal X axis*

Next, perform the same work process that you did for the PropH class and create a **PropV** class that sets the **isFlipV** property to **true**, and implements the **spriteFrame.setScaleY(-1);** method call, as shown in Figure 14-15.

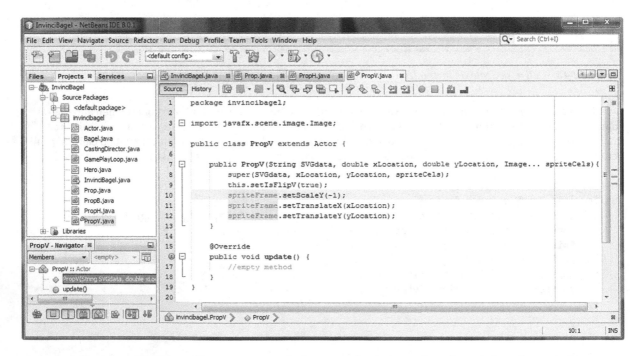

Figure 14-15. *A completed PropV() constructor method creates a fixed PropV object flipped along the vertical Y axis*

Next, perform the same work process that you did for the PropV class, and create the **PropB** class. This class will set **both** the **isFlipV** and **isFlipH** properties to **true**, and implement a **spriteFrame.setScaleX(-1);** method call, as well as a **spriteFrame.setScaleY(-1);** method call. Your Java class structure for this last PropB class, which will mirror fixed prop imagery along both an X and Y axis, can be seen in Figure 14-16 and will look like the following code:

```java
public class PropB extends Actor {
    public PropB(String SVGdata, double xLocation, double yLocation, Image... spriteCels) {
        super(SVGdata, xLocation, yLocation, spriteCels);
        this.setIsFlipH(true);
        spriteFrame.setScaleX(-1);
        this.setIsFlipV(true);
        spriteFrame.setScaleY(-1);
        spriteFrame.setTranslateX(xLocation);
        spriteFrame.setTranslateY(yLocation);
    }
}
```

As you can see in Figure 14-16, the code is error-free, and you now have a PropB class, which will create fixed objects for your Scene that are flipped or mirrored around both the X and the Y axis at the same time! Having these four different fixed Prop classes will allow us to quickly and easily design Scene (and eventually, game levels) elements, without having to do anything but declare the correct prop class, and reference the correct Image asset and X,Y locus (location) and collision polygon SVG data.

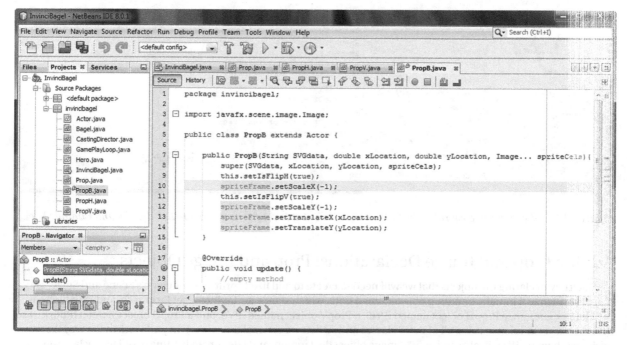

Figure 14-16. *A completed PropB() constructor method creates a fixed PropB object flipped along both the X and Y axis*

Now we are ready to use these four new fixed sprite classes, and learn how to add Scene (Stage) elements.

Using the Prop Class: Creating Fixed Scene Objects

Before we get into the coding in our InvinciBagel.java class, which you should have open in its own tab in NetBeans already, and use these Prop classes to add fixed sprite design elements to our game, I wanted to show you how to get rid of those pesky little **wrench icons** next to your file names. You may have several of these on your IDE screen right now, after creating these four new props-related classes, so let's learn how to make these vanish! As you can see in Figure 14-17, if you right-click on the file name next to the wrench icon, and select the **Compile File** menu option, or use the **F9** function key, the wrench will disappear. Essentially the wrench signifies that you are in the process of working on that file, that is, you have made changes to the code in that file, and have not made that code permanent, by compiling it to check it for errors as well as to save it.

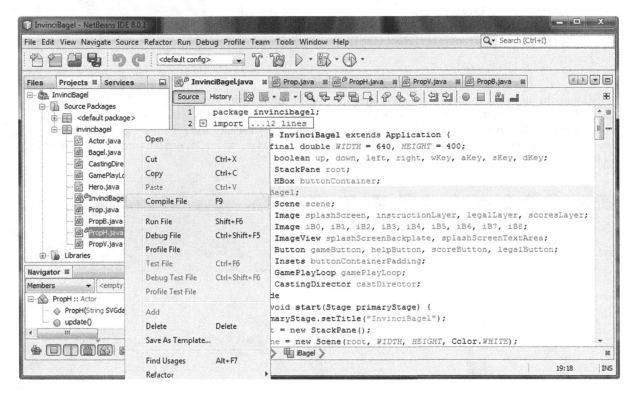

Figure 14-17. *If you want to get rid of the little wrench icon next to the file name, right-click the file, and Compile File*

Adding Prop and Image Declarations: Prop and Image Objects

Let's start by declaring the objects that we will need to create to add fixed sprites to our game's Scene and Stage objects, which will initially be a Prop object named iPR0, which stands for InvinciBagel Prop zero, and eventually as the chapter goes on, a PropH object named iPH0, a PropV object named iPV0, and a PropB object named iPB0, just so that you have experience using all of these classes and so that we can make sure that they all work in the way that we designed them to. We will also add an iP0 Image object declaration, and later on an iP1 Image object declaration, to the end of the Image iB0 through iB8 declarations. The Java statements are shown in Figure 14-18, and look like this:

```
Prop iPR0;
private Image iB0, iB1, iB2, iB3, iB4, iB5, iB6, iB7, iB8, iP0;
```

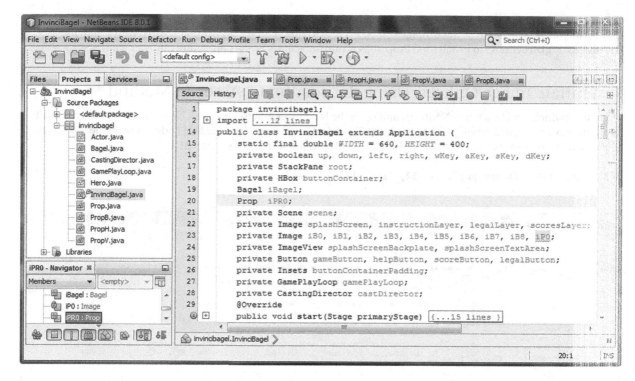

Figure 14-18. *Add Prop object declaration, name it iPR0 (invincibagel Prop zero), and add an iP0 to Image declaration*

Before we can instantiate the Image objects, we need to copy the Image assets into the /**src** folder, so use a file management software package (I used Windows Explorer) to copy the **prop0.png** and **prop1.png** PNG8 image files in with the other dozen or so image assets you have installed in the game project already, as is shown in Figure 14-19.

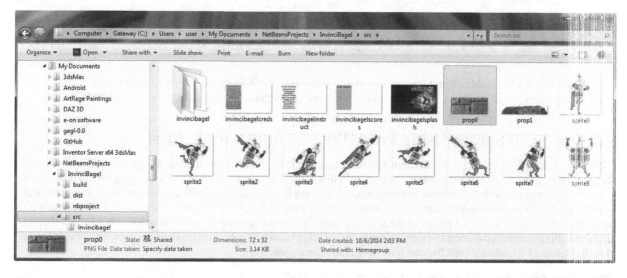

Figure 14-19. *Use your file management software to copy the prop0 and prop1 PNG8 files into the project /src folder*

Next, let's instantiate the Image object that holds one of the prop images, a tileable brick, so that we can use our four InvinciBagel.java methods, **.loadImageAssets()**, **.createGameActors()**, **.addGameActorNodes()**, and, finally, **.createCastingDirection()** to install fixed Prop objects into our game's Scene object, and onto our game's Stage object.

Instantiate Image Objects: Using the .loadImageAssets( ) Method

Open the InvinciBagel.java tab in NetBeans and open the loadImageAssets() method. Now add an iP0 Image object instantiation statement referencing the prop0.png file and its 72x32 pixel size. The Java code to create the iP0 Image object, which you can see in Figure 14-20, should look like the following Java statement:

```java
iP0 = new Image("/prop0.png", 72, 32, true, false, true);
```

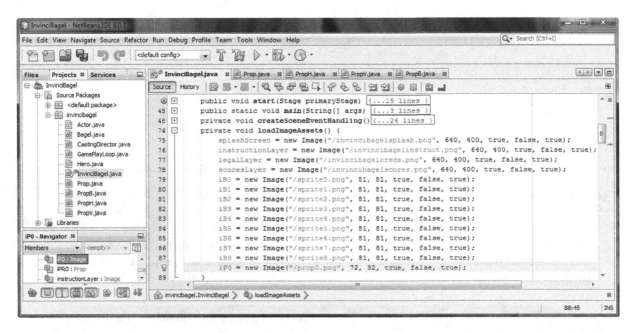

Figure 14-20. *Add the iP0 Image object instantiation using the prop0.png file name and the 72 by 32 pixel image size*

Now we're ready to add our first Prop object to our game to add a fixed sprite, which will allow us to create our game design using classes that we're putting into place in our invincibagel package code base during this chapter.

Adding Fixed Sprites Using Prop Objects: .addGameActors( )

After your .loadImageAssets() method there are three other method "containers" that we designed for our use during the game design process, for adding Actor objects into this game. These are called in the order that we need to utilize them for this process, so let's continue to be organized, and use them in that order. The first instantiation that we will need to perform creates a new (using the Java **new** keyword) Prop object. We will use our "dummy" SVG shape data again for now, as well as the 0,0 center of the screen X and Y locations, and finally, the **iP0** Image asset, which we just declared and instantiated during the previous sections of this chapter. The Java instantiation statement, which can be seen in Figure 14-21, should look like the following line of Java code:

```java
iPR0 = new Prop("M150 0 L75 200 L225 200 Z", 0, 0, iP0);
```

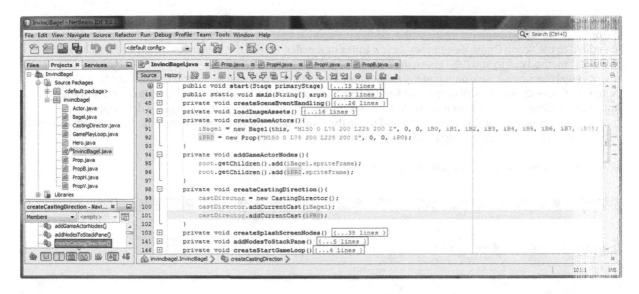

Figure 14-21. *Instantiate an iPR0 Prop object, add it to the root Scene Graph, and add it to the CurrentCast List<Actor>*

The next step is to add the ImageView **Node** object for the iPR0 Prop object to the Scene Graph **root** object. This is done using a **.getChildren().add()** method chain, which references the **spriteFrame** ImageView object, inside of the **iPR0** Prop object **using dot notation**, using the following Java statement, which is also shown in Figure 14-21:

```
root.getChildren().add(iPR0.spriteFrame);
```

Next, use an .addCurrentCast() method to add an iPR0 object to a castDirector object, seen in Figure 14-21:

```
castDirector.addCurrentCast(iPR0);
```

Next, test the code using a **Run ➤ Project** work process. The results are seen on the left side of Figure 14-22.

Figure 14-22. *Testing InvinciBagel 0,0 prop placement (left) and changing the z-index in .addGameActorNodes() (right)*

As you can see, the InvinciBagel character is behind the Prop object, which means that we need to change the order of the Java statements inside of the .addGameActorNodes() method, since the order that Node objects are added to the Scene Graph determines their **z-index** or **z-order**. As you can see in Figure 14-23, I have moved the .add() method call to add iPR0 above the one for iBagel, so as you can see on the right side of Figure 14-22, the InvinciBagel character is now on top of the Prop object. Once we add collision detection this will not be an issue, of course. Let's use the same work process and add a PropH object into the scene, so that I can show you how this tile image can be flipped and mirrored to create seamless tileable constructs for your Java 8 game development.

Let's use the same naming convention and name the PropH object iPH0. The Java instantiation statement, which can be seen in Figure 14-23, should look like the following line of Java code:

```
iPH0 = new PropH("M150 0 L75 200 L225 200 Z", 0, 0, iP0);
```

Figure 14-23. *Instantiate an iPH0 PropH object, add it to the root Scene Graph, and add it to a CurrentCast List<Actor>*

Our next step in adding a fixed sprite prop, is adding the ImageView **Node** object for the iPH0 PropH object, into the Scene Graph **root** object. This is accomplished using the **.getChildren().add()** method chain, which references the **spriteFrame** ImageView object that lives inside of the **iPH0** PropH object, by using dot notation. This is done using the following Java statement, which is also shown in Figure 14-23:

```
root.getChildren().add(iPH0.spriteFrame);
```

Finally, we will use the **.addCurrentCast()** method that we created in Chapter 10, to add this **iPH0** object to the CURRENT_CAST List<Actor> ArrayList object, inside of the castDirector CastingDirector object, using the following line of Java code, also shown at the bottom of Figure 14-23:

```
castDirector.addCurrentCast(iPH0);
```

As you can see in Figure 14-23, I have also changed the **0,0** coordinates for the Prop object to **0,148**, and the coordinates for the PropH object to **72,148**. This will place the **Y-axis mirrored PropH** object seamlessly to the right of the Prop object. If you want to see the seamless tiling effect now, you can use your **Run ➤ Project** work process. If you don't have your NetBeans 8 IDE running currently, and you want to look ahead to Figure 14-26, you can see this tiling (mirroring) effect now. Eventually, I'm also going to integrate the PropV and the PropB classes (objects) into this tiling.

Let's use the exact same work process, and add a **PropV** object into the scene, so that we can see how this tile image can be flipped and mirrored around the X axis, to create even more complex seamless tileable constructs for your Java 8 game development. Let's use the same naming convention, and name this new PropV object **iPV0**. Your new Java instantiation statement, which can be seen in Figure 14-24, should look like the following line of Java code:

```
iPV0 = new PropV("M150 0 L75 200 L225 200 Z", 0, 0, iP0);
```

The next logical step to adding a fixed sprite prop, is to add the ImageView **Node** object for this iPV0 PropV object into the Scene Graph **root** StackPane object. This is accomplished using the **.getChildren().add()** method chain, which references the **spriteFrame** ImageView object, which lives inside of the **iPV0** PropV object, using dot notation. This can be accomplished by using the following Java programming statement, which is also shown in Figure 14-24:

```
root.getChildren().add(iPV0.spriteFrame);
```

Finally, we will use the **.addCurrentCast()** method, that we created in Chapter 10, to add this **iPV0** object to the CURRENT_CAST List<Actor> ArrayList object, inside of the castDirector CastingDirector object, using the following line of Java code, which is also shown at the very bottom of Figure 14-24:

```
castDirector.addCurrentCast(iPV0);
```

***Figure 14-24.** Instantiate an iPV0 PropV object, add it to the root Scene Graph, and add it to a CurrentCast List<Actor>*

Finally, let's add a **PropB** object into the scene, so that I can show you how your tileable image can be flipped (mirrored) around **both** the X and the Y axes at the same time. We'll follow our naming convention, naming the PropB object iPB0. The instantiation statement, which can be seen in Figure 14-25, should look like the following Java code:

```
iPB0 = new PropB("M150 0 L75 200 L225 200 Z", 0, 0, iP0);
```

Figure 14-25. *Instantiate an iPB0 PropB object, add it to the root Scene Graph, and add it to a CurrentCast List<Actor>*

Next, let's add the ImageView **Node** for the iPB0 PropB object into the Scene Graph **root** object. This is done using a **.getChildren().add()** method chain. This references a **spriteFrame** ImageView object, which is inside of the **iPB0** PropB object, using dot notation. This is done using the following Java statement, which is also shown in Figure 14-25:

```
root.getChildren().add(iPB0.spriteFrame);
```

Finally, we'll use the **.addCurrentCast()** method that we created in Chapter 10 to add this **iPB0** PropB object to a **CURRENT_CAST** List<Actor> ArrayList<Actor> object, inside of the castDirector CastingDirector object, which can be seen at the bottom of Figure 14-25, and which uses this following single line of Java code:

```
castDirector.addCurrentCast(iPB0);
```

Now that we've put all four of the Actor subclasses that we have created during the first half of this chapter into service, we can test the application and see what the different X and Y axis mirroring does to the prop0.png brick.

Use **Run ➤ Project** and test the game to see how each brick is mirrored differently, as shown in Figure 14-26.

Figure 14-26. *Run ➤ Project; Prop, PropH, and PropV shown at the left, and all four Prop subclasses shown at the right*

Next, let's take a look at how to use large Scene Prop objects to composite background elements on a Stage.

Using Larger Scene Props: Compositing with JavaFX

One thing that is really nice about these four Prop Actor subclasses that we have created is that they allow us to leverage the PNG8 (background image assets) and PNG32 (true color compositing images with alpha channels) image assets to do digital image compositing right in our game Scene and Stage objects. If we do not use a fixed prop with a motion sprite game character by implementing collision detection, and if we keep these fix props in the background, by watching what we're doing inside of our .addGameActorNodes() method as far as Actor z-index goes, we can optimize game visual elements using the same compositing engine we have developed for characters and obstacles. We might not have to use any background image plates for our game at all. At the very least, this allows us to add simpler background image plates, such as a basic sky with clouds, or a sunset. These compress better, due to their simplicity, and can use PNG8 images with pristine results. Let's add a larger fixed sprite prop next, one that has nearly 500 pixels of width and nearly 100 pixels of height. The first thing that we'll need to add, as shown in Figure 14-27, is another Prop object that we'll name iPR1, and another Image object that we'll name iP1, using the following code:

```
Prop iPR0, iPR1;
private Image iB0, iB1, iB2, iB3, iB4, iB5, iB6, iB7, iB8, iP0, iP1;
```

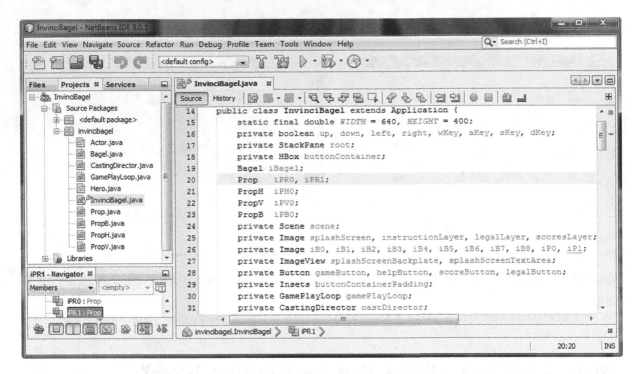

Figure 14-27. *Add an iPR1 Prop declaration (shown with all other PropH, PropV and PropB declarations) and iP1 Image*

Copy your iP0 Image instantiation, creating an **iP1** Image, referencing **prop1.png**, as shown in Figure 14-28.

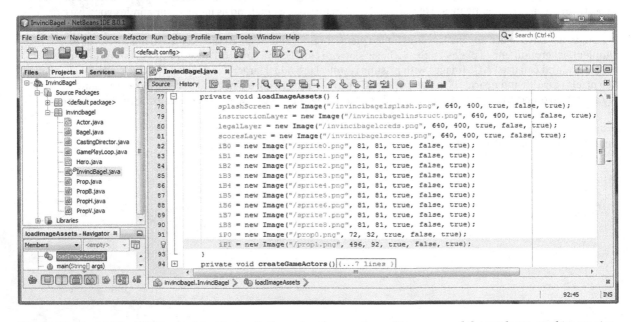

Figure 14-28. *Add the iP1 Image object instantiation using the prop1.png file name, and the 496 by 92 pixel image size*

Copy your iPR0 object instantiation and addition code, and create an **iPR1** object, as shown in Figure 14-29.

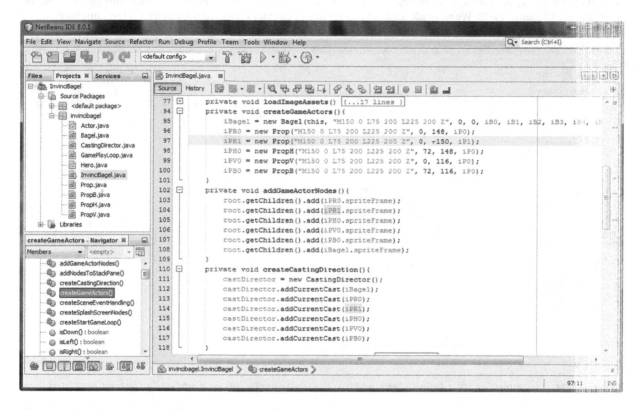

Figure 14-29. *Instantiate an iPR1 Prop object, add it to the root Scene Graph, and add it to the CurrentCast List<.Actor>*

To put a moss rock at the top of the screen, I used the **0,-150** screen coordinates in my constructor method call. Now use the **Run ➤ Project** work process to take a look at the results, which are shown on the left in Figure 14-30.

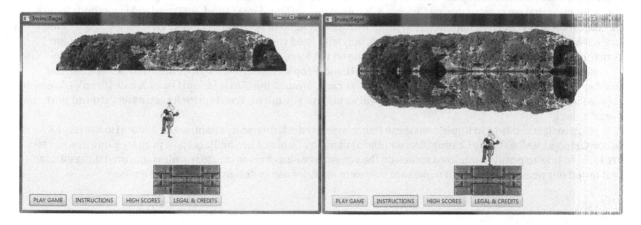

Figure 14-30. *Run the project; the Prop iPR1 is shown at the left, and iPV1 PropV mirrored object is shown at the right*

You can also "flip" large props, creating some very cool effects. Create an **iPV1** declaration and instantiation, as seen in Figure 14-31, and create a PropV object, which will mirror the moss rock, along the X axis. This can be seen on the right side of Figure 14-30. We've made a lot of progress in this chapter using fixed sprite Prop class capabilities.

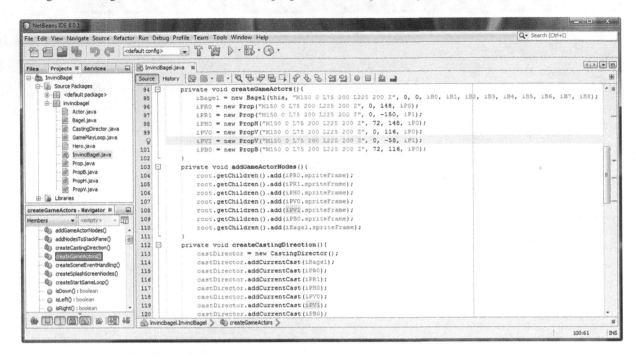

Figure 14-31. *Instantiate an iPV1 PropV object, add it to the root Scene Graph, and add it to a CurrentCast List<Actor>*

Summary

In this fourteenth chapter, we created our fixed sprite "prop" classes that allow us to design our game scenes and the fixed objects that our motion sprite Actor objects will interact with. We first created the **Prop** class, which extends the Actor class that we created during Chapter 8. We used the .setTranslateX() and .setTranslateY() methods to take the xLocation and yLocation parameters in the constructor method to position the ImageView on the Stage, similar to what we did with the .moveInvinciBagel() class, only with fixed sprites a move is only made once, inside of the constructor method, to position the prop in the Scene on the Stage.

Next we created even more complicated **PropH** and **PropV** classes, which in addition to positioning the fixed sprites in the Scene, also mirror them automatically, around the Y axis (PropH) and X axis (PropV). We also created a PropB (B stands for Both) class that will automatically mirror fixed sprite Image assets around both the X and Y axes.

Next, we learned how to implement these Prop classes by declaring, instantiating, and adding (to the JavaFX Scene Graph as well as to the CastingDirector object) them inside of our InvinciBagel.java primary game design class. We learned how to position our fixed sprites on the screen, as well as how to create seamless mirrored tiling effects, and tested our new Prop classes to make sure they were ready for use in designing game play levels.

Finally, we tested two of these four new fixed sprite classes with larger props, which, if we do not define the fixed sprite objects for use in collision detection by adding them into the CastingDirector object, could conceivably be used for scene background compositing. This would help reduce the data footprint for the game, by minimizing use of large PNG24 background imagery, allowing us to replace these data heavy images with far smaller PNG8 background images. These could depict scene "settings," such as a rainy day, a cloudy sky, or a vivid sunset.

In the next chapter, we are going take a look at how to add a digital audio sound effects engine to our game code. This audio engine will use the JavaFX AudioClip class to add sound effect sequencing capabilities to the game, so that we have all of the basic new media elements (fixed and motion imagery, and audio feedback) to work, with when we get into adding things such as like physics and collision detection. In this way, we can start to add in multimedia that will utilize all of our player's senses in the game play (user) experience.

Implementing Game Audio Assets: Using the JavaFX AudioClip Class Audio Sequencing Engine

Now that we have created both motion sprite and fixed sprite classes using our abstract Actor (fixed sprites) and Hero (motion sprites) superclasses, we need to put the code into place that will play our game audio assets. Although generally not thought of as being as important as the digital image (visual) assets, digital audio (aural) assets can be quite important to the quality of your game play. In fact, you would be surprised how much that great audio assets can add to the perceived value of your Java 8 game products. We will be learning how to optimize and implement digital audio assets for your Java 8 game development during this chapter, using open source tools such as Audacity 2.0.6.

Fortunately for us, the JavaFX **AudioClip** engine (actually, it is a class in the **javafx.scene.media** package) can bring a lot of power to our games development. This is because this class has essentially been designed to be an audio sequencing engine, able to control every aspect of the audio asset performance, as well as to create new audio assets using 6 octave (three up, and three down) pitch shifting capabilities. We'll be learning about this class in detail, during the beginning of this chapter, and then implementing it in our primary InvinciBagel.java class, as well as using it in our Bagel.java class in a new **.playAudioClip()** method, which we'll code and call in that class's primary .update() method.

After we look at the JavaFX AudioClip class is detail, we will get into using the popular **Audacity 2.0.6** digital audio editing (and audio effects) software, which we installed in Chapter 1, when we installed all of your open source game development software tools. We'll go through an audio asset creation and optimization process using Audacity. We will use the concepts that we learned in Chapter 5 covering new media content creation concepts, and optimize digital audio files to achieve an 800% data footprint savings. We will do this so that our digital audio assets do not use more than 64KB of our system memory; in fact, we will get six 16-bit digital audio assets to use less than 62KB of data.

Once we have created the six audio assets, which will match up with the six different keys that we are using to control our InvinciBagel character, we will create the **.loadAudioAssets()** method in the InvinciBagel class and learn how to declare AudioClip and **URL** objects. Inside of the .loadAudioAssets() method we will then use these two classes (objects) together in order to create our digital audio assets for the game and install them into the player's computer system (or consumer electronics device) memory.

Once these six AudioClip objects are in place, we will then have NetBeans create six Setter methods for the AudioClip objects and then "morph" these .setiSound() methods into the .playiSound() methods that we require. After this is done, we will go into our Bagel.java class, and add a .playAudioClip() method. Inside of this method, we will call the six .playiSound() methods, based upon which keys the player is pressing.

We have a lot of ground to cover during this chapter, so let's get started by taking an in-depth look at the JavaFX AudioClip class and its various properties and methods that we can invoke impressive audio sequencing with! After we get that out of the way we can get into the fun stuff and start using Audacity 2.0.6 and NetBeans 8 to create!

JavaFX AudioClip Class: A Digital Audio Sequencer

The **public final** AudioClip class is part of the **javafx.scene.media** package, and is essentially a digital audio sample playback and audio sequencing engine that is designed to use short audio snippets or "samples" to create more complex audio performances. This is why this class is the perfect digital audio media playback class to use for your Java 8 game development. As you can see by the Java inheritance hierarchy shown below, the JavaFX AudioClip class is a direct subclass of the java.lang.Object master class. This signifies that the AudioClip class has been "scratch coded" specifically for the purpose of being a digital audio sequencing engine.

```
java.lang.Object
  > javafx.scene.media.AudioClip
```

Your AudioClip objects will each reference one **digital audio sample** in memory. These can be triggered with virtually zero latency, which is what makes this class the perfect class to use for Java 8 games development. AudioClip objects are loaded similarly to Media (long-form audio or video) objects, using URL objects, but have a vastly different behavior. For example, a Media object cannot play itself; it will need a MediaPlayer object, and also the MediaView object, if it contains digital video. Media objects would be better suited for long-form digital audio assets (like music), which cannot fit in memory all at the same time, and must be streamed for optimal memory utilization. A MediaPlayer will only have enough decompressed digital audio data "pre-rolled" into memory to play for a short amount of time, so a MediaPlayer approach is much more memory efficient for long digital audio clips, especially if they are compressed.

The AudioClip object is usable immediately upon instantiation, as you'll see later on during this chapter, and this is an important attribute to have when it comes to Java 8 game development. AudioClip object playback behavior can be said to be "fire and forget," which means that once one of your playiSound() method calls is invoked, your only operable control at that point over the digital audio sample is to call the AudioClip .stop() method.

Interestingly, your AudioClip objects may also be triggered (played) multiple times, and AudioClips can even be triggered simultaneously, as you will see a bit later on during this chapter. To accomplish this same result by using a Media object, you would have to create a new MediaPlayer object for each sound that you want to play in parallel.

The reason that the AudioClip object is so versatile (responsive) is because your AudioClip objects are stored in memory. The AudioClip object uses a raw, uncompressed digital audio sample representing the entire sound. This is placed into memory in its raw, uncompressed state, which is why in the next section of the chapter we're going to use the WAVE audio file format. This audio format applies zero compression, and thus, the resulting file size for optimized digital audio samples will also represent the amount of system memory that each of these samples will utilize.

What is really impressive about the AudioClip class, however, is the amount of power it gives developers via its properties and the three overloaded .play() method calls. You can set up sample playback priorities, **shift the pitch** (frequency of the sound) up to 8 times (higher octaves) or down to 1/8th (lower octaves), **pan** the sound anywhere in the spatial spectrum, control the left and right **balance** of the sound, control the **volume** (or amplitude) of the sound, and control the **number of times** the sound is played, from once to forever, using the AudioClip **INDEFINITE** constant.

Besides the getter and setter methods for these AudioClip properties, there are .play() and .stop() methods as well as three (overloaded) .play() methods: one for simple (default) playback; one where you can specify volume; and one where you can specify volume, balance, frequency rate (pitch shifting factor), panning, and sample priority.

The key to controlling the AudioClip object is to call one of the three .play() methods based upon how you want to control the sample playback. Use **.play()** for straightforward playback, as we will be doing during this chapter; or use **.play(double volume)** to play your AudioClip object at a relative volume level from 0.0 (off) to 1.0 (full); or use the **.play(double volume, double balance, double rate, double pan, double priority)** to play your AudioClip object at a relative **volume** (0.0 to 1.0), a relative **balance** (-1.0 left, 0.0 center, 1.0 right), pitch shift **rate** (0.125 to 8.0), relative **pan** (-1.0 left, 0.0 center, 1.0 right); and **priority** integer, which specifies which samples get played over others, which, due to low resources and low priority, may not get played. Let's get into using Audacity to optimize our samples next!

Creating and Optimizing Digital Audio: Audacity 2.0.6

Launch the latest version of Audacity—at the time of this writing that would be 2.0.6, and use your microphone to record your voice saying the word "left." Fortunately my NetBeans 8 and Java 8 development workstation is also my Skype workstation, and I have a basic Logitech adjustable microphone on a stand that I can use to make the basic audio files that we will need to put audio files into place for each of our different sprite movements that we put into place in Chapter 13. I will go through the digital audio file "scratch creation" and optimization work process in this section of the chapter, and you can do this yourself, for each of the six digital audio files we will need to use in the coding sections of this chapter. You can also use the six audio files included with this book's software repository if you want to simply get onto the Java 8 coding part of digital audio asset implementation using the JavaFX AudioClip class. I would recommend going over how to optimize uncompressed audio for use in system memory, as we're about to take 113KB of raw source audio data, and knock 99KB of data off of it, and reduce it another 88% to be only 14KB.

As you can see in the left side of Figure 15-1, I have **recorded** the spoken word "**left**," and used the Audacity **selection tool** to select only that portion of the recording session, seen in a darker gray shade, that contains the audio data. Since you can see the digital audio waveform representation in the Audacity waveform editing area, you can see the portion of your recording where the data that you just recorded is contained. The portion of your audio recording that does not contain any digital audio data will just look like a straight line.

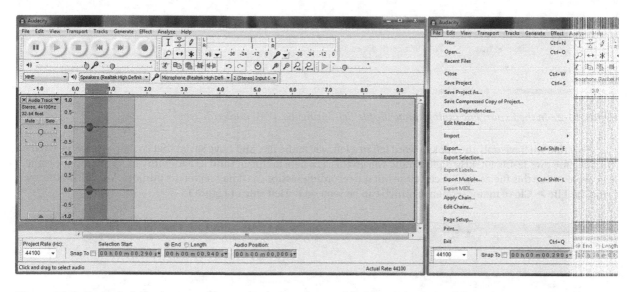

Figure 15-1. *Launch Audacity, record your voice saying the word "left," and then select the wave and Export Selection*

The fastest way to get only the raw digital audio data, which is all that we really want inside of our .WAV file anyway, and is the only data that we want to be optimizing using Audacity, is to use the **File ➤ Export Selection** menu sequence. This will allow us to directly write the selected audio data into the **left.wav** file using the WAVE PCM digital audio format. After we do this, we can then start a new Audacity editing session and simply open up that file and start the digital audio content optimization process.

After you use the Export Selection menu option in Audacity, you will get the **Export File** dialog, which is shown in Figure 15-2. Type **left** in the **File name:** field, seen in the bottom of the dialog, and click the **Save** button.

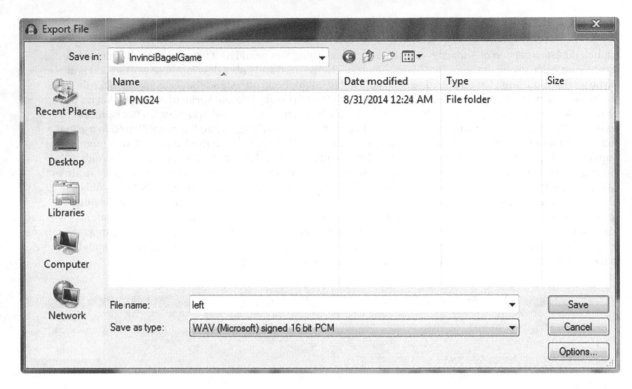

Figure 15-2. *In the Export File dialog, name the file "left" using the .WAV audio file type*

Now that we have only the spoken word left in a left.wav audio file, and have saved that so that we can see what this baseline raw 32-bit 44.1kHz digital audio will give us as a data footprint (and as a memory footprint for our game, if we were to use this file as-is), we can close out the recording session, as it has served its purpose. We will do this by using the **File ➤ Close** menu sequence, which can be seen on the left side of Figure 15-3.

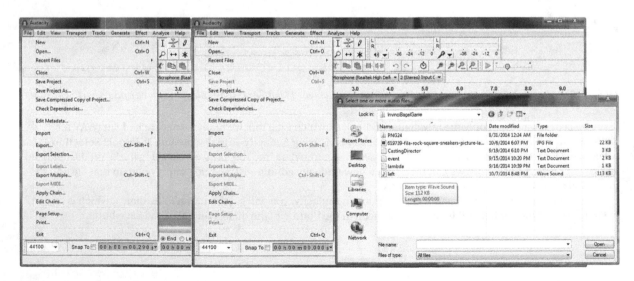

Figure 15-3. *Close the current editing session, then Open the "left" file, noting its raw file size, for further optimization*

The next thing that we will do is to go back and use the **File ➤ Open** menu sequence to open the **left.wav** file that contains only the segment of digital audio data that we wish to optimize. This is seen in the middle of Figure 15-3 (the menu sequence), and on the right side of the screenshot you can see a **Select one or more audio files** (File Open) dialog. Notice that the left.wav file shows what its raw (original) data footprint is (113 KB).

We can use this original data footprint as a **baseline** to see how many times we reduce the data footprint (it will eventually be 8.8 times smaller, once we are done) during this optimization process we are about to embark on.

When you click on the **Open** button and open a file for the first time in Audacity you'll get a **Warning** dialog, which is shown in Figure 15-4. This will advise you that you can make a copy of your original file for use in your editing session, instead of using the original. This is what is called "non-destructive" editing in the multimedia industry, and is always a very good idea, since it essentially provides you with a **back-up** file (the original), as part of the work process.

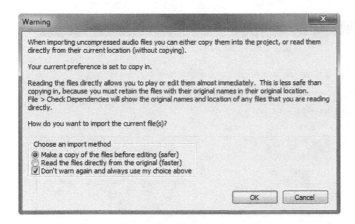

Figure 15-4. *Enable non-destructive audio editing in Audacity*

Select the "**Make a copy of the files before editing (safer)**" radio button option, and check the "**Don't warn again, and always use my choice above**" checkbox, which will turn Audacity 2 into a non-destructive non-linear digital audio editing software package. Click on the **OK** button and we'll be ready to start your digital audio data optimization work process. We will be optimizing our digital audio data, but not compressing it, and I will get into why that is next.

Optimization Versus Compression: The Audio Memory Footprint

You might be wondering why I am using the uncompressed, pulse code modulated (PCM) Wave (.wav) file format instead of the industry standard .MP3 file format that many of you use for your digital audio music file storage. I will cover the reason for this up front, before we start the optimization process. In digital audio, there are really two stages to data footprint optimization. First you optimize the sample resolution (32-bit original recording, 24-bit HD audio, 16-bit CD Quality audio and 8-bit lower quality audio) and the sample frequency (44.1kHz, 22.05kHz, 11.025kHz are the primary frequency levels that still maintain enough data for a quality result), and then you apply the compression. The compression affects your file size; in this case it is your .JAR (Java Resources) file.

So, why are we not compressing our files into MP3 format, to make our .JAR file a few kilobytes smaller? A primary reason for this is because MP3 is a "lossy" format, which throws away original data (and quality) for the audio sample. Since the JavaFX AudioClip class is going to take our digital audio assets and **decompress** them into memory, if we use MP3, that memory will contain **lower quality** audio data that if we use WAV format. Given that we are going to get at least an 8X data footprint reduction during the sample optimization work process that we are about to learn in the next section of the chapter, and that all our digital audio assets are going to be optimized to between 4KB and 14K of data footprint, MP3 compression is not going to give us any real JAR file data footprint reduction relative to the reduction in sample quality that it will "cost" us. Game audio is short-burst sound effects and musical loops, so we can use WAV file format and still get a good result, and not have to use **any compression**. The other advantage is the data size of the WAV file that you see in our file management software is also the amount of memory the sample will use.

Audio Sample Resolution and Frequency: Optimizing for Your Memory Footprint

The first step in the memory data footprint reduction process will be to take the raw 32-bit data sampling rate and reduce that by 100%, from 32-bit floating point data to 16-bit PCM data, as is shown in Figure 15-5 on the bottom left of the screenshot. Find the drop-down arrow in the gray information panel on the left side of the Audacity sample editing area, which I have circled in red in this screenshot as it is kind of difficult to find if you are not used to using it. This will give you a menu that allows you to set the data display (Waveform or Spectrogram) and set your Sample Data Format, which is the submenu that we want to use to select the **16-bit PCM** option rather than the 32-bit float option. Do not set your sample rate using this menu, as it will slow down your voice (you can try this if you want to use this as a special effect later on). Next, we will be looking at the correct work process for setting the sample rate.

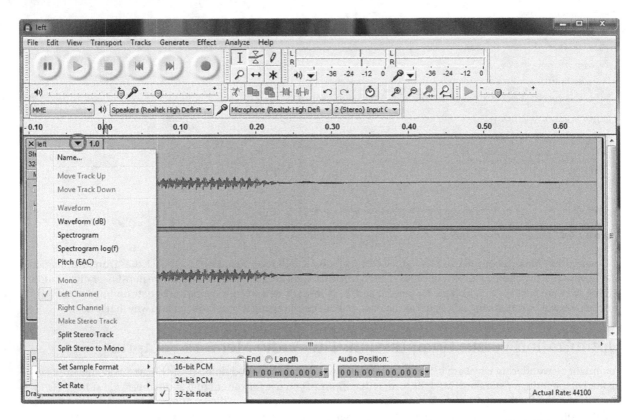

Figure 15-5. *Click the drop-down menu arrow at the left and select the Set Sample Format ➤ 16-bit PCM setting option*

It is important to note that if you save your file out after making this data bit-level change, your file size will not have changed! As you may have noticed, the Export File dialog is saving your file in 16-bit PCM WAVE format, so it is doing this same adjustment that you are doing here in memory, for your file size on disk. I am simply including this step here so that you get a comprehensive overview of the entire process, starting with a sample data rate reduction, and then reducing the sample frequency rate, which we are going to do next, and finally addressing the stereo versus mono sample consideration, which will be our final step later on in this section of the chapter.

Each of these "optimization moves" can reduce the file size (and memory footprint) by 100% or more, upon each application of the work process. In fact, when we reduce the sampling frequency next from 44,100 to 11,025 we will be reducing the data footprint by 200% (100% from 44,100 to 22,050, and then 100% from 22,050 to 11,025).

Setting the Audio Sample Frequency: Reducing Your Memory Data Footprint by Another 200%

The proper way to set the **digital audio sampling frequency** for your project in Audacity is to use the drop-down dialog for the project's sample frequency setting. This can be seen in the lower left corner of Figure 15-6, highlighted inside of a red box. Select the **11025** frequency setting, which reduces the audio data (think of these as vertical slices of the sound wave) sampling rate from 44,100 times per second, to 11,025 data slices per second, or a 4X reduction in audio data sampled in the first place, which is a 200% reduction in data footprint due to this sample frequency step in the data (in this case, you should look at this as memory used, more than file space used) optimization work process.

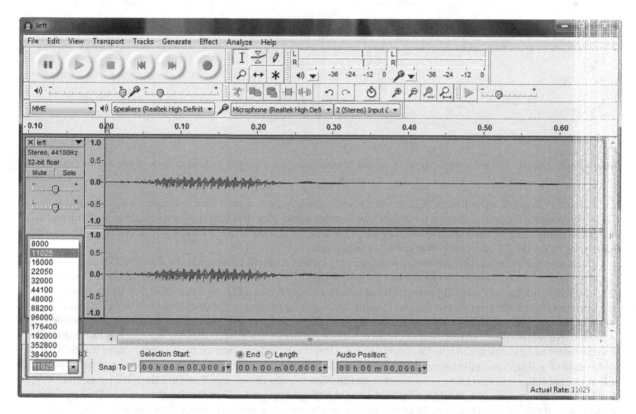

Figure 15-6. *Reduce audio sampling frequency by four times by reducing it from 44100 per second to 11025 per second*

You can play around with these seven different settings, between the 44,100 and 8000 sample frequency rates, as each of them will have a different quality level, with 8000 being too low of a quality to use for voice samples, but which might work well with a "dirty" or "noisy" sound, such as an explosion.

If you want to hear what these different settings sound like, after you select each one of course, click on the green play (right facing triangle) in the audio transport buttons shown at the top-left of Figure 15-6. You will see that the 32,000 frequency sounds just like the 44,100 frequency rate, as does the 22,050 frequency. The 16,000 or 11,025 frequency rates do not sound as "bright" but are still usable, so I used the 11,025 rate, to get an even 4X downsample of the data. This is because downsampling by an **even** 2X (100%) or 4X (200%) will always provide the best result. This is because of the math involved leaving no "partial" samples (or pixels, since the same concept applies with imaging).

Next, let's use the **File ➤ Export** work process. If you want to see this on a menu, this menu sequence can be seen in Figure 15-1, and is shown on the File menu, above Export Selection option. In the Export File dialog, which can be seen in Figure 15-7, you can save the new version of the file using a **different file name**, so that you have both the original uncompressed data in the left.wav file and the new compressed (stereo) data in the leftstereo.wav file. Name this file **leftstereo**, and click on the **Save** button, to save it as an uncompressed **16-bit PCM WAV** file, as shown on the left side of Figure 15-7.

Figure 15-7. *Use the File ➤ Export dialog, name the file leftstereo, Save the file, then use File ➤ Open to check its file size*

The next thing that we will want to do is use the same work process shown back in Figure 15-3, and use the **File ➤ Open** menu sequence, to open the **Select one or more audio files** dialog, shown on the right side of Figure 15-7, which will allow us to mouse-over the **leftstereo.wav** file and see that the size is **28.0 KB**, which is four times less data than the original 112 KB source file size, just as we expected!

Therefore, we've reduced our memory requirements for this audio file that states the word "left" from one-ninth of a megabyte (112 KB), to one-thirty-sixth of a megabyte (28KB). This means that you can have **36** audio assets of this size, and still be using only one single megabyte of system memory! When I created the other five audio assets, this one turned out to be the largest, and the smallest (up and s, as you may have guessed) were less than 4KB each!

The last stage of our digital audio optimization work process is the **conversion** of this data from a stereo file to a mono file. We will do this because we don't need two copies of the same spoken word for our game audio assets. This is also true for most game audio special effects, such as laser blasts and explosions; mono audio works just fine in these types of audio sound effect situations. This is especially true because the JavaFX AudioClip class and its pan and balance capabilities will also allow us to simulate stereo effects, using mono digital audio assets, if we want to.

This will also reduce our data footprint by another 100%, giving us a 14KB audio file. We could fit **72** digital mono audio assets of this size into one megabyte of system memory, so using mono (monaural) audio assets instead of stereo digital audio assets is a great thing to do whenever you can, which is why we are going to cover this next.

Stereo Versus Mono Audio: Reducing Your Memory Footprint Another 100%

The last stage of our digital audio optimization work process is the conversion of our digital audio data from using a stereo audio asset into a monaural audio asset. We will do this because we don't need two copies of the same spoken word for our game audio asset in this case. This is also true for most game-related digital audio special effects, such as laser blasts and explosions. Monaural audio will work just as well as stereo audio in these types of audio sound effect situations. This is especially true because the JavaFX AudioClip class gives developers audio panning and balance capabilities. These will allow developers to simulate stereo effects using mono audio assets. Audacity has an ability to **combine** stereo audio asset (two tracks, one left and one right) data into one mono audio asset that sounds the same.

If we combine our two stereo audio tracks into one mono track, using the Audacity **Tracks ➤ Stereo Track to Mono** algorithm which is shown in the menu sequence in Figure 15-8, it will reduce the digital audio data footprint by another 100%, giving us a 14KB audio file. We could fit 72 digital audio assets of this size into one megabyte of system memory. As it is, using the (uncompressed, no less) digital audio data footprint optimization that I have shown during this section of the chapter, I have managed to get all six digital audio assets into less than 62 KB of memory footprint.

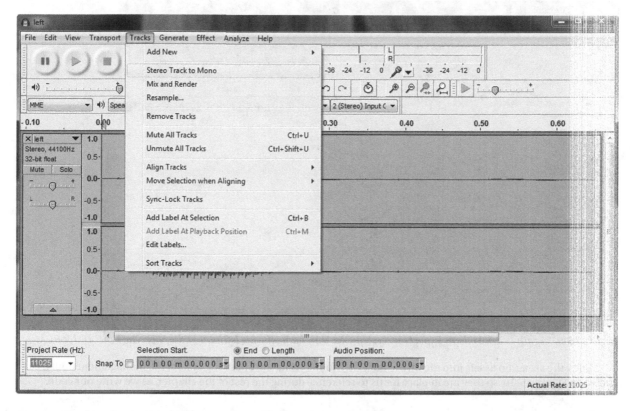

Figure 15-8. *Use the Tracks ➤ Stereo Track to Mono algorithm to combine the stereo samples into one Mono sample*

What I want you to do before you use this stereo-to-mono algorithm is to click on the **Play** transport button at the top of Audacity, and listen to the stereo audio asset carefully, a couple of times. Next, go ahead and invoke this stereo-to-mono track merging algorithm, using the menu sequence shown in Figure 15-8. After you see a single mono audio asset, which you can look ahead and see in Figure 15-9, click on the Play transport button again, and then listen to the audio sample, now that it is monaural, and see if you can detect any difference whatsoever.

This difference is even more difficult to detect (if you even can) with specialized sound effects. The Audacity 2.0.6 software package is a fully professional digital audio editing, sweetening, and sound effects program, and as you can see here, you can achieve professional game audio development results using the correct work process with this software, which is why I had you download and install it during Chapter 1. To make sure you have the most powerful version of Audacity 2.0.6 possible, make sure that you have all of the **LADSPA**, **VST**, **Nyquist**, **LV2**, **LAME**, and **FFMPEG** plug-ins downloaded, and then install them in the **C:\Program Files\Audacity\Plug-Ins** folder, and restart Audacity.

Preparing to Code: Exporting Your Assets and Copying Them into Your Project

Let's export the final monaural file and name it **leftmono.wav** using the **File ➤ Export** menu sequence, as is shown in Figure 15-9. You can record the other five files using the same work process, or use assets I have created if you prefer.

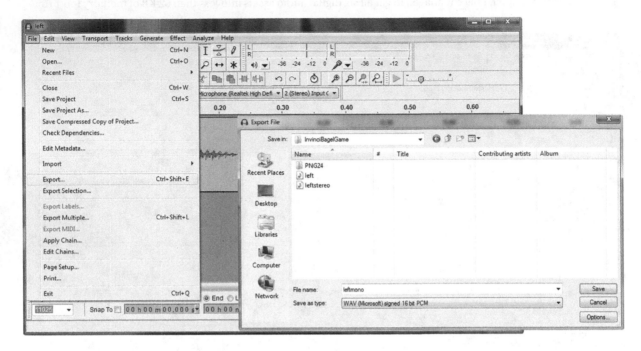

Figure 15-9. *Again use the File ➤ Export menu sequence and name the file leftmono and select the WAV 16-bit PCM*

Copy the six audio assets into the InvinciBagel/src folder using the operating system file management utility, as shown in Figure 15-10, so they are in place for us to reference during the rest of the chapter, as we write our code.

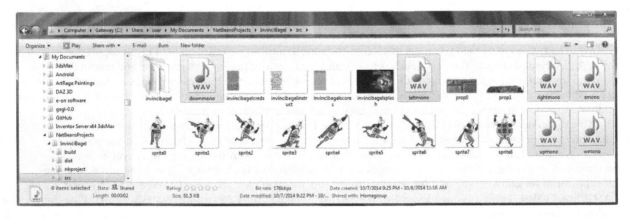

Figure 15-10. *Use your file management software to copy the six .WAV files into the InvinciBagel/src project folder*

Now we're ready to get back into Java 8 coding. First, we will add code in our InvinciBagel.java class in order to implement six AudioClip objects, which will reference our audio assets, and later, in the Bagel.java class, where we will utilize the assets in a new .playAudioClip() method that we will add to our Bagel class's primary .update() method.

Adding Audio to InvinciBagel.java: Using AudioClip

The first thing that we need to do to implement the AudioClip sound engine is to declare six private AudioClip objects, using a compound declaration statement at the top of the InvinciBagel.java class. I will name these iSound (stands for InvinciBagel Sound) zero through five, as shown in Figure 15-11, using the following single line of Java code:

```
private AudioClip iSound0, iSound1, iSound2, iSound3, iSound4, iSound5;
```

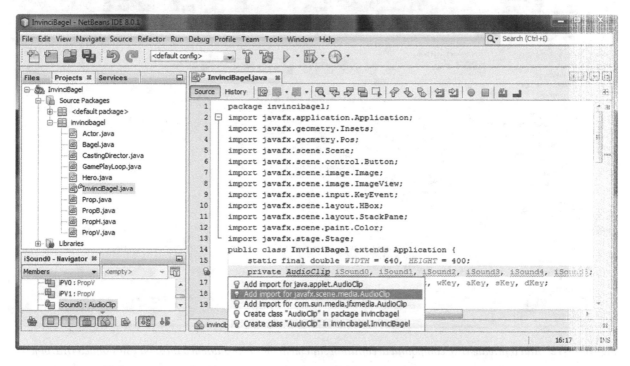

Figure 15-11. *Add the private AudioClip compound declaration statement for your iSound0 through iSound5 objects*

As you can see in Figure 15-11, you will have to use the **Alt-Enter** work process, and select the "Add import for javafx.scene.media.AudioClip" option, and have NetBeans 8 write your AudioClip class import statement for you.

Referencing AudioClip Assets: Using the java.net.URL Class

Unlike Image objects in JavaFX, which can be referenced using a simple forward slash character and the file name, digital audio assets are not as simple to reference, and require the use of the **URL** class, which is part of the **java.net** (network) package. The URL class is used to create a URL object, which provides a Uniform Resource Locator (URL) file reference, which is essentially a "pointer" to a "data resource," which is usually a new media asset, and in the case of our Java 8 game development, it is a WAVE audio file in our /**src** folder.

Like the AudioClip class, the URL class was also scratch coded to provide URL objects, as you can see from the Java class hierarchy, which looks like the following:

```
java.lang.Object
  > java.net.URL
```

The second step in our implementation of our six AudioClip objects is the declaration of six **private** URL objects named iAudioFile0 through iAudioFile5 at the top of the InvinciBagel.java class using a compound declaration statement, which can be seen in Figure 15-12, and looks like the following single line of Java code:

```
private URL iAudioFile0, iAudioFile1, iAudioFile2, iAudioFile3, iAudioFile4, iAudioFile5;
```

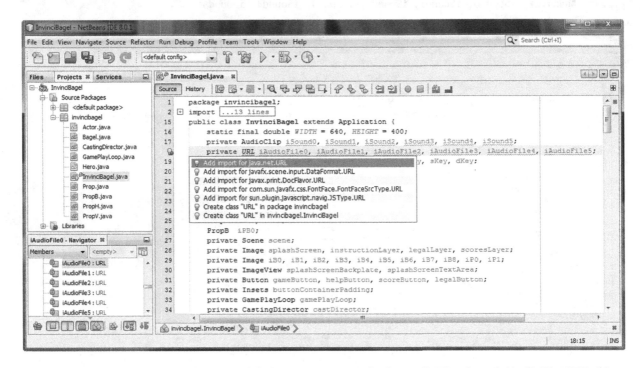

Figure 15-12. *Add a private URL compound declaration statement for the iAudioFile0 through iAudioFile5 URL objects*

As you can see in Figure 15-12, you will have to again use the **Alt-Enter** work process, and select the "Add import for java.net.URL" option, and again have NetBeans 8 write your URL class import statement for you.

Now we are ready to write the Java code that loads our URL objects, and then uses these to instantiate our AudioClip objects. To maintain our high level of code organization using custom methods inside this class, let's add a **loadAudioAssets()** method into our .start() method next, and then create a **private void** loadAudioAssets() method to hold our AudioClip related code, in case we want to add more than six digital audio assets into our game in the future.

It is important to note that due to the versatility of the AudioClip class as far as **pitch shifting** and **2D spatial** (left to right) audio movement is concerned, you should not need as many audio assets as you might think, because you can turn even six well-designed audio assets into literally hundreds of different sound effects for your game play.

Adding Your Audio Asset Loading Method: .loadAudioAssets( )

Create a method call inside of your start() method, as seen in Figure 15-13, called **loadAudioAssets();** and place it in the logical method order right before the **loadImageAssets();** method invocation. To get rid of the wavy red error highlighting, add a **private void loadAudioAssets(){}** empty method after the createSceneEventHandling() method. In this way, your digital audio assets will be referenced and loaded into memory right after your KeyEvent handling is set up, and right before your digital image assets are referenced and loaded into memory.

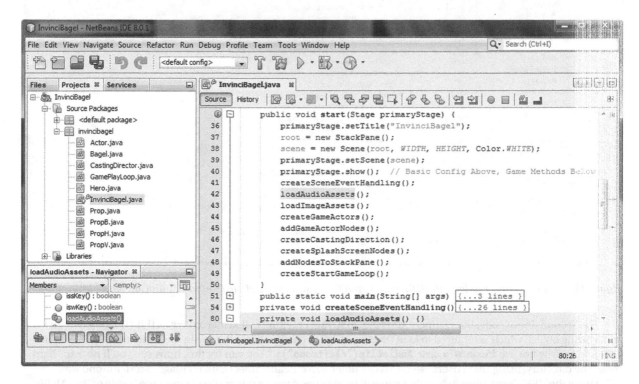

Figure 15-13. *Create the private void .loadAudioAssets() method to hold the AudioClip object instantiation statements*

Inside of your .loadAudioAssets() method body, your will have two Java code statements, as loading a digital audio asset is a little bit more involved than referencing digital image assets. First, you will load your first **iAudioFile0** URL object, using the **getClass().getResource()** method chain. This method chain loads the URL (uniform resource locator) object with the digital audio sample resource that you want to use, and will do this for your Class object (in this case, this is the InvinciBagel class, since that is the Java class which we are writing this code in).

The resource that you are looking to get the URL for goes inside of the .getResource() method call, and uses the same format as the resource references that you used for your digital image assets, which in this case would be a "/leftmono.wav" file reference, which is converted by the .getResource() method into a binary URL data format. This Java code can be seen in Figure 15-14, and looks like the following Java method body:

```java
private void loadAudioAssets() {
    iAudioFile0 = getClass().getResource("/leftmono.wav");
    iSound0 = new AudioClip(iAudioFile0.toString());
}
```

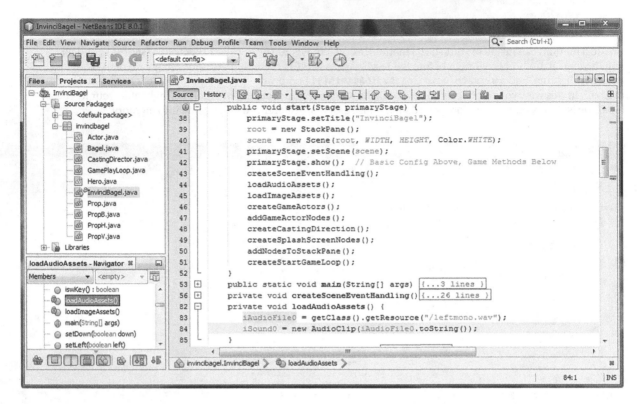

Figure 15-14. *Instantiate and load the URL object, and then use it inside of the iSound0 AudioClip object instantiation*

The second line of code, interestingly, uses the **.toString()** method call, which converts this URL object right back into a String object, which is required to load the AudioClip() constructor method with the audio asset URL. You may be thinking: why not use **iSound0 = new AudioClip("/leftmono");** ? You can try this, however, you'll have to "hard code" the directory, using "file:/Users/users/MyDocuments/NetBeansProjects/InvinciBagel/src/leftmono.wav."

I used the URL object approach so that you will be able to reference this audio file from the inside of the JAR file, instead of using the approach shown above that **requires** an "absolute" location on a hard disk drive. Therefore, this **getClass().getResource()** method chain is adding "relative" reference data into this URL object. Your InvinciBagel class needs this relative reference data to be able to reference your WAV audio resource files from the inside of your NetBeans 8 project **InvinciBagel/src** folder, as well as from the inside of your JAR file for your Java 8 game application.

Next, use your trusty programmer's shortcut, and copy and paste these two lines of code five more times underneath themselves, which is the easy way to create your other five AudioClip objects. Change the zero on both iAudioFile0 and iSound0 to iAudioFile1 through iAudioFile5 and iSound1 through iSound5 respectively. Then change the WAV audio file name reference to **rightmono.wav**, **upmono.wav**, **downmono.wav**, **wmono.wav** and **smono.wav** respectively. Your completed loadAudioAssets() method should then look like the following Java method body, which is also shown in Figure 15-15:

```
private void loadAudioAssets() {
    iAudioFile0 = getClass().getResource("/leftmono.wav");
    iSound0 = new AudioClip(iAudioFile0.toString());
    iAudioFile1 = getClass().getResource("/rightmono.wav");
    iSound1 = new AudioClip(iAudioFile1.toString());
    iAudioFile2 = getClass().getResource("/upmono.wav");
    iSound2 = new AudioClip(iAudioFile2.toString());
```

```java
    iAudioFile3 = getClass().getResource("/downmono.wav");
    iSound3 = new AudioClip(iAudioFile3.toString());
    iAudioFile4 = getClass().getResource("/wmono.wav");
    iSound4 = new AudioClip(iAudioFile4.toString());
    iAudioFile5 = getClass().getResource("/smono.wav");
    iSound5 = new AudioClip(iAudioFile5.toString());
}
```

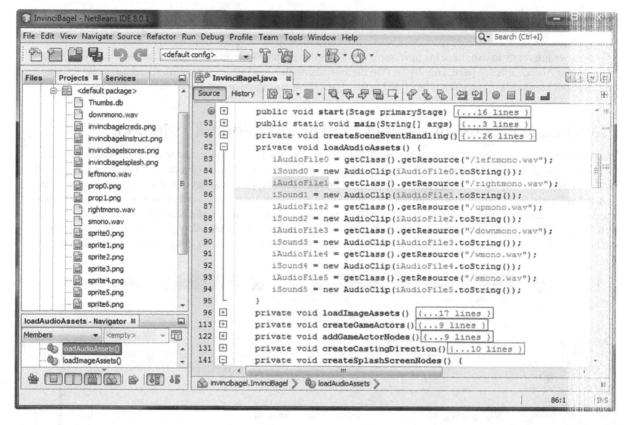

Figure 15-15. *Create more AudioClip objects referencing the rightmono, upmono, downmono, wmono, and smono files*

Since we've made our AudioClip objects **private**, we need to create methods inside of the InvinciBagel class, which can be called from our Bagel.java class (and other classes as well, later on in development) using method calls.

Use your **Source ➤ Insert Code ➤ Generate ➤ Setters** work process to open the **Generate Setters** dialog, seen in Figure 15-16, and select the iSound0 through iSound5 objects, so that NetBeans creates six **.setiSound()** methods.

Figure 15-16. *Use the Generate Setters dialog and create six .setiSound() methods*

Now we are ready to use these six new .setiSound() methods that NetBeans has coded for us, which we do not need, as our AudioClips are permanently "set" in memory using the .loadAudioAssets() method, to create the six .playiSound() methods that we do in fact need to play back these six digital audio assets. Let's do that next.

Providing Access to Your AudioClip: The .playiSound( ) Methods

What we are about to do is what I consider another programmer's shortcut, but instead of copy and paste, I used NetBeans **Source ➤ Insert Code** function to create Setter methods for the iSound objects that I am going to change from **.setiSound()** to **.playiSound()** methods, so that I do not have to type out all six of these method bodies. As you can see in Figure 15-17, NetBeans created six complete method bodies for us, and all that we have to do is to remove the AudioClip iSound references inside of the method parameter areas, change the setiSound() to be playiSound(), and finally change the **this.iSound0 = iSound0;** statement to be **this.iSound0.play();** instead. We will do this for each of the six .setiSound() method bodies, which will allow us to quickly create six .playiSound() method bodies.

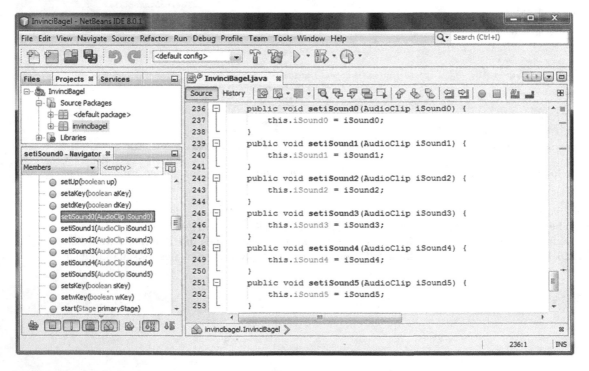

Figure 15-17. *Edit these six .setiSound() methods, created by NetBeans, at the bottom of the InvinciBagel.java class*

The edit process is relatively easy: select the set part of setiSound and type "play" over the set; select the inside of the parameter area (**AudioClip iSound#**), and hit the **delete** or **backspace key** to remove that; and finally, select the " = **isound**" part of the Java statement, inside of the method between this.iSound and the ; semicolon and type in **.play()** instead. The completed Java method bodies are shown in Figure 15-18 and should look like the following:

```java
public void playiSound0() {
    this.iSound0.play();
}
public void playiSound1() {
    this.iSound1.play();
}
public void playiSound2() {
    this.iSound2.play();
}
public void playiSound3() {
    this.iSound3.play();
}
public void playiSound4() {
    this.iSound4.play();
}
public void playiSound5() {
    this.iSound5.play();
}
```

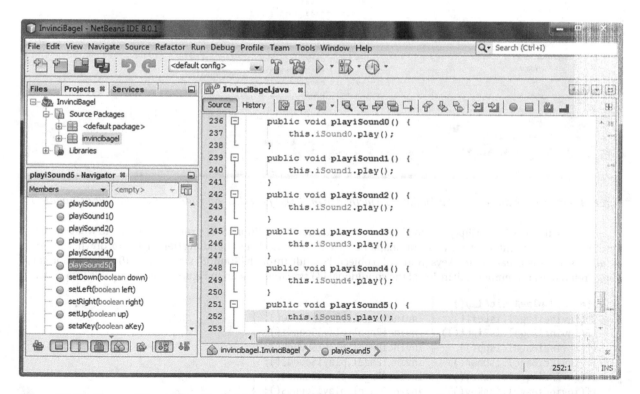

Figure 15-18. *Turn .setiSound() methods into .playiSound() methods by adding calls to the AudioClip .play() method*

Triggering the .playiSound() Methods in Bagel.java: The .playAudioClip() Method

Now that we have declared, universal resource located (referenced), and instantiated our AudioClip objects, and created .playiSound() methods that will allow us to trigger each of these digital audio samples from "outside" of the InvinciBagel.java class, we can go into the Bagel.java class, and write some code that allows us to trigger these audio objects, to see how well the AudioClip class works. The best way to do this with our existing code is to use the event handler code we are using to move our motion sprite object to also allow us to trigger one of these sounds for each of the KeyEvents that we have set up currently for our game. This is why I named these files with the keys that they will be triggered by. The first thing that we need to put into place in the Bagel.java class, similar to what we did in the InvinciBagel class, is a method call to a playAudioClip() method inside of the .update() method that references an empty private void playAudioClip() method. This method call and empty method body can be seen in Figure 15-19.

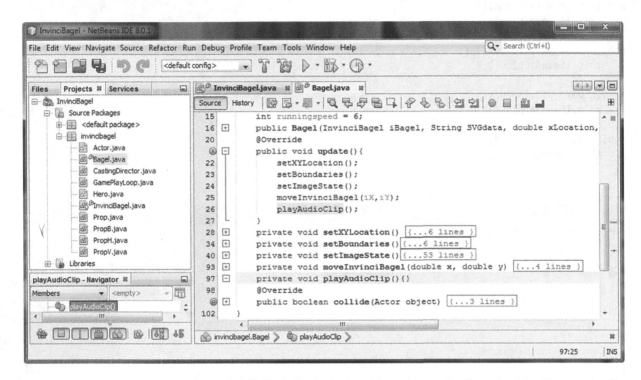

Figure 15-19. *Create an empty .playAudioClip() method in the Bagel.java class and add a call to it inside of .update()*

Inside of the playAudioClip() method body, we need to create conditional if() structures, similar to what we did for the sprite movement that we created in Chapter 12. We'll match KeyEvent handling (left, right, up, down, w, s) to audio files that speak each of the keys (AudioClip objects iSound0 through iSound5) via an invinciBagel.playiSound() object reference and method call inside of the conditional if() statements, seen in Figure 15-20, using this Java code:

```
private void playAudioClip()    {
    if(invinciBagel.isLeft())  { invinciBagel.playiSound0(); }
    if(invinciBagel.isRight()) { invinciBagel.playiSound1(); }
    if(invinciBagel.isUp())    { invinciBagel.playiSound2(); }
    if(invinciBagel.isDown())  { invinciBagel.playiSound3(); }
    if(invinciBagel.iswKey())  { invinciBagel.playiSound4(); }
    if(invinciBagel.issKey())  { invinciBagel.playiSound5(); }
}
```

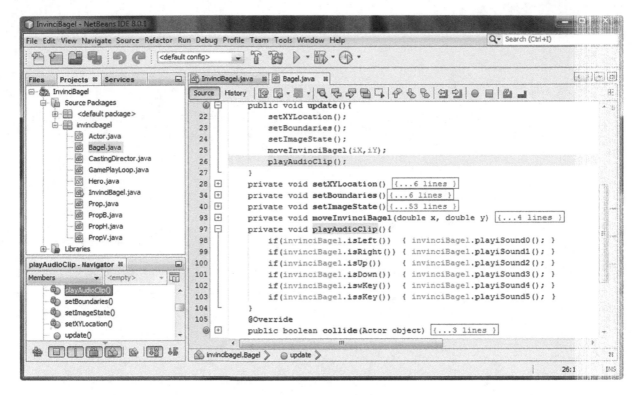

Figure 15-20. *Add conditional if() statements to the .playAudioClip() method that call the correct .playiSound() method*

Now we have added digital audio to our game engine infrastructure, and all we have to do later is swap out the voiceovers with sound effects, and we will have the digital audio portion of our game development completed. If you use a **Run ➤ Project** work process and test the code, you will find that audio samples trigger rapidly using JavaFX.

Summary

In this fifteenth chapter, we changed our focus from how our game looks to our eyes (visual) and addressed how it sounds to our ears (aural), and took a chapter to implement the code for the AudioClip class so that we can trigger **digital audio sound effects**.

First we took a look at the JavaFX **AudioClip** class. We learned why it is perfectly suited for use in our game development for audio, including short musical loops (using the **INDEFINITE** constant setting) or rapid sound effects.

Next, we learned how to optimize digital audio assets using **Audacity 2.0.6**. We learned the work process for optimizing digital audio so that it takes only a dozen or so kilobytes of system memory, and how to optimize audio so well that we do not even have to apply compression, especially since audio compression codecs supported by Java 8 are "lossy" codecs and can degrade the quality of the audio data once they are decompressed into system memory.

Finally, we implemented AudioClip objects in our InvinciBagel.java class using a **.loadAudioAssets()** method, and then created six **.playiSound()** methods to allow external classes to access and play these digital audio assets. We also added a **.playAudioClip()** method in our Bagel.java class that triggered the audio samples based on which keys were being pressed. In the next chapter, we are going take a look at how to add **collision detection** to our game code.

■ ■ ■

Collision Detection: Creating SVG Polygons for the Game Actors and Writing Code to Detect Collision

Now that we have implemented digital audio for our game sound effects and short-loop music, as well as implemented our digital imaging related classes that create motion sprites (characters) and fixed sprites (props), we will now delve into the other major genre or area of new media: **vectors**. Vectors are utilized in 2D illustration software (InkScape) as well as 3D modeling and animation software (Blender), and use math to define the shapes that are used to create the 2D or 3D artwork. This makes vectors the perfect solution for defining **custom collision shapes** that perfectly encase our sprites, so that instead of using a complex array of pixels to detect collision, we use a far simpler (and far more memory and processor efficient) **collision polygon**, that will perfectly surround our sprite.

Fortunately for us, the JavaFX **SVGPath** class in the **javafx.scene.shape** package allows us to use custom SVG Path (Shape) data to define our sprite collision boundaries. Not only that, but this SVGPath class (object) is also highly efficient, as it has zero properties, only a few methods, and a simple SVGPath() constructor method, as you have seen already in Chapter 8. This means that using the SVGPath class (object) is relatively **memory and processor efficient**. In fact, the only method that we will need to use is the **.setContent()** method that we used in our Actor class constructor method in Chapter 8. Since we'll do this once, at game start-up, the SVG Path collision data will be loaded into system memory and will be used in our collision detection routines, which we will be putting into place later in this chapter.

In this chapter we'll take a detailed look at how the SVG Path data can be defined. This is specified by World Wide Web (W3) Consortium (also known as W3C), the body who defines HTML5. This specification is on their w3.org website, and is located at the `http://www.w3.org/TR/SVG/paths.html` URL, if you want to view it in further detail.

After we look at the SVG or **Scalable Vector Graphics** (in case you are wondering what this stands for) data format in detail, we will get into using the popular **GIMP 2.8** digital image editing software, which you installed in Chapter 1, and learn how to create collision polygons. We will also take a look at how to use the **PhysEd** (PhysicsEditor) collision polygon generation software. This is from a company called **CodeAndWeb** GmbH, who makes professional, and affordable, game assets creation software.

We will go through a collision polygon vector asset creation and optimization process using GIMP 2.8, using both the quick and dirty work process, which allows GIMP to 100% create the collision polygon shape for you, as well as a more "involved" work process, where you create your own collision polygon yourself, by hand, using GIMP's Path tools. After we have learned how to create collision polygons that are compatible with the JavaFX SVGPath class, we will spend the remainder of the chapter on Java 8 game programming, creating the collision detection engine (code) that will allow us to detect when our InvinciBagel character comes into contact with any of the other Actor objects in the game environment (Scene and Stage objects). This is where the book will start to become more advanced (useful).

The SVG Data Format: Hand Coding Vector Shapes

There are ten different letters that can be utilized with the numeric (X,Y data point location in 2D space) data in an SVG data string. Each has an upper case (absolute referencing) and a lower case (relative referencing) version. We will be using absolute referencing as we need these data points to match up with pixel locations in the sprite imagery that we are going to "attach" or group these SVG Path data strings with to provide collision detection data guidelines. As you can see in Table 16-1, the SVG data commands provide you a great deal of flexibility in defining custom curves for your Java 8 game development. You could even combine all of these scalable vector commands with your Java 8 code to create interactive vector (digital illustration) artwork that has never before been experienced, but since this is a game development title, we're going to use this information to develop highly optimized **collision polygons** that only use a dozen X,Y data points (somewhere between 12 and 15) to define a relatively detailed collision polygon that will encase our sprite imagery, and provide highly accurate (from the game player's viewpoint, at least) collision results.

Table 16-1. *SVG data commands to use for creating SVG path data string (source: Worldwide Web Consortium w3.org)*

SVG Command Name	Symbol	Type	Parameter	Description
moveto	M	Absolute	X, Y	Defines a **Start Of Path** at the X,Y using **absolute** coordinates
moveto	m	Relative	X, Y	Defines a **Start Of Path** at the X,Y using **relative** coordinates
closepath	Z	Absolute	None	**Close SVG Path**, by drawing line from last to first coordinate
closepath	z	Relative	None	**Close SVG Path**, by drawing line from last to first coordinate
lineto	L	Absolute	X, Y	**Draws a Line** from the current point to the next coordinate
lineto	l	Relative	X, Y	**Draws a Line** from the current point to the next coordinate
horizontal lineto	H	Absolute	X	**Draws a Horizontal Line** from current point to next coordinate
horizontal lineto	h	Relative	X	**Draws a Horizontal Line** from current point to next coordinate
vertical lineto	V	Absolute	Y	**Draws a Vertical Line** from current point to next coordinate
vertical lineto	v	Relative	Y	**Draws a Vertical Line** from current point to next coordinate
curveto	C	Absolute	X,Y, X,Y, X,Y	**Draws a cubic Bezier curve** from current point to next point
curveto	c	Relative	X,Y, X,Y, X,Y	**Draws a cubic Bezier curve** from current point to next point
shortandsmoothcurve	S	Absolute	X,Y, X,Y	**Draws a cubic Bezier curve** from current point to next point

(continued)

Table 16-1. *(continued)*

SVG Command Name	Symbol	Type	Parameter	Description
shortandsmoothcurve	s	Relative	X,Y, X,Y	**Draws a cubic Bezier curve** from current point to next point
quadratic Bezier curve	Q	Absolute	X,Y, X,Y	**Draws a quadratic Bezier curve** (current point to next point)
quadratic Bezier curve	q	Relative	X,Y, X,Y	**Draws a quadratic Bezier curve** (current point to next point)
short quadratic Bezier	T	Absolute	X,Y	**Draws a short quadratic Bezier** (current point to next point)
short quadratic Bezier	t	Relative	X,Y	**Draws a short quadratic Bezier** (current point to next point)
elliptical arc	A	Absolute	rX, rY, Rot	**Draws an elliptical arc** from current point to next point
elliptical arc	a	Relative	rX, rY, Rot	**Draws an elliptical arc** from current point to next point

The best way to see how to use the powerful SVG data "path drawing" commands is to get down to learning the work process for creating SVG data-based collision polygon paths. We will learn how to do this using GIMP 2.8.14, using a "quick and dirty" approach, which lets GIMP do 100% of the path creation work. After that, we'll learn another way to do this by hand using GIMP. A second approach gives you 100% of the path creation control. At the end of this SVG topic, I will also show you how to use another dedicated collision and physics development tool called **PhysEd** from an innovative game development software tools company, located in Ulm, Germany, called **CodeAndWeb GmbH**.

Creating and Optimizing Collision Data: Using GIMP

Fortunately for us, the popular open source digital image editing software package called GIMP, currently at version 2.8.14, has enough Path capabilities, and the ability to export this as SVG datasets, to allow the software to be used as a full-fledged collision polygon creation tool. The GIMP software supports paths using a **Path Tool** (shown as an old-fashioned **fountain pen** tip next to a curve data point with Bezier handles coming out of it), which you can see in Figure 16-1 (second icon from the left in the second row of the Toolbox Icons). The reason GIMP supports paths, as it is not generally a **vector** (path-based) software package, but instead a **raster** (pixel-based) software package, is because the ability to create a path and then "convert" it to a **selection area** is a very useful one to the digital image compositing artisan. In fact, we will be using GIMP's ability to do just the opposite of this: that is, convert an algorithmically created selection set into path data, which will form the foundation of our fully automated, "quick and dirty" SVG Path data creation process. We will take a look at this first, since it is fast, simple, and effective (but "data heavy"). Let's get started by launching GIMP, and using the **File ➤ Open** process to open the **sprite1.png** PNG32 digital image asset that is in your project **/src** folder. As you can see in Figure 16-1, I have zoomed into the image. This allows me to see the collision data path (initially, this will be a **selection**) that we're about to create using the GIMP **Toolbox**.

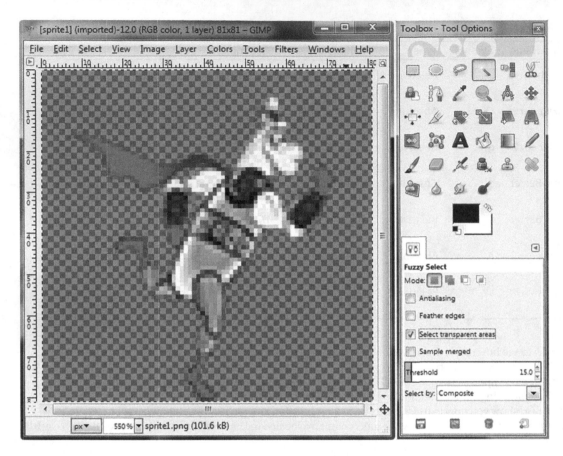

Figure 16-1. *Launch GIMP, and use File* ➤ *Open to open the sprite1.png file*

Click on the GIMP **Fuzzy Selection Tool** (icon looks like a sparkler or a magic wand), which is shown selected (depressed, as in "sunk in," not sad) in Figure 16-2. Click on any area of the image that shows a **checkerboard pattern**, which always signifies **transparency** in any digital imaging software package, as well as many other types of software, such as the game asset creation software packages from CodeAndWeb GmbH, for instance. As you see, in Figure 16-2, you'll get an animated, "crawling ants" outline around the transparent areas of the image, since the transparent areas have just been selected by the Fuzzy Selection Tool algorithm, which selects areas of **contiguous color values**.

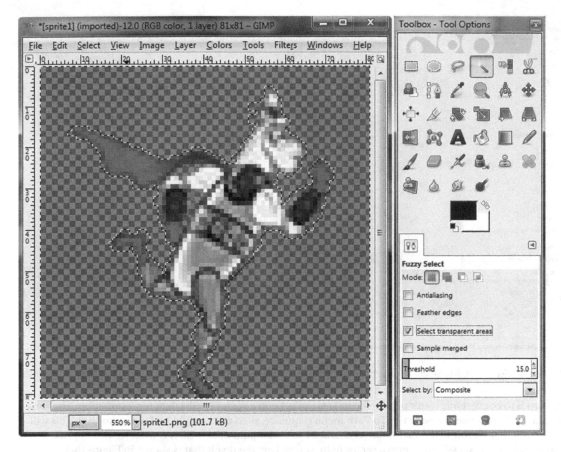

Figure 16-2. Click in a transparent area using Fuzzy Select Tool to select Actor

In this case, the Fuzzy Select tool is selecting transparency values. In fact, you should notice that you have to select an option to select transparent areas in an image, using the Fuzzy Select Tool Options dialog, which can be seen at the bottom of the Toolbox Tool Options floating palette. As you can see, I have instructed GIMP to not only "look" at the RGB plates in the image, but also to look at the Alpha plate, by selecting the "Select transparent areas" option.

Now that we have that selection set that contains everything except the sprite character that we wanted to select, we need to figure out a way to get the opposite of what we now have selected. Selecting the transparent areas was admittedly much easier than trying to select the different colored areas of the InvinciBagel character! Fortunately GIMP has an algorithm that **inverts** the selection completely, selecting everything that is not selected, and deselecting everything that is selected.

Under the GIMP 2.8 **Select** menu, find the **Invert** option, or, use the **Control+I** keyboard shortcut, shown on the menu next to the Invert option, all of which can be seen on the left half of Figure 16-3. Once you do this you will notice that the animated "marching ants" no longer march around the square perimeter (extents) of the digital image and that they are only around the InvinciBagel character, which means that the selection has been inverted and what we wanted to select is now contained in the selection set.

347

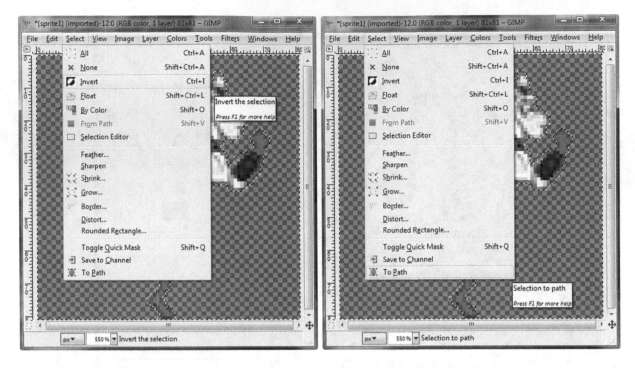

Figure 16-3. *Invert selection using Select ➤ Invert, so only Actor is selected (left); use Select ➤ To Path to convert to path*

The next step is to convert this raster pixel selection set (array) into a vector (path) data representation. The way that we do this in GIMP is to use the **Select ➤ To Path** menu sequence, seen on the right half of Figure 16-3. This will convert the selection that is around the InvinciBagel character to vector path data, which is what we want to cull.

Once you convert the pixel selection into a vector path, you will get the result that is shown in Figure 16-4.

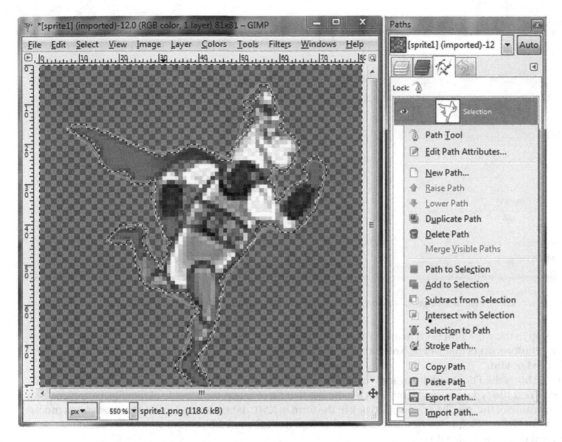

Figure 16-4. *Right-click on Selection Path in Paths Palette, and Export Path*

In the other floating palette, click on the **Paths Tab**, shown on the right side of Figure 16-4. GIMP has two, primary floating tool windows; one is the GIMP **Toolbox**, containing **Tools**, **Options**, **Brushes**, **Patterns**, and **Gradients**, and the other contains **four tabs**, which represent your digital image's compositing **Layers**, **Channels**, Selection **Paths**, and even an **Undo Buffer**, which gives you a "history" of every "move" you have made in GIMP since you launched it.

Select the Path named **Selection** (the Path layer named Selection will then turn blue). Next right-click on the Path named Selection, and at the bottom of that menu of things that you can do to the Selection Path, you will see an **Export Path** menu option. This is another one of the key GIMP algorithms that enables this collision polygon creation and output work process for us.

Selecting this Export Path option will export the current InvinciBagel character Selection Path data for us, as a text-based (XML) file containing SVG data, which is what we need to use in our Bagel() constructor method call. This data will be contained in the first **String SVGdata** parameter, and will replace our "dummy data" that we have been using as a placeholder thus far.

Once you invoke the Export Path menu option, you will see the Export Path to SVG dialog, which is shown in Figure 16-5. As you can see, I've selected the "Export the active path" option, at the bottom of the dialog, since I only want to have one collision polygon path data object, and I am naming this file **sprite1svgdata.svg**, and I am saving it in my **C:\Clients\BagelToons\InvinciBagelGame\Shape_Data** folder.

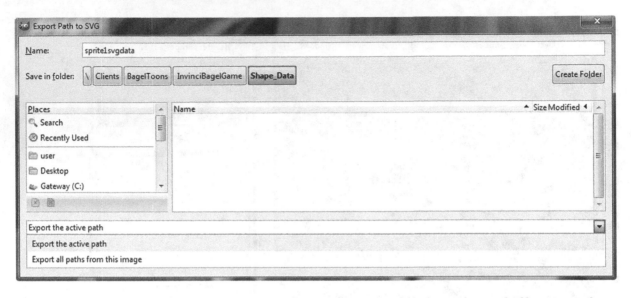

Figure 16-5. Select "Export the active path" option, in the Export Path to SVG dialog, and name the file sprite1svgdata

The next step in the work process is to open the **sprite1svgdata.svg** file that we are exporting in Figure 16-5 in a text editor: for Windows users that will be **Notepad**, for Macintosh users that will be **TextEdit**, and for Linux users it will probably be **vi** or **vim**.

Figure 16-6 shows the File **Open** dialog for Windows Notepad, and you may notice that by default, Notepad will look for the **.txt** (**Text file type**) file extension, which indicates that there is **text data** inside of that file. However, there is also text data inside of the .svg file extension (type), in the form of XML data. We need to use the drop-down menu at the bottom right of the dialog to tell Notepad to look at all files that are available, and to allow us to decide which of them contain text data, and which do not.

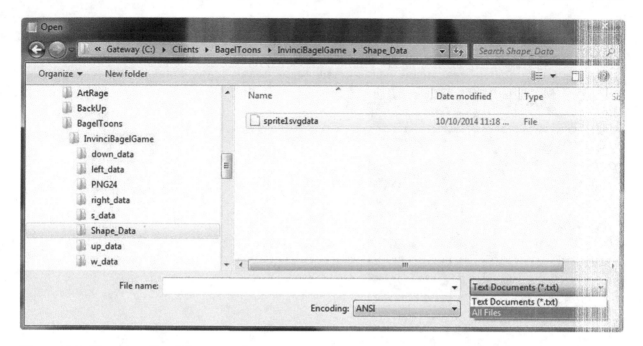

Figure 16-6. *Use a text editor (like Notepad) and select "All Files" option and Open sprite1svgdata*

Once you select the "All Files" option, you will see the **sprite1svgdata** file, and you can double-click on it to open the file (or single click on it to select it, and then click on the **Open** button).

If you want to use this data in your Java code, simply select the part after the **d = (data equals)** in quotation marks, including the quotation marks, which you will need to denote a String, as seen selected in blue in Figure 16-7.

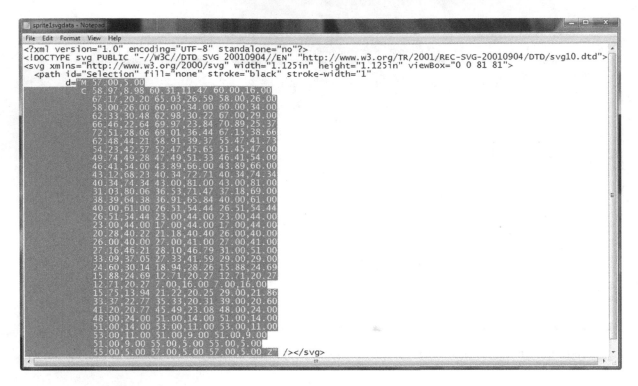

Figure 16-7. *Select the SVG data (including quote characters) for the SVG Path representation, and use it in your code*

As you can see in Figure 16-7, there are 32 times 3 data pairs, which is close to 100 data points, which is a lot of data to process, especially if two objects that both have SVGPath collision detection data defined are colliding!

If you look at the InvinciBagel character in Figure 16-4, we really should be able to define a collision polygon around the character using 14 to 16 lines that perfectly encapsulate the character, and use many times less (16 times less, in fact, as you will see during the next section of the chapter) data, which equates to 16 times less memory, and 16 times less processing (1600% higher efficiency) overhead, if not more.

For that reason, I want to show you the more complex work process in GIMP for defining your own **custom** collision polygon SVG data shape object, using as few lines (between data points) as possible. This essentially equates to **collision detection SVG Path shape data optimization**, and since I've been showing you the data optimization work process for other new media elements, there is no reason to stop that trend now! So next, let's take a detailed look at how to reduce our collision detection SVG Path shape data overhead by 1600% in the next section of this chapter.

Creating an Optimized Collision Polygon: Using the Path Tool

Let's start over, either by closing the previous project, and using the **File ➤ Open** to reopen the **sprite1.png** file, or by deleting the previous Selection Path in the Paths palette. This time, instead of the Fuzzy Select Tool, use the **Paths** Tool, and select the **Design Edit Mode** in the options (bottom) part of the Toolbox, and select the **Polygonal** checkbox option. This will keep our lines nice and straight, like the polygons you see in 3D modeling packages such as Blender. Click in the InvinciBagel character's hair, and then click another point on his left shoulder, as shown in Figure 16-8. This will automatically draw a line segment (polyline) between the two points for you. Click a third point at the elbow, a fourth point at the wrist, a fifth point at the toe, a sixth point at the knee, a seventh point at the thigh, an eighth point at the heel, and so on, to create an outline using straight lines that perfectly contains the InvinciBagel run state.

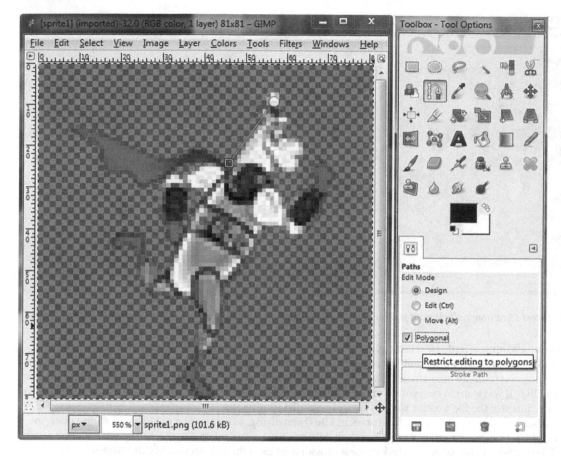

***Figure 16-8.** Open sprite1.png, select the Paths Tool, and start to draw a simple Path*

As you can see in Figure 16-9, I created the collision polygon using only **15 points**. You can leave the polygon open, and simply add the **Z** character you learned about in the first section of the book, to create a **closed polygon**. As you can see on the right side of Figure 16-9, the polygon conforms closely to the sprite, so during game play the result of a collision will look like it happened with the pixels of your sprite rather than with the collision polygon, which even though the collision polygon path data is visible here in GIMP, will be invisible during your game play.

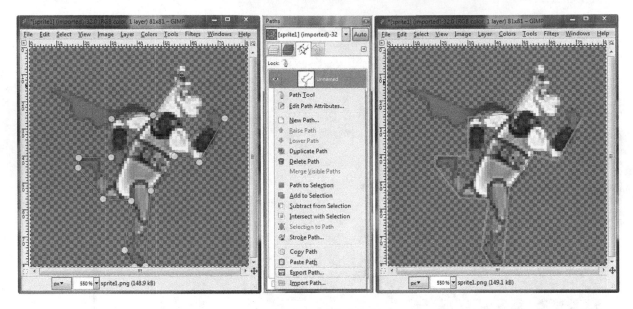

Figure 16-9. *Insert 15 strategically placed points to define a collision shape and use the Export Path to export SVG data*

Export your hand-drawn path, by selecting, and right-clicking on the **Unnamed Path** shown in the middle of Figure 16-9, and use the **Export Path** menu option to export it as the file **sprite1svghand.svg**, just like you did back in Figure 16-5. If you want to name the path in GIMP, you can double-click on the path name in the path dialog, and give it a name, if you like. If you want to save your work in the native GIMP **.xcf** file format, you can also use the **File ➤ Save** menu sequence, and give the file a name, such as **sprite1svgpath15points.xcf**.

Next, use your Text Editor's (Notepad, for instance) **File Open** dialog, as was shown in Figure 16-6, and open the latest **sprite1svghand.svg** file, so you can see how much data you have saved relative to the nearly 100 data point pairs that the GIMP Fuzzy Select Tool selection work process provided for us in the first section of this chapter.

As you can see in Figure 16-10, there are 14 times 3 (42) data pairs, which is less than half of the amount that we had in the previous work process. This is strange, because theoretically, there should only be **15** data pairs, so let's do some investigative work, and see what might be going on with this data.

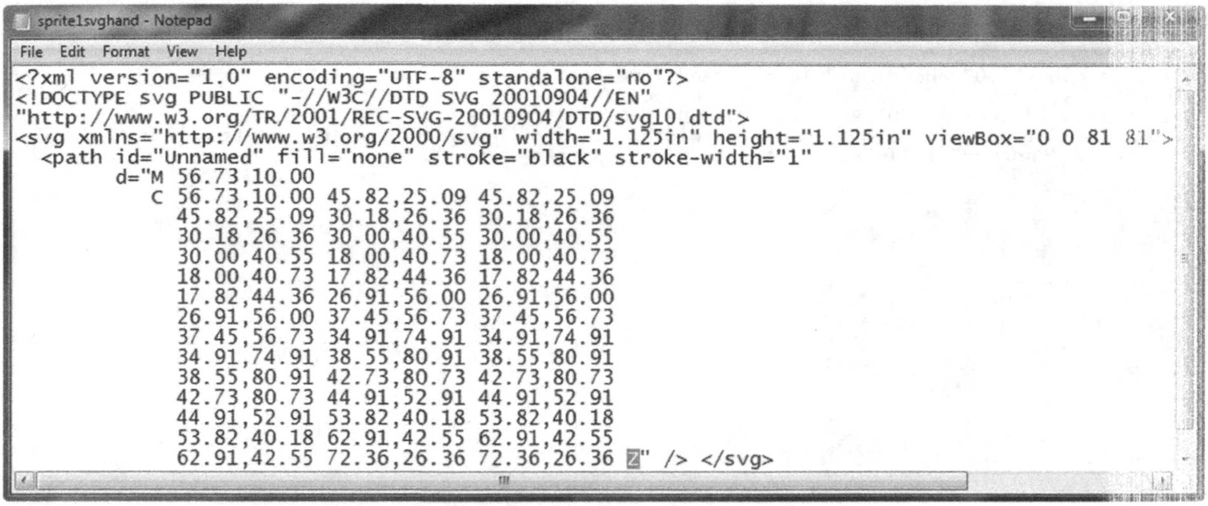

```
sprite1svghand - Notepad

File  Edit  Format  View  Help
<?xml version="1.0" encoding="UTF-8" standalone="no"?>
<!DOCTYPE svg PUBLIC "-//W3C//DTD SVG 20010904//EN"
"http://www.w3.org/TR/2001/REC-SVG-20010904/DTD/svg10.dtd">
<svg xmlns="http://www.w3.org/2000/svg" width="1.125in" height="1.125in" viewBox="0 0 81 81">
    <path id="Unnamed" fill="none" stroke="black" stroke-width="1"
          d="M 56.73,10.00
             C 56.73,10.00 45.82,25.09 45.82,25.09
               45.82,25.09 30.18,26.36 30.18,26.36
               30.18,26.36 30.00,40.55 30.00,40.55
               30.00,40.55 18.00,40.73 18.00,40.73
               18.00,40.73 17.82,44.36 17.82,44.36
               17.82,44.36 26.91,56.00 26.91,56.00
               26.91,56.00 37.45,56.73 37.45,56.73
               37.45,56.73 34.91,74.91 34.91,74.91
               34.91,74.91 38.55,80.91 38.55,80.91
               38.55,80.91 42.73,80.73 42.73,80.73
               42.73,80.73 44.91,52.91 44.91,52.91
               44.91,52.91 53.82,40.18 53.82,40.18
               53.82,40.18 62.91,42.55 62.91,42.55
               62.91,42.55 72.36,26.36 72.36,26.36 Z" /> </svg>
```

Figure 16-10. Open SVG Path data in a text editor and add a Z "close polygon" command to the end of the data

Just as NetBeans 8 does not always utilize the "optimal" or correct work process to suit our particular Java 8 game creation goals, it is possible that we are having the same type of problem with GIMP. If this is the case here, we will have to take matters into our own hands, and intervene by adding our own custom work process steps to achieve the precise results that we know that we need for our Java 8 game development. Luckily this SVG Path data uses text data, inside of an XML "container," so we should be able to add our own steps into this work process if we need to. In the end, you will find that developing a professional Java 8 game is not as easy an endeavor as playing the game itself!

Upon closer examination of the SVG data (the part after d=), the first thing that you will see is that the level of **numeric precision** that is being utilized is not necessary for this application. Since we are trying to match collision data point precision to pixel precision, we can use **integer** numbers, rather than the **floating point** numbers that are being utilized for this SVG data. Let's take matters into our own hands and round the decimal portion of these floating point numbers up or down to the nearest **whole integer number**. Doing this will get rid of the floating point precision that is currently being utilized. This will be our second round of optimization (the first being hand drawing a polygon). Also, add a "Z" close path command at the very end of the data, as shown in Figure 16-10, to form a closed polygon.

As you can see in Figure 16-11, the first round of optimization will give you significantly less data, simplifying the collision data considerably. However the question is, if we put this SVG data back into GIMP 2.8, will your collision polygon still look exactly the same? Next let's take a closer look at the work process that can answer this question. Save this file as **sprite1svghandintegerxml.txt**, so that we have the optimized data, shown in 16-11, when we need it.

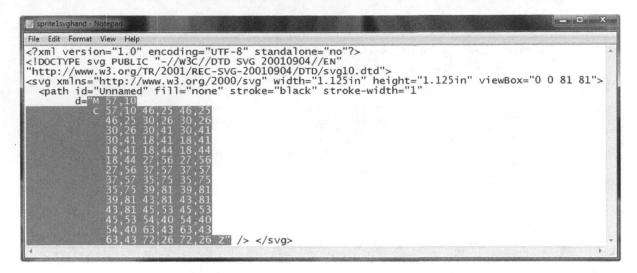

Figure 16-11. *Remove the floating point values, by rounding them up or down, to the nearest integer values*

Refining SVG Path Collision Shapes in GIMP: Using Import Path

Let's start over yet again, either by closing the previous project, and using the **File ➤ Open** to reopen the **sprite1.png** file, or by deleting the previous Selection Path in the Paths palette. As you can see in Figure 16-12, the Paths palette is empty, and we can **right-click** inside the empty area of the palette, and select the **Import Path** option, at the bottom.

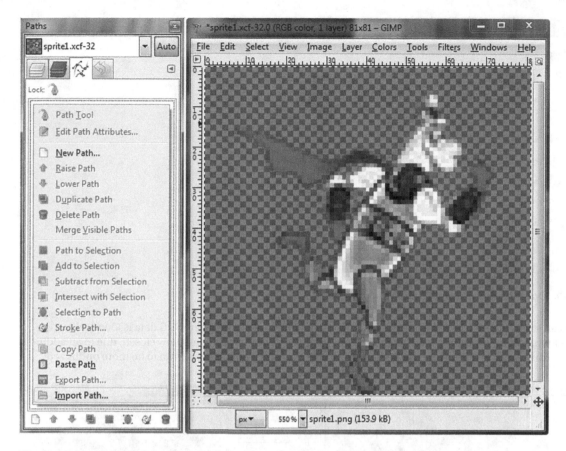

Figure 16-12. *Right-click in empty Paths palette, select Import Path option*

Once you click on the **Import Path** menu item seen in Figure 16-12, you will get the **Import Paths from SVG** dialog. Select the "All files (*.*)" drop-down menu option, and then click on the **sprite1svghandintegerxml.txt** file and then click the **Open button**, as shown in Figure 16-13. This will open up the edited integer collision path data in GIMP.

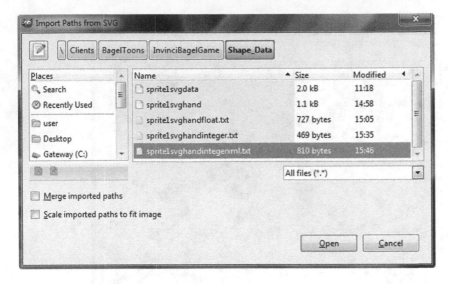

Figure 16-13. *Open the sprite1svghandintegerxml.txt file*

As you can see in Figure 16-14, this integer representation of the collision polygon SVG data is identical to a floating point representation, which was shown in Figure 16-9. The collision polygon is now closed, due to an addition of an SVG "Z" command, at the end of the SVG data string. We are getting our collision data to be more optimized!

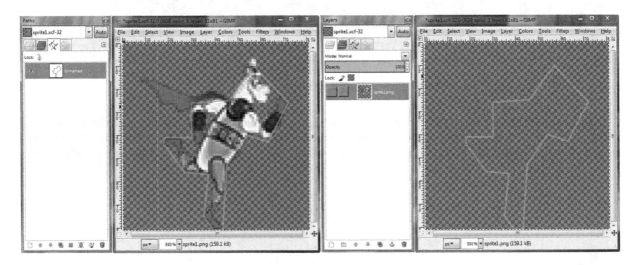

Figure 16-14. *Collision polygon is correct using integer data (left); deselect visibility in Layers Palette (right) to see SVG*

You may have noticed that there are three identical X,Y data point coordinate values for every point, except for the starting and ending point, for which we have data point pairs instead of data point triplets. If you recall back in Table 16-1, the only SVG command that uses triplet (three) X,Y data point pairs is the **C**, or Cubic Bezier (Spline) Curve. Sure enough, as you see in Figure 16-15, right under the **M** (moveto) opening SVG command is the C command. This explains why GIMP put three data points in each point in your polygon. The reason all the data point triplets have the **same value** is because we checked the **polygon** option in GIMP. This puts the spline curve control handles "away" or out of sight, directly on top of the X,Y data point. This defines zero curvature, or the square polygon structure seen in Figure 16-14.

Let's export the SVG data with the triplets removed, which is shown in Figure 16-15, and see what the result looks like in GIMP, using our newfound Import Path work process, primarily for learning purposes, as we are not quite finished with the optimization work process.

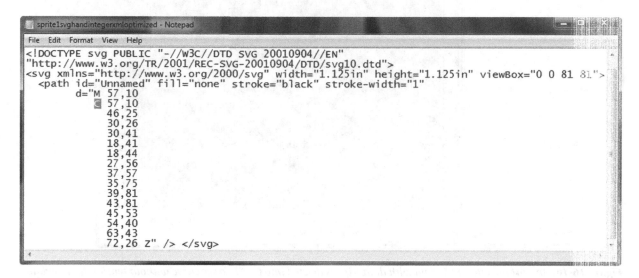

Figure 16-15. *Remove duplicate point data for those points in the interior of the collision polygon, to further optimize*

Save the XML data shown in Figure 16-15 as **sprite1svghandintegerxmloptimized.txt** and then use the same Import Path work process, shown in Figures 16-12 and 6-13, to import this further optimized SVG data set into GIMP. As you can see in Figure 16-16, removing those cubic Bezier curve control handles from the data set also removes the polygonal nature of your collision polygon. So, we will need to do some further work on our SVG data to correct this.

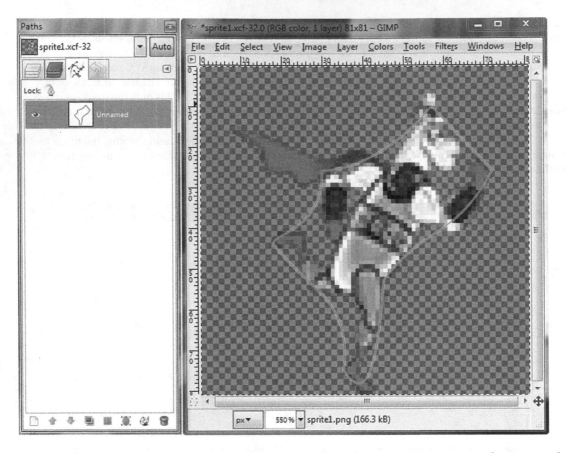

Figure 16-16. *Import the latest SVG data with data triplets deleted into GIMP to see curve without tension handle data*

The solution to turn these non-conforming (to the sprite outline) curves into the same collision polygon that we had before is quite simple, and you may have already guessed what it is. Since we want **straight lines** between our data points, we need to change this "**C**" to an "**L**." This will turn a **curveto** SVG command into a **lineto** SVG command.

As you can see in Figure 16-17, our collision polygon data is almost where we expected it to be, containing 16 data point pairs and a Z closing command to create a 16-sided collision polygon. We can remove the first duplicate data pair, reducing the data set to 15 data point pairs, which is what we "laid down" in GIMP. Next, let's again use our **Import Path** work process in GIMP, and see if we get the same square polygon result that is shown in Figure 16-14.

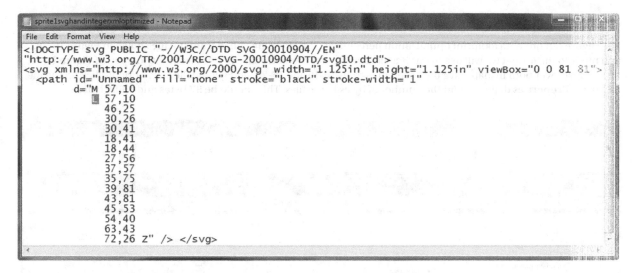

Figure 16-17. *Change your SVG Path data from using the C (curve) data type to the L (line) data type representation*

The final SVG data set is shown in Figure 16-18, and you can copy and paste that data into your Java code as well as into an empty Notepad document and save it as its own file, named **iBshape1svg.txt**, so that we can do some math next, and see exactly how much data we have reduced our collision polygon from the automatic GIMP created collision polygon, to our hand-optimized custom collision polygon. If you import the collision data shown in Figure 16-18 in GIMP, you will get the desired collision polygon shown in Figure 16-14 with 15 data point pairs, instead of 100!

Figure 16-18. *To use optimized SVG Path data set, select the part after d= (including quotes), and paste into the code*

Ascertaining Collision Data Optimization: Calculating Data Footprint for SVG Data

Let's figure out our data footprint optimization percentage. The SVG data culled from the file shown in Figure 16-18, and put into the format we will use in our Bagel() constructor method call, can be seen in the top part of Figure 16-19.

Mouse-over both iBshape1svg files, seen in Figures 16-19 and 16-20, and get the file size, or right-click on the file, and use a **Properties** dialog to find the number of bytes in the files. This should be **97** bytes and **1,605** bytes.

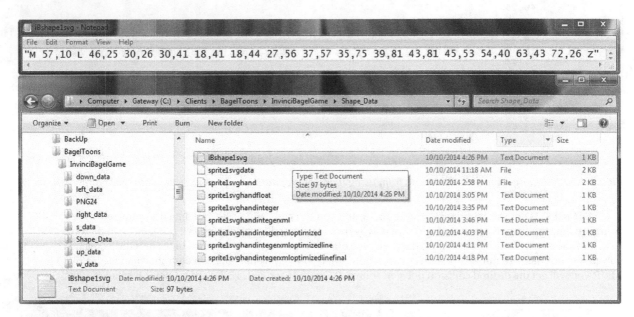

Figure 16-19. *Open folder in your workstation containing the SVG data, and mouse-over file to see the number of bytes*

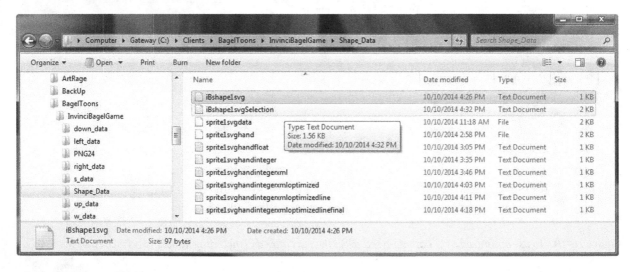

Figure 16-20. *Mouse-over the original Fuzzy Select Tool generated SVG data to get the data footprint, and do the math*

To find out the data footprint optimization, simply divide these numbers into each other. If you divide 97 by 1605 (97/1605=0.0604) you find that 97 is 6% of 1605, giving you a **94%** reduction in data footprint. If you divide 1605 by 97 (1605/97=16.546) it means you have reduced the file by 16.546 times, giving a **16.55X** data footprint reduction. These are the inverse (1/x) of each other on the calculator, so you can look at it from either direction. So 1605 bytes is 1,655% more data than 97 bytes, or 97 bytes is 6% (or 94% less data) of 1605 bytes. Any way that you look at it, you have just saved your game a whole lot of memory, processing, and JAR file data footprint, and that is only for one of the sprites! Remember that optimizing your collision polygon to use more than 16 times less memory as well as 16 times less CPU processing overhead can be very significant to the smoothness of your game play once you implement collision detection in your game logic, which we are going to do after we take a look at CodeAndWeb's PhysEd tool.

Creating and Optimizing Physics Data: Using PhysEd

I want to take a couple of pages to show you an alternative to GIMP that incorporates both physics and collision into a unified game development tool offering that is extremely affordable relative to all that it does for game development. **PhysicsEditor**, or PhysEd (or PE) is from **CodeAndWeb GmbH**, a company owned by another Apress author, **Andreas Loew**, who writes about iOS Game Development. Let's take a quick look at how we would define our sprite's collision polygon using this professional game development tool, and then we will be ready to get to collision detection coding. Install and launch PE using the green cube PE icon, and use the Import Sprite button shown in Figure 16-21 to open up your sprite1.png file, and use the zoom slider at the bottom of the screen to zoom in **600%**, just like we did in GIMP.

Figure 16-21. *Launch PhysicsEditor and use the Add Sprites button to open the sprite1.png file and zoom into it 600%*

Next click on the **tracer icon** at the top of the sprite editing area (it is the middle icon, that looks like a magic wand), which will open the **Tracer** dialog, shown in Figure 16-22. In this dialog you can set the zoom, tracing algorithm tolerance, **Trace Mode** and **Frame mode**, and see the resulting vertex count as a result of these settings.

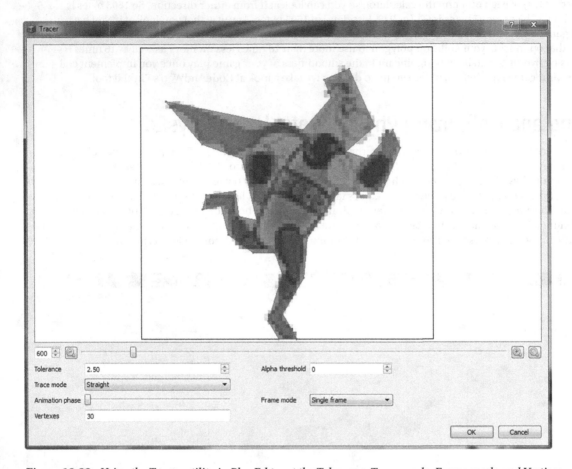

Figure 16-22. *Using the Tracer utility in PhysEd to set the Tolerance, Trace mode, Frame mode and Vertices*

Once you have the visual result that you're looking for, which is accomplished by tweaking the various Trace dialog settings, click on the **OK** button, and you will be taken back to the PhysicsEditor primary user interface window.

You can then refine your collision polygon structure data point by data point, by clicking and dragging these points with your mouse, as seen in Figure 16-23. If you compare the collision polygon in Figure 16-22 with the one in Figure 16-23, you can see I that have refined several of the data points to better conform to the outline of the sprite.

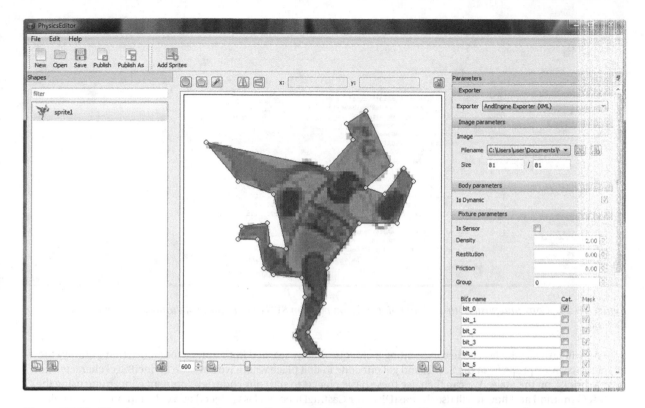

Figure 16-23. *Fine-tune your vertex placement for the collision polygon in the PhysicsEditor, then select your Exporter*

The closer you can get the collision polygon to the outline of the sprite, optimally you would want to put it right on top of the anti-aliasing that is on the pixel-edge between the sprite pixels and the transparency, or even right inside of the anti-aliasing if you want a more challenging game play. Ultimately, your collision polygons will have to be tweaked during your game development and game testing cycles, so that you get the most realistic result during your game play. If you're developing for powerful platforms such as game consoles, you can add data points to the collision polygon, and if you're developing for single or dual processor platforms, such as HTML5 phones or iTVs, use less data.

Replacing Dummy Collision Data: InvinciBagel.java

Next, let's make some changes to your Java code in the **InvinciBagel.java** class, so that you are actually using this highly optimized collision polygon data that we just developed during this chapter. We will use the data set that has only 15 data points, so that we can see all of our collision polygon data in our NetBeans 8.0 code editing pane. As you can see in Figure 16-24, we will need to put the Bagel() constructor method call on three different lines: one for the **iBagel = new Bagel(this)** part of the instantiation, another for the **collision polygon SVG data String object**, and another for the xLocation, yLocation and Image object List. We will also be using our knowledge of SVG commands, which we learned from Table 16-1, to create the collision polygon data for our tileable brick elements. We will be using these brick "Prop" elements to develop our collision detection Java code later on in the chapter. We will create these simpler collision polygons using only our brains, by implementing numeric logic that relates to the resolution of the brick image, and where the corner pixel locations would be in X,Y coordinate space, in conjunction with the SVG path drawing commands that we learned about in Table 16-1. You are becoming quite a game development professional!

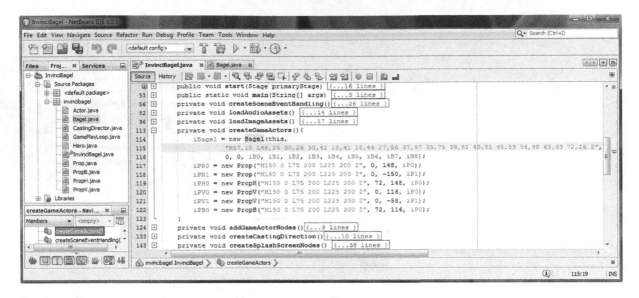

Figure 16-24. *Copy and paste your 15 data point collision polygon SVG data in place of dummy data in Bagel()*
method

We will also use the Java code commenting technique that we learned in Chapter 3 to remove (temporarily) the
larger mossy rock props from the Scene, and get our code to that place where we have the InvinciBagel character, and
several bricks, on the Stage. We can then use these basic objects to start our code development concerning using the
.collide() method and how it will use the **castDirector** CastingDirector class (object) as a collision processing guide.

If you want to see the iPR1 and iPV1 objects temporarily removed from your **.createGameActors()** as well as your
.addGameActorNodes() and **.createCastingDirection()** methods, you can see this Java code commenting in place
in Figures 16-25 and 16-26. Next, let's copy and paste the SVG collision polygon data set that you created earlier in the
chapter. Open the **iBshape1svg.txt** file, shown in Figure 16-20, and select and copy the SVG data, using the **Edit ➤
Copy** menu sequence or **CTRL-C** keyboard shortcut. Be sure to including the quotation marks. Paste the data in your
Bagel() method in the **.createGameActors()** method where the dummy SVG data used to be, as seen in Figure 16-24.

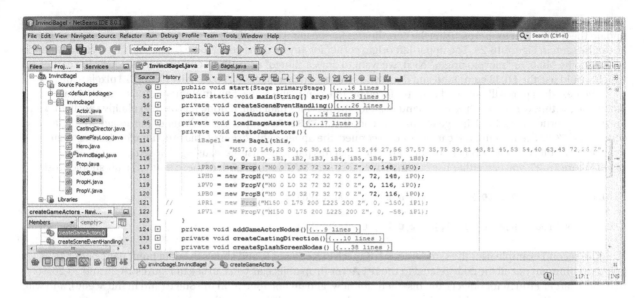

Figure 16-25. *Create collision polygon SVG data for the iP0 fixed Actor props using a prop0.png image 32×72 resolution*

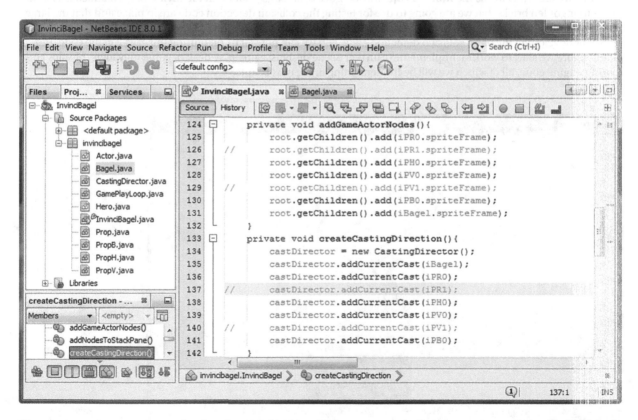

Figure 16-26. *Comment out code related to iP1 object in addGameActorNodes() and createCastingDirection() methods*

After you update your iBagel Bagel() constructor method, with accurate SVG data for your collision polygon, update the iP0 fixed Actor props, using the coordinates for the four corner pixels, to create a square collision polygon, as can be seen in Figure 16-25. The upper-left origin corner for any image is going to be **0,0**, so the first SVG command is going to be **M0,0**, or "moveto origin." Next, we want to draw a "lineto" using the **L** command, the lower-left corner, which would use the **L0,32** command and data set, since this brick image is 32 pixels tall (Y), and 72 pixels wide (X).

The next data pair will not need to be prefaced by an **L** command, since any implementation of an SVG data parsing algorithm will assume the command used for the previous data pair, if none has been explicitly specified. Your lower-right corner of the brick image will use X,Y coordinate **72,32**. The upper-right corner of this image would use X,Y coordinate **72,0**. The **Z** command can be used to connect the upper-right corner of this prop image with the origin, so that we have collision detection on the top of the brick, in this particular use-case, using a closed polygon. As you can see in Figure 16-25, you can either use commas or spaces with SVG data, so both of these method calls should work:

```
iPR0 = new Prop("M0 0 L0 32 72 32 72 0 Z", 0, 148, iP0);
                                                    OR:
iPR0 = new Prop("M0,0 L0,32 72,32 72,0 Z", 0, 148, iP0);
```

The second example uses the same amount of space in NetBeans 8, and shows the data point pairs better. I am going to comment out all the code related to the **iP1 Actor Prop** object, as you can see in Figures 16-25 and 16-26, so that these larger Prop Actor objects are "disabled" for now, and do not appear on the Stage (and in the Scene), and will not interfere with our basic code development for implementing collision detection.

Now we are ready to use the **Run ➤ Project** work process, and make sure that the InvinciBagel character, as well as the four golden bricks that we are going to use for testing the collision detection code are in place and that the large mossy rock objects are no longer anywhere to be seen on the Stage. As you can see in Figure 16-27, we have the Scene set up for developing the basic collision detection code, and we can now focus on putting this Java 8 game code into place, before we start to work on implementing further Scene designs, game play design, game play logic, physics and scoring engine code, all of which we will be implementing in the next chapter 17.

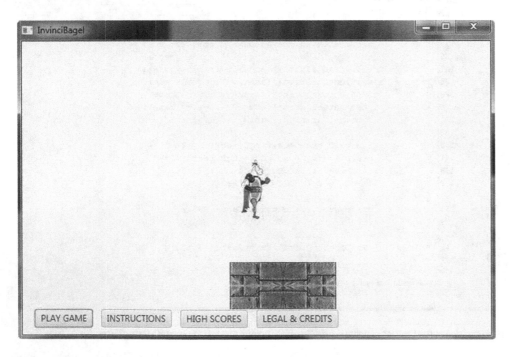

Figure 16-27. *Use the Run ➤ Project work process and test the game*

There are one or two basic changes that we'll need to make in the InvinciBagel.java class, before we switch over into the Bagel.java class to implement collision detection. Since we are going to use the CastingDirector object in the collision code, we'll have to remove the **private** access control keyword in the **CastingDirector castDirector;** declaration, as shown in Figure 16-28. We are trying to keep as many of the variables in our InvinciBagel class private as possible, and later make them package protected if we need to access them from another class, such as Bagel.java.

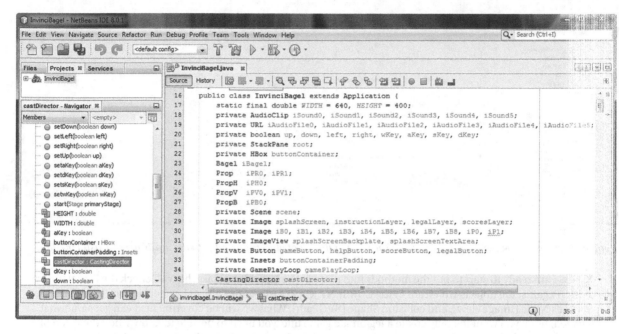

Figure 16-28. *Remove the private access control modifier keyword for CastingDirector castDirector object declaration*

The next thing that we'll want to do is to remove the **iBagel** object from the **.addCurrentCast()** method call parameter list in the createCastingDirection() method. We are doing this so that the InvinciBagel, who we are going to be checking for collision against the rest of the Actor objects, which are contained in the **CURRENT_CAST List<Actor>** object, does not check for collision against itself! The new shorter method call (minus the iBagel object) should look like the following Java code, which is shown highlighted at the bottom of Figure 16-29:

```
castDirector.addCurrentCast(iPR0, iPH0, iPV0, iPB0);
```

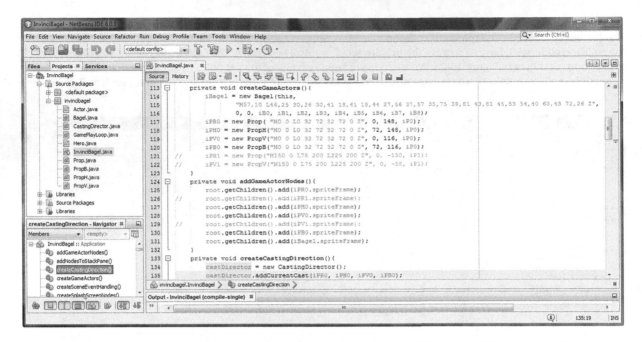

Figure 16-29. Remove the iBagel object from the front of the list of objects passed into the .addCurrentCast() method

Now we are ready to start to put the methods into place in the **Bagel.java** class that will check the iBagel object for collision against the objects which are in the CURRENT_CAST List<Actor> object by checking the boundaries for each object's Node (ImageView), and collision Shape (SVGPath). What we will be covering next can get somewhat complicated, but if you want to really create a legitimate game title, you need to be able to know when the game play elements **intersect** (called collide in game development terminology) with each other. Let's dive into that Abyss now!

Bagel Class Collision Detection: .checkCollision()

Right-click on the Bagel.java class in the Projects pane shown in Figure 16-29 and select the Open option and open up the Bagel.java tab in NetBeans 8. Go into the .update() method, and **comment out** the playAudioClip() method call, using two forward slashes at the beginning of the line of code. This will effectively turn off the audio for the KeyEvent (KeyCode) KeyPressed constant call-outs that we have in place. The reason I am doing this is because I am going to use this audio to "call out" a detected collision in the code that we're about to create. Next, create a **.checkCollision()** method call at the end of the methods that are called inside of the .update() method. This method will call collision detection Java code, which we are about to put into place during the remainder of this chapter, on every pulse event that is processed. This is in keeping with the logical sequence of game code processing inside of the .update() method.

The new .update() method, which is seen in Figure 16-30, should look like the following Java method body:

```java
public void update() {
    setXYLocation();
    setBoundaries();
    setImageState();
    moveInvinciBagel();
//  playAudioClip();
    checkCollision();
}
```

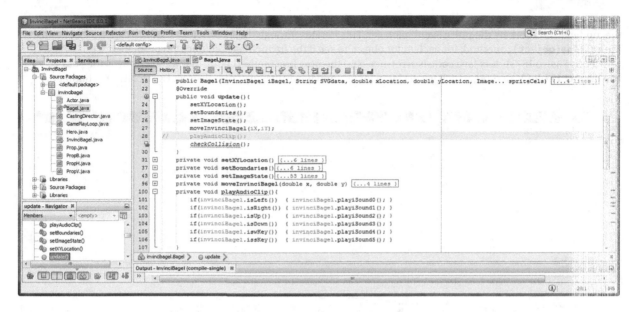

Figure 16-30. Comment out the playAudioClip() method call to turn off all audio and add a checkCollision() method call

Create an empty **public void checkCollision(){}** method body, which will remove that wavy red error highlighting that you see in Figure 16-30, so that we can begin to put the code into place that will look through the CURRENT_CAST List<Actor> object, so that we can ascertain if any of the cast members **intersect** (have collided with) the primary InvinciBagel character on the game Stage.

Inside of this **.checkCollision()** method, we will need a Java **for "counter" loop** structure. This structure will be used to traverse through your CURRENT_CAST List<Actor> array of objects; in this case, these are **Prop** objects, to check for any collisions (intersections) with the InvinciBagel object. The first part of the for loop is the iterator variable declaration and initialization, in our case, **int i=0;** to declare the integer type **iterator** variable named "i," initialized to a count value of zero.

The second part of the for loop is the **iteration condition**, which, in this case, is "iterate until you reach the end of the CURRENT_CAST List<Actor> object, or **i<invinciBagel.castDirector.getCurrentCast().size()** that represents the size of (and thus, the last item in) the List. The third part of the for loop statement condition is the amount to iterate by, and since we want to go over each object in the List<Actor> to check for collisions, we will use the familiar **Java ++ operator** on the "i" variable, or **i++**. Inside of the for loop {...} curly braces are the things that we want to perform during each iteration of the loop; in this case, this would be for each Prop Actor object that is in the List<Actor> object. This is a good construct to use to iterate any List objects from the first element to the last element.

Inside of the for loop, we are going to create a "local" Actor object reference variable, which we are going to set equal to the **current element** in the List(i), using the **invinciBagel.castDirector.getCurrentCast().get(i)** method chain. Java method chains are a cool way to create compact Java code structures, aren't they? Once we have loaded that Actor object with the CURRENT_CAST(i) cast member object, we will then call the **.collide()** method, using the collide(object); Java statement. Remember that we installed this abstract .collide() method in our Hero superclass, so we are going to have to "Override" and code that method next, after we learn more about the **Node** and **Shape** classes, and a couple of their key methods and properties that can be used to determine intersections (collisions).

```java
public void checkCollision() {
    for(int i=0; i<invinciBagel.castDirector.getCurrentCast().size(); i++) {
        Actor object = invinciBagel.castDirector.getCurrentCast().get(i);
        collide(object);
    }
}
```

This is the first (easy) part of determining collisions, in this first checkCollision() method, called from inside of the .update() method, by the pulse event manager. This iterates through the List<Actor> CURRENT_CAST and calls the **collide(object);** method, for each Actor object, to see if the InvinciBagel character has collided with it. As you can see in Figure 16-31, this Java code is error-free, and the next Java method body that we will code is the **public boolean collide()** method, which we declared for use previously inside of our abstract Hero class, in Chapter 8.

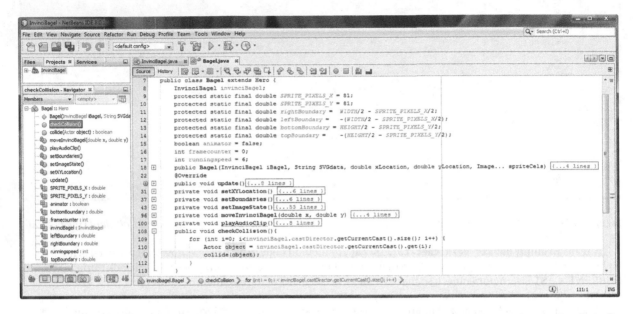

Figure 16-31. *Add a for loop, counting from 0 to number of objects in the CURRENT_CAST using .getCurrentCast().size()*

Before we code the .collide() method, which is one of the more difficult method bodies that we'll be coding during this entire book, we'll need to look at some of the more complex topics relating to the **javafx.scene** package's **Node** class, and its **Bounds** property, and **.getBoundsInLocal()** and **.getBoundsInparent()** method call. We will also be looking at the **javafx.scene.shape** package's **Shape** class, and its **.intersect(Shape shape1, Shape shape2)** method call. We will be using all of these inside of our **public boolean collide(Actor object) {...}** method, so we will need to have this advanced knowledge in place first, before we write this complex and dense (but exciting) Java structure.

Locating a Node Object: Using the Bounds Object

The first thing that we need to look at regarding collision detection is the **javafx.geometry** package's **Bounds** class. This **public abstract** class (and the objects that it creates) is utilized in the **javafx.scene** package's **Node** class to hold the **boundaries** for the Node. As you may have surmised, this is one of the things that we will leverage to determine collision detection, in conjunction with our collision SVGPath Shape data, which we will get into after we take a look at how this Bounds object, and its related **.getBoundsInLocal()** and **.getBoundsInParent()** methods, can work for us.

This Bounds class was created from scratch, using the java.lang.Object master class, and contains **X**, **Y**, and **Z** coordinates, as well as **width**, **height**, and **depth** values. Since we will be working in 2D, we will be using the X and Y, as well as the width and height, values (properties) of the Bounds object. The Bounds class has a single direct known subclass, called BoundingBox. In case you are wondering, a "direct subclass" means the BoundingBox class declaration says BoundingBox **extends** Bounds, and a "known" class is one that has been **officially** added into the Java 8 JDK.

An example of an "unknown" class would be one of your own customized Bounds subclasses, if you were to write one, that is. The Java 8 class hierarchy for the javafx.geometry.Bounds class would look like the following:

```
java.lang.Object
  > javafx.geometry.Bounds
```

The Bounds class is used to create Bounds objects. These are used to describe the Bounds of a Node object, which as we know are JavaFX Scene Graph Node objects. An important characteristic of a Bounds object is that it can have a **negative** width, height, or depth. A negative value for any of the Bounds object attributes (properties) is used to indicate that the Bounds object is **empty**. We will be using this in our code later on to ascertain when a collision has **not** occurred. As I pointed out earlier in this book, sometimes you have to take the "opposite" approach to finding the solution, or the proper work process, for achieving your game design and programming objectives.

Using Node Local Bounds: The .getBoundsInLocal() Method

One of the important methods in the JavaFX Scene Graph Node class is the **public final Bounds .getBoundsInLocal()** method. This method is the getter method that retrieves the value of the boundsInLocal property. The boundsInLocal property is "read-only" and holds a rectangular Bounds object for the Node it is contained in. The data that it contains represents **untransformed** (original) local coordinate space for a Node. Untransformed means the Node coordinates prior to their being **rotated**, **translated**, or **scaled**, which represents the Node object's original (default) coordinates.

For a Node class (object) that extends the Shape class (which our ImageView Node does not), the local Bounds will also include the space required to implement a non-zero Shape (or Path) **stroke**, as this might extend "outside" of the Shape geometry, which is being defined by these position and size attributes. A **local Bounds** object also includes any **clipping path** areas that you may have set, as well as the extents of any **special effects** that you may have set.

The **boundsInLocal** property will always have a **non-null** value, and it is important to note that this method does not take the Node object's visibility into account, so the computation is based on the geometry of the Node only. The boundsInLocal property is automatically computed whenever the geometry of a Node object changes.

We will be using the .getBoundsInLocal() method on an intersection of our InvinciBagel SVGPath Shape data with our other Scene Actor Prop SVGPath collision Shape data, in order to ascertain if the width of the intersection is negative one, as -1 in a Bounds object, as we have learned, is empty, or **no intersection**, which signifies **no collision**. Next, let's take a look at the **boundsInParent** property, which contains the boundsInLocal data plus transformations.

Using Node Parent Bounds: The .getBoundsInParent() Method

Another one of those important methods to understand in the JavaFX Scene Graph Node class is the **public final Bounds .getBoundsInParent()** method. This method is the getter method that retrieves the value of the boundsInParent property. The boundsInParent property is a "read-only" property that holds the rectangular Bounds object for the Node it is contained in. The data that it contains represents the **transformed** (modified) coordinate space for a Node. Transformed means the Node coordinates plus any transforms that have taken place since the Node object's default, initial or original state. It is named "boundsInParent" because the Bounds object rectangle data will need to be relative to the Parent Node object's coordinate system. This represents the 'visual' bounds of the Node object, as in what you see on the screen, after the Node has been **moved**, **rotated**, **scaled**, **skewed**, and so on.

The **boundsInParent** property is calculated by taking a local Bounds, defined by the boundsInLocal property, and applying all of the transforms that have taken place, including any calls to .set() methods for the following Node properties: **scaleX**, **scaleY**, **rotate**, **layoutX**, **layoutY**, **translateX**, **translateY**, and **transforms** (the Java ObservableList). Just like the boundsInLocal property, this boundsInParent property will always contain a **non-null** value.

A resulting Bounds object will be contained **inside of** the **coordinate space** of a Node object's Parent object, however, the Node object need not have a Parent (it can be the Scene Graph root of the Scene) in order to be able to calculate the boundsInParent attribute. Just like the .getBoundsInLocal() method, this method does not take the Node object's visibility into account, so don't make the mistake of thinking you can circumvent your collision detection code by "hiding" your Actor Node, which, in our case, is an ImageView Node subclass named **spriteFrame**.

Since it computes changes to the boundsInLocal property, it is logical that the boundsInParent property will be computed whenever the geometry of a Node changes, or when any transformations of that Node object occur. For this very reason it would be a mistake to compute any of these values in a Node based on an expression that depends upon this variable. For example, the X or Y variables of a Node object, or translateX, translateY shouldn't be computed using this boundsInParent property for the purpose of positioning the Node, since prior positioning data is included in this property, and thus would create a **circular reference** (somewhat akin to the infamous infinite loop scenario).

Using Node Intersection: The .intersects(Bounds object) Method

Another important method in the JavaFX Scene Graph Node class where collision detection is concerned is the **public boolean intersects(Bounds localBounds)** method. This method will return a true value if the Bounds object that specifies the local coordinate space for the Node object that this method is being called "off of" intersects the Bounds object passed into the method using the parameter, which is the Bounds object of the Node that you are trying to determine intersection with. For instance, to determine if the ImageView Bounds that contains the InvinciBagel sprite intersects the ImageView Bounds that contains one of the Prop sprites, we would use the following Java code format:

```
iBagel.spriteFrame.getBoundsInParent().intersects(object.getSpriteFrame().getBoundsInParent());
```

It is important to note that just like the .getBoundsInLocal() and .getBoundsInParent() methods, this method also does not take the Node object's visibility attribute into account. For this reason, an intersection test will be based on **geometry** for the Node objects in question only, and for our ImageView spriteFrame Node objects, which would be the geometry (dimensions) of their **square** (InvinciBagel) or **rectangular** (Prop) Image containers. The default behavior of the Node class **intersects(Bounds localBounds)** function is to check and see if local coordinates for a Bounds object that is passed into this method call intersects with the local Bounds coordinates of the Node that the .intersects() method call is being called "off of." Next, let's take a closer look at the Shape superclass, and its .intersect() method.

Using Shape Class Intersect: The .intersect() Method

Just like a Node class (object) has an intersection method called .intersects() that is used to determine when Node objects intersect, the Shape class also has an intersection method, which you can use for Shape object intersection. This method is called **.intersect()** (rather than intersects), so that these methods use different naming conventions. This was probably done so developers won't be quite as confused between Node.intersects() and Shape.intersect() methods. We will be using both of these in our collision detection code later on in the chapter—first to detect when an ImageView Node overlaps another ImageView Node, and then to do a Boolean intersection operation between our SVG data collision polygons (SVGPath objects named spriteBounds within each Actor object).

The **static** method format for the Shape class's .intersect() method takes two Shape objects in its parameter list, and this method returns a new Shape object. The new Shape object that is created represents an intersection of (between) two input shapes. As you can imagine, you can also use this method to do Boolean intersection generation for your vector artwork if you are using the Shape class and its subclasses for this purpose. The format for the method is **static Shape intersect(Shape shape1, Shape shape2)**, and the way that we're going to use it looks like this:

```
Shape shape = SVGPath.intersect(invinciBagel.iBagel.getSpriteBound(), object.getSpriteBound());
```

The reason that the Shape class's .intersect() method works so well for our collision detection application is because we can later use a **.getBoundsInLocal().getWidth()** method chain, to determine if a collision has occurred, or rather, if it has **not** occurred by looking for a **-1 empty** value. We'll call this method chain that looks for a -1 off of this new Shape object, which we will name **intersection**, in our **.collide(object)** method, using the following line of code:

```
if (intersection.getBoundsInLocal().getWidth() != -1) { collisionDetect = true; }
```

The way this .intersect() method works is that it only processes the **geometric data** that occupies your input shapes, which in our application is the **spriteBound** SVGPath object inside of our Actor objects. This is why we're using an SVGPath Shape object (for maximum collision cage or polygon definition), purely for its geometric data values, and why we've installed this spriteBounds SVGPath Shape object container in our Actor object design, because we intend on using this geometric data for our collision detection, and not for vector illustration artwork (we are not stroking, or filling, the SVGPath, for instance, and please, no subtle jokes here folks, we're learning game development right now).

What this means is that the geometric areas of the input Shape objects being considered by the algorithm in the .intersect() method is "math based" only. This means the algorithm is independent of the type of Shape (subclass) being processed, as well as independent of configuration for the Paint object being used for filling or stroking (please, again briefly resist the temptation to snicker one more time, for the sake of learning Java 8 game development).

Before the final intersection calculation, the areas of the input Shape objects are transformed to the Parent Node object's coordinate space (think: boundsInParent). In this way, the resulting shape will only include those areas (mathematical geometric areas, more precisely) which were contained in the areas of the two input Shape objects passed into the method using the parameter list. Therefore, if there's any data (something other than a -1 empty data value) in the resulting Shape object, which we will be calling intersection in the code we will be writing next, there has been some level of intersection, and even a small area of intersection (overlap) needs to signal a detected collision.

Now we are ready to use the technical Java 8 class and method information that we have learned over the past several pages of the chapter to create the core collision detection logic using only around a dozen lines of Java code. We'll add another dozen lines of code before the end of the chapter, to process the collision for our game play.

Overriding the Abstract Hero Class: .collide() Method

Finally the time has come to **override** and implement the **public boolean collide (Actor object)** method that we installed in our abstract Hero class back in Chapter 8. This is a critical method to our game play, as it determines when our primary InvinciBagel character comes into contact with other elements in the game. The result of this contact is scoring, as well as things changing visually on the game screen, so it becomes pivotal to everything that we will be doing in the next chapter to implement game play elements into the InvinciBagel game. The first thing we want to do is to install a Boolean "flag" variable called **collisionDetect**, and set it equal to a **false** value (collision not detected) at the top of the .collide() method. The Java code for this statement setting up the collisionDetect flag should look like the following:

```
boolean collisionDetect = false;
```

The next step in determining if a collision has occurred is to use a Java conditional if() statement. This allows us to test if the ImageView Node objects that contain the sprite Image assets have intersected by using the Node class .intersects() method call in conjunction with the .getBoundsInParent() method call off of each spriteFrame ImageView Node object. The first spriteFrame.getBoundsInParent() method call is the one that we method chain the .intersects() method call off of, since what we are trying to do is to ascertain collision with our primary game character. Since we want to reference the invinciBagel object (InvinciBagel class) and its iBagel Actor object, this construct would take the form of an **invinciBagel.iBagel.spriteFrame.getBoundsInParent().intersects()** method call structure. Since the Bounds object from the Actor object that we are testing for collision needs to be inside of the .intersects(Bounds localBounds) method call, we need to use the **.getSpriteFrame()** method call we developed in

Chapter 8. Off of the Actor object we pass into the .collide() method we will method chain the .getBoundsInParent() method call, resulting in the **object.getSpriteFrame().getBoundsInParent()** structure, which is then placed on the inside of an .intersect() method call. The complete conditional if() construct looks like this:

```
if( invinciBagel.iBagel.spriteFrame.getBoundsInParent().intersects(
    object.getSpriteFrame().getBoundsInParent() ) ){second level of collision detection in here}
```

This first level of collision detection code will check for the intersection of the iBagel spriteFrame ImageView Node with the spriteFrame ImageView Node object that is contained in each Actor object that will be passed into this .collide(Actor object) method call that we are coding currently.

This part of the code will check for a "top level" ImageView Node proximity (collision) before we call a more "expensive" Shape intersection algorithm, which we are going to implement next, in order to confirm more definitive collision occurrence (SVGPath collision polygon intersection). Remember that the code we're putting into place inside of this .collide() method will be processed for each iteration of the for loop (for each cast member) that is calling this collide(Actor object) method.

The Java code inside of this first conditional if() statement creates a **Shape** object, named **intersection**, and sets it equal to the result of an **SVGPath.intersect()** method call that references the iBagel SVGPath Shape object and an SVGPath Shape object passed into the collide(Actor object) method. Both objects call a **.getSpriteBound()** method, which we created back in Chapter 8, to access the SVGPath Shape objects needed for the **.intersect(Shape1, Shape2)** method call format. Your Java code, formatted using two lines of code, for readability, should look like the following:

```
Shape intersection = SVGPath.intersect( invinciBagel.iBagel.getSpriteBound(),
                                         object.getSpriteBound() );
```

After we have this intersection data, we will use another conditional if() statement to see if that intersection Shape object contains any collision data, and if it does (that is, if it doesn't contain a -1 value) a collision has occurred.

The second nested if() statement will utilize the **.getBoundsInLocal().getWidth()** method chain, called off of the intersection Shape object, and will check to see if it is empty (returns a -1 value), or if a collision has occurred. The collision detection will occur if the intersection Shape object's Bounds object contains any data value other than -1. In the body of the if() statement, collisionDetect Boolean flag is set to true of any data is present (signified by != -1). The Java code for the conditional if() statement should look like the following:

```
if(intersection.getBoundsInLocal().getWidth() != -1) { collisionDetect = true; }
```

To test the collision code, I put the **invinciBagel.playiSound0()** method call inside of the **if(collisionDetect){}** conditional statement. This is why I commented out that .playAudioClip() method call in the .update() method, so that the only thing that I will hear during a collision is the audio playback. This is a quick, easy, and effective way to test the collision code, at least for now. Since this is the **public boolean collide(Actor object)** method, I am also going to put a **return true;** line of code at the end of the if() body, that returns a **true** value from the method call. I am placing the statement inside of this conditional if() construct, so that if needed, we can use this true Boolean value returned from the .collide() method call in the .update() method for other processing, if we want to. The very nature of this .collide() method is to detect if a collision has occurred and then **return** a value, so we could do further processing inside of the .collide() method, or more efficiently do this on-collision processing inside of the .checkCollision() method, using an **if(collide(object)=true){invinciBagel.playiSound0();}** construct, instead of the way that we are doing this here with the statement processing inside of the .collide() method. The reason I am doing it this way, at least for now, is because I am testing this .collide() method, so I'm putting the statements that allow me to test the .collide() method inside of that .collide() method since that is where I'm working within the IDE right now. The Java code looks like this:

```java
if(collisionDetect) {
    invinciBagel.playiSound0();
    return true;
}
return false;
```

The complete .collide(Actor object) method structure, before we get into manipulating the CastingDirector class and object List<Actor> objects, should look like the following, which can also be seen in Figure 16-32:

```java
@Override
public boolean collide(Actor object) {
    boolean collisionDetect = false;
    if ( invinciBagel.iBagel.spriteFrame.getBoundsInParent().intersects(
        object.getSpriteFrame().getBoundsInParent() ) ) {
            Shape intersection =
            SVGPath.intersect(invinciBagel.iBagel.getSpriteBound(), object.getSpriteBound());
            if (intersection.getBoundsInLocal().getWidth() != -1) {
                collisionDetect = true;
            }
    }
    if(collisionDetect) {
        invinciBagel.playiSound0();
        return true;
    }
    return false;
}
```

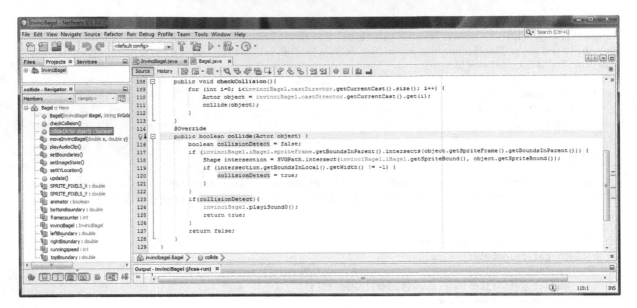

Figure 16-32. *Creating the basic collision detection code and testing it using the invinciBagel.playiSound0() method call*

Now we're ready to add the Java code that manages the CastingDirector object, to remove the Actor object.

If Collision Detected: Manipulating the CastingDirector Object

Add a line of code under the .playiSound0() method call, accessing the CastingDirector object, **invinciBagel. castDirector**. Next type a **period** key, to access a method helper pop-up, seen in Figure 16-33, and select **.addToRemovedActors()**.

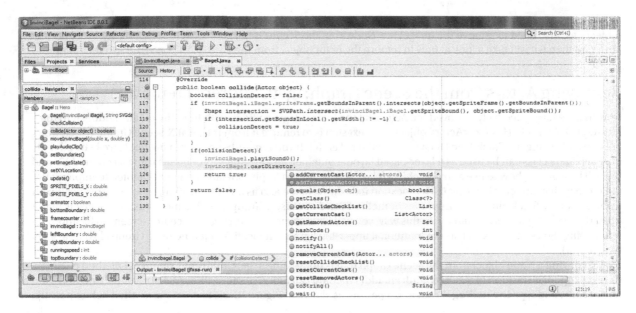

Figure 16-33. *Add a line of code under the .playiSound0() method call, and type invinciBagel.castDirector, and a period*

After you double-click on the **.addToRemoveActors(Actor... actors)** option in this pop-up helper dialog, you will need to pass the Actor object, aptly named **object**, into the method call using the parameter list area inside of the parentheses, as shown highlighted at the bottom of Figure 16-34. This will add this Actor object that was just involved in a collision (luckily, no one was hurt) to the REMOVED_ACTORS HashSet<Actor> object.

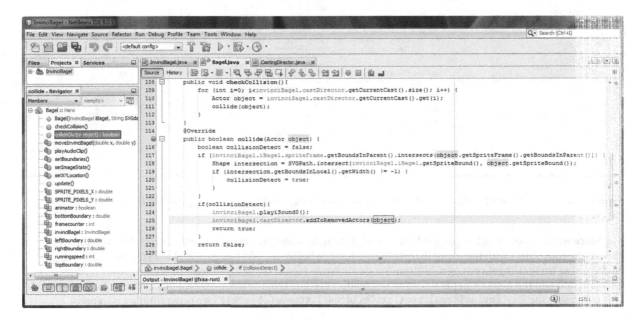

Figure 16-34. *Add Actor object that was passed into the .collide() method to parameter list of addToRemovedActors()*

Not only do we need to remove this collided Actor object from the game cast using the CastingDirector class (object), we also need to remove the ImageView Node from the Scene Graph root as well. Let's look at how to do that next, and then we will take a look at how to remove the Actor object from the CURRENT_CAST List<Actor> after that.

Removing Actors from the Scene Graph: .getChildren().remove()

Now that we have effectively removed the Actor that the InvinciBagel collided with from the cast by adding it to the REMOVED_ACTORS HashSet<Actor> object, the next step is to remove it from the JavaFX Scene Graph, which we are currently using the StackPane UI layout container class for. If you remember earlier in the book, we learned that the StackPane class can be used as a layer-based layout container, and arranges its contents using a centered XY grid. We will be learning how to use a **Group** object (class) as our Scene Graph root later on in the chapter, to implement the more typical upper-left corner 0,0 XY location indexing scheme and as an optimization, as we are not specifically using any of the StackPane class properties or methods, and because a Group class is a more basic class that is higher up in the Node superclass hierarchy. In this way, you will have experienced using both center screen 0,0 location referencing (StackPane), as well as the traditional upper-left 0,0 screen location referencing (a Group class as a Scene Graph root).

Removing a Node object from the Scene Graph root is done using a **.getChildren().remove()** method chain, in the exact opposite fashion of the **.getChildren.add()** method call found in the .addGameActorNodes() method. Add a line of code, and type **invinciBagel.root** and a **period**, as shown in Figure 16-35, to open the method helper pop-up.

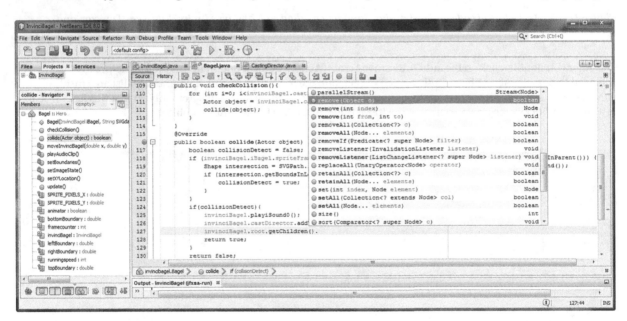

Figure 16-35. *Add a line of code under an .addToRemovedActors() method call and type invinciBagel.root and a period*

Since we are doing this ImageView Node removal from the Bagel.java class, we will use Java dot notation to preface the root object with the invinciBagel object reference before we add the .getChildren() method call, using the following **invinciBagel.root.getChildren()** code shown in Figure 16-35. Double-click on the **remove(Object o)** selection and add the object you passed into the .collide() method into the .remove() method, as seen in Figure 16-36. This will create the final **invinciBagel.root.getChildren().remove(object);** Java programming statement.

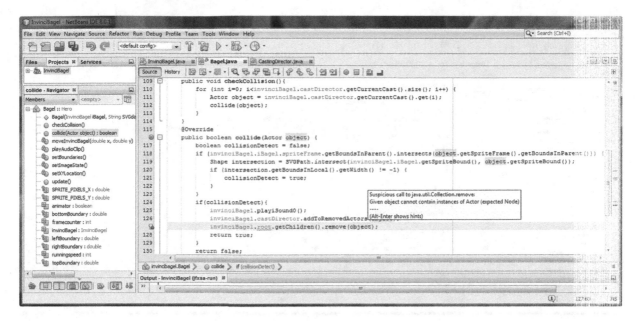

Figure 16-36. *Investigate red error highlight under the Scene Graph root StackPane object reference in the method call*

Mouse-over the warning highlighting, and you will see that NetBeans sees that we are passing our custom Actor object to the .getChildren().remove() method chain, instead of the ImageView Node object. The error message also tells us that the **private StackPane root;** declaration in our **InvinciBagel.java** class will not allow us to access this object, until we remove this **private** access control modifier keyword. Let's fix the most serious (error) problem first, and then fix the "Suspicious method call to java.util.Collection.remove" after that by using an **object.getSpriteFrame()** method call, inside of the current .remove() method call.

Click on the InvinciBagel.java editing tab in NetBeans and remove the **private** keyword from the front of the **StackPane root;** object declaration, as is shown highlighted in Figure 16-37.

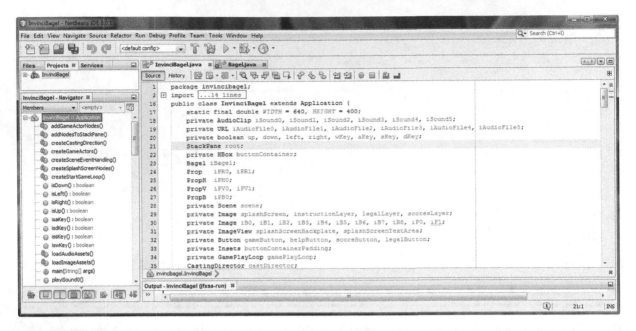

Figure 16-37. *Remove the private access control modifier keyword from in front of the StackPane root; Java statement*

Once you make this modification, you will see the wavy red error highlighting in your current programming statement in the Bagel.java disappear, as shown in Figure 16-38, and all we have to worry about now is removing the warning highlighting that pertains to passing an Actor object to be removed from the Scene Graph rather than a Node object (a spriteFrame ImageView) that it is expecting. This is because the JavaFX Scene Graph manages Node classes, as well as Node subclasses such as ImageView, and does not accept non-Node-subclasses, such as the Actor class that we designed in Chapter 8, and have implemented during subsequent chapters. Our Actor class (object) does contain a Node object, an ImageView Node subclass, inside of it, so we have to include a reference to this object, using Java dot notation, so the .remove() method can effectively look "inside" of our Actor object to reach (access) this Node object.

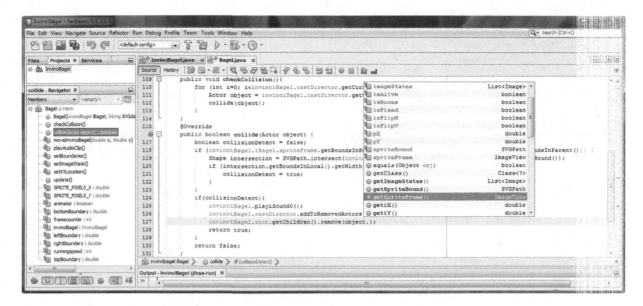

Figure 16-38. *Add a period after object in the .remove() method to open method helper and select .getSpriteFrame()*

Place your cursor after the object reference that is inside of the .remove() method call that we are working on implementing, and type a **period**. This will bring up the attribute (property) and method helper pop-up, shown in Figure 16-38. Double-click on the **getSpriteFrame()** method, which we created back in Chapter 8, to call it off of the current Actor object which has been passed into the .collide() method. This will pass an ImageView Node object over inside of the .remove() method call, as expected, and the warning highlighting will also disappear, leaving clean code.

As you can see in Figure 16-39, all of your Java code is error-free, and you have now played a sound, added this Actor object to the HashSet<Actor> REMOVED_ACTORS data set, and removed the spriteFrame ImageView Node object for this Actor from the JavaFX Scene Graph root (currently a StackPane layout container). We are now ready to remove this Actor object from the CURRENT_CAST List<Actor> object, by using a **.resetRemovedActors()** method call.

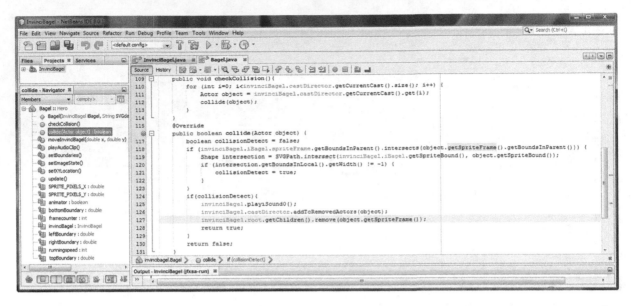

Figure 16-39. *Remove the currently collided with Actor object ImageView Node from the Scene Graph using .remove()*

After we update the CURRENT_CAST List, we will have done our basic collision management coding, and we can take a look at how we can optimize the .checkCollision() and .collide() methods to work together more efficiently.

Reset the Removed Actor List: .resetRemovedActors() Method

The final thing that we need to do in the series of programming statements that need to happen when a collision occurs is to reset the REMOVED_ACTORS HashSet<Actor> object. As you recall from Chapter 10, this method removes the removed actors from the CURRENT_CAST List<Actor> object, so that the Actor object is completely removed from the game entirely. Besides the .playiSound0() method call we are using to test this method using our ears, this is one of the simplest Java programming statements that we will have to code, and should look like the following Java code:

```
invinciBagel.castDirector.resetRemovedActors();
```

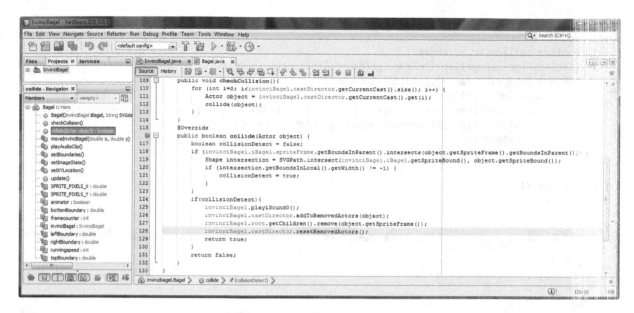

Figure 16-40. *The finished .collide() method is error-free and only 19 lines of code, and is ready for further optimization*

If you use a **Run ➤ Project** work process, and test your game code now, you will not only hear the audio, you will also see the Prop objects disappear upon collision with the InvinciBagel object. I'm going to leave the audio in this code for now, so you can test to see if these Actor objects are really gone by have the InvinciBagel run (or fly) over the area where the Prop object was to make sure (using your ears) that it's really gone. Next, we'll optimize the code even more, by implementing the **if(collide(object))** approach that I mentioned earlier, having the .collide() method simply return a **true** (collision detected) or **false** (no collision detected) value, as a properly behaved Boolean method should.

Optimizing Collision Detection Processing: if(collide(object))

To optimize the collision detection process, we'll move code that is executed on collision up to the **.checkCollision()** method, inside of an **if(collide(object)){}** conditional if block of Java code. This allows us to eliminate a Boolean **collisionDetect** variable from the collide() method, making it much more streamlined. All we are doing now in the .collide() method is pass the **return true;** statement back up to the calling entity, in this case, the .checkCollision() method, if a collision is detected. This also allows us to completely eliminate the **if(collisionDetect)** structure as well.

Before this optimization, we had 6 lines of code in the **.checkCollision()** method, and 19 lines of code in the .collide() method. After the optimization, we have 5 less lines of Java code, with 10 lines of code in each method. The new Java structures for these methods are error-free, as shown in Figure 16-41, and look like the following Java code:

```java
public void checkCollision() {
    for(int i=0; i<invinciBagel.castDirector.getCurrentCast().size(); i++) {
        Actor object = invinciBagel.castDirector.getCurrentCast().get(i);
        If (collide(object)) {
            invinciBagel.playiSound0();
            invinciBagel.castDirector.addToRemovedActors(object);
            invinciBagel.root.getChildren().remove(object.getSpriteFrame());
            invinciBagel.castDirector.resetRemovedActors();
        }
    }
}
```

```
}
@Override
public boolean collide(Actor object) {
    if (invinciBagel.iBagel.spriteFrame.getBoundsInParent().intersects(
        object.getSpriteFrame().getBoundsInParent() ) ) {
            Shape intersection =
            SVGPath.intersect(invinciBagel.iBagel.getSpriteBound(), object.getSpriteBound());
            if (intersection.getBoundsInLocal().getWidth() != -1) {
                return true;
            }
    }
    return false;
}
```

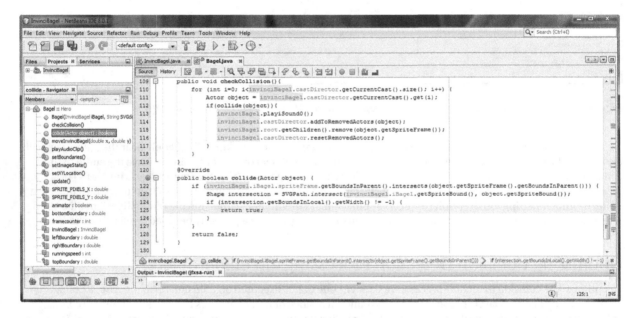

Figure 16-41. *Optimizing the interaction between the collide() method and the checkCollision() method*

Use the **Run ➤ Project** work process to make sure the code works as it did before the method optimizations.

Optimizing the Scene Graph: Using the Group Class

Since we're not really using the StackPane for image layer compositing or UI design, other than the splashscreen use, let's add another optimization, and use a **Group** class (object) for our game, since it is further up the class hierarchy, and closer to the Node superclass than the more specialized StackPane class (object) is. Rather than using a class that uses the more complex **Object ➤ Node ➤ Parent ➤ Region ➤ Pane ➤ StackPane** hierarchy, we will use the much shorter and simpler **Object ➤ Node ➤ Parent ➤ Group** hierarchy. The significance of this optimization is that using a Group root Node uses a lot less code (properties and methods) in system memory. Since we are not specifically using any of the highly specialized StackPane properties or methods, we can perform a major optimization by using a Group class. A Group object (class) uses **fixed** object positioning, so we will have to redo the code for our **HBox** and Actor objects, but only after we use the **Run ➤ Project** work process to see exactly how using a Group differs from using a StackPane. After all, it's all about learning how these classes work! The Java code for changing a StackPane object's import, declaration, and instantiation into a Group object should look like the following Java code, which is also shown in Figure 16-42:

```
import javafx.scene.Group;                    // replaced StackPane import with Group
public class InvinciBagel extends Application {  // all other object declarations omitted
    Group root;
    public void start(Stage primaryStage) {      // all other object instantiations omitted
        root = new Group();
```

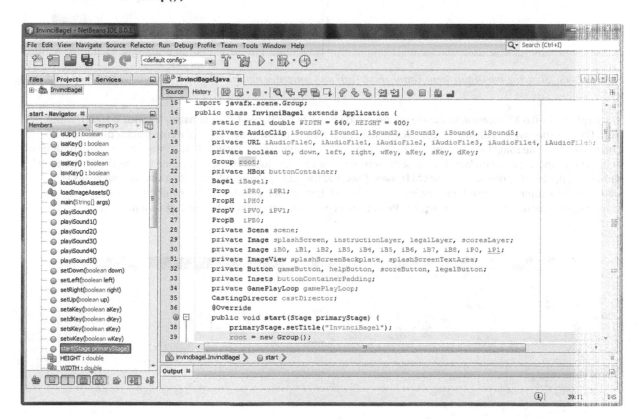

Figure 16-42. *Replace the StackPane UI container with the Group (Node subclass) import, declaration and instantiation*

After you make these changes and **Run ➤ Project**, you'll see the result shown on the left half of Figure 16-43. The game is now using an upper-left 0,0 origin, so we'll have to modify the rest of the existing code. Let's do that now.

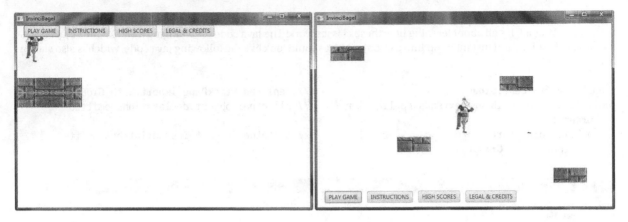

Figure 16-43. *Showing the Group Scene Graph result (left) and corrective modification to HBox, iBagel and Prop (right)*

Replace the 0,0 XY location in the iBagel instantiation call to the Bagel() class constructor with **WIDTH/2** and **HEIGHT/2** respectively. This uses screen size constants and calculation code inside of a constructor method call, which will place the iBagel at the center of the screen. Add some different numbers in the Prop object instantiations as well, to place these tiles at different areas of the screen so we can develop some scoring code next as the InvinciBagel picks them up. Finally, replace the **.setAlignment(Pos.BOTTOM_LEFT);** method call with a **.setLayoutY(365);** method call to implement fixed positioning of the HBox UI Button elements back where they were before when we were using StackPane. If you use the **Run ➤ Project** work process, you will see the result shown on the right half of Figure 16-43.

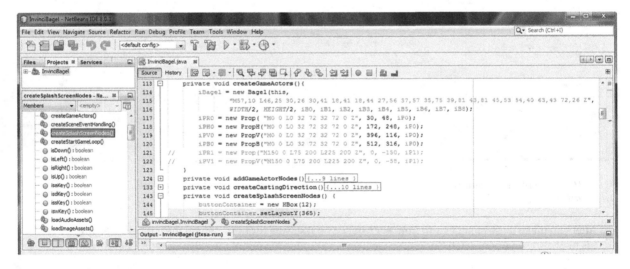

Figure 16-44. *Use .setLayoutY() method to position HBox, WIDTH/2 and HEIGHT/2 to position iBagel, and new Prop X,Y*

When you test your collision code, you will find that you cannot get to some of these tiles! Let's fix this next.

Go into the Bagel.java class and modify the screen boundary constants at the top of the class so that the left and the top boundaries use the 0,0 origin values, since the Group class uses the upper-left corner of your screen as its point of reference, rather than the center of the screen, as the StackPane does. To calculate the **rightBoundary** value, you would take the **WIDTH** of the screen and subtract the width of the sprite using the **SPRITE_PIXELS_X** constant. A similar approach would be used for the bottomBoundary value, which will take the **HEIGHT** of the screen and subtract the height of the sprite using the **SPRITE_PIXELS_Y** constant. As you can see in Figure 16-45, we don't have to change the .setBoundaries() method at all, thanks to the modular, logical and organized way that we have set up our code.

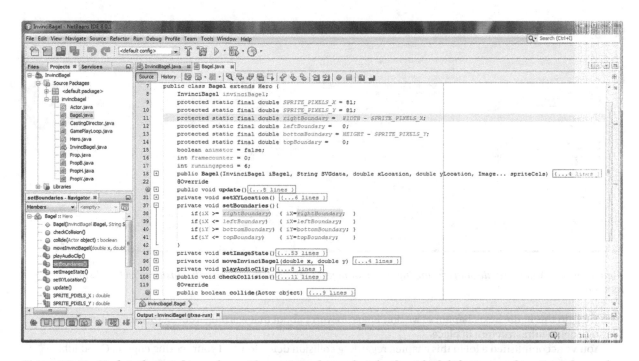

Figure 16-45. *Update the Bagel.java class with new Boundary values for the right, left, bottom and top Boundary value*

Before we finish up with the chapter, let's add a scoring engine framework to our game, so that this collision detection routine calls a scoringEngine method, in addition to playing a sound and removing the Actor from the game.

Creating a Scoring Engine Method: .scoringEngine()

Before we finish up with this chapter, let's put a framework in place for the scoring engine, so we can focus the entire next chapter on game play. Create a **private void scoringEngine(Actor object){}** empty method right after the checkCollision() method, and add a **scoringEngine(object);** method call at the end of the **if(collide(object))** conditional if() structure, inside of the checkCollision() method. As you can see in Figure 16-46, you will get one wavy gray warning highlight under the Actor object reference inside of the .scoringEngine() method declaration. This is because the object reference has not been implemented inside of the method body.

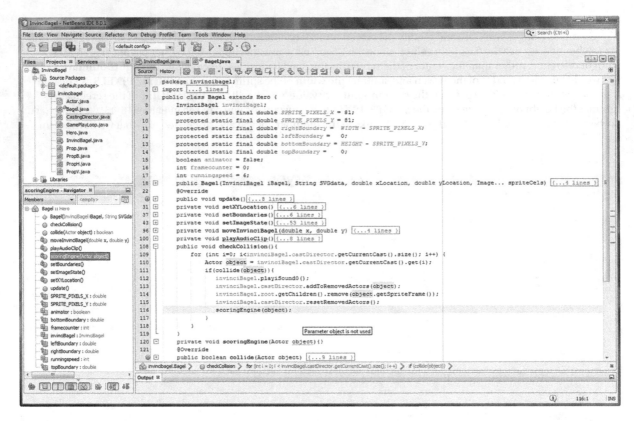

Figure 16-46. *Add a private void scoringEngine(Actor object) empty method, and call if inside .checkCollision() method*

We'll do this in the next chapter, so we don't have to worry about that warning from NetBeans, and we have our scoring engine infrastructure in place.

You've accomplished a lot in this chapter, regarding collision detection and your scoring engine. Good Job!

Summary

In this sixteenth chapter, we started in on some of the more advanced topics that we will be covering during the last couple of chapters in this book. **Collision detection** is one of the foundational topics of game development, whether this is using Java 8, or any other platform, for that matter. In this chapter we learned about the **SVG data format** specification, so that we can leverage the JavaFX **SVGPath** class, which allows us to access **custom path shapes**, often called **polygons**, if they are closed, and which collision shapes, or **collision polygons**, usually are. We looked at the seven primary commands within the SVG specification, all of which can be used in **absolute** or **relative mode**.

Next we took a detailed look at how to get GIMP 2.8 to create custom collision shape SVG data strings for us using a fully automated process that uses only GIMP tools (algorithms) to allow us to simply click on transparent areas and have GIMP generate the selection set. We converted the selection set into a collision path, and then exported the path as SVG data. This work process allows us to generate complex collision polygons with transparent (alpha channel data) areas within any of the game asset digital images.

This auto-generated collision data is very "heavy," so we looked at a more involved work process, allowing us to create collision polygons by hand using fewer data point pairs. This process involved using the Path Tool in GIMP to create a collision polygon by hand, which gave us far more control over generating as few data points as possible. We also looked at the CodeAndWeb PhysicsEditor software, which can be used across all game development platforms.

In the next chapter, we are going take a look at how to implement enhanced game play elements into a game, including the scoring engine, adversaries, treasure, an auto-attack engine, and physics simulation.

CHAPTER 17

■ ■ ■

Enhancing Game Play: Creating a Scoring Engine, Adding Treasure and an Enemy Auto-Attack Engine

Now that we've implemented collision detection for our game, as well as putting the foundation in place for a scoring engine, let's finish coding the scoring engine that is called from the **.checkCollisions()** method, and then add some more game play elements to take advantage of this scoring engine, as well as to make the game play more interesting. To implement our scoring engine display, we will create a **gameScore** integer variable and **scoreText** Text object in our InvinciBagel.java class. We will also create a **scoreFont** Font object, and use it to style the scoreText Text object, to make it stand out better. We will also learn how to use the Java **instanceof** evaluator in the conditional if() statement in the **.scoringEngine()** method that we will be creating, and use this to determine what type of Actor object the InvinciBagel has collided with. Of course, we will then increment our gameScore variable accordingly.

We'll also create a **Treasure.java** class, so that we can add valuable bounty to the game for our InvinciBagel character to pick up, while he is evading constant Enemy attacks from the **InvinciBeagle**, or iBeagle for short, who can shoot both deadly bullets (iBullets) as well as Cream Cheese Balls (iCheese) Projectile objects. We will also be creating these **Enemy.java** and **Projectile.java** classes during this chapter, so we will be using all of the knowledge that you've learned during this book to create some very advanced Java 8 classes and methods during the course of this chapter.

Once we have the Enemy and Projectile classes in place, the real challenge comes in creating an **auto-attack engine**, so the game itself plays against the player, so that we can create a **single-player** version of this game. We will do this by wiring the Enemy.java class into the GamePlayLoop.java class, by calling the Enemy class **.update()** method from the GamePlayLoop class **.handle()** method, which will allow us to harness the JavaFX pulse timing engine for the iBeagle Enemy object. Once this is done, we can code the Enemy object, and give it a life of its own, having it appear randomly on the screen, and attack the InvinciBagel by shooting deadly bullets, or scrumptious cream cheese balls.

We will build this auto-attack engine logically and gradually, first by making the iBeagle Enemy appear on either side of the screen, and flip around to face the iBagel character correctly. Then we will add programming logic that will animate the iBeagle onto the screen, and then back off of the screen. Then we will make him shoot a bullet or cream cheese ball, and then we will add some timing code in order to make his movement far more realistic.

After that, we will add **randomization** to the appearance, locations, and movement, so that the game player cannot tell where an iBeagle attack is going to come from. After that we will add physics simulation so that the bullets and cream cheese balls are affected by drag and gravity, all of which will make the game play more and more realistic, as the chapter progresses on, through the end of the book!

I hope that you have enjoyed your learning experience during the book, as much as I have enjoyed writing it for you. Now let's get into making our game play more and more challenging and professional, as we learn even more about Java 8 and JavaFX classes and programming techniques.

Creating the Score UI Design: Text and Font Objects

The first thing that we need to do to implement a display for our scoring engine is to open the InvinciBagel.java tab in NetBeans, and add an **integer** variable to hold a numeric score accumulation, and a **Text** UI element object, to display the score on the bottom of the screen, alongside our other UI elements. The Text class in JavaFX is used to work with text elements in your games, and even has its own **javafx.scene.text** package, because text is an important element in applications. The integer data type allows your game players to score well into the billions of points, so this should be adequate for holding any magnitude of numeric score your game player can rack up. We will place these Java variable and object declarations, which can be seen highlighted in Figure 17-1, at the very top of the InvinciBagel.java class, right after the WIDTH and HEIGHT constant declarations, and the Java code should look like the following:

```java
int gameScore = 0;
Text scoreText;
```

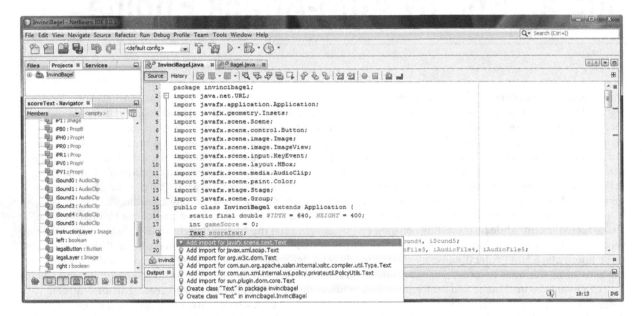

Figure 17-1. *Add an integer variable named gameScore and initialize it to 0, then add a Text object named scoreText*

Mouse-over the wavy red error highlighting, and click next to the line of code containing this error, to select it (which is shown using a light blue color). Next, use an **Alt-Enter** work process to bring up the error resolution helper pop-up, shown at the bottom of Figure 17-1, and double-click on the "Add import for javafx.scene.text.Text" option to have NetBeans write this Text class import statement for you.

Now we are ready to open the **.createSplashScreenNodes()** method, and instantiate this Text object named **scoreText**, using a Java **new** keyword and the **Text()** constructor method. After you do this, you can call the **.setText()** method, and reference the **gameScore** integer, using the **String.valueOf()** method, as well as positioning it in your UI layout design, using the **.setLayoutX()** and **.setLayoutX()** methods, using the following Java code shown in Figure 17-2:

```java
scoreText = new Text();
scoreText.setText(String.valueOf(gameScore));
scoreText.setLayoutY(365);
scoreText.setLayoutX(565);
```

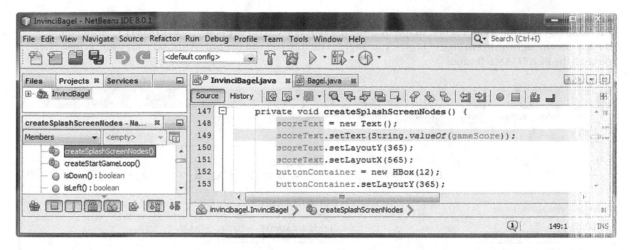

Figure 17-2. *Instantiate a scoreText object using a Java new keyword and call the .setText() and .setLayout() methods*

For now, we are going to use the X,Y position value of **365,565**, as you can see in Figure 17-2. To be able to style this Text object, we will need to declare a **private Font** object, named **scoreFont**, as seen in Figure 17-3. Use the **Alt-Enter** work process again on the red error highlight, and select the "Add import for javafx.scene.text.Font" option.

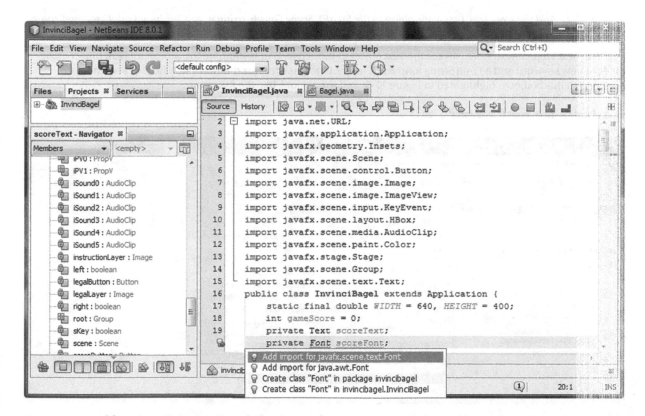

Figure 17-3. *Add a private Font scoreFont declaration and use Alt-Enter and select "Add import javafx.scene.text.Font"*

Before we can use this scoreFont Font object to style the scoreText Text object, we will need to add this scoreText Text Node object to the JavaFX Scene Graph by using the **root.getChildren().add(scoreText);** Java statement, which is shown highlighted in Figure 17-4. If you forget to do this, you will see only white on your game screen after you click the PLAY GAME Button!

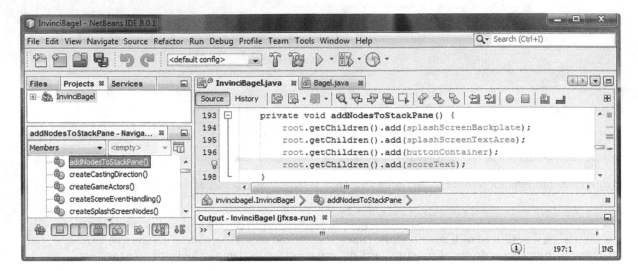

Figure 17-4. *Add the scoreText Text Node object to the JavaFX Scene Graph, using a .getChildren().add() method chain*

The next step, now that we can see the Text object in the Scene, is to instantiate the scoreFont Font object using the Java new keyword and a Font(String fontName, int fontSize) constructor method call. The Java statement to accomplish this is shown highlighted in Figure 17-5, and should look like the following:

```
scoreFont = new Font("Verdana", 20);
```

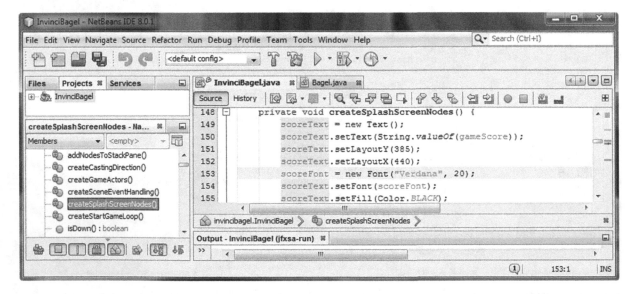

Figure 17-5. *Instantiate scoreFont object with a Java new keyword and Font(String fontName, int fontSize) constructor*

The next step in the work process is to "wire" the scoreText Text object into the scoreFont Font object using the **.setFont()** method, which is called off of the scoreText object and sets the Text object to utilize the scoreFont Font object using the following code, which is shown in the bottom part of Figure 17-5. You can also use a **.setFill()** method called off of the scoreText Text object to set the color of the Text object; for now, we will use a **Color.BLACK** constant.

```
scoreText.setFont(scoreFont);
scoreText.setFill(Color.BLACK);
```

Now we can test the scoreText Text object placement, and refine our X,Y screen location values, so that the score is right next to the HBox UI Button bank. I found that I had to move the Y location down twenty pixels to a pixel location of 385, while I had to move the X location five pixels to the right, to a pixel location of 445, as is shown in Figure 17-6, in the left half of the screen shot, in the bottom right of the InvinciBagel game, next to the Legal Button.

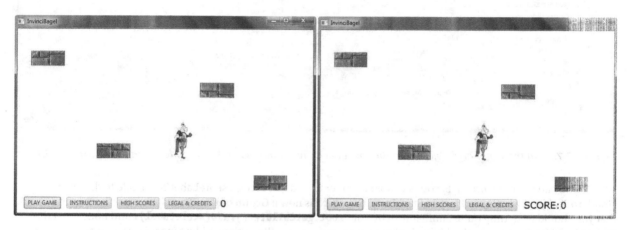

Figure 17-6. *Test the scoreText and scoreFont objects using the Run ➤ Project work process to refine their placement*

We will be adding a Text object label that says "SCORE:" in the next section of the chapter to label our score for the player. The result of this second round of coding is shown in the right half of Figure 17-6, at the bottom right.

Creating a SCORE Label: Adding the Second Text Object

Instead of just having a number on the right side of the UI Button bank (HBox), let's add a Text label that says SCORE: to the front of the scoreText Text object. We will create a scoreLabel Text object and use the same Font object that we created in the previous section to style that Text object. I am going to change the numeric part of the score text to be blue, using the **scoreText.setFill(Color.BLUE);** Java statement, and make the SCORE: label black, using the following Java code, which can also be seen in Figure 17-7:

```
scoreText.setFill(Color.BLUE);
scoreLabel = new Text();
scoreLabel.setText("SCORE:");
scoreLabel.setLayoutY(385);
scoreLabel.setLayoutX(445);
scoreLabel.setFont(scoreFont);
scoreLabel.setFill(Color.BLACK);
```

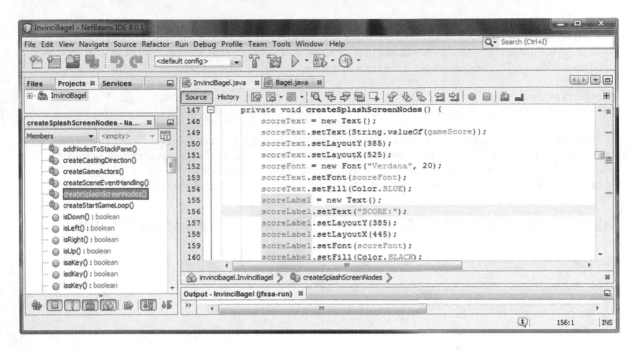

Figure 17-7. *Add the scoreLabel object instantiation and configuration method calls underneath the scoreText object*

As you can see in Figure 17-8, you need to remember to add this second scoreLabel Text Node to the Scene Graph root object, which used to be a StackPane, but which is now a **Group** object. This is done using a method chain, that you should be getting quite familiar with by now: **root.getChildren().add(scoreLabel);** and notice that the addNodesToStackPane() method is beginning to see more use now that we are adding more UI elements to the game. Even though the gameScore variable will be updated dynamically during game play, these Text objects will be **static** in nature, since they are declared, instantiated, configured, and positioned at start-up, just like your other UI elements.

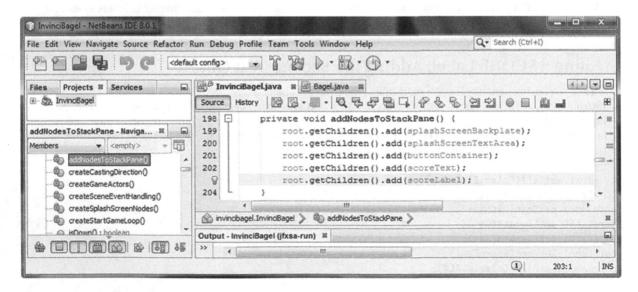

Figure 17-8. *Add the scoreLabel Text Node object to the JavaFX Scene Graph using a .getChildren().add() method chain*

Creating the Scoring Engine Logic: .scoringEngine()

What I want to base scoring on in this game is the **type** of Object, as we are going to have fixed Actor subclass objects for the InvinciBagel to score against, such as Prop, PropV, PropH, PropB, Treasure, Projectile, Enemy, and similar. Since the switch-case structure does not support using an Object in its evaluation logic, we are going to have to use conditional if() statements, along with the Java **instanceof** operator, which, as you can tell from its name, is used to determine object type or instance; in this particular case, to start with, if the **Actor** object **is an instance of** the Prop, **PropV**, **PropH**, or **PropB** class. The basic Java code structure for the **scoringEngine()** method evaluates one if() for each Actor object type, and then sets the **gameScore** variable, which is displayed by the scoreText Text object, inside of the **invinciBagel** object. This programming logic can all be seen in Figure 17-9. The Java code should look like this:

```java
private void scoringEngine(Actor object){
    if(object instanceof Prop)  { invinciBagel.gameScore+=5; }
    if(object instanceof PropV) { invinciBagel.gameScore+=4; }
    if(object instanceof PropH) { invinciBagel.gameScore+=3; }
    if(object instanceof PropB) { invinciBagel.gameScore+=2; }
    invinciBagel.scoreText.setText(String.valueOf(invinciBagel.gameScore));
}
```

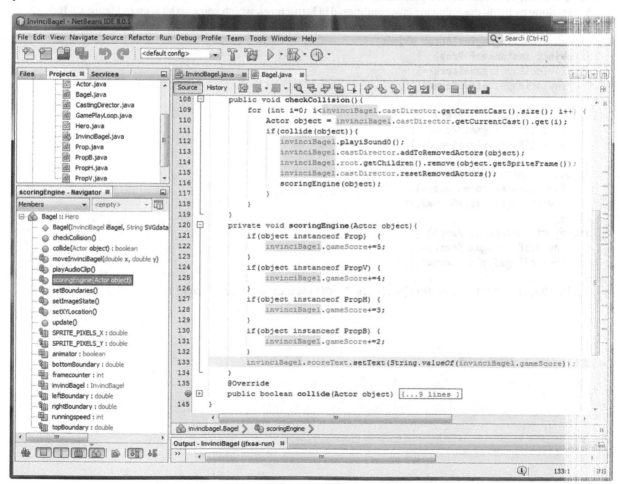

Figure 17-9. *Code basic conditional if() statements inside of the .scoringEngine() method using instanceof*

Be sure not to call a **invinciBagel.scoreText.setText(String.valueOf(invinciBagel.gameScore));** statement, which updates the scoreText UI element using a **.setText()** method, inside of each of these conditional if() statements. Instead, notice that I am placing it at the end of the method, after all of these evaluations are completed. I am doing this so I only have to call this one line of code one time, at the end of the conditional if() object processing structure. That said, the Java code will still work if you place this scoreText object score update statement inside each of the conditional if() statement code body structures. However, I'm trying to show you how to write code that does a lot of work by using relative few (a dozen or less) lines of code to accomplish major Java 8 game development tasks.

Next, we are going to take the .playiSound0() method call out of the .checkCollision() method, and we'll put it inside of the scoringEngine() method instead. As long as it is in one of these two methods, it's going to get called on collision, one way or the other. The reason that I am going to do it this way is because we will probably want to play a different sound effect when a player finds a treasure, or is hit by a projectile. In this way, your audio is associated with scoring and game play when different types of collisions are detected, rather than just playing audio for any collision.

Our conditional if() structure code bodies use curly braces, which allows us to add Java statements into each type of collision (scoring) object instance (type). So in addition to incrementing (or decrementing, as we will add later) the score, we can also use different sounds (audioClips) for different objects. Let's add the .playSound() method calls into these conditional if() code blocks next, so that we have the code in place to trigger sound effects when a treasure is picked up by the primary character or when he is hit by (or catches) a projectile shot by an enemy (an InvinciBeagle) character, or when he collides with a prop in the scene.

This is done by using the following Java conditional if() structures, which can also be seen in Figure 17-10:

```java
private void scoringEngine(Actor object) {
    if(object instanceof Prop)  {
        invinciBagel.gameScore+=5;
        invinciBagel.playiSound0();
    }
    if(object instanceof PropV) {
        invinciBagel.gameScore+=4;
        invinciBagel.playiSound1();
    }
    if(object instanceof PropH) {
        invinciBagel.gameScore+=3;
        invinciBagel.playiSound2();
    }
    if(object instanceof PropB) {
        invinciBagel.gameScore+=2;
        invinciBagel.playiSound3();
    }
    invinciBagel.scoreText.setText(String.valueOf(invinciBagel.gameScore));
}
```

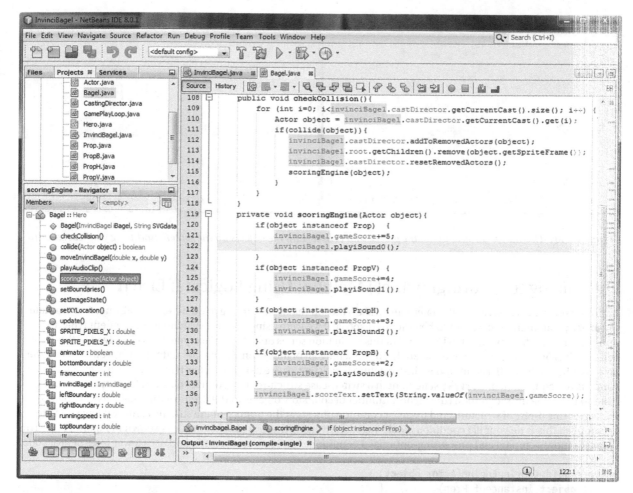

Figure 17-10. Add .playiSound() method calls in each if() statement body to play different audio for each type

Now we have even more game play interaction in place, as the scoreboard will instantly update correctly on each collision, and will play an audioClip at the same time, to indicate that a collision has been detected, the type of collision that has occurred (good or bad), and that the scoreboard has been updated, since after all, this programming logic is contained in the scoringEngine() method and thus should pertain to the act or scoring in some way or another.

After we test this conditional if() programming logic and make sure that everything works as anticipated, we can take a look at how to add optimization into this .scoringEngine() method, and then we will be ready to add some more Actor types, such as the Treasure.java class, which we will be adding next. After that, we can add some enemies (adversaries) to the InvinciBagel game, as we continue to add features that make our game play more fun and exciting during the course of this chapter.

Test the game, using the **Run ➤ Project** work process. As you can see in Figure 17-11, the scoreboard works!

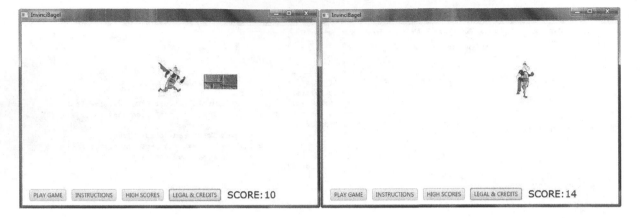

Figure 17-11. *Use Run ➤ Project to test the game, and collide with the objects on the screen, updating your scoreboard*

Optimizing the scoringEngine() Method: Using Logical If Else If

Although the previous series of if() statements will do the job that we are trying to do here, we really need to emulate the **break;** statement that we would have at our disposal if we were using the Java switch-case statement type. To optimize this method, we want to break out of this evaluation series once the object type that is involved in the collision has been determined. We can do this by attaching all of these conditional if() statements together, using the Java **else-if** capability. If a condition in this structure is satisfied, the rest of the **if-else-if** structure is not evaluated, which is the equivalent of a **break;** statement in a switch-case structure. To optimize this even further, you would want to place the most common (the highest number of collidable objects in the Scene of that object type) objects at the **top** of this if-else-if structure, and the least common objects at the bottom of the structure. All you have to do to accomplish this is tie your if() condition blocks together by using the Java **else** keyword, as shown in Figure 17-12. This creates a more compact and processing-optimized conditional evaluation structure, and uses fewer lines of Java code:

```java
private void scoringEngine(Actor object) {
    if(object instanceof Prop)        {
        invinciBagel.gameScore+=5;
        invinciBagel.playiSound0();
    } else if(object instanceof PropV) {
        invinciBagel.gameScore+=4;
        invinciBagel.playiSound1();
    } else if(object instanceof PropH) {
        invinciBagel.gameScore+=3;
        invinciBagel.playiSound2();
    } else if(object instanceof PropB) {
        invinciBagel.gameScore+=2;
        invinciBagel.playiSound3();    }
    invinciBagel.scoreText.setText(String.valueOf(invinciBagel.gameScore));
}
```

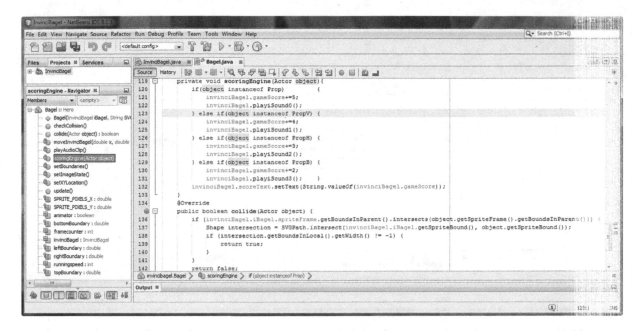

Figure 17-12. *Make all the previously unrelated if() structures into one if-else-if stucture by inserting else in between ifs*

Adding Bounty to the Game: The Treasure.java Class

To make our game play more exciting, let's add a **Treasure.java** class, so that our game players have something to look for during game play that allows them to add points to their score now that the scoring engine is in place. This type of Treasure object will take advantage of the **hasValu** and **isBonus** boolean flags, which we installed in the abstract Actor class, and we will set these to a **true** value in the Treasure() constructor method, which we will code next, along with overriding the required .update() method, so that later on in development we can add animation and treasure processing logic. Like the Prop, PropV, PropH, and PropB classes, this class will use the xLocation and yLocation parameters to set the translateX and translateY properties for the spriteFrame ImageView Node object, which will live inside of this Treasure object (Actor object type, also Actor subclass) as part of the Treasure() constructor method programming logic. The Java code for this class, which can also be seen in Figure 17-13, should look like the following:

```java
package invincibagel;
import javafx.scene.image.Image;
public class Treasure extends Actor {
    public Treasure(String SVGdata, double xLocation, double yLocation, Image... spriteCels){
        super(SVGdata, xLocation, yLocation, spriteCels);
        spriteFrame.setTranslateX(xLocation);
        spriteFrame.setTranslateY(yLocation);
        hasValu = true;
        isBonus = true;
    }
    @Override
    public void update() {    // Currently this is an Empty but Implemented Method    }
}
```

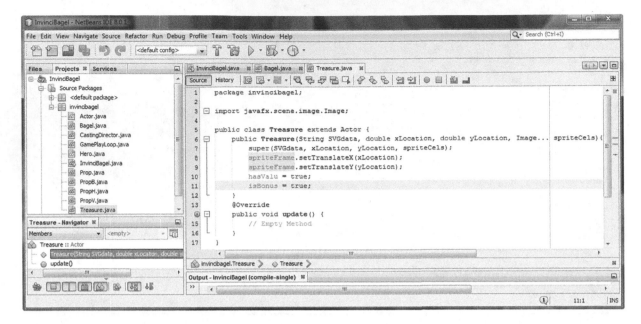

Figure 17-13. *Create a new Java class named Treasure.java extends Actor and create Treasure() and update() methods*

Using the Treasure Class: Create Treasure Objects in the Game

Now that we have a Treasure.java class, we can create Treasure objects for the game. As you know, this will be done in the InvinciBagel.java class. Declare **package protected** (since we're going to reference them outside of InvinciBagel, in Bagel.java) Treasure objects, and name them **iTR0** and **iTR1** (stands for InvinciBagel Treasure). Add **iT0** and **iT1** Image object declarations to the end of your private Image objects compound declaration. Instantiate the iT0 and iT1 Image objects using the Java **new** keyword, the **Image()** constructor method, and the **treasure1.png** and **treasure2.png** image assets, respectively. After that, you can create the iTR0 and iTR1 Treasure objects, using the **Treasure()** constructor method, SVG path data of 0,0, 0,64, 64,64 and 64,0 and locations of 50,105 and 533,206 respectively. Make sure that you add these new Treasure object's spriteFrame ImageView Nodes to the JavaFX Scene Graph, using the **.getChildren().add()** method chain, called off of the root Group object. As you can see in Figure 17-14, the code is error-free, and we are now ready to test the new Treasure.java class and the Java code that we have added to the InvinciBagel.java class to see if we can get Treasure in the game Scene. Your Java code should look like the following:

```
Treasure iTR0, iTR1;     // These Object Declarations go at the top of the InvinciBagel class
private Image iB0, iB1, iB2, iB3, iB4, iB5, iB6, iB7, iB8, iP0, iP1, iT0, iT1;

iT0 = new Image("/treasure1.png", 64, 64, true, false, true);  // .loadImageAssets() Method
iT1 = new Image("/treasure2.png", 64, 64, true, false, true);

iTR0 = new Treasure("M0 0 L0 64 64 64 64 0 Z", 50, 105, iT0);  // .createGameActors() Method
iTR1 = new Treasure("M0 0 L0 64 64 64 64 0 Z", 533, 206, iT1);

root.getChildren().add(iTR0.spriteFrame);
root.getChildren().add(iTR1.spriteFrame);
```

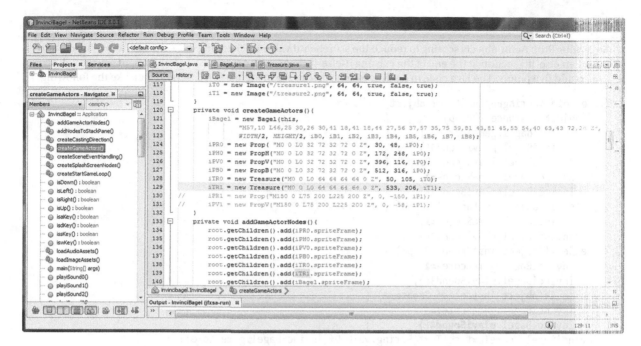

Figure 17-14. *After adding declarations at the top of the class, instantiate the objects, and add them to a Scene Graph*

Let's take a moment and use a **Run ➤ Project** work process and see if our Treasure Actors are on the screen!

As you can see in the left half of Figure 17-15, all Treasure objects are visible in the Scene, and we're ready to start enhancing our .scoringEngine() method, to support **negative scoring** as well as add in **Treasure scoring** values.

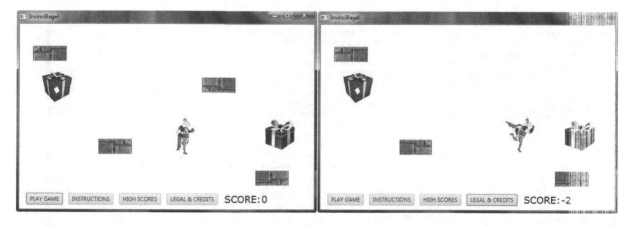

Figure 17-15. *Check Treasure placement (left) and test negative collision values (right) and Treasure collision detection*

As you'll soon see (and is seen on the right side of Figure 17-15), a Java int (integer) data type supports negative values, so all you have to do in your **.scoringEngine()** method is to change += to -= for Actor objects that you want the game player to avoid. In our development scenario here, we'll use collision with Prop objects to give a negative score.

Adding Treasure Collision Detection: Updating .scoringEngine()

Change your Prop Actor objects scoring to reduce the scoreboard value by changing the += values to -=1 or -=2, and then add an else-if{} section at the end of the existing if-else-if chain, to support Treasure objects, which we will score at +=5, to add five points. The Java code to do this, which you can see in Figure 17-16, should look like the following:

```java
private void scoringEngine(Actor object)  {
    if(object instanceof Prop)              {
        invinciBagel.gameScore-=1;
        invinciBagel.playiSound0();
    } else if(object instanceof PropV) {
        invinciBagel.gameScore-=2;
        invinciBagel.playiSound1();
    } else if(object instanceof PropH) {
        invinciBagel.gameScore-=1;
        invinciBagel.playiSound2();
    } else if(object instanceof PropB) {
        invinciBagel.gameScore-=2;
        invinciBagel.playiSound3();
    } else if(object instanceof Treasure) {
        invinciBagel.gameScore+=5;
        invinciBagel.playiSound4();         }
    invinciBagel.scoreText.setText(String.valueOf(invinciBagel.gameScore));
}
```

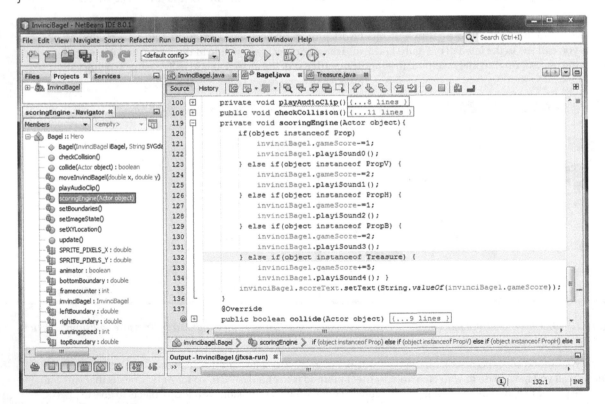

Figure 17-16. *Add a Treasure else-if structure to end of the .scoringEngine() method conditional if() structure*

You will need to remember to add the Treasure objects to the **castDirector** object, as seen in Figure 17-17, because the collision detection engine uses this **CastingDirector** class (object) to manage a collision detection process. If you do not do this step, the InvinciBagel will go right over the Treasure objects without seeing (colliding with) them!

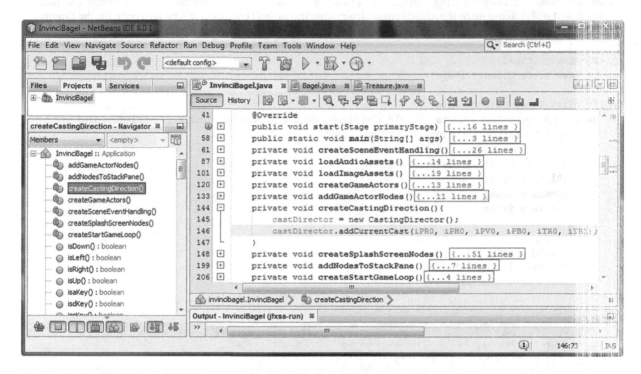

Figure 17-17. *Add iTR0 and iTR1 Treasure objects inside the .addCurrentCast(Actor. . .) method call*

Now that we have added these two Treasure objects to the castDirector CastingDirector object, the collision detection programming logic will "see" them, and collisions with the Treasure objects will occur, triggering the scoring engine to score the game correctly. Test the final code for implementing Treasure in your game, and make sure that it works, and then we can move on to adding **adversaries** and have them shoot projectiles at the InvinciBagel character.

Adding Enemies: The Enemy and Projectile Classes

Now that we have added positive (Treasure) elements to our game, let's add some negative (Enemy and Projectile) elements to the game, so that we remain "balanced" in our development work process. We are going to use the Actor superclass, rather than the Hero superclass, to create the Enemy and Projectile classes (objects). This is because by doing it this way, we have a more optimized game, as we are only using **one single .collide() method** (remember that each Hero object has a .collide() method implemented) for our JavaFX pulse event engine to process. When I convert this game into a **multi-player** game (the code for this is beyond the Beginner nature of this title), I would want to make the Enemy class a Hero subclass, so that the Enemy character could collide with things, such as Treasure and Projectiles, just like the InvinciBagel can. Since the Enemy class still has an .update() method, it can be moved around on the screen, where it can (and will) come out of hiding and shoot bullets (negative effect) and balls of cream cheese (positive effect) at the InvinciBagel character. The only thing that differentiates the Hero class is the .collide() method, and for this version of the game, having one .collide() method to process per pulse allows us to optimize the game play processing, while still having a game with the different game features that an arcade game would include. As you can see in the **Enemy()** constructor method, the Enemy character **isAlive**, **isBonus**, and **hasValue**, and so all of these properties or characteristics of the Enemy will be set to a boolean value of **true** inside of the constructor method, after the sprite location has been set using .setTranslateX() and .setTranslateY(), and after the SVG data, Image, and initial X,Y location data is passed up to the Actor() constructor using the super() constructor. The Java code for the Enemy.java class can be seen error-free in Figure 17-18, and should look like the following Java class structure:

```java
package invincibagel;
import javafx.scene.image.Image;

public class Enemy extends Actor {
    public Enemy(String SVGdata, double xLocation, double yLocation, Image... spriteCels) {
        super(SVGdata, xLocation, yLocation, spriteCels);
        spriteFrame.setTranslateX(xLocation);
        spriteFrame.setTranslateY(yLocation);
        isAlive = true;
        isBonus = true;
        hasValu = true;
    }
    @Override
    public void update() {
        // Currently Empty Method
    }
}
```

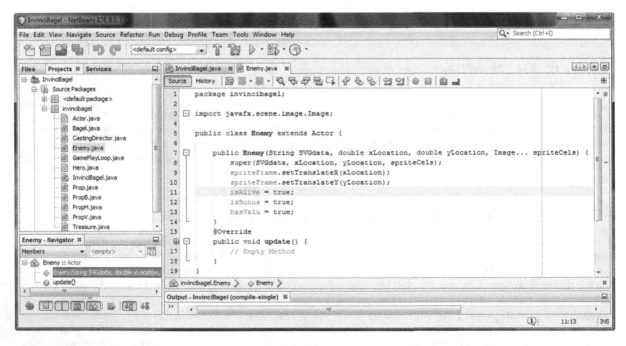

Figure 17-18. *Create an Enemy.java class, override the .update() method, and code your Enemy() constructor method*

The next step in the work process is to use GIMP to create the **collision polygon** for the Enemy object, as is seen in Figure 17-19, using only nine data points. Use the SVG data creation work process you learned in Chapter 16.

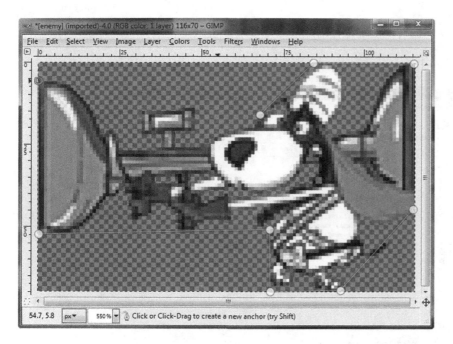

Figure 17-19. *Use GIMP to create a nine-point collision polygon for your Enemy Actor*

Before we go into the InvinciBagel.java class to declare and instantiate an Enemy object named iBeagle, let's create the **Projectile.java** class, so that our Enemy object has Projectile objects to shoot at the InvinciBagel character!

Creating Cream Cheese Bullets: Coding a Projectile.java Class

Now that we have added positive (Treasure) elements to our game, let's add some negative (Enemy and Projectile) elements to the game, so that we remain "balanced" in our development work process! Create a **Projectile.java** class and constructor method that sets **isFixed** to **false** (since projectiles fly) and **isBonus** and **hasValu** to true, so the object properties are set. The Java code for this Projectile.java class can be seen in Figure 17-20, and looks like the following:

```
package invincibagel;
import javafx.scene.image.Image;
public class Projectile extends Actor {
    public Projectile(String SVGdata, double xLocation, double yLocation, Image... spriteCels) {
        super(SVGdata, xLocation, yLocation, spriteCels);
        spriteFrame.setTranslateX(xLocation);
        spriteFrame.setTranslateY(yLocation);
```

```
        isFixed = false;
        isBonus = true;
        hasValu = true;
    }
    @Override
    public void update() {    // Empty Method    }
}
```

Figure 17-20. *Create a Projectile.java class, override the .update() method, and code a Projectile() constructor method*

Adding an Enemy and Projectiles to the Game: InvinciBagel.java

Open the InvinciBagel.java tab in NetBeans and declare an **Enemy** object, named **iBeagle**, and two **Projectile** objects, named **iBullet** and **iCheese**, underneath the iBagel Bagel object, as shown highlighted in Figure 17-21. Next, declare three Image objects, **iE0**, **iC0**, and **iC1**, by adding the object names at the end of the second private Image declaration.

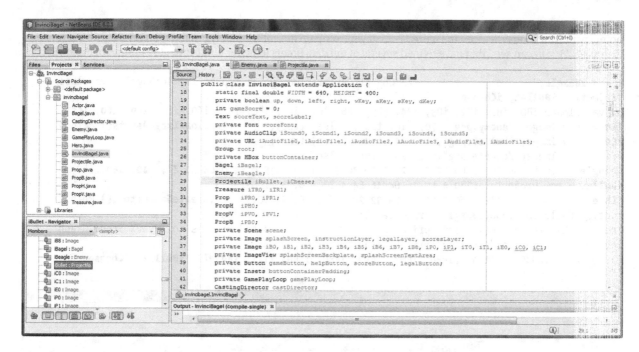

Figure 17-21. *Declare iBeagle, iBullet, iCheese (Enemy and Projectile) objects, and iE0, iC0, iC1 (Image) objects*

Copy the **enemy.png**, **bullet.png** and **cheese.png** image assets into the **/src** folder, as shown in Figure 17-22.

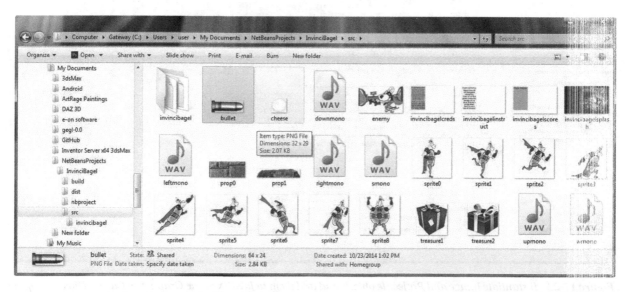

Figure 17-22. *Copy the enemy.png, bullet.png, and cheese.png image assets into your InvinciBagel/src project folder*

You can then refine your collision polygon structure data point by data point, by clicking and dragging these points with your mouse, as seen in Figure 17-23. If you compare the collision polygon in Figure 17-22 with the one in Figure 17-23, you can see I that have refined several of the data points to better conform to the outline of the sprite.

```
Enemy iBeagle;                       // Object Declarations go at top of InvinciBagel.java class
Projectile iBullet, iCheese;
private Image iB0, iB1, iB2, iB3, iB4, iB5, iB6, iB7, iB8, iP0, iP1, iT0, iT1, iE0, iC0, iC1;
iE0 = new Image("/enemy.png", 70, 116, true, false, true);        // .loadImageAssets() Method
iC0 = new Image("/bullet.png", 64, 24, true, false, true);
iC1 = new Image("/cheese.png", 32, 29, true, false, true);
iBeagle = new Enemy("M0 6 L0 52 70 52 70 70 70 93 115 45 115 0 84 0 68 16 Z", 520, 160, iE0);
iBullet = new Projectile("M0 4 L0 16 64 16 64 4 Z", 8, 8, iC0);
iCheese = new Projectile("M0 0 L0 32 29 32 29 0 Z", 96, 8, iC1); // .createGameActors() Method
root.getChildren().add(iBeagle.spriteFrame);
root.getChildren().add(iBullet.spriteFrame);                      // Add Objects to JavaFX Scene Graph
root.getChildren().add(iCheese.spriteFrame);
castDirector.addCurrentCast(iPR0, iPH0, iPV0, iPB0, iTR0, iTR1, iBeagle, iBullet, iCheese);
```

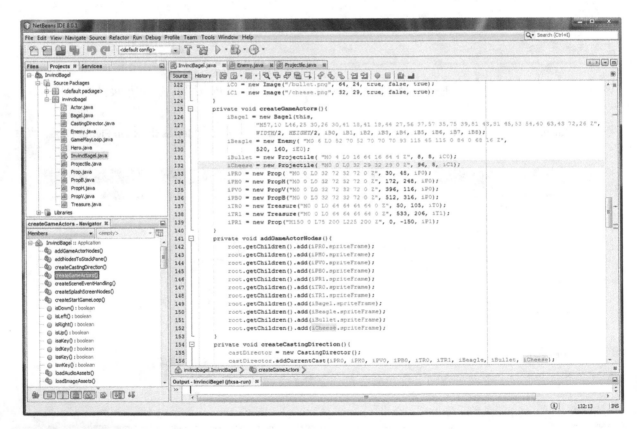

Figure 17-23. *Instantiate Image and Projectile objects and add them to JavaFX Scene Graph and CastingDirector object*

While we are adding game design elements to the game, let's go ahead and learn how to use a splashscreen ImageView Node object to implement a game background image plate. We will do this so that our white iBeagle, and (Cream) iCheese and iBullet objects, stand out to the game player better, using an enhanced blue background color.

Adding a Background Image: Using .toBack() Method

Before we get into coding the collision and scoring routines for the Enemy and Projectile objects, let's add an Image asset (object) to use in the background plate, while we are in the process of adding objects to our game. Copy the **skycloud.png** 8-bit PNG8 image asset, seen in the bottom-left corner of Figure 17-24, from the book repository into the NetBeansProjects/InvinciBagel/src folder. After you do this, add a skyCloud Image object declaration to the end of the private Image object declarations for the splashscreen related image assets, as seen at the top of Figure 17-24. As you can see, there will be a warning highlight under this object until you implement (use) it in your Java code. Next, instantiate a skyCloud object in .loadImageAssets(), as seen at the bottom of Figure 17-24, using the following code:

```
private Image splashScreen, instructionLayer, legalLayer, scoresLayer, skyCloud;
skyCloud = new Image("/skycloud.png", 640, 400, true, false, true);
```

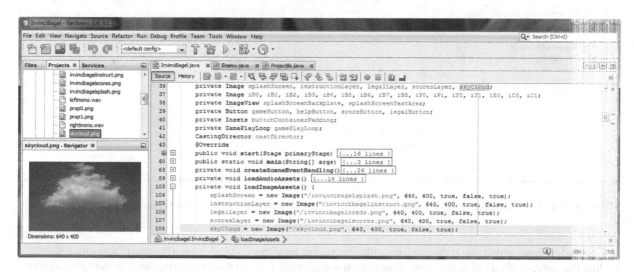

Figure 17-24. *Declare and instantiate a skyCloud Image object that references a skycloud.png background image asset*

Now you have a skyCloud object, so use a **.setImage()** method to set a SplashScreenBackground ImageView Node, to use this image asset inside the gameButton.setOnAction(ActionEvent) code block, so that when you click the PLAY GAME Button, this image is set as the backplate image. Also, make sure to use the **.setVisible()** method call with a value of **true**, so that the ImageView Node will be visible. The Java code, shown in Figure 17-25, should look like this:

```
splashScreenBackground.setImage(skyCloud);
splashScreenBackground.setVisible(true);
```

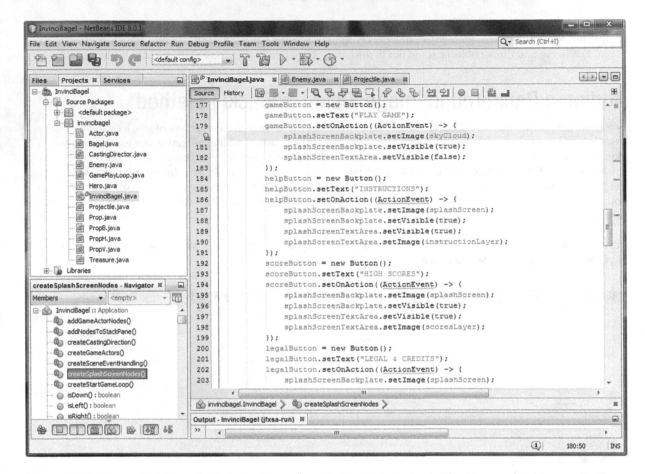

Figure 17-25. *Use a splashScreenBackplate.setImage() method call to install a skyCloud Image object in gameButton*

Since you have added this code to the gameButton's event handling code, you must "counter" this move, by adding the same method call to the other three Button event handlers to set the image asset back to the splashscreen image asset, using the following Java code, shown in the other three Button event handling methods in Figure 17-25:

```
splashScreenBackground.setImage(splashScreen);
```

Use **Run ➤ Project** to test the code. As you can see on the left side of Figure 17-26, we have a z-index issue!

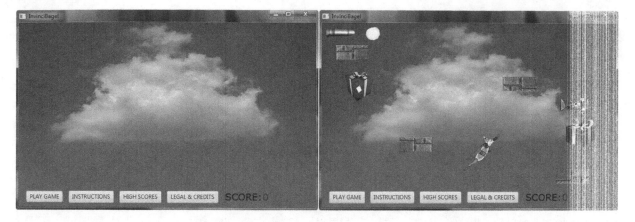

Figure 17-26. *Install the skyCloud background Image (left), and use a .toBack() method call to set proper z-index (right)*

Since we want to have our background image at the lowest (zero) z-index so it will be behind all of our game play assets, but also have all the splashscreen assets at the highest z-index, so that those image plates will cover (be in front of) all of our game play assets, we normally would have to implement yet another ImageView compositing plate, to be able to do this. However, there is a handy set of z-index related **Node** class methods that will allow us to use the SplashScreenBackplate ImageView object to hold both the game splashscreen and a game background image plate at the same time! This is one of the ImageView Node optimizations that I wanted to implement to keep our game Nodes at a minimum, to reduce memory and processing overhead. The code to place the ImageView behind our game assets will call the **.toBack()** method off of the **SplashScreenBackplate** ImageView Node object, which relocates that Node to the Back (Bottom layer) of the JavaFX Scene Graph Node Stack. This is the equivalent of setting this Node's z-index to **zero**. The Java statement can be seen highlighted in light blue at the top of Figure 17-26, and the completed Java code for your **gameButton.setOnAction((ActionEvent)->{}** event handling structure should look like the following:

```
gameButton.setOnAction((ActionEvent) -> {
    splashScreenBackplate.setImage(skyCloud);
    splashScreenBackplate.setVisible(true);
    splashScreenBackplate.toBack();
    splashScreenTextArea.setVisible(false);
});
```

As you probably realize by now, we'll need to "counter" this move in the other three Button event handling structures. We will use the opposite of the .toBack() method call, which is of course the **.toFront()** method call. As you can see, we need to not only call the .toFront() method off of the **splashScreenBackplate** ImageView Node object, but also off of the **splashScreenTextArea** ImageView object, and the **buttonContainer** HBox object that is holding our UI Button controls. We will need to call this method off of all of these Splashscreen and UI objects so that all of these are brought back to the front of the JavaFX Scene Graph Node Stack. The Java code, shown in Figure 17-27, looks like this:

```
helpButton.setOnAction((ActionEvent) -> {
    splashScreenBackplate.setImage(splashScreen);
    splashScreenBackplate.toFront();
    splashScreenBackplate.setVisible(true);
    splashScreenTextArea.setVisible(true);
    splashScreenTextArea.setImage(instructionLayer);
    splashScreenTextArea.toFront();
    buttonContainer.toFront();
});
```

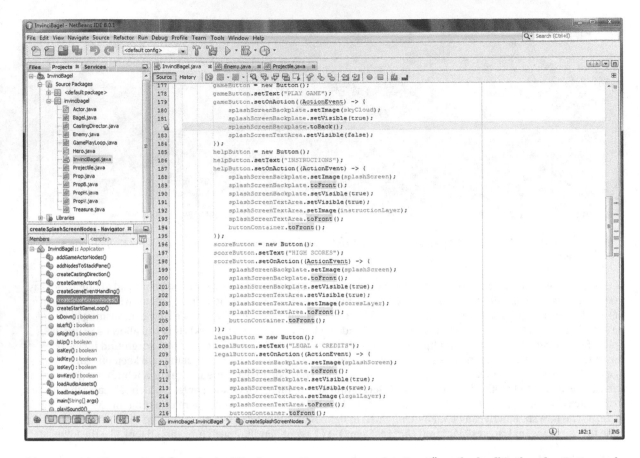

Figure 17-27. *Use a .toBack() method call in the gameButton code, and .toFront() method call in the other Button code*

Using Random Number Generators: java.util.Random

The **java.util** package contains programming **utilities** that you can use for your Java 8 games development, as you may have guessed from the package name. One of the most important Java utilities for game programmers is the **Random** class, and its **Random()** constructor method. This class can be used to create **Random Number Generator** objects, which generate random number (or boolean) values for use inside your game programming logic. We will be using this class to generate both **int** (integer, for random screen locations) and **boolean** (for "guess where the Enemy is coming from next" functions) random values. These will make sure the game player cannot anticipate the game by recognizing **patterns** during the game play. The Java 8 Random class was scratch-coded specifically to generate random numbers using the Java Object master class. The class hierarchy for the Random class looks like the following:

```
java.lang.Object
  > java.util.Random
```

The Random class has two constructors, a **Random()** constructor, which we will be using, and an overloaded **Random(long seed)** constructor, where you can specify the **seed value** for the Random Number Generator that this class implements. Once you have a Random object, you can call one of almost two dozen (22) methods that generate different types of random values. The method calls we'll be using during this chapter are the **.nextInt(int bound)** and **.nextBoolean()** method calls. In case you are wondering, there is also a .nextInt() method, but we need to generate a random number inside of a **specific range** (zero to bottom of screen), and the .nextInt(int bound) allows generation of a random number range from zero to the specified integer bound (boundary) passed over inside of the method call.

We will be using the Random class for our Enemy attack strategy (and code) in the Enemy.java class. Let's go ahead and declare and instantiate a Random object named **randomNum** at the top of the Enemy.java class, as shown in Figure 17-28, using the following compound (declaration plus instantiation) Java 8 programming statement:

```
protected static final Random randomNum = new Random();
```

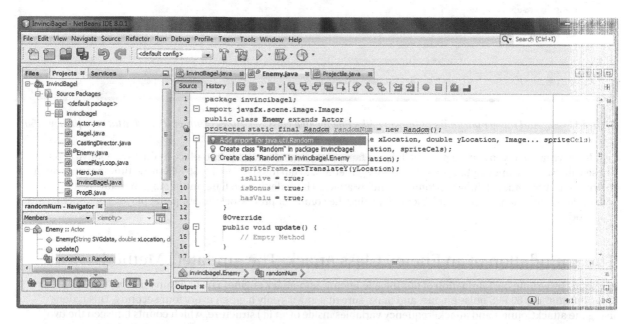

Figure 17-28. *Declare and instantiate a Random Number Generator at the top of the Enemy.java class using Random()*

We will be using this Random (number generator) object throughout the remainder of this chapter to add random attack positions, sides, and bullets for our Enemy iBeagle object, so that he can try his best to take down the InvinciBagel character (the game player), or at least cause him to generate lots of negative scoring points if he can!

Mounting the Attack: Coding the Enemy Onslaught

First we need to declare **counter variables**, seen highlighted in Figure 17-29, using the following two Java statements:

```
int attackCounter = 0;
int attackFrequency = 250;
```

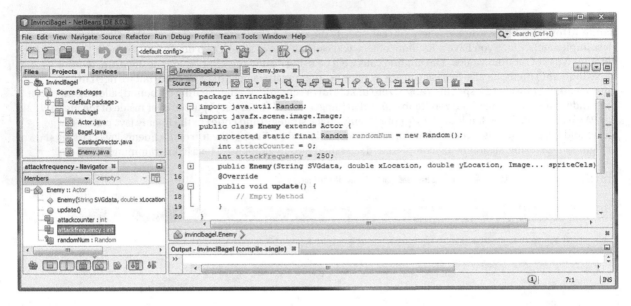

Figure 17-29. *Add integer variables at the top of the Enemy.java class; set attackCounter=0, and attackFrequency=250*

Now we are ready to start to put a half dozen fairly complicated methods into place in the **Enemy.java** class. These will use the GamePlayLoop class's **.handle()** method, to tap into the JavaFX 60 FPS pulse timing event engine, to drive a fully automated, fully randomized Enemy attack. The code that we'll be putting together during the remainder of this chapter is the equivalent of turning the computer processor into our game player's opponent. Let's write code!

The Foundation of an Enemy Class Attack: The .update() Method

Let's start by writing the foundation of our iBeagle Enemy auto-attack engine. The first thing that we want to do is to "throttle" the 60 FPS pulse engine, and make sure that attacks only happen every four seconds. This is done using the attackCounter and attackFrequency variables inside of an if() structure, which counts between the two variables. If the attackCounter reaches **250**, it is reset to **0** and an **initiateAttack()** method is called. Otherwise (else) the attackCounter is **incremented** using +=1. You could also use **attackCounter++** to accomplish this. The code for the basic conditional if() structure, which can be seen highlighted in the middle of Figure 17-30, should look like the following Java method:

```java
public void update() {
    if(attackCounter >= attackFrequency) {
        attackCounter=0;
        initiateAttack();
    } else {
        attackCounter+=1;
    }
}
```

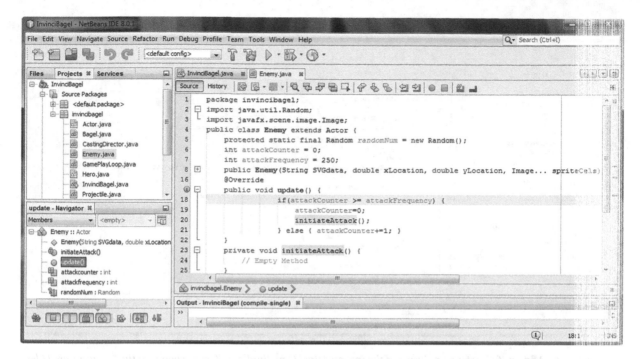

Figure 17-30. *Create a conditional if using attackCounter inside the .update( ) method that calls initiateAttack( ) method*

Most of this "auto-attack" code we will be writing during this admittedly advanced chapter will leverage this .update() method, which will be called from the .handle() method that runs our game from the GamePlayLoop class. The reason I installed this .update() method that you need to override in every Actor subclass, is in case you wanted to animate things in the game. If an Actor is static, the .update() method simply exists as an empty or unused method.

Attacking on Both Sides of the Screen: .initiateAttack() Method

The way to make your attack come from both sides of the screen is to have a boolean variable that can be set to right (true) or left (false), which we will call **takeSides**. Declare this variable at the top of the Enemy class, and then create an empty **private void initiateAttack(){}** method structure underneath your .update() method. Inside of this .initiateAttack() method, create an empty if-else structure **if(takeSides){}else{}** to hold your attack programming logic, so **private void initiateAttack(){if(takeSides){}else{}}** if you are into writing super compact Java code (this is valid Java code, but does absolutely nothing thus far). If you follow the industry standard Java 8 code formatting practices, the Java method body that you would use to implement this empty infrastructure can be seen in Figure 17-31, and should look like the following:

```java
boolean takeSides = false;
private void initiateAttack() {
    if(takeSides) {
            // Empty Statement
    } else { // Empty Statement }
}
```

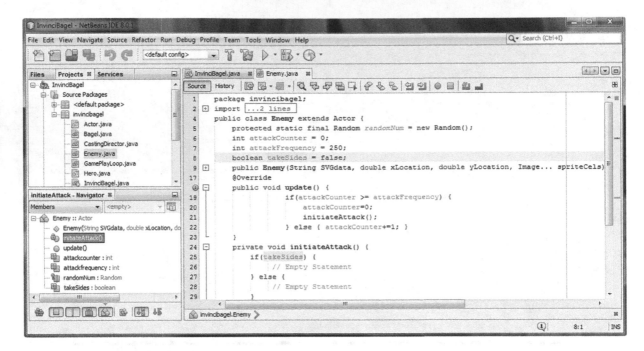

Figure 17-31. *Add an if-else structure inside of the initiateAttack() method, to alternate between the left and right sides*

Inside the if(takeSides){} structure set the Enemy object (which we named iBeagle in the InvinciBagel class) to an X location of 500, by using **spriteFrame.setTranslateX(500);** and to a **random height** on the screen, using a **spriteFrame.setTranslateY()** method call in conjunction with the random number generator object we installed in the previous section of the chapter. If you type in your **randomNum** object name and then hit the period key, you will be presented with a number of method call options, which is shown in Figure 17-32. Double-click the **nextInt(int bound)** option, and insert that method call off of the randomNum object inside the .setTranslateY() method.

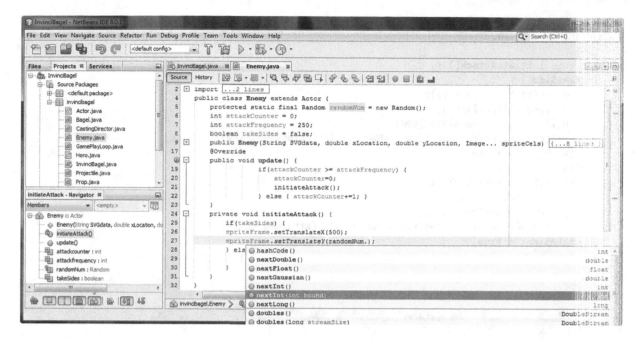

Figure 17-32. *Use a randomNum Random object inside of the .setTranslateY() method and use a period to call selector*

The next thing that you will want to do is to declare an **integer** variable named **attackBoundary** that will be referenced inside of your **.nextInt()** method call, so that you can change your Y axis (bottom of screen) boundary later on if you wish, in one easy-to-edit location at the top of the Enemy.java class. The Java statement should look like this:

```
int attackBoundary = 300;
```

Now we're ready to finish writing the Java code that flips the iBeagle Enemy Actor (sprite) so he is facing the correct direction, and then we can test the code. It is important to write complex Java code in logical, digestible steps. In this way, you can test your code as you write it, making sure that each component of the programming logic works, before adding additional complexity. You will see this work process during this chapter, as we develop a robust auto-attack algorithm inside of the Enemy.java class. This auto-attack code can be used for any of the Enemy objects that you create in the future; thus the code that you're writing during this chapter will cover a plethora of bad guy attacks!

It is important to note here that since takeSides is boolean and can only have two values – true or false, we'll only need to implement a simple conditional if-else structure. This is because if our if(takeSides) condition equates to being true, then we know that the false value (else condition) logic structure will handle the takeSides=false scenario.

Inside of both of these if{} and else{} attack logic processing structures, we'll flip the sprite image around the Y axis, remembering to set the **isFlipH** variable for future use, set the sprite X location, to one side of the screen or the other, set the sprite Y location to a **random height** value on the screen and then set the **takeSides** boolean variable to the opposite of its current true or false data value. In this way, the iBeagle Enemy Actor object will **alternate** between the left and right sides of the screen. Later, we'll use the **.nextBoolean()** method, from the **Random** class, to make the attack unpredictable. Remember that we are starting simple, and adding complexity as we develop this code. The Java code for the basic initiateAttack() method body is shown error-free in Figure 17-33, and should look like the following:

```java
private void initiateAttack() {
    if(takeSides) {
        spriteFrame.setScaleX(1);
        this.setIsFlipH(false);
        spriteFrame.setTranslateX(500);
        spriteFrame.setTranslateY(randomNum.nextInt(attackBoundary));
        takeSides = false;
    } else {
        spriteFrame.setScaleX(-1);
        this.setIsFlipH(true);
        spriteFrame.setTranslateX(100);
        spriteFrame.setTranslateY(randomNum.nextInt(attackBoundary));
        takeSides = true;
    }
}
```

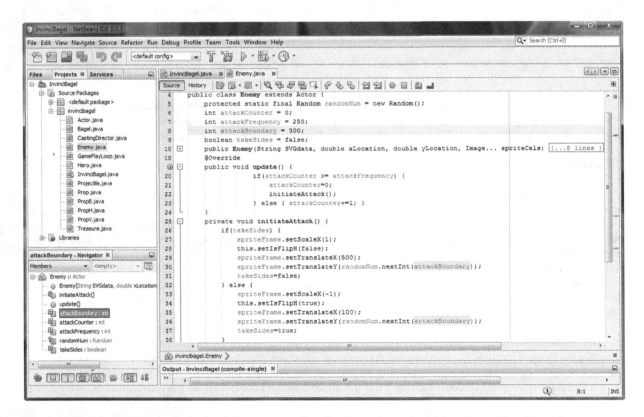

Figure 17-33. *Add the logic inside the if-else structure that flips the sprite and positions it on either side of the screen*

Powering the Enemy .update() Method: Using the GamePlayLoop .handle() Method

Before we can start to test the code inside the Enemy.java class .update() method, we must "wire it up" to the **.handle()** method in the GamePlayLoop.java class. As you know, this method is our doorway into the JavaFX pulse timing event processing engine that drives our game at a lightning fast 60 FPS. Now our GamePlayLoop .handle() method will be updating both an **iBagel** InvinciBagel character as well as the **iBeagle** Enemy auto-attack programming logic. It is easy to see why InvinciBagel and InvinciBeagle are enemies; it's an identity crisis of sorts, kind of like one of those misspelled domain name disputes! Your Java code, seen error-free in Figure 17-34, will look like the following:

```java
@Override
public void handle(long now)     {
    invinciBagel.iBagel.update();
    invinciBagel.iBeagel.update();
}
```

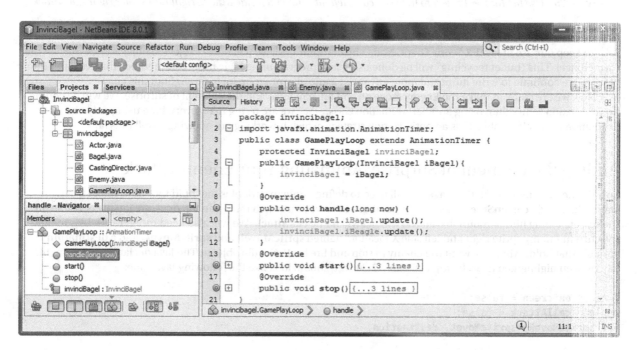

Figure 17-34. *Add a call to the invinciBagel.iBeagle.update() method inside of the GamePlayLoop .handle() method*

Use the **Run ➤ Project** work process to test your first round (level) of Enemy auto-attack Java code. As you can see in Figure 17-35, the InvinciBeagle appears on both sides of the screen, in **random locations** along the **Y axis**, and alternates between the left side of the screen and the right side of the screen. I left the Bullet and Cream Cheese Ball Projectile Actor objects visible on the screen for now, in the upper-left corner. We will eventually place these off-screen, and will shoot them at the InvinciBagel every few seconds using the InvinciBeagle's powerful bazooka.

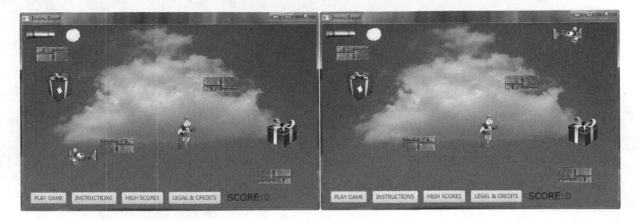

Figure 17-35. *Use the Run ➤ Project to test your code; left half shows left side attack, right half shows right side attack*

To keep our use of JavaFX Scene Graph Node objects optimized, we will reuse Projectile objects once they hit the InvinciBagel. This "bullet recycling" will be done using Java programming logic in several methods that we'll put into place as we continue to write more and more advanced game play program logic throughout this chapter.

Now we are ready to make the Enemy move on and off-screen, to add the element of surprise. We will be coding this animation rather than using another Animation class, since we are trying to do everything using only one AnimationTimer class (object) as an optimization strategy, which is working out amazingly well thus far.

Adding the Element of Surprise: Animating Your Enemy Attack

To animate our Enemy onto the Stage we will need to define **boolean** variables that hold the "on-screen off-screen" state, which I will call **onScreen**, as well as one that will serve as a switch that I can flip once the Enemy is visible on the screen, telling him to mount his attack, which I will name **callAttack**. We will also need **integer** variables to hold the current Enemy sprite right and left side X location, named **spriteMoveR** and **spriteMoveL**, and a **destination** variable that holds where we want the Enemy to stop and fire his Projectile objects. The Java declaration statements can be seen highlighted near the top of Figure 17-36, and should look like the following Java code:

```
boolean onScreen = false;
boolean callAttack = false;
int spriteMoveR, spriteMoveL, destination;
```

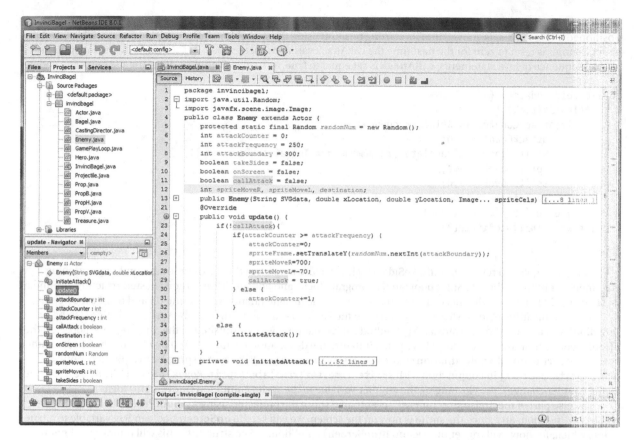

Figure 17-36. *Add callAttack, spriteMove and destination variables and an if(callAttack)-else programming structure*

The first thing that we'll need to do, inside the **.update()** method, is add an **if(!callAttack)** if-else conditional structure around the **if(attackCounter >= attackFrequency)** structure that we already have in place. We will leave the **attackCounter = 0;** initialization statement inside of this inner loop, and we will add a **spriteMoveR = 700;** and a **spriteMoveL = -70;** initialization statement. These will place the Enemy sprite off-screen on either side of the Stage.

A callAttack **boolean flag** allows us to communicate between the .update() and the .initiateAttack methods, as you can see, in the .update() method, after the attackCounter (timer) has allowed the player enough time to collect his wits after enemy attacks, this callAttack variable is set to a true (attack) value. In a more complex version of your .initiateAttack() method, you will set this callAttack variable to a false (delay attack) value, starting the attackCounter.

Let's also make a Java code optimization and take the .setTranslateY() method call that we have twice in the initiateAttack() method, and make just a single method call (which represents a 100% savings on usage of the Random object's .nextInt() method call). Once all these programming statements are in place, you can finally set the **callAttack** boolean variable to a **true** value, so that the next time that the **if(!callAttack)** conditional if-else structure is called, the else portion at the bottom of the structure will execute and will call an **initiateAttack()** method. This method is where the real heavy lifting is done, as far as **animating** the iBeagle Enemy character onto the screen, having him **pause** and fire off a shot, and then **retreat** off-screen before the InvinciBagel can execute (collide with) him, gaining ten valuable scoring points.

The **else** part of this if-else programming structure will call the initiateAttack() function, once the callAttack variable has been set to a true value inside of the attackCounter timer section of your conditional programming logic.

Once your conditional if() timer logic has expired (completed its countdown), your Enemy sprite is randomly positioned along the Y axis, moved into its starting position using the spriteMoveR and spriteMoveL variables, and the attackCounter is reset to zero for the next time the callAttack variable is set to false. At the end of the "set-up initiate attack" sequence of Java statements, **callAttack** is set equal to **true**, as seen in Figure 17-36, using the following code:

```java
public void update() {
    if(!callAttack) {
        if(attackCounter >= attackFrequency) {
            attackCounter = 0;
            spriteFrame.setTranslateY(randomNum.nextInt(attackBoundary));
            spriteMoveR = 700;
            spriteMoveL = -70;
            callAttack = true;
        } else { attackCounter+=1; }
    } else { initiateAttack(); }
}
```

Next we're going to rewrite our if(takeSides) logic structure to remove the Y axis random number positioning statements, reposition the takeSides boolean flag program logic, and add an **if(!onScreen)** nested structure, around a .setTranslateX() method call. This will allow us to animate the iBeagle Enemy Actor sprite on and off of the screen.

Inside of the if(!takeSides) structure, you'll keep the first two statements that set the sprite mirroring (facing direction), but remove the .setTranslateY() method call as that is now accomplished in the .update() method. Add the if(!onScreen) conditional structure, where you'll initialize the destination location to **500** pixels, and then nest another counter **if(spriteMoveR >= destination)** structure, inside of which you'll move the sprite by two pixels per pulse using **spriteMoveR-=2;** in conjunction with **spriteFrame.setTranslateX(spriteMoveR);** to actually move the sprite as the counter changes, thus leveraging the counter variable in the sprite animation (movement) logic.

The else part of the if-else structure will (eventually) shoot the projectile using a **.shootProjectile()** method we will be coding soon, and since the sprite is now on the screen, we will set the **onScreen** boolean flag variable to a **true** value, which, for now, will trigger the second **if(onScreen)** conditional logic structure. This will remove the Enemy sprite from the screen using half the velocity (move one pixel per counter iteration) that it came onto the screen with.

The logic for the second nested conditional if(onScreen) structure is quite similar to the first. You will set the **destination** to **700** pixels (putting the Enemy sprite back off-screen, and again out of view), and this time, you'll iterate using **+=1** instead of -=2, which will not only move the Enemy in the opposite direction, due to a plus instead of minus, but will also use half the initial velocity used to mount an attack, because you're moving by one pixel rather than two.

The real difference in the if(onScreen) conditional if-else structure is in the **else** portion of the programming logic, where we not only set the **onScreen** boolean flag variable back to **false**, but we'll also set the **takeSides** boolean variable to **true**, so that the Enemy will use the other side of the screen for his next attack attempt.

Finally, since the attack sequence is completed, we will also set the **callAttack** boolean flag variable to **false**. As you know, this will start up the attackCounter program logic in the .update() method, which will give your player a few seconds to recover from being attacked. The Java structure for the entire **if(!takeSides)** conditional structure, and its nested **if(onScreen)** conditional structures, is shown highlighted in Figure 17-37, and should look like the following:

```java
private void initiateAttack() {
    if(!takeSides) {
        spriteFrame.setScaleX(1);
        this.setIsFlipH(false);
        if(!onScreen) {
            destination = 500;
            if(spriteMoveR >= destination) {
                spriteMoveR-=2;
                spriteFrame.setTranslateX(spriteMoveR);
```

```java
    } else {
        // ShootProjectile();
        onScreen = true;
    }
    if(onScreen) {
        destination = 700;
        if(spriteMoveR <= destination) {
            spriteMoveR+=1;
            spriteFrame.setTranslateX(spriteMoveR);
        } else {
            onScreen = false;
            takeSides = true;
            callAttack = false;
        }
    }
}
```

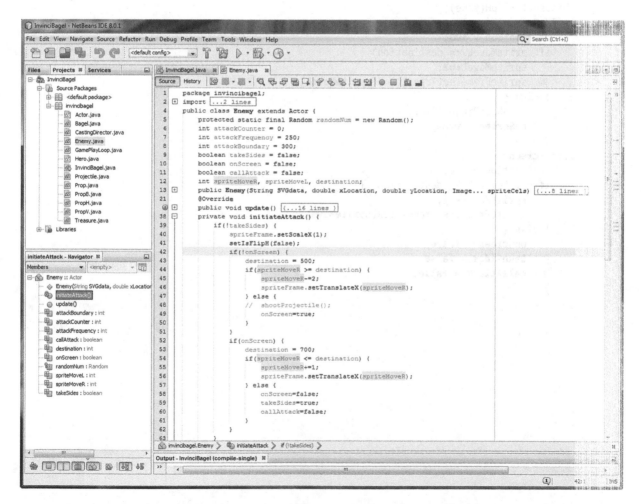

Figure 17-37. *Add an if(onScreen) level of processing inside the if(!takeSides) logic to animate sprite from the right side*

Inside the second **if(takeSides)** structure, in the if(!onScreen) structure, initialize the destination location to **100** pixels, and nest another counter **if(spriteMoveL <= destination)** structure. This time, you will move the sprite by two pixels per pulse using **spriteMoveL+=2;** in conjunction with **spriteFrame.setTranslateX(spriteMoveL);** to move the sprite in the opposite direction. In the else portion, set the **onScreen** boolean flag variable to a **true** value.

The logic for the second nested conditional **if(onScreen)** structure is again similar to the first. You'll set your **destination** to -70 pixels, and this time, you'll iterate using -=1 instead of +=1. In the **else** portion of the programming logic, we will again set the **onScreen** boolean flag variable back to **false**, and we'll set the **takeSides** boolean variable back to **false**, so that the Enemy will again alternate sides and use the other side of the screen for his next attack.

Finally, since an attack sequence is completed, we will again set the **callAttack** boolean flag variable to **false**. As you know, this will start up the attackCounter program logic in the .update() method, which will give your player a few seconds to recover from being attacked. The Java structure for this entire **if(takeSides)** conditional structure, and its nested **if(onScreen)** conditional structures, is shown highlighted in Figure 17-38, and should look like the following:

```java
if(takeSides) {
    spriteFrame.setScaleX(-1);
    this.setIsFlipH(true);
    if(!onScreen) {
        destination = 100;
        if(spriteMoveL <= destination) {
            spriteMoveL+=2;
            spriteFrame.setTranslateX(spriteMoveL);
        } else {
            // ShootProjectile();
            onScreen = true;
        }
    }
    if(onScreen) {
        destination = -70;
        if(spriteMoveL >= destination) {
            spriteMoveL-=1;
            spriteFrame.setTranslateX(spriteMoveL);
        } else {
            onScreen = false;
            takeSides = false;
            callAttack = false;
        }
    }
}
```

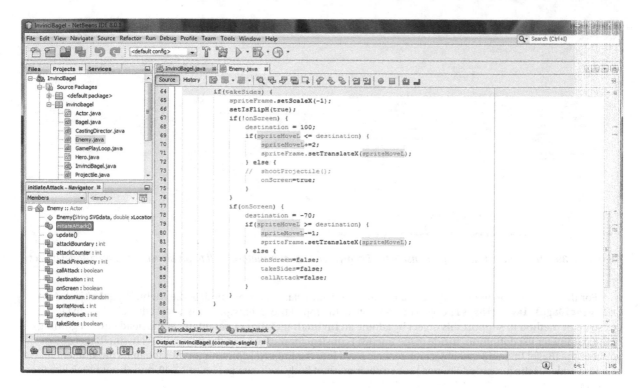

Figure 17-38. *Add an if(onScreen) level of processing inside the if(takeSides) logic to animate a sprite from the left side*

Weaponizing the Enemy: Shooting Projectile Objects

Now that we have the Enemy animating onto (and off of) both sides of the screen, the next level of complexity that we need to add is the shooting of Projectile objects. We'll first implement **iBullet** objects (negative score generation) and later **iCheese** objects (positive score generation), both of which will require our Enemy.java class to have visibility into the InvinciBagel class. Thus, the first thing that we'll need to do is to modify the **Enemy()** constructor method to accept an InvinciBagel object using the Java **this** keyword, much like we did with our Bagel() constructor method. Go into the InvinciBagel.java class and add a this keyword to the front end of (beginning of) your Enemy() constructor parameter list, as shown highlighted in Figure 17-39, using the following amended Enemy() constructor method call:

```
iBeagle = new Enemy(this, "MO 6 LO 52 70 52 70 70 70 93 115 45 115 0 84 0 68 16 Z",520,160,iEO);
```

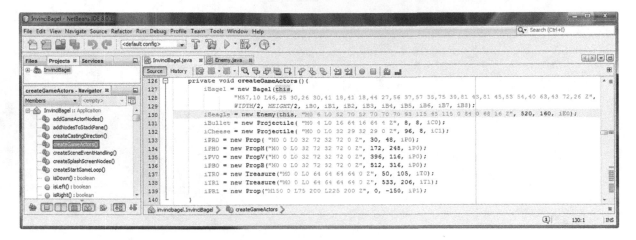

Figure 17-39. *Add a Java this keyword inside the Enemy() constructor method call to pass over the InvinciBagel object*

For this to work, you need to also update your Enemy.java class to accommodate the **InvinciBagel** object. Add an **InvinciBagel invinciBagel;** object declaration, at the top of the Enemy.java class, and edit your Enemy() constructor method to support this object by adding an **InvinciBagel iBagel** parameter at the head end (beginning) of the parameter list definition. Inside of the Enemy() constructor method, set the invinciBagel InvinciBagel object equal to the iBagel InvinciBagel object reference passed into the Enemy() constructor method in its parameter list. The Java code for the amended Enemy() constructor method body is shown in Figure 17-40, and should look like the following:

```
InvinciBagel invinciBagel;
public Enemy( InvinciBagel iBagel,
            String SVGdata, double xLocation, double yLocation, Image... spriteCels) {
        super(SVGdata, xLocation, yLocation, spriteCels);
        invinciBagel = iBagel;
        spriteFrame.setTranslateX(xLocation);
        spriteFrame.setTranslateY(yLocation);
        isAlive = true;
        isBonus = true;
        hasValu = true;
    }
```

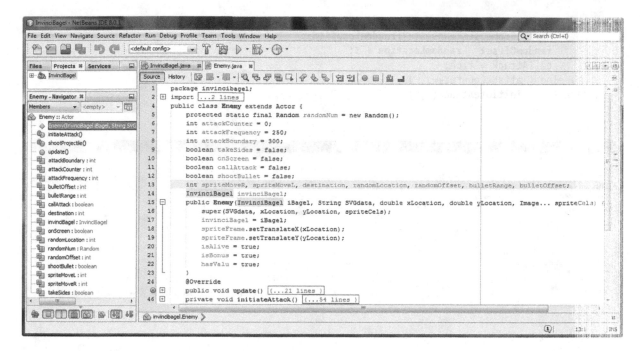

Figure 17-40. *Modify the Enemy() constructor method in the Enemy class to add an InvinciBagel object named* iBagel

Now that the Enemy class (object) can see into the InvinciBagel class (object), we're ready to add projectiles.

Creating a Projectile Infrastructure: Adding Projectile Variables

To add projectile support to the Enemy class we will need to declare four new variables at the top of the class. These will include randomLocation, a new variable that we'll use for both the Enemy character and the projectile he shoots; randomOffset, a new variable that will hold the vertical (Y) offset that allows us to fine-tune position the projectile so that it comes out of the bazooka barrel; and the bulletRange and bulletOffset allowing us to do X positioning. We will set the **randomLocation** variable equal to the **randomNum.nextInt(attackBoundary)** logic, which used to be inside of the **.setTranslateY()** method call, and add **5** to this variable, to create the **randomOffset** variable data value. The new Java structure for these methods is error-free, as shown in Figure 17-41, and should look like the following Java code:

```
int spriteMoveR, spriteMoveL, destination;
int randomLocation, randomOffset, bulletRange, bulletOffset;
public void update() {
    if(callAttack) {
        if(attackCounter >= attackFrequency) {
            attackCounter=0;
            spriteMoveR = 700;
            spriteMoveL = -70;
```

```
            randomLocation = randomNum.nextInt(attackBoundary);
            spriteFrame.setTranslateY(randomLocation);
            randomOffset = randomLocation + 5;
            callAttack = true;
        } else { attackCounter+=1; }
    } else {     initiateAttack(); }
}
```

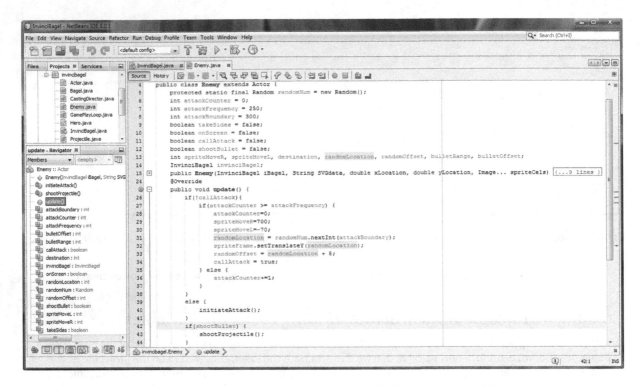

Figure 17-41. Add randomLocation, randomOffset, bulletRange, and bulletOffset variables to control bullet placement

Also notice, at the bottom of Figure 17-41, we've also added an **if(shootBullet){shootProjectile();}** conditional if structure to the bottom of the .update() method, as well as adding a **boolean shootBullet = false;** declaration at the top of the Enemy.java class. Before we code the .shootProjectile() method, let's add the shootBullet flag settings to the .initiateAttack() method, as well as setting a **bulletOffset** X location for the bullet, in **if(!onScreen)**.

Invoking a .shootProjectile() Method: Setting shootBullet to True

Inside each of the if(takeSides) conditional if-else structures, in the else portion of the statement, add a bulletOffset variable setting (**480** or **120**) and set **shootBullet** equal to **true**. The Java code, seen in Figure 17-42, will look like this:

```java
if(takeSides) {
    spriteFrame.setScaleX(1);
    this.setIsFlipH(false);
    if(!onScreen) {
        destination = 500;
        if(spriteMoveR >= destination) {
            spriteMoveR-=2;
            spriteFrame.setTranslateX(spriteMoveR);
        } else {
            bulletOffset = 480;
            shootBullet = true;
            onScreen = true;        }
```

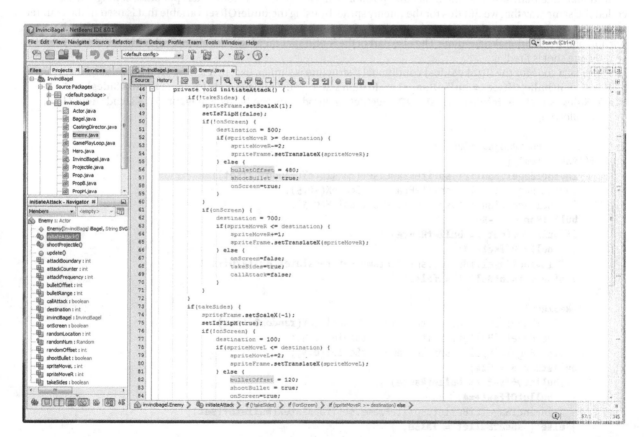

Figure 17-42. *Add bulletOffset values and shootBullet=true statements into the sprite-reached-destination else body*

Now that you have set up the variables and if(shootBullet) structure in the .update() method, which will call the .shootProjectile() method to launch the Projectile objects out of the iBeagle Enemy Actor bazooka, we can start to create the code that will animate the iBullet object (and later, the iCheese object as well) in a similar way to how we created our Enemy animation functionality.

Shooting Projectiles: Coding the .shootProjectile( ) Method

If you have not already created an empty **private void shootProjectile(){}** method structure to get rid of those wavy red error highlights in your code, you can do so now. Inside of this method, we will again have the **if(!takeSides)** and **if(takeSides)** conditional structures, to segregate the different logic for each side of the Stage. This is similar to what we did to animate the Enemy character onto the screen in the .initiateAttack() method. The first Java statement will position the Y location, this time using the **randomOffset** variable inside of the .setTranslateY() method call off of an iBullet.spriteFrame ImageView object. The randomOffset variable adjusts bullet placement relative to the bazooka barrel. The next two .setScaleX and .setScaleY() method calls reduce the bullet image scale by half (0.5) and also flip the bullet using the -0.5 value. It is interesting to note here than any negative value, not just -1, will mirror around an axis. The next line of code sets the **bulletRange** variable to -50, before the **if(bulletOffset >= bulletRange)** conditional statement animates the bullet into position using a high velocity four pixels per pulse setting. This is coded the same way that we did this for the Enemy sprite, by using the **bulletOffset** variable that is used in the counter logic inside of the **.setTranslateX()** method call off of the **iBullet.spriteFrame** ImageView object inside of the if portion of the conditional statement. The else part of the if-else statement sets the **shootProjectile** variable to **false**, so only one shot is fired!

The Java code for the **if(takeSides)** conditional if structure is similar, except it uses +=4, a bulletRange of **624**, and an **if(bulletOffset <= bulletRange)** evaluation statement. Your Java code for these **if(!takeSides)** and **if(takeSides)** structures inside of the **shootProjectile()** method body can be seen in Figure 17-43, and should look like the following:

```java
private void shootProjectile() {
    if(!takeSides) {
        invinciBagel.iBullet.spriteFrame.setTranslateY(randomOffset);
        invinciBagel.iBullet.spriteFrame.setScaleX(-0.5);
        invinciBagel.iBullet.spriteFrame.setScaleY(0.5);
        bulletRange = -50;
        if(bulletOffset >= bulletRange) {
            bulletOffset-=4;
            invinciBagel.iBullet.spriteFrame.setTranslateX(bulletOffset);
        } else { shootBullet = false; }
    }
    if(takeSides) {
        invinciBagel.iBullet.spriteFrame.setTranslateY(randomOffset);
        invinciBagel.iBullet.spriteFrame.setScaleX(0.5);
        invinciBagel.iBullet.spriteFrame.setScaleY(0.5);
        bulletRange = 624;
        if(bulletOffset <= bulletRange) {
            bulletOffset+=4;
            invinciBagel.iBullet.spriteFrame.setTranslateX(bulletOffset);
        } else { shootBullet = false; }
    }
}
```

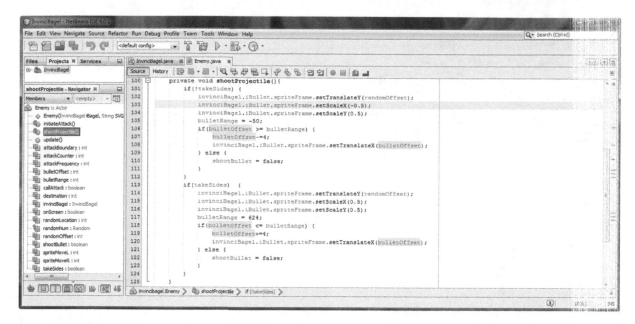

Figure 17-43. *Add private void shootProjectile() method and code the if(!takeSides) and if(takeSides) if-else statements*

If you now use your **Run ➤ Project** work process you will see your iBeagle animate on screen, shoot a bullet, and retreat quickly back off-screen. The next level of realism that we need to add into our code is to have the iBeagle pause for a second while he aims and shoots the bullet, because currently it looks like he is hitting an invisible barrier and bouncing back off-screen. We will do this by adding counter logic into the if(shootBullet) conditional statement in the .update() method. Let's do that next, so that we have a completely professional Enemy auto-attack sequence!

Making the Enemy Pause Before Firing: pauseCounter Variable

To make the Enemy pause on screen, so that his shooting action looks more realistic, and so that the InvinciBagel character has some time to try and tackle him (which we are going to assign ten scoring points to a bit later on), let's add an integer **pauseCounter** variable and a boolean **launchIt** variable at the top of our Enemy.java class, as is shown highlighted in Figure 17-44. Inside of the if(shootBullet) conditional statement, after the shootProjectile() method call, place an **if(pauseCounter >= 60)** conditional structure, and inside of it, set **launchIt** equal to **true**, and reset the **pauseCounter** variable to **zero**. In the else part of the condition, increment the pauseCounter by one using **pauseCounter++** and then all we have to do is to implement the launchIt boolean flag into our initiateAttack() method and we will have an Enemy character who takes his time when he aims and shoots at the InvinciBagel character. Your Java code for this if(shootBullet) if-else structure can be seen in Figure 17-44, and should look like the following code:

```
if(shootBullet) {
    shootProjectile();
    if(pauseCounter >= 60) {
        launchIt = true;
        pauseCounter = 0;
    } else { pauseCounter++ }
}
```

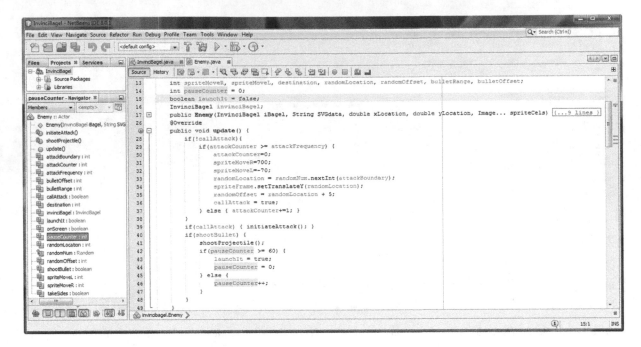

Figure 17-44. *Add a pauseCounter variable to create a timer, creating a one-second delay, so Enemy doesn't bounce*

Shoot the Bullet: Pulling the Trigger Using the launchIt Variable

Inside of each of your **if(takeSides)** and **if(!takeSides)** conditional if structures, modify the if(onScreen) structure to be an **if(onScreen** && **launchIt)** structure instead, and then add a **launchit = false;** statement into the else portion of this modified structure. The Java code for the new if() structure is shown in Figure 17-45, and looks like the following:

```
if(onScreen && launchIt) {
    destination = 700;
    if(spriteMoveR <= destination) {
        spriteMoveR+=1;
        spriteFrame.setTranslateX(spriteMoveR);
    } else {
        onScreen   = false;
        takeSides  = true;      // This will be false if inside of the if(takeSides) structure
        callAttack = false;
        launchIt   = false;  }
}
```

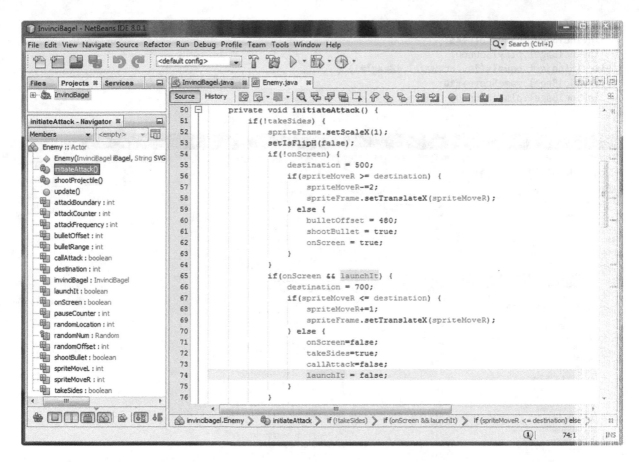

Figure 17-45. *Add a launchIt flag to the if(onScreen) condition to make that code structure wait for the pauseCounter*

For the **if(takeSides)** version of this if(onScreen && launchIt) structure, make sure to change the destination to -70, make the counter **if(spriteMoveL >= destination)** and the counter update **spriteMoveL-=1;** and the takeSides equal to **false** in the **else** portion of this conditional structure. Next, let's update our **scoring engine** in the Bagel class.

Update the .scoringEngine() Method: Using .equals()

Let's use a different approach for these last three object scoring else-if structures, and instead of using an if(object instanceof Actor) for more general object type comparisons, we will use the more precise .equals() method that allows us to specify the object itself, such as **if(object.equals(invinciBagel.iBullet)**. You can see the complete if-else structure in Figure 17-46, and the Java code for the last three Enemy objects looks like the following:

```
} else if(object.equals(invinciBagel.iBullet)) {
    invinciBagel.gameScore-=5;
    invinciBagel.playiSound5;
```

```
    } else if(object.equals(invinciBagel.iCheese)) {
        invinciBagel.gameScore+=5;
        invinciBagel.playiSound0;
    } else if(object.equals(invinciBagel.iBeagle)) {
        invinciBagel.gameScore+=10;
        invinciBagel.playiSound0;   }
```

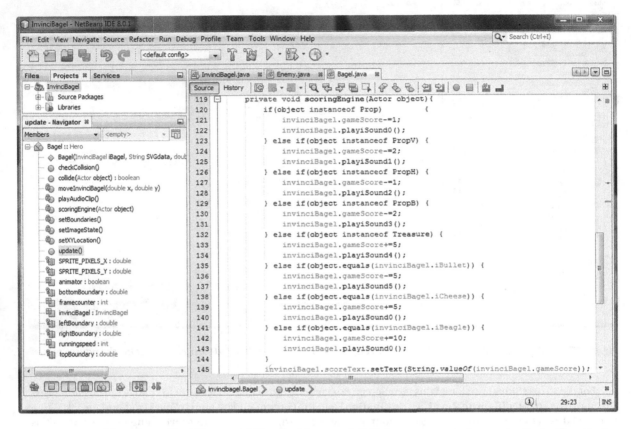

Figure 17-46. *Adding the iBullet, iCheese and iBeagle object.equals() if-else structures to the .scoringEngine() method*

At this point, if you use a **Run ➤ Project** work process, you should have an iBeagle shooting a Bullet or Cream Cheese Ball. When you catch the iBeagle with the InvinciBagel character, you should score ten points, or, if you catch a Cream Cheese Ball, you should get five points. If you get hit by a Bullet, you should lose five points.

You will notice as you test the InvinciBagel game application that once you get hit by a Bullet, Cream Cheese Ball, or when you catch the iBeagle, that they do not come back! This is because the collision detection programming logic removes an object from the game once an InvinciBagel collects it (Treasure) or collides with it (Prop or Projectile).

So the next step in our development will be to add in the programming logic that adds an iBullet, iCheese or iBeagle object back into the castDirector object once they have been removed by the collision detection programming logic that you put into place in Chapter 16. To do this, we'll have to code an enhancement to the **CastingDirector.java** class, code the new .loadEnemy(), .loadBullet() and .loadCheese() methods at the bottom of the Enemy.java class, and add the appropriate programming logic implementing these three new methods into the .initiateAttack() method.

Adding Bullets to a Clip: Updating .addCurrentCast()

Since we are going to add single (one at a time, not unmarried) Actor objects back into the CURRENT_CAST List, we will need to modify the .addCurrentCast() method as it currently only takes an Actor . . . series of objects and we need it to accommodate a single added Actor object, like the addToRemovedActors() method does currently. You can see the .addToRemovedActors() method at the bottom of Figure 17-47. The .addCurrentCast() method was designed to be used **statically** in the InvinciBagel.java class, in the start() method, to add all of the cast members at one time (remember static versus dynamic). Now I am going to show you how to redesign it to allow "one off" additions during gameplay, which is a dynamic use of the method, as the List<Actor> will be modified **dynamically** in real-time during gameplay. To upgrade the .addCurrentCast() method, simply "wrap" the .addAll() method call inside of the method with an if(actors.length > 1) if-else structure, with the original code inside of the if() portion and a **CURRENT_CAST. add(actors[0]);** statement inside of the else portion to accommodate single Actor method calls. The Java code for the new method structure can be seen in Figure 17-47, and should look like the following:

```java
public void addCurrentCast(Actor... actors) {
    if(actors.length > 1) {
        CURRENT_CAST.addAll(Arrays.asList(actors));
    } else {
        CURRENT_CAST.add(actors[0]);
    }
}
```

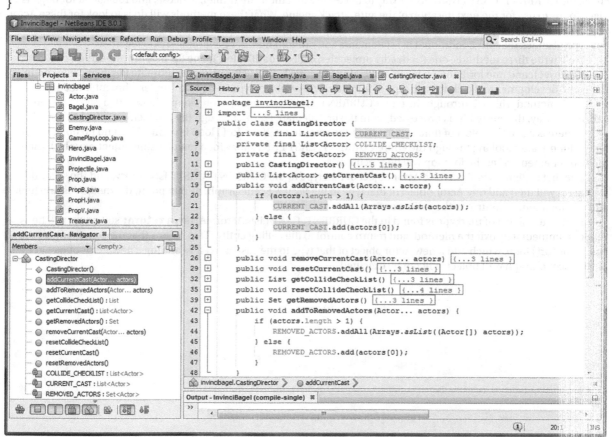

Figure 17-47. *Upgrade addCurrentCast() method in the CastingDirector class to accept a single object in parameter list*

It is important to note that we could also accomplish this objective by **overloading** this .addCurrentCast() method as well. If you wanted to do this in this fashion, the Java code would look like the following method bodies:

```java
public void addCurrentCast(Actor... actors) {
        CURRENT_CAST.addAll(Arrays.asList(actors));
}
public void addCurrentCast(Actor actor) {
        CURRENT_CAST.add(actor);
}
```

Once your game design becomes more advanced and you have decorative Actor objects on the Stage, you can implement the COLLIDE_CHECKLIST in your if() structures that need to iterate through (only) the Actor objects in your Scene that need to be processed for collision.

At this point in our game design, we are processing all of the Actor objects for collision, thus, we don't yet need to implement the COLLIDE_CHECKLIST List<Actor> Array. I've included it in the class design to be thorough and because I design foundational classes for games by looking out into the future toward what I will need in order for me to create an advanced (complete) game engine. That said, we may not have enough pages in this Beginner title to get that advanced, but the functionality is there if you needed to use it in your games, and after this chapter you will have plenty of experience using if() structures!

Now that we can add cast members on an individual basis, it is time to write the methods that will allow us to check the CURRENT_CAST List<Actor> Array to make sure that there are iBullet, iCheese, and iBeagle Actor objects in place for us to use for the next iteration of the auto-attack engine. What these methods will do is to look for these Actor objects in the CURRENT_CAST List, and if they are not present, will add one of them to the List so that it is ready for any type of attack that our conditional if() statements and random number generator create together!

We'll write three methods, one for deadly projectiles, called **.loadBullet()**; one for healthy projectiles, called **.loadCheese()**; and one for Enemy objects, called **loadEnemy()**. This will give us the ultimate flexibility, later on in our game development, of calling each type of functional Actor object type in its own "replenishment function."

Each method will look through the entire CURRENT_CAST List, using a for() loop, along with a .size() method call. In this way, the entire List is processed, from the first element (zero), through the last element (the List's size).

If there is no Actor object of that type found in the cast, that is, if the for() loop is completed, and no object of that type is found, after looking through the entire CURRENT_CAST List<Actor> for a match using **object.equals()**, then the two statements after the for loop will be executed.

The first statement will add one Actor object of that type to the CURRENT_CAST List<Actor>, and the second statement will then add one Actor object of that type to the JavaFX SceneGraph. At that point, the method is finished, and will then return control to the calling entity.

If an Actor object of that type is found in the CURRENT_CAST List<Actor> Array, a **return;** statement will be called to immediately exit the method, and return control to the calling entity. This means that the statements at the end of the for() loop, which add a new Actor object of that type to the cast, as well as adding a new Actor object to the JavaFX Scene Graph root object, will not be executed.

This **return;** statement is a central component to making this method work, because if any Actor object of that type exists, a duplicate one will not be added to the List<Actor> Array, which would cause an error to occur. This is a great way to make sure that we only use one Node for each type of Projectile and Enemy object, which allows us to optimize both memory and processor overhead. The Java 8 programming structures for all three of these methods is quite similar, and can be seen in Figure 17-48. The three **private void** method bodies should look like the following:

```java
private void loadBullet() {
    for (int i=0; i<invinciBagel.castDirector.getCurrentCast().size(); i++) {
        Actor object = invinciBagel.castDirector.getCurrentCast().get(i);
        if(object.equals(invinciBagel.iBullet)) {
            return;
        }
    }
    invinciBagel.castDirector.addCurrentCast(invinciBagel.iBullet);
    invinciBagel.root.getChildren().add(invinciBagel.iBullet.spriteFrame);
}

private void loadCheese() {
    for (int i=0; i<invinciBagel.castDirector.getCurrentCast().size(); i++) {
        Actor object = invinciBagel.castDirector.getCurrentCast().get(i);
        if(object.equals(invinciBagel.iCheese)) {
            return;
        }
    }
    invinciBagel.castDirector.addCurrentCast(invinciBagel.iCheese);
    invinciBagel.root.getChildren().add(invinciBagel.iCheese.spriteFrame);
}

private void loadEnemy() {
    for (int i=0; i<invinciBagel.castDirector.getCurrentCast().size(); i++) {
        Actor object = invinciBagel.castDirector.getCurrentCast().get(i);
        if(object.equals(invinciBagel.iBeagle)) {
            return;
        }
    }
    invinciBagel.castDirector.addCurrentCast(invinciBagel.iBeagle);
    invinciBagel.root.getChildren().add(invinciBagel.iBeagle.spriteFrame);
}
```

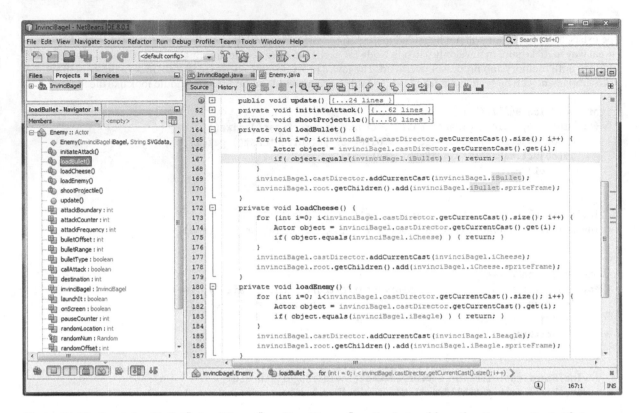

Figure 17-48. *Create loadBullet(), loadCheese() and loadEnemy() methods, to add another Enemy or Projectile to game*

Now that all these methods are in place, we can call them inside of the .initiateAttack() auto-attack method body and put them to work checking to see if we need to add a Projectile or Enemy object before we mount the next attack. The proper place to invoke these method calls would be after the Enemy object is onScreen, and the Projectile object has been launched, which means that these method calls need to go at the end of the if(onScreen && launchIt) structure's **else{}** body of code. The Java code for implementing these three method calls can be seen in Figure 17-49, and should look like the following:

```java
if(onScreen && launchIt) {
    destination = 700;
    if(spriteMoveR <= destination) {
        spriteMoveR+=1;
        spriteFrame.setTranslateX(spriteMoveR);
    } else {
        onScreen    = false;
        takeSides   = true;     // This will be false if inside of the if(takeSides) structure
        callAttack  = false;
        launchIt    = false;
        loadBullet();
        loadCheese();
        loadEnemy();
    }
}
```

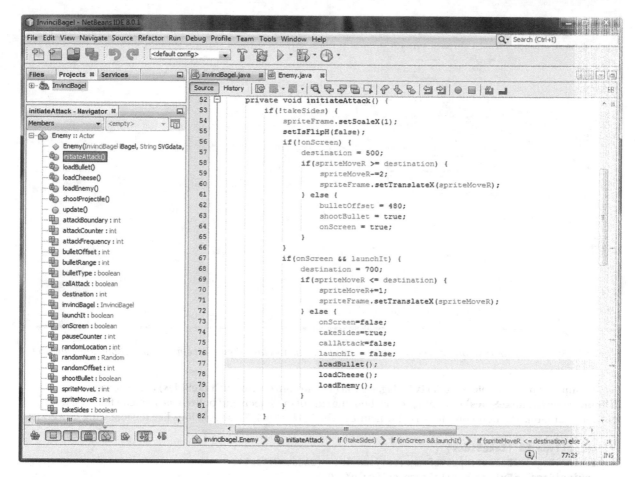

Figure 17-49. *Add calls to loadBullet(), loadCheese() and loadEnemy() to end of "move Enemy offscreen" else structure*

Next, let's add a unique twist to our game play, and have a Projectile object, in the form of a Cream Cheese Ball, that will generate positive points if the InvinciBagel is able to put himself in a position to get hit by it.

Shooting Cream Cheese Balls: Different Bullet Types

To accommodate different types of projectiles, we will need to declare a new boolean variable, which we will name **bulletType**, so that we can have deadly projectiles (iBullet) and healthy projectiles (iCheese). In the .update() method, right before you set callAttack equal to true to start the attack sequence, you will set this bulletType variable equal to the result of a call to the .nextBoolean() method made off of the randomNum Random object. The Java code, which is shown highlighted in Figure 17-50, should look like the following Java statements:

```
boolean bulletType = false;

bulletType = randomNum.nextBoolean();
```

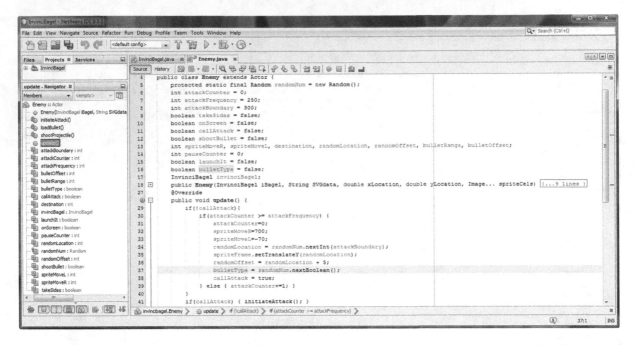

Figure 17-50. *Add a boolean bulletType variable at top of the Enemy class, then set it equal to .nextBoolean() method*

To implement this boolean bulletType flag, we will need to convert your **if(!takeSides)** evaluator to be an **if(!bulletType && !takeSides)** evaluator, so that both the side of the screen and bullet-type boolean flags are taken into consideration. The new conditional if() structures, seen in Figure 17-51, should look like the following Java code:

```java
if(!bulletType && !takeSides) {
    invinciBagel.iBullet.spriteFrame.setTranslateY(randomOffset);
    invinciBagel.iBullet.spriteFrame.setScaleX(-0.5);
    invinciBagel.iBullet.spriteFrame.setScaleY(0.5);
    bulletRange = -50;
    if(bulletOffset >= bulletRange) {
        bulletOffset-=4;
        invinciBagel.iBullet.spriteFrame.setTranslateX(bulletOffset);
    } else { shootBullet = false; }
}
if(!bulletType && takeSides) {
    invinciBagel.iBullet.spriteFrame.setTranslateY(randomOffset);
    invinciBagel.iBullet.spriteFrame.setScaleX(0.5);
    invinciBagel.iBullet.spriteFrame.setScaleY(0.5);
    bulletRange = 624;
    if(bulletOffset <= bulletRange) {
        bulletOffset+=4;
        invinciBagel.iBullet.spriteFrame.setTranslateX(bulletOffset);
    } else { shootBullet = false; }
}
```

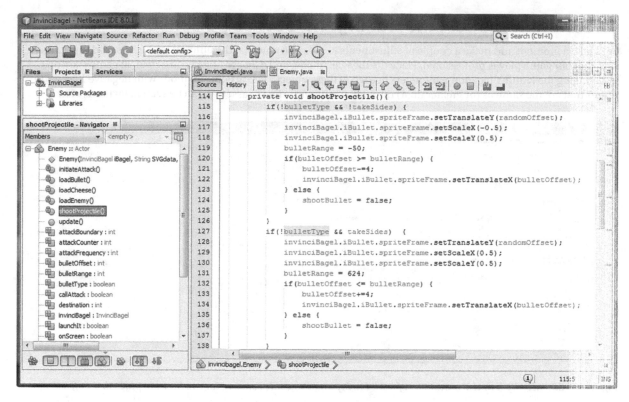

Figure 17-51. Add bulletType to conditional if statement evaluation in shootProjectile() method, to shoot cream cheese

Next we need to do the same conversion for the bulletType equals true value. This will signify use of Cream Cheese as a Projectile object type. Once we put these conditional if() structures into place, we'll have one if() structure for each logical combination of takeSides and bulletType. The last two conditional if() structures should look like this:

```
if(bulletType && !takeSides) {
    invinciBagel.iCheese.spriteFrame.setTranslateY(randomOffset);
    invinciBagel.iCheese.spriteFrame.setScaleX(-0.5);
    invinciBagel.iCheese.spriteFrame.setScaleY(0.5);
    bulletRange = -50;
    if(bulletOffset >= bulletRange) {
        bulletOffset-=4;
        invinciBagel.iCheese.spriteFrame.setTranslateX(bulletOffset);
    } else { shootBullet = false; }
}
if(bulletType && takeSides) {
    invinciBagel.iCheese.spriteFrame.setTranslateY(randomOffset);
    invinciBagel.iCheese.spriteFrame.setScaleX(0.5);
    invinciBagel.iCheese.spriteFrame.setScaleY(0.5);
    bulletRange = 624;
    if(bulletOffset <= bulletRange) {
        bulletOffset+=4;
        invinciBagel.iCheese.spriteFrame.setTranslateX(bulletOffset);
    } else { shootBullet = false; }
}
```

Tweaking a Game: Fine-Tuning the User Experience

Let's take a moment and make a couple of adjustments to the code now that the auto-attack logic is working, to make sure that our game play is professional. Place the iBeagle, iBullet, and iCheese objects off-screen at game start-up, by changing the X and Y location parameters in each of these object's constructor methods with negative X location values that are the same as (or greater than) the width of the sprite image asset, as can be seen in Figure 17-52.

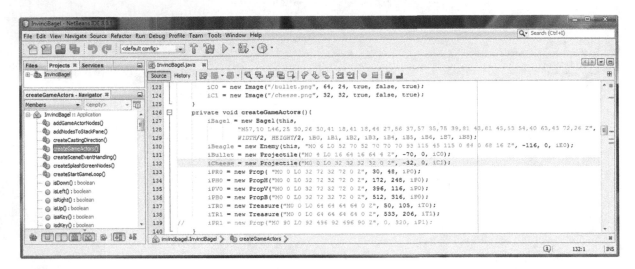

Figure 17-52. *Modify X and Y parameters for all Enemy and Projectile constructor methods, to place them off-screen*

You also may have noticed that the Projectile objects are on top of the Enemy's bazooka, so let's change the **z-index** of the iBeagle object, so the projectiles come from behind the gun. To do this, put your .add() method call for the iBeagle after iBullet, and before iBagel, at the end of the .addGameActorNodes() method, as seen in Figure 17-53.

Figure 17-53. *Change z-index of iCheese and iBullet in the addGameActorNodes() method so they're before iBeagle*

Now let's add even more realism to this auto-attack game play, by **randomizing** which side the Enemy sprite emerges from, so that the game player does not know what to expect. Currently, we are alternating sides, so we need to add a randomization of the **takeSides** boolean flag at the strategic place within our code. Let's write this code next.

Randomizing an Auto-Attack: Using .nextBoolean with takeSides

Even though we set the takeSides boolean flag right before we exit our initiateAttack() method after completing an attack, there is nothing that says we can't set it again before we call an attack by setting callAttack equal to true in the **if(attackCounter >= attackFrequency)** structure, which you can see I have done in Figure 17-54, using the following Java statement:

```
takeSides = randomNum.nextBoolean;
```

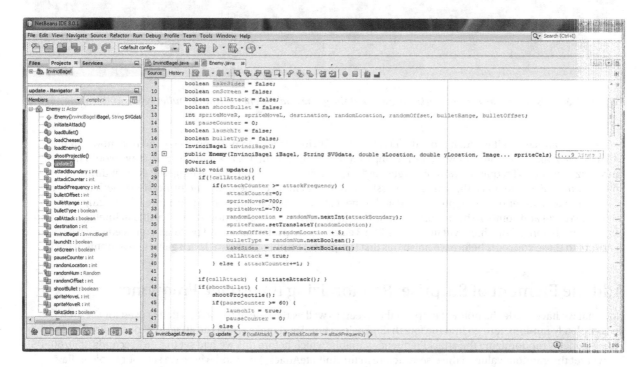

Figure 17-54. *Set the boolean takeSides variable to use a .nextBoolean() method call off a randomNum Random object*

Now that you have set the takeSides boolean flag variable in this way inside the Enemy .update() method, you can further optimize your code by removing the **takeSides = true;** and **takeSides = false;** statements, which are currently located inside your if(onScreen && launchIt) else statement (reference Figure 17-45).

Since those alternating boolean values will now be subsequently replaced by the .nextBoolean() method call in the **if(!callAttack)** structure, they can be safely removed, because the if(!callAttack) conditional structure randomly sets these two boolean values. The result of this is that now the iBeagle Enemy Actor object will randomly appear from out of either side of the screen, and the game player cannot anticipate where the attack is coming from anymore.

Use a **Run ➤ Project** work process, and play and test the game, which is seen in Figure 17-55. The first thing that you will notice is that all of our **z-index character layer ordering** is correct. You will also see that your Enemy and Projectiles are not visible at game start-up, which is another step toward a professional end-user experience.

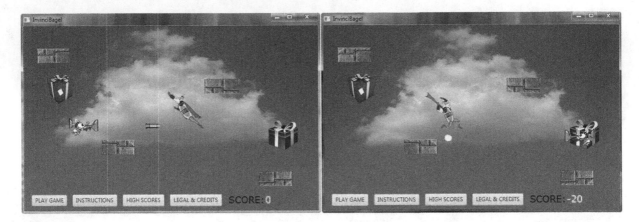

Figure 17-55. *Use a Run ➤ Project work process to test the game and the enemy attack, bullet types, and scoring engine*

You will notice that it is much more difficult to get the InvinciBagel into position, as you do not know where, when, or what direction the enemy attack is going to come from! Well, that is not entirely true, as we would need to randomize the attackFrequency variable to get the "when he appears" part to not be triggered at even time intervals. Since our objective is to make this game progressively more and more challenging and professional, let's do this next!

For the remainder of the chapter we will add some features that make the game play more challenging and realistic. We will add some of the important game design elements such as randomization, artificial intelligence, and physics simulation, all of which will make your Java 8 games more professional and popular. You need to have some exposure to these concepts before we finish this first (beginner) round of our core Java 8 games development cycle.

Add the Element of Surprise: Randomizing the Attack Frequency

Now that we have made the point of entry on the screen as well as the side of the screen that is used for the attack to be completely random, let's go into the fourth dimension (time) and make when the attack will occur also random. This is done by randomizing the attackFrequency variable, which before this we had set to 4.167 seconds (250/60FPS). We will set this random value in the else structure in the .initiateAttack() method where we set your boolean flag settings and call the .load() methods that we created to make sure the auto-attack engine always has Enemy and Projectile objects to work with. We will put a Java statement that inserts a random value into the attackFrequency variable at the end of this else portion of the if(onScreen && launchIt) conditional structure, so that a new random time is in place when the .update() method starts using this variable for its attack delay counter programming logic. Since the .nextInt(int bounds) method call structure gives us a random integer between zero and the upper bounds, in order to get a range of attack delay between one second (60) and nine seconds (60+480), we will need to add 60 to the value generated by the **randomNum.nextInt(480)** part of the statement, and then set the attackFrequency variable equal to that value. The Java code for this attackFrequency randomization statement can be seen in Figure 17-56 and should look like the following:

```
attackFrequency = 60 + randomNum.nextInt(480);
```

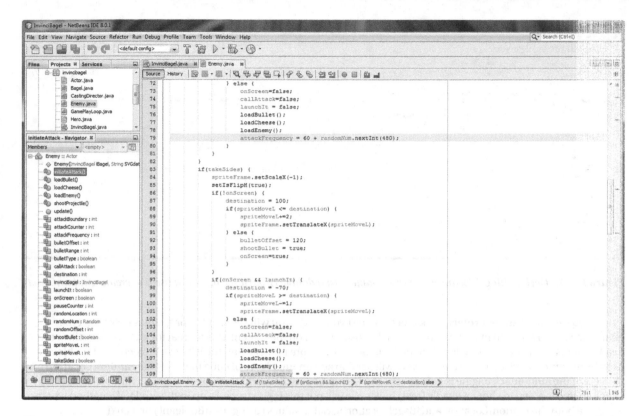

Figure 17-56. *Add an attackFrequency statement incorporating a .nextInt(bounds) method in if (onScreen && launchIt)*

As you can see when you use the **Run ➤ Project** work process, you no longer can calculate when any given Enemy attack will commence! Let's make the auto-attack engine more intelligent, by telling it where the InvinciBagel character is located (Y coordinate) on the screen, so that the auto-attack engine can more effectively target him!

Targeting the InvinciBagel: Adding Enemy Artificial Intelligence

The next thing that we should do to make game play more challenging is tell the auto-attack engine where the iBagel is located on the screen, an artificial intelligence gathering mission, made easier because we control all of the Java code! To do this, instead of using the randomLocation random Y screen height location value, we will create a variable that will hold the InvinciBagel Y screen height location value, giving the Enemy inside information regarding where the iBagel object is on the screen. This is done using the iY attribute of the iBagel Hero object, which we access using the .getiY() getter method, and then use in the .setTranslateY() method call. We are using integer (rather than double) as the iBagelLocation data type, so we'll need to "cast" the double data value we get from the .getiY() method, so that it is compatible with the iBagelLocation variable. The Java code, shown in Figure 17-57, should look like the following:

```
int iBagelLocation;
iBagelLocation = (int) invinciBagel.iBagel.getiY();
spriteFrame.setTranslateY(iBagelLocation);
randomOffset = iBagelLocation + 5;
```

449

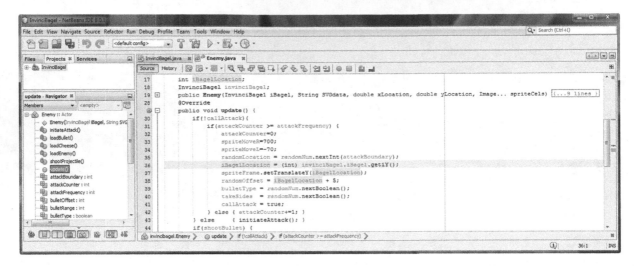

Figure 17-57. *Declare iBagelLocation integer variable, cast a double iY variable to it, and use it to create randomOffset*

If you use your **Run ➤ Project** work process to test your code, you will see that the projectiles now target the InvinciBagel character, no matter where you might position him on the screen! This is great for attacks that utilize the deadly iBullet Projectile Actor object, but makes it too easy to score points when the iCheese Projectile Actor object is used by the auto-attack engine. Therefore, we will need to add another layer of code that uses the **randomLocation** variable, if the auto-attack engine is going to shoot a Cream Cheese Ball, and the **iBagelLocation** variable, if the auto-attack engine is going to shoot a deadly (real) bullet. We will put this logic structure up in the .update() method where we create both the randomLocation and iBagelLocation variable values (using .nextBoolean() or .getiY() method calls), right after the bulletType is determined, using a .nextBoolean() method call off of the randomNum Random object.

The **if(bulletType)** conditional if structure that we are going to create will use a .setTranslateY() method call, passing a randomLocation parameter, if bulletType equates to a true value (iCheese), and will use the .setTranslateY() method call passing the iBagelLocation parameter, if the bulletType equates to a false value (iBullet), using the else{} portion of the if-else structure. In a second line of code inside each section of the if-else structure, we'll remember to set the randomOffset variable, to add five pixels to the randomLocation variable inside the if portion of the structure, or to add five pixels to the iBagelLocation variable, inside the else portion, using the following code, shown in Figure 17-58:

```
if(attackCounter >= attackFrequency) {
    attackCounter=0;
    spriteMoveR = 700;
    spriteMoveL = -70;
    randomLocation = randomNum.nextInt(attackBoundary);
    iBagelLocation = (int) invinciBagel.iBagel.getiY();
    bulletType = randomNum.nextBoolean();
    if(bulletType) {
    spriteFrame.setTranslateY(randomLocation);
    randomOffset = randomLocation + 5;
    } else {
    spriteFrame.setTranslateY(iBagelLocation);
    randomOffset = iBagelLocation + 5;
    }
    callAttack = true;
} else { attackCounter+=1; }
```

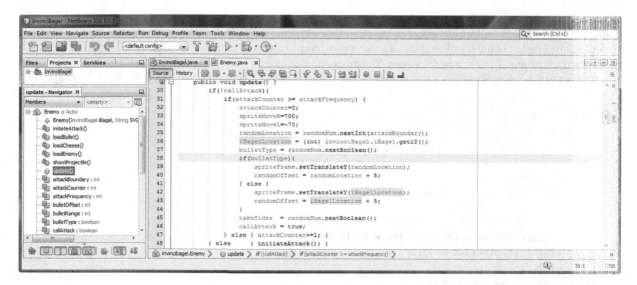

Figure 17-58. *Add an if-else structure after the bulletType, randomLocation, and iBagelLocation to locate by* bulletType

Adding Gravity to the Bullets: Intro to Game Physics

Since physics calculations tend to use fractional numbers rather than integers, we need to pull the randomOffset out of the compound integer declaration and make it a **double randomOffset;** declaration, as seen in Figure 17-59. Also, you'll need to declare **double** variables for **bulletGravity** and **cheeseGravity**, and set them equal to **0.2** and **0.1** values.

Figure 17-59. *Declaring bulletGravity and cheeseGravity double variables, and converting randomOffset to a* double

What we want to do is to add a bulletGravity (or cheeseGravity) factor to the randomOffset (Y location) on each frame, so we get a slight "tailing off" effect on the shot. This will simulate gravity pulling the Projectile down to Earth. We will put this inside of the if(bulletOffset >= bulletRange) counter loop so that gravity factor is only applied when the projectile is visible flying across the screen. The Java code that incorporates bulletGravity and cheeseGravity adjustments to the Projectile object's trajectories can be seen in Figure 17-60, and should look like the following code:

```java
private void shootProjectile() {
    if(!bulletType && !takeSides) {
        invinciBagel.iBullet.spriteFrame.setTranslateY(randomOffset);
        invinciBagel.iBullet.spriteFrame.setScaleX(-0.5);
        invinciBagel.iBullet.spriteFrame.setScaleY(0.5);
        bulletRange = -50;
        if(bulletOffset >= bulletRange) {
            bulletOffset-=6;
            invinciBagel.iBullet.spriteFrame.setTranslateX(bulletOffset);
            randomOffset = randomOffset + bulletGravity;
        } else { shootBullet = false; }
    }
    if(!bulletType && takeSides) {
        invinciBagel.iBullet.spriteFrame.setTranslateY(randomOffset);
        invinciBagel.iBullet.spriteFrame.setScaleX(0.5);
        invinciBagel.iBullet.spriteFrame.setScaleY(0.5);
        bulletRange = 624;
        if(bulletOffset <= bulletRange) {
            bulletOffset+=6;
            invinciBagel.iBullet.spriteFrame.setTranslateX(bulletOffset);
            randomOffset = randomOffset + bulletGravity;
        } else { shootBullet = false; }
    }
    if(bulletType && !takeSides) {
        invinciBagel.iCheese.spriteFrame.setTranslateY(randomOffset);
        invinciBagel.iCheese.spriteFrame.setScaleX(-0.5);
        invinciBagel.iCheese.spriteFrame.setScaleY(0.5);
        bulletRange = -50;
        if(bulletOffset >= bulletRange) {
            bulletOffset-=4;
            invinciBagel.iCheese.spriteFrame.setTranslateX(bulletOffset);
            randomOffset = randomOffset + cheeseGravity;
        } else { shootBullet = false; }
    }
    if(bulletType && takeSides) {
        invinciBagel.iCheese.spriteFrame.setTranslateY(randomOffset);
        invinciBagel.iCheese.spriteFrame.setScaleX(0.5);
        invinciBagel.iCheese.spriteFrame.setScaleY(0.5);
        bulletRange = 630;
        if(bulletOffset <= bulletRange) {
            bulletOffset+=4;
            invinciBagel.iCheese.spriteFrame.setTranslateX(bulletOffset);
            randomOffset = randomOffset + cheeseGravity;
        } else { shootBullet = false; }
    }
}
```

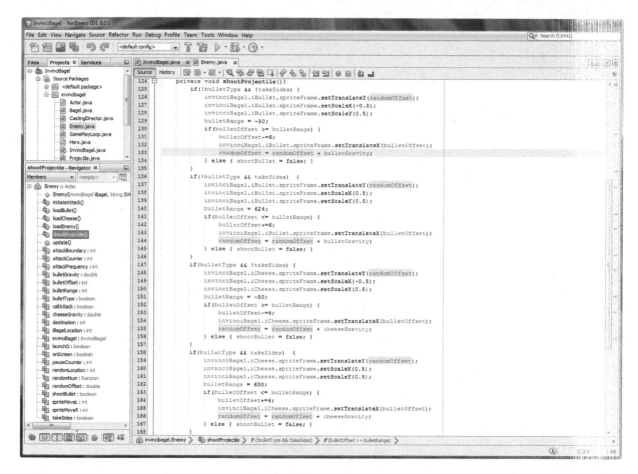

Figure 17-60. *Adding physics simulation of gravity to the Projectile object's trajectory in the .shootProjectile() method*

Summary

In this seventeenth and final chapter, we used all of the foundational elements of our game engine(s) that we have been building during the course of this book, and created the basic game play for the InvinciBagel game, including a scoring engine and an auto-attack engine, as well as random attack strategies and basic physics simulation to enhance realism. We learned how to use the JavaFX 8.0 Text and Font class to create scoreboard output on the game, and how to use the Java 8 Random class as a random number generator to make our auto-attack engine seem like it had a life of its own. We also added bounty to the game by coding a Treasure.java class and created a .scoringEngine() method to track and organize our scoring algorithm. We learned more about optimization, using if-else-if loops with **break;** and learned how to use **return;** to break out of a method prematurely as well, and we used both of these techniques to great benefit in our game play logic. We added Enemy characters and Projectile objects to the game, and learned how to implement a background plate behind the game play. I've tried to go beyond a basic beginner Java 8 book and show you the work process involved in creating a game engine infrastructure, including the design thought process, how to leverage key classes in Java 8 and JavaFX 8.0, and how to use new media assets and optimization techniques.

Index

A

ActionEvent object, 193
Actor superclass, 165, 168, 299
   Actor() constructor method, 169, 173
   boolean data variables, 172
   double data variables, 171
   getter and setter methods, 174
   overloaded method, 169
   Prop subclasses (*see* Prop subclasses)
   setContent() method, 169
   update() method, 170
addGameActorNodes()
      method, 237–238, 248
addNodesToStackPane()
      method, 128, 143, 238, 241
addStackPaneNodes() method, 138
Antialiasing, 110
ArrayList, 208
   class, 209
   object, 209
      addAll() method, 215
      addCurrentCast() method, 214
      COLLIDE_CHECKLIST, 218
      getCurrentCast() method, 214
      removeCurrentCast() method, 215
      resetCurrentCast() method, 216
ASDW keys function
   coding, 289–290
   Getter and Setter methods, NetBeans
      Insert Code, 291, 293
   jump and evade animation, 293–294
   WSAD keys, 290
Audacity, 13
AudioClip, 323
   Audacity
      Export File dialog, 325
      non-destructive audio editing, 327
      waveform representation, 325

class, 324
InvinciBagel.java class
   loadAudioAssets() method, 335
   playAudioClip() method, 340
   playiSound() methods, 338
   URL class, 333
loadAudioAssets() method, 323
memory footprint, 327
   export assets, 332
   PCM, 327
   resolution, 328
   sampling frequency, 329
   stereo *vs.* mono audio, 331
object, 324
playAudioClip() method, 323
setiSound() methods, 323
Auto-attack engine, 393, 417
   addGameActorNodes() method, 446
   boolean variables, 424
   constructor methods, 446
   GamePlayLoop .handle() method, 423
   getter method, 449
   handle() method, 418
   iBagelLocation variable, 450
   if-else structure, 425
   initiateAttack() method, 419, 447
   nested if conditional structures, 426
   nextBoolean() method, 421, 447
   nextInt() method, 421
   randomNum.nextInt() method, 448
   shootProjectile() method, 426
   update() method, 418

B

Background image
   loadImageAssets(), 413
   setImage() method, 413
   setVisible() method, 413

Background image (*cont.*)
    toBack() method, 415
    toFront() method, 415
Bagel.java class, 223
    Bagel() constructor method, 224
    collide() method, 225
    update() method, 225
Blank white screen, 187
Blender, 15
bulletGravity, 451
Bullet types, 443
Button object instantiation, 53

C, D

Captive *vs.* streaming audio, 118
CastingDirector.java class
    ArrayList (*see* ArrayList)
    CastingDirector() constructor method, 222
    CURRENT_CAST object, 216
    HashSet class, 208, 213
    HashSet Object
        addAll() method, 221
        addToRemovedActors() method, 220
        getRemovedActors() method, 219
        removeAll() method, 221
    List<E> public interface, 210
    Set<E> public interface, 212
    threading, 217
cheeseGravity, 451
Codecs, 114–115
Collision detection, 343
    bounds object, 372
        getBoundsInLocal() method, 373
        getBoundsInParent() method, 373
        intersects(Bounds localBounds) method, 374
    CastingDirector object, 378
    checkCollision() method, 370, 385
        boolean collide() method, 372
        update() method, 370
    getBoundsInParent() method, 376
    getChildren().remove() method, 380
    InvinciBagel.java class, 365
        addCurrentCast() method, 369
        collide() method, 366
        iBagel Bagel() constructor method, 368
        parsing algorithm, 368
        private access control keyword, 369
        testing, 368
    invinciBagel.playiSound0() method, 376
    object.getSpriteFrame() method, 381
    PhysicsEditor (PhysEd), 363
    resetRemovedActors() method, 383–384
    scoringEngine() method, 389
    Shape class intersect() method, 374

    SVG Path data (*see* SVG Path data)
    SVGPath.intersect() method, 376
    using Group class, 386
        setBoundaries() method, 389
        setLayoutY() method, 388
        StackPane UI container, 387
createActorCollisionData() method, 236
createCastingDirection() method, 238
createGameActors() method, 235
createSceneEventHandling() method, 231
createSplashScreenNodes() method, 128, 240
    addNodesToStackPane() method, 137
    configuration code, 136
    .getChildren().addAll(), 136
    Java code, 136
createStartGameLoop() method, 239

E

EditShare Lightworks, 14
empty constructor method, 132
Enemy() constructor method, 408, 429
    if() structure, 436
    pauseCounter variable, 435
    randomLocation variable, 431
    shootProjectile() method, 433
extends keyword, 149

F

Framecounter, 281–282
FXML UI design
    CSS styles, 120
    definition, 121
    HelloWorld, 121
    Inspector panel, 120
    Scene Builder Kit API, 120

G

Game design
    concepts
        collision detection, 104
        physics simulation, 104
        sprites, 104
    digital audio
        amplitude, 116
        analog audio, 117
        baseline file format, 118
        captive *vs.* streaming, 118
        codecs, 118
        digital audio, 117
        frequency, 116
        optimization, 119
        pulse wave, 116

saw wave, 116
sine wave, 116
digital image
8-bit transparency gradient, 113
alpha channel transparency value, 108
antialiasing, 110
banding, 111
blending modes, 108
color values, 107
dithering, 111, 113
dot patterns, 111
graphics interchange format (GIF), 106
hexadecimal notation, 109
Joint Photographic Experts Group (JPEG), 106
masking, 109
portable network graphics
(PNG\; pronounced "ping"), 106
resolution, 107, 111
digital video, 113
codecs, 114–115
data packets, 114
dropping frames, 115
frames, 114
high definition (HD), 114
standard definition (SD), 114
ultra high definition (UHD), 114
foundation
GamePlayLoop class, 124–125
Java class structure, 125
JavaFX Scene Graph (*see* JavaFX Scene Graph)
JavaFX UI classes (*see* JavaFX UI classes)
primary game functional screens, 124
optimization, 103
static *vs.* dynamic, 102
types
dynamic games, 105
static games, 105
strategy games, 105
Game Development Environment, 1
Audacity, 13
Blender, 15
GIMP, 12
Inkscape, 11
JDK 8 installation, 6
license agreement, 4
Lightworks, 14
NetBeans IDE 8.0
directory suggestions, 9
installer dialog, 8
license agreement, 9
percentage dialog, 10
summary dialog, 10
workstation, 2
programs and features, 2
uninstall button, 3

Game Play Loop
handle() method
abstract methods option, 151
NetBeans coding, 150
@Override keyword, 150–151
UnsupportedOperationException, 151
java class creation, 147
javafx.animation package, 145
JavaFX pulse system (*see* JavaFX pulse system)
NetBeans Profiler
menu sequence, 153
Threads tab, 154
pulse control, 152
pulse engine, 162
.start() and .stop() methods
empty method, 157–158
handle() method, 156–157
InvinciBagel.java tab, 155–156
Live Results Profiler tab, 158
@Override keyword, 154
super keyword, 154
Threads tab, 159
UI container, 160
getChildren().addAll() method, 132
GIMP, 12
Graphics interchange format (GIF), 106

■ H

HashSet class, 213
HashSet Object
addAll() method, 221
addToRemovedActors() method, 220
getRemovedActors() method, 219
removeAll() method, 221
Hero superclass, 165
collide() method, 178
getter and setter methods, 182
Hero() constructor method, 177
setContent() method, 177
sprite control, 179
compound declaration, 181
initialization statements, 180
variable declarations, 181
update() method, 178

■ I

if() statement, 274
Image() constructor methods, 133
ImageView() constructor methods, 134
Inkscape, 11
InvinciBagel animation
fly state, 277
isFlipH Property

InvinciBagel animation (*cont.*)
    Java coding, 295
    testing, 295
  isLeft() method, 278
  isRight() method, 278
  run cycle (*see* Run cycle)
  run state, 276
  setImageState() method, 274
  setScaleX() method, 278
  wait state, 274–275
InvinciBagel application, 123
  buttons
    pulse efficiency, 142
    .setOnAction() event-handling
     structure, 140–141
    UI design, 142
  .setImage() method, 139
  splashScreenTextArea.setImage() method, 140
  StackPane, 139
InvinciBagel diagram, 159–160
InvinciBagel.java class, 229, 252, 333, 365
  actor object creation
    handle() method, 242
    update() method, 243
  addCurrentCast() method, 369
  addGameActorNodes(), 237–238
  castDirector, 233
  collide() method, 366
  contextual information, 254
    Bagel() constructor method, 255
    createGameActors() method, 256
    is() methods, 257
    protected access, 255
    update() method, 257
  createCastingDirection(), 238
  createGameActors() method, 235
  createSceneEventHandling() method, 231
  createSplashScreenNodes(), 240
  createStartGameLoop() method, 239
  creation, 230
  enemy object, 410
  GamePlayLoop() constructor method, 258
  iBagel Bagel() constructor method, 368
  loadAudioAssets() method, 335
  loadImageAssets() method, 234
  logical methods structures, 230–231
  moveInvinciBagel() method, 265
  playiSound() methods, 338
  private access control keyword, 369
  Projectile object, 410
  remove static modifier
    boolean KeyEvent variables, 252
    Getter and Setter dialog, 253
  setBoundaries() method, 267
  setXYLocation() method, 266

  StackPane object, 261
  start() method, 230
  static keyword, 233
  SVG data parsing algorithm, 368
  testing, 246, 270, 368
  URL class, 334
InvinciBagel Prop zero (iPRO), 310
InvinciBagel sprite images, 167
isDown() method, 277
isUp() method, 277

■ J

Java 8, 43
  APIs level, 47
  classes
    extends keyword, 48
    init() method, 49
    inner classes, 50
    InvinciBagel class, 49
    modifier keywords, 48
    nested class, 50
    stop() method, 49
  code blocks delimiters, 46
  conditional control structures, 65
    decision making, 66
    looping, 68
  data field
    constants, 56
    variables, 55
  data types
    primitive data types, 60
    reference data types, 61
  Javadoc comment, 45
  methods
    constructor method, 54
    object method, 53
    start() method, 52
  modifier keywords (*see* Modifier keywords)
  multiline comments, 44
  objects
    GamePiece() constructor method, 73
    InvinciBagel object, 69
  operators, 61
    arithmetic operators, 62
    assignment operators, 64
    conditional operators, 65
    logical operators, 64
    relational operators, 63
  semicolon, 45
  single-line comment, 44
JavaFX 8 API, 75
  animation class, 85
    AnimationTimer class, 87–88
    collision detection, 88

Interpolator class, 86
KeyFrame objects, 86
pulse management system, 87
Timeline object, 86
transition class, 86
Camera class, 81
concurrent package, 97
event class, 97
geometry class, 95
Glass Windowing Toolkit, 76
JVM layer, 77
LightBase class, 81
overview, 76
popup class, 89
prism bridges, 77
Quantum Toolkit, 76
SceneAntialiasing class, 81
scene class, 79
scene graph, 76, 79
scene subpackages, 82
javafx.scene.control, 83
javafx.scene.effect, 83
javafx.scene.image, 83
javafx.scene.input, 83
javafx.scene.layout, 83
javafx.scene.media, 83
javafx.scene.paint, 83
javafx.scene.shape, 83
javafx.scene.text, 84
javafx.scene.transform, 84
javafx.scene.web, 84
screen class, 89
SnapshotParameters class, 81
StackPane class, 79
stage class
initStyle() method, 90
setBackground() method, 93
setFill() method, 91
setTitle() method, 90
top-level packages, 84
WebKit, 76
window superclass, 89
JavaFX pulse system, 145
AnimationTimer class, 147
frame rate, 147
handle() method, 147
javafx.animation package, 146
javafx.animation.Transition
class, 146
KeyFrame class, 146
KeyValue class, 146
PathTransition class, 146
JavaFX Scene Builder (*see* FXML UI design)
JavaFX Scene Graph, 123
.addStackPaneNodes() method
java code, 138

composite images, 126
createSplashScreenNodes() method, 136
addNodesToStackPane() method, 137
configuration code, 136
.getChildren().addAll(), 136
Java code, 136
InvinciBagel class code, 127
node hierarchy, 126
start() method
composite ImageView assets, 129
creation, 128
usage, 126
JavaFX UI classes
HBox class, 131
Image class, 132–133
ImageView class, 134
Insets class, 130
Pos class, 130
TableView class, 135
types, 129
Java interface, 209
Joint Photographic Experts Group (JPEG), 106

■ **K**

Keyboard event handling, 187, 195
ActionEvent class, 196
ASWD keys, 197, 204
character variable, 198
controllers, 195
import statements, 203
javafx.event package, 196
JavaFX events, 196
javafx.scene.input package, 196
java.util package, 196
KeyEvent class, 197
lambda expression, 201
setOnKeyPressed() method, 199, 202
switch-case statement, 200
update() method, 205

■ **L**

Lambda expressions, 187, 191
Lightworks, 14
loadImageAssets() method, 234, 241

■ **M**

Masking, 109
Memory footprint
export assets, 332
PCM, 327
resolution, 328
sampling frequency, 329
stereo *vs.* mono audio, 331

Modifier keywords
  access control modifiers
    package private access
      modifier, 58
    private access modifier, 58
    protected access modifier, 57
    public access modifier, 57
  nonaccess control modifier, 58
    abstract modifier, 59
    final modifier, 59
    static modifier, 59
    synchronized modifier, 60
    volatile modifier, 60
moveInvinciBagel() method, 295

N

NetBeans IDE 8.0, 19
  attributes
    code indenting, 20
    code refactoring, 20
  code optimization, 22
  debugger, 22
  extensible, 20
  InvinciBagel game project, 23
    application class
      creation, 26
    compilation, 28
    compile progress bar, 29
    description pane, 25
    Finding Feature dialog, 25
    package statement, 27
    profile menu (*see* Profile menu)
    Quick Launch icon, 23
    run project, 29
    start page tab, 24
  Navigator pane, 21
  Project pane, 21
  UI design, 22

O

Object declaration, 53
Object instantiation, 53
Open-source software
  packages, 16

P

PhysicsEditor (PhysEd), 363
Portable network graphics
  (PNG; pronounced "ping"), 106
Profile menu, 32
  analyze performance, 33
  calibration process, 34

memory usage
  Record stack, 38
  Telemetry tabs, 40
  Threads tab, 39
profiler tab
  garbage collection, 36
  output pane, 37
  telemetry section, 36
project utility, 32
Windows firewall, 35
Projectile.java class, 409
Prop subclasses, 300
  addCurrentCast() method
    iPB0 PropB object, 316
    iPH0 PropH object, 314
    iPR0 Prop object, 313
    iPV0 PropV object, 315
  addGameActorNodes() method, 317
  class declaration, 302
  error highlights, 300
  helper dialog, 301
  image declarations, 310
  Java Class dialog, 300
  loadImageAssets() method, 312
  moveInvinciBagel() method, 303
  PropB class, 309
  Prop() constructor method, 302
  PropH class, 304
    PropH() constructor method, 308
    setIsFlipH method, 306
    setScaleX() method, 307
  PropV class, 308
  setTranslateX() method, 303
  setTranslateY() method, 303
  UnsupportedOperationException(), 301
  update() method, 302
  wrench icons, 310
Public abstract class, 166
Pulse code modulated (PCM), 327

Q

Quick Launch icons, 17

R

Random number generators, 416
Run cycle
  fly and land states, 286
  Nested If-Else structure, 279
  throttle program logic, 281–282
  triple Nested If-Else
    Java code, 285–286
    ScaleX property, 284
    structures, 283

■ S

Scalable Vector Graphics (SVG), 343
Scoring engine, 394
    addCurrentCast() method, 439
      COLLIDE_CHECKLIST, 440
      if else method, 442
      loadBullet() method, 440
      loadCheese() method, 440
      loadEnemy() method, 440
      private void method, 441
      return statement, 440
    code implementation, 399
    createSplashScreenNodes() method, 394
    equals() method, 437
    getChildren().add() method, 396
    if-else-if structure, 402
    if() structures, 400
    playiSound0() method, 400
    private Font object, 395
    scoreLabel Text object, 397
    setFill() method, 397
    setFont() method, 397
    setText() method, 400
    String.valueOf() method, 394
.setImage() method, 134
setImageState() method, 274, 295
setTitle() method, 128
setTranslate() methods, 245–246
setVisible() method, 232
Stereo *vs.* mono audio, 331
SVG Path data, 344
    using GIMP, 345
      Export Path, 349
      Fuzzy Selection Tool, 346
      invert selection, 348
      pixel selection, 348
      quotation marks, 351
      text editor, 351

    using Import Path, 356
      Bezier curve control, 359
      collision polygon, 358
      data footprint optimization, 362
      floating point
        representation, 358
      integer collision path, 357
      remove duplications, 359
      Z closing command, 360
    using Path Tool, 352
      close path command, 355
      numeric precision, 355
      optimization, 355
      Unnamed Path, 354

■ T

TableView() constructor method, 135
Treasure.java class, 393
    code implementation, 403
    collision detection, 406
    Image() constructor method, 404

■ U, V

UnsupportedOperationException(), 158
update() method
    If statements, 243–245
    import static statements, 243
    setTranslate() methods, 245–246

■ W, X, Y, Z

White background
    ImageView, 190
    setVisible() method, 189
    testing, 190
Width and height
      variables, 187–188

Get the eBook for only $10!

Now you can take the weightless companion with you anywhere, anytime. Your purchase of this book entitles you to 3 electronic versions for only $10.

This Apress title will prove so indispensible that you'll want to carry it with you everywhere, which is why we are offering the eBook in 3 formats for only $10 if you have already purchased the print book.

Convenient and fully searchable, the PDF version enables you to easily find and copy code—or perform examples by quickly toggling between instructions and applications. The MOBI format is ideal for your Kindle, while the ePUB can be utilized on a variety of mobile devices.

Go to www.apress.com/promo/tendollars to purchase your companion eBook.

Apress®
THE EXPERT'S VOICE™

All Apress eBooks are subject to copyright. All rights are reserved by the Publisher, whether the whole or part of the material is concerned, specifically the rights of translation, reprinting, reuse of illustrations, recitation, broadcasting, reproduction on microfilms or in any other physical way, and transmission or information storage and retrieval, electronic adaptation, computer software, or by similar or dissimilar methodology now known or hereafter developed. Exempted from this legal reservation are brief excerpts in connection with reviews or scholarly analysis or material supplied specifically for the purpose of being entered and executed on a computer system, for exclusive use by the purchaser of the work. Duplication of this publication or parts thereof is permitted only under the provisions of the Copyright Law of the Publisher's location, in its current version, and permission for use must always be obtained from Springer. Permissions for use may be obtained through RightsLink at the Copyright Clearance Center. Violations are liable to prosecution under the respective Copyright Law.